The Year Book 1971

Cover Pictures. *Front:* Edward Heath at Number 10; Leila Khaled; hijacked aircraft blown up on Dawson's Field, near Amman; Lunokhod 1 on the Moon; victims of East Pakistan cyclone and tidal wave disaster; Bobby Moore; the World Cup. *Back:* Brandt and Kosygin signing non-aggression pact; Pope Paul VI on his tour of the East and Australia; London production of *Oh! Calcutta!*; Gen. de Gaulle; Iain Macleod; President Nasser; Bertrand Russell; shooting of students at Kent University, Ohio.

Endpapers. "Minaret", one of the hand-printed wallpaper designs by Osborne & Little Ltd., London, that received a British Council of Industrial Design award in 1970.

ISBN 0 7172 7802 6

© **THE HOUSE OF GROLIER, 1971**
Head Offices: Star House, Potters Bar, Herts, England

Made and printed in Great Britain by Butler and Tanner Ltd., Frome and London

The Year Book

a record of the events,
developments,
and personalities
of 1970

GROLIER · LONDON

Contents

*Detailed contents are given on each
sectional title page*

Pictorial Features

Editor-in-Chief	ROBERT H. HILL
Assistant	David Tinkler
Art Editor	KENNETH POWELL
Picture Research	Derek Gilby
Fact Digest	ELIZABETH HOGARTH

The Year in Headlines

January

**Capricorn (The Goat),
December 21–January 19**

1 S. Vietnam Buddhist Church claims number of civilians allegedly killed by U.S. troops in "Pinkville" (March 1968) was nearly 600—highest estimate so far.

U.K. holidaymakers' £50 foreign travel limit, introduced in July 1966, is abolished.

2 Federal Nigerian troops clear two vital roads through Biafra, cutting it into three parts.

Hurricane in Canary Islands causes damage later assessed at £12½ million.

4 **Sunday** Capt. William Bright and Capt. Frank Buxton arrive in Sydney in their twin-engine Britten-Norman Islander to win 11,500-mile air race from London.

5 Mud and water from burst dam sweep through Mendoza City in Andean foothills, Argentina, killing at least 36.

Four-day inquest into death of Mary Jo Kopechne (July 18, 1969) opens in Massachusetts.

6 One thousand five hundred anti-apartheid demonstrators clash with police at Springboks v. Midland Counties (West) at Coventry.

Johnny Famechon, Australia, retains world featherweight title when he knocks out Masahiko (Fighting) Harada, Japan, in Tokyo.

7 Israeli planes bomb targets 18 miles from Cairo.

Massive failure of public transport in Glasgow following city's coldest night for 30 years; in Carnwath, Lanarkshire, 38 degrees of frost reported.

Farmers demonstrate in Exeter when Cledwyn Hughes, Minister of Agriculture, addresses stormy meeting of Devon National Farmers' Union.

8 U.S. army charges two more soldiers, Pte. Gerald Smith and Sgt. Charles Hutto, in connection with alleged "Pinkville" massacre.

9 About 1,000 farmers demanding greater financial support for agriculture break through police at Monk's Wood, near Huntingdon, to present petition to Harold Wilson.

In U.K. influenza has killed 2,850 people in past week—highest weekly figure for 19 years—bringing number of deaths in past five weeks to over 7,000.

11 **Sunday** As Federal Nigerian government announces capture of Owerri all organized resistance in Biafra collapses, and Biafran leader Gen. Ojukwu flees by air to Ivory Coast.

12 Gen. Gowon accepts Biafra's surrender in midnight broadcast, asking all Nigerians to welcome former rebels as brothers.

Start of two-week teachers' strike in 450 schools throughout the U.K. involving 4,500–5,000 N.U.T. members.

13 Israeli jet planes attack Egyptian base at El Khanka, 13 miles north-east of Cairo.

Following discovery of hole in dam of Lluest Wen reservoir in Rhondda Fach Valley, Glamorgan, which contains 242 million gallons of water, firemen and water board men pump out water to reduce level and 2,000 people are evacuated from their homes.

Two hundred farm vehicles in demonstration at Pershore, Worcs.

Alan Jacques jailed for four years after pleading guilty to maliciously setting fire to Anne Hathaway's Cottage, Stratford-on-Avon (Nov. 22, 1969).

14 Gen. Gowon bans all relief aid from France, Portugal, S. Africa, Rhodesia, and other countries "studiously hostile" to Nigeria, but accepts medical aid from Great Britain. Nigerian Federal troops complete their occupation of Biafra.

Agriculture, commerce, and industry reported to be at a standstill in many areas of Portugal after worst floods for many years.

15 Biafra's official surrender document is handed to Maj.-Gen. Gowon.

Labour M.P., William James Owen, is charged with offence under Official Secrets Act.

P. and O. liner *Oronsay* held in Vancouver while 26 cases of typhoid among passengers and crew are investigated.

Tenants of 117-ft.-high blocks of council flats in Kidderminster given immediate notice to leave because high winds might cause buildings to collapse.

16 William Owen accused of passing secret information in London between Aug. 26, 1961, and Dec. 1969.

Militant farmers from 22 counties meet at National Farmers' Union h.q., London, and set up committee to co-ordinate

action in event of unfavourable price review.

17 Cyclone hits north-east Queensland.

Cathy McGowan, "pop girl", marries Hywel Bennett, actor, in Norbury, London.

18 **Sunday** U Thant, United Nations secretary-general, flies to Lagos for talks with Federal Nigerian leaders.

Israeli jets bomb military targets on outskirts of Cairo.

19 Walter Ulbricht, East German chief of state and Communist party leader, gives his first international press conference for nine years.

Lt. William Calley charged with murder of civilian in S. Vietnam six weeks before alleged "Pinkville" massacre.

20 Queensland's cyclone blows itself out, having caused 11 deaths and damage estimated at £4,600,000. Winds of over 100 m.p.h. and 40 in. of rain in 24 hours were recorded.

Damage to 12 cricket grounds in England and Wales by anti-apartheid demonstrators in campaign to stop S. African cricket tour of Great Britain.

A thousand Madrid University students riot in centre of city, on first anniversary of suicide of law student while held by police.

Archbishop of Canterbury preaches in Greek Orthodox Cathedral, London, an unprecedented occasion and part of universal week of prayer for Christian unity.

In Warsaw, U.S.A. and Communist China resume formal ambassadorial talks after two-year suspension.

21 Israeli commando force, backed by tanks and aircraft, makes 19-hour attack on Jordanian positions near Sedom, on the Dead Sea.

Sixteen people executed in Baghdad for plotting to overthrow the Iraq government.

Fraserburgh lifeboat capsizes off Aberdeenshire coast; one survivor picked up by Russian ship.

22 Israeli paratroop force captures Egyptian-held island of Shadwan in Red Sea.

Gen. Gowon allows relief supplies to be flown into Port Harcourt, Enugu, and Calabar airports, but refuses to put Uli airport into service.

Pan American's first jumbo-jet Boeing 747 to carry fare-paying passengers arrives at London Airport from New York, seven hours late, after an overheated engine had forced change of planes at Kennedy Airport.

23 From Shadwan island (Jan. 22) a radar station is dismantled and ferried to Israeli-held Sinai by helicopter before troops leave after 32-hour occupation.

Outside Turin University, Italy, 1,550 members of left-wing and right-wing student movements fight, and are separated by several hundred police.

International Publishing Corporation and Reed Group announce agreed terms for merger, with market value of over £225 million.

Farmers halt traffic in centre of Haverfordwest, Pembrokeshire, for 1½ hours with tractors, cars, and farm machines.

25 **Sunday** Harold Wilson leaves London Airport for Ottawa on first part of N. American visit.

In clash with about 2,000 anti-Vietnam demonstrators in Whitehall, London, three policemen are injured, and 11 men arrested.

Lluest Wen reservoir (Jan. 13) is certified safe.

26 Harold Wilson leaves Ottawa and arrives in New York.

Ten thousand mourners attend funeral of five Fraserburgh lifeboatmen (Jan. 21).

27 Harold Wilson and President Nixon meet at White House for two hours of talks.

Protestant and Catholic extremists roam Belfast for fourth successive night; in Falls Road a 500-strong mob faces troops guarding peace line.

Further 6,000 members of N.U.T. at 400 schools come out on strike, bringing total number of teachers called out on official strike since Nov. 1969 to 15,000.

28 Israeli fighter-bombers attack targets in Cairo suburb of Maadi, killing three civilians and injuring 12.

Lubomir Strougal becomes Czechoslovakia's prime minister, following resignation of Olrich Cernik.

One hundred and fifty feared killed when avalanches fall on 30–40 mile stretch of Haraz road to Caspian coast, about 50 miles from Teheran.

Thirty-two children killed when express train crashes into stalled school bus on level crossing 20 miles south of Johannesburg, S. Africa.

29 Nigerian magistrates' court in Port Harcourt sentences 20 Roman Catholic missionaries—17 Irish and three British—to six months' jail for illegal entry.

Fifth consecutive night of confrontation between troops and militants in Belfast.

30 Lesotho government declares state of emergency following defeat of ruling National party by Pan-Africanist Congress party in general election of Jan. 27, and Chief Jonathan, prime minister and leader of National party, announces dusk-to-dawn curfew.

El Salvador proclaims state of emergency after border incidents with neighbouring Honduras.

Typhoid outbreak on P. and O. liner *Oronsay* (Jan. 15), during which 82 confirmed or suspected cases were taken to hospital, expected to cost company over £200,000.

31 Chief Jonathan, prime minister of Lesotho, admits seizing power, and says King Moshoeshoe II has "technically abdicated".

In Belfast, bomb thrown from speeding car blasts 5-ft. hole in wall of army post.

At Twickenham during Springboks' last match of tour anti-apartheid demonstrators use smoke and flour bombs.

In Cardiff, James Callaghan, Home Secretary, is jostled and booed by farmers taking part in nation-wide campaign.

28th . . . Avalanche near Teheran, Persia

23rd . . . Israelis airlift Egyptian radar station

27th . . . Wilson arrives at Washington

12th . . . Joy in Lagos at Biafra's surrender

February

Aquarius (The Water-Carrier),
January 20–February 18

1 **Sunday** Fierce fighting on Syria–
Israel border, involving aircraft,
tanks, and artillery.
At least 300 people killed and more
than 500 injured when Argentine
express train runs into back of stationary
local train 22 miles from Buenos
Aires.

2 About 150 farmers besiege
ministry of agriculture in London,
and go to House of Commons to lobby
their M.P.s.

3 Federal Nigerian government
releases 25 Irish, six British, and
one American Roman Catholic missionaries held in Port Harcourt in jail and
under house arrest, and flies them to
Lagos for deportation.

4 Twenty-two Welsh nationalists
invade High Court, London,
demonstrating against jailing of Dafydd
Iwan, pop singer, on Jan. 28. Fourteen
who refuse to apologize are sentenced
to three months in jail, and eight others
are fined £50.

5 Egyptian commandos cross Suez
Canal and destroy two tanks and
other Israeli military vehicles. King
Hussein arrives in Cairo for talks with
President Nasser.
U.K. teachers told they will not be
given interim pay rise on April 1 unless
agreement has been reached with
Burnham committee, or they are
prepared to go to arbitration.
In Sydney, N.S.W., the first sale for
41 years of Merino rams for export is
held.

6 After Egyptian frogmen sink 960-
ton Israeli ship in Eilat harbour,
Israeli planes raid targets along Suez
Canal and bomb and sink 700-ton
Egyptian minelayer in Red Sea.
Stones thrown at British troops in
Londonderry when Roman Catholic
demonstrators attempt an attack on
Rev. Ian Paisley's supporters.

7 Armed troops stand by to reinforce
police in Belfast when rival mobs
of civil rights demonstrators and
militant Protestants roam the city.
Demonstrations in 10 towns and cities
of Northern Ireland.
Police investigating disappearance of
Mrs. Muriel McKay (Dec. 29, 1970)
question two brothers, and start search
of farmhouse and land near Stocking
Pelham, Herts.

8 **Sunday** Arctic hurricane with
winds of over 130 knots destroys
10 houses and two public buildings, and
causes damage to all others in
Angmagssalik, East Greenland.

9 Communiqué jointly issued by
Egypt, Syria, Iraq, Jordan, and
Sudan at end of three-day Cairo
summit talks reaffirms Arab determination
to liberate territories occupied by Israel
after 1967 war.
Pre-trial hearing of ''Pinkville'' case
opens at Fort Benning, Georgia, U.S.A.
Masked raiders escape with £200,000
from Barclay's Bank, Ilford, Essex.

10 Three Arab commandos armed
with revolvers and hand grenades
attack airport bus at Munich airport,
killing one passenger and injuring 11
people.
Japanese ore carrier, *California Maru*,
34,001 tons, sinks in Pacific; all 29
crew reported missing.
Brothers Arthur and Nizamadeen
Hosein, of Rooks Farm, Stocking
Pelham, Herts, charged with murder of
Mrs. Muriel McKay, whose body has
not been found.

11 Japan launches her first successful
satellite from Uchinoura.
The Prince of Wales takes his seat in
House of Lords.
National Union of Teachers choose
Birmingham, Waltham Forest, and
Southwark for indefinite strikes by
teachers (4,850 in Birmingham to be
called out on Feb. 18; 950 in Waltham
Forest on Feb. 23; and 1,400 in
Southwark on Feb. 25).
Eleven Welsh students freed by Court
of Appeal from sentences imposed in
High Court (Feb. 4), and bound over to
keep the peace. Three others similarly
jailed do not appeal.

12 Israeli planes bomb metal factory
at Abou Zabal, on outskirts of
Cairo, killing 70 workers and injuring 98.
U.S. army announces that charges
have been brought against Capt. Thomas
Willingham for crimes committed at
Song My village, S. Vietnam, in
March 1968.
U.K. Cricket Council announces that
S. African cricket tour is to be reduced
to 12 matches on eight grounds.
Four destructive avalanches in Val
d'Isère, France.

13 Cambridge students fight with
police, and smash hotel windows,
in demonstration against evening of
Greek entertainment. Six are arrested.
At least seven people die in fire caused
by arson at Jewish old people's home,
Munich.
Two men die in fire at Exeter city
hospital, and several others injured.

15 **Sunday** U.K. Ford motor company workers, in free vote,
overwhelmingly defeat militant shop
stewards who wanted to call strike at all
21 plants from Feb. 16, all except
Swansea workers accepting company's
pay rise offer.

16 Dominican DC-9 airliner crashes
after take-off from Santo Domingo
killing all 102 people on board.
Strike at Ford's Swansea plant
threatens to halt production at all other
Ford plants.
Joe Frazier becomes new heavyweight
champion of the world by defeating
Jimmy Ellis on technical knock-out in
fifth round, at Madison Square Garden,
New York.

17 At least 100 Muslims die, and
scores are injured, when their
train plunges off embankment south of
Kaduna, Nigeria.
About a third of the 12,000 workers
at Ford's Halewood plant go on strike.
Wife of U.S. army officer, Capt. Mac-
Donald, and their two daughters, aged
six and two, beaten and stabbed to death
in their home at Fort Bragg army base,
North Carolina, by three men and a
woman. MacDonald is also stabbed.

18 More than half the primary
schools and over a third of the
secondary schools in Birmingham close
as members of N.U.T. begin their
indefinite strike.

19 Another massacre in S. Vietnam
in which U.S. soldiers killed 100
civilians is alleged in N.B.C. broadcast to
have taken place in Quang Nam province
on same day as alleged ''Pinkville''
incident in March 1968.

20 Five-year jail sentences imposed
by U.S. Federal Judge Hoffman
on five persons for inciting riots during
1968 Democratic party convention in
Chicago; demonstrations against
sentences in Washington, New York,
Boston, and Los Angeles.
U.K. Post Office clerical staff stage
lightning strikes throughout the country
in protest against management's withdrawal of 8·5 per cent pay increase offer.
Ford workers at Swansea plant agree
to return to work.

21 Swiss Coronado jet plane bound
for Tel Aviv crashes near Swiss–
German border, killing all 47 people
aboard. Sabotage is suspected.

Report that Communist forces, sweeping down from N. Vietnam, have captured Plain of Jars in Laos.

22 Sunday Many national airlines, including BOAC, BEA, Air France, Swissair, KLM, and Lufthansa, ban freight deliveries to Israel following yesterday's crash.

Guyana becomes a co-operative republic: the first Caribbean country to sever link with the British Crown.

Explosion in Roman Catholic-owned public house in Belfast.

23 Inaugural run of Sydney—Perth "Indian-Pacific" transcontinental passenger express train in Australia. (Regular service began on March 1.)

Mitja Ribicic arrives in London on first visit by a Yugoslav prime minister to Great Britain since the Second World War.

More than 150 students at Oxford University break into administration building looking for personal dossiers, following allegations that a student was rejected by Warwick University after a letter from his headmaster had revealed his political interests.

24 Pres. Pompidou of France arrives in Washington, U.S.A., for talks with Pres. Nixon.

Avalanches at French ski resort of Lans Le Villard, where six people are killed, four injured, and others missing, and at Reckingen, Switzerland, where 11 are killed and 18 missing.

25 Over 1,400 teachers in S. London join the 6,000 teachers already on indefinite strike. Two hundred thousand children now without education in Birmingham, Southwark, and Waltham Forest.

Vice-Chancellor of Manchester University issues writs against five students to prevent them organizing occupation of university's administrative block to search for personal dossiers.

26 It is announced that five U.S. marines have been charged with murder of 16 Vietnamese women and 11 children on Feb. 20 at Lamlet, 27 miles south of Da Nung.

During the second night of rioting by about 2,000 students at University of California, Santa Barbara, a branch of Bank of America is gutted.

One thousand students occupy Manchester University's offices, demanding enquiry into personal dossiers.

Five people injured when terrorist explosion wrecks Belfast club.

"Indian-Pacific" train (Feb. 23) arrives in Perth, having crossed Australia from Sydney in 65 hours 45 minutes.

Rupert Murdoch dismisses Stafford Somerfield, editor of *News of the World*.

Ann Jones, Wimbledon champion, announces in TV programme that she will not defend her title.

27 National Guardsmen move into Santa Barbara, California, after three nights of student rioting.

After London meeting between university vice-chancellors and representatives of National Union of Students a statement is issued that universities are not interested in, and should not keep, files on students' political or religious opinions or affiliations.

Seven of 11 men trapped for 80 hours after a railway tunnel cave-in in the Kaimai Mountains, 60 miles from Hamilton, New Zealand, are brought to safety through a steel pipe pushed 55 ft. through wall of rock and earth.

15th . . . Ford's Dagenham workers defeat the militants and vote against a strike

12th . . . Bombed factory on outskirts of Cairo

24th . . . Search for avalanche victims at Reckingen

March

**Pisces (The Fishes),
February 19–March 20**

1 Sunday Israeli air raids on central and southern sectors of Suez Canal kill 32 Egyptian soldiers and civilians.

Austrian general election won by Socialist party, who take 81 of National Assembly's 165 seats.

5,000 Orangemen march peacefully through Belfast in Reformation Day parade.

Pres. Pompidou arrives in Chicago.

2 Rhodesia becomes a republic at one minute past midnight (local time), ending 80-year link with Britain.

Willy Brandt, W. German chancellor, arrives in London for official two-day visit.

Pres. Pompidou cancels meeting with Jewish leaders in New York because of demonstrations against French policy in Middle East; Pres. Nixon flies to New York to apologize.

Sit-in by Oxford undergraduates (Feb. 23) ends when about 400 students march out carrying banners and red flag.

Unofficial strikes by firemen at London Airport (Heathrow) twice close airport to passenger traffic.

3 U.K. teachers' dispute settled: they will receive interim increase of £120 p.a. from April 1.

Pres. and Mme. Pompidou leave New York at end of state visit.

Heathrow airport closed for 12 hours by unofficial strike of firemen.

Sixty policemen injured in five-hour clash with left-wing students at Nanterre, Paris.

4 Blizzards sweep nearly the whole of Great Britain, bringing worst road chaos since 1963, cutting off towns and villages, and closing airports; in Kent, power failure, putting winding gear out of action at three pits, traps 688 coal-miners 3,000 ft. underground.

French submarine, *Eurydice*, officially reported lost with all 57 men on board during exercise off Toulon.

Queen, Duke of Edinburgh, and Princess Anne arrive in Suva, Fiji, on 24-hour visit.

In fighting with students at Nanterre, Paris, 125 policemen are injured.

5 Nuclear non-proliferation treaty formally comes into effect after ceremonies in London, Washington, and Moscow.

U.K. bank rate reduced from 8 to $7\frac{1}{2}$ per cent.

6 Heathrow airport closed at 8 p.m. for fifth night running by firemen's strike.

William Owen committed to stand trial for breach of Official Secrets Act (Jan. 15).

German bank rate raised from 6 to $7\frac{1}{2}$ per cent.

7 Queen arrives in Tonga (Friendly Isles).

At Wembley, Football League Cup is won by Manchester City who defeat West Bromwich Albion 2–1 in extra time.

8 Sunday Archbishop Makarios survives attempt to assassinate him by machine-gunning his helicopter from roof in Nicosia.

9 For first time in a week Heathrow airport opens for night-flying when striking firemen temporarily return to work.

20,000 shopkeepers and workmen driving at 3 m.p.h. in buses and cars disrupt traffic on Paris's outer ring motorway, in demonstration of dis-content.

Sussex University officials agree to allow students to see their personal files and to destroy confidential material not open to student inspection.

10 Capt. Ernest Medina charged with murder in connection with alleged "Pinkville" (My Lai) massacre, and new charges of murder or intent to murder are brought against one other officer and three enlisted men.

Sidney Genders, aged 51, arrives in Antigua, West Indies, after rowing across the Atlantic from Cornwall in 143 days.

11 Cambodian students and workers sack the North Vietnamese and Vietcong embassies in Phnom Penh, capital of Cambodia.

12 Bomb explosions damage New York offices of three major U.S. corporations.

Kurdish leader Mullah Mustafa Barzani signs agreement with Iraq, ending 9-year war.

Bridgwater by-election (first in which 18-year-olds have been able to vote) won by Conservatives.

13 Heathrow firemen walk out again at 1 a.m.

15 Sunday Opening of Expo 70 at Osaka, Japan.

Polycarpos Georghadjis, former Cypriot minister of the interior, assassinated by gunmen in Nicosia.

In explosion at Breza, near Sarajevo, Yugoslavia, 49 coalminers are killed and 10 injured.

16 Half Heathrow airport staff leave work to attend mass meeting protesting against service contract given by British Airports Authority to Canadian-based company.

Series of explosions shake New York's World Trade Centre.

17 U.S. army charges 14 officers, including major-general in charge of training academy at West Point, with offences relating to alleged "Pinkville" massacre.

18 Cambodia's head of state, Prince Norodom Sihanouk, is ousted in bloodless right-wing coup. He leaves for Peking, and Cheng Heng, a lawyer, is installed as new head of state.

U.K. farmers remain unappeased by record £85 million in farm price review.

Heathrow again closes at 8 p.m. because of firemen's dispute.

19 W. German Chancellor Willy Brandt and E. German Chancellor Willi Stoph meet at Erfurt, East Germany, the first meeting of heads of government of the two parts of Germany. After talks the two agree to resume discussions at Kassel, W. Germany, on May 21.

20 Labour party retains South Ayr-shire in by-election.

Heathrow airport strike ends when firemen vote by 35 to 34 to resume normal working.

Queen's Visit to New Zealand

March

12 Arrives in Wellington; unveils memorial plaque to Capt. Cook.

13 State opening of Parliament.

15 Re-enactment of Capt. Cook's landing at Ship's Cove, near Picton.

16–17 Christchurch.

18 Dunedin.

19 Lamb race at Invercargill; end of tour of South Island.

20 Concert in New Plymouth; visit to Massey University, Palmerston.

21 Napier.

22 Maori greeting in Gisborne.

23–24 Arrives in Auckland.

24 State banquet in Auckland at end of visit.

30 Leaves by air for Australia.

21 Outside S. African embassy, Trafalgar Square, London, anti-apartheid demonstrators re-enact Sharp-ville massacre of 1960.

It is announced that Alexander Dubcek has been suspended from the Czecho-slovak Communist party.

23 For third night in succession troops clash with bottle- and stone-throwing crowd in Bogside, Londonderry. Bernadette Devlin leads group of civil rights supporters in 23-hour sit-in outside 10 Downing Street.

On sixth day of strike by over 100,000 U.S. postal workers Pres. Nixon declares state of emergency and orders troops in New York City to ensure essential mail services.

Arthur Chung sworn in as first president of republic of Guyana.

Attempted coup in Congo (Brazzaville) fails.

Protest march by 10,000 farmers in Melbourne, Australia.

24 Mail service in New York City paralysed for eighth day, but postal workers in rest of U.S.A. return to work.

Pay increase of up to 26 per cent for British nurses agreed by Whitley council.

At Wembley, Henry Cooper regains British heavyweight title, beating the holder, Jack Bodell, on points over 15 rounds.

25 Israeli jets strike at Egyptian radar stations in three raids.

U.S. postal strike ends as men vote to accept 12 per cent pay increase.

Several leading U.S. banks cut their prime lending rate from $8\frac{1}{2}$ to 8 per cent.

26 New York City postal workers return to work.

27 **Good Friday** Palestinian guerrillas and Falangist militiamen fight in and around Beirut, Lebanon, for third successive day; number of deaths in three days is over 30.

Israeli attempts to destroy Sam-3 missile system being constructed west of the Nile; five Egyptian planes shot down.

Signor Rumor, Italian prime minister, forms new centre-left coalition cabinet.

28 One of the biggest recorded earthquakes hits many Turkish towns, from Kutahya to the Aegean Sea at Izmir; in Gediz at least 300 die.

Violence in Londonderry, N. Ireland, following parade of 5,000 people in Easter Rising commemoration; 12 soldiers injured.

Cambridge wins University boat race for third year in succession.

29 **Easter Day** British troops clash with rioters besieging police barracks on outskirts of Bogside, Londonderry.

30 **Bank Holiday** Crowd of youths stone security forces in Armagh, N. Ireland.

Southend police arrest over 50 "skin-heads" for assaulting police, having offensive weapons, and damaging property.

National Union of Teachers annual conference decides by 162,052 votes to 74,577 to seek affiliation to Trades Union Congress.

31 Terrorists kidnap West German ambassador, Count Karl von Spreti, in Guatemala City.

Following Junior Orangemen's parade in Belfast, army units clash with stone-throwing crowds: seven soldiers injured.

Japanese "Red Army" students hijack airliner on flight from Tokyo at sword-point, demanding to be taken to N. Korea; plane lands near Seoul, S. Korea, and women and children are allowed to leave, but 106 male passengers and crew are held.

Egyptian civilians killed and injured by Israeli fighter-bomber attacking Mansoura, 60 miles N. of Cairo.

Series of earth tremors kill at least 200 in Kutahya province, W. Turkey; deaths since March 28 stated to be about 3,000.

A thousand farmers march and drive tractors and trucks through Perth, Western Australia, in protest over farm prices.

12th . . . First 18-year-old to vote in Great Britain

12th . . . Queen Elizabeth decorates Maori Queen Te Ata-I-Rangikaahu Ariki nui with the D.B.E.

19th . . . Willy Brandt and Willi Stoph meet at Erfurt, East Germany

31st . . . Protest procession by farmers in Perth, Western Australia

April

Aries (The Ram),
March 21–April 20

1 U.S. army charges Capt. Medina with premeditated murder of all civilians reported killed by his company in alleged "Pinkville" massacre of March 1968.

Immam al-Hadi al-Mahdi, spiritual leader of Sudanese Umma party, killed while trying to escape to Ethiopia after attempted revolt against regime of Maj.-Gen. Jafaar al-Nimeiry.

Moroccan airliner en route from Agadir to Paris crashes at Casablanca, killing 61 of 82 people on board.

Everton become Football League First Division champions.

2 Troops in Belfast use CS gas to repel rioting mobs.

3 Passengers and crew freed from Japanese plane at Seoul (March 31) in exchange for Japanese deputy minister of transport who has offered himself as hostage in their place, and plane flies him and the hijackers to Pyonyang, N. Korea.

Guatemala refuses rebels' demands for $700,000 and the release of 25 political prisoners in exchange for W. German Ambassador, Count Karl von Spreti (March 31).

Israeli jets penetrate 50 miles into Egypt's Nile delta region, and attack Sam-2 missile bases.

Gen. Sir Ian Freeland, N. Ireland security chief, warns that anyone manufacturing, carrying, or throwing petrol bombs is liable to be shot dead.

4 Troops in Belfast use CS gas to disperse Protestant football crowds attempting to march into Catholic districts; three bomb explosions in centre of city.

Gay Trip, ridden by Pat Taaffe, wins Grand National.

5 **Sunday** Count Karl von Spreti (March 31, April 3) is killed by kidnappers, and his body is found 10 miles north of Guatemala City.

Hi-jacked Japanese airliner (April 3) brings Japanese deputy minister of transport back to Tokyo.

In Belfast, shots are fired following a brawl between Catholic and Protestants, and bomb explodes outside block of old people's flats.

6 Two bombs explode in Belfast, and Stormont government doubles to £10,000 its reward for information on bombing.

7 Earthquake in Philippines kills at least seven and injures over 175.

8 Thirty children killed and 50 injured when bomb from Israeli aircraft hits primary school in Nile delta.

Underground gas explosion causes fires and damage in Osaka, Japan, killing 73 people and injuring 282.

9 Twenty people drowned and 38 injured when 15,800-ton British ore-carrying ship, *London Valour*, sinks in heavy seas outside Genoa harbour after hitting breakwater.

10 Ian Smith's Rhodesian Front party wins 47 of the 50 European seats in first republican election.

In Greater London Council elections Conservatives keep control of Council, but lose control of Inner London Education Authority.

W. German chancellor Willy Brandt arrives in Washington on two-day visit.

11 U.S. spacecraft Apollo 13 launched at 8.13 p.m. B.S.T. with astronauts Capt. James Lovell, Fred Haise, and John Swigert, for intended landing on Moon.

F.A. Cup Final at Wembley between Chelsea and Leeds United results in a 2–2 draw after extra time, for first time since 1912.

12 **Sunday** Apollo 13 over half-way to Moon.

At least 90 Vietnamese men, women, and children held in compound in Cambodian town of Prasot are killed by machine-gun and automatic rifle fire during Vietcong attack.

13 Greek composer Mikis Theodorakis arrives in Paris, after release by Greek government.

14 Disaster strikes Apollo 13 when, at 4.15 a.m. B.S.T., Capt. Lovell reports an explosion, followed by gas venting into space. Moon landing is cancelled, and manoeuvres are plotted at Houston to swing spacecraft round Moon and bring it back to Earth. Lovell and Haise transfer to lunar module.

U.K. Budget gives to the lower-paid tax reductions amounting to £220 million a year.

15 Crippled Apollo 13 rounds the Moon and re-establishes radio contact at 1.45 a.m. B.S.T.

16 Apollo 13 passes half-way mark on return to Earth.

Second round of SALT (Strategic Arms Limitation Talks) between U.S.A. and U.S.S.R. opens in Vienna.

Clifford Dupont sworn in at Salisbury as first president of Rhodesian Republic.

Riot police clash with students and others on University of California campus at Berkeley, California: hundreds of windows in university buildings are smashed, and many arrests made.

Rev. Ian Paisley is elected to Stormont parliament in Bannside by-election, and Rev. William Beattie, his associate, is elected for South Antrim.

30th . . . South Vietnamese and American tanks roll forward to invade Cambodia

Queen's Visit to Australia

March
30 Arrives at Sydney, N.S.W.
31 Garden party at Government House, Sydney.

April
2 Arrives at Hobart, Tasmania.
4 Launceston, Northern Tasmania.
5 Arrives at Melbourne, Victoria.
6 Opens Captain Cook bicentenary exhibition at National Gallery of Victoria.
7 Swan Hill and Portland, Victoria.
8 Sets sail for Brisbane, Queensland.
10 Calls at Port Kembla, N.S.W., and visits Newcastle and Broadmeadow.
11 Coff's Harbour, N.S.W.
12 Arrives in Brisbane.
14 Assembly of school-children at Lang Park football ground, Brisbane.
15 Leaves by air for Longreach and Mt. Isa, Queensland.
16 Broadcasts from the Royal Flying Doctor Service base at Mt. Isa; leaves by air for Mackay and sails for Barrier Reef.
20 Day in Townsville, North Queensland

21 Visits underwater observatory at Green Island.
22 Re-enactment of landing of Capt. Cook at Cooktown Jetty.
23 Arrives at Cairns and flies to Canberra; reception at Parliament House.
25 Attends Anzac Day parade, inaugurates Capt. Cook memorial at Regatta Point on Lake Burley Griffin, and unveils model of H.M.S. *Endeavour* at National Library.
26 Opens carillon on Aspen Island to mark Canberra's golden jubilee.
28 Flies from Canberra to Sydney, via Armidale, N.S.W.
29 Re-enactment of landing of Capt. Cook at Botany Bay.
30 Arrives by train at Orange, N.S.W., flies to Richmond, and visits Parramatta.

May
1 Returns to Sydney.
2 Concert at Sydney Town Hall.
3 Opens Sydney Airport's new national terminal before leaving for London.

14th . . . Royal family greeted in Brisbane

Seventy-two people, including 56 boys, killed in landslide which strikes a sanatorium at Plateau d'Assy in the French Alps.

17 To relief of millions watching on TV, capsule of crippled Apollo 13 safely splashes down in Pacific at 7.7 p.m. B.S.T., $3\frac{1}{2}$ miles from recovery ship, *Iwo Jima*, and only five seconds late.

18 $A9$\frac{1}{2}$ million Australian tanker, *Amanda Miller*, being built in Whyalla shipyards, is burnt out in biggest fire in shipyard's history.

19 **Sunday** The three Apollo 13 astronauts are re-united with their families in Honolulu, and decorated with the Medal of Freedom by Pres. Nixon.

20 Opening of trial of former Labour M.P. William Owen (Jan. 15, March 6) on charges under the Official Secrets Act.

21 Police fire on hundreds of Black Power supporters in Port of Spain, Trinidad, when they loot and set fire to shops.
Alan Rudkin retains his British bantamweight title, and also takes the vacant bantamweight championship of British Empire, by defeating Johnny Clark.

22 British and U.S. warships converge on Trinidad, where fighting is taking place between government troops and mutineers who have seized army's main arsenal and are attempting to enter Port of Spain.
In S. African general election, National party loses nine seats to United party, but maintains overall majority of 70 seats.

23 President Duvalier's palace at Port-au-Prince, Haiti, is shelled by mutinous crews of coastguard vessels.
Gang armed with shotguns snatch diamonds worth £128,000 from two postmen in Hatton Garden, London.

24 China launches 380-lb. earth satellite.
During first papal visit to Sardinia for over 17 centuries, stones are hurled at cars in Pope's procession.
Gambia is proclaimed a republic, and Sir Dauda Kairaba Jawara, the prime minister, named as country's first president.
Collapse of Trinidad's army mutiny; 80 soldiers are in custody.

27 Soviet Union puts eight satellites into earth orbit from single rocket.
Three policeman injured in clash with Black Power supporters at Oxford Circus, London.

28 Rhodesia's Christian churches unite in defiance of Ian Smith's new race laws.
At Highbury, London, Arsenal win European Fairs Cup by defeating Anderlecht (Belgium) 3–0 (4–3 on aggregate).

29 Italian labour unions stage nationwide 24-hour strike, stopping trains, closing schools, and suspending postal services.
In replay at Manchester, Chelsea win F.A. Cup by defeating Leeds 2–1 after extra time.
In Vienna, Manchester City win European Cup-Winners' Cup by defeating Gornik (Poland) 2–1.

30 Pres. Nixon announces that U.S. and S. Vietnamese troops have launched attack in Cambodia against h.q. controlling Communist military operations in S. Vietnam.

19th . . . Pres. Nixon congratulates Apollo 13 crew on their safe return

May

**Taurus (The Bull),
April 21–May 20**

1 Left-wing students join in demonstration in Grenoble, France, after sentence on militant shopkeepers' leader, Gerard Nicoud, has been confirmed by appeal court.

2 Twenty thousand young people stage week-end demonstrations in New Haven, Connecticut, U.S.A., against murder trial of Bobby Seale, chairman of Black Panther party, and eight other Panthers.

4 National Guard troops open fire on student demonstrators from Kent State University, Ohio, U.S.A., protesting against extension of Vietnam war into Cambodia, killing four of them.

5 While student protests take place throughout the country, Pres. Nixon promises that U.S. troops will leave Cambodia within seven weeks.
Petrol bombs thrown into U.S. embassy in London.

6 William Owen acquitted on all eight charges under Official Secrets Act (April 20), but will have to pay costs.

Jack Lynch, prime minister of Irish Republic, announces that he has called for resignations of Neil Blaney, minister of agriculture and fisheries, and Charles Haughey, minister of finance, who are alleged to have been involved in the illegal importation of arms.
In Milan, Feyenoord (Netherlands) win European Champions' Cup by defeating Celtic 2–1 after extra time.

7 U.S. troops claim capture of vast arms base in Cambodia.

8 While over 200 U.S. colleges and universities are reported to be closed and hundreds more at virtual standstill because of student strikes and demonstrations, Pres. Nixon states that he agrees with students' aims, and again promises that all U.S. troops will be withdrawn from Cambodia by the end of June.
Tens of thousands of Australians stage peaceful demonstrations in all State capitals, calling for withdrawal of foreign forces from Vietnam and for the repeal of Australia's National Service Act.

9 Pres. Nixon drives to Lincoln Memorial in Washington just before 5 a.m. and talks to students spending the night there. At least 100,000 students gather round White House, which is protected by 3,000 police and 5,600 troops, while 28,000 other troops stand by.
In London, 60 policemen are hurt when 5,000 demonstrators against U.S. action in Cambodia attempt to break into U.S. embassy.
In Rome, Vicente Saldivar (Mexico) regains world featherweight championship by defeating champion Johnny Famechon (Australia) on points.
At Wembley, Castleford retain Rugby League Cup by defeating Wigan 7–2.

10 **Sunday** Bomb attempts, preceded by telephone warnings, made against Spain's Iberia Airlines in

Geneva, Frankfurt, Amsterdam, and Heathrow: no one is hurt.
Demonstrations against U.S. action in Cambodia in W. Berlin, Paris, Helsinki, Toronto, and Vancouver.
During 16 hours of violence in Belfast, troops use tear gas to control mobs.

11 Wife of Mikis Theodorakis (April 13) announced to have escaped from Greece with her two children.
U.K. National Farmers' Union begin week-long ban on marketing of livestock.
Tornado hits Lubbock, Texas, U.S.A., killing at least 23, injuring 1,000, and rendering 10,000 homeless.

12 Israeli tanks and infantry invade Lebanon to attack Arab guerrilla bases on Mount Hermon.
In Augusta, Georgia, U.S.A., six negroes are shot dead in guerrilla warfare in which 50 stores are ruined or heavily damaged; 1,000 National Guardsmen patrol streets.
Harry Houghton and Ethel Gee, sentenced in 1961 to 15 years' imprisonment for their part in Portland spy case, are freed on parole.
Inauguration of first Swiss atomic power station at Bexnau-Döttingen.
At Wembley, Mark Rowe becomes British and Commonwealth middleweight champion by defeating Les McAteer.

13 At Hiroshima, police sharpshooter kills man who has hijacked Japanese ferry, *Prince Maru*, and forced it to make 17-hour voyage on Japan's Inland Sea.
Two members of first Japanese Everest expedition reach summit.

14 Syria-supported Palestinian guerrillas enter Lebanon.
Pre-election violence in Santo Domingo, Dominican Republic, has caused death of 28.
Pierre Trudeau, prime minister of Canada, arrives in Brisbane, Australia, on official visit.

4th . . . Kent State University students shot dead

22nd . . . Children killed in Israeli school bus

15 S. Africa is expelled from Olympic Games movement, the first nation ever to be so treated.

Two negro students shot dead and others wounded when police open fire at predominantly negro Jackson State College, Mississippi.

In Italy, 600,000 municipal and provincial office workers return to work after wage agreement, but secondary school teachers strike over pay and promotion prospects.

16 Israeli air force planes sink Egyptian destroyer and missile vessel at naval base of Ras Banas on W. shore of Red Sea.

Pres. Joaquin Balaquer and his Reformist party win Dominican Republic elections.

18 CS gas used by troops after petrol bombs are thrown in Ardoyne, N. Ireland; bank premises are shattered and three soldiers injured.

Bernadette Devlin, M.P., receives three-month prison sentence, suspended for two years, and is fined £20, for her interruption of Omagh Urban Council meeting last week.

Italian printers go on nation-wide seven-day strike.

David Ben Gurion resigns seat in Israeli parliament.

Fire in Press-Association-Reuter building in Fleet Street, London, stops all news services for three hours.

19 U.K. Cricket Council states that it has decided that S. Africa tour will take place as planned, but that in all future tours teams must be selected on multi-racial basis.

20 It is announced that Rumania's worst floods for centuries have killed at least 200 people, left thousands homeless, and destroyed vast areas of farmland.

Millions of Italians, including farm-hands, railwaymen, civil servants, and firemen, continue to strike, and in Taranto 30 people are injured in fighting between strikers and non-strikers outside a navy shipyard.

Pierre Trudeau, prime minister of Canada, leaves Australia at end of five-day visit.

21 E. German chancellor Willi Stoph arrives in W. Germany for second round of talks with Willy Brandt, but leaves after a day of demonstrations and wrangling.

One hundred thousand construction workers demonstrate in New York in support of U.S.A.'s Vietnam war effort.

22 Children and adults killed and injured when Israeli school bus is attacked by bazooka rocket on Israeli–Lebanese border. Israelis shell four Lebanese border villages in retaliation.

S. Africa cricket tour of Great Britain cancelled by Cricket Council, at request of James Callaghan, Home Secretary.

23 Fire seriously damages the entire half-mile length of the Britannia railway bridge across the Menai Strait.

24 **Sunday** In Milan, over 2,000 right-wing demonstrators clash with police following public meeting held by Neo-Fascist party (MSI).

25 **Bank Holiday** Rumania's flood situation worsens with further torrential rain; deaths known to be 200, and 250,000 are homeless.

England's soccer captain, Bobby Moore, accused of stealing a gold bracelet from hotel jewellery shop in Bogotá, Colombia, is ordered to remain in the city.

Nearly 100 "skinheads" arrested at seaside resorts in U.K.

26 Russian TU-144 airliner flies at 1,336 m.p.h.—twice the speed of sound—at height of nearly 10 miles, for several minutes.

General strike in Lebanon in protest against lack of protection of border villages against Israeli attacks

Police in Rome use tear gas to break up student demonstration protesting against Nato council meeting in the city.

27 British cars take nine out of first 10 places at finish of *Daily Mirror* World Cup Rally in Mexico City.

28 Bobby Moore is provisionally released, and rejoins England team in Guadalajara, Mexico.

Neil Blaney and Charles Haughey, ministers in Republic of Ireland government, are arrested on arms charges (May 6).

U.S. charges two officers of attempted murder of unspecified number of people in Vietnam in June 1969.

In Paris 1,000 left-wing students fight running battles with police in protest against jailing of two Maoists.

State opening of Rhodesia parliament by Pres. Clifford Dupont.

29 Former Argentine president, Lt.-Gen. Pedro Atamburu, is kidnapped by "National Liberation" commandos, who say he will be shot within two hours.

30 British team reach summit of Himalayan peak Annapurna, by previously unclimbed south-face route.

31 **Sunday** More than 30,000 people die in earthquake which devastates northern Peru; town of Huaras, with population of 80,000, suffers 5,000 deaths.

Israel admits heaviest single-day casualties since 1967 war, sustained during two Egyptian commando raids.

Arkle, famous steeplechaser, is put down, aged 13.

Opening ceremony of World Cup football tournament in Mexico City.

25th . . . Rumania suffers devastating floods

31st . . . Peruvian town erased by earthquake

June

Gemini (The Twins),
May 21–June 20

1 It is announced that a Russian Soyuz 9 spacecraft is in earth orbit, carrying Col. Andrian Nikolayev (pilot) and Vitaly Sevastyanov (flight engineer).

Arab rockets fired from Jordan hit school in Israeli town of Beit Shean, killing a girl and wounding eight other people.

2 Peruvian mountain city of Yungay obliterated by flooding following earthquake; deaths estimated at 50,000.

River Danube, swollen to three times normal size, floods all 18 ports along its course in Rumania. Rumanian deaths from flooding remain at 200, in 39 provinces.

Collapse of part of a £3½ million bridge construction at Pembroke Dock, Milford Haven, kills four men.

Bruce McLaren, racing driver, killed when car at Goodwood explodes.

3 Four Israelis killed and 28 injured in Arab rocket and artillery attacks on Beison and Tiberias.

Derby won by Nijinsky, ridden by Lester Piggott.

4 In Dublin, Kevin Boland, former Irish minister of local government, is expelled by 60 votes to 11 from Fianna Fail party.

Tonga becomes independent after 70 years as British protectorate.

8 Argentine armed forces' commanders claim to have deposed Pres. Juan Carlos Ongania.

Eight Czechs hijack a Czech airliner on flight from Karlovy Vary to Prague, and force crew to fly it to Nuremberg, W. Germany.

In Kirghizia, near Russian border with Chinese province of Sinkiang, 5,000 homes are destroyed by earthquake.

9 King Hussein's car comes under hail of bullets in Amman street battle between Palestinian guerrillas and Jordanian troops.

Pres. Juan Carlos Ongania of Argentina submits to military leaders of yesterday's coup.

10 Strike by printing unions shuts down all national newspapers printed in London and Manchester.

Seventy hostages are held in Amman hotels by Arab guerrillas in retaliation for artillery attack by Jordanian army on Palestinian refugee camps.

11 Fighting between Palestinian guerrillas and Jordanian army in Amman continues, and Pres. Nasser appeals to both sides to stop fighting. P.F.L.P. (Popular Front for the Liberation of Palestine) threatens to blow up hotel in which foreigners are held hostage.

In Rio Janeiro, W. German ambassador to Brazil, Herr Ehrenfried von Holleben, is kidnapped, his captors demanding release of political prisoners held by Brazilian government in exchange for his life.

Mr. Vorster, S. African prime minister, arrives in Paris on his European tour, after "private visit" to Portugal and Spain.

Many injured in train collision 27 miles west of Copenhagen.

Australia's second-biggest money robbery in Melbourne: $A289,000 payroll stolen from a security company carrying it for Ford Motor Co.

12 Evacuation by air of 500 foreign nationals from Amman begins, and hostages are released from two hotels, as fighting dies down.

Israeli troops enter Egypt north of Kantara and blow up two miles of Egyptian front-line fortifications.

British newspaper strike settled by increased pay offer.

It is now considered certain that ex-Pres. Aramburu of Argentina (May 29) is dead; note is found saying that he was shot at 7 a.m. on June 1.

13 Brazilian government agrees to release 40 political prisoners in exchange for W. German ambassador von Holleben (June 11).

W. German government accepts Oder–Neisse line as W. border of Poland.

World's largest restaurant—Lyon's Coventry Street Corner House, London—closes, the site having been sold for £7,400,000.

U.S. retains Wightman Cup, 4–3.

14 **Sunday** Nearly half W. German population go to polls in three Länder—North Rhine-Westphalia, Lower Saxony, and Saarland. Results show substantial gains for Christian Democrats.

Argentine military junta names Brig.-Gen. Roberto Marcelo Levingston as new president.

Mr. Vorster, S. African prime minister, arrives in Geneva for a meeting of S. African ambassadors in Europe.

In N. Ireland, Catholic youths throw stones and bottles at a parade of 1,000 Orangemen in Dungiven.

First British national newspapers published since June 9.

In quarter-finals of World Cup, England is defeated by W. Germany 3–2 after extra time, the full-time score being 2–2.

15 At 2.35 p.m. B.S.T. Nikolayev and Sevastyanov in Soyuz 9 (June 1) break space endurance record of 330 hrs 35 mins set up by Borman and Lovell in Gemini 7 in Dec. 1965.

Paris paralysed by 24-hour strike of bus and Metro workers.

Rumanian president, Nicolae Ceausescu, arrives in Paris on his first state visit to a W. European country.

Further floods in S. Hungary and N.W. Rumania. Rumanian flood casualty figures now given as 200 dead, 250,000 evacuated, 11,000 houses destroyed and 30,000 damaged.

Opening of Sharon Tate murder trial in Los Angeles: Charles Manson, another man, and three young women are accused.

U.S. Supreme Court allows, by 5–3 vote, conscientious objection to military service on deeply held moral or ethical (as well as religious) grounds.

16 Israeli helicopter-borne task force lands deep inside Syria and shells an army camp 44 miles N.E. of Damascus, the capital.

Forty released Brazilian political prisoners arrive in Algiers, and W. German ambassador to Brazil is set free unharmed.

Martial law for a month imposed in Istanbul, as 50,000 workers demonstrate against new labour union law.

First negro mayor of Newark, N.J., U.S.A., is elected.

17 U.S. Congress approves Civil Rights Bill giving the vote to 18-year-olds in 1971.

18 U.K. general election, resulting in surprise victory for Conservative party with overall majority of 31 seats.

W. German parliament vote to reduce voting age from 21 to 18 as from next general election—expected in 1973.

19 Harold Wilson resigns, and Edward Heath becomes U.K. prime minister.

Soyuz 9 and crew land safely, after orbiting the earth for 17 days, 16 hrs, 59 mins.

20 James Bailey, aged 40, sails into Old Harbour, Rhode Island, after a 45-day solo Atlantic crossing in home-made catamaran.

21 **Sunday** Train loaded with compressed gas is derailed at Crescent City, Illinois, and two-thirds of the town of 600 inhabitants is destroyed by fire.

Tony Jacklin (G.B.) wins U.S. Open golf championship, the first Englishman to take the title for 50 years.

Brazil wins World Cup by defeating Italy 4–1.

Piers Courage, British racing driver, killed in Dutch Grand Prix at Zandvoort.

22 Sir Alec Douglas-Home, U.K. foreign secretary, removes embargo on arms sales to S. Africa imposed by Labour government.

Over a million Japanese attend country-wide rallies in protest against renewal of U.S.–Japan security treaty.

N. Ireland Court of Appeal dismisses appeal by Bernadette Devlin, M.P., against sentence of six months' imprisonment imposed on her at Londonderry in December 1969.

José (Urtain) Ibar (Spain) retains European heavyweight title by defeating Jurgen Blin (W. Germany) on points in Barcelona.

23 U.K. cabinet decides to send 4,000 more troops to N. Ireland in next seven days.

Transport and General Workers Union call national dock strike from July 14, in support of claim for higher national basic rate of pay.

Oldrich Cernik, former Czechoslovak prime minister, resigns from ministry of technical and investment development.

24 It is announced that Alexander Dubcek has been dismissed from his post as Czechoslovak ambassador to Turkey.

25 Cambodian government decrees general mobilization and makes all men and women between 18 and 60 eligible for call-up.

William Rogers, U.S. secretary of state, announces peace proposals to end the Arab–Israeli conflict.

26 Riots in Londonderry, Armagh, and Belfast following re-arrest of Bernadette Devlin, M.P.

Alexander Dubcek is expelled from Czechoslovak Communist party.

27 Five people shot dead in Belfast riots; injured include 10 soldiers and over 200 civilians (54 by shooting).

28 **Sunday** Gen. Sir Ian Freeland, G.O.C. N. Ireland, announces that any civilian seen carrying or using firearms is liable to be shot without warning. More troops are flown to N. Ireland.

Jean-Jacques Servan-Schreiber, Radical party secretary-general, is elected to French national assembly as member for Nancy.

29 Last U.S. troops leave Cambodia, 24 hours ahead of Pres. Nixon's promised deadline.

Pres. Nasser of Egypt arrives in Moscow for talks with Russian leaders on Middle East conflict.

Harold Wilson re-elected leader of U.K. Labour party.

Tens of thousands of Italian-Americans rally in New York in protest against alleged harassment by the F.B.I. and department of justice.

Mrs. Caroline Thorpe, wife of British Liberal party leader, Jeremy Thorpe, killed in car crash.

30 Reginald Maudling, U.K. Home Secretary, starts two-day visit to N. Ireland. Under legislation placed before Stormont parliament, rioters, looters, and gelignite bombers now face automatic prison sentences ranging from one month to five years.

In Luxemburg, Anthony Barber, chancellor of the duchy of Lancaster, opens negotiations for British entry to the European Economic Community.

16th . . . Forty Brazilian political prisoners freed

19th . . . Edward Heath enters Number 10

21st . . . Tony Jacklin with U.S. Open trophy

25th . . . Cambodia starts general mobilization

July

**Cancer (The Crab),
June 21–July 20**

1 Reginald Maudling ends his two-day visit to N. Ireland. In Belfast scuffles between troops and crowds follow rehearsal by 6,000 Orangemen for July 12 and 13 processions.

Hanoi rejects Pres. Nixon's appeal for ''just peace'' in Indo-China.

2 Announcement that insufficient evidence has been found to send former Irish minister of agriculture, Neil Blaney, to trial for importing arms illegally into the Republic.

Prince of Wales leaves for Canada. After visits to Toronto, Ottawa, and Eganville, he will join royal family at Frobisher Bay on July 5.

3 Over 1,500 British troops under fire in Belfast; they return fire and four civilians are killed and 50 people injured. Army imposes curfew in area.

Comet airliner, en route from Manchester to Costa Brava, crashes into mountain near Barcelona, killing all 112 people aboard.

Eight Cambridge students sentenced to imprisonment for their part in riotous anti-Greek demonstration at hotel (Feb. 13).

In Wimbledon's longest-ever women's singles final of 2½ hours, Margaret Court beats Billie-Jean King, 14–12, 11–9.

4 Troops searching Falls Road area of Belfast, following night of rioting and violence, discover arsenal of weapons.

John Newcombe wins men's singles title at Wimbledon, beating Ken Rosewall, 5–7. 6–3, 6–2, 3–6, 6–1.

5 **Sunday** Thousands of women carrying food supplies march into Falls Road area of Belfast after curfew is lifted, in protest against alleged food shortages caused by curfew, and in defiance of ban on parades.

At Phom Penh, Prince Norodom Sihanouk of Cambodia is sentenced to death in his absence for crimes against the state.

All 108 people aboard Air Canada DC-8 airliner killed when it crashes in flames on landing at Toronto airport.

Bomb explodes in Dublin Castle, and in Paris bombs damage British and Irish Republic embassies.

Racing driver Jochen Rindt wins French Grand Prix.

6 Dr. Hillary, minister for external affairs in the Irish Republic, pays secret visit to Falls Road area of Belfast in order to ''relax tension''.

Signor Mariano Rumor, Italian prime minister, on eve of threatened general strike, announces his government's resignation.

7 Sir Alec Douglas-Home describes Dr. Hillary's secret visit yesterday to Belfast as ''a serious diplomatic discourtesy'', and invites him to call at Foreign Office in London.

Roman Catholic Mass is held in precincts of Canterbury Cathedral—the first for 400 years—to mark the 800th anniversary of the death of St. Thomas Becket.

8 Roy Jenkins is chosen deputy leader of U.K. Labour party.

9 Continuing dispute over increase in basic minimum wage leads Transport and General Workers' Union to call official dock strike for July 14.

Airport workers in Jersey join 1,000 local government staff already on unofficial strike, shutting down airport at 5 p.m.

10 State of emergency declared in Jersey after 1,200 government manual workers refuse to end their strike.

Bjarni Benediktsson, Icelandic prime minister, his wife, and his 4-year-old grandson are killed in fire which destroys his summer residence.

12 **Sunday** Strike of public employees in Jersey ends.

Thor Heyerdahl arrives at Bridgetown, Barbados, at end of 57-day voyage across Atlantic in his papyrus boat Ra 2.

13 National dock strike in U.K., due to start tomorrow, is deferred after new pay offer by employers.

Day of marching by 100,000 Orangemen in N. Ireland ends almost without incident, after biggest internal security operation ever mounted in U.K.

14 About 29,000 U.K. dockers go on unofficial strike, in defiance of trade union's decision to defer stoppage.

15 By 48 votes to 32, U.K. dockers' delegates decide to strike, in spite of trade union's plea to accept employers' offer as basis for negotiations.

It is announced that 2,000 troops are to be withdrawn from riot duty in N. Ireland.

16 At Meadowbank, Edinburgh, Duke of Edinburgh opens Commonwealth Games, in which 1,900 representatives of 41 countries will participate.

Thirty-one people injured after bomb explosion in Belfast bank.

Fourth consecutive night of rioting in Reggio Calabria, Italy, in protest against the naming of Cantanzaro instead of Reggio as capital of Calabria region: one person killed and 300 injured.

Prince Charles and Princess Anne arrive in Washington for three-day stay at White House.

Members of three Australian trade unions now on strike bring all container cargo terminals to a halt.

17 Body found at remote farmhouse 240 miles west of Buenos Aires is identified as that of ex-President Aramburu of Argentina (May 29, June 13).

Troops in N. Ireland are issued with new type of rubber bullet to be fired by pistols used for CS gas.

Jochen Rindt wins British Grand Prix at Brand's Hatch, after first being disqualified.

19 **Sunday** 448 passengers and 271 crew from Norwegian cruise liner *Fulvia* rescued unharmed after eight hours adrift in lifeboats when the vessel catches fire 140 miles off Canary Islands. (The ship sank on July 20.)

20 Death of Iain Macleod, chancellor of the exchequer in new U.K. government, aged 56.

West German airliner carrying 95 passengers lands safely in N.E. Spain after mid-air collision with Piper Club aircraft in which all three occupants are killed.

Queen's Visit to Canada's North-West Territories and Manitoba

5 Arrives at Frobisher Bay, Baffin Island, airport; cuts the first sod for new cathedral.

7 Visits Arctic Eskimo settlement in Resolute Bay, and Yellowknife, capital of the Territories.

9 Banquet in Yellowknife; and broadcast to the people.

11 Open-air gathering in the Pas Indian reservation, Manitoba.

15 Addresses Manitoba legislature in Winnipeg.

16 Returns to Great Britain.

22 Arab guerrillas hijack Olympic Airlines Boeing-727 en route from Beirut to Athens with 47 passengers and eight crew, and force promise from Greek government that seven of their colleagues, imprisoned for attack on Israeli jet, will be freed on Aug. 22.

Settlement of oil refinery dispute in Melbourne, Australia, ends two-week strike, which has caused severe petrol shortage.

23 Egypt announces acceptance of U.S. Middle East peace initiative.

N. Ireland government imposes six-month ban on all parades.

M.P.s flee from Commons debating chamber after two CS gas canisters are thrown from Strangers' Gallery; a man is later taken into custody.

24 Fire causes damage estimated at £250,000 in St. Ives, Cornwall, town centre.

25 Anthony Barber is named as new U.K. chancellor of the exchequer.

Emilio Colombo (Christian Democrat) agrees to try to form new Italian coalition government.

Last day of 1970 Commonwealth Games in Edinburgh.

26 **Sunday** Armed riot police fire from top of church on members of Black Power organization in Houston, Texas, killing group's leader, wounding six others, and making about 70 arrests.

It is revealed that Sultan Said bin Taimur, 60-year-old ruler of Muscat Oman, has been deposed by his son, Sheikh Qabus bin Said.

28 Geoffrey Rippon, former minister of technology, is named to succeed Anthony Barber as chancellor of duchy of Lancaster in charge of E.E.C. negotiations, and John Davies takes Mr. Rippon's place.

At free "rock" concert in Grant Park, Chicago, thousands of youths fight with police; three youths are shot and wounded, 100 people, including 24 policemen, are injured, and 148 arrests are made.

29 U.K. national dock strike called off by 51 votes to 31 at trade union delegate conference; the 46,500 dockers will return to work on Aug. 3.

30 Population of Reggio Calabria unanimously support a general strike called by "agitation committee" demanding recognition of Reggio as capital of Calabria region.

175 people killed and 120 injured in earthquake in N.E. Iran.

31 Israel accepts U.S. Middle East peace proposals, with a truce of at least three months confined to her front with Egypt.

In Belfast, a 19-year-old youth holding a petrol bomb is shot dead by army marksman after three warnings that troops will open fire if fire-bombing continues. Water cannon used to break up subsequent rioting in Roman Catholic area.

Peter Thomas, secretary of state for Wales, is chosen chairman of Conservative party, succeeding Anthony Barber.

Daniel Mitrione, U.S. security expert advising Uruguayan police, is kidnapped in Montevideo by terrorist Tupamaro organization.

Her Majesty's Theatre, Sydney, Australia, first opened in 1927 as Empire Theatre, is destroyed by fire.

13th . . . Orange Day parades in Northern Ireland

16th . . . Prince and Princess at Washington

15th . . . Start of U.K. dockers' strike

16th . . . Wild rioting in Reggio Calabria

August

**Leo (The Lion),
July 21–August 21**

2 **Sunday** Troops use CS gas against continuing demonstrations and rioting in N. Ireland; government increases from £10,000 to £50,000 reward offered for information leading to conviction of anyone using explosives. Belfast women and children besiege an army barracks.
World's first hijacking of Boeing-747 jumbo jet, carrying nearly 400 people, when armed man diverts plane to Cuba.

3 In Belfast 25 soldiers are injured in riots between Catholics and Protestants. An 8 p.m. curfew on sale of alcohol is imposed.

4 Sixth successive night of rioting in Belfast.
160 m.p.h. Hurricane Celia hits parts of S. Texas, killing 32 people, destroying 9,000 houses, and doing estimated £25 million damage to crops.
Nine people are killed and 29 injured by gale in S.W. France.

6 New Italian government, under premiership of Emilio Colombo (July 25), is sworn in at Rome.

7 U.S. secretary of state William Rogers announces 90-day cease-fire between Israel and Egypt, starting at 11 p.m. B.S.T.

Thunderstorm in which 1·7 inches of rain falls in 30 minutes causes traffic chaos, floods five theatres, and disorganizes underground and bus services in London.

9 **Sunday** Seventeen policemen injured when about 200 Black Power demonstrators march through West London in protest against police treatment of coloured people in the district. Nineteen people are arrested.
When Peruvian Lockheed Electra airliner explodes and crashes after take-off at Cuzco on flight to Lima, all but one of 99 passengers and crew are killed.
Earth tremor, lasting about four seconds, shakes five counties of northern England.
At least 50 passengers killed when two trains crash head-on near Bilbao, Spain.

10 Daniel Mitrione (July 31) is found shot dead in car in Montevideo suburb.
Torrential rain in Austria, where six people are killed and many injured in ensuing floods; in Belgium; and in Germany, where the Oberammergau passion play is halted when water pours into hall.

11 Major Chichester-Clark, prime minister of N. Ireland, receives unanimous support from his government to continue programme of reforming policies.
In N. Ireland two policemen are killed by booby-trap in stolen car.
Floods in Czechoslovakia and central Switzerland after torrential rain and hailstorms.
Boiler-room fire cripples P and O liner *Oriana* an hour after she leaves Southampton at start of world cruise.

12 Russo-German non-aggression treaty signed in Moscow by Willy Brandt, W. German chancellor, and Mr. Kosygin, Soviet prime minister.
In spite of ban, the Londonderry Apprentice Boys' march takes place:

2,000 marchers clash with troops on Craigavon bridge in hand-to-hand fighting, and troops use CS gas; Dr. Conor O'Brien, Irish Republic Labour M.P., is injured at Belfast rally.

13 Israel government complains that Egypt has violated cease-fire agreement by moving Russian Sam missiles closer to Suez Canal.

14 Second phase of SALT talks ends in Vienna.
Full diplomatic relations between Yugoslavia and the Vatican resumed after a break of 18 years.

15 Eighteen-year-old U.S. marine found guilty at Da Nang, S. Vietnam, of murdering 15 Vietnamese women and children in February 1969.
Heaviest rainfall recorded in N. Ireland since 1927 floods Belfast and puts 12,000 telephones out of order.

16 **Sunday** Bomb planted in London West End cinema seriously injures young couple who unknowingly take it away in their car.
Storms cause havoc in U.K.: many ships and yachts in distress, flooding in parts of Scotland and in N. Ireland.

17 London offices of Spanish Iberia Airways damaged by explosion.
Explosion wrecks third floor of department of zoology building at Cambridge University, causing damage estimated at £100,000.

18 After weeks of controversy, 67 tons of U.S. nerve gas is sunk in old ship scuttled in water 3 miles deep in Atlantic, 283 miles off Cape Kennedy, Florida.
Colombia's police intelligence service says that it has concrete proof of Bobby Moore's innocence of alleged theft of bracelet (May 25).

19 Court of Appeal quashes conviction of one of eight Cambridge students (July 3), but dismisses appeals of others. Riotous behaviour inside and outside court.

2nd . . . British troops fight Belfast women

15th . . . Belfast women bless British troops

20 Colombia's Superior Court exonerates Bobby Moore on bracelet theft charge (Aug. 18).

Four killed and several injured when a French and S. African submarine collide off French naval base at Toulon.

Hurricane kills 10 people in Canadian city of Sudbury, Ontario, and renders thousands homeless.

Floods in Midlands, N.E. Wales, and parts of S. England, and for second day in Scotland.

21 In S. Japan, Typhoon Anita kills 20 and injures 300, damages 56,000 houses, and renders over 4,500 homeless.

In Martinique, West Indies, Hurricane Dorothy kills 24 people and injures hundreds.

24 Fierce battle when police try to clear hundreds of "hippies" from Dom Square, Amsterdam, which they had turned into an encampment.

Armed detectives seize five sub-machine guns and about 5,000 rounds of ammunition at Hilton Hotel, London, and later arrest an American and two Lebanese.

Over 20,000 British car workers laid off because of unofficial pay strike at GKN-Sankey components factory, Wellington, Shropshire, and at Dunlop tyre works, Coventry.

Wedding of Peter Sellers and Miranda Quarry at Caxton Hall, London.

25 Middle East peace talks begin at U.N. headquarters, New York.

Industry throughout Australia comes to virtual halt as 750,000 workers strike against Federal budget.

26 Large dumps of guns, ammunition, bombs, and booby-traps seized in London and S. England during nation-wide action by regional crime squads; several men and women are arrested.

Robert Porter, N. Ireland minister for home affairs, resigns, and Prime Minister Major Chichester-Clark takes over his duties.

Opening of pop music festival at Freshwater, Isle of Wight.

27 In U.S.A., Women's Liberation Front march through major cities with banners saying "We Demand Equality", to mark 50th anniversary of women's suffrage.

28 In Amman, Jordan, Palestinian guerrillas' organization rejects Middle East peace proposals which have been accepted by King Hussein.

Fighting between guerrilla commandos and government troops.

Five thousand strikers at GKN-Sankey factory (Aug. 24) unanimously reject offered pay increase and continue unofficial stoppage.

At least six people drown in floods in Eastern Cape Province, S. Africa, after 96 hours of continuous rain, but in northern Cape Province and Orange Free State fodder is moved in by army to relieve animals suffering from severe drought.

30 **Sunday** Split between General Dayan, Israeli defence minister, and members of cabinet over reaction to alleged Egyptian violations of Middle East cease-fire.

31 **Bank Holiday** Armed Amboinese separatists seize Indonesian ambassador's residence at The Hague, Holland, and hold his family hostage for 12 hours, after shooting a policeman dead.

Police and troops in Belfast collect hand grenades, ammunition, pistols, a shot gun, materials for home-made bombs, and nearly 500 petrol bombs from houses in the city.

Freshwater, Isle of Wight, pop festival closes.

9th . . . Black Power marches in West London

18th . . . U.S. nerve gas sunk in Atlantic

26th–31st . . . Quarter of a million attend "pop" festival at Freshwater, Isle of Wight

September

Virgo (The Maiden),
August 22–September 22

1 King Hussein of Jordan escapes unhurt when convoy of cars is ambushed on way to Amman airport.
Concorde 002 makes its first supersonic flight over land.

3 U.S. state department publicly accuses Egypt of violating Middle East cease-fire agreement by moving Russian missiles nearer to Suez Canal.
French finance minister Giscard d'Estaing announces a 5 per cent reduction in direct income tax next year and introduction of P.A.Y.E. system to stop tax evasion.
Pres. Suharto of Indonesia arrives at The Hague on state visit reduced to one day by recent anti-Indonesian demonstrations.

4 Israeli troops invade Mount Hermon area of Lebanon, attacking Palestinian guerrilla bases.
Presidential election in Chile is narrowly won by Marxist Salvador Allende.
Pres. Suharto arrives in Bonn, W. Germany, on three-day state visit.
Natalia Makarova, Russian ballerina in London with the Kirov ballet, is given asylum in the U.K.

5 Following deaths of 200 in last few days in Jordan in confrontation between guerrillas and army, both sides order a stand-down.
Jochen Rindt, 1970 world champion racing driver, is killed in practice at Monza, Italy.

6 **Sunday** Three transatlantic airliners are hijacked by Palestinian guerrillas of the P.F.L.P. group: two (a Swissair DC-8 and a TWA Boeing-707) are made to fly to "Revolution Airfield", 45 miles from Amman, and one (a Pan Am Boeing-747 jumbo jet) to Beirut and then to Cairo. A fourth hijacking (of an El Al Boeing-707) fails, a male hijacker being killed by El Al security guards and a girl (Leila Khaled) overpowered, and

the aircraft makes emergency landing at Heathrow, where the girl is taken into custody.
Fighting between Palestinian guerrillas and Jordanian army recurs, at Ma'an, S. Jordan. Israeli troops withdraw from Lebanon.
Israel suspends participation in U.N. Middle East peace talks because of Egyptian breach of cease-fire agreement.

7 Hijacked Pan Am jumbo jet is destroyed with explosives at Cairo airport, minutes after passengers and crew have left it. In the two airliners in Jordan, non-Israeli women and children are released, but 174 passengers and crew are held hostage, the guerrillas demanding release by 3 a.m. on Sept. 10 of three Arabs held in W. Germany, three in Switzerland, and Leila Khaled.
Renewed fighting in Amman between guerrillas and Jordanian army.

8 Israel formally withdraws from U.N. Middle East peace talks.
Opening at Lusaka, Zambia, of third conference of heads of state of 25 "non-aligned" countries.

9 BOAC VC-10 airliner, flying from Bombay to London, is hijacked by P.F.L.P. guerrillas and flown to Beirut and on to Revolution Airfield; 105 passengers and 10 crew are held hostage for release of Leila Khaled. Hostages in Jordan now number 289 in airliners and 127 in Amman hotels. Fighting between guerrillas and army in Amman, Irbid, and Ma'an brings Jordan to brink of civil war.
U.S.A. decides to sell 16 Phantom jet fighter-bombers to Israel to help maintain arms balance in Middle East.

10 The five countries whose nationals are held hostage in Jordan decline guerrillas' terms, and the latter extend their ultimatum.
World's biggest jewel robbery in Boston, Mass., where £1½ million worth of gold, silver, and diamonds is taken from the strong-room into which thieves have tunnelled from next-door premises.
Wedding of André Previn and Mia Farrow at Hampstead, London.

11 Pres. Nixon orders a 6th Fleet task force to sail to within air-strike distance of Jordan.
Armed men steal £20,000 worth of silver bars from a bullion lorry at Enfield, N. London.
Tornado strikes Venice area and Padua, injuring 245 and killing 41, including 27 passengers of a ferry on Venice lagoon which is sucked into air and dropped back into water. 1,000 buildings in Venice lose their roofs.
Typhoon in N. Philippines kills 140, and renders 15,000 homeless in Quezon City.

12 The three hijacked airliners at Revolution Field, Jordan, are blown up, 15 minutes after last hostages have been removed. All but 54 hostages are allowed to go free.
Russian unmanned satellite Luna 16 is launched at 2.26 p.m. B.S.T., to "explore the Moon and near-Moon space".

13 **Sunday** Severe fighting in Irbid, N. Jordan, between guerrillas and army.
Closing day of Expo 70 at Osaka, Japan, the most successful world fair yet held, and the first ever to make a profit.

14 Start of Old Bailey trial of Trinidad-born Indian brothers Hosein for murder of Mrs. Muriel Mackay (Feb. 10).
At midnight 350,000 members of Union of Automotive Workers in U.S.A. go on strike against General Motor Corporation.

15 One hour after peace agreement with Palestinian guerrilla movement (P.L.O.) the Jordanian government resigns.
Mr. Vorster, prime minister of South Africa, offers non-aggression pacts to all black African states.
A just-completed eight-storey block of flats at Almeria, Spain, crumbles and falls, entombing 52 men.
In Sydney, N.S.W., thieves steal four million doses of stimulant drug amphetamine, worth $A2 million on black market.

16 King Hussein of Jordan appoints a completely military government and hands his own command of forces to Field-Marshal Habes al-Majali. Palestinian guerrillas appoint Yasser Arafat their c.-in-c. and readmit P.F.L.P. to their central committee. Renewed fighting in Amman.
Two of three men arrested after discovery of arms at London Hilton Hotel (Aug. 24) are released; third is remanded.
Mrs. Golda Meir, Israeli prime minister, flies to Washington for talks with Pres. Nixon.

17 Full-scale civil war breaks out in Jordan; army attacks guerrillas with tanks, artillery, and rockets in Amman, Irbid, and Zarqa. Fate of 54 hijacked hostages still in guerrilla hands is unknown.
Shop stewards at GKN-Sankey car components factory, Wellington, Shropshire, vote 51–37 in favour of ending the six-week unofficial strike that has crippled the British car industry and made 40,000 workers idle.
Russian spacecraft Luna 16 (Sept. 12) is in Moon orbit, circling 70 miles above surface.

18 Major offensive by Jordanian army against guerrilla supply routes in north of Jordan.

Mass meeting of 5,000 workers at GKN-Sankey factory accept yesterday's shop stewards' vote and agree to return to work on Monday, Sept. 21.

Many thousands demonstrate in all Australian State capitals against Vietnam war; 300 arrested.

19 Sixth successive day of renewed rioting and street battles with police at Reggio Calabria (July 16 and 30).

20 **Sunday** Syrian forces invade northern Jordan to assist Palestinian guerrillas; they are defeated in battle with Jordanian army and retreat back to Syria.

French prime minister, Jacques Chaban-Delmas, wins Bordeaux by-election with over 63 per cent of votes.

Luna 16 soft-lands on Moon in Sea of Fertility.

21 Leaders of eight Arab countries hold summit meeting in Cairo.

Luna 16, having gathered samples of Moon rock, blasts off automatically from Moon to return to Earth.

23 Journalists "imprisoned" in hotel by fighting in Amman since Sept. 17 are flown to Cyprus. Heavy fighting continues in Jordanian civil war.

24 Pres. Nimeiry of Sudan heads a mediation mission to Amman in attempt to end civil war in Jordan.

Luna 16, with its sample of Moon rock, safely lands by parachute in Kazakhstan.

25 King Hussein and Yasser Arafat accept cease-fire proposals of mediation mission. Sixteen of the 54 hijacked hostages are released from Palestinian refugee camp outside Amman.

U.S.A. defence department reveals indications of construction of a Russian submarine base at Cienfuego, Cuba.

Zambia's worst mine disaster, at Mufulira copper mine, where collapse of workings kills 90 men.

26 Thirty-two more of the 54 hijacked hostages are released by Palestinian guerrillas.

In Belfast rioting after football match, CS gas and rubber bullets are used, and 39 policemen, 17 soldiers, and over 100 civilians are injured.

In Puerto Rico, Ken Buchanan (Scotland) wins world lightweight championship by defeating Ismael Laguna (Panama).

27 **Sunday** At Cairo summit meeting of leaders of Arab countries, King Hussein and Yasser Arafat sign agreement to end Jordanian civil war.

Pres. Nixon arrives in Rome at start of eight-day, five-country tour of Europe.

After three days of the worst bush fires ever known in Southern California, 220,000 acres have been devastated, 289 houses destroyed and thousands more damaged.

28 In Cairo, Pres. Nasser of Egypt dies of a heart attack, immediately after closing ceremony of Arab leaders' summit meeting that ended the Jordanian civil war.

Pres. Nixon is received in audience by the Pope.

29 Remaining six hijacked hostages in Jordan are released.

Start of series of strikes by local authority manual workers in U.K., with withdrawal from work of dustmen, sewage workers, ambulance drivers, etc., in parts of London; improved basic rate of pay is demanded.

30 Now that all the hijacked hostages have been released and flown out of Jordan, Leila Khaled (Sept. 6), the three Arabs held by W. Germany, and the three held by Switzerland are all freed and flown to Cairo.

Pres. Nixon arrives in Belgrade for three-day visit to Yugoslavia.

Local authority workers' strike spreads to many more London districts and to Midlands.

12th . . . Hijacked airliners blown up by Palestinian guerrillas at "Revolution Airfield"

14th . . . General Motors strike

20th . . . Chaban-Delmas wins

27th . . . Hussein and Arafat agree to end civil war

October

**Libra (The Scales),
September 23–October 22**

1 In Cairo, four million demonstrate hysterical grief at Pres. Nasser's funeral.

Parade of tens of thousands in Peking in celebration of 21st anniversary of founding of Communist China.

2 Pres. Nixon arrives in Madrid for talks with Gen. Franco.

Strike by local authority manual workers involves all London's sewage treatment works, and similar works in various parts of the U.K.

3 Pres. Nixon visits England for a few hours, during which he lunches with Mr. Heath and the Queen at Chequers, and then flies to Dublin.

4 **Sunday** About 20,000 demonstrators for military victory in Vietnam march through Washington.

Millions of gallons of untreated sewage pour into rivers Thames and Avon, as consequence of continued strike by local authority manual workers.

Distribution of national newspapers starts to return to normal in Greater London, following provisional pay settlement yesterday.

Tony Densham, British engineer, sets up new land speed record of 207·6 m.p.h., driving a Dragster powered by a supercharged 6·3-litre Ford engine.

5 In Montreal, four armed terrorists of the Front de la Libération du Québec (F.L.Q.) kidnap British trade commissioner James Cross, demanding $500,000 ransom and release of fellow separatists in prison for criminal acts.

Acting Egyptian president Anwar el Sadat unanimously nominated by Arab Socialist Union to succeed Pres. Nasser (approved by National Assembly on Oct. 7).

Pres. Nixon visits Timahoe, co. Kildare, home of his Irish Quaker ancestors, sees Pres. de Valera, and leaves Dublin for Washington at end of his European tour.

Worst bush fires in memory in S. France kill 11, and destroy dozens of homes and cars. Bush and timber fires in California have since Sept. 25 devastated half a million acres and killed 14 people.

6 Pres. Pompidou of France arrives in Moscow for important talks.

Following proclamation of Gen. Juan Torres as president of Bolivia, air force planes attack presidential palace in La Paz.

Canadian government refuses to meet ranson demands made by kidnappers of James Cross (Oct. 5).

The brothers Hosein sentenced to life imprisonment for murder of Mrs. Muriel McKay (Sept. 14).

7 In a television address Pres. Nixon proposes a cease-fire in Vietnam, Laos, and Cambodia, and an international peace conference to settle S.E. Asia conflict.

Gen. Torres drives right-wing rebels from La Paz, Bolivia, and sets up military government.

Prince of Wales leaves on a 25,000-mile tour of the Pacific and Caribbean.

8 In Genoa, flooding kills at least 18 and injures hundreds.

9 Cambodia is proclaimed the Khmer republic.

Pres. Torres of Bolivia appoints 17-man left-wing cabinet.

British customs post on N. Ireland–Eire border at Mullan, 14 miles from Enniskillen, is blown up.

10 Quebec Labour Minister Pierre Laporte is kidnapped by F.L.Q. terrorists, who threaten to murder him on Oct. 12 unless their demands are met.

The Prince of Wales represents the Queen at Fiji's independence ceremony, ending 96 years of British rule.

11 **Sunday** Letter from Pierre Laporte to Quebec premier Bourassa urges agreement to ransom demands.

Troops seal off Bogside, Londonderry, and disperse mobs with CS and tear gas and rubber bullets: 40 soldiers and six police hurt during weekend.

12 Pres. Nixon announces additional withdrawal of 40,000 U.S. troops from Vietnam by Christmas 1970.

Reggio Calabria paralysed and cut off from rest of Italy on sixth consecutive day of rioting.

Mob of youths stone troops in Londonderry and throw petrol bombs at police station.

13 In Moscow, M. Pompidou and Pres. Podgorny sign a protocol including provision for regular half-yearly consultations by the foreign ministers of Russia and France.

Negotiations with Quebec terrorists for release of Pierre Laporte and James Cross.

After bomb explosions at Reggio Calabria, Italian government decides to reconsider its choice of Catanzaro as capital of region of Calabria.

14 Police using bulldozers, mobile cranes, and pneumatic drills force their way through barricades at Reggio Calabria, and free the port from rioters.

15 A 382-ft. section of the £18 million new West Gate bridge across the river Yarra at Melbourne collapses, killing 31 and injuring 18, 11 others being reported missing.

16 Canadian government invokes War Measures Act, suspending civil liberties; police and troops comb Montreal and Quebec and arrest 250 separatists and sympathizers.

Republic of Ireland introduces immediate statutory price and income control. Until Dec. 31, 1971, there will be a limit of 6 per cent on pay increases, and firm control of prices.

Italian government moves 3,000 troops into Reggio Calabria as fighting between police and demonstrators continues.

At Inglewood, California, Chucho Castillo becomes world bantamweight champion by defeating Ruben Oliveras on technical knockout.

17 Central and Quebec governments broadcast offer to F.L.Q. kidnappers of safe conduct to Cuba if Mr. Laporte and Mr. Cross are returned unharmed.

Anwar el Sadat takes oath of office as president of Egypt.

Explosion destroys world's largest aircraft, the U.S. military transport plane C5A Galaxy, during refuelling at Marietta, Georgia.

18 **Sunday** Pierre Laporte found murdered in boot of taxi at St. Hubert military airport, Montreal.

Reggio Calabria almost normal after three months of insurrection; about 500 people have been charged with disorderly behaviour, and 116 gaoled.

19 Egypt agrees to extension of 90 days to present cease-fire with Israel, provided that talks are resumed at U.N.

End of six-month-long strike by bank employees in Eire, but banks remain closed until backlog of work is cleared.

In Philippines, Typhoon Kate kills 13 (29 missing) and renders hundreds homeless.

20 Funeral of Pierre Laporte in Montreal, after thousands file past his body lying in state.

Farm workers in England and Wales receive wage increase for one hour per week less work.

Prince of Wales arrives in Bermuda for 350th anniversary of first meeting of island's parliament.

Bodies of five people found in swimming pool at burning home of eye surgeon at Santa Cruz, California; there is another multiple killing near Paso Robels, 120 miles away.

21 Bernadette Devlin, M.P., released from Armagh prison (May 18).

Deaths in Philippines, struck by typhoons Joan and Kate, reach 759; half a million are homeless.

22 Prince of Wales leaves Bermuda for Barbados.

23 Collision with tanker *Allegro* sets tanker *Pacific Glory* ablaze from stem to stern off Isle of Wight: five seamen are killed, and eight missing.

Necessary two-thirds majority for official national strike is not obtained in ballot of Britain's 292,000 miners.

Charles Haughey, Eire's former finance minister, and three other men are acquitted of gun-running by Dublin court.

James Frazier, 24-year-old mechanic, arrested for murder of three adults and two children at Santa Cruz, California (Oct. 20).

London is now littered with piles of refuse as result of local authority manual workers' strike. In Tower Hamlets, troops move refuse designated as ''health hazard''.

New land speed record of 622·407 m.p.h. set up at Bonneville salt flats, Utah, by Gary Gabelich of California in *Blue Flame* rocket car.

24 Greek athlete Christos Pepenicolaou sets new world pole-vault record of 18 ft. 0½ in. at Athens.

25 **Sunday** Fire extinguished on *Pacific Glory*, and attempts made to prevent the spilling of her 77,000 tons of crude oil.

Gen. Schneider, Chilean army c.-in-c., dies of wounds received in ambush by right-wing extremists.

Fifteen Black Panthers surrender to police after 9-hour siege in Detroit building following shooting of two policemen.

Fighting at Trafalgar Square, London, meeting in protest against proposed sale of arms to S. Africa causes injury to 26 policemen and 65 arrests.

26 Admiralty writ issued to prevent *Allegro* from leaving British waters, but she is released next day on £1½ million security bond.

In England and Wales, almost 65,000 local authority manual workers are now on strike.

At Atlanta, Georgia, Muhammad Ali (Cassius Clay) in his first match for 3½ years defeats Jerry Quarry in third round.

27 Anthony Barber, U.K. chancellor of the exchequer, announces first instalment of new government's economic programme, including reductions in income tax and other taxes, changes in various health and welfare charges, and other economies, expected to save a total of £330 million a year.

National executive of National Union of Mineworkers by 13 votes to 11 recommend acceptance of National Coal Board offer of pay increases of up to £3 a week.

28 Tanker starts to pump oil from stranded *Pacific Glory*.

29 South Africa's ruling National Party loses several seats in provincial election.

30 Delegates representing 35,000 miners from 52 South Wales pits decide to strike in protest against N.C.B.'s pay offer. In Yorkshire some 19,000 miners from 14 pits, and in Scotland 2,000 miners, are already on unofficial strike.

Demonstrators throw stones, eggs, and bottles at Pres. Nixon's car and entourage at election rally in San Jose, California.

31 Fourteen soldiers injured in Belfast rioting during which gelignite bombs and machine-guns are used. Fighting also breaks out in London-derry.

About 1,000 people in Hackney, London, protesting about uncollected rubbish near their homes, pile it in road and block traffic.

1st . . . Frenzied grief at Nasser's funeral in Cairo

3rd . . . The Nixons lunch with the Queen and Mr. Heath

15th . . . Collapse of section of Melbourne's new bridge

23rd . . . Strike leaves London streets piled with garbage

November

**Scorpio (The Scorpion),
October 23–November 22**

1 **Sunday** Death of 142 young people in fire at dance hall in St. Laurent-du-Pont, near Grenoble, France. Only about 30 escape, some badly burned, two of whom die later.

Zygfryd Wolnick, Polish deputy foreign minister, arriving on state visit to Pakistan, is among four people killed at Karachi airport when they are deliberately run down by airport baggage van; driver is later charged with murder.

2 Violence again erupts in Belfast after hundreds protest against higher bus fares, and stones and petrol bombs are thrown as troops move in.

Miners' unofficial pay strike spreads as pits in S. Wales and Scotland join those already on strike in Yorkshire; over 48,000 men are on strike.

SALT talks re-open in Helsinki.

3 In U.S. mid-term Congressional elections Republicans fail to win control of the Senate, and lose ground in House of Representatives; Democrats capture many State governorships.

Mass funeral of 142 victims of St. Laurent-du-Pont fire (Nov. 1) during which prayers are said by Moslem, Jewish, Roman Catholic and Protestant ministers.

In U.K. severe gales with gusts of well over 100 m.p.h.—one of 150 m.p.h. is recorded in the Isle of Man—and heavy rain, cause widespread damage.

4 Egypt announces her acceptance of 3-month extension of Middle East cease-fire.

Mrs. Golda Meir arrives in England for talks with British government.

The Queen opens first meeting of the new General Synod of Church of England.

5 Municipal manual workers' strike called off, following publication of report of inquiry by Sir Jack Scamp, which proposes basic pay increases little less than trade union's demand.

First 3-month cease-fire agreement between Israel and Egypt expires at midnight.

6 Two bombs explode in Tel Aviv's central bus station, killing one and injuring 35 others.

Emperor Haile Selassie arrives in Rome on 4-day state visit to Italy.

7 In Rome, Carlos Monzon (Argentina) wins world middle-weight championship by knocking out holder, Nino Benvenuti (Italy), in 12th round.

8 **Sunday** In *Land* election in Hesse, West Germany, Social Democrats obtain 45·9 per cent, Christian Democrats 26·4 per cent, and Free Democrats 10·1 per cent of the vote, so strengthening the Social Democrat–Free Democrat central coalition government.

Announcement that the Earl of Cromer, former governor of the Bank of England, is to replace John Freeman as Great Britain's ambassador in Washington.

9 Death by heart failure of Gen. de Gaulle at Colombey-les-Deux-Églises, aged 79.

Number of miners on unofficial strike in U.K. rises to 174,000 at 119 pits.

British aircraft carrier *Ark Royal* collides with Russian destroyer observing R.A.F. and naval exercises in eastern Mediterranean 350 miles from Malta; several Soviet sailors are missing.

Emperor Haile Selassie calls on the Pope.

10 Russian unmanned spacecraft, Luna 17, is launched towards the Moon at 3.44 p.m. B.S.T.

At Wembley, Henry Cooper (Great Britain) regains European heavyweight championship by defeating Jose Urtain (Spain).

11 Most wanted British criminal, John McVicar, who broke out of security wing of Durham prison in 1968, is recaptured in Blackheath, S.E. London.

Announcement that troops in Belfast are being reduced by 1,000, leaving 1,500 on duty there, and 6,000 in N. Ireland as a whole.

12 Burial of Gen. de Gaulle in churchyard of Colombey-les-Deux-Églises is attended only by relatives, parishioners, and members of Order of the Liberation. Memorial service in Notre Dame, Paris, is attended by heads of state and political leaders.

National executive of National Union of Mineworkers decide, by 14 votes to 9, with one abstention, to hold a pithead ballot on the wages agreement with the National Coal Board, and to call for a national delegate conference.

Nation-wide 36-hour strike in Argentina against government's economic policies starts at noon; during demonstrations one man is killed and 210 people are arrested.

The Archbishop of Canterbury starts tour of South Africa.

13 In worst natural disaster of the century, 150 m.p.h. cyclone and 30-ft.-high tidal wave sweep over islands in Ganges delta, East Pakistan, causing deaths later officially estimated at 175,000, and unofficially at about half a million.

3rd . . . Mass funeral, conducted by ministers of four denominations, of 142 young victims of French dance-hall fire

Syrian army, led by defence minister Lt.-Gen. Hafiz Asad, takes control of country, putting head of state and prime minister, Dr. Nureddin-al-Atasi, under house arrest.

More violence at Reggio Calabria where 3,000 students, accusing government of indecision about Calabrian capital, clash with police.

Leaders of 17,000 Yorkshire miners at 22 pits vote to return to work.

14 DC-9 of Southern Airways crashes in West Virginia killing all 75 people on board; they include 37 members of a local university football team.

15 Sunday Archbishop of Canterbury preaches at multi-racial rally of 20,000 people in Cape Town, S. Africa.

Egyptian prime minister, Dr. Mahmoud Fawzi, submits resignation of his government and is given mandate by Pres. Anwar Sadat to form a new one.

Luna 17 (Nov. 10) reported to be circling the moon.

16 Virtual collapse of unofficial miners' strike in England and Wales, as 41,000 return to work, and Scottish miners' leaders order 18,000 to do so.

Twelve people killed and 71 wounded in clashes between Jordanian forces and Palestinian guerrillas in northern Jordan.

17 Court martial of Lt. William Calley, accused of killing 102 of 175 S. Vietnamese civilians at My Lai ("Pinkville") on March 16, 1968, opens at Fort Benning, Georgia.

Luna 17 lands an eight-wheeled automatic vehicle, Lunokhod 1, loaded with scientific equipment, on the surface of the Moon.

Banks in Irish Republic re-open for first time in 6½ months.

18 Foreign ministers of W. Germany and Poland initial in Warsaw draft treaty giving *de facto* recognition of Oder-Neisse line.

Pope's Tour of the East and Australia

November

26 Leaves Rome and visits Teheran, Iran.

27 Visits Dacca, E. Pakistan, and arrives at Manila, Philippine Islands.

29 Leaves Manila and visits Pago Pago, Western Samoa.

30 Arrives at Sydney, N.S.W.

December

3 Leaves Sydney and arrives at Jakarta, Indonesia.

4 Leaves Jakarta and visits Hong Kong and Colombo, Ceylon.

5 Returns to Rome.

In Detroit, Joe Frazier retains world heavyweight title by knocking out Bob Foster in second round.

19 At least 38 people killed, more than 300 injured, and thousands left homeless in Philippines by typhoon Patsy.

20 U.S. helicopter landings 20 miles from Hanoi, N. Vietnam, in abortive attempt to rescue American prisoners of war.

In Vienna, Ralph Charles (England) wins European welterweight championship by knocking out holder, Hans Orsolics (Austria).

21 U.S. war-planes resume large-scale bombing of N. Vietnam. Sgt. David Mitchell, first soldier to be put on trial in connection with alleged My Lai ("Pinkville") massacre, is acquitted of charges of assaulting 30 Vietnamese civilians with intent to kill.

22 Sunday Pres. Sekou Touré of Guinea says his country has been invaded by foreign mercenaries from neighbouring Portuguese Guinea. After day of street fighting, government troops regain control of the capital, Conakry.

Archbishop of Canterbury conducts a multi-racial service at the City Hall, Durban, at which over 2,000 Anglicans celebrate Communion.

24 International relief operations in East Pakistan now fully under way, with arrival of Royal Navy flotilla sent with supplies from Singapore.

Viscount Hall, first chairman of the U.K. Post Office Corporation, is dismissed by the minister of posts and telecommunications.

25 Nearly 50,000 U.K. post office workers stage 24-hour protest strike over dismissal of Lord Hall.

Yukio Mishima, Japanese author and actor, commits hara kiri after leading an abortive raid on army h.q. in protest against disappearance of Japan's former military might.

26 U.K. miners delegate conference vote to accept National Coal Board's £38 million pay offer, giving them £3 a week increase, and to postpone their demand for a £20 a week minimum wage.

Rhodesian government publishes draft bill aimed at introducing a form of residential apartheid.

A thousand London School of Economics students barricade street outside the college in protest against road accident which occurred there yesterday.

27 At Manila airport, Bolivian artist, Benjamin Mendoza y Amor Flores, dressed as a priest, attempts to stab the Pope, but is seized and arrested.

28 Three thousand members of the N. Ireland Civil Rights Association stage march, in defiance of ban on parades, in Enniskillen, co. Fermanagh, and 700 soldiers, 650 policemen, and 28 helicopters are called out to disperse them.

12th . . . Funeral of General de Gaulle at Colombey-les-Deux-Églises

27th . . . Attempt to stab the Pope

December

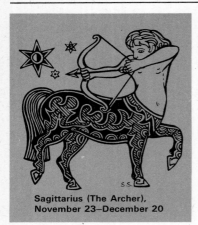

**Sagittarius (The Archer),
November 23–December 20**

1 Dr. Michael Ramsey, Archbishop of Canterbury, at end of 3-week tour, calls on S. Africa's white Christians to rid country of "racial inhumanity and injustice".

Indian mobs alleged to have raided East Pakistan enclave on West Bengal border, killing 300 men, women, and children. Pakistan government later (Dec. 6) lodged protest with India.

2 Eugen Beihl, West German honorary consul in San Sebastian, Spain, kidnapped by Basque nationalists; message from E.T.A. separatist organization says his fate depends on that of 16 Basques going on trial tomorrow for murder and treason.

In Brisbane, first Test match between England and Australia ends in draw.

3 Trial by military court of 16 Basque separatists opens in Burgos, and demonstrations and strikes take place throughout Spain.

James Cross is freed after house where he is held is surrounded by police and troops.

In Syracuse, N.Y., Billy Backus (U.S.A.) wins world welterweight championship by defeating Jose Napoles (Mexico).

4 Eire government announces reactivation of Special Powers Act and orders preparation of internment camps, following evidence of a kidnapping conspiracy linked with plans for armed bank raids.

Merger of giant tyre companies of Dunlop and Pirelli announced in London and Milan.

Armed gang hijacks van containing £105,000 gold and diamond bullion at Hyde Park Corner, London.

5 Gen. Franco orders 3-month state of emergency in Basque province of Guipuzcoa, centred on San Sebastian.

James Cross is flown to Great Britain.

In Rome, Carlos Duran (Italy) wins back European middleweight championship by outpointing Tom Bogs (Denmark).

6 **Sunday** Huge explosion shatters Humble Standard oil refinery at Linden, New Jersey, U.S.A.; possibility of sabotage is investigated.

Fighting in Amman between Palestine guerrillas and Jordanian army.

7 Pakistan's first general election: in West, Zulfikar Ali Bhutto's People's party wins 94 of the 138 seats; in East, Sheikh Mujibur Rahman's Awami League wins 149 out of 153 seats. Voting in nine cyclone-devastated constituencies delayed until early 1971.

As overtime ban and work-to-rule by U.K. power-station staff begins over pay dispute, power supplies are cut, trains run late, road chaos occurs at traffic lights, hospitals cancel operations, and large areas are blacked out for hours.

Swiss ambassador, Giovanni Bucher, is kidnapped in Rio de Janeiro, Brazil, by terrorists demanding release of 70 political prisoners.

Muhammad Ali (Cassius Clay) defeats Oscar Bonavena on technical knock-out in 15th round at Madison Square Garden, New York.

8 In Warsaw, Willy Brandt, W. German chancellor, and Josef Cyrankiewicz, Polish prime minister, sign draft treaty recognizing the Oder–Neisse line.

U.K. electricity supply situation worsens; at evening peak, reduction in supplies is 31 per cent; in Northern Ireland, state of emergency is declared.

Twenty-four hour strike, officially estimated to involve 350,000 people, against Industrial Relations Bill, takes place throughout U.K.; no national newspapers are published.

In Brussels, Great Britain takes major step towards entering Common Market by accepting proposals giving her 5 years for adjustment to Market's industrial and agricultural rules.

9 Leaders of power-station workers refuse appeal of secretary for employment to take their pay dispute to arbitration; in Northern Ireland, government prohibits industrial use of electricity.

In Burgos, trial of 16 Basque separatists ends; announcement of judgment is postponed.

10 Railways in U.S.A. brought to a standstill by national strike over pay claim; Congressional order makes strike illegal, and three of four unions involved order their members to return to work.

Demonstration by thousands of Parisians and Spanish exiles in Paris in support of Basque nationalists.

Earthquake in northern Peru and southern Ecuador causes 74 deaths, with at least 1,000 injured.

11 At least 32 people killed when Budapest–Berlin express crashes near Brno. At least 13 killed when passenger trains collide at Sacavem, Portugal.

13 **Sunday** Both sides in U.K. power-station dispute agree to submit to public court of inquiry.

Three hundred intellectuals and artists, including Joan Miro, stage sit-in in monastery near Barcelona, in protest against trial of Basque nationalists.

Announcement that Olrich Cernik, prime minister of Czechoslovakia under Alexander Dubcek, has been expelled from Communist party.

14 Power-station workers' unions decide to return to normal working as "act of faith", pending findings of court of inquiry.

Fifteen trade unions representing 60,000 airline and airport workers start work-to-rule at U.K. airports, following rejection of their demand for $4\frac{1}{2}$ per cent pay rise from Jan. 1, 1971.

15 Industrial Relations Bill passes second reading in House of Commons by 324 votes to 280, with support of Liberals and abstention of at least two Labour back-benchers.

Edward Heath leaves for Ottawa for talks with Mr. Trudeau.

Place de l'Étoile in Paris is renamed Place Charles de Gaulle.

16 Reports of two days of rioting over food and fuel price increases in north Polish ports of Gdansk (former Danzig), Gdynia, and Sopot; tanks in action, six said to be dead and many injured, and 6 p.m.–5 a.m. curfew imposed.

South Korean ferryboat in Korean Strait sinks, killing all but 12 of 320 on board.

17 Poland's premier, Josef Cyrankiewicz, issues "shoot to kill" orders in attempt to quell riots in Gdansk and Gdynia; up to 300 reported killed and several hundred wounded.

Gen. Franco addresses tens of thousands demonstrating their loyalty to him outside the royal palace in Madrid.

Edward Heath arrives in Washington from Ottawa, for talks with Pres. Nixon.

U.K.'s 27,000 firemen declare nation-wide work-to-rule after their trade union turns down $5\frac{1}{2}$ per cent wage offer.

18 Tens of thousands of demonstrators battle with soldiers and police, supported by tanks, in Szczecin (former Stettin), Poland.

Pres. Nixon and Edward Heath end 2 days of talks with informal 2-hour session at Camp David.

19 Six hundred workers evacuated from Nevada underground nuclear test range following accident which leads to massive leak of radiation.

20 **Sunday** Wladyslaw Gomulka, Poland's Communist party leader, is replaced as first secretary by Edward Gierek, and four other members of 12-man Politburo are relieved of their posts.

At Naha, Okinawa, 2,000 rioters set fire to 80 vehicles at U.S. air base and burn guard-room and an office, after U.S. driver has knocked down and injured an Okinawan; troops use tear-gas; at least 25 people are injured, and 21 arrested.

Arab guerrillas fire two Russian-made rockets into heart of Jerusalem, damaging buildings.

21 Following yesterday's conciliatory broadcast by Edward Gierek, many shipyard workers return to work in Gdansk and Gdynia, but strikes continue in Szczecin.

22 Franz Stangl, war-time commandant of Treblinka extermination camp, sentenced to life imprisonment by Düsseldorf court for murder of at least 400,000 Jews.

23 In government reshuffle in Poland Marshal Marian Spychalski replaced as head of state by Josef Cyrankiewicz, and Piotr Jaroscewicz, former deputy prime minister, becomes prime minister; the latter pledges a 2-year "freeze" in food prices.

Regis Debray, French Marxist writer, freed from Bolivian prison, after serving 3 years of 30-year sentence imposed for his support of Che Guevara.

24 At Leningrad trial of 11 people for attempted hijacking of plane at Smolny airport on June 15, two (both Jews) are sentenced to death. World-wide protest marches are held over next 7 days.

25 **Christmas Day** Eugen Beihl, W. German diplomat (Dec. 2), is released.

British banker, David Johnston, is freed by Chinese after 28 months' detention.

28 Israeli forces reported to have wiped out buildings used as terrorist centre in north Lebanon, in one of biggest raids for several months.

Three principal suspects in the kidnapping and murder of Pierre Laporte (Oct. 18) arrested at St. Luc, 25 miles south of Montreal.

In Leningrad, sentences of 4–15 years in labour camps are passed on remaining nine persons (seven of them Jews) accused of hijacking attempt.

Death sentences for murder and treason announced for six of 16 Basque nationalists tried at Burgos, and jail terms ranging from 12 to 16 years on nine others. One woman is acquitted.

Israel ends her 4-month boycott of U.N. peace talks, suspended on Sept. 6.

29 As world protest against sentences on Basque nationalists continues with attacks on Spanish embassies in Brussels, Paris, and Rome, over 20,000 workers in San Sebastian and 3,000 in Bilbao go on strike. Gen. Franco holds meeting of council of the realm.

30 Gen. Franco commutes death sentences on six Basque nationalists to 30-year prison sentences.

Troops help to rescue estimated 10,000 people trapped in Rhône valley in one of worst snow storms in memory; at least 12 reported killed.

31 Death sentences imposed in Leningrad on Jewish hijackers (Dec. 24) are commuted to 15 years' imprisonment.

Edward Gierek, Poland's new leader, announces financial aid worth £128 million, in form of wage increases, family allowances, and pensions, for over 5 million people hardest hit by food price increases.

Seventy people feared killed and another 130 seriously hurt when two trains collide near Ardekan, Iran.

Explosion in mine near Hyden, Kentucky, U.S.A., kills 38 miners.

6th . . . Explosion at oil refinery in New Jersey

8th . . . Strike against U.K. Industrial Relations Bill

10th . . . Another severe earthquake in Peru

26th . . . Tel Aviv protest over sentences on Russian Jews

The Tower of the Sun, one of the figures in the Symbol Area, was 198 ft. high.

Progress and Harmony at

EXPO 70

BRENDA RALPH LEWIS

To DESIGNERS, architects, planners, engineers, and other artists limited by the demands of finance, utility, and public opinion, a world exposition is like time out of school. Here they can put aside for a while the controversies of professional life and let the imagination free. This is certainly what happened at Expo 70, Asia's first world exposition, which was held near Osaka, Japan, from March 15 to September 13.

The 815-acre site was a wonderland of invention, a place where no one was surprised to find walls made of mirrors, fences of slender blue rods, roofs floating on cushions of air, domes decorated with a tracery of steel, a yellow and red tunnel resembling a mammoth caterpillar, or a stylized tree made of steel lattice-work topped by 35,000 electric light bulbs. These were only some of the many spectacular ideas to be found in Expo's 122 air-conditioned pavilions, which were visited by 64,218,770 people, including 1,700,000 non-Japanese and a daily average of 300,000 Japanese.

About 35 pavilions represented commercial and industrial interests, such as gas, chemicals, automobiles, or telecommunications. The rest were national pavilions, where countries from the five major continents put their talents and achievements on display. Some of the smaller countries shared facilities, as in the joint pavilion of Costa Rica, Cyprus, Dominica, Ecuador, El Salvador, Malta, Mauritius, Monaco, and Nicaragua. At the other end of

the scale, Russia emphasized its size—it occupies one seventh of the world's land surface—by producing the biggest pavilion at Expo: a procession of red and white steel panels marching up to a peak topped by a hammer-and-sickle. This even dwarfed the 412-ft. Expo tower, which was built to provide a panoramic view of the site.

Expo's Noble Themes

Expo 70 was set in an excavated bowl at the foot of the Senri Hills, in the heart of the Kansai district. Here idealism had its head for a brief six months as the nations came together to express their interpretations of Expo's theme: "Progress and Harmony for Mankind." Under this hopeful heading were four supporting themes: fuller enjoyment of life, depending on peace and mutual respect between peoples; getting the most out of the world's natural resources; using science to improve life without dehumanizing it; and better understanding between the nations.

With these ideas in mind, the organizers of Expo 70 placed at its centre an elaborate Symbol Area, which included a Tower of the Sun, 198 ft. high, flanked by two smaller towers symbolizing Motherhood and Youth. Within the Tower of the Sun, visitors could view a panorama of human history, from the prehistoric past to what it is evidently hoped will be a trouble-free future. Within the Symbol Area was the Festival Plaza, over 7,000 yards square, with three main theatres for live entertainment. Here, too, was the Expo Museum of Fine Arts, containing some 750 exhibits.

The Symbol Area was covered by a spectacular transparent roof, the world's largest, which experts have hailed as a considerable triumph for chief Expo architect Kenzo Tange. As Expo publicity put it, Tange and his fellow designers "envisaged the site as a great tree with the Symbol Area as its trunk; the moving sidewalks extending from it in four directions are the branches, the plazas and service centres the leaves; and the pavilions flowers of imagination and originality".

Practical Lessons for the Future

However, seeing the continuing furore of the international scene, it is rather more logical to assume that Expo's practical rather than moral pointers to the future will become reality first. In this, Expo 70 fulfilled a recognized function of exhibitions of its type. Modern architecture and town planning have constantly taken cues from these melting pots of ideas.

The glimpses of the future at Expo were not, of course, uniformly welcome. Several pavilions earned themselves uncomplimentary nicknames. The Australian pavilion, with its blunt-ended column rearing forward to support a structure of steel webbing and flanged base panels, was dubbed "a dinosaur eating spaghetti". The U.S.A. pavilion, a modest translucent dome, was called "a giant burrowing turtle", and those who viewed the Expo

A feature of the opening ceremony was this huge robot, accompanied by dancing children.

scene with horror rather than delight called the whole site "the valley of monsters".

But whatever view one takes, Expo will have an inevitable influence on the shape of things to come. For example, the advantages for housing offered by the "Vinyshell" method of dome

In contrast, children and others from a hundred nations twirled flower-decorated hoops as they processed past the Emperor of Japan, who opened Expo.

construction were on display at Expo in the American pavilion and that of the Fuji Group, which represented 36 Japanese industrial and commercial firms. The American dome was made of synthetic rubber sheets filled with a layer of concrete and supported by compressed air. The Fuji structure—the "mammoth caterpillar" already referred to—consisted of 16 air beams with several domes, each nearly 40 ft. wide. Depending on size, the time taken to inflate a dome was between 10 and 20 minutes. An example of speedy building was also offered by the prefabricated sections of the Takara pavilion, another representative of industry and commerce. This consisted of a framework of steel piping with steel-covered capsules plugged into it. The three-storey structure took only a week to assemble.

Novelties in Transport

Town planners and those responsible for the transport of the future could glean plenty of ideas from Expo 70. The exposition was laid out on the grid street system, with the main pavilions placed on the perimeter where the crush of visitors would cause least congestion. Around the perimeter, too, there ran an automatically operated monorail, with six trains circling the site in 15 minutes. Rather slower, but no less futuristic, methods of travel were the air-conditioned moving sidewalks, and battery-powered runabout cars. Moving at $1\frac{1}{2}$ miles per hour, the sidewalks were elevated above the display area and were sheltered by a transparent covering. The battery-driven cars, which cost about £1,000 each, could keep going for almost eight hours without recharging, and took visitors round the exposition at up to 5 miles per hour. Visitors could also view Expo in panorama by taking a $7\frac{1}{2}$-minute ride in one of the rotating gondolas, which were slung from ropes placed diagonally across the area.

Expo 70 indicated some of the possible future uses of the computer. Five large electronic computers provided visitors with information about vehicle congestion and how many of the 20,000 car spaces and 1,500 bus spaces were available, and even let them know where to locate mislaid children. The computers handled, too, information about special performance charges at Expo's theatres, and controlled the moving stages. Here, there was accommodation for 18,000 people, and the entertainments they saw were a veritable feast of talent. There were performances by famous orchestras from Berlin, Cleveland, Leningrad, and New York and by the Canadian National Ballet and Bolshoi Opera. There were a song-and-dance spectacular and a special staging of

Expo 70 was remarkable for the bizarre architecture of the various national pavilions. Top of facing page: an aerial view shows a kaleidoscope of multi-coloured dishes, domes, cones, and, of course, pagodas. The British pavilion was patriotically prominent from the air. Bottom left: suitably calm and aquatic, the futurist Dutch pavilion subtly suggested a picturesque Dutch hamlet by a pleasing unity of spire and oblongs. Centre right: unfurled somewhat stiffly, the Russian pavilion ambitiously symbolized the red flag. Bottom right: suspended from a "sky-hook", a swirl of concrete worthy of the nation building the Sydney Opera House, the Australian pavilion comprised a 160-ft.-diameter circular arena and a 230-ft.-long "space tube".

the Ed Sullivan show. As well as these well-established favourites, performances also featured some as yet undiscovered talent, in the form of giant robots. One of them was 70 ft. high, and all were controlled by computer.

Audiences in one of the theatres found themselves in rather unfamiliar surroundings: their seats were wrapped in transparent coloured material, giving them an impression of being suspended in space. Other performances, staged on a floating platform in the middle of a lake, could be observed through a gigantic wall of glass.

Display of National Traditions

Among all this inventiveness, the traditional and familiar were not forgotten. For example, the designers of the Japanese pavilion, which consisted of five precast concrete drums, deliberately set out to imitate the five petals of the cherry blossom: this is a traditional symbol of Japan and was the symbol, too, of the exposition. Traditional, too, was the Japanese garden, which covered 64 acres and incorporated bamboo groves, flowering shrubs, fountains, springs, waterfalls, and groupings of boulders recalling early places of Japanese nature and spirit worship.

Other nations followed the example of the host country in displaying aspects of their own history and culture. The centre-point of the Burmese pavilion, for example, was an ancient royal palace built on to a dragon-headed catamaran. In an annexe built like a Burmese farmhouse, gourmets could eat traditional Burmese food, as a change from the meals served in Expo's 210 other restaurants. The Vietnamese, Malaysian, and Argentinian pavilions also offered traditional national fare.

The Tanzanian pavilion featured four round wooden houses symbolizing a typical African village. The Dutch featured the geographical character of Holland by building their pavilion over water, with the two paths leading up to it placed below surface level. The Hawaiians

"The Generation Gap" at Expo 70

Among the many exhibitions of art at Expo 70 was a collection of sculptures in steel, of which three of the most striking examples are shown here. A dozen avant-garde artists all over the world were invited to submit works to illustrate the theme—"Discontinuity: the Generation Gap". Above is "Birthday Table", by the German Heinrich Brummack, in which the empty chairs may have a sad significance. At left is a gate of polished steel, entitled simply "Work No. 5—'69", by the Japanese Kazuo Yujara. A gate both divides and joins. The apparent scrapheap of machinery, resembling an aircraft in outline (below), is the work of a Swiss, Jean Tinguely, who gave it the title "Kamikaze" (Japanese for "wind of the god"), which was the name given to Japan's suicide dive-bomber pilots during the Second World War. This perhaps symbolizes the gap between the war-time and the post-war generations.

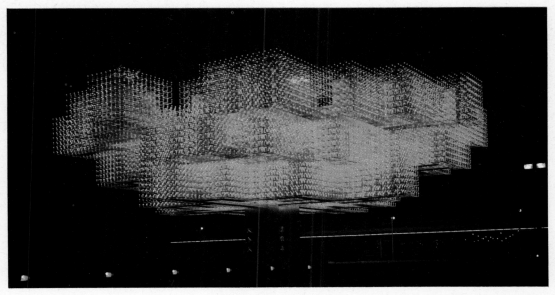

The golden tree of the Swiss pavilion was made glorious at night by the glow of 35,000 electric lamps. This was one of the loveliest of the national buildings.

emphasized the dominating feature of their island—five volcanic mountains—by shaping their pavilion in the form of a volcano. The Ceylonese suspended batik-work banners from the ceiling. The Latin American concourse, built to be shared by nations from that continent, included a Plaza of the Sun, commemorating the sun worship of the Incas. The great white blocks of the Algerian pavilion closely resembled the typical native houses of North Africa.

The British pavilion was no exception. On entering the building, which had room for 2,000 people, visitors first saw the floral emblems of the United Kingdom enamelled on metal—the rose of England, the daffodil of Wales, the thistle of Scotland, and the flax of Northern Ireland. Then, set in a 16-ft. high stainless steel sculpture, there was an illuminated and animated map of Britain as a foreground to a colour-slide audio-visual presentation of the country in all its variety. Next, in the first of four exhibition halls, the British pavilion opened up for visitors a panoply of the past, in the fields of democratic development, literature, science, the arts, industry, and communications. Visitors emerged through glazed corridors into a second and third hall demonstrating Britain's contribution to the progress of mankind, and plans for the world of the future. In the fourth and final hall, a panorama was laid out of what Britain is like today, in its landscape, recreations, family life, sports, and crafts.

All this was contained in a structure made of wall panels of built-up plywood faced with aluminium foil and painted white. Four red box-section masts, each 112 ft. high, "lifted" the pavilion off the ground by means of 24 steel ropes, giving it a night-time appearance of floating in the air. The pavilion covered an area of 48,600 ft. The £800,000 spent on it was not an unusual amount at Expo.

Time-Capsule Reminders

Expense on this scale, added to the considerable amount of time, skill, and energy that goes into such events, makes its basic impermanence rather regrettable. After six months on display, most of the Expo buildings were dismantled and taken home, probably never to be erected again. In the course of time, the whole effort will largely fade into a memory.

However, the Japanese were determined that a rather more durable reminder should be left behind and, to commemorate the exposition, two time capsules, containing records and small objects, were buried in the south-western corner of the site. Both were filled with inorganic gas to preserve their contents, and one will be dug up in the year 2000 to check on their condition. The other is intended to remain in the earth for 5,000 years. In A.D. 6970, some enterprising archaeologist may dig it up, and discover through the microcosm of Expo 70 the ideas, inspirations, and aspirations of a long-vanished world.

Centenary Occasions of 1970

ELIZABETH HOGARTH

Schoolchildren taking part in the parade in Moscow's Red Square in honour of the centenary of Lenin's birth on April 22.

PROBABLY THE MOST widely celebrated centenary of 1970 was that of the birth of Vladimir Ilyitch Ulyanov, who in 1901 adopted the name of Lenin. He was born on April 22, 1870. In Russia, new issues of his writings were printed by the million; newspapers carried special pages devoted to his life's work; new feature-length films dealing with episodes in his life as a revolutionary were shown; and special medallions bearing his portrait were awarded "For Heroic Labour". On April 21 and 22 a special meeting of the Central Communist Party and the Supreme Soviet of the U.S.S.R., attended by many foreign guests, was held in the Kremlin, and on the 22nd leaders of the government and the party took part in a wreath-laying ceremony at his tomb in Red Square, Moscow. In all communist countries, lectures, exhibitions, and other events dedicated to Lenin and his work were held throughout the year. In London, exhibitions at the Marx Memorial Library and the British Museum included examples of his work; there was a book display at the National Book League; and a special season of films showing various aspects of his life was held at the National Film Theatre.

A number of commemorative events took place in South Africa in celebration of the centenary of the birth of Field-Marshal Smuts, the chief one being at his old home in Doornkloof, near Pretoria, where he spent 40 of his 80 years. Here, on May 24, his birthday, during a ceremony attended by distinguished guests, the president, J. J. Fouché, unveiled a plaque to his memory and declared the house a national monument. Celebrations in England in honour of two famous literary figures took place during the year, for William Wordsworth was born on April 7, 1770, and Charles Dickens died on June 9, 1870. These are mentioned on page 156.

The earliest historical event to be commemorated in 1970 was the assassination on December 29, 1170, of Archbishop Thomas Becket in Canterbury Cathedral. On September 23, 1970, performances of T. S. Eliot's *Murder in the Cathedral* began at Canterbury. At Bramfield, near Hertford, a festival commemorating the archbishop was held from June 11 to June 21, for he was the first known rector of the church there.

Postcards and Waxworks

The postcard first saw the light of day on October 1, 1870, when the first one—plain, prepaid, and with a printed violet stamp—was issued officially by the Post Office. During the first year 75 million were sent through the post. A fascinating exhibition, "50 Years of Post Cards, 1870–1920", with about a thousand valuable cards on view, was staged at the Victoria and Albert Museum, London, from early December till the end of January 1971. The cards ranged from posed "pin-up" pictures of Edwardian actresses to the patriotic sentimental cards of the First World War, and included the work of such well-known artists as Charles Dana Gibson, Bruce Bairnsfather, Alphonse Mucha, and Donald McGill.

On March 5, 1770, Dr. Philippe Curtius, a qualified physician, opened his display of models in wax to the public at the Palais Royal, Paris. His niece, Madame Marie Tussaud, an indomitable lady who is known to have taken death masks of Marie Antoinette and others after their deaths by guillotine, brought the exhibition to England in 1802. To celebrate its 200th anniversary a silver-coloured card, costing 75p, allowed people to visit Madame Tussaud's as often as they wished during 1970 except in peak holiday periods, and a dinner for 150 distinguished people, many of them portrayed in wax in the exhibition, was held in the building's Grand Hall.

Lloyd and Lauder

Two music-hall artists born in 1870 were Marie Lloyd (on February 12) and Sir Harry Lauder (on August 4). A musical, *Sing a Rude Song*, with Barbara Windsor playing the part of the great star, had its première at the Garrick Theatre on May 26. Two memorial services to Marie Lloyd took place—one on May 4 at St. Paul's, Covent Garden, where many famous theatrical personalities saw her sister unveil a memorial plaque and heard Wee Georgie Wood give the address; and the other, on February 15, at the Holy Trinity Church, Hoxton.

The Edinburgh city fathers should have unveiled a small bronze plaque set in the wall of 3, Bridge Street, on August 4, for it was here that Sir Harry Lauder, most famous of all Scottish music-hall artists, was born. Unfortunately—but perhaps Sir Harry would have appreciated the joke—it was discovered that the date of his death engraved on the plaque was given as February 26, 1949, instead of July 26, 1949, and the ceremony was postponed. In any case, the cottage is due for demolition in a redevelopment plan, and some other home will have to be found for the plaque.

On May 9, 1970, celebrations went on all day at Covent Garden market, to mark the tercentenary of the opening of the first market by King Charles II at its present home behind the Strand. Organized by men and women employed in the market and café owners and publicans who rely on the market for their trade, the festivities included Punch-and-Judy shows, a boxing tournament, dancing, and basket-carrying races. The Duke of Edinburgh was the guest of honour and, during his visit, gave the signal for a test drilling to start at the market's new site 2 miles away, thus ironically marking the beginning of the end of the Garden while in the act of celebrating its foundation.

Australian Personalities

A week of celebrations to commemorate the death of the bushranger Frederick Ward, popularly known as "Captain Thunderbolt", was held at Uralla, N.S.W.—where his grave is a tourist attraction—from May 16 to May 24. Eighty members of the town's Wild Colonial

This famous sculpture, "The Lion of Lucerne", was the work of Bertel Thorwaldsen, who was born on November 19, 1770.

Days Society re-enacted the scene of his death. Thunderbolt "held the roads" between Newcastle and the Queensland border from 1864 until he was shot by Constable Walker on May 25, 1870. The constable's heroism was also recognized, for a plaque to his memory was unveiled during the week. Australia also marked the centenary of the tragic death of Adam Lindsay Gordon, the famous Australian poet, who committed suicide at Brighton, a Melbourne suburb, on June 24, 1870. The Brighton Historical Society organized several commemorative events, including a display

In honour of the 800th anniversary of the murder of St. Thomas Beckett, T. S. Eliot's play, *Murder in the Cathedral,* was performed in Canterbury Cathedral. Below is the murder scene in the play.

depicting his life and works, and the showing of two biographical films.

History and Art

The Hudson's Bay Company celebrated its 300th birthday with many events, including a tour of Eastern Canada by a replica of the *Nonsuch* (the company's first ship) which arrived in Montreal from England on April 6, and culminating in a day of festivities on May 2—the date in 1670 on which the company was granted its royal charter by Charles II—when employees enjoyed a fête, festival, carnival, ball, and birthday party.

The first centenary of the capture of Rome from the French and papal forces, which completed the unification of Italy, fell on September 20. A programme of special ceremonies throughout the country started at the beginning of September, and were to continue until April 1971.

On April 13 the Metropolitan Museum of Art, New York, had its 100th birthday, for it was on that day in 1870 that it was granted its charter of independence by the New York Legislature. On April 14 a day of anniversary events included a centennial ball and the opening of five special exhibitions. To commemorate the 200th anniversary of the founding of the Spode porcelain factory an exhibition held at the Royal Academy, London, displayed 497 examples of its work, covering the whole period of its production. One section of the

200 years of Spode porcelain was celebrated in 1970. This artist is at work in the Spode factory, still at Stoke on Trent.

exhibition showed the practical work involved in producing a piece of Spode.

The Fit and the Fat

The Rugger season of 1970–71 celebrated the foundation of the Rugby Football Union on January 26, 1871. At Cambridge in September 100 delegates from nearly 50 Rugby-playing countries attended a congress. A series of special matches followed, the first between England and Wales on one side, and Scotland and Ireland on the other; played at Twickenham on October 3, the match resulted in a 14–14 draw.

The year also marked the bi-centenary of the birth of the unfortunate Daniel Lambert, who, although we are told he led an active and abstemious life, weighed 32 stone when he was aged 23. Born in Leicester on March 13, 1770, he died in 1809, by which time his weight had increased to $52\frac{3}{4}$ stone.

Half-Centenaries

While not strictly centenaries, two very different events were so enthusiastically remembered that they deserve mention. Five-month-long celebrations to mark the 350th anniversary of the sailing of the *Mayflower* from Plymouth for America took place in Plymouth, starting with a luncheon on May 2 when a boy from Provincetown, Massachusetts, presented the lord mayor of the city with a Bible. Southampton, where the ship actually started out, also celebrated the occasion. During the weekend of July 18–19 the village of Selborne in Hampshire celebrated the 250th anniversary of the birth on July 18 of its most illustrious inhabitant, the Rev. Gilbert White, author of *The Natural History of Selborne*, with lectures, concerts, poetry readings, and a garden party in the garden of his old home, The Wakes, which is being restored in his honour.

Other Anniversaries of 1970

Births

Henry Handel Richardson, Australian authoress (Jan. 3, 1870); George Canning, British statesman (April 11, 1770); Franz Lehar, Hungarian composer (April 30, 1870); Hilaire Belloc, British poet (July 27, 1870); Bransby Williams, British actor (Aug. 14, 1870); Maria Montessori, Italian educationalist (Aug. 31, 1870); Christopher Brennan, Australian poet (Nov. 1, 1870); Viscount Samuel, Liberal statesman (Nov. 6, 1870); Hector Hugh Munro ("Saki"), British short-story writer (Dec. 18, 1870).

Deaths

Sir James Simpson, Scottish "father" of anaesthetics (May 6, 1870); Mark Lemon, editor of *Punch* for 27 years (May 23, 1870); Jules de Goncourt, French novelist (June 20, 1870); Thomas Chatterton, British poet (Aug. 24, 1770); Robert E. Lee, U.S. confederate general (Oct. 12, 1870); Alexander Cruden, compiler of the Concordance to the Bible (Nov. 1, 1770); Alexander Dumas *père*, French author of *The Three Musketeers*, etc. (Dec. 5, 1870); Gustavo Becquer, Spanish poet (Dec. 22, 1870).

Events

Irish Land Bill (Aug. 1, 1870); foundation of the British Red Cross Society (Aug. 4, 1870); U.K. Elementary Education Act (Aug. 9, 1870); birth of Australia's sugar industry (Sept. 6, 1870); Germany declared a united empire (Dec. 10, 1870).

Science and Power

Three of the comets observed in 1970 are illustrated
here. At left is the White-Ortiz-Bolelli comet, first
spotted by an Australian student, Graeme White, on May 18.
The planet Venus is at the
top of the photo.

A New Look at Comets and Meteors

A. G. BROWNE
who is Science Correspondent of the
Press Association

THE SCIENCE of astronomy remains a practical delight for many amateurs, and the discovery of comets is one field in which they do particularly well. Of the seven discovered in 1968 six were first noted by people under 21 years of age; a 16-year-old schoolboy at Bishop, Texas, found one on his third night of comet-hunting. By 1969 the Japanese amateur Minoru Honda had discovered 12. In 1970 four naked-eye objects were reported in the first few months. A typical discovery was the White-Ortiz-Bolelli comet, named after the first three people whose reports reached the International Astronomical Union's central bureau for telegrams in Cambridge, Mass. This was 1970f, the sixth discovery of the year. First to see it, on May 18, was Graeme L. White, a 22-year-old Australian university student of Barrack Point, New South Wales, who was using binoculars. Three evenings later, Emilio Ortiz, an Air France pilot, saw it while flying over the Indian Ocean. That same evening it was first noted by a professional, Carlo Bolelli, at the Cerro Tololo Inter-American Observatory in Chile. This comet passed within 1 million miles of the sun.

The most valuable work on comets in 1970, however, was done by professional investigators of two magnificent comets discovered by amateurs towards the end of the previous year. These were the Tago-Sato-Kosaka comet, reported by three Japanese on October 10 and 12, 1969, and the Bennett comet, found on almost the last day of the year by John C. Bennett, of Pretoria, South Africa.

The Tago-Sato-Kosaka became the first comet to be observed from outer space when, on January 14, the American satellite OAO-2, equipped with instruments to ascertain the distribution of hydrogen in space, studied it by ultra-violet light. This revealed a cloud of hydrogen stretching out a million miles from the nucleus, which is one and a quarter times the size of the Sun. It was the first time that free hydrogen had been detected in a comet, and further studies by the spacecraft also showed the presence of hydroxyl (HO). Bennett's comet was an even more magnificent object, the finest comet for many years, likened by some to Halley's in 1910. Observations from another spacecraft, OGO-5, indicated that its hydrogen cloud measured 8 million miles across. Ground studies of the Tago-Sato-Kosaka revealed for the first time the presence of cyanogen in a comet, and an extensive range of free radicals and charged particles were found in both comets.

The presence of free radicals in the coma of comets, known for some time, is something of a puzzle. The classic theory about comets is that they consist of a small nucleus, some tens of miles across, made up of ice of various compounds, including water and ammonia. As the nucleus comes within the orbit of Jupiter the heat from the Sun causes it to stream off gas and dust to produce the comet's head. Inside the orbit of Mars the tail appears, stretching away from the Sun whether the comet is approaching or receding, carried by the solar wind. Comets are luminous, according to theory, because the gases fluoresce in the Sun's light. But the energy from radiation should not alone be enough to produce free radicals in the quantities believed to exist. If the density of the head is greater than appears from its visibility from Earth, the necessary energy may be provided by collisions between particles; this belief was supported by observations during the year. It is not unlikely: radiation from many of the chemicals is absorbed in the Earth's atmosphere, and the rate of collisions between molecules need only be of the order of one per second or less.

Right: Bennett's comet, first seen by South African John Bennett on Dec. 28, 1969; this photo was taken three months later. Below: the Tago-Sato-Kosaka comet, photographed at Mount Palomar observatory on Jan. 26. It is moving from left to right, its tail being "blown" ahead by the solar wind.

Considerable quantities of the material in a comet are lost as it passes near the Sun. New calculations during the year suggested that between a half and one astronomical unit from the Sun (one astronomical unit is the mean distance between Earth and Sun, 93 million miles) a large comet loses from 10^{30} to 2×10^{31} molecules per second. This amounts to around 10^{15} grammes, or a thousand million tons, during one passage near the Sun. Yet even at this rate a comet should be able to survive several thousand passages.

Cosmic Dust and Meteors

Such losses of matter must continually add dust to the solar system, and probably an equal amount comes from collisions between asteroids. The presence of dust is shown by the zodiacal light, the faintly illuminated zone stretching across the sky about twilight. What is added, however, probably just makes up for what is lost either by being streamed out of the system by the solar wind or, in the case of larger particles, falling into the Sun. Particles of matter that fall to the Earth as meteors are usually burnt up as they pass through the atmosphere, being visible as "falling stars". Most meteors are probably cometary in origin, since showers occur when the Earth passes through the orbits of known comets. It seems fairly certain that cometary material does not survive its incandescent journey through the atmosphere, so that the composition of comets cannot be studied on the Earth. This is one reason for a suggestion that space-probes should be sent up to sample comets.

The material which does survive the journey through the atmosphere to arrive on the Earth's surface as meteorites probably comes from the asteroids. Almost 2,000 meteorites have been collected. A 23-lb. specimen which

landed at Lost City, Oklahoma, on January 3, was the first to be found by computing its trajectory from photographs taken during its passage through the atmosphere. Appearing as a fireball brighter than the full Moon, it was photographed by the automatic cameras of the Smithsonian prairie network, which was set up in 1965 for just such an event. Four fixed cameras, covering the whole sky, are switched on by twilight sensors at each station of the network. A special shutter intercepts a meteor's track 20 times per second, and if a meteor is seen from two stations its position in space, its velocity, and its deceleration can all be determined. As soon as the Lost City meteor's trail was observed aircraft took off to pick up material left by its passage, a feat which had been successfully attempted twice before. From the photographs it was computed that a 1 kilogram object had landed in the vicinity of the small farming community of Lost City. The manager of the prairie network set out by car through heavy snowfalls to try to get the local residents to help look for it. Fortune favoured him. He found the meteorite lying in the middle of the road less than half a mile from the position calculated.

That meteorite proved to be a far better detector of cosmic rays than any man-made spacecraft. Bombardment by cosmic rays as it orbited the Sun, out to 2·35 astronomical units, had resulted in the production of radioactive isotopes with half-lives of 5 days to 2 million years. Study of these showed that during the 35 days before it hit the Earth the cosmic-ray flux had been only one third of the average of the past 270 years.

Origin of Comets and Planets

Meteorite trajectories can now be computed to find their origin. Cometary orbits have been worked out for centuries, but their origin is still a matter of speculation. Some comets are on elliptical orbits, well within the solar system. Others appear to come from far outside to make one passage round the Sun and then disappear. Those travelling on elliptical orbits within the system have probably been perturbed as they passed near a planet. One suggestion is that all comets come from a cloud of cometary material, perhaps a light year distant from the Sun. This theory was supported by mathematical studies reported during the year from the Leningrad institute of theoretical astronomy, where computers were fed with data concerning all known comets. The theory suggests that the cloud, probably containing enough material for about 100,000 million cometary nuclei, could be the remnants of matter which went to make up the planets and was thrown by centrifugal force to the periphery of the solar system.

One can speculate how this accords with the trend of theories on the origin of the solar system. There has recently been a revival of interest in theories about a "hot" origin for the planets, i.e. that they formed from matter emitted from the Sun. Professor Fred Hoyle produced his version of what could have happened during the International Astronomical Union's 1970 meeting in England. A contracting proto-Sun, with a surface temperature of 3,500°C, spinning more rapidly as it shrank, would reach instability around the orbit of Mercury, he calculated. A disc of matter would be thrown off, consisting of elements in the same proportion as they appeared in the Sun—largely hydrogen and helium. Only Saturn and Jupiter have constitutions anything like this, so a theory has to be found to account for differential separation of the material.

At the terrestrial orbit, argued Professor Hoyle, the temperature would have dropped sufficiently for the main constituents of the Earth—iron and silicates—to condense, the iron appearing slightly earlier to concentrate in the core. Beyond the orbits of Saturn and Jupiter some process has to be postulated for speeding up molecules of hydrogen and helium so they escape into space, leaving behind the carbon, oxygen, and nitrogen of which Uranus and Neptune seem to be composed. Sonic effects at the temperature reached by cooling from that initial 3,500° might be the explanation. Any continuing centrifugal effect could presumably account for the remote cloud of cometary material.

Professor Thomas Gold, of Cornell University, U.S.A., pointed out to the same conference that if planets are formed by the aggregation of lumps of matter—either collected as cold dust by a star or condensing from gas emitted from it—then the continual collisions between them will result in a large-scale "swapping" of their chemical ingredients. Professor Zdenek Kopal, of Manchester, reported that such an aggregation may be going on in one giant system 4,000 light years away. This is the binary system called epsilon Aurigae, a bright super-giant, probably only 1 million years old but 20 times as big as the Sun. The second part of it now appears to be a cold flattened disc, 40 astronomical units across, apparently made up of coarse solid matter with fragments possibly as large as small planets. This is the first reported such planetary system in the making, if indeed it is that—which impels Professor Kopal to the view that such systems must be rare, and therefore life in the universe must be rare, too.

More about the Moon

A further year's discussion of the new information on the Moon obtained by the Apollo flights has still not produced any generally accepted reassessment of theory. The mysterious 50-minute reverberation of the Moon caused when the Apollo 12 ascent stage was hurled back to the surface led at the time to suggestions that the Moon must be a completely cold body. Several other explanations for the reverberation appeared during 1970. A. K. Mukhamedzhanov, a Russian astronomer, produced detailed computations of trajectories of debris thrown up by the impact, which showed that it would have fallen for up to 22 minutes afterwards and that the cascade effect would have carried on long enough to account for 50 minutes of moonquake.

Some evidence that the Moon is still warm beneath its surface came from magnetism studies sent back by instruments left behind by Apollo 12, supporting radio studies previously made from Earth. Study of the moon-rocks left little doubt that the Moon was very hot in the past. Professor G. Malcolm Brown, the British geologist who was one of those chosen to examine the rocks, gave it as his opinion that, although the Earth and Moon were formed at the same time, they were not formed from the same materials. Most probably the Moon was formed from a ring of cosmic dust which surrounded the primeval Earth.

The interior of the Moon probably consisted of a rock called pyroxenite, which could melt to form lava similar to that erupted from Earth's volcanoes. The rocks Professor Brown examined were chiefly volcanic lava, but there were also material apparently carried down from the lunar highlands and glassy material formed by meteoritic impacts. The main meteorite activity probably occurred during the first 1,000 million years of the Moon's existence. The youngest lavas, about 3,500 million years old, had been relatively unaffected until picked up by the astronauts. Much of the material brought back appears to have condensed from a molten condition in the complete absence of oxygen or water.

The Puzzling Pulsars

Pulsars continue to puzzle astronomers. By the time of the International Conference 55 of them had been found. Professor Vitali Ginzburg, a Russian theoretical physicist, suggested that maser action could account for their radio emissions. That view might not be universally approved, but there is widespread acceptance of the belief, which he also expounded, that a pulsar is a rapidly rotating magnetized neutron star with its rotational axis oblique to its magnetic symmetry axis. The physical laws of bodies with densities of a million tons, or tens of millions of tons, per cubic centimetre are going to take a good deal of working out. Professor Ginzburg postulated

conditions of superconductivity and superfluidity within them.

Some findings from Jodrell Bank suggest that all pulsars are slowing down, at rates which would give a life-time of 2,500 years for the pulsar in the Crab Nebula, but 140 million years for certain others. The Crab pulsar seems in some ways to be unique, probably because it appears to be the remnant of the nearest and most recent supernova in our galaxy. The energy released by its slowing down is probably sufficient to account for all the energy radiated from the nebula. Timing of this pulsar can be made to differences of millionths of a second per year, and one jump in its period has been said to correspond to a decrease in its radius of one hundredth of a millimetre. The gravitational energy released by this minute change, however, is said to be enough to supply the kinetic energy of one of the wisps of matter seen to be moving outwards from it.

A major astronomical event of 1970 was the total eclipse of the sun on March 7, which was observable only in Central and North America. The map shows the path of totality along the eastern seaboard of the U.S.A. Below is a photo sequence, of ten separate exposure on one piece of film, showing the eclipse (not quite total) as it appeared over Washington, D.C., landmarks.

The pictures in this and the facing page all show new means of getting about that came into use in 1970. At left is the Ameise battery-operated runabout or "personnel-carrier". Although here seen on the road, it is intended primarily for use in factories, some of which are so extensive that walking about in them can become very fatiguing.

Putting

At right is the B.S.A. Ariel 3, the world's first three-wheeled moped. A 50-c.c. two-stroke engine between the two rear wheels gives a top speed of 30 m.p.h. with a petrol consumption of about 150 miles per gallon. Up to 50 lb. of shopping can be carried in the basket mounted over the engine. The cost of this useful little vehicle is just over £100.

Below left is a Japanese invention—a baby carriage fitted with rubber caterpillar tracks that make it easy to negotiate steps or push the pram over snowy or swampy ground. The hiker at right below is carrying a small computer that takes note of every step in whatever direction it is taken, so that at any time it can work out his exact map position. Correct setting of the instrument before starting is all that is necessary. The equipment has been tried out by U.S. troops on jungle patrol in Vietnam.

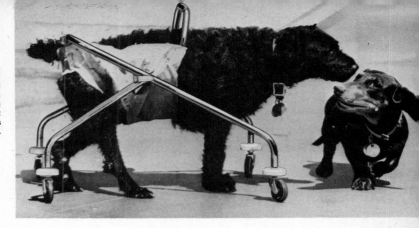

Human beings in need of assistance in locomotion were not the only species to benefit from the ingenuity of inventors and engineers during 1970. A wheeled walking frame with canvas body-sling for a dog recovering from a broken leg or similar ailment was welcomed by the canine world. This patient is suffering from a slipped disc.

Science to Work

RONALD
SHARP

Undoubtedly one of the greatest inventions of modern times has been plastics. It is difficult to realize that less than 50 years ago the only man-made material of the kind we know as plastics was a brittle substance of very limited use. Modern plastics are virtually indestructible, and have been adopted for an infinite variety of uses. This, however, has its drawbacks, particularly in the disposal of unwanted plastic articles such as empty containers. Refuse disposal departments of cities and towns have become quite alarmed at the growing problem of plastic litter. They can unload it on to rubbish dumps or bury it, but neither is a real solution, because plastics do not decompose.

For this reason, borough engineers and their refuse disposal experts have been looking with great hope at a series of experiments which were undertaken during 1970 by scientists at an English university who have actually found a way of making plastic rot and reducing it to dust. Basically, the method uses coloured dyes which cause the plastics to break down physically when subjected to sunlight. Professor Gerald Scott, head of the team at Aston University where the experiments were carried out, explained that after being left in daylight for a few weeks, the dyed plastics become embrittled and then crumble. One difficulty was to prevent the premature destruction of plastic articles that are meant to be exposed in a shop window. With this in mind, dyes were devised which are immune to the feebler light rays that penetrate window glass.

The versatility of plastics continues to attract inventors, scientists, and engineers in many fields. In the U.S.A., horses have started wearing plastic shoes, and cows are now treading on plastic carpets, which have been found to make excellent floor-covering for milking barns. It will soon be possible to raise sunken ships with plastics, thanks to a new technique developed in 1970. This involves pumping urethane foam into the wreck under high pressure. The foam, expanding to many times its original size, becomes buoyant enough to lift the vessel to the surface.

On land, plastic car bodies are already in use. In the air we have yet to see the all-plastic aircraft, but we shall not have long to wait. Already plastics are used on a large scale for the interior fitting, and manufacturers have begun to use them in structural applications to provide aircraft with the ideal of rigidity without weight. 1970 saw the first test flights of a four-seater aircraft with fuselage, wings, and tail assembly all made of reinforced epoxy plastic. The strength of plastics can be combined with natural materials to provide hitherto unattainable strengths. The Bureau of Mines in Washington developed a special type of plastic which can strengthen rock and heal cracks in it. This is particularly valuable in reinforcing mine roofs, which can get progressively weaker as mining continues. The new plastic will allow mining engineers to extract the maximum amount of mineral from a deposit before abandoning the mine.

Lasers and Batteries

Another new aid to mining is the laser. Each year brings some new application that adds to the versatility of this remarkable beam of light. One of the new uses in 1970 was a special-purpose laser for use in civil engineering,

43

construction work, surveying, and mining. Known as the SL4T, it is a helium-neon laser attached to a telescope. The laser head has a separate power supply that allows it to operate directly from 240 volts AC or almost any DC voltage from 12 upwards. The SL4T, which was devised by a British company, will simplify many otherwise tedious operations, such as sampling, measuring, and close-up inspections.

American scientists developed a new inspection laser, which combines an infra-red laser with a microscope. The device can look into materials which are opaque to visible light, and can be used for all materials that are transparent to infra-red. The laser sweeps a pinpoint of 3,390-Angstrom frequency infra-red radiation over an area of about 2 in. Passing through the sample, the radiation is detected by an infra-red cell behind it. A video-scanner picks up the transmitted infra-red and displays it on an oscilloscope, giving a picture of the transmission and absorption pattern of the sample.

Another electrical device that saw life in 1970 and will live on into the next century is a lead-acid battery designed to last at least 30 years. It was devised by an American research laboratory. Its long life is due to the fact that its performance actually improves during most of its life-span. It is intended for use by telephone companies in stand-by power applications, but it could also be used in motor-cars. In most conventional batteries, the grids are rectangular frames smeared with a paste of lead-oxide, and standing side by side. They are floated in a sulphuric-acid bath through which an electric current flows from the positive to negative poles. The batteries gradually deteriorate as corrosion widens the lattice of the grid, separating it from the lead-oxide paste and breaking the contact. In the new 30-year battery, the grids consist of a series of concentric rings connected by radial spokes. Even when these corrode, the distance between the rings remains constant, and they do not separate from the energy-producing paste. Since corrosion has the effect of increasing the amount of lead-oxide paste, the battery's capacity becomes greater with age, until it eventually wears out.

Inventions to Help the Sick

An intriguing device designed to ease insomnia, headaches, migraine, and almost every discomfort of the head that prevents sleep is the Somnor, developed by British scientists specializing in electronic health instruments. This is a battery-powered unit giving out carefully measured and controlled impulses which are applied to the head through a headband. During hospital tests, it was found that the Somnor relaxed the patient and encouraged a state that has become known as "electrosleep", which is not actual sleep but a state of absolute mental relaxation. Somnor is not a futuristic device—it can be bought now, for about £130, with a doctor's approval.

The Somnor was one of many humanitarian inventions to appear in 1970. Another produced by scientists at the Temple University, Philadelphia, was an artificial arm that is al-

An artificial arm that responds to directions from the brain in much the same way as a natural arm was demonstrated in the U.S.A. during 1970. Below: a specialist marks the places on the patient's back (left) where the electrical impulses from the brain that travel along the nerves to the muscles can be picked up by electrodes attached to the skin (right).

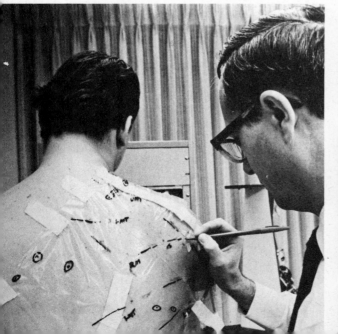
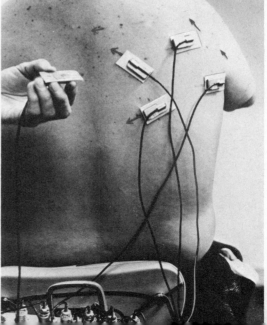

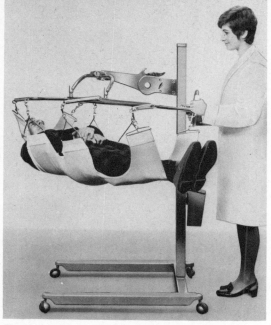

The "Ambulift", a combination of chair, sling, and stretcher by means of which one nurse can lift a heavy patient in and out of bed or bath.   *Mecanaids Ltd., Gloucester*

most as good as the real thing since it responds to directions from the brain in much the same way as a natural limb. Instead of being controlled by the conventional but cumbersome harness and pulley system, the new arm is controlled by muscles in the chest, shoulder, and back. Tiny electrical pulses generated by the brain travel along the spinal cord to the ends of the nerves in the muscles, where electrodes attached to the skin pick up the signals and decode the brain's commands, which are then

Transformed into electric currents, the impulses activate four small motors which move the arm.
Temple University, Philadelphia, Pa.

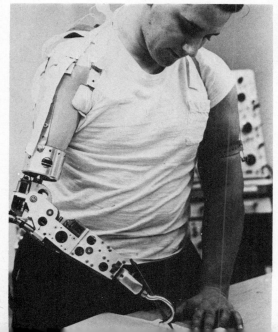

carried out by four small motors. With the new device, it is possible to make eight different limb movements, from finger manipulations to elbow bending.

A manipulator of another kind is the Mecanaids Ambulift, developed by British engineers and first demonstrated by the Royal Society of Health in 1970. It is a combination of chair, lift, stretcher, and sling, and with it one nurse can move heavy patients in and out of bed with almost no effort. The versatility of the device knows no bounds. For the incontinent, a commode pan can be clipped on to the chair unit. In the bathroom, forks are positioned around the bath, and the chair is lowered into the water, and after immersion the patient can be raised to a convenient height for drying. To get a patient out of bed, the chair is removed from the frame and inserted under the patient so that he can be rolled on to it and raised to a sitting position. Once the patient is inside the encircling fold-away arm-rests, he can be rotated on the chair into the correct position for elevation from the bed. In these days of staff shortages in hospitals, the Ambulift will prove invaluable in the speedy and effortless handling of patients.

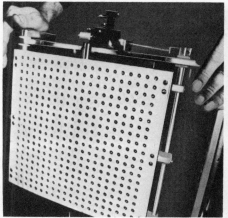

Plastic pins on a back-board (left) are raised to form recognizable patterns by impulses from a television camera held by a blind person (right).
University of the Pacific, San Francisco

A new device for the blind is one which can help a sightless person to see through the skin of his back. Developed by scientists at the University of the Pacific in San Francisco, the system includes a back-board fitted with rows of plastic pins. The pins are activated in a pattern dictated by a television camera as it scans different objects. The user learns to identify the objects from the pattern felt on his back.

At the Stanford University School of Medicine in California, Dr. Donald C. Harrison used ultrasonic "sonar" (echo-sounding) to

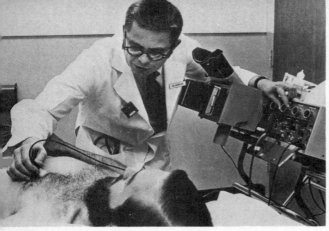

A new method of examining the heart and lungs is by an ultrasonic "echo-sounding" device invented by an American medical scientist. *Stanford University School of Medicine, U.S.A.*

study the functioning of the human heart and obtain fundamental information on heartbeats and blood circulation. Unlike conventional methods, Dr. Harrison's invention can be carried out in minutes by any well-trained person, either in a doctor's consulting room or at the bedside. It is safe, simple, and painless, and can monitor patients with suspected heart disease by measuring the exact amount of blood which is pumped out of the heart at each contraction—which is something that standard monitoring systems cannot do. Dr. Harrison claimed that one of the most important advantages of his ultrasonic method is that it also measures the heart size and any backward blood-flow that would indicate a defective heart.

Another listening device with a humanitarian objective of a different kind is a new teaching method called Individually Prescribed Instruction (IPI), in which young children are taught such subjects as arithmetic by means of re-

"Individually Prescribed Instruction" is a method of teaching children, at their own speed of learning, by means of recordings and headphones. *University of Pittsburgh, Pa.*

cordings while the teacher merely looks on and follows their progress. The system is based on the use of thousands of worksheets, each with specific instructions how to do the problems, and its big advantage is that it allows each child to proceed at his own pace. Not all the worksheets call for a written answer. Some tell the pupil to listen to a tape recording; others may tell him to measure a room, or find a certain book in the library, or play a certain game. If a child finds the worksheet too difficult, the teacher is on hand to prescribe a simpler one. IPI is being used in nearly 200 schools in the U.S.A., and is proving so successful that it is almost certain to spread to other countries.

Making Millions of Faces

An improvement on an established device is the "Photo-Fit" identity system devised to assist the police in the identification of wanted persons. Most people are familiar with the established "Identikit" system, in which portraits are built up piece by piece by means of drawn sketches. "Identikit" has the drawbacks which all sketches impose, particularly a lack of reality and a tendency for every built-up face to have some degree of similarity. "Photo-Fit", as its name implies, uses photographs instead of sketches, and is much more realistic.

"Photo-Fit" was invented by Jacques Penry, an Englishman whose lifelong interest in facial topography has resulted in several books on the subject. Mr. Penry maintains that a face can be distinguished from another by only the slightest difference in a single feature—the chin or jaw, perhaps, or the slope of the forehead, the curve, length, or breadth of the nose, the shape of a lip, and so on. With "Photo-Fit" it is possible to assemble realistic composite faces by means of photographed facial sections which cover the whole human range, regardless of age, sex, or nationality. To maintain complete anonymity of the photographic models, great care was taken to ensure that the 510 parts or sections in the system do not include more than one feature from the same face. The number of possible combinations is endless. If one operator built up 10,000 faces a day, seven days a week, 365 days a year, without a break it would still take many years to build every face made possible by the system. The total possible number of faces is, in fact, 5,400 million.

The 510 pieces of "Photo-Fit" include 169 foreheads and hairlines, 81 pairs of eyes, 70 noses, 86 mouths, 64 chins and cheek outlines, and a variety of moustaches, beards, spectacles, and headgear. "Photo-Fit", which costs only about £80 a set, was adopted by the British police in April 1970, and is expected to be taken up by Interpol and police forces all over the world.

Another new invention taken up by the British police is an underwater metal detector that can locate an article as small as a nail even if it is buried in more than a foot of mud. Called the "Elsec" detector, it functions by transmitting a high-powered magnetic pulse from a coil and analysing the resulting eddy currents in surrounding objects. The "Elsec" can be used by an aqualung diver, and the engineers who developed it envisage its increasing use among underwater archaeologists, treasure hunters, salvage operators, and pipeline technologists. Indication of a buried object is given on an internal meter seen through a window in the device. There is also an output socket to allow readings to be taken externally, e.g. aboard accompanying ships or by a diver wearing an earphone. The maximum detection distance depends on the size, shape, and electrical conductivity of the object. The detector can function at depths up to 650 ft. It can locate a penny buried under 20 in. of mud, or a 9-in.-diameter pipe from a distance of 8 ft.

New Ways of Cutting Metal

Many of the inventions that come to light in the course of a year are concerned with metal in one way or another. In 1970, British engineers perfected a new cutting gas capable of eating its way through 9 in. of steel. Called "Apachi", the new gas proved itself in one of the most arduous cutting jobs ever undertaken —the dissection of a series of derelict forts around Portsmouth. Known as Palmerston's Follies, the iron forts were built in the 1830s and never fired a shot. The iron is worth up to £1,000 a ton because of its purity and low radioactivity, but it has always proved too difficult to cut. With the "Apachi" gas, the iron was removed from the forts at the rate of 4 tons a day, which was more than could be achieved in a month by other methods. A methyl acetylene-based liquid petroleum gas, "Apachi" is used in an admixture with oxygen to provide the very high temperatures needed for cutting.

Metal cutting has also benefited from the improved development of the gas laser. Contrary to popular belief, solid-state lasers, such as the ruby laser, have not been capable of many of the miracles attributed to them by science-fiction enthusiasts, because their peak power is available for only short periods. For this reason, the application of ruby lasers in metalwork has been limited to spot-welding and drilling single holes. The development of the carbon dioxide gas laser has removed these limitations by giving continuous power outputs of 50 to 75 watts per metre length of laser tube. This makes it a valuable tool for both continuous seam-welding and cutting. By using a jet of oxygen on the workpiece, materials which are normally difficult to cut even in a straight line can now be cut to quite complicated shapes. The actual ability to cut is not the only benefit, for cutting speed has proved much greater than anyone had envisaged, while the cut edge is so smooth that for many applications it needs no further finishing.

While the power of the laser is one of its recommendations, its delicacy is another.

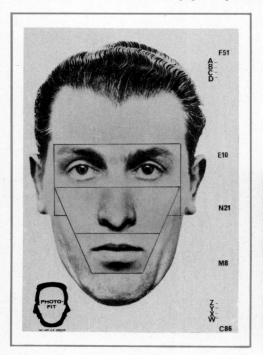

"Photofit" is a new means devised by a British inventor of building up a composite photograph (left) of a wanted person from a set of 510 pieces. Below: the inventor, Jacques Penry, making faces.
John Waddington Ltd., England

British scientists succeeded in developing a laser technique so delicate that it can be used to machine extremely thin metal films of the kind used in micro-electronic circuits, without the risk of chemical contamination which can result from "photo-resist" etching methods. The new method uses a pulsed laser which gives a high resolution and definition at a lower cost than either "photo-resist" or computer-controlled laser etching. The pulsed laser operates under controlled conditions in which unmasked portions of the metal film are progressively reduced, not blasted away. Complex profiles, straight lines, and small numerals can easily be produced with precise definition, but where a high degree of accuracy is unnecessary, profiles can simply be sketched on a clear glass plate.

Novel Uses for Computers

Every year brings a new crop of computer applications. Dr. P. Broadbent, of the North of Scotland College of Agriculture, with the collaboration of the medical physics department of Aberdeen University, applied the computer to the feeding of farm animals. Research is constantly being undertaken into the best kinds of food to give to farm animals at different stages of their lives and under different conditions. With cattle, such research requires work on large herds if a scientifically acceptable answer is to be obtained, and at the same time in many cases it also demands individual feeding of each animal. The chief obstacles have always been that individual feeding calls for separate pens—which is hardly ever possible—while, in the case of cows, the animals always eat better when they are together than when alone.

Dr. Broadbent's individual feeding device provides each animal with a "key" which unlocks its own feeding pen and no other. The key is in the form of a tuned coil which, as the animal nears the feedboxes, activates a similarly tuned oscillator that then draws a solenoid bolt on the appropriate door. The device can be programmed by computer to operate automatically, but the only power needed to work the components is a car battery to open the door. As the animal pushes with its head against the now unbolted door, the door swings open vertically in such a way that it bars access to the neighbouring feedbox.

Computers are also being used to feed Texan cattle. The interesting point is that the computers are actually 1,500 miles away, in Atlanta, Georgia. A firm of feed manufacturers mixes the rations in Texas; to prevent blends which would be unpalatable or indigestible to cattle, restrictions on the amounts of the ingredients are programmed into the computer, which then considers the costs of various types of feed and prints out the cheapest mixture to meet nutritional standards. The data are fed into the computer by a push-button console at the Texas end of a telephone line to Atlanta. Local feed prices are punched in on the buttons, and the optimum mixture of feed is printed out in about six minutes.

A computer was used in 1970 to detect lung disease in human beings. The idea came from a British scientist, Dr. Roy Bentley, while he was working at the Biomedical Computer Laboratory at Washington University in St. Louis, Missouri. The new method, which can detect lung disorders four months before they show up on traditional X-rays, involves measuring the amount of radioactivity passing through a patient's chest as he breathes, and using a computer to analyse the results. The patient stands between a disc of radioactive material about 15 in. in diameter, and a scintillation camera. He inhales, holds his breath for several seconds, and then exhales for several seconds. More radioactivity rays get through the lungs during inhalation because the lungs

Pulsed laser as used in machining extremely thin metal films spread on a glass plate. Here the pattern to be etched is represented by an S.

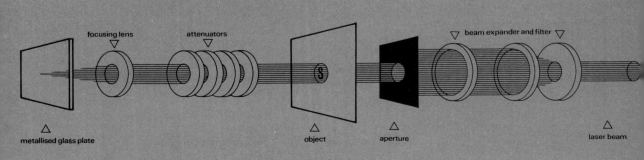

focusing lens   attenuators   beam expander and filter

metallised glass plate   object   aperture   laser beam

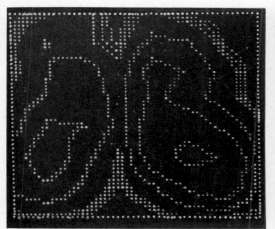

Computerized oscilloscope pictures of lung density during breathing: left, normal lung; right, lung of emphysema patient.

are filled with air and are therefore less dense. When the patient exhales, the lung tissue, contracting to expel the air, becomes more dense, and therefore less radioactivity passes through to be detected by the camera recording the positions of the rays as they pass through the chest. The electrical information from the camera is converted to numerical values which can be analysed by the computer into measurements of the difference in density in a given period of time for 64 different regions of the chest. The technique can be carried out in just 20 seconds. It is not intended to replace the X-ray in general use, and is being considered only for screening patients suspected of lung disorders.

Reading meters by computer is not a new idea, but the need to provide some link—physical or by radio—between the meter and the computer has prevented it from being used on a large scale. In 1970, American engineers perfected a system in which water, gas, or electricity meters in every home could be read through a telephone line. (Whether it can be

Cutting metal by means of a gas laser.
Laser photos, National Research Development Corporation, London

done economically will be decided as a result of tests to be carried out over large areas during 1971.) A connection is made between the gas or electricity company's computer and special equipment in the telephone exchange. When the computer calls the subscriber's phone number the call is connected to the meter in the subscriber's house. The householder does not answer the phone because it does not ring—the bell is muted by using special electrical currents and circuits. An encoder and modulator attached to the meter convert the mechanical dial readings into electrical pulses or tones which are transmitted through the telephone line to the gas or electricity company's office. There, a data communications terminal, controlling the entire process, receives the meter signals and directs them to the computer, which works out the amount of gas or electricity used and prints out the bill. The whole process, from connection to recording, takes only a few seconds. In fact, the part of the sequence involving the home telephone is so fast that it does not even interrupt a call in progress.

Even behind an ordinary telephone call lies a vast and complex system which carries the human voice across the street or across the world faster than the blink of an eye. In 1970, on a windswept former Royal Air Force station in Suffolk, a team of British Post Office scientists did some unusual things with the voice. They developed a telephone system based on radio waves beamed through hollow copper tubes buried in the ground. Known as the waveguide system, it can transmit up to 400,000 telephone conversations simultaneously through a small copper tube not much wider than a car's exhaust pipe.

Waveguides use extremely high radio frequencies never before used for communications.

On this automatic train track laid between the carriageways of a motorway in Chicago, 150 small traincars, like the one seen here, can travel at 70 m.p.h.

Until now the equipment to deal with these has not been available. But with suitable electronic devices now on the market, the scientists believe they have found an ideal means of data transmission. The technique is like a fantastically fast form of telegraphy—so fast that it could transmit the entire Bible in a fraction of a second, provided, of course, that there was a machine capable of picking it all up at the other end.

Innovations on Rail and Road

The year 1970 proved to be particularly prolific in new ideas in the field of transport. Experiments were carried out in London recently with driverless trains, but so far the idea has not been wholly put into practice. The nearest thing to driverless trains can be found in the U.S.A., where there are now automatic trains in the sense that the "man up front" has no hand in controlling the train. He sits at a console of buttons, lights, and telephones. He pushes two buttons, one of which rings a warning bell and the other closes the doors. After that, control passes to a man at a control centre which can be several miles away. The control centre illustrated below directs as many as 19 trains at a time, automatically accelerating some to keep them

Control centre at which one man can direct as many as nineteen driverless trains at one time.

Delaware River Port Authority, U.S.A.

apart, slowing them to the correct speed for curves, stopping and starting them at stations. With this system, it is possible to accelerate to 75 m.p.h. in 75 seconds, and a journey of 15 miles, with 10 intermediate stops, takes 23 minutes. In Chicago, an automatic train track has been laid down between the carriageways of a motorway. About 150 stainless steel carriages are capable of travelling 70 miles on continuous welded rails, faster than the road traffic on either side.

More futuristic is a rocket train developed by electrical engineers for the U.S. Atomic Energy Commission. In its present form it is a magnetic sled, but engineers believe it could be the first step towards speeding commuters to work in a rocket-powered subway train suspended by magnetism. The sled, now used for testing atomic-energy components, is capable of development into a larger-scale mass transportation system, one reason being that the faster it goes the more stable and efficient it is.

While American engineers are remotely controlling trains, their British counterparts are doing the same with road traffic. From 12 control centres situated at strategic points along 800 miles of motorways, police sit at television-type consoles; tapping the keys they can set up signals to warn of hazards ahead, and instruct motorists to slow, stop, or change lanes. Input information is picked up by sensors along the motorways and fed to computers—two each at each control centre—which exercise the appropriate control function and store the overall picture of what is happening all along the length of the section.

Gas-fuelled cars are not new—they were used to a limited extent during the 1939–45 War, when petrol was rationed. They could return to the roads if the efforts of scientists at the University of California reach fruition. Their gas is propane, and they have perfected a propane-powered car which is now in daily use. Claimed as a small contribution towards cleaner air, the car is cheaper to run than a petrol-engine vehicle, with savings on oil, sparking plugs, points, and other conventional ignition components. The car is also expected to need fewer maintenance checks. Conversion to propane involved changing a carburettor and adding a vaporizer and special fuel tanks. The tanks hold 33 gallons of the liquid gas, giving the car a range of over 400 miles. The converted vehicle needs no warming up and accelerates to 50 m.p.h. in six seconds.

Cars powered by steam are likewise nothing new. In fact, the steam car was the predecessor of the petrol-driven version. In 1970, the steam car made its reappearance as another possible answer to air pollution. It has a num-

An experimental steam-driven motor car devised to obviate the evil of pollution by exhaust gases.

ber of advantages over the petrol engine—no starter motor, carburettor, or cooling system; no complex wiring or transmission system. The mechanics of fitting a steam engine into a modern car are quite simple. Almost any type of burnable fuel—including paint thinners—can be used to produce the steam in boilers filled with fine coiled tubing. The steam is injected into an engine which can be of either the piston or the turbine type. A condenser liquefies the steam for recirculation through the system.

More down to earth was a simple development which passed almost unnoticed, despite the fact that it occurred in London's busy streets. It was the first-ever installation of radio-telephones in London's red double-decker buses. For a start, 25 buses were fitted, as part of a scheme to improve operational control, particularly during periods of heavy traffic congestion. The driver is able to report his position to a central control point, who can advise him on the measures he should take to meet whatever situation he finds himself in.

A form of vehicle that could be useful to men on the Moon is the eight-wheeled "Twister", although it was not devised with the lunar surface in mind. The "Twister" is really two vehicles in one (it has two bodies and two engines) and it can do what no other vehicle can do—clamber over walls and climb almost any type of obstacle. It will be used for hauling men and supplies over rough country, making short work of craters, trenches, and fallen trees.

Seagoing Inventions

One of the most revolutionary inventions of 1970 was a two-man submarine known as the X2. It was designed and built by George Cooke at the Royal Aircraft Establishment, Farnborough, England, who spent two years on the project before the submarine was successfully put through its proving trials. There is nothing new about two-man submarines—they were used to penetrate enemy defences during the 1939–45 War—but there are two unusual things about Cooke's. It is made of fibreglass, and it is powered by a car battery—and it can cruise at five knots at depths of up to 150 ft.

Automatic devices such as radar have reduced the number of seagoing hazards dramatically in recent years, and 1970 was no exception. It took a team of American radio engineers to come up with one of the year's most imaginative ideas—an automatic boat that can find its own way about, without a crew if necessary. Known as SKAMP (Station Keeping And Mobile Platform), the boat can sail to any part of the world's oceans over a period of many months and then find its way back to port. It is radio-controlled and can keep its position to within one tenth of a mile; it has two lightweight plastic sails and contains a mass of electronic components. SKAMP is being used for charting ocean currents and for navigational experiments. It will also be used in experiments with a navigational satellite in Earth orbit. And, of course, it can be used as a homing device to save lives at sea.

Another seagoing invention of 1970 is an automatic fish surveillance device which has been hailed as a major advance in fishery research. It is an automatic electronic eye that keeps a constant watch on edible fish and other marine life. The device consists of a remote-controlled underwater photographic sled equipped with film and television cameras, which can be towed to any part of the ocean and positioned at any height above the seabed.

The eight-wheeled "Twister", with two bodies and two engines, can climb over walls and similar obstacles.

This piece of apparatus, ready to be lowered into the sea, is an underwater sled carrying film and television cameras for watching the movement and development of fish.

U.S. Department of the Interior

On its first assignment, the device produced remarkable photographs of vast concentrations of scallops in their natural habitat, and in the spring of 1970 observations were made of young scallops in the Atlantic off Cape Kennedy in order to predict future harvest areas for commercial scallop fishermen.

Improving Air Safety

In aviation almost every invention is associated with safety. Gatwick, in England, became the first airport in Europe to have a fully automated visibility measuring system. Developed by British electronics engineers, the system eliminates human assessment of visibility conditions and in addition to increasing safety margins will also raise traffic-handling capacity.

Most airports rely on visual judgment, which is no more than an eye-count of the number of runway lights that can be seen. While this gives some idea of landing conditions, it does not approach a pilot's split-second view as he touches down. The automated system takes readings every $1\frac{1}{2}$ seconds from a number of points along the runway, so that an overall, up-to-the-second picture can be obtained of the visibility conditions as experienced by the pilot in the vital seconds before touchdown.

Light is measured by photo-electric cells along the runway, and the information is passed to a data-processing unit in the control tower and then to a number of indicators on the control consoles. To ensure that measurements are consistent, a film of filtered dry air is maintained over the receiving unit to prevent condensation and contamination, which could give misleading readings. The data are transferred through normal telephone lines incorporating a security check to protect against interference. In making its final assessment of runway visibility, the system also takes into account the level of runway lighting, which is measured directly from the lighting control gear, and the general background light, which

is monitored separately. The installation at Gatwick is the first phase of a programme designed by the National Air Traffic Control Services organization under which every major airport in the United Kingdom will be automated in this way. Next on the list will be Heathrow, Manchester, Liverpool, and Glasgow.

Developments in Metallurgy

One of the year's most important developments in the field of metallurgy was a plasma arc spraying method which can provide tough skins on soft metals, however complex their shape. The method involves blowing a stream of powdered material through an electric arc in a gas jet which turns the powder into molten droplets. Alumina and tungsten carbide can be deposited on the periphery of grinding wheels to form a dense and extremely hard surface which is very much cheaper than diamond grit and, in some ways, superior.

American metallurgists have perfected a method of patting metal into shape, as butter used to be apportioned by grocers. The metal pat-shaper is a mould, the sides of which move in and out, patting the hot metal which has been brought to a plastic state. The pat-a-cake action of the mould moves the solidifying metal through a series of progressive shape-changing moulds without any form of pulling or handling equipment. The system has given continuous casting speeds of up to 50 ft. per minute, and a 2 in. by 2 in. copper bar was cast in a single piece 430 ft. long.

The metal is cooled in a long tube with water pumped in at the midpoint so that it surrounds the moulded shape and emerges at each end of the tube. This prevents the entry of air and reduces the oxidation of certain metals. The water-cooled mould has two moving sides and two stationary sides. The moving sides have an elliptical motion, both in-and-out and up-and-down; this motion moves the still plastic metal through the mould, at the same time avoiding tension which could rupture the outer skin of the casting. The in-and-out action is one hundredth of an inch at 1,000 strokes a minute, while the up-and-down action is one tenth of an inch. During the patting action, the sides need not be parallel, which means that a tapered length of metal can be easily produced.

The Drilling and Spilling of Oil

Spectacular developments have been taking place in finding and bringing up oil and natural gas from under the sea. These offshore riches are expected to benefit from a development which took place in 1970 off the Canadian coast of British Columbia, where experiments involved men living in "cellars" on the seabed, 1,000 ft. down. The experiments are particularly important to engineers working in the North Sea gasfields because there are serious economic difficulties in extracting oil and gas from depths greater than 400 ft., and much of the North Sea area now awaiting development or due to be licensed is much deeper than that.

Wells will continue to be drilled by surface rigs but, once this has been done, steel "cellars" 21 ft. high will be fitted permanently over the well heads, and men will work in them. The system was tried out in the Straits of Georgia between Vancouver Island and the mainland of British Columbia. The men travelled between ship and cellars in steel capsules operated by a vessel on the surface, and an umbilical cable links ship and cellars at all times. The cable supplies air and other essentials, and the men can work in shirt-sleeve conditions. On the surface is a semi-submersible vehicle known as a "manifold centre" into which the oil or gas is pumped from the well head, to be partially refined before being pumped to transport vessels or sent by pipeline to the shore.

European Conservation Year helped to concentrate attention on the problems of oil pollution of the sea. A simple method of recovering spilled oil was achieved by French engineers. It uses a propeller to create a rotary movement below the surface of the water on which the oil is floating. This results in a vortex which collects the oil in a cone-shaped pocket from which it is then pumped out. Apparatus no more than 3 ft. in diameter succeeded in recovering 1,600 gallons of crude oil, spread in a layer 1 in. thick over an area of about 350 square yards—and it took only 90 minutes.

An American device was an enormous vacuum cleaner consisting of two tugs pulling an 800-ft. length of pipe which bent between the tugs to form a "V" at the pipe's vortex where a barge collects the oil.

For very large oil spills, a liquid called Polycomplex A-11 was developed for spraying on to oil slicks. The chemical, which is harmless to sea life, combines with the oil, breaking it up into microscopically small particles, which are dispersed by winds, currents, and tides and later decompose through the natural action of bacteria in the water. Paradoxically, the decomposed oil could eventually help to nourish sea life rather than destroy it.

Detection of Gas Leaks

From oil spills to gas leaks. Detecting the presence of explosive gases and vapours in

A simplified mass spectrometer, with coarse mesh wire screens in place of electrodes, can be used to detect gas leaks, monitor air pollution, and diagnose blood and respiratory diseases.
General Electric Company, U.S.A.

multi-storey buildings, chemical works, gasworks, oil tankers, and fuel storage depots is of vital importance. A remote gas and vapour detection system was invented by British electronics engineers. Known as the Becorit RMS4, it is fully automatic and gives visual and audible alarms. Detectors are placed at strategic points, and in the event of a leak, a signal is relayed to a control panel which can be fitted with a variety of equipment, such as fans and power-point cut-offs. Incorporated in the detectors are pellistor filaments which were invented by the Safety in Mines Research Establishment. Diffusion takes place through a bronze disc which acts as a flame arrester, and an active carbon filter is used to filter out filament poisons. Two filaments are connected to a bridge circuit; this is in balance at normal times, but when gas is present one of the filaments becomes heated by reaction with a catalyst, and the circuit becomes unbalanced and sends a signal to the control panel.

Another new way of monitoring leaks of gas and chemical vapours is by means of the mass spectrometer. This instrument employs a magnetic field to analyse gases at low pressure by sorting out charged atoms and molecules according to their mass. Conventional mass spectrometers are complicated and costly since they require electrodes carefully machined to precise tolerances. A new simple yet highly sensitive type utilizes three small screens of coarse wire mesh in place of the high-precision electrodes. Weighing less than 2 ounces, it is particularly effective in analysing gases in weak concentrations when they have been diluted with other vapours and are consequently under almost unnoticeable pressure.

The device is ideal for use aboard spacecraft where instrumentation must be compact as well as accurate, while in industry it could serve as an air pollution monitor. In addition, medical laboratories could use it in the analysis of blood and the diagnosis of respiratory disease. In the new spectrometer, a variable magnetic field is set up by a combination of direct and alternating radio-frequency voltages. Charged particles—gas ions—are injected into the field. Ions with unstable trajectories escape, but ions of a particular mass are trapped within the field and strike a detector which measures their number. Ions of any given mass can be detected by applying different combinations of direct and alternating voltages.

Increasing the World's Food

Food production is a field in which science is called upon to produce some extremely novel ideas. One that made its appearance in 1970 was a merry-go-round for milking cows. Conventional cow-milking systems are laid out on a "herring-bone" pattern which can accommodate up to 50 cows an hour. The rotary system can milk as many as 70 cows an hour, and can easily be used on herds of 80–150 cows in one manageable milking session. Basically, the machine comprises a circular frame 24 ft. in diameter, carrying eight stands which are about 3 ft. from the floor. It is powered by an electric motor through reduction gearing and a friction roller which drives the platform. A cow is positioned on the platform, and the operator prepares its udder and puts on the cups; he then presses a foot pedal which rotates the platform to allow another cow to enter the next stand. As the first cow gets off another one gets on, so that there are always eight cows being milked at one time. The milk is passed from a recorder jar at each of the eight stands to a separate container each time the machine rotates, and from the container it passes through a pipeline to the dairy.

Australian engineers developed a completely automatic method of producing cheddar cheese. The system combines curd separation, fusing, cheddaring, milling, salting, and hooping. Known as the "Lact-o-matic" system, it involves a synchronized line of machines which can produce 3,500 lb. of cheese an hour, with only two operators. Electronic weighing ensures that the correct amount of salt is used, and airborne contamination is avoided by the use of fitted covers over every stage of the process.

A food of the future is a substance known at present simply as "A35". When eaten, it tastes like rice, *or* beef stew, *or* meat pie filling, *or* chicken curry. In fact, the scientists who developed it claim that with another four years of research—and about £3 million to spend on their work—they can make it taste like almost anything—which is no mean achievement when one learns that "A35" is, in fact, fungus. It was produced at the laboratories of a British firm of flour millers. The fungus contains 50 per cent protein (compared with the 15 per cent protein in beef), but can be sold at a fraction of the cost of meat. The scientists are keeping secret its constitution and the way they make it grow. Professor Arnold Spicer, head of the team of scientists who developed it, revealed that in its raw state the fungus is colourless, tasteless, and powdery, but by adding colouring and flavouring it can be made to taste like and resemble any form of food.

If Professor Arnold completes his research during 1971, he may help to feed the hungry half of the world at a fraction of the expected cost. For example, "A35 meat" would cost only 5p a pound, yet would have twice as much protein as real meat. First to taste "A35" will be British housewives, who will buy it under "mock" guises because Professor Arnold feels that they would rather buy "mock steak" than "a piece of genuine synthesized protein."

A new system of controlling vital freshwater resources was presaged by the work of Dr. Larry Huggins and Dr. E. J. Monke, of Purdue University, Lafayette, Indiana, who developed a technique for predicting rainfall distribution, thereby laying the groundwork for an economic and feasible approach to the planning and design of reservoirs, drainage

Drs. Huggins and Monke with the rainfall simulator that they used, in combination with a computer, to predict the distribution of rainfall on the ground.

Purdue University, Lafayette, Indiana, U.S.A.

systems, and other structures used in water conservation. By using computers and a rainfall simulator, they developed a mathematical model for predicting what happens to surface run-off water—how much sinks into the ground, how much runs off, and how long it takes for the water to reach a reservoir or lake. Having constructed a watershed with a series of tiny sections, they then mathematically defined the run-off in each section according to the amount and intensity of rainfall. From these data, which were analysed by a computer, they developed a general model for use in predicting surface run-off patterns. Laboratory testing was carried out with the help of a simulator which can produce rainfall at almost any rate and impact. Huggins and Monke are now refining their mathematical model for greater accuracy, and they hope to have it available for practical use within three years.

Rainfall prediction will be of great help to farmers and crop growers. So will a new automatic cotton picker which was introduced in America in 1970, since it is a device that can be adapted for most kinds of crops. Cotton-growers all over the world, facing strong competition from man-made fibres, are always looking for any new ideas which will help to reduce production costs. The automatic cotton picker is a self-propelled machine which can pick two rows at a time, matching harvesting speed to crop and field conditions.

Manufactured Diamonds

Diamond miners are likewise wondering about future competition from manufactured

Self-propelled automatic mechanical cotton picker, an American invention to save labour costs. It can pick two rows at a time.

These one-carat gem-sized diamonds are manufactured from graphite, but are indistinguishable from the natural product.

General Electric Company, U.S.A.

diamonds. Synthetic diamonds have been made for several years in South Africa, Ireland, Sweden, and the U.S.A., by a process which, in a matter of hours, simulates the tremendous heat and pressure that produce natural diamonds over millions of years. The only difference between natural and synthetic diamonds —both kinds are genuine diamonds in every sense—is that natural diamonds come in all sizes and a variety of colours and grades of perfection, whereas synthetic diamonds have until now been made only in the form of "grit"—microscopic particles which, although of perfect shape individually, are too small to be of any value except as an industrial medium for grinding wheels.

In 1970, however, the picture changed when an American company succeeded in synthesizing diamonds of gem size and quality. One-carat diamonds were produced from graphite, the substance which is used in pencil leads. The synthetic gems have all the attributes of natural diamonds—hardness, colour, and clarity—and they can be cut and polished in the normal way. The only drawback is that, for the time being at least, they are more costly to produce than those which come from the diamond mines.

Diamonds were associated in 1970 with an interesting development in Japan where scientists perfected a method of foiling diamond thieves with a device called the "Miwa Brilliant ID Scope". This, in effect, fingerprints cut diamonds by photographing the patterns created by refracted light from the stones. Even the minutest variations in the facets of a diamond alter these light patterns, and it is therefore possible to keep a record of all known diamonds. The device, which is about the size of a portable radio, can also distinguish between real diamonds (natural or synthetic) and "paste".

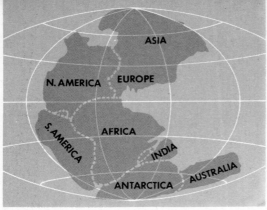

In the Permian period (225 million years ago).

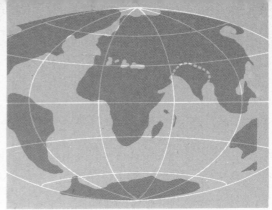

The positions to which the continents have drifted today.

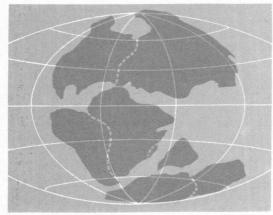

In the Triassic period (200 million years ago).

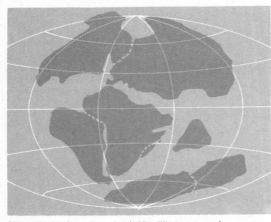

Above: in the Jurassic period (135 million years ago).

Below: in the Cretaceous period (65 million years ago).

The Drifting Continents

P. D. J. HOLLAND, M.A.

UNDOUBTEDLY THE GREATEST geological interest has been generated and the greatest advances have been made in confirming the hypothesis of what is commonly called "continental drift" or, more recently, "sea-floor spreading". Evidence has been gathered from sites all over the world, including the East and West Indies, the Atlantic Ocean, the Mediterranean, Africa, and South America, and from such different branches of study as biology, geophysics, and geology.

The theory of continental drift, first suggested at the beginning of the 20th century by a German meteorologist, Alfred Wegener, is briefly that at one time all the present separate land masses of the earth formed one huge solid area, which has subsequently split up and its portions drifted apart to form the continents that we know today. The concept of sea-floor spreading, first put forward in 1960 as the means by which continental drift takes place, was confirmed beyond reasonable doubt in 1969 by the results of the first phase of the Joint Oceanographic Institutes' deep-sea drilling project. Using techniques developed for the abandoned Mohole project, the drilling ship, *Glomar Challenger*, stays within a circle of 100-ft. diameter for the several days it takes to complete a drilling. By September 1970 12 phases had been completed, 50,000 miles travelled, over 160 holes bored, and more than 4 miles of oceanic sediments recovered. The next site is to be the Mediterranean, while further cruises are planned until August 1972.

The basic premise of the sea-floor spreading theory—and no sediments collected by the drilling programme have contradicted it—is that material from the Earth's mantle rises, emerges from mid-oceanic ridges, becomes magnetized in the direction of the geomagnetic field, and moves away from each side of the ridge. This, together with the occasional reversals of the Earth's magnetic field (*see* Advances in Physics and Chemistry, p. 80), results in a series of normally and reversely magnetized zones running parallel to the ridge.

Plate Tectonics

Taking these theoretical considerations a step farther is the concept of plate tectonics, which incorporates the hypotheses of both continental drift and sea-floor spreading. It is now accepted that the Earth's crust is composed of a number of "plates", large and small, which are rigid sections in constant motion, with deformation taking place only around their edges. They are bounded by oceanic ridges, by ocean trench and continental mountain systems, and by what are called transform faults (seismically active frac-

tures in the Earth's crust). The map of the Earth's major plates (below) shows that they include both continental and oceanic areas, and that is why the term "continental drift" is inappropriate, for the continents are merely passengers on the plates which are carrying them. Deep trenches, such as those on the east and west sides of the Pacific, are formed by the downward drag of plates meeting and plunging at an angle of about 45 degrees. These become the centres of deep-seated earthquakes. The relative lightness and buoyancy of the continents prevents them from being consumed beneath the trenches, but it is said that the compression results in the formation of mountain systems, which are indeed commonly associated with ocean trenches.

It has been estimated that the rate of movement of sea-floor spreading averages about 2 centimetres a year, although variations from 1 centimetre a year near Iceland to 9 centimetres a year in the equatorial Pacific Ocean have been recorded. On this basis, it seems that perhaps 50 per cent of the present deep sea floor, constituting one third of the surface area of the Earth, was formed in the last 65 million years, and that none of the ocean floors is older than 225 million years. The

The latest theory of continental drift is that the Earth's crust comprises a number of moving "plates" (the coloured and shaded areas in the map below), upon which the continents are carried. At their edges are active ridge crests, transform faults, deep oceanic trenches, and zones of compression, some of which are the sites of earthquakes and some of mountain systems. In the map, the six major plates are named. Minor ones are numbered, as follows: 1, Arabian; 2, Philippine; 3, Cocos; 4, Nasea; 5, Caribbean; 6, Scotia. The arrows indicate the directions of sea-floor spreading, and by their size the speed of the movement, which varies from 1 centimetre per year near Iceland to 9 centimetres per year in the equatorial part of the Pacific Ocean.

Reproduced by permission of F. J. Vine, School of Environmental Sciences, University of East Anglia, and of "Nature", London

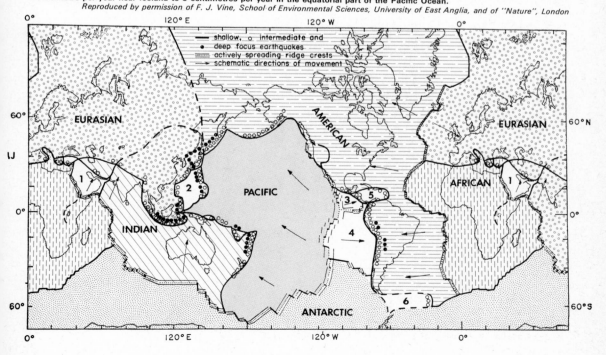

The *Glomar Challenger*, the American ocean-floor drilling ship, which can bring up samples of rock from 2,500 ft. beneath the sea floor which is itself 20,000 ft. below the surface.

oldest rock brought up so far by the drilling programme is 160 million years old. It was obtained near the Bahamas, and fits in well with other calculations that the east coast of the U.S.A. separated from north-west Africa 180–190 million years ago.

Further supporting evidence is provided by the discovery of shallow-water fossils in the deepest part of the Atlantic Ocean, at the base of a 25,000-ft.-high limestone cliff off the eastern end of the Dominican Republic. The history of the oceans earlier than 225 million years ago can be studied only by analysis of the rocks of present land masses. It was recently calculated that the differences between the east and west coasts of North America—differences of rock types and of volume of sediments—can be explained by the westward movement of the continent.

Cores recovered from Orphan Knoll, an isolated sea mount just beyond the continental shelf near Newfoundland, support earlier evidence from the Rockall plateau that the split between North America and Europe was not as clean as that between South America and Africa. It is thought that the eastern Canary Islands of Lanzarote, Fuerteventura, and Concepcion Bank are continental fragments left by the break-up of Gondwanaland (the name given by geologists to the southern land mass before it broke up and drifted apart). The western Canary Islands, however, are typical cones built from sea-floor vents.

Fossil Evidence

Evidence from many sources was considered before the computerized fit of the southern continents was produced. There are many geological links between Africa and South America, a newly discovered one being a thick pre-Cambrian series in the Bahia region of Brazil, which extends into central Gabon in Africa. There are also a number of striking geological links between Australia and Western Antarctica. The best estimate of the time of the break-up is probably given by evidence of fossil fauna: the joins of South America with Africa, Africa with Madagascar, and Madagascar with India are the most certain fits on this basis. It seems from this evidence that plate margins were established in Gondwanaland in Jurassic and Cretaceous times, and that dispersal took place in Upper Cretaceous and Tertiary times. This created the continental fragments of South America, Africa, Arabia, Madagascar, India, Australia, New Zealand, and Antarctica. Indications from geomagnetism, however, suggest that the South Atlantic began to open in Triassic times (about 200 million years ago), and that it was half open by Cretaceous times (65 million years ago).

It is apparent that, although the main argument regarding the truth or falsity of the continental drift theory is at an end, research and discussion will continue about the issues of fit and timing. What is more, geologists are no farther in their understanding of the heat mechanisms that produce the moving force.

Corollaries of the Theory

With the radical re-thinking about the Earth's structure it is not surprising that ideas central to geology are being re-examined. One of them is the theory of mountain building referred to. The hypothesis recently put forward is that lumps of crustal material are added to the bottom of the continental crust. This addition leads, by the principle of isostasy (which states that the Earth's crust must be in a state of balance), to the buckling of the crust and the placing of material above the earlier additions. The oceanic material comes from the oceanic crust, which is dragged down when the lithosphere, some 40–45 miles thick, slides beneath a continent. This is said to explain, for example, the relationship between the Andes, the trench off the South American coast, and the lithospheric current descending beneath it.

Glaciation is another topic about which ideas are being revised by recent developments. The latest part of the drilling programme brought up, from a depth corresponding to 3 million years ago, rock fragments which are thought to have been dropped by melting icebergs. This puts back by over a million years the previously estimated beginning of the glacial period. (Incidentally, beneath the glacial debris were found subtropical organisms which show that before the glaciation the North Atlantic Drift or "Gulf

Stream" was probably warming the coast of Labrador and not that of Britain.)

More important is the recent theory that continental drift is the *cause* of ice ages. Changes in the distribution of land and sea affect the circulation of the air-ocean system and, therefore, the climatic zoning of the Earth and the mean annual temperatures at various points. A fall of only 3–10°C is sufficient to reduce the amount of heat absorbed by the Earth and so further lower the temperature.

In Cambrian and Ordovician times the South Pole lay below what is now North Africa. The central Sahara was widely glaciated, and many features, such as glaciated valleys, erratic boulders, eskers, and tillites, have been identified in the Gautier Mountains on the Niger–Libya borders. The area to the north became at times a meltwater plain strewn with glacial debris, traces of which have been found in the Hassi Messaoud oilfield some 600 miles away. In the Carboniferous the South Pole underlay South Africa, and in the Permian it was under eastern Antarctica and Australia. It seems that the South Pole was glaciated for over 400 million years altogether. Glaciation is thus not the isolated or rhythmic occurrence it was thought to be.

Earthquakes and Volcanoes

A study of earthquakes as indicators of earth movement is central to the understanding of plate tectonics. One of the most catastrophic earthquakes ever known occurred on May 31, 1970, in the Peruvian Andes, where over 50,000 people were killed. The epicentre was some 15 miles off the Peruvian coast west of Chimbote. Two thirds of the people who died were living in buildings made of adobe (sun-dried clay and straw) which collapsed on them. The other deaths resulted from the triggering off by the earthquake of an avalanche of ice and rock from the 21,860-ft. mountain Nevados Huascaran. The avalanche, moving on a cushion of air at 250 m.p.h., travelled 9 miles in under 3 minutes. One branch of it rode over a 600-ft.-high ridge and descended upon two small towns. Earlier, on March 28, 1970, another severe earthquake had killed 1,000 people and made 80,000 homeless in the upper reaches of the Gediz river in Turkey.

These events have given impetus to research into the forecasting and control of earthquakes. It has been suggested that the severity of earthquakes could be modified in two ways. Observation that they sometimes follow the infilling of reservoirs has suggested that the injection of water into the rocks might release strain by reducing frictional resistance to fracturing. Alternatively, setting off a nuclear explosion might have a similar effect.

Meanwhile, instrumentation in the area of earthquake prediction is becoming more and more sophisticated. For example, at least four new types of laser seismometers, which are strain-measuring devices, have been designed in the last two or three years. Further, instrumental coverage of the world is increasing rapidly. There is a growing feeling that earthquake control is becoming more of a real possibility. The prediction of volcanic eruptions is also getting more fruitful. Recent research in New Zealand, following eruptions at Mounts Ruapehu and Ngauruhoe, suggests

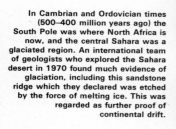
In Cambrian and Ordovician times (500–400 million years ago) the South Pole was where North Africa is now, and the central Sahara was a glaciated region. An international team of geologists who explored the Sahara desert in 1970 found much evidence of glaciation, including this sandstone ridge which they declared was etched by the force of melting ice. This was regarded as further proof of continental drift.

strongly that magnetic changes are normal features of volcanic eruptions. The most rapid occur during the eruption itself, but notice of impending eruption is given by smaller changes over a period of a few hours to a few days beforehand.

Even Great Britain had her earthquake in 1970. The shock—on August 9—was felt in Cumberland, Durham, Lancashire, Yorkshire, and Westmorland, the epicentre being near the town of Kirkby Stephen. With a magnitude on the Richter scale of between 4·5 and 4·7, it was one of the largest ever recorded in the country. It is thought that the movement took place along either the Dent or the Craven fault. There have also been several earthquakes in the last two years with a magnitude of up to 4·0 in the Bangor area, associated with the faults along the Menai Straits.

Uranium in Scotland

Mineral prospecting in and around the British Isles has continued with increasing momentum. It was disclosed in August 1970 that deposits of uranium ore in northern Scotland are considerably more widespread than had previously been thought. They are located in Caithness and Sutherland, around Ousdale, Helmsdale, and Brawlbin. It is not yet certain whether they are sufficiently large to justify exploitation, but a zone over half a mile long has been found in the Ousdale area. It is planned to continue the survey until 1972.

Two new prospecting techniques are helping in the intensified prospecting proceeding in Great Britain. Very low frequency radio waves can penetrate land up to 500 ft. below the surface, and are distorted by changes in the magnetic and electrical properties of the material through which they pass. An airborne

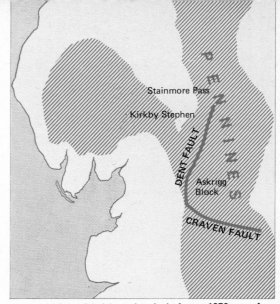

The site of Great Britain's earthquake in August 1970, one of the largest ever recorded in the country.

detector system analyses the distortions to produce a map of underground metallic and non-metallic deposits which would not be apparent from the surface. Sand, gravel, and underground water, for example, can be found in this way. Another development is the mercury-vapour "sniffer", which can detect mercury vapour in the air at a concentration as low as one part in a billion. Its importance lies in the fact that mercury vapour is given off by many ore bodies, notably gold and silver.

The first long-term drilling project to study the geology and the mineral content of the British continental shelf started in the Irish Sea in July. It is known that the geological structures below Cardigan Bay are similar to the gas-bearing areas of the North Sea. Drilling will therefore take place in Cardigan Bay, and then move on to the northern Irish Sea, the Moray Firth, and the Firth of Forth.

Some micro-fossils have been found in pre-Cambrian Torridonian chert in north-west Scotland. While these do not compare in age with the 3,000-million-year-old micro-fossils of South Africa, at something over 963 million years old they are the oldest micro-fossils found in Britain.

Another survey, with implications beyond geology, was the taking of 60,000 samples of fine sediments from small streams, about one sample to every square mile of England and Wales. The aim is to produce an atlas of 25 trace elements, including copper, molybdenum, cobalt, and manganese, which play an important part in life processes. It is expected that the completed atlas will reveal correlations between plant, animal, and human deficiency diseases that are at present unsuspected.

Searching with a scintillometer for uranium in Scotland.
United Kingdom Atomic Energy Authority

TOWARDS THE GLOBAL VILLAGE

PAT HAWKER

IN THE FIRST YEAR of this new decade, the most significant feature of telecommunications was the massive nature of their expansion. The world over, the constant babble of telephone chatter, the rattle of Telex messages, and the discreet purr of computer communicating with computer grow apace, throwing up statistics that stagger the imagination.

There are now well over 250 million telephones in the world—rather more than 100 million of them in the U.S.A., over 20 million in Japan, 14 million in the United Kingdom. Each U.S. subscriber now averages over 700 telephone calls per year, and the Canadians are only a fraction less talkative. International telecommunications traffic is growing at the rate of 25 per cent per year. In Great Britain, the Post Office is investing in new plant at a rate of £300 million annually, catering for more than a million new subscribers in each 12-month period, with Telex subscribers,

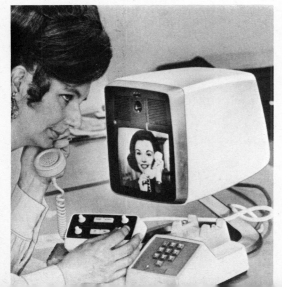

The long-promised television-telephone at last became a reality for some subscribers in Pittsburgh, U.S.A., when the Bell Telephone Co. started their "Picturephone" service on July 1, 1970.

having passed the 30,000 mark, increasing at the rate of 12 per cent per year. British computer data terminals (Datel services) double each year; now over 14,000, they are expected to reach 50,000 by 1973. More and more countries are linked by high-quality telephone circuits via communications satellites in space or cables snaking beneath the oceans. A single subscriber trunk dialling call depends on the functioning of some 140,000 components.

Broadband "Highways"

To cope with this insatiable demand for local, inter-city, and international facilities, engineers are planning new forms of broadband "highways" along which thousands of calls can be transmitted simultaneously. For example, during 1970 the British Post Office announced plans for installing new 60 MHz coaxial-cable routes between London and Birmingham during the next few years. These systems will have nine pairs of coaxial cables, each capable of carrying 10,800 simultaneous two-way telephone circuits—making possible a route total of 97,200 conversations. Large though this total is by present standards, it can be expected to cope for only a few years with the estimated requirement of 12,000 additional circuits each year on this busy route.

For the future, even these new systems will seem meagre in comparison with the proposed technique of piping enormous numbers of circuits through "waveguides" (see page 49). Another alternative is based on the idea of concentrating the enormous traffic capabilities of laser light beams along hair-thin glass fibres; although it is unlikely to be operational for a number of years, experimental work on this system is making progress. During 1970, it was announced that research engineers at Standard Telecommunications Laboratories in the United Kingdom had succeeded in developing a tiny laser, about $\frac{1}{2}$ mm long, that gives adequate continuous output of light even at normal room temperatures. This device, called a "double heterostructure gallium arsenide laser", is seen as a vital step towards the realization of practical optical fibre transmission systems which could provide links capable of carrying up to 100 television channels on each tiny fibre.

Australian Developments

The year proved to be of particular significance to the growth of Australian telecommunications. In May, the automatic Telex service, already available to Great Britain, Canada, Hong Kong, Japan, and New Zealand, was extended to 11 countries of western Europe. In July, the country's largest single project, 1,430 miles of broadband microwave systems linking Western Australia into the national network of telephone and television distribution circuits, was officially opened. For some months before this, many Sydney–Perth telephone calls were being routed via Intelsat III satellites. Early in 1971, the Australian Post Office will complete another major broadband trunk project in Western Australia: a 530-mile coaxial cable system between Carnarvon and Port Hedland. The broadband network will then stretch down the west coast, across to Adelaide, Melbourne, and Hobart, and up the entire east coast to Cairns, linking all the capital cities and hundreds of provincial centres. It was also announced during 1970 that Darwin and other northern centres would be linked into the national network in 1972 by the building of a new microwave system between Mount Isa and Townsville, Queensland.

The Australian Post Office are also establishing a nation-wide common-user data network using computer-based switching centres to be located in Sydney, Melbourne, Brisbane, Adelaide, and Perth. This service will become available during 1971. A contract was also awarded in June for the supply of Australia's first computer-controlled trunk telephone exchange, which will be in Sydney. Among the many additional facilities made possible by such exchanges are automatic redirection of calls and much easier tracing of malicious and annoying calls.

Computers Are Taking Over

Computers are fast becoming an essential component in the operation and administration of telecommunications. Systems for telephone accounting and customer billing, traffic analyses, fault analyses, the assembling of commercial data, network planning, the production of telephone directories, and computer-controlled telephone and Telex exchanges are all coming into general usage. The Apollo moon-flight communications network relies on the direct use of 48 computers at 14 ground-based centres, tracking sites, and instrumentation ships. The flight controllers and astronauts have the benefit of the fastest international network facilities ever linked together; in total more than 70 general-purpose computers at 25 sites are involved. Their importance was underlined during the unlucky Apollo 13 flight; much of the credit for the safe return of the astronauts belongs to the smooth functioning of the communications systems.

In the future there will probably be two-way telephone conversations between people and computers. The computer will "hear" the speaker's words and will, in a sense, interpret them. It will then compose an appropriate reply and respond in spoken words. Bell Telephones in the U.S.A. are already investigating systems which would allow a computer to "reply" to a subscriber who dials a non-working number. For example, soon such a subscriber may receive from the computer the message: "The number you have reached, 555-2638, has been changed. The new number is 555-3598. Please make a note of it. . . ."

Communication by Satellite

The international space communications network, at present based on the use of Intelsat III satellites, continued to grow throughout 1970, carrying an ever-increasing proportion of long-distance telephone conversations, reaching more countries, and attracting rising revenues. Few months went by without the entry into service of another giant dish antenna or the announcement of more to come. Goonhilly 2, in Cornwall, officially opened in January, links the U.K. directly with, for example, Ceduna (Australia's fourth civil earth station) which was opened early in the year. The opening, inaugurating the first single-hop satellite circuits between the U.K. and Australia, was marked by a relay of live colour television pictures.

The 1,200-channel Intelsat IIIF, launched on January 14, was insured with Lloyd's of London until it reached geostationary orbit, to protect Comsat stockholders against 75 per cent of the potential losses, for the two previous Intelsat satellites had failed to reach orbit in 1968–69. Intelsat IIIG, which followed on April 23, suffered from a premature shutdown of the second-stage engine, which placed it in a lower orbit than planned, but this was subsequently corrected and it entered commercial service on May 8. Intelsat IIIH, launched on July 23, was placed over the Pacific Ocean; this 330-lb. satellite has a hydrazine thruster so that it can be moved over the Indian Ocean, if necessary, as a back-up satellite. By the end of 1970 there were 45 ground stations in 32 countries using the Intelsat III satellite system.

Rather more difficulties were experienced in the course of the long and complex negotiations for the definitive arrangements for the International Telecommunications Satellite Consortium (Intelsat). This body, set up on an interim basis in 1964, now includes more than 75 different countries. Originally it had been expected that the final arrangements, including such matters as voting powers and day-to-day management—which has been the concern of Comsat (the U.S. Communications Satellite

Weather satellites increased in number and efficiency in 1970. Above: testing the TV camera carried by a Tiros satellite. Right: programming the computer that handles the data transmitted by ITOS-1; the satellite itself is in the foreground. ITOS-1 took the photo in page 138.

Corporation)—would be reached in 1969 or 1970. However, differences of opinion between American and European administrations delayed an agreement, in spite of compromise proposals put forward by the Australians and Japanese. Operationally, however, Intelsat has proved itself one of the world's first true and successful international partnerships of independent nations.

The Russians launched three windmill-shaped Molniya satellites during the year: the latest, Molniya IQ, which entered orbit on September 25, brought the total in the series to 15. Molniya satellites have six "sails", weigh about 2,200 lb., and are placed in cigar-shaped orbits with a 12-hour period, which makes them ideally suited to provide continuous radio and TV coverage throughout the Soviet Union.

Two 1970 space communications anniversaries deserve notice. Early Bird (Intelsat I), launched on April 6, 1965, completed five years in space; although now "retired" and no longer used except for emergency service, this world's first commercial communications satellite was still capable, when needed, of providing useful facilities—a remarkable example of the reliability of modern unattended electronics. April 1970 also saw the tenth anniversary of the introduction of weather satellites, which provide cloud cover pictures by means of novel techniques. In the ten years the Americans have placed in orbit 23 meteorological satellites (the Tiros, Nimbus, Essa, and Itos series). Over a million pictures of the earth's cloud cover and other data for weather forecasting and research have been transmitted. Since 1963, the use of the automatic picture transmission (APT) system has allowed cloud

photographs to be received on relatively simple equipment, and a number of radio amateurs and schools have even built and operated their own receivers.

Operational coverage by U.S. weather satellites was more than doubled with the launch of ITOS-1 on January 23. This box-shaped satellite carries four TV cameras and two infra-red cameras for taking day and night cloud-cover pictures in the visible and infra-red wavelengths. Nimbus 4, which followed on April 8, expanded the capability of measuring a complete vertical atmospheric structure—showing temperature, ozone, and water vapour. This is done by means of an interferometer spectrometer which measures the infra-red energy coming from the Earth. The satellite also collects data by radio from remote weather balloons, buoys, ships, and inaccessible locations, providing increased information on atmospheric circulation. Russian weather satellites included four in the Meteor series, launched in March, April, June, and October respectively, to maintain global TV observation of the Earth's weather, cloud cover, ice and snow, and thermal emissions from the day and night sides. Nowadays, weather satellites transmit cloud pictures and other detailed weather data to more than 500 receiving stations in 50 countries.

Australian experimenters and amateurs

Model of Goonhilly 3, the new British Post Office aerial designed to work with the Intelsat IV generation of communications satellites.

the year at Birmingham University. In September 1970, the British Post Office announced plans for Goonhilly 3. It will have a 97-ft.-diameter aerial providing a capacity for 1,800 telephone channels and a colour television channel in readiness for the next generation (Intelsat IV) high-capacity communications satellites, the first of which is expected to be launched during 1971.

More Undersea Cables

Despite the rapid growth of space communications, the insatiable demand for more facilities has brought about an equally spectacular spread of submarine cable systems. In five years the traffic capacity of such systems has been trebled. By the end of 1970, some 94 cable systems, comprising 85,000 route miles and no less than 14·2 million circuit miles, were in operation.

The year saw the opening of another Transatlantic telephone cable system, TAT-5, from the U.S.A. to Spain and Portugal, and, via another new cable, MAT-1, to Italy, which added a total of 740 simultaneous telephone circuits to this important route. It has been estimated that by 1980 there will be a need for between 10,000 and 20,000 telephone circuits across the Atlantic, plus many data and Telex circuits: thus there seems an assured future for both satellite and cable systems.

To cope with the rapidly increasing international traffic, a new international switching centre—which may become the largest "gateway" exchange of its kind in the world—is being built in the City of London. Ultimately, the exchange will be able to connect up to 200,000 calls an hour, using more than 20,000 cable, satellite, and terrestrial telephone circuits. To be named Mondial House, the building is expected to be completed in 1972, when installation of equipment will begin. The present 30 million international calls made each

scored a success when a small satellite "Australis Oscar 5", built by enthusiasts at Melbourne University, was launched in January 1970 from California by NASA. The satellite, which carried beacons operating in the 29 and 144 MHz amateur bands, was heard by many hundreds of amateurs throughout the world, during about 300 "operational" orbits.

Experimental work in this field continues. A large 90-ft.-diameter antenna at Chilbolton, Hampshire, is used by the British Radio and Space Research Station specifically for wave-propagation study, and is being improved to allow its use up to 20,000 MHz. Research at even higher frequencies is possible with a new high-accuracy radio telescope opened during

Artist's impression of Mondial House, fronting the Thames (right), which will be perhaps the largest international telephone exchange in the world, capable of connecting as many as 200,000 calls per hour. The building will be completed in 1972.

year from the U.K. are expected to increase to about 70 million by 1975. The U.K. has direct circuits to about 75 countries, and other countries can be reached through intermediate centres. At present about half of all international calls are dialled directly by the users, and this is expected to increase soon to 70 per cent. In March 1970 it became possible for subscribers in London and New York to dial one another directly. International dialling is still in its infancy, but all the indications are that before long telephone users will literally have the world at their fingertips.

Dialling a TV Programme

In January 1970 the British company Rediffusion Research publicly demonstrated for the first time a "Dial-a-Programme" wired-television system now under development. When completed, it could give viewers the choice of not three, five, or ten programme channels, but an almost unlimited number. Dialling into a local "TV programme exchange"—akin to a local telephone exchange—would bring back along the subscriber's wire any one of twenty, thirty, or even fifty programmes. For urban viewers such an ambitious wired-television system is by no means out of the question from a technical viewpoint; it is less certain whether in most countries it would be possible to overcome the many complex legal and financial problems involved. However, in the U.S.A., where some urban viewers already have the choice of over ten channels from local stations or via the rapidly growing number of CATV (community antenna television) systems, a field trial of the new British system began in mid-1970, providing some 300 viewers with a choice of twenty different channels.

Both in the U.S.A. and the U.K. the number of viewers who now receive programmes by wire, instead of direct from broadcasting stations, is considerable. Well over one million homes in the U.K. obtain their television signals not from their own aerials but by various types of wire networks. The network operators, who can erect elaborate master receiving stations on favourable sites, are often able to supply good pictures in weak signal areas. Moreover, some local authorities dislike the appearance of a mass of TV aerials on housing estates under their control, and have opted for community systems in which all houses on the estate are wired to the network.

There are two main systems in use in the U.K. In one, the signals come along coaxial cables as a series of very high frequency signals (from about 50 to 200 MHz); in the other (developed in the U.K.), the programmes are distributed at high frequency (between about 3 and 12 MHz) using pairs of wires (similar to normal telephone wires) rather than special coaxial cable, with a separate pair of wires for each programme. The proposed "Dial-a-Programme" system is based on the high frequency approach. But instead of the present multi-core cables containing up to about twelve pairs of wires going to each home, it would be based on cheap four-core (two pairs) cable—one pair of wires to carry all vision signals, the other for the sound signals and for control purposes.

A Procession of Programmes

In the conventional multi-core system, all the channels are brought continuously to the viewer's home, and he selects his choice of programme with his switch. But some years ago Rediffusion, investigating ways in which remote villages and farmhouses could be wired up more economically, developed a system in which only one signal at a time is carried to the house, and the viewer decides by means of his switch which programme it shall be. It was soon realized that this principle could be extended to more elaborate networks, and would open the way to a greater choice of programme than could ever be offered by merely increasing the number of cores in the multi-core distribution cables. It is now proposed that only one programme at a time should come to a viewer, but by means of a local "programme exchange" he could be "plugged into" any of a large number of programmes available at the exchange. Each exchange would serve up to a maximum of 5,000 urban viewers. Under such a system direct "on air" broadcasting could cease, or at least could be limited to providing main transmitters working to master receiving aerials. And the old problem of fitting enough television channels into the radio spectrum would thus be solved.

Demonstrating the new "Dial-a-Programme" system developed by Rediffusion for viewers who receive their TV by wire.

WILLIAM MORSE, B.Sc., M.I.Mech.E., P.Eng.

CONSTRUCTION
IDEAS AND ACHIEVEMENTS

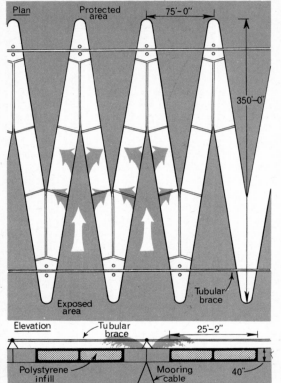

Plan — Protected area — 75'-0"

350'-0"

Exposed area — Tubular brace

Elevation — Tubular brace — 25'-2"

Polystyrene infill — Mooring cable — 40"

Floating Runways have been suggested as a means of providing the increased airport facilities required all over the world, without using up vast areas of valuable land near great cities. In connection with a plan for creating a new airport at Foulness near the mouth of the Thames the "Seadrome" scheme was devised by consulting engineers Archibald Shaw & Partners and Harris & Sutherland, under the sponsorship of Shell U.K. Limited. The artist's impression above shows a floating airport in use.

The Seadrome scheme is based on floating runways of concrete, made up of separate elements precast on shore and prestressed together. Hollow, buoyant slabs of concrete, 100 ft. square, would be cast on shore; ten of them would be placed end to end, and high-strength wires fed through the whole length, tensioned-up, and anchored. A runway would consist of a number of such strips placed side by side, held together with tensioned wires passed through transverse holes. The result would be a large expanse of concrete, made up from a number of identical square slabs.

The whole would resemble a series of egg-boxes of concrete, with a top slab, a bottom slab, and concrete partitions running in two directions parallel to the sides. Such a box will float if water is kept out of the compartments, but, to be on the safe side, they would be filled with expanded polystyrene (a very light, foamed material having a vast number of tiny closed cells) to exclude the water permanently. Such a pavement is not likely to crack under any foreseeable combination of load and temperature difference.

Instead of a vertical breakwater acting as a barrier to the waves, a horizontal floating barrier would be used, on which the waves would break as if on a beach and so spend themselves. The design suggested consists of a compressed zigzag structure, shown at left in plan and elevation. The waves would run in, in the direction of the arrows, and break laterally. Their energy would be progressively dissipated along the breakwater, and consequently the mooring forces could be comparatively small. The drawing below shows how the airport and breakwater would be moored.

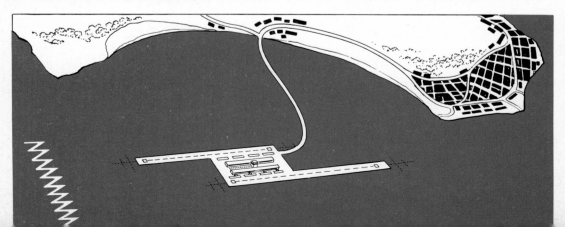

Desert Island Tower. The bulbous-looking tower below, built during 1970 in the Arabian Gulf state of Abu Dhabi, carries half a million gallons of desalinated water. With a height of 106 ft., a spheroidal diameter of 61 ft., and a base diameter of 28 ft., it is visible for miles across the 25,000 square miles of the territory.

The tower was fabricated by the Thompson Horseley Division of the John Thompson Group for the O.T.A.C. Company of Beirut. After trial erection in Britain, the tower was shipped to the Gulf, and the segments transported to the shore in Arab dhows, which alone could navigate the shallow waters of the harbour.

Landmark Tower. The 200-ft tower above is being constructed as a landmark for ships at Millers Point, N.S.W., Australia, by the Maritime Services Board and is expected to be in operation by July 1971.

Natural-Draught Cooling Towers. The twin cooling towers of the power station of the State Electricity Commission at Yallourn, Victoria, are the first hyperbolic natural-draught towers in Australia. They are large enough at the base, where the diameter is 295 ft., to take a soccer pitch. The height is 375 ft., and the minimum diameter 158 ft. at about 68 ft. from the top. Each tower cools 7 million gallons of water an hour, from a temperature of 99°F to 75°F, under normal conditions.

The decision to use towers of this design was influenced by the limited space, which made it impossible to dredge an artificial cooling lake on the site. The idea of employing induced draught towers was rejected because their comparatively low-level emission could have caused severe fog.

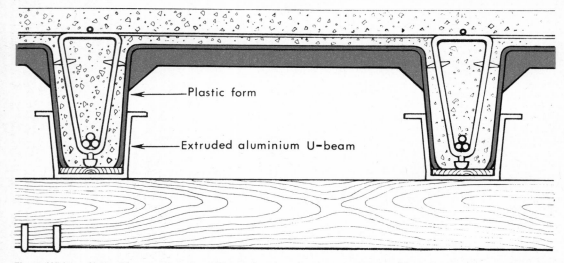

Floors Without Nails. The award-winning Ajab system of casting concrete flooring decks, devised by Ake Norlander, is a cheap and simple way of house-building. It consists of extruded aluminium U-beams, on which light-weight plastic forms are rapidly erected. The forms are fixed in place by the pressure of the concrete poured into them, so that nails and other fasteners are unnecessary.

By courtesy of "Sweden Now"

Shipbuilding in All Weathers. A fully weatherproof shipbuilding factory, equipped with sophisticated shipbuilding machinery, was opened in 1970 on the river Torridge, near Bideford, Devon, England, by Appledore Shipbuilders Ltd., part of the Court Line group. The 390 ft. × 110 ft. dock, which is really a dry dock that can be flooded, is covered by a main hall, measuring 400 ft. × 110 ft., with provision for an extension in length to 800 ft. All types of vessel up to 10,000 tons deadweight can be constructed here, uninterrupted by the weather. This represents a great saving, since most yards suffer a 20 per cent loss of productivity in the winter.

The whole system is designed to produce ships logically and efficiently under safe and comfortable conditions; the dock, buildings, cranes, offices, workshops, and machines are all planned accordingly. In many instances, when construction work on one vessel is completed, the dock is flooded and the ship floated across to the other side for fitting out, so that building of another vessel can go forward in the vacated space.

Viaduct at Lake Geneva. Civil engineers are increasingly adopting segmental concrete construction for bridges, using joints made with Araldite-based epoxy resin formulations. An instance is the 1½-mile elevated section of the N 9 highway along the north-eastern shore of Lake Geneva, between Chillon and Villeneuve. Mounted on slender piers 145 ft. high, the deck of the road consists of prefabricated concrete segments bonded together with Sikadur, an adhesive based on CIBA epoxy resin and made by SIKA International. Each T-section segment measured 10 ft. along the roadway, and weighed between 45 and 75 tons. A giant gantry crane, 135 yds. long and weighing 150 tons, placed each segment in position.

The box-section elements were manoeuvred into position as shown at right, and an operator, working on a platform slung from the gantry, applied adhesive to both sides of the joint. The element was then moved into its final position for stressing, the adhesive at this stage acting as a lubricant and aiding fine manipulation.

Over 50,000 cubic yards of concrete and 5,000 tons of steel were used in the project, which cost £3 million. A special concrete works—one of the largest of its type in Europe—was built to supply the material.

Japanese Pipeline Bridge. Part of an 8-mile pipeline system that carries industrial water from the Fuji river No. 2 hydroelectric power station to industrial areas in Shizuoka prefecture consists of a 1,138-yd. pipeline bridge, one of the longest in the world, across the river below Fujiyama (below). Two 7·2-ft.-diameter pipelines run across the ten arches of the bridge, with a total capacity of 1·41 million tons of water a day. Construction was by the steelmaking firm Nippon Kokan Kabushiki Kaisha.

World's Largest Bascule Bridge. This bridge (right) forms part of the 11,000-ft. bridge across the Bay of Cadiz in southern Spain, the steel structure for which was erected by Stahlbau Dortmund of Rheinische Stahlwerke, in co-operation with Spanish companies.

Ships up to 72 ft. high can pass through the closed bridge, but to allow the passage of large ocean-going ships the 220-ft. leaves of the bridge can be raised hydraulically in three minutes.

New Rochester Bridge. An ingenious engineering project has been carried out at Rochester, Kent, where an old disused railway bridge over the river Medway was converted into a modern road bridge which was opened in 1970. The diagram below shows the sequences of operations: 1. The old bridge, consisting of three parallel continuous wrought-iron plate girders, one in the centre and one on each side. 2. Two new steel box-girders were slid into place within the old bridge structure, and supported at the abutments and piers on temporary piers. 3. Slots were cut in the old plate girders, through which rolled steel joists, called needles, were passed, to carry the weight of the old bridge. 4. The outside

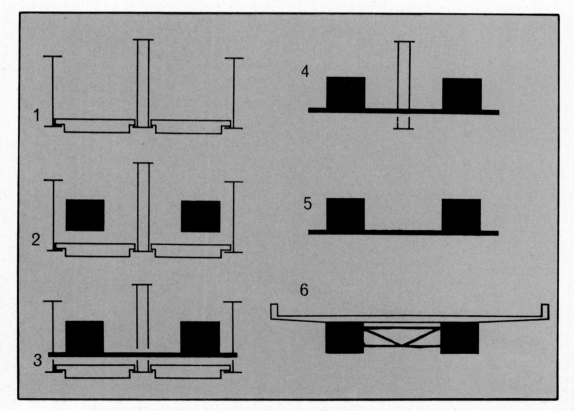

girders were cut into convenient pieces and removed. 5. The same was done to the centre girder, and it was removed. 6. The new girders were lowered about 8 ft. and the reinforced concrete deck erected on it.

The photo at top of the facing page shows the two new box-section girders (totalling 412 tons) in position between the old wrought-iron girders (totalling 973 tons). In this page, above left, the old wrought-iron girders are being burnt away; the slot for one of the "needles" can be seen just below the shadow of the ladder. Above right, the new box girders are being lowered to the correct level in a series of 5-in. stages, with the aid of sixteen 100-ton mechanical jacks. Meanwhile, the old piers and abutments were removed and temporary military trestling installed to carry the weight while all this work was done. The temporary supports were then removed and new abutments and piers built. Below are seen the new reinforced concrete piers supporting the box girders on rubber bearings; the varying depth of the new girders is well brought out in this photograph.

Finally, the reinforced concrete deck was constructed.

This deck acts compositely with the steel girders, and extreme care was needed in placing it, to avoid distortion and overstressing in the steel and to make due allowance for shrinkage.

Above is a general view from the Rochester side of the new road bridge and its approaches, showing the completed bridge deck. The new bridge stands between two existing bridges—a road bridge to the left, and a railway bridge still in use to the right. Below is the last stage in the construction—waterproofing the concrete deck and applying the hand-laid mastic asphalt. The photo shows the completed main deck, with kerbs, balustrading, and lighting columns already in position.

The new bridge was constructed for the Rochester Bridge Trust, and the approaches for the ministry of transport. A separate welded steel bridge to carry pipes and cables across the river was built for the various public utility service authorities. The consulting engineer for the whole project was J. Kenneth Anderson, M.A.(Cantab.), C.Eng., F.I.C.E., M.Cons.E., of Beckenham, Kent, who provided all the illustrations reproduced here and approved the written description.

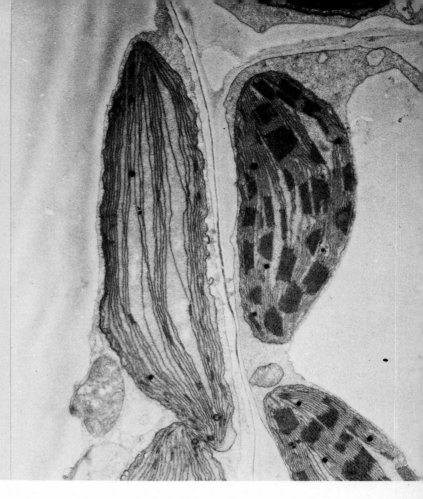

Two chloroplasts of maize seen under the electron microscope. Typical stacks of membranes (right) contrast with the loosely packed membranes (left) found in tropical grasses.

Progress in Biology

F. E. G. COX, B.Sc.,Ph.D.

Reader in Zoology in the University of London

MOST BIOLOGISTS would agree that one of the most important areas of biological research at the present time is the study of photosynthesis. It has been known since the 19th century that green plants use the energy of sunlight to convert carbon dioxide and water into oxygen and carbohydrates such as sugar. The energy from the sun is first absorbed by chlorophyll, which is contained in chloroplasts consisting of stacks of membranes enclosed in an envelope.

Much of the work on the initial biochemical steps in photosynthesis was carried out with isolated chloroplasts which, in fact, are unable to assimilate much carbon dioxide. Dr. D. A. Walker, of Imperial College, London, reported, in the journal *Nature*, that isolated chloroplasts lose 95 per cent of their ability to fix carbon dioxide, and that this can be correlated with the loss of the outer envelope, which is selectively permeable to various substances involved in the initial processes of photosynthesis. It is also now known that there are two different kinds of chloroplasts, the kind with stacks of membranes and another

in which these stacks are reduced. Two Australian workers, Drs. M. D. Hatch and C. P. Slack, demonstrated that the latter occurs in certain tropical grasses, and that in these grasses the initial stages of photosynthesis are very different from the classically accepted pattern. Such plants do not give off much carbon dioxide during respiration if the air taken in is free of this gas, and grow as well in air as in 3 per cent oxygen—features which distinguish them from the majority of plants. The initial biochemical pathway in such plants has been referred to as the Hatch-Slack pathway, by Dr. Michael Black of Queen Elizabeth College, London, to distinguish it from the Benson-Calvin pathway hitherto thought to be universal.

Better Cereals and Grasses

How this pathway can be correlated with the two kinds of chloroplasts is obscure. In an article in the *New Scientist*, Dr. Black and his colleague Ian Spooner pointed out that the biochemical processes in these tropical grasses are much more efficient than the

Benson-Calvin pathway, and that such plants grow more quickly and have a higher yield than temperate grasses closely related to them. The significance of these observations is two-fold. First, they will have a major effect on the selection and cultivation of grasses and cereals to feed an ever-increasing population; and, secondly, they indicate that such plants are physiologically adapted to an atmosphere low in carbon dioxide, and thus well able to live in the man-made atmosphere of today.

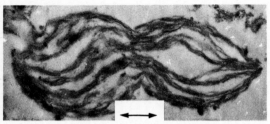

A chloroplast of a broad bean dividing, under the electron microscope. Arrows indicate one thousandth part of a millimetre.

Equally exciting work has been carried out on isolated chloroplasts by Stuart Ridley and Rachel Leech at the University of York. It has been known for some time that chloroplasts can remain alive in a variety of conditions outside plants, including snail and mammalian cells. It has been suspected that such isolated chloroplasts divide in their unnatural surroundings as they do in nature, but until the work of Ridley and Leech this had never been proved. Ridley and Leech managed to demonstrate it with chloroplasts of the broad bean maintained in a highly complex medium. This work also has important practical and theoretical considerations. Practically, the isolation of dividing chloroplasts might well be applied to the large-scale artificial production of sugars and other carbohydrates. Biologically, the possibility that chloroplasts might be regarded as symbiotic entities must again be considered. The assimilation of photosynthetic material into an animal must give it a tremendous evolutionary advantage, and such relationships have been encountered in coelenterates, flatworms, and molluscs. This is clearly an expanding area of research.

A New Kind of DNA

Nearly the whole of molecular biology for the past 10 years has been based on a single simple concept: that the structure of protein is entirely determined by the sequence of bases in the nucleic acid DNA (deoxyribonucleic acid). In other words, the information necessary for the synthesis of protein comes from the nucleus, and protein cannot form other protein or nucleic acid. Discoveries made

during 1970 have resulted in a critical reconsideration of the situation. Basically, the nucleus of a cell contains the nucleic acid DNA, which consists of paired long chains of four bases. The sequence of bases is repeated, directly or indirectly, in three forms of the nucleic acid RNA (ribonucleic acid): ribosomal-RNA, messenger-RNA, and transfer-RNA. What happens is this. The sequence of bases in the DNA is copied by the messenger-RNA, and this information is used when amino acids are brought from an amino-pool by transfer-RNA and assembled in long chains to form proteins at the ribosomes. The sequence of amino acids in any protein is therefore determined by the sequence of bases in the DNA in the nucleus. The questions that have been asked are whether this type of process holds for all cells, and whether it is the whole story.

Dr. Eugene Bell of the Massachusetts Institute of Technology found a new kind of DNA in the cytoplasm of certain animal cells. He suggested that the nuclear DNA is transcribed into messenger-DNA (not RNA) called information-DNA, which passes to the cytoplasm where it is transcribed into messenger-RNA. If this is true for all cells, it would answer a question that has been troubling molecular biologists for some time: does messenger-RNA occur in the nucleus, and, if it does, how does it get into the cytoplasm?

The most significant discovery in this area of molecular biology, however, has been that the flow of information from DNA to RNA is not always one-way. Drs. Howard Temin and Satoshi Mizutani of Wisconsin and David Baltimore of Massachusetts reported independently that certain RNA tumour viruses contain an enzyme which uses the RNA as a template for DNA synthesis. Dr. S. Spiegelman and his colleagues at New York confirmed the presence of a similar enzyme in all seven tumour viruses which they have examined. The New York scientists have also shown that the DNA produced is complementary to the viral RNA.

A considerable field of research has thus suddenly opened, and great efforts will be made to characterize the enzyme involved. The fact that all the viruses concerned produce tumours may be the biggest discovery in cancer research for many years. But it is important, when faced with discoveries of this magnitude, not to be carried away by them, and Dr. Francis Crick of Cambridge was quick to point that out. Writing in *Nature*, he suggested that there are three general transfers of information that occur in all cells: DNA→DNA, DNA→RNA, and RNA→protein. There are also, he wrote, three special transfers: RNA→RNA,

RNA→DNA, and possibly DNA→protein. The first two of these have been demonstrated only in cells infected with viruses. It seems sensible at the present time to accept the three general transfers as being common to all cells, and to await the discovery of the special transfers in cells other than those infected with viruses.

Isolation and Synthesis of a Gene

All biological activities are controlled by genes, and many attempts have been made to isolate genes and to synthesize them. A gene may be considered to be a length of DNA, and usually a group of genes operates together to bring about a particular process. In the bacterium *Escherichia coli*, three genes operate in a sequence to bring about the synthesis of three enzymes, which in turn enable the bacterium to make the sugar lactose. The first of these genes is called z and is associated with two small units, a promoter and an operator which regulate its activity. Dr. Jon Beckwith and his colleagues at Harvard succeeded in isolating this gene, and found that it consists of a helix of DNA containing 3,700 pairs of bases, of which 410 are in the operator and promoter region.

When one considers that the whole DNA molecule is about 3 million base pairs long, the immensity of the task facing the scientist who hopes to synthesize a particular gene is obvious. Nevertheless, this has been done, and the achievement must go down as one of the highlights of molecular biology. The successful scientists work in a team at Wisconsin, headed by Dr. H. G. Khorana. The particular gene synthesized is the one responsible for the transfer of the amino acid alanine from the amino-acid pool to the ribosome in a yeast. As genes go it is a small one, consisting of 77 base pairs. It was synthesized bit by bit. The structure and base sequence of the gene responsible for alanine transfer-RNA was known from the structure of the transfer-RNA itself. The gene was divided into three parts, and fractions of each part were synthesized chemically. The fragments were joined together, and the whole gene finally synthesized by taking advantage of the regions of overlap.

So far this synthetic gene has not been shown to be functional. The main problem is that, as has already been said, most genes are much larger than this particular one, but this should not deter scientists of the calibre of Dr. Khorana. It is highly likely that in a very short time problems raised by observations such as those on the passage of information from DNA to RNA (or from RNA to DNA!) may be solved by using synthetic genes.

A more sensational report of biological synthesis came in November from the State University of New York, Buffalo, where "the first artificial synthesis of a living and reproducing cell" was claimed. For some time it has been known that the nucleus of an amoeba can be transplanted to another amoeba from which the nucleus has been removed, and will take over the role of the removed nucleus. What Dr. J. F. Danielli and his colleagues at Buffalo did was to assemble a new amoeba from the nucleus of one, the cytoplasm (or "flesh") of another, and the outer membrane (or "skin") of a third. The hybrids lived and divided quite happily for generations. It was a beautiful technique, which may have theoretical and practical implications, but was far from the "creation of life" suggested by newspapers.

Evolution of Birds and Man

Important discoveries in vertebrate palaeontology are concerned either with the origin of major groups or with the evolution of man. Advances were made in both these fields during the year. The reptiles gave rise to both the birds and the mammals, and although there are many remains which throw light on the origin of the mammals, the transition between reptiles and birds is marked by only two upper Jurassic forms, both belonging to the genus *Archaeopteryx*. The lower jaw of *Archaeopteryx* is usually regarded as being typically reptilian, but Dr. Joel Cracraft of the American Museum of Natural History re-examined the evidence and reached the conclusion that the jaw is in fact a mosaic of primitive and advanced characters. This suggests that *Archaeopteryx* had advanced farther along the evolutionary line to the birds than was previously thought, and calls for another estimation of the time that birds first evolved.

A number of remains belonging to the genus *Australopithecus* were found in limestone quarries at Swartkrans, South Africa, among them bones of a more advanced hominid hitherto known as *Telanthropus capensis*. Drs. R. J. Clarke, F. Clark Howell, and Charles Brain examined further fragments, including most of a skull, and reached the conclusion that these fossils are quite different from *Australopithecus* and should be classified as *Homo erectus*. So yet another old fossil can now be assimilated into the general pattern of man's evolution.

Two biologists at Berkeley, Drs. A. C. Wilson and V. M. Sarich, questioned the timing of the stages in human evolution as determined by the usual method of interpreting the fossil record. The approach they used was to deter-

Archaeopteryx, an early fossil bird almost completely preserved in a lithographic rock. Even the feathers can be seen.

mine the state of mutational differences between various primates. They estimate that one amino acid in the haemoglobin molecule is replaced every 3·5 million years. Using this information, Drs. Wilson and Sarich found that primates and horses are separated by 90 million years, which is within 15 per cent of the figure obtained from the fossil record. Man is related to gorillas and chimpanzees as closely as horses are related to donkeys. The Old World monkeys diverged from the line leading to apes and man about 30–40 million years ago. Man diverged from the Old World apes 5–7 million years ago, which is 7–14 million years more recently than suggested by the fossil record. If these studies are accepted, many widely held beliefs will have to be abandoned. It seems strange that studies on amino acids should shake a long-established science like palaeontology, but observations such as these cement rather than fragment the science of biology.

New Breed of Cattle

At a time of population explosion an important problem is the breeding of cattle for milk and meat in the tropics. Dr. John Francis of the University of Queensland came up with some suggestions that might do much to alleviate protein deficiency in the tropics. There are two basic kinds of cattle, the European (*Bos taurus*) and the Indian (*Bos indicus*), and there is evidence to suggest that new breeds resulting from crosses between these cattle would provide the kind of cattle required. Unfortunately, traditionalists among cattle breeders and geneticists in general are reluctant to make progress in this direction. Dr. Francis advocated the wide use of semen from *Bos taurus* dairy bulls, and that this use should proceed simultaneously with detailed trials, as in the English Charolais trials. Thus it seems that the methods of cattle-breeding used in England in the 18th century might be more productive than waiting for the outcome of 20th-century genetics.

"Droughtmaster" cattle, bred in Australia from European and Indian ancestors.

Advances in Physics and Chemistry

R. E. H. STRACHAN, M.A.

A NOTABLE STIMULUS was added in 1970 to the search for new superheavy transuranic elements. While a degree of doubt still remains about the claimed production of the elements of atomic number 103 and 104, workers at the University of California, Berkeley, announced the synthesis of the element of atomic number 105—to which the name *hahnium* was provisionally allotted. The isotope produced was stated to contain 155 neutrons.

Dr. Albert Ghiorso of the Lawrence radiation laboratory in the University of California reporting on April 27 the discovery of element 105 (hahnium).

It is now widely accepted that an increase in the number of neutrons in the nucleus of a superheavy element will tend to increase its stability, or at least to produce isotopes with long half-lives, stable enough to be detected. It has been predicted that a region of stability may occur in elements which have nucleii containing between 110 and 114 protons and 184 neutrons.

In the meantime, Professor P. H. Fowler of Bristol was conducting a series of experiments on cosmic rays in an area of the U.S.A. where the strength and direction of the earth's magnetic field is such as to diminish the degree to which cosmic rays are deflected away from the Earth's surface. He considered that there is a real chance that he will be able to confirm traces of superheavy elements, and that these may even include the element of atomic number 110 and mass number 294. A possible source of these elements in cosmic rays was suggested by Dr. P. Bandyopadhay and Dr. P. R. Chaudhuri of the Indian Statistical Institute, who concluded that the physical conditions in the newly discovered "radio" stars called pulsars might be such as to promote their synthesis. It is suspected that pulsars are principally made up of exceedingly tightly packed neutrons. In these conditions a core temperature of some 10^9 deg C would be needed, and this is thought to be a distinct possibility.

Other work in this field proceeded along more conventional lines—the bombardment of uranium with heavy nuclei accelerated to high energies. Present accelerators cannot give the necessary energy to nuclei heavier than argon, the difficulty being that the heavier the accelerated nucleus the greater its positive charge and so the greater its energy must be if it is to enter the positively charged nucleus of the target uranium atom against the electrostatic repulsion between charges of similar sign. Attempts were made by researchers at the University of California and by others at the High Voltage Engineering Corporation, Massachusetts, to surmount this difficulty. They used fission fragments of the element californium 252. These are emitted spontaneously with energies of about 80 MeV, and by using a Van der Graaf generator this can be increased to 200 MeV (there is a further possibility that some relatively small modifications

 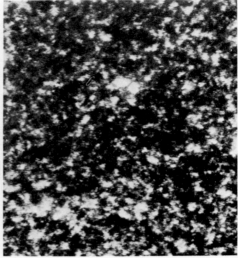

Enlarged 5 million times by an electron microscope, individual atoms were photographed for the first time in 1970.
Left: Prof. A. V. Crewe of Chicago University pointing to white dots (the smallest in the photo) which are single atoms of thorium.
Right: the pair of relatively bright dots in the upper centre of this photograph are two uranium atoms.

will extend this to 600 MeV). With this sort of energy, the fission products, which include isotopes of silver, cadmium, iodine, and bismuth, might well be used to produce a number of new superheavy elements.

High Energy Particle Accelerators

The largest accelerator operating in Europe is the 28 GeV proton accelerator owned by CERN and sited in Geneva. The European Committee for Future Accelerators proposed as long ago as 1963 that CERN should build a new accelerator to produce protons of energy 300 GeV. The proposal has met with repeated set-backs. First of all, it was not supported by the U.K.; then, when it was modified to produce a smaller and less expensive version, there was disagreement between the various

Quarks Queried

Since his claim in September 1969 that he had found five quark tracks in 50,000 bubble-chamber photographs, Professor Charles McCusker of the University of Sydney has had to meet sharp criticism of his evidence for the existence of these still hypothetical sub-atomic particles which, if they exist, are the ultimate building blocks of the universe. The prime characteristic by which a quark could be recognized is the charge that it possesses—either one third or two thirds of the electronic charge. When a quark enters a bubble chamber the number of ions it will produce will be less than the number produced by particles of equal velocity but greater charge; and McCusker attributed the low density of the bubbles in his five tracks as being due to this cause. His deduction was criticized on the ground that an individual charged particle's low rate of ion-production might be due to an unusually low speed rather than to an unusually low charge.

This criticism encouraged McCusker to re-examine the remainder of his 50,000 photographs to see if there was evidence of enough variation in the density of ion-production to suggest a sufficiently great variation of particle speed to allow for the production of his five tracks. After analysing 300 "normal" tracks he concluded that the variations in velocity which they exhibit are insufficient to account for the five tracks which he still considers are due to particles of lower charge—that is, quarks.

A shred of encouragement was received from the Argonne National Laboratory in the U.S.A., where physicists from Ohio State University and from the University of Kansas discovered a single track, caused by a particle in a cosmic ray shower, which could be attributed to a quark. A single example is not conclusive evidence but, coming from an independent team of observers, it was welcome corroboration for McCusker.

countries (including Austria, Belgium, West Germany, France, Italy, and Switzerland) about the country in which it should be sited.

But in 1970 the nations of CERN were examining a new proposal advanced by the Director, Dr. John Adams of the U.K. He submitted a design for a system which could eventually produce protons with an energy of 800 GeV, and which would not only cost much less but also occupy less space and could accordingly be constructed on the present site near Geneva. The existing facilities and accelerator would largely be incorporated in the new system, and the design is such that present research projects could continue during and after the construction of the new facilities. Further, at various stages of the construction, experiments could commence at energies of 150 GeV, then 300 GeV, and later possibly 550 GeV and even 800 GeV. All this could be done for an expenditure of £110 million, compared with the £190 million needed for the original 300 GeV project. Extension beyond the 300 GeV range

conductor was being developed by Dr. Peter Smith in the Rutherford Laboratory at Oxford. The strands of niobium-titanium wire used in the coil windings are first twisted, then embedded in a cupro-nickel alloy and finally in copper. Both the twisting and the alloy reduce the size of the currents induced by the changing field, and so reduce the energy expended. The copper cladding acts as a heat sink, which is needed to maintain an operating temperature near 4 deg K. A possible difficulty may be the susceptibility of these Ni-Ti superconductors to radiation damage; if this is confirmed their use will be restricted to those parts of the accelerator in which the radiation is small.

The accompanying diagrams show the relationship between the principal components of Dr. Adams's new system. C.P.S. is the existing 28 GeV accelerator. This feeds the I.S.R. (the proton intersecting storage rings), which is already in process of construction. From the I.S.R., which will be re-filled with protons each morning, beams of 20 to 28 GeV protons

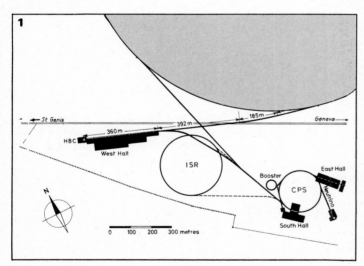

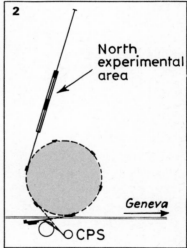

involves the use of superconducting magnets, for which the design allows. The reduction in the size of the machine is based partly on this, but also on the employment of separate systems of magnets for bending and focusing the beam.

Superconductivity in metals occurs at temperatures very close to absolute zero. The actual temperature at which the resistance of a metal vanishes not only varies between different metals but is also affected by changes in physical conditions. One important condition is the rate of change of magnetic field strength, and it is because of this effect that the so-called "twisted wire" type of super-

could be extracted for direct experiment at West Hall, or alternatively beams of 10 GeV protons could be injected into the new 300 GeV accelerator. The output of this accelerator would be examined in West Hall and later, when even higher energies are available, in a new building to be constructed in the North Experimental Area.

Direction of Earth's Magnetic Field

It is a well-known property of a bar magnet that if it is freely suspended it will settle with one end, called its North-seeking pole, pointing towards the North. This fact is the basis of magnetic compasses. The needs of navigators have ensured that much has been found out about the periodic minor variations which are known to occur in the direction and size of the forces controlling the position of the magnet. What is less well known, perhaps, is that there is evidence that, at certain times in the geological past, the direction of the Earth's field has been completely reversed, so that the North-seeking poles of compasses would have pointed in an approximately southerly direction.

Evidence for past reversals must be sought in rocks laid down at various periods. Palaeomagnetists from the University of Colorado published in 1970 the results of a detailed analysis of separate lava piles lying some 55 miles apart. Lavas contain what are effectively tiny magnets, and as the lavas solidified the magnets tended to set themselves in the direction of the magnetic field at the place where the solidification occurred. Examination of the degree and direction of these natural magnets provides evidence of the strength and direction of the magnetic field and the time and place of solidification. Local magnetic effects were eliminated by examining samples from well-separated sites, which gave similar results. Variations in fossil magnetism at different heights in one site gave evidence of variation of the Earth's magnetic field over the geological time period during which the lava deposit was laid down. The conclusion was that the switch-over in the direction of the field took place by a relatively rapid reduction in value in one direction, followed by a comparable rise in the other.

Measuring Very High Pressures

A standard technique for the measurement of pressures of the order of thousands of atmospheres is to employ the established relation between the freezing point of mercury and the pressure to which it is subjected. At a pressure of 1 atmosphere, mercury freezes at about -39 deg C, but the freezing point rises to 0 deg C when the pressure is raised to 7,470 atmospheres. Thus a measurement of the freezing point of mercury can be used to deduce pressure. A new practical approach was successfully made by physicists at the Commonwealth Scientific and Industrial Research Organization, Australia. A small amount of mercury is contained in polyethylene within a steel capillary tube which has one end blocked while the other is inserted into the enclosure where the pressure is to be measured. The change in state of the mercury is recognized by the absorption or rejection of the very small amount of latent heat involved. The system can be used to make about 15 measurements per hour with a high degree of reproducibility.

Keeping Catalysts Pure

A catalyst is a material which promotes a particular chemical reaction but takes no part in the reaction and accordingly is not consumed as the reaction proceeds. Finely divided platinum is a well-known catalyst for a number of important reactions. A major difficulty, however, is the liability of the catalyst—particularly platinum—to be poisoned by impurities in the reacting ingredients. The poisoning effects of the sulphur content of crude oil is an important example.

The problem has been approached in a variety of ways, but work in England by B. J. Cooper and D. C. Trimm in 1970 culminated in the production of a platinum catalyst system which is not affected by poisons, including sulphur. The principle is to disperse the platinum in a material which has extremely fine pores, the actual material used being a form of micro-porous carbon. A number of other metallic catalysts have also been incorporated into these micro-porous molecular sieves, so that a whole range of stable and chemically inert catalysts may well be made available to the chemical industry. What Cooper and Trimm did is to develop a technique for producing a practical molecular sieve, and to demonstrate that it can be made effective in protecting the catalyst from impurities.

"Polywater" in Question

EVIDENCE for the existence of polymerized water molecules of large molecular weight was published in 1969. In 1970, further research at the Los Alamos Scientific Laboratory in the University of California not only gave rise to grave doubts about the existence of such polymers, but provided a more likely explanation for the differences in physical behaviour between the so-called polywater molecules and ordinary water. It had been suspected that the differences in viscosity, refractive index, and density might have been due to absorption of material from the surfaces of the quartz capillaries in which the polywater was made. In 1970 it was shown that the process of making the material did indeed involve the picking up of traces of contaminants such as sodium, boron, and oxygen, and, further, that by adding traces of these substances to pure water, the resulting liquid exhibits many of the characteristics of the postulated polymer.

The Human Sciences

A Hundred Years On

BARBARA LOWTHER

THE YEAR 1970 was something of a landmark in education. Designated by UNESCO as International Education Year, it was also the centenary of W. E. Forster's Elementary Education Act of August 9, 1870, which introduced into Great Britain the idea that the state is responsible for education. The Montessori Society met on July 25 to honour the centenary of the birth of Maria Montessori, the educationist who developed the principle of learning through activity and experience that is so much in evidence today.

The centenary celebrations survived well into the autumn. In May, about 80 schools and colleges from all parts of England and Wales contributed towards the exhibition "Learning for a Purpose", at the Central Hall, Westminster. There were celebrity speakers, concerts by the London Schools Symphony Orchestra and young musicians from all parts of the country, and films displaying the work of various schools. This sparked off a national programme of events. Those mentioned in the calendar prepared by the department of education and science totalled over 200.

Money Matters

The year's outburst of enthusiasm for education in Britain was oddly paralleled by the teachers' continued militant policy. The second week in January saw nearly 5,500 teachers on strike in 419 schools. This was followed by a run of one-week strikes in Manchester, the West Riding of Yorkshire, and Birmingham. The four-months-old pay dispute was settled on March 3 after trade union leaders had won a £2·30 a week interim award (totalling £39 million), with an agreement that this was to be added to in the period

from January to April 1971 within a new salary structure. The pay increase left £45 million to play with, of which £3 million were available before April 1971 and £42 million for the following year. The question of restructuring teachers' salaries brought two unions, the National Union of Teachers and the National Association of Schoolmasters, almost to blows. The 250,000 strong N.U.T. called for a basic rise of £225, of which £160 was earmarked as priority for the basic scale. The N.A.S. produced its own restructuring scheme which would cost £152 million and would put greater emphasis on a career structure. The management panel of the Burnham committee responded with a sketch plan for restructuring based on a hypothetical £47 million. They invited the teachers' panel to join a working party to demand more money to improve this "purely illustrative" scale.

The proud Labour party claim that public expenditure on education in 1970 had exceeded that on defence (though cynics pointed out that this was largely a result of cuts in the defence budget) was still ringing ominously in a good many ears when it was rumoured that the treasury had asked the department of education to cut its budget by £100 million. There were many speculations as to where the axe would fall to prune the mammoth bill, which amounted to £2,300 million in 1970.

Changing Votes in Mid-Stream

During the year the tide of comprehensive education in the U.K. swelled with increasing numbers of devotees and converts. With more than 30 per cent of the secondary school population in comprehensive schools, Edward Short, Labour secretary of state for education, crested the wave and produced Circular 10/69, *Organization of Secondary Education*. This requested local education authorities to submit

Top of page: A feature of British teachers' peaceful demonstrations for higher pay was this slogan-plastered double-decker bus. In February it blocked the entrance to Downing Street while a petition to the prime minister was handed in at Number 10.

their own schemes for comprehensive education in secondary schools. It was an effective move. Those authorities that had been dithering on the brink were given a gentle push, and most of them took the plunge. By the beginning of March, 110 of the 163 authorities in England and Wales had had their reorganization schemes approved. Comprehensive education was an established fact, although it was uncertain whether "banding" or drawing up strict catchment areas should be employed to ensure a good social cross-section in the schools. The Donnison report recommended that the 178 direct grant and independent schools should be either integrated into the comprehensive system or deprived of support from government funds. In June, Edward Short's "mini-Bill", designed to make non-selective secondary education compulsory, was defeated in the Commons after a precarious course through two readings and the committee stage.

Education played only a peripheral part in the general election campaign. Nevertheless, June 18 was a decisive day for education, and one that was destined to delay the cause of comprehensive education in a way that might have persuaded even W. E. Forster to listen to those opposers of the 1870 Education Act who had insisted that education should be "above politics". The Conservative secretary of state for education and science lost little time in withdrawing Circular 10/69, replacing it with Circular 10/70. This allows education authorities to select their own schemes for secondary education, provided that they take into account "educational considerations in general, local needs and wishes in particular, and the wise use of resources". There were some rapid changes of plan. In Surrey, where several comprehensive schools were already well advanced, the education committee was asked to revert to an earlier plan, which included selection at 11-plus and had been rejected by the department of education and science in 1966. Children and parents in Surrey demonstrated against the continuance of early selection, setting up an S.T.E.P. (Stop the Eleven-Plus) campaign. Surrey teachers threatened to boycott the 11-plus examinations if the county did not forge ahead with comprehensive plans.

France also had its financial problems: 24,000 new teachers were admitted to the profession in comparison with 48,000 in 1969. The dual theme of finance and democratization was admirably presented by Tom Roper of the National Union of Australian University Students in his booklet *The Myth of Equality*—one of the many efforts of a union campaign to remove from Australia "all vestiges of inequality". According to the author, most educational grants in Australia were awarded to the children of the nation's top 20 per cent wage-earning population. City schools were often out of date and badly equipped. Children in rural areas were neglected educationally, and a national survey was urgently needed. But recent attention to educating aborigines was at last producing results, with 11 at universities in 1970. A 1970 survey in Australia described morale among teachers as "low" because "they are not accorded sufficient respect by the government". When Ronald Gould, retiring as president of the World Congregation of Organizations of the Teaching Profession in August, spoke at the annual conference held in Sydney, there were demonstrations for "more schools and fewer armaments".

Dilemmas of Higher Education

In Britain other aspects of education were less radically affected by political events than

The immense range of and contrast in education is well illustrated in these two photographs. Left: with infinite patience a London teacher tries to make an autistic child familiar with the names of common objects and animals. Right: the mathematics master at Sion Manning Comprehensive School, North Kensington, London, had no such problems with the team of girls who built a computer of his design, containing 2,500 resistors and 600 transistors, and capable of storing 5,000 pieces of information and retrieving them at 2,500 a second.

was secondary education. Priority was to be given to primary school development. Independent schools were promised assistance. The building programme for polytechnics was on schedule, with 26 of the 1970 quota of 30 completed by August.

One of the outstanding features of education in 1970 was the sudden mushrooming of these large centres of higher education, defined in the White Paper of May 1966 as "comprehensive and academic communities catering for full-time sandwich and part-time students at all levels of higher education, including those below degree level". In 1970 nearly 20,000 students were taking first-degree courses run by the Council for National Academic Awards. Universities in 1970 accepted approximately half of the 57,000 applicants. The fact that some 463 fewer engineers and 850 fewer scientists were admitted than in 1969 could mean that a large number had applied to polytechnics in preference to universities.

There were widely differing views on polytechnics. Should they be geared to supply immediate social and economic needs, or should they compete with universities in pursuing a high level of academic achievement? Many authorities advocated combining all forms of higher education—universities, polytechnics, and colleges of education—into a "comprehensive university". The dilemma was world-wide. A school of education opened at La Trobe University, Australia, with a diploma

Student demonstrations, chiefly in protest at the way universities are run and studies organized, continued in 1970, though less violent than in 1968 and 1969. These members of the French students' union were showing their disapproval in March of the suppression by police of earlier demonstrations at Nanterre.

in education course for graduates and one running concurrently with the four-year Bachelor degree course.

The National Foundation for Educational Research in England and Wales produced a shock report in February about teacher education. It accused the colleges of education of adhering to a pre-war structure, of giving negligible tuition in the teaching of the basic skills of reading and mathematics, and condemned the "deplorable level of mathematical knowledge and ability" of students in the colleges. Throughout the year there were more proposals for reform than there were colleges to put them into effect. It was decided that a short intensive government-sponsored enquiry should be set up in 1971.

Student Protest Activities

Perhaps the 126,000 students attending the colleges of education would welcome the opportunity of participating in the notorious student activities. One of the highlights of 1970 was the discovery in February at Warwick University of confidential files on the political activities of some staff and students. This provided large numbers of the student population with the exciting new pastime of file-hunting. The rules were simple: students cajoled authorities, staged "sit-ins", raided archives, and stole dossiers. Eventually an enquiry into the confidential information contained in students' files revealed 55 cases which were thought worthy of comment, of which 26 contained some "unfortunate remarks" about students' social backgrounds. In all it was a disappointing conclusion. A protest against "Greek Week" culminated in a violent demonstration at the Garden House Hotel, Cambridge, in February, and there were anti-apartheid demonstrations at Essex University. Sit-ins, vandalism, nude bathing, petrol bombs, fires, and lots of red paint completed the lively student scene at Keele University.

In general, however, British universities lacked the sound and fury of their French counterparts. A fierce battle in January between leftist militants in Paris and their opponents at the law faculty of Nanterre provoked brutal police intervention which resulted in 145 arrests. The creation of 13 Paris universities was announced early in the year; university staff criticized the inadequate planning and finance that had been applied to such an ambitious development. In West German universities, which experienced a fairly peaceful year, the first steps were taken towards integrating colleges of education with comprehensive universities, where educational method is to be studied jointly with other

REV. KENNETH SLACK
Minister of the City Temple, London

On July 7, Protestant extremists, led by Ian Paisley, demonstrated (facing page) in Canterbury against the Roman Catholic Mass celebrated there (left) in commemoration of the 800th anniversary of the murder of St. Thomas Becket. The first Roman Catholic Mass to be said in the Cathedral precincts for 400 years, it was conducted by the Archbishop of Southwark and attended by 5,000 Catholics.

on the non-Catholic partner to give an undertaking that all children of the union should be brought up as Roman Catholics. This demand has been removed.

Paisley the Unappeasable

Such small moves as this did nothing to assuage the militant anti-Romanism of such men as Ian Paisley, the Ulster Protestant extremist, who in the course of the year had the encouragement of being elected to the parliaments of both Stormont and Westminster. He led objections to the celebration of a Roman Mass within the precincts of Canterbury Cathedral on the occasion of the 800th anniversary of the martyrdom of Thomas Becket, and his supporters were to the fore in noisy and repeated protests against the official visit of Cardinal Marty, Archbishop of Paris, to London in February.

Not only Rome was the target of such vehement objections. Once again Pastor Glass, Ian Paisley's Scottish lieutenant, forced a suspension of the sitting of the General Assembly of the Church of Scotland when a distinguished delegation of Orthodox churchmen, including the Patriarch of Alexandria, was being received.

Moves towards Church Unity

Despite all this noise and fury, always apt to be overestimated because its telegenic character gives it wide publicity, quite a little occurred during 1970 to encourage those committed to the search for Christian unity. The Methodist Church showed no sign of being discouraged in its support for the Anglican–Methodist unity proposals by the failure of the Church of England to secure the requisite 75 per cent majority in 1969. All the English

Methodist synods (to which all major proposals for change have to be remitted) voted in support, and the 1970 Conference slightly increased its positive majority of the previous year. In 1970 it was 79·4 per cent.

Further encouragement came as a result of a law-suit during the summer. Two representatives of the unofficial group leading opposition to the proposals, "The Voice of Methodism Association", sought a declaration from the High Court that the action of the 1969 Conference was contrary to the Deed of Union, which established the Methodist Church as it is today by the union of three Methodist bodies in 1932. The judgment went wholly in favour of the high officials of the Methodist Church who were named as defendants in the suit, and the superintendent minister and solicitor who sued became liable for damages estimated at £4,000. Since the threat of legal action has been much used by opponents of the scheme, the judgment may be regarded as highly encouraging to the enthusiasts for union.

Any reintroduction of the scheme for a further vote by the Church of England had to await the coming into being of the General Synod in November 1970. The effect of the change from Church Assembly to General Synod is to give the laity for the first time a vote in matters affecting doctrine (which unity proposals are considered to be). Previously such matters were reserved for the bishops and clergy meeting in the Convocations of Canterbury and York. It remained to be seen whether this substantial change in the government of the Church of England would produce any different judgment from that which was given in 1969.

It was expected that 1970 would see the decisive, if not the final, vote regarding the full union of two smaller English Free Churches, the Congregational Church in England and Wales and the Presbyterian Church of England. Considerable delays in the preparation of legal documents prevented this, but late in the year a fairly substantial volume was published containing all the material on which a judgment must be made at the 1971 assemblies of the two Churches. It includes the text of a private parliamentary bill which will be promoted if the decision to go forward

When Cardinal Marty, Roman Catholic Archbishop of Paris, visited London in February, he was joined in an ecumenical service at the French church off Leicester Square by the Archbishop of Canterbury (left). The Cardinal also visited Buckingham Palace. Outside the Palace (below), a group of sixteen extremist Protestant clergy held up cards which read "Betrayal—No Popery"—a further demonstration that the moves towards amity between the Anglican and Roman Churches were by no means universally popular in the British Isles.

is made. These two Churches are obviously determined to run no risks in the High Court.

North of the Border proposals for Congregational-Presbyterian union failed by narrow margins to secure the necessary support. One factor undoubtedly was the great disparity of size in the two Churches. The Church of Scotland has one and a quarter million members, the Congregational Union of Scotland but thirty thousand: union would have seemed like absorption. Even so, reluctance was shown on both sides. COCU (The Conference on Church Union) in the U.S.A. produced a report in March which laid a draft scheme of union before the nine denominations which have been taking part in the discussions over the last few years on proposals originally brought forward by Dr. Eugene Carson Blake (now General Secretary of the World Council of Churches) and the late James Pike, then Bishop of California.

In Pakistan on All Saints' Day, November 1, a most significant church union was inaugurated, which (following the example of the Church of South India almost a quarter of a century before) brought Anglican and major non-episcopal traditions together in one Church. An identical plan for the Churches of North India hit objections during the year from the largest of the negotiating bodies, the Methodist Church of Southern Asia. The inauguration of the united Church took place without the Methodists on Advent Sunday, November 29. Six Churches joined, of which the Anglican was the largest, with 300,000 members. At the world level two pan-confessional bodies (i.e. organizations representing world-wide denominations) merged during 1970. They were the International Congrega-

tional Council and the World Alliance of Reformed and Presbyterian Churches. The union assembly of the two bodies took place in Nairobi, Kenya, in August. Many of the member Churches of the two bodies have united or are negotiating to do so.

Questions of Finance

In recent years there have been increasing suggestions that the major motive for church union is economic. This may be doubted, although wise stewardship of resources and a refusal to waste them in sectarian competition are not sub-Christian motives. Certainly 1970 saw an increase of anxiety regarding finance and the pressures of continuing and accelerating inflations on bodies which depend substantially or even wholly on voluntary giving. That giving is often from the section of the population gaining least from wage increases and also diminishing in numbers.

Even the Church of England with an endowment that (thanks to the skilful policies of the Ecclesiastical Commissioners) has produced an income that has risen with inflation faces sharp difficulties. The new General Synod started its life knowing that the Church's departments are only being maintained at their present pruned level by raiding reserves. A 25 per cent rise in giving over the next three years has been stated to be essential. A report published during the year calculated that some £2 million is being spent on essential pastoral expenses out of the clergy's own pockets. Thus the harder a parson works the poorer he makes himself. No resources were visible to end this disturbing state of affairs.

The situation in the Free Churches, wholly dependent on free-will offerings, tends to be even more anxious. The demand for the stationing of Methodist ministers is reduced by the inability of circuits to pay them. The report of a commission of the Baptist Churches, *Ministry Tomorrow*, boldly suggested that it might be necessary to reduce the number of ministers from the present 1,200 to 400. Such a report did not command universal support, and its reception showed once again the tension between radicals and traditionalists. It remains clear that short of some most unlikely reversal of trends (either in church attendance and support, or in money values) such predictions may well find fulfilment within the decade. Certainly 1970 saw no change in the downward line of the graph of entrants to the seminaries of virtually all Churches.

Financial problems were not only to be seen in Britain's still beleaguered economy where the Churches are in seemingly irreversible decline. Even Churches in North America, so long the envy of less affluent communions, showed signs of strain. The Anglican Church in Canada and the Episcopal Church in the U.S.A. both had to make severe budgetary cuts in the course of the year. In the latter Church a fifth of the central staff was declared to be redundant, and for the first time since 1948, when the World Council of Churches came into full being, the Church had to cut its grant to that ecumenical body.

Radicals and Racialism

One factor that some have discerned in the failing support for the central work of the Episcopal Church in the U.S.A. has been the forthright stand of its bishops and councils on divisive issues like civil rights for the American negro, and reparations to the black community. Church conferences, and notably meetings of the National Council of the Churches of Christ in the U.S.A., have resounded with the demands of black militants, and Episcopal leaders have been to the fore in advocating positive response to them. They have not always commanded the support of the silent laity, who have in effect voted through the offertory bag. Once again the radical-traditionalist tension emerges.

A similar division probably accounts for the strange situation in Rhodesia. There legislation, notably in regard to land tenure, which was felt to disadvantage the African met almost unanimous and outright condemnation from the leaders of the Churches. (The only exception was the small Dutch Reformed Church.) But if these leaders are really being followed by members of their Churches the equally almost unanimous support for Mr. Smith's regime by the white electorate is hard to understand. Further tension was generated on this issue when on September 3, 1970, the World Council of Churches granted $200,000 (£83,330) from a special fund set up to combat racialism to 19 groups including the British Anti-Apartheid Movement, the African National Congress of South Africa, and FRELIMO, the anti-Portuguese guerrilla movement operating in Mozambique. The British Council of Churches in October voted in support of this action although the Archbishop of Canterbury disapproved.

Another issue which divided British Christian opinions sharply in 1970 was the proposed South African cricket tour. Some Christian leaders, like Bishop David Sheppard of Woolwich (a former Test cricketer) and Bishop Trevor Huddleston of Stepney, led outright

The idea of popularizing and modernizing church services in order to attract a new congregation from among young people gained ground in 1970. At a Roman Catholic church in New York, where the morning service of the Broadway Congregational Church of New York City was being ecumenically held (above), two groups of coloured pop artists entertained one Sunday in June. In April, even ballet was performed at a Eucharistic service in Southwark Cathedral (right). The music was Grieg's *New Life Through Spring*, and the dancers were supplied by the Arts Education Trust.

opposition to it. The British Council of Churches unanimously pleaded for it to be stopped, and, by a small majority, urged Christians to join in peaceful demonstrations if it went forward. Others, like the Bishop of Peterborough, Dr. Eastaugh, were horrified by such action, regarding it as uncharitable. Yet others, when the government successfully exerted pressure on the Cricket Council to cancel the tour, regarded this as a disturbing surrender to the forces of disorder, and felt that the part of Christian leaders in it was disgraceful. A similar division of church opinion was occasioned by the opposition expressed by the Archbishop of Canterbury and many others to the new Conservative government's decision to end the embargo on the sale of arms to South Africa. The Archbishop displayed both courage and diplomacy by visiting South Africa in November, after an exchange of politely disagreeing letters with Mr. Heath.

Losing Faith?

Tension also made itself felt in regard to the degree in which the Churches must recognize the shift of British society away from religious conviction. Controversy attended the report *The Fourth R* by a group under the chairmanship of the Bishop of Durham, Dr. Ian Ramsey, in June. This was produced by an independent commission of Anglicans to enquire into religious education in schools. Members of other Churches served in a co-opted capacity. Urgency was given to its work by the knowledge that the new government would be certain to bring in a new Education Bill. The commission startled many by calling for the repeal of the rigid provisions of the 1944 Act in regard to religious instruction and school worship. Its report said: "To press for acceptance of a particular faith or belief system is the duty and privilege of the Churches and other similar religious bodies. It is certainly not the task of a teacher in a county school".

The ever growing "permissiveness" of society, notably in sexual matters and their portrayal in literature and the other arts, again accentuated the polarization referred to at the beginning of this article. Plaintive correspondents to church papers complained that clerics appearing on TV with Mrs. Mary Whitehouse, leader of the "Clean Up Television" campaign, criticized her rather than giving her the support which (in the opinion of the correspondents) she deserved. Many Christian leaders contrasted the traditional concentration of Christian moral concern on sex with the absence of sufficient concern with racialism and world poverty. But many Christian lay people feel that essential moral positions are being lightly given up by those who should feel pledged to maintain them, and that social and political concerns are being substituted for the simple morality of the Ten Commandments. It seems unlikely that this tension between radical and conservative will diminish in the immediate future.

The tension expressed itself at many other points than those which have been mentioned. The Oberammergau Passion Play, to which great crowds from all over the world flocked during the year, was dismissed by some as "Victoriana" (using a British term scarcely applicable to Bavaria), while others found its traditional presentation of the Cross the more moving for not making too many concessions to the present day. Priests and ministers more conscious of the multitudes untouched by worship are enthusiastic for the changes in it which might make it more meaningful to the outsider, while those who have grown up in the old forms tend to resent change. This also showed itself among some Catholics in regard to the Mass in the vernacular. The Methodist Conference took the first steps towards admission of women to the ministry, declaring that there could be no doctrinal objection to it; but some saw it as an unwarranted departure from tradition that would create fresh obstacles in the path of reunion.

Certainly the religious scene could not be accused of dullness in 1970. Institutional religion has never been under sharper challenge, but many called to leadership within the Churches are proving more prepared for change than many of the laity. They could perhaps take comfort from a saying of that great journalist, Lord Northcliffe: "A leading article is never a following article." They may feel that the business of a leader is not to count heads but to obey convictions.

FIGURES BASED on a 1968 international survey by the American Institute of Public Opinion, covering 12,000 adults in 12 countries, published in April 1970, showed that only 38 per cent of British people believe in life after death compared with 73 per cent in the U.S.A. and 41 per cent in West Germany. In 1948, when a previous survey was conducted, 49 per cent in Great Britain held this belief, and 68 per cent in the U.S.A. The number of believers in the Netherlands had declined from 68 per cent in 1948 to 50 per cent in 1968; in France from 58 per cent to 35 per cent; in Sweden from 49 per cent to 38 per cent; and in Norway from 71 per cent to 54 per cent.

In 1968 in the U.S.A. 60 per cent believed in the devil, but only 21 per cent in Britain and Sweden and 17 per cent in France shared this belief. On the basic question "Do you believe in God?", 98 per cent of Americans answered "Yes", which put the U.S.A. at the top of the 12 countries; Great Britain came ninth with 77 per cent, and Sweden bottom with 60 per cent.

Transport

Motoring's Big Question Marks

STUART BLADON
Assistant Editor of *Autocar*

WILL THERE BE any petrol-driven cars in production in the U.S.A. after 1974? Are safety belts for cars soon to be obsolete? Is the cost in human life becoming too high a price to pay for Grand Prix racing, and will any backers survive to pick up the financial bills of motor sport? Will car production ever again be really profitable in Great Britain? Will any other manufacturer succeed in breaking Porsche's domination of sports car racing? How long will it be before a car breaks the sound barrier on land? These are some of the important questions posed by the motoring events of 1970.

It was a testing year for the British motor industry. American firms with big-investment subsidiaries in Britain were wondering about the prospects of future profitability, and considering how long they could prop up the losses if they continued at the same rate. Some of the worst results were announced just before the June election. Vauxhall had the worst year in the history of the company, with a loss of £2 million in the first half of the year, following a long history of buoyant trading. Rootes lost £7½ million in the six months to January 31—a higher loss than Vauxhall's, though not so unexpected. In July, the transfer of Rootes to Chrysler ownership was marked by a change of name—to Chrysler (U.K.) Ltd.—and a prediction of an £11 million loss for the year. At British Leyland the half-year's profit was down to a mere £1·1 million on sales of £458 million. Even Ford reported a fall of £4·9 million in pre-tax profits, after losing 60,000 units during their February–March strike.

Higher Wages—Higher Prices

There was no lack of demand; indeed, waiting lists grew to almost 1946 lengths for some models. British design ingenuity was proved by such awards as the "best all-round car" accolade by *Modern Motor*, Australia's top circulation motoring magazine, to the Jaguar XJ6. The problems arose directly from industrial troubles, often affecting suppliers of components rather than car manufacturers directly,

and, while production lingered, costs soared. Car prices went up by leaps and bounds. When new models were announced there was a good case for trying to buy the superseded version to avoid the inevitable price increase. For example, the total price for an unchanged model like the Jaguar XJ6 4·2 rose from £2,475 to £2,690 during the year, while a revised hood and an ashtray for the MG Midget were accompanied by price rises from £818 to £906 between January and October.

Wage demands appeared to be going completely out of control, but in the end management had to take a firmer stand. Strikers at the Wellington factories of Guest Keen and Nettlefolds (GKN-Sankey) brought almost the entire Midlands car production to a halt for four weeks, but finally agreed to go back to work on terms offered three weeks earlier.

Expansion and investment in the British motor industry ground to a halt, but in March it was announced that British Leyland are to invest £14 million in Australia by 1972, and aim to double their sales there by 1974. Their plans include a new all-Australian car, to be on sale by the end of 1972. In spite of the depressed trading conditions, the year saw some significant production landmarks both at home and abroad, among them the one millionth Mini and Cortina for export, and the millionth Citroen DS and Simca 1000. A name that disappeared from the scene, however, was Singer, ended by Rootes from April 1.

America's Anti-Pollution Rules

Britain's was not the only car production in the doldrums; the American first quarter output was the lowest for nine years. All development work was concentrated on overcoming the Federal pollution laws. President Nixon set the pattern in his January 1970 State of the Union message, in which he said: "The automobile is our worst polluter of air. Adequate control requires further advances in engine design and fuel composition. We shall intensify our research, set increasingly strict standards, and strengthen enforcement procedures—and we shall do it now." U.S. regulations for the further control of pollution after 1974 seem impossible to meet with existing car engines.

A good-condition 1966–67 car with no emission control may be expected to give off 600–800 parts per million of unburnt hydrocarbons of petrol, and 3–4 per cent of carbon monoxide. By 1975 this is to be reduced to 40–50 parts per million of unburnt hydrocarbons, while the CO content is to be reduced to 0·2 per cent; and between 1975 and 1980, still more stringent controls are to be introduced. In October, Ford issued a paper stating the impossibility of meeting these stiffer controls in the time allowed. The paper stated that the amended Clean Air Act could prevent the continued production of cars after January 1, 1975, or, if it did not stop production, it could lead to huge increases in the price of cars. "Some of the changes in the bill," the paper went on, "could have a tremendous impact on all of American industry and could do irreparable damage to the American economy." Ford claim that they stand by their promises to achieve products and manufacturing processes that do not significantly contaminate the atmosphere, waters, or landscape, but declare that the provisions of the Act would produce minimum improvements in air quality at maximum cost to the public.

The paper stated that a 70 per cent reduction in carbon monoxide had already been achieved, and that total air pollution from cars has passed its peak and is now on the way down. The latest proposed standards would demand exhaust emission reductions from pre-1968 levels of 98 per cent in hydrocarbons, 97 per cent in carbon monoxide, and 90 per cent in oxides of nitrogen and what are called particulates. Ford said that these levels are unrealistic for 1975, and in any case would produce a very small improvement in air quality.

The problem is further aggravated by the intense efforts at present being made by the American industry to compete with imported cars, which captured 17 per cent of the U.S. market in September. Importers face the same pollution regulations, but their labour costs are between a half and a quarter of American costs. Although the answer to the question "Will car production in the U.S.A. continue beyond 1974?" is almost certain to be "Yes", no one could see in 1970 what the solution would be. But the health and well-being of the American nation call for pollution control as a matter of urgency, and President Nixon signed the anti-pollution legislation into law on December 31, 1970.

Safety Devices Required by Law

American designers also have to contend with what is rather pompously called the passive passenger restraint problem. This means preventing injury to the occupants of a vehicle in the event of a crash, without the need for the occupants to take any active safety measure, such as fastening a seat belt. "Passive" means that the restraint is done automatically for them. This may sound impossible, but it is on the way, and will be required by law as from January 1973. So the answer to the question "Are safety belts becoming obsolete?" is definitely "Yes"—at least in the U.S.A.

American anti-pollution rules demand modifications to the engines of cars made in Europe for export to the U.S.A. These photos show work on the British Jaguar E-type. Left: the required ignition control equipment in the form of a bridge carrying exhaust heat from the left side of the engine to heat the incoming mixture. Right: testing the exhaust while the car "runs" on a roller dynamometer.

The answer to the restraint problem is to be the self-inflating air bag. Only a few years ago this was regarded as a joke. It is deadly serious now, and development was proceeding apace in 1970. In March it was announced that as from January 1, 1972, every car produced would have to be fitted with an air-bag system. The industry pointed out the impossibility of redesigning facias and front ends and completing the necessary development in so short a time. The National Highways Safety Bureau listened to them and grudgingly allowed another year. The air bag is on the way, as surely as the pollution-free car.

Ford researchers found as long ago as 1966 that compressed gas could be released through an explosive valve in the four hundredths of a second which is the maximum time allowable if the inflated bag is to afford any protection. Gradually the feasibility of the idea was accepted, but enormous problems remain. The bag must absorb the energy of the occupants as they leave their seats and hurtle forward into it in an accident; yet at the same time it must not give them a neck-breaking blow. Further, what is right for an adult could throw a child backwards and out of the rear window; and without doubt there will have to be legislation to ensure that no child ever stands at the front in a car equipped with an air bag, since if it went off either inadvertently or as result of an accident, the result would almost certainly be fatal.

One may wonder why the authorities are so anxious to introduce passive restraint. The answer is that research and safety experts have claimed that it could bring about a saving of 20,000 lives or more in a year's road accidents in America. If this claim is justified, one can understand why the National Highway Safety Bureau insists that in two years' time every car must be so equipped. One may also wonder whether success of the air bag in America may bring in a similar requirement in Europe. The problem is less urgent here, partly because of the smaller size of the cars in general use, and partly because of a greater acceptance of conventional safety belts. In November, the U.K.

General Motors Corporation of U.S.A.'s experimental self-inflating air bag, to provide "passive passenger restraint".

IMPACT + 0 SECOND

IMPACT + 1/30 SECOND

IMPACT + 2/30 SECOND

IMPACT + 4/30 SECOND

A new world land speed record of 622·407 m.p.h. was put up at Bonneville salt flats on October 23 by Gary Gabelich of Long Beach, California. After his triumph, the driver (right) held up seven fingers to indicate that he means to reach 700 m.p.h. in 1971. His rocket-propelled car, *Blue Flame*, was slowed (above) by a braking parachute.

Road Research Laboratory published details of experiments with an automatic safety-belt system which fastens itself as the car doors close. This system, or perhaps some device that would prevent the engine from starting until safety belts have been fastened, seems a more probable solution in Europe.

Speed Records and Limits

The salt flats at Bonneville, Utah, were the scene of a new land speed record, which raised Craig Breedlove's 600·6 m.p.h. to a new figure of 622·407 m.p.h. The record was set by Gary Gabelich, driving his liquid-fuel rocket-propelled car *Blue Flame*. Unlike Craig Breedlove's *Spirit of America*, which has three wheels, Gabelich's is a four-wheeler with the front wheels mounted only 9 inches apart. The maximum thrust of the rocket engine is 22,000 lb. Apparently, only 13,000-lb. thrust would be sufficient for a speed of 700 m.p.h., and the design has been tested in a wind tunnel at 900 m.p.h. So it is only a question of time before the sound barrier—which is 760 m.p.h. at sea level—is broken by a car.

Regarding speeds at a lower level, the British minister of transport industries retracted in November his earlier intention to raise the 70 m.p.h. speed limit because of the bad accident record on motorways. Logicians were quick to draw attention to the anomaly that, when the 70 m.p.h. experiment was brought in, it was declared that it would not be kept in force if it did not reduce accidents, whereas now failure to reduce accidents was being used as an argument to retain the limit. More significant was the sensible decision to install crash barriers on motorway centre reservations progressively, and make them universal by 1975.

In motorway construction in Britain, the year brought completion of the important and beautiful section of the M6 between Lancaster and Penrith, which avoids the A6 route over Shap Fell. In the Birmingham area the Midlands motorway link between M5 and M6 was completed, and work continued on the extension of the M6 to join the M1 east of Coventry (the east–west part of the link). The M5–M6 join-up and the northern extension of the M6 to the Penrith by-pass made a continuous motorway from the Ross Spur near Tewkesbury all the way to the north of Penrith; and construction was in hand to take it to Carlisle and onward to Scotland. July saw the opening of London's £30 million Westway elevated motorway, attended by angry demonstrations from householders along the route. More extensive property purchase and demolition may accompany future urban motorway construction, to ensure that householders are not too near the noise and smell of new major roads.

Sad Year for Motor Sport

In the world of motor sport 1970 was a tragic year. Three top-line drivers gave their lives in the cause of racing, and the question how long Grand Prix racing can be allowed to continue was raised again. Motor sport has a tremendous following, and it would be sad indeed to see it banned everywhere, as it is in Switzerland, but no one can doubt the concern with which the authorities must regard the loss of life. Bruce McLaren's fatal accident on June 2 was not in racing, but in testing at Goodwood the new McLaren car for the Can-Am series. It is believed that the tail section came loose and blew off. The car went out of control on the Lavant Straight and struck an observer's hut at a speed estimated at about 170 m.p.h. Later in the same month, Piers Courage was killed in the Dutch Grand Prix. The third tragedy was the accident which killed

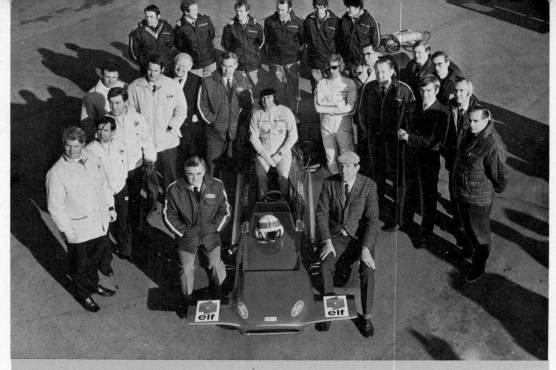

The high cost of supporting motor racing and rallying caused some manufacturers to announce their withdrawal from such competitions in future. An idea of the number of people involved in putting and keeping a racing car on the circuit is given by this photograph of Jackie Stewart on his new Formula 1 car, the March-Ford. At left are the Dunlop tyre designer and his team, with, next to them, the Dunlop racing manager and the engine designer. At rear are Stewart's six mechanics. At right is Stewart's No. 2 driver, with representatives of the companies making equipment—instruments, brakes, shock absorbers, sparking plugs, and electrics. On the wheels are a director of Ford (left) and "team boss" Ken Tyrell.

Jochen Rindt in practice for the Italian GP at Monza.

Motor sport lost some important supporters during 1970. Dunlop and Ford of America both announced that they would no longer participate in racing, and an even greater surprise was the retirement of British Leyland from rallying as from August.

The 1970 world championship began with the South African GP in March when, in spite of a minor accident in which Jochen Rindt's Lotus drove over his front wheel, Jack Brabham drove his new monocoque Brabham-Ford BT33 to victory at 111·7 m.p.h. Denny Hulme was second in the McLaren M14. In the Spanish GP in April, Jackie Stewart gave the March-Ford its first victory, at 87·2 m.p.h. An accident on the opening lap resulted in the destruction of Oliver's BRM and Ickx's Ferrari; Ickx was slightly burnt and had a broken arm, while Oliver was unhurt. Graham Hill, back in the cockpit after his 1969 accident, finished a creditable fourth behind McLaren and Andretti. Rindt's car went out with mechanical trouble, but he was not so unlucky in the next GP—at Monte Carlo in May—which he won at 81·75 m.p.h.

The Belgian GP at Spa in June went to Rodriguez driving a BRM; he won at 149·94

m.p.h. Amon was second, and Beltoise third. Rindt won again with his Lotus 72 in the Dutch GP at the end of June, with a speed of 112·95 m.p.h. Jackie Stewart in the March-Ford was second, and Ickx (Ferrari) third, but the event was overshadowed by Courage's fatal accident.

Jochen Rindt was hit in the face by a flying stone in practice for the French GP at Clermont Ferrand, and had to have three stitches, but he went on to his third GP win in the race, the Lotus 72 now seeming very reliable and extremely fast. At one time Beltoise (Matra-Simca MS 120) was in the lead, but tyre failure robbed him of victory. The British GP at Brands Hatch in July will long be remembered for the dramatic last-lap misfortune which cheated Jack Brabham out of a win. His Brabham BT33-Cosworth took on 39 gallons of fuel for the 80-lap race, but on Clearways Corner at the last lap he ran out of petrol. Close behind him, Rindt was able to nip in front to his fourth GP win of the season, while Brabham free-wheeled across the line just in front of Denny Hulme.

Just before the British GP, came the startling news that the German GP was to be cancelled because the GP Drivers' Association had demanded alterations to the Nürburgring circuit which could not possibly be completed in the time. But it was held at Hockenheim instead, and was one of the most exciting races of the season, with a thrilling battle between Rindt's Lotus 72 and Jackie Ickx's Ferrari, fought wheel to wheel to the very last lap. Rindt's win, his fifth for the year, gave him a clear lead for the championship. He must have hoped to be successful in his home country, Austria, at the *Grand Prix von Österreich* on August 16, but his engine blew up and the race went to Ickx and Regazzoni (Ferraris). Then came the disastrous practice session for the Italian GP at Monza when Rindt's car spun wildly out of control and hit the crash barrier twice. Jochen died in the ambulance. In the race itself, Regazzoni (Ferrari) won at 147 m.p.h.; Jackie Stewart was second, and Beltoise third. Ferrari's third win in succession came when they took the Canadian GP; this time Ickx won, and Regazzoni was second.

The United States GP was significant for Jackie Ickx's failure to win—because he alone could have beaten Rindt's total of 45 points in the championship, if he had won this and the Mexican GP. After a pit stop to replace a broken fuel system union, Ickx finished fourth, and Rindt became the first posthumous champion in the history of the title. Emerson Fittipaldi (Lotus-Ford) won at 126·79 m.p.h. The season ended with the Mexican GP, marred by deplorable crowd behaviour; again Ferrari were first and second (Ickx first, Regazzoni second).

Porsche Triumph Again

In sports car racing Porsche had a magnificent season, and nine victories gave them as assured a win for the world manufacturers' championship as any make has ever achieved. Porsche also took the first three places in the 86-hour *Marathon de la Route* at the Nürburgring with a team of VW-Porsche 914/6s. Porsche also excelled in the world of rallying, winning the Monte Carlo and the Swedish (for the third time in succession). But their triumph of the year was victory, after so many years, in the Le Mans 24-hour race (Hans Herrmann and Richard Attwood), at 119·249 m.p.h. Porsche took the first three places, and had five cars in the first seven.

The rally of the year was undoubtedly the *Daily Mirror* World Cup Rally from London to Mexico, which ran through May, covering 16,000 miles. It resulted in a splendid victory for a Ford Escort driven by Hannu Mikkola and Gunnar Palm. B. Culceth's Triumph 2·5 PI, which won the Scottish Rally, was second, and Ford had no fewer than five Escorts in the first eight places. The highest-placed non-British car was a Citroen DS21, which finished seventh. Another Citroen crashed and caught fire in the closing stages, killing the driver, Ido Marang. (See also pp. 370, 371.)

New and Improved Models

Despite the problems facing the world's motor industry, it was a good year for new

Above: the new Triumph Toledo.
Below: the 3½-litre Range Rover.

Above: the Triumph 3-litre Stag.
Below: the new Marcos Mantis coupé.

models. First was the highly praised Hillman Avenger, on which so much of the future of Chrysler U.K. depends. In Italy, the exciting Alfa Romeo Montreal with 2½-litre vee-8 engine was introduced, and Maserati and Citroen combined to produce the very fast Citroen SM. Another thrilling newcomer was the world's most expensive two-seater, the Monteverdi Hai (German for "shark"). In Germany, Volkswagen declared their intention to build the NSU K-70 front-wheel drive car as a sister to the Audi. Thus the K-70 will see the light of day after all; invitations to its launching had gone out a few years before, but when Volkswagen took over NSU, the project was killed—until its revival in 1970.

In their efforts to withstand the threat of the imported car, American Motors introduced the Gremlin, and Ford the Pinto, while from GM's Chevrolet came the Vega; these are all so-called sub-compacts, about equivalent in size to the British Victor or Cortina. June saw the arrival of the Triumph Stag, with vee-8 3-litre engine, and featuring a removable hardtop on a fixed roll-over support; the Bond Bug, as a new concept in three-wheelers with a 700-c.c. water-cooled four-cylinder engine at the front; and the Range Rover. Powered by the all-aluminium Rover-Buick 3½-litre vee-8 engine, the Range Rover was one of the most interesting new cars of the year, combining estate-car space and 90 m.p.h. performance with constant four-wheel drive and cross-country

ability. Most revolutionary car of the year, however, was the Citroen GS, announced in August. It has an air-cooled flat-four engine of 1,015 c.c., mounted at the front and driving the front wheels. The all-independent suspension uses hydro-pneumatic units interconnected at front and rear. Chrysler (France) introduced their new 160 model, a larger Simca replacement. Volkswagens came in for some important suspension and minor body modifications, and Germany also produced two new Opels—the Manta coupé with 1·6- or 1·9-litre engine, and the Ascona estate car and medium-size saloon.

Announcements at the British Motor Show in October included the Vauxhall Viva with a new and handsomely styled body and many valuable improvements, the Triumph Toledo and 1500, and the new Ford Cortina. In an entirely new body shape offering much more accommodation, and with wishbone front suspension and a coil-spring back end, the Cortina is offered with improved versions of existing 1,300 and 1,600 ohv engines, or with new overhead camshaft engines of 1,600 and 2,000 c.c. A host of valuable improvements included the far better Austin Maxi 1750, the revised Rover 2000 and 3500, the Volvo 144 Grande Luxe with fuel injection, the Hillman Hunters, and the Simca 1204 Special. New sports cars included the Skoda S110R coupé, the Marcos Mantis, and the Lamborghini vee-8.

Above: the Ford Cortina GXL.
Below: the improved Vauxhall Viva.

Above: the new Hillman Avenger.
Below: Citroen's revolutionary new GS.

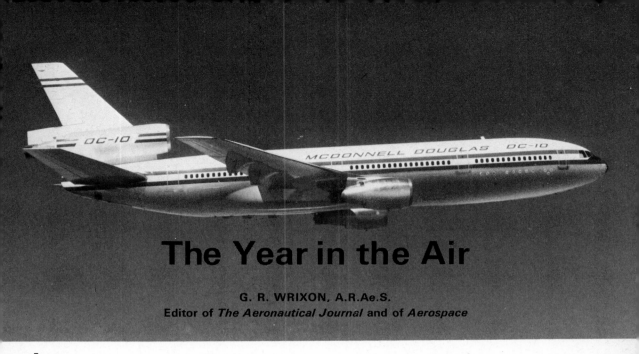

The Year in the Air

G. R. WRIXON, A.R.Ae.S.

Editor of *The Aeronautical Journal* and of *Aerospace*

I T IS NO exaggeration to say that aviation made more of a mark on the general public during 1970 than in any 12 months since the end of the Second World War. Aircraft noise and the pollution of the atmosphere were widely discussed, the Concorde made its first supersonic test flights under severe public criticism, and—perhaps worst of all—passengers had to submit to "frisking" and long delays due to security precautions which the rash of hijacking imposed.

The year should have seen the start of a new era of air transport as the first Boeing 747 jumbo jets gave the public a foretaste of the wide-body configuration of the passenger cabins of tomorrow. But although the 747s quickly appeared on the long-haul routes, there were stories of disappointing load factors and doubts about the reliability of their engines. Many people said they were worried about flying in an aircraft carrying such a large number of passengers. BOAC received its first 747s in good time for a big argument over pilots' pay, which prevented their going into operation.

Rolls-Royce, with a large stake in the new generation of wide-body jets, ran into difficulties over the financing of the development programme for the RB.211 three-spool turbofan engine which powers the Lockheed TriStar. The U.K. government had to step in with the promise of a further £42 million of launching aid, making their total contribution £89 million towards the £135 million the engine is now expected to cost. Increasing costs of material and labour, as well as technical problems, were given as the reasons for the escalation. The carbon-fibre fan blades developed by Rolls-Royce had to be replaced by titanium ones because of the difficulty of overcoming rain and sand erosion problems. In the U.S.A. the Lockheed company also nearly overreached themselves financially and measures had to be taken to salvage them from their troubles. Despite these anxieties, the flight engines for the first TriStar were delivered on time, and the graceful new airliner took to the air for the first time on November 16, exactly in accordance with the tight schedule laid down 2½ years before. McDonnell Douglas, who were ahead in the race to build a wide-body jet, had got theirs airborne 11 weeks previously, on August 29, and test flights proceeded very satisfactorily. Their jumbo, the DC-10, is powered by American turbofans built by U.S. General Electric.

With their big-diameter fuselage cross-sections, these new generation aircraft are characterized by an unusual interior cabin arrangement; seven or more passengers are seated abreast, and twin aisles between the rows of seats allow easy access by the cabin staff. In Europe, both the Airbus (A.300B) and the BAC Three-Eleven projects followed the new trend in cabin arrangement, and throughout the world the overall diameters of the fuselages closely correspond. This should make for easy standardization of freight pallets and containers designed for storage in the capacious holds below the cabin floor.

Airbus Politics

Politics were more closely involved in decisions about the A.300B and the Three-Eleven

The wide-bodied fuselage of the newest airliners is typified in this mock-up of the first-class section of the McDonnell Douglas DC-10. In the "coach" (economy) class, passengers are seated eight abreast. The DC-10 made its first test flight on August 29, 1970; it is seen in flight at the top of the preceding page.

than in even the Concorde or the RB.211 engine of the TriStar. Great Britain was anxious not to put a foot wrong with the French, in view of her application to join the Common Market. Despite the fact that the U.K. had officially withdrawn from the project, the French had already decided to go ahead with the A.300B Airbus with American engines, and were cutting metal for a prototype. Hawker-Siddeley on their own initiative came back into the project, to build the Airbus wings, and staked £30 million of their own money on the aircraft. France and Germany both wanted Britain back as a paying partner, and tried to achieve this in a series of high-level meetings in London and Paris. The German Dornier company withdrew during the autumn.

Meanwhile BEA, who would operate these high-capacity short-haul jets, came out strongly in favour of the home-designed BAC Three-Eleven, the specification of which fitted their requirements more satisfactorily. Both the previous and new British governments were aware that the indigenous design was of great importance to the country if it is to have a strong aircraft industry. Taken as a whole including airframe, engines, and ancillary manufactures, the Three-Eleven could have had a profound effect on the balance of payments. More than 85 per cent of it would have been manufactured in Britain, and it would have been powered by RB.211–61 engines similar to those being developed for the TriStar but more powerful—and needing further capital for development. The Airbus was offered with U.S. General Electric CF-6 engines, which replaced the Rolls-Royce turbofans on which Britain had insisted when she was a party to the pro-

The Lockheed L-1011 TriStar, powered by three Rolls-Royce RB.211 engines, took to the air on its first test flight on November 16.

ject. Later the French said that the RB.211–61 could be offered easily as an alternative power-plant for customers who want Rolls-Royce engines—and, in fact, at the Farnborough Air Show a special Rolls-Royce-powered A.300B was proposed specifically to meet BEA requirements. It was a difficult position for the new British government, but on December 2 it published its decision: no money would be provided to support either the Three-Eleven or the A.300B. Too much had already been spent on Concorde and the RB.211 engine, and the country could not afford the £144 million that would be needed to support the Three-Eleven and the RB.211–61. BEA were advised to buy the Lockheed TriStar or the A.300B when it became available. The decision naturally dismayed BAC, where several thousand workers faced redundancy because of the abandonment of the Three-Eleven.

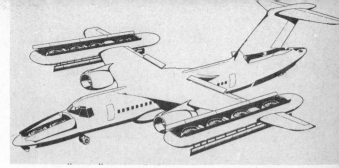

Jump-jet Passenger Planes

The Concorde and the wide-body jets all need very long runways—at least as long as any to be found at the major airports of the world. Although the idea is taking time to reach fruition there is little doubt that these acres of concrete will eventually be made redundant by the V/STOL (Vertical or Short Take-off and Landing) passenger airliner. During 1969–70 some notable new projects were announced which indicated that many people were thinking along these lines. First of all, the German government launched a design competition, and towards the end of 1969 the first details began to emerge of the military or civil VTOL transport projects which they were considering. Basic requirements, prepared by the German Air Force and by Lufthansa, were for an 80–100 seat aircraft which could be ready for service in 1977–78.

Basing their design on their experimental Do 31 prototypes, the Dornier company met the specification with the Do 231, which like its forebear would have podded wing-mounted lift engines and separate underwing propulsion engines. Like some other new VTOL aircraft, the Do 231 would have no fewer than twelve Rolls-Royce RB.202 lift engines, each

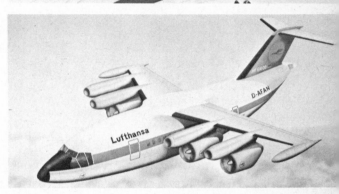

Important to airport planners in 1970 was the trend towards vertical or short take-off and landing passenger planes. A West German government competition produced four designs, shown at right. From the top: Dornier's Do 231, with wing-mounted lift engines; the Messerschmitt-Bölkow-Blohm Bö 140, a tilting wing design; the same company's HFB 600, with the same engines providing lift and flight; and the VC 180 by Vereinigte Flugtechnische Werke, with ten engines for lift and three for flight. Bottom: Hawker Siddeley's HS.141 V/STOL liner, with swivelling lift engines.

delivering something like 13,000 lb. of thrust. The proposed propulsion power-plants are two Rolls-Royce RB.220 turbofans, each rated about 24,000 lb. of thrust. The wing-span of the Do 231 would be 85 ft. 4 in. and its length 118 ft. 9 in., and it would have a maximum take-off weight of 129,000 lb. Carrying a payload of about 22,000 lb., it would cruise at some 458 knots. The military version is planned to have a deeper rear fuselage, with freight-loading doors.

By contrast the Messerschmitt-Bölkow-Blohm Bö 140, although designed to the same specification, is a tilt-wing aircraft powered by four 11,400 s.h.p. U.S. General Electric GE1/S1 turboshaft engines, driving four-bladed propellers of no less than 27 ft. diameter. When tilted vertically on the wing, these huge fans would fulfil the same function as the rotors of a helicopter. MBB plan to build the blades of a glass-fibre-reinforced plastic core enveloped by a carbon-fibre skin. They have been developing a special rigid helicopter rotor for several years, and the fans would be based on this. In its civil configuration the Bö 140 would span 116 ft. 1 in. and would be 88 ft. 7 in. long. The maximum take-off weight is planned to be 107,140 lb., and the aircraft would cruise at 489 m.p.h. with a payload of 19,250 lb.

The Hamburger Flugzeugbau Division of MBB devised yet another solution to meet the same specification. Their project is called the HFB 600. Half its lift for vertical take-off is derived from four GE1/10 gas generators which, besides giving forward thrust for cruising flight, produce vertical lift by means of cascade deflectors. The remaining lift is provided by four gas generators and four lift fans under the cabin floor. Control fans, one at each wing tip and two in the rear fuselage, provide additional control for hovering. The HFB 600 spans 78 ft. and is 101 ft. long. It would weigh 122,750 lb. at its maximum take-off weight, and would cruise at 600 m.p.h. with 35,200 lb. of payload.

Two further designs were proposed by the Vereinigte Flugtechnische Werke. One, the VC 180, is powered by ten 20,500-lb.-thrust Rolls-Royce RB.202–25 bypass lift engines mounted in wing-tip pods, and three rear-fuselage-mounted 16,980-lb.-thrust U.S. General Electric C-type twin-spool turbofans for forward flight. The other, the VC 181, would have no fewer than twelve 14,330-lb.-thrust bypass lift engines of RB.202–25 type housed in the fuselage, and four 13,010-lb.-thrust U.S. General Electric C-type turbofans mounted in pairs in underwing pods. The less sophisticated of the two—the VC 180P in its civil form—would be able to carry a 22,000-lb. payload

and cruise at 485 knots. The maximum take-off weight would be 121,250 lb.

Meanwhile, Lockheed-Georgia revealed that they were studying a 100-passenger Mach 0·8 V/STOL transport, lighter in weight than the German designs at only 76,000 lb., which would have four lift fans each of about 20,000-lb. thrust and four propulsion turbofans, two in wing pods and two in the tail. By using the lift fans to provide low speed roll control and the propulsion engines to provide pitch control, the number of lift fans needed is kept to a minimum. According to Lockheed, the lower weight and reduced number of engines would help to reduce costs considerably. Great Britain came into the picture when details were revealed at the 1970 Hanover air show of the 10,000–20,000-lb.-thrust Rolls-Royce RB.202 lift fan specified for the so-called discrete fan lift aircraft projects, the Do 231, VC 180P, and Britain's own Hawker Siddeley HS.141. Probably 16 of these engines would lift the HS.141; they would swivel to give acceleration during transition from vertical to horizontal flight. The design submitted to the ministry of aviation supply covers a 100-passenger aircraft capable of cruising at over 600 m.p.h., with a range of 150–1,300 miles. Propulsion would be by twin Rolls-Royce turbofans, possibly RB.220s.

The one thing that emerged from all these studies is that, even if the designs varied radically, they tended to be about the same size throughout the world, and capable of much the same order of performance. Civil V/STOL has yet to come, but 1970 saw the emergence of the first really considered designs. It will offer benefits to the passenger of time-saving and convenience, and for society it offers a transport system which will preserve community amenities.

Death of Handley Page and Beagle

Among other aviation developments in 1970, probably most significant was the loss to Britain of two more airframe manufacturers. The final collapse of Handley Page Ltd. came on February 27, just as it appeared that there was real hope again for the Jetstream project. In October 1969 the company was in process of being salvaged by the American Craven Corporation, with the assistance of the ministry of technology. Its Jetstream was to have been a small twin turboprop airliner, which it had been hoped would turn the fortunes of this famous old British company, denied the opportunity to tender to the government for new military aircraft because it refused to merge into the bigger airframe groups. The Jetstream was expected to carry a 1,000-lb. payload over a range of 1,500 miles. In the event, its performance fell far short of this target. CSE, the Oxford aircraft sales company, severed their connections, and the U.S.A.F. order for 11 aircraft was cancelled. On the company's airfield at Radlett stood 18 R.A.F. Victor V-bombers awaiting conversion to flight refuelling tankers, but the ministry contract was never placed. Craven's finance was not forthcoming, so the Victors went to Hawker Siddeley at Manchester for conversion, and the remaining Jetstreams were sold off by Shackleton Aviation on behalf of the receiver.

While Handley Page was slowly dying the government announced that it could provide no more aid to keep Beagle Aircraft alive. This active company, centred at Shoreham, was building the Pup light aeroplane for club and private use, and had begun the development flying of a strengthened military version called the Bulldog. The company went into liquidation while the Bulldog prototype, subject of an order for 58 from the Swedish Air Force, was undergoing cold-weather trials on skis in Sweden beyond the Arctic Circle. The Swedes were convinced that it was the perfect trainer aircraft for their purposes, and high-level negotiations eventually resulted in the taking over of Bulldog production by Scottish Aviation at Prestwick. The Scottish company, however, decided not to undertake any production of the Pup.

The Bulldog military trainer, manufacture of which was taken over from the defunct Beagle Aircraft company by Scottish Aviation, Prestwick.

Three Military Aircraft

Troubles continued to beset the General Dynamics F-111 aircraft—grounded for long periods because crashes have thrown some doubt on the engineering of its swing-wing pivot joint—and Australia is still in a quandary regarding its order for this aircraft. But two successful military aircraft consistently hit the headlines: the Jaguar, subject of co-operation between BAC and the French aircraft industry, and the Hawker Siddeley Harrier, the jump-jet of the R.A.F. The first British-assembled example of the Jaguar flew on October 12, 1969, and thereafter both British and French prototypes quickly built up a lot of flying hours. One of them even completed deck-landing trials on the French aircraft carrier *Clemenceau*, and two thrilled the crowds at the Farnborough Air Show in September 1970.

The Harrier, which is being built in considerable numbers for the R.A.F. at Kingston, attracted so much attention during the 1969 *Daily Mail* Transatlantic air race, when it landed vertically in the heart of New York, that it won big orders from the U.S. Marine Corps. Twelve Harriers were being completed at

The Anglo-French Jaguar, tactical support military aircraft, on deck-landing trials on the French carrier *Clemenceau* in July.

Kingston for the U.S.M.C., and it began to look likely that at least another 18 will be built for them in the U.K.—if not the whole 114 which it is believed the U.S.M.C. will eventually order. Some of these were to have been built under licence in the U.S.A. by McDonnell Douglas, but this possibility was thought to be fading.

Concorde Goes Supersonic

The Concorde completely confounded many of its critics during the year by the steady and successful expansion of its capabilities in the course of the flight test programme. The British-assembled 002 exceeded the speed of sound for the first time on March 25. During the summer both the French and British prototypes were grounded for considerable periods while the up-rated Rolls-Royce Bristol Olympus 593-3B series engines were fitted and modifications were made to their air-intake systems. The 002 was ready first, and after a short series of trials over the North Sea the aircraft began its supersonic flights over the specially chosen route along the western seaboard of the U.K. In November, both 001 and 002 reached the Mach 2 design speed, and all reports indicated that there were few problems of control or handling at the elevated speeds at which this aircraft will be operated. Few can now believe that Concorde will be unable to reach or exceed the guarantees of performance which have been given.

Ten Concordes have been authorized by the British and French governments—001 and 002 already flying, 01 and 02 the pre-production aircraft, and two batches of production Concordes, 03, 04, 05, and 06, 07, 08. A final decision whether after all the effort and expense the Concorde can be ordered into production has to wait until both governments are satisfied that the performance requirements, particularly in terms of payload and range, can be adequately met.

Meanwhile, in Oban, Pembrokeshire, and Cornwall people living along the west coast route anxiously waited for the Concorde to make its sonic booms, which they believed might cause damage to buildings and property and unnecessary suffering to human beings and animals. Flights began in September, and the whole 800 miles had soon been covered at speeds up to about 1,300 m.p.h. The boom turned out to be an anticlimax: very few complaints were received from the $1\frac{1}{2}$ million people living along the route who heard it. In any case, the government had largely anticipated criticism by announcing in a White Paper of May 28 that when the Concorde and other SSTs really come into service supersonic overflying will not be permitted in Great Britain. This brought the U.K. into line with the U.S.A., Canada, the Netherlands, West Germany, Norway, Sweden, Switzerland, and the Irish Republic, which had all already announced that they would not permit supersonic flight over their land.

The U.S.A. has now fallen well behind in the race for supersonic transport. Some £35 million was available for starting work on a prototype of the Boeing 2702 during 1970, and in the summer a full scale mock-up was completed of the 286-ft.-long SST (which had reverted to a delta-wing layout in place of the questionable swing-wing layout originally proposed). But when the F.A.A. asked for £130 million of public money to spend on it in 1971, the U.S. Senate unexpectedly turned down the request. As the year ended, President Nixon was seeking a way out of the impasse, but valuable time had been irretrievably lost.

Mergers in France and Britain

In France a big merger took place of Sud-Aviation, the Concorde's manufacturer, Nord-Aviation, and Sereb. The resulting company, SNIAS (Société Nationale Industrielle Aerospatiale), became the sole nationalized French company building military and civil aircraft, helicopters, missiles, and rockets. It employs no fewer than 42,500 people, its capital stands at more than £30 million, and the joint turnover was said to be almost £200 million in 1968.

In Britain, the government decided that if the nation were to take full advantage of the rapidly increasing inclusive tour charter business, there was a real need for a so-called "second force" airline. Towards the end of 1970 this came into being, perhaps a little more quickly than had at first been foreseen. Suggestions that British United should be taken over by BOAC fell through in March, but eventually protracted negotiations resulted in a merger of BUA with Caledonian Airways in October. This commercially inspired merger created the large second-force airline the government had in mind, and, against considerable opposition from managements and trade unions, certain routes were to be withdrawn from the nationalized BOAC and BEA for Caledonian-British United to operate. The government also announced in November that the decision had been finally taken for the two corporations to come jointly under an Airways Board by 1972, and that a new Civil Aviation Authority would at the same time absorb the functions of the air transport licensing board, the air registration board, the air safety board, and the civil air traffic control organization.

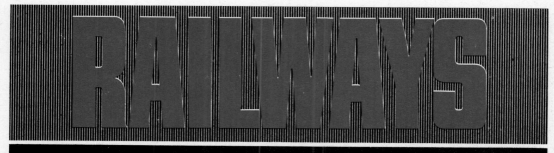

RAILWAYS
FACE THE FUTURE
CECIL J. ALLEN, M.Inst.T., A.I.Loco.E.

THE YEAR 1970 was one of great significance in the history of Australian railways. The Australian States began their railway construction with three different gauges—3 ft. 6 in. in Queensland and Western Australia; 4 ft. 8½ in. in New South Wales; and 5 ft. 3 in. in Victoria and South Australia. At last this short-sightedness was corrected by the completion (with the help of the Commonwealth government's 1,051-mile Trans-Australian line between Port Augusta and Kalgoorlie) of a unified 4 ft. 8½ in. gauge route right across the continent from Brisbane in Queensland to Perth and Fremantle in Western Australia. Thus, on March 1, 1970, the first regular through passenger train service began to operate between Sydney and Perth, twice weekly in each direction. This is the *Indian Pacific* (so named because of the two oceans which it connects) which covers the 2,461-mile journey in 65 hours. The service proved so popular that during the year it was fully booked for weeks in advance. Fortunately it will shortly be joined by a second *Indian Pacific*, thus providing four through trains each way every week.

Travel in the *Indian Pacific* is quite an experience. First-class passengers have the use of individual or twin-bedded rooms, with armchair accommodation by day, and their own toilets and showers. The earlier Trans-Australian custom of providing a coach in the train as a kind of social centre has been continued in a more luxurious form with a piano, observation lounge, and cocktail bar. For the through journey between Perth and Sydney the charge, including lavish meals, is about £41 first class and £31 economy class.

Even with all the improvements that have been carried out, the average rail speed across Australia still does not quite reach the 40 m.p.h. mark. This is understandable as much of the route is over former minor lines with relatively light tracks and much curvature, laid out in the first place without an expectation of future high-speed running. By contrast the Trans-Australian line achieves a world record with a dead straight section no less than 297 miles in length. But as this for the most part is over almost completely uninhabited arid country, to keep it in first-class order for high-speed running would be an expense altogether disproportionate to the limited amount of traffic passing over it. In other parts of Australia, of course, much higher speeds are run, particularly by the *Spirit of Progress* and *Southern Aurora* expresses between Sydney and Melbourne, now also using 4 ft. 8½ in. gauge track throughout.

Tokaido Line Extension

The New Tokaido line in Japan, with its regular service of electric flyers covering the 320 miles between Tokyo and Osaka in 3 hours 10 minutes, at an average of 101 m.p.h., still remained the fastest stretch of railway in the world during 1970. This was also a case of substituting a 4 ft. 8½ in. for a 3 ft. 6 in. gauge, but the Japanese, regardless of expense, laid out a completely new line throughout, with the track and all equipment designed for speeds up to 130 m.p.h. Such has been the outstanding success of this notable project that the New Tokaido line was being extended during 1970 from Osaka to Kobe and Okayama, again with entirely new trackage (including one 10-mile and two 5-mile tunnels) adapted for even higher speeds. Meanwhile the Japanese ministry of transport authorized a further extension: from Okayama through Hiroshima to Hakata and Fukuoka, again with some lengthy tunnels, including one under the Kanmon Strait to reach the island of Kyushu. It is planned to cut the present time of 12 hours from Tokyo to Hakata (using the New Tokaido line as far as Osaka and the existing 3 ft. 6 in.

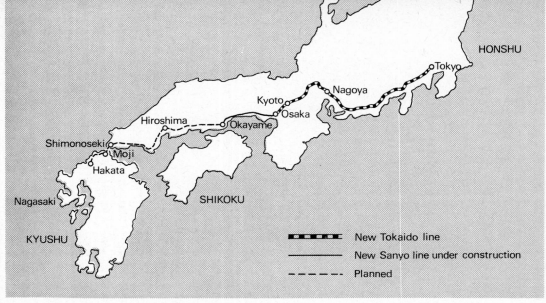

So successful has the New Tokaido line been that the Japanese are extending it, under the name of New Sanyo Line, from Osaka to Okayama, and plan to take it all the way to Hakata in Kyushu.

narrow gauge line from there onwards) to 6 hours 40 minutes.

The fact that the Japanese are prepared to spend £560 million on the 350 miles of new line from Osaka to Hakata, in addition to the £400 million already expended on the 320-mile New Tokaido line, is evidence of their unbounded faith in railways.

U.S. Failures and Successes

This is in strong contrast with what has been happening in the U.S.A., where the position of the railways has been going steadily from bad to worse. Air and road competition have now robbed the American railways of most of their passenger traffic—famous long-distance trains like the *Twentieth Century Limited* and the *Broadway Limited* have disappeared. Some railways have abandoned passenger operation completely, and during 1970 the largest railway system in the country —the Penn Central—formally declared itself bankrupt.

Nevertheless the increasing congestion on American motorways and airways is persuading Americans to look closely at the facilities offered by railways for moving passengers at speed between city centres. The traffic problem

The new Metroliner electric train service of the "formally bankrupt" Penn Central Line runs from New York to Washington (a distance of 226 miles) in 2½ hours.

between the cities of New York, Philadelphia, Baltimore, and Washington has become so acute in recent years that the Federal government had to step in to help financially in establishing the ultra-high-speed *Metroliner* service between New York and Washington which began in 1968 and has been improving ever since. This provides the nearest approach in speed to the Japanese standard that the rest of the world has yet seen. The enormous expense involved in building an entirely new line, however, could not be justified, and it has been necessary to make the best use possible of the existing Pennsylvania main line between New York and Washington.

With each coach of an electric *Metroliner* developing 1,200 h.p., the total of 7,200 continuous h.p. per 448-ton train (and considerably more over short periods) permits some quite fantastic acceleration. Indeed, the specification for these trains laid it down that on level track they should be able to reach 125 m.p.h. in two minutes from a standing start, and 150 m.p.h. in three minutes, and that their maximum speed capacity should be 160 m.p.h. Even with speed restrictions through Philadelphia and Baltimore, the fastest time scheduled over the 226½ miles between New York and Washington, with one intermediate stop, is 2½ hours, requiring an average speed of 90 m.p.h. The *Metroliners* have proved very popular, and usually run filled to capacity, but there have been many teething troubles, and as yet it has not been possible to introduce anything like the full service originally proposed.

One interesting experiment in connection with these trains has been the installation at New York, Philadelphia, and Washington of the world's first computer-controlled ticket-selling machines. A passenger wanting to know if a seat is available in a *Metroliner* deposits a "quarter" (of a dollar, value 10p) in the slot of a machine marked "inquiry", then presses a button for his destination and another to indicate if he wants a "Metroclub" (first class) or a "Coach" (second class) seat. Within 20 seconds, an illuminated panel advises him if a seat is available and the time of departure, also the cost. If the reply is satisfactory, he then deposits the correct fare into the machine, which prints and issues his ticket and returns his "inquiry" deposit. Reservations can be made up to a month ahead, and are stored in the "memory" of the computer in New York until the day of travel.

Speeding Up British Rail

In Great Britain the most notable decision of 1970 affecting the railways was the ministry of transport decision that the electrification of

The first consumer-operated, computer-controlled ticket-issuing machine in the world, installed in conjunction with the Metroliner service.

the main line of the London Midland Region out of Euston may be extended from Weaver Junction, north of Crewe, where the main line forks and a line strikes out to the north, for 227 miles to Glasgow Central. With electrification, curves will be smoothed out wherever possible, to permit higher speeds. There will also be a rearrangement of the lines at various points to facilitate operation, and all-electric signalling will be installed. Electrification between Euston and Birmingham, Liverpool, and Manchester has proved such an outstanding success that at last the government recognized the heavy expenditure on this extension as justified. The high-speed Inter-City passenger services of British Railways, which—in their combination of frequency, systematic even-interval times, and 100 m.p.h. speeds—are superior to any others in the world, have proved that over medium distances the railways can still beat air transport.

As a curtain-raiser to this electrification extension, in May 1970 the London Midland and the Scottish Regions decided to show what they could do with diesel power over the main line that is to be electrified. A new timetable was brought into force, with accelerations on an almost unprecedented scale. The times of the day trains from Euston to Glasgow were cut by an average of no less than 64 minutes, and of the up trains by an average of 44 minutes, bringing the average time of the 401½-mile London–Glasgow journey down to about 6 hours in each direction. The new acceleration, of course, takes place entirely north of Crewe, as already these trains were timed at not far short of 80 m.p.h. between Crewe and

London. This has been made possible by using Class 50 diesels in pairs, with a combined horsepower of 5,400. By using multiple-unit control each pair is under the control of a single crew.

The locomotive performance needed to maintain the new times exceeds anything previously known on the West Coast main line. On the first day of the accelerated service, railway enthusiasts who had bought tickets on the down *Royal Scot* were impressed when the twin diesels lifted the 13-coach train, some 460 tons in weight, from just above sea level on passing Carnforth to the 915 ft. Shap Summit, in the Westmorland fells, at an *average* speed of 85 m.p.h. Allowing for several out-of-course signal and permanent-way delays, with electric power from Euston to Crewe and diesel power from there onwards, the net average speed from Euston over the 299 miles to the Scottish border at Carlisle was 81·5 m.p.h.

Coming up two days later, the *Royal Scot* covered the 401½ miles from Glasgow to Euston in an actual time of 5 hours 54 minutes —36 minutes less than the fastest scheduled time that has ever operated previously (the 6½ hours of the steam-hauled pre-war *Coronation Scot*). It is true that in November 1936, on an experimental run, the steam Pacific *Princess Elizabeth* ran from Glasgow to Euston in just under 5¾ hours, but this was non-stop with a train of eight coaches only, and practically unchecked. The *Royal Scot*'s 5 hours 54 minutes included 4½ minutes standing at Carlisle and 15 minutes at Crewe, as well as a number of out-of-course checks, and was with an 11-coach load of 390 tons—a much harder proposition of haulage.

Moving a River to Save Three Minutes

On the East Coast main line there was also considerable expenditure during 1970 in smoothing out curves in order to permit 100 m.p.h. speeds over as much of the route as possible. The biggest task was to straighten out the sinuous stretch of the main line where it borders the River Ouse at Offord, just south of Huntingdon. Here the course of the river was diverted, and the tracks moved up to 26 ft. from their original position to permit an increase in maximum speed from 70 to 100 m.p.h., even though this expenditure will not save more than two or three minutes at most in running times.

As a result of these and other track improvements throughout the route, the fastest time over the 268¼ miles between King's Cross and Newcastle upon Tyne has now come down to 3 hours 35 minutes, including a stop at Darlington. The shortest time between London and Darlington (232¼ miles apart) is now 2 hours 59 minutes, requiring an average speed of 77·8 m.p.h. This is performed by 3,300 h.p. *Deltic* diesels with eight-coach trains of 290 tons, which these remarkable locomotives can work even up 1-in-200 gradients at 100 m.p.h. speeds.

During 1970 developments in other directions were taking place. New designs for British main-line coaches were prepared, and construction began. These will be the longest yet built for service in Great Britain, 75 ft. overall compared with the previous standard of 67 ft., and so will be able to accommodate 48 compared with 42 passengers in each first class coach, and 72 instead of 64 in each second class coach.

A great improvement will be air conditioning, while double windows and acoustic blanketing will make for silent running. Improvements in coach suspension will also provide smooth travel at speeds up to 125 m.p.h. New types of seating and lighting will add further to the comfort of passengers, and public address facilities will be provided in each coach. Looking farther ahead, there is the

During the spring of 1970 British Rail diverted the river Ouse at Offord, Hunts, to straighten out a curve. Below left: the tight curve before improvement. Right: work in progress on the diversion of the river.

Advanced Passenger Train project which was being worked out during the year at British Rail's Derby research centre. This project aims at speeds of 150 m.p.h., but no details of the design had been made public as the year ended.

In pursuit of safety, 1970 saw attention being paid in greater degree than ever before to the reliability of the rails over which trains run. Several derailments in recent years have given unpleasant reminders of what can happen if rails break, and that such breakages can result from flaws in steel which looks completely sound. For a good many years past flaw detectors of the type first developed by the American Sperry Company have been in use, but with hand operation patrolling tracks for this purpose has been a slow business. Now, however, British Railways have built a rail flaw detector car, which can automatically detect and record internal rail fissures when travelling at a speed of up to 25 m.p.h. This will permit far more frequent and systematic flaw detection than hitherto and make a valuable contribution to safety.

28-mile Tunnel through the Alps?

Finally, the year saw an important railway development in Switzerland, another country which has unbounded faith in the future of its railways, and is continually spending money on a massive scale to improve their efficiency and carrying capacity. Recently completed Swiss projects include the complete reconstruction of the main station at Berne; the doubling of remaining single-line sections of main-line tracks; the beginning of some costly work to shorten the main line between Berne and Zürich; and vast new marshalling yards at Basle and Chiasso, on the French–German–Swiss and Swiss–Italian frontiers respectively. These are at the two ends of the principal main line between South Germany and North Italy —the Gotthard—over which a vast and increasing freight traffic flows constantly.

Much has been done in previous years to improve the Gotthard, by doubling and fly-overs at Brugg and Rotkreuz, but it still has to pass through the massive barrier of the Alps, and this means a lengthy and steep climb from both directions to the 3,786-ft. summit level in the $9\frac{1}{4}$-mile Gotthard tunnel. Through this tunnel an enormous flow of traffic passes, complicated by trains carrying motor-cars which want to avoid climbing to the 6,916-ft. altitude of the Gotthard Pass. The tunnel is automatically signalled throughout, and can pass trains through at two-minute intervals but, even so, the limit of the Gotthard main line's capacity is approaching, and during 1970 it became apparent that something drastic must soon be done to ease the situation.

Proposals emerged, therefore, to bore a new tunnel from Amsteg, in the Reuss valley just south of where the long climb to Göschenen begins, to Giornico, near the foot of the southern ramp from Airolo, which would enable trains to thread the main Alpine chain practically on the level, and thus make possible both increased line capacity and considerably shortened travelling time.

This most ambitious project would constitute a tunnel through rock no less than 28 miles in length, and at its deepest probably some 8,000 ft. below the surface. Huge engineering problems would have to be solved to enable tunnelling to proceed for so long at such a depth. But Swiss engineers were already working on a 9-mile road tunnel during 1970, and as with the Swiss the word "impossible" does not seem to exist, it may well be that before many years have elapsed the boring of the Gotthard Base Tunnel will be added to the list of the world's most notable railway achievements.

Below: last stage in the straightening of the Offord curve by diverting the Ouse.

Motorists who want to avoid climbing 7,000 ft. to the Pass go by train through the Gotthard Tunnel.

SHIPS

MICHAEL CONNOR
of *Lloyd's List*

The 100,000-ton Norwegian bulk carrier *Hoegh Rainbow*, the largest dry cargo ship ever to discharge at a British port, unloading iron ore at Port Talbot, in August.

IN 1970 THE WORLD'S SHIPPING and shipbuilding industries entered what could be one of the most exciting decades in maritime history. Not only was a vast and growing market clearly evident, but revolutionary ideas in ship design pointed to both a booming and an exciting future. World sea transport already accounts for more than three quarters of international cargo movements, and world trade generally is increasing in tonnage and, more significantly, in ton-mileage. Every indication—population, economic development, and rising standards of living—shows that it will continue to expand. During 1970 shipping and ship-building companies, both British and foreign, grasped these tremendous opportunities and laid the foundations for almost certain long-term prosperity.

The oil and dry bulk trades became more and more dominated by the economies of huge ships as the year progressed. In the liner trades the container and other unit-load ships set new standards for the efficient movement of goods. In Britain's shipping industry in particular a remarkable change-round in

fortune was seen, due, to a larger extent than has been appreciated, to favourable government legislation in recent years regarding investment grants and the like. The massive amount of new shipping ordered by United Kingdom shipowners—almost 20 million tons, worth in the region of £950 million—means that a "new" British merchant fleet will soon be plying the world's ocean trade routes. And this fleet will consist of giant tankers, container ships, and bulk carriers—the types of vessel which will capture most of the world's future trade. Scandinavian and Continental shipping lines were not content to watch Britain scoop the trade pool. Joint services or mergers became the rule rather than the exception; for it is now recognized that only large groups of companies can compete in the fierce fight for trade.

Cruising Holidays

Rising standards of living have meant changes in holiday habits. Shipowners, who are generally very shrewd businessmen, anticipated that cruising holidays would probably become one of the most popular ways of "getting away from it all". During the year the Cunard company's beautiful liner *Queen Elizabeth 2* proved to be a highly successful investment for the British company. Indeed Cunard are so convinced that more and more people will want to go cruising that they ordered another two liners—smaller than the *Q.E. 2*—from a Dutch shipyard. Norwegian and Greek shipowners were also anxious to enter the cruise field and either ordered new ships or snapped up second-hand ones.

Oddly enough, the only country to lay up many of its passenger ships was the U.S.A. The high costs of manning and running an American vessel are blamed for this unhappy situation. European cruise-liner operators, of course, took full advantage of this lack of American competitors, and 1970 saw them flocking to U.S. ports to gain this lucrative passenger trade.

Trisec—a New Design

Although the United States merchant shipping and shipbuilding industries continued to

for the SEVENTIES

decline as they had done over a number of years, it was, ironically, from America that most of the exciting technological developments came during 1970. Litton Industries' research staff designed the Trisec ship: a new competitor to enter the race to fill the transportation gap between aircraft and conventional ships with speeds of up to 35 knots. This gap in the transportation spectrum is also the preoccupation of hovercraft and hydrofoil designers. Thus the year saw the proposed trans-Atlantic hovership challenged by the proposed Trisec.

The Trisec concept is really a sophisticated catamaran which will be powered by aircraft-type gas-turbine engines, and thus reach speeds of up to 80 knots. The proposed ship has three basic sections: underwater pontoon hulls, above-water hull struts, and a main connection hull for cargo, passengers, or troops and military equipment. It is, of course, because the resulting form is trisected, that Litton designers have christened this new type of ship the Trisec.

Litton claim that the design results in high speeds together with surprising fuel economy, and that the ship would be competitive with jet aircraft: a trans-Atlantic Trisec liner could cut the crossing time by sea from five days to two. Container ships and general cargo vessels could also be made more competitive with this design. And the Trisec would use only 50 per cent of the power needed by a ship with a conventional displacement-type hull. The Trisec's twin hulls rest on torpedo-shaped pontoons, greatly reducing wavemaking resistance—one of the greatest speed limitations for conventional vessels. The pontoons, which provide the major portion of buoyancy, are submerged, with the waterplane area of the dual-hull struts reduced to a minimum.

If the Trisec can do all that Litton claim for her, and if the design does not suffer from the stress problems which have affected previous attempts to build cargo-carrying catamarans, then this new type of vessel may well live up to her designers' hopes, and have an impact on sea travel comparable to the impact of the commercial jet on air travel.

The All-Purpose Seabee

In 1971 the first Seabee ship is scheduled to enter service and during 1970 some outstand-

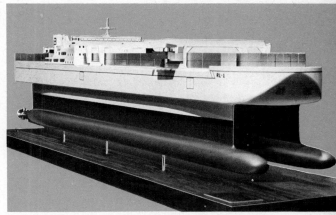

Model of the twin-hull gas-turbine-powered Trisec, a projected 35,000-ton ship 700 ft. long and 108 ft. wide, with a speed of 50 knots, being developed by Ingalls West, a division of Litton Industries, U.S.A.

ing claims were put forward for this new type of barge carrier. Enthusiastic American representatives of Lykes Lines were confident that the project will be proved viable despite its immense cost. Both shipping and cargo-handling experts agreed that the Seabee carriers under construction for Lykes represent a totally new system of ocean freight transportation. During the year three 27,183-ton Seabees were being built at General Dynamics Corporation's shipyard at Quincy,

Artist's impression of the U.S. General Dynamics Corporation's 27,000-ton barge-carrying vessel, the Seabee, with one of her barges being towed to its destination. The first Seabee is scheduled to enter service during 1971.

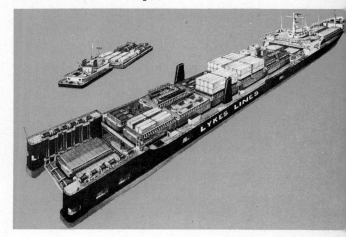

A new method of transporting cars was adopted in 1970 by Renault, who sent hundreds of cars in flat double-deck river barges from Paris down the Seine to Rouen and Le Havre. A tug can push four barges at a time.

Mass. Together with their fleet of barges the Seabees will cost well over $100 million. Initially they will operate between Lykes terminals on the United States Gulf and terminal ports in Continental Europe and the United Kingdom. The Seabee barge units— 38 per vessel—are the real cargo carriers in the total service concept of the Seabee system. They will link two of the world's greatest inland waterway systems, the Mississippi and its tributaries, serving the vast Mississippi Valley area of the U.S.A., with the Rhine, which serves the heartland of Europe.

The Seabees will be the largest American cargo ships ever built, and probably the most flexible vessels ever conceived. The design encompasses the advantages of the barge carrier, the container ship, the drive-on drive-off ship, the break-bulk ship, and, to some degree, the small tanker. Each Seabee ship will have a 2,000-ton stern elevator able to load barges containing cargo on to the "mother" ship; and these barges will be huge by comparison with other barge carriers.

The barge-carrying ship stimulating most interest from maritime nations during 1970 was the LASH (Lighters Aboard Ship) vessel. At the end of 1969 the *Acadia Forest*, the first LASH ship, delivered her first trans-Atlantic cargo of loaded lighters from the U.S. Gulf to Europe. Since then she has been plying the Atlantic in a regular service closely watched by the world's shipowners. Indeed, by the end of 1970 a number of LASH-type ships had been ordered by Scandinavian and Continental companies, and a loan of $A12 million had been promised by the Australian Federal government to the Western Australian government to equip the State shipping line with two barge-carrying vessels, probably based on the LASH system. These two ships, which have been designed by a Chicago firm of naval

architects, are expected to enter service in 1972. Although no mention was made during the year concerning which service they will operate on, reports have referred to north-western Australia between Fremantle and Darwin.

Unloading through Pipes

Early in March 1970, the bulk carrier *Marconaflo Merchant* delivered 41,000 tons of Canadian iron-ore concentrate to a steel company in Portland, Oregon, U.S.A., and in doing so made history. The ore was unloaded without the use of cranes, bucket, or conveyor belts, and without dust or spillage. In fact, the entire operation could have been completed even without the ship's docking. The arrival of the 51,046-ton *Marconaflo Merchant* marked the first time a large-scale commercial cargo had been delivered using a new process which loads and discharges granular bulk materials as a slurry—yet ships them as solids. Developed by the international Marcona Corporation, the process is called Marconaflo. With this new process dry bulk materials are placed into liquid suspension and then moved by pipelines.

There is therefore no need for costly shore installations made up of docks, railhead, chutes, cranes, or conveyors. The only shore facilities needed are a pond or tank for slurrying or slurry storage, and an underwater pipeline to an offshore mooring buoy. According to mining industry experts, this technique demonstrates a tremendous potential for bulk transport in a number of fields—opening up previously inaccessible mining areas, widening the distribution and increasing the number of smelters and refining plants in ore-importing countries, and increasing the capacity and altering the design of bulk carriers. The impetus behind this revolutionary design, with all its implications for other industries, is simply the hope of reducing the cost of loading and discharging bulk raw materials by up to 90 per cent.

Submarine Tankers?

Tankers dominated the world's headlines throughout 1970. A number of 200,000-tonners were involved in puzzling disasters: tragedies which as the year ended had still not been fully explained. But these ships were only a small part of the huge fleet of giant tankers hauling massive loads of crude oil around the world's oceans. Although one shipowner ordered a 400,000-ton tanker from a Japanese shipyard, most oil firms seem content to settle their ship-sizes at around 250,000 tons. The British and Continental ownership of tanker tonnage has grown at an astounding rate, matched by only a few other nations. Current world orders for new tankers are in excess of 63 million tons, of which well over 9 million tons are expected to operate under the British flag. Most of this new U.K. tonnage consists of super-tankers. The epic North-West Passage voyage, in September 1969, of the American tanker *Manhattan* to discover whether it would be feasible to move oil from the new Alaskan oil fields to the eastern United States, was still being evaluated during 1970. Meanwhile, General Dynamics in the United States released designs for the construction of 170,000-ton nuclear-powered tanker submarines to move Alaskan oil under the ice to an ice-free North Atlantic port, where the oil could be transferred to a conventional vessel. Such submarines would be 900 ft. long, with a beam of 140 ft., and a speed of 18 knots. It is contended that these vessels could ship oil at an appreciably lower cost per ton than ice-strengthened surface tankers.

More and More Container Ships

One of the most dynamic sectors of the world's shipping industry has been the container field. Enormous sums of money have been invested by British, Australian, Continental, and Scandinavian shipping companies to utilize this concept fully. And so far the idea of carrying cargo in a box on a ship has proved extremely successful. In the course of 1970 extensive containerization of general cargo on the North Atlantic route between Western Europe and the U.S. eastern and western seaboards was achieved. Container services between the United Kingdom and the Continent and Australia and New Zealand were also opened. There were also new container links between North America and Australia. It now seems certain that container ships will largely replace conventional liner shipping on the major inter-continental sea routes between Europe, North America, Japan, and Australasia.

There were, however, some misgivings voiced during 1970 to the effect that there may soon be too many container ships available for the amount of cargo to be carried. A tremendous amount of container shipping has been ordered from the world's shipyards. It must be remembered that each container ship has a much greater capacity than the conventional cargo ship it displaces. Moreover, it is faster and

The container ship trade from the new terminal at Tilbury, London, at last got moving in 1970 after over two years' delay due to labour troubles. Left: three British container ships at the new dock. Below: the long-awaited Clyde-built *Jervis Bay*, received by her owners, Overseas Containers Ltd., on May 15, became a fortnight later the first container ship to leave Tilbury on the Australia run.

therefore capable of more round trips a year. As the ports at either end are equipped for the fast handling of containers as an integral part of the new services, the turn-round time is cut from 3 weeks to 3 days and this further increases the carrying capacity of the fleet. But, despite the fact that the deep-sea container business could be in an unhappy position during 1971, shipyards were busy during 1970 drawing up plans for even more economic container vessels with anything up to three times the capacity of those in use at present. It did not pass unnoticed that fast container ships of about 40,000 to 50,000 tons would require much the same kind of propulsion systems as medium-speed 500,000-ton tankers. Britain's giant Vickers concern disclosed details of design studies for nuclear-powered systems which would be applicable to big container ships or 500,000-ton tankers.

Shipbuilders in the Red

Most of the world's shipyards have overflowing order books but, paradoxically, they have either been losing money or just breaking even. This strange situation—which became apparent at the beginning of 1970 and lasted throughout most of the year—is caused by inflation, which eats away most of the shipyards' anticipated profits. To counter their losses the yards introduced an escalation clause on new contracts during the year. In other words, if a shipbuilder's costs go up while he is building a vessel the client for whom the ship is under construction pays the extra money. As profits from shipping operations in 1970 were extremely good most shipowners were more than happy to agree to escalation clauses.

Still far ahead of every other nation in the shipbuilding league is Japan, which continues to produce an enormous amount of new tonnage for shipowners of every country. West Germany, Sweden, and Great Britain occupy the next positions in the "league". A most disappointing shipbuilding performance came from Australia during 1970. Although many of the shipyards in the country have adequate facilities and expertise to build the complicated vessels required in these days, demand has fluctuated so much that a steady level of employment has been lacking. Even the Australian National Line's first big container ships were built abroad. Nevertheless, Australian shipbuilders maintain that if only home demand is stimulated they will build their industry into a powerful force, able to combat tough foreign competition.

Dutch, German, and French shipbuilders followed the lead of British and Scandinavian companies by merging their yards into strong, viable units. The new groups that appeared on the Continent during the year are, in some cases, so strong that even Japanese firms have expressed fear for the future. The British shipbuilding industry had a mixed year. Like their foreign counterparts, the yards had full order books but were still making losses on fixed-price contracts. This will alter when the new escalation-clause orders are dealt with. In addition the shipbuilding companies were turning more and more to standard-type ships during the year: vessels which are cheap to produce and easy to sell.

Less Oil on the Beaches?

It was, of course, European Conservation Year, in which everyone, including shipowners, endeavoured to fight the threat of pollution of the environment. Most of the pollution of the seas originates ashore. Detergents, chemical wastes, and untreated sewage are poured into rivers, lakes, or direct into the sea itself. Oil also escapes into the sea, not only from ships but by accidental spills from oil refineries and even from underwater oil wells. Such pollution can cause wholesale destruction of birds, fish, and other marine life. The seafarer is well aware of this and is just as annoyed as other members of the public by the oil washed ashore on holiday beaches and the damage to wild life. Each industry has a duty to reduce its own pollution, and shipping has accepted the task of doing as much as possible to cut down all types of pollution from vessels in port or on the seas.

There are two main ways by which oil finds its way on to the waters from ships: by washing cargo oil tanks at sea (which is now much less prevalent than it once was); and by accidents to tankers or other vessels carrying oil as cargo or fuel. The reason that operational discharge of tank washings was widespread until recently was that, as with many other forms of pollution, there was no satisfactory alternative method of disposal. Now, thanks to the initiative of leading tanker owners, there is the "load-on-top" system which, in most trades, offers a safe, economic way of avoiding pollution. The load-on-top system is estimated to have avoided the discharge of over 2 million tons of pollutant oil per annum. Accidental pollution can obviously be reduced by avoiding accidents. The British and Continental schemes for ship traffic separation in narrow waters, which came into effect during the year, were already yielding dividends by its end, and of course the increasing availability and reliability of aids to navigation are playing their part.

Nature

The World has become . . .

A Poisonous Place to Live In

WILLIAM KEAL

By 1970 THE WORLD was awakened to the problems of the pollution of the environment. People began at last to ask why they should have to live surrounded by filth and noise. They at last queried whether technological progress need go hand in hand with a less pleasant environment. In America they joked about it ("I'm moving. My doctor recommends a change of pollution.") In France, Canada, and other countries they legislated against it. In Japan they went on strike against it (four million workers downed tools in a demand for action). In Britain, the Labour government set up the traditional royal commission on it, and the Conservatives lumped together the ministries of housing, transport, and public works as a department for (the year's "in" word) Environment. Europe had its Conservation Year, and U Thant, secretary general of the United Nations, called for a world organization to deal with the problem.

The term pollution covers smoke (or smog), sewage, noise, poison by pesticides, waste (industrial and domestic), exhaust fumes (from cars and aircraft), and radioactive contamination. It increases at a rate exactly as fast as a population is industrialized, as Lord Kennet, the Labour parliamentary secretary at the ministry of housing and local government, said in his pamphlet, *Controlling Our Environment*. There is nothing new about pollution. Man has always polluted his environment since he piled up his kitchen midden outside his cave. Open sewers and drains in early times led to the plague; the industrial revolution brought on the pea-souper fogs.

In Great Britain, the rapid change from an agrarian-based economy in the 18th century to a science-based one in the 19th brought with it tremendous quantities of industrial pollution over which there was no control or experience of control. The Alkali Act of 1863 and the Factory Acts provided some curb, but in general very little was done about the problem. Many thought that little needed to be done. There are some authorities who still think that extreme views on pollution are unnecessarily alarmist.

For example, in his 1970 report to the U.K. minister of housing and local government the chief inspector of the alkali inspectorate, the organization that monitors atmospheric discharges by industry, strongly criticized those who predict that pollution of the environment will end in catastrophe. Their gloomy prophecies, the report said, need to be put into proper perspective. The fear that carbon dioxide, building up from the burning of fossil fuels, will result in a rise in the Earth's temperature and melt the Polar caps, thus flooding many coastal towns, is highly speculative, the report said. And the fear that the temperature will also rise because of a belt of dust in the atmosphere is just as speculative.

The report maintained that there is no sign of global changes caused by man's interference with nature. Sulphur dioxide from burning fossil fuels is regarded as one of the most significant pollutants. But we must not, the report said, be misled into believing that its elimination would end most of the health and amenity problems caused by acid gases. Man's efforts cause the emission into the air of 120 million tons of gases a year, compared with 600 million tons from natural causes. Astronomical figures are frequently quoted for the cost of the effects of air pollution. But there is no rush by the alleged sufferers to finance the prevention of pollution at source, although, on the face of it, there should be a phenomenal return for the outlay. The chief reason why a degree of pollution is tolerated is economic, said the report, and it is important that the financial resources available should be directed primarily towards abatement in the correct order of priority.

Nevertheless, people have begun to rebel against living conditions that seem to be getting nastier, and there is a genuine fear of what further technological advances will lead to. Sea birds died in their thousands in the Irish Sea—perhaps from the effects of waste products of the plastics industry, but no one knows for certain. DDT traces have been found in seals in the Baltic and in pelicans in the Antarctic. That does not prove that DDT is harmful to man: no one really knows, but many countries have banned it. The dumping of nerve gas in sealed containers into the depths of the Atlantic and the storing of radiation waste from nuclear power stations at the bottom of disused mines were stated by experts to be perfectly safe. But what, people wondered, might happen if there was an earthquake? How safe should we be then?

The skies generally seem to be getting darker. The Greek chamber of technology said that, unless radical measures were taken immediately to combat air pollution, Athens would have to be abandoned within 10 years. Already atmospheric pollution there is increasing so rapidly that in a few years the Acropolis will be invisible from below. It is not only the industrial areas that suffer from the gases of chimneys and exhaust pipes. In Hawaii, far from any major industrial area, atmospheric turbidity has increased by 30 per cent in 10 years, and in the Caucasus the increase in 40 years is 1,900 per cent! The cloud cover over the North Atlantic is now 10 per cent above normal, thanks to the condensation trails of jet aircraft. It has been stated that the coming of general supersonic air travel could lead to the permanent clouding over by the year 2000 of the Atlantic, together with much of North America and Europe. The cloud could reflect the sun's heat away from the Earth's surface and start a new Ice Age, said one scientist. Others took the view that a catastrophic *rise* in temperature is imminent because of the heat which industry generates into the atmosphere.

The Fate of the Oceans

Equally dire prospects have been forecast for the world's waters. Commander Jacques Cousteau, the expert in underwater exploration, declared that the oceans, vast though they are, are dying because of over-fishing and pollution. Fishing techniques have improved dramatically in the past decade. Modern nylon nets and lines are almost invisible to fish, and tracking devices have discovered so many of their migration routes and feeding grounds that they will soon be hunted to extinction. Sir Hugh Mackenzie, director of the Atlantic salmon research trust, has stated that unless high-seas fishing is ended within the next three years the Atlantic salmon will have passed the point of no return on its way to extinction.

Of equal menace are the disastrous oil spills, such as arose from the wreck of *Torrey Canyon*. During his crossing of the Atlantic in his papyrus boat *Ra 2*, Thor Heyerdahl reported that a continuous stretch of 1,400 miles of the journey was polluted by lumps of solidified oil. He observed them uninterruptedly every day for 27 days. Another danger at sea is the possible spillage of the cargoes of biocides, chemicals such as the DDT group, which ships regularly carry across the oceans.

Examples of world-wide protest. Left: in May, young demonstrators cycled through Stockholm wearing respirators against car exhaust fumes. Right: English anglers marched through an April shower to Downing Street to present a 200,000-signature petition against river pollution.

Already the international council for the exploration of the sea has stated that the Baltic Sea is becoming a dead sea. Pollution by sewage discharges from Leningrad and Copenhagen, by industrial discharges from the wood-pulping industries of Finland and Sweden, and by general industrial wastes and pesticides has brought a marked decrease in the oxygen content of the water. The council forecast that if these developments continue unchecked the whole water mass below the halocline will probably turn into a lifeless oceanic desert such as is found in the Black Sea. The halocline is the level of sharp change in salinity which impedes the exchange of water below and above a depth of some 180 ft.

DDT concentration in Baltic seals is in some cases ten times as high as in North Sea seals, and the reproductive ability of some species may have been reduced. Bans have been imposed on the consumption of fish from some parts of the Baltic, because of mercury pollution. The main danger to the sea is that the reduction of oxygen is closely related to the generation of the poisonous gas hydrogen sulphide, which has been detected in deep waters. The gas arises when phosphates from sewage, detergents, and other wastes stimulate the growth of marine plant life which absorbs oxygen from the water. At the end of its life cycle, the plant matter sinks to the bottom, where it absorbs still more oxygen as it decomposes and thus produces the poisonous gas.

The problems of the Baltic are not isolated. Marine biologists in Edinburgh have found that the decline in the population of a dozen species of plankton in the Atlantic could have catastrophic effects on the ecology of the sea. It is by no means the big things which cause trouble. Scottish trout fed on shrimp larvae imported from the Great Salt Lake died because each shrimp contained a tiny amount of pesticide which had got into the lake. The pesticide was not enough to kill a shrimp, but it proved lethal to a trout after it had eaten a few hundred shrimps. Human beings could be similarly affected. Already, it has been stated, the milk of American mothers contains so much DDT that their babies should not be breast-fed.

Saltier Mediterranean

Harmful environmental change does not always derive from wilful negligence. The salt content of the eastern Mediterranean, for instance, is increasing as a result of the building of the new Aswan high dam. This is having a detrimental effect on the fish population. The water is saltier because less fresh water is reaching the Mediterranean from the Nile, by reason of evaporation from storage reservoirs and irrigation works. And the Nile water that does flow into the Mediterranean is itself saltier because its use in irrigation is drawing salt out of previously uncultivated land. The river's waters also contain fewer nutrients because so much of the flood of muddy water which used to wash down from the agricultural land of Egypt is now trapped behind the dam. The Nile flood used to begin a new life cycle among the plant matter in the Mediterranean, enriching the food supply for all creatures in the sea. One example of the change is that

Two of the world's worst car-polluted cities showed their citizens what urban life could be like when they closed a few main streets to traffic for a day. In Tokyo (left), the Ginza on an August Sunday was thronged by thousands just walking and breathing. On "Earth Day" (April 22), New Yorkers ambled up and down a stretch of Fifth Avenue (right), enjoying the forgotten taste of carbon-dioxide-free air.

Pollution-conscious organizations keep a continuous watch and check on the manifold activities that make life unbearable for human and animal creatures. Above left: at the Bureau of Sport Fisheries and Wildlife 200 miles north of San Francisco, closed-circuit television monitors the state of the Sacramento river and the health of the fish that swim in it. Right: a Greater London Council official with microphone and decibel-meter carrying out a noise test on a hovering helicopter at a site in the disused St. Katharine's Dock.

Most countries have regulations controlling the amount of permissible emission of poisonous gases by petrol-driven vehicles, but too often the rules are not enforced. In 1970 public agitation made authorities more vigilant, and checks on exhaust fumes were more strictly applied. These photographs show a few examples of official action against atmospheric pollution in great cities of the West and the East. Upper left: a free test of exhaust provided for motorists by the Paris police; right, compulsory measurement of carbon monoxide in a car's exhaust by Tokyo police. Lower left: one of Madrid's buses undergoing a toxicity test; right, testing the air in a Stockholm street.

Egypt's sardine catch, which was 18,000 tons in 1965, has now been reduced to a few hundred tons a year.

In Alaska, a road to the newly discovered oilfields at Prudhoe Bay, although cut only a few inches deep in the winter ice and fragile tundra, so unbalanced the thermal regime of the permafrost that the following summer it was one long bog. The Arctic environment is the most delicately balanced in the world. At the same time, the Arctic is the source of thermal and weather influences which affect the whole of the earth. Since our knowledge of these matters is sparse we can never be certain of the effects of human activities in the area.

"Dying" Rivers and Lakes

The great lakes and rivers of the world are no less seriously affected than the seas. In Great Britain virtually all the river fisheries are threatened, not by crude sewage and industrial pollution, which are gradually being overcome, but by eutrophication, or over-enrichment of the water. This comes about through the replacement of natural spring water with fully treated sewage effluent and the run-off from the land treated with artificial fertilizers. The drainage of these chemicals into the rivers results in a superabundance of algal growths, particularly in the fast streamy rivers of the rich chalk country of the south. The process, which gets under way during spring and early summer, is greatly aided by increasing sunlight.

Before long the surface of the water becomes completely covered, shutting out all light from the river bed and stifling the growth of natural weed. In due course, the unnatural surface weed breaks away and floats downstream in such quantities that the river turns black. Where it collects at obstructions in the river it rots and begins to smell. The water becomes silted, covering the clean gravels, and most of the natural life common to waters disappears. Thus the water becomes sterile through "over-feeding".

A Cleaner Thames

Although too many local authorities take the view that there are no votes in sewage and rubbish and that rivers exist to be open drains and the seas giant cesspits, much is being done to combat water pollution. Poisonous rivers are often associated with large towns, but a study of the Thames shows that this need not be. Anti-pollution measures, which have cost the Greater London Council and their predecessors the London County Council £20 million since 1949, resulted in the return of fish to the lower reaches for the first time since the 1920s. An expert from the Natural History Museum identified 31 marine species, as well as the usual fresh-water ones. He reported that in January 1970 there were a considerable number of haddock between Purfleet and Dartford, and large shoals of herrings and sprats had been identified. The capture at Fulham of a smelt, a sand goby, and a flounder which had come up from the sea through what would be considered the worst polluted areas of the river was another significant pointer. The smelt, a small member of the salmon family, is a migratory species and enters rivers to spawn.

London has also shown the way to a healthier life by its implementation of the Clean Air Act of 1956. With the introduction

Years of effort and expenditure on anti-pollution measures in the Thames at last paid a dividend in 1970. In July, teams of anglers fished between Blackfriars and Chelsea to prove the return of fish with cleaner water. Fifty species are now known to inhabit London's river.

of smokeless fuels and penalties for those who cause the emission of black smoke, the dirt from millions of chimneys and the killer fogs and smogs of two decades ago have been eliminated. The cleaner air has attracted back many species of birds, and in the square mile of the City of London 200,000 plants a year now thrive in several hundred varieties, where a mere 10 years ago only privet, laurel, and plane trees could grow.

According to Professor J. K. Page of the department of building science at Sheffield University, Great Britain can in due time have not only clean air everywhere but also the capability of creating recreational spaces that could be the environmental equivalent of the West Indies, even in winter. This could be brought about by the use of electricity to create an artificial outdoor climate. The natural climate would decline in importance—at least in city areas.

The Nuisance of Noise

Evidence is accumulating to show that the assault on our ears by the noise of modern life can lead to substantial physical and psychological harm. Deafness for many of the world's factory workers is an occupational hazard; for instance, a survey of British cotton mills showed that 25 per cent of loom workers are on the verge of needing hearing aids. Traffic noise has become a major nuisance in cities. When she was minister of transport Mrs. Barbara Castle calculated that the noise level in streets was increasing at a rate of one decibel a year (decibels are a measurement of noise level). It has been shown that a level of 80–85 decibels can cause physical damage to the ears, and the noise level in many factories, busy streets, and airports considerable exceeds that.

Some countries impose limits on noise. In France, car noise must not exceed 83 decibels; Switzerland has a limit of 70 decibels; and Japan limits the noise level to 50 decibels in residential areas. In Great Britain the government set up a series of discussions with the motor industry on a phased and precise programme of noise reduction. Research has shown that it is possible to produce heavy lorries which make no more noise than the average car, and that all family cars can be made as quiet as the quietest of cars today. One of the worst increasing sources of noise is aircraft. In future, in Great Britain subsonic jet planes will need a low-noise certificate before being allowed to operate, and supersonic aircraft such as the Concorde will probably be banned from flying over land at above the speed of sound.

Under the Clean Air Act, the City of London has been a smokeless zone for three years. This photo, taken on a breezy but cloudy March day, shows the complete absence of chimney smoke that London now enjoys.

These plans for the limiting of noise were set out in a white paper (*Protection of the Environment*), which showed how the government proposed to tackle every aspect of pollution. "Although public health must be the most important criterion in determining the priorities for action, it is not the only one," the paper declared. "Increasingly we must pay attention to pollution which, while it does not harm public health, yet does harm amenity and the enjoyment of life. . . . It is not necessary that people should be made ill by pollution before the government acts. Government must also increasingly act where people are offended or annoyed by pollution, and this new phase of government activity is already well under way."

Sweeping up Oil Slicks

An example of this activity is the elaborate set of arrangements for dealing with oil slicks which makes Britain the first major maritime nation with a nationally organized system for coping with that problem. Stocks of detergents and the equipment for spreading them have been set up at some 50 points round the coastline. The equipment, which is to be available for attachment to sea-going tugs as the need arises, consists of booms that spray the detergent on the oil. It is then mixed into it by wooden surface breakers on tow behind the booms. This device can be on its way to the scene in less than six hours, and can cope with an eighth of a square mile per hour.

Private industry, too, is playing its part in the fight against pollution. Rolls-Royce became the first company to produce a diesel engine which complies with the stringent

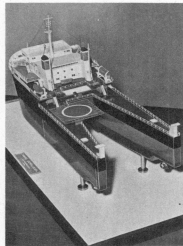

CLEARING OIL FROM THE SEA

A few of the many ingenious new inventions for clearing oil slicks from inshore waters are shown here. Above: left, model of a French ship with a divided hull, in the V of which the oil is collected and, after separation, stored in the hold, while the water is pumped back into the sea; centre, "skimmers", invented in the U.S.A., which sweep and suck up oil from the surface; right, another American device, a boom to trap oil and prevent it from spreading. Right: invented by Shell Oil, these booms jutting from a ship's side shower a slick with tons of sand treated with an ammonia derivative to which the oil attaches itself and then sinks to the bottom. Below: if all these and similar devices fail and the oil comes ashore, clearing of the beaches is a slow job with shovel and bucket or a slightly quicker one with fire.

anti-pollution standards set by the British Standards Institution three years ago. These standards are expected to form the basis of new government regulations for diesel engines. In the U.S.A., where smog from vehicle exhaust is at its worst, the legal limitation of exhaust fumes, first introduced in California, will become nation-wide in 1971. Experiments with steam-driven and electrically powered cars are continuously proceeding in an attempt to make an exhaust-free vehicle.

Towards a Nicer World

But most of all in 1970 private individuals and the public at large in some countries began to play their part in the anti-pollution movement, recognizing that it could not be left to governments and industrialists alone. April 22 was "Earth Day"—climax of "Earth Week" —throughout the U.S.A., and massive demonstrations took place in most of the big cities. In New York a section of Fifth Avenue was closed to traffic, and large throngs paraded or promenaded in the carbon-monoxide-free air. (Also in New York a state department of environment conservation was set up in June.)

In Great Britain there was less noticeable public participation, and the autumn of European Conservation Year was unfortunately marked by a nation-wide series of strikes by dustmen, sewage workers, and grave-diggers, which made nonsense of the year's efforts to reduce pollution. Some impact was made by a BBC2 television programme, *The Country We Are Making*, introduced by Prince Philip, and by another on the preservation of Europe's

wild life introduced by Prince Bernhard of the Netherlands.

Everywhere in Europe, indeed, the media were active; it remained to be seen whether their efforts would produce any long-term effect. Certainly technologists were made aware of their responsibilities towards their fellow inhabitants of the Earth—human and animal—and much scientific experiment was begun. If as much human ingenuity can be applied to cleansing the world as has been put into inventions that have made it a dirty place to live in, the anti-pollution fanfare that marked European Conservation Year will not have been sounded in vain.

Both the Duke of Edinburgh and the Prince of Wales have spoken out forcefully on pollution. The cartoon cover of *The Engineer* in May (right) showed them knee-deep in effluent under a smog-filled sky, with the Duke saying: "One day, my son, all this will be yours." Below: the Duke in the front row listening to the Prince's address to the "Countryside in 1970" conference in London's Guildhall in October.

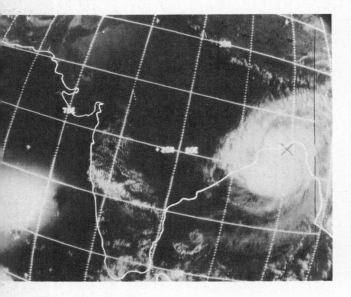

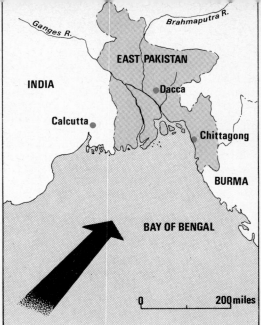

The Violence of Nature

JOHN GROGAN

THE YEAR 1970, in which the worst earthquake for nearly half a century was overshadowed by an even more terrible disaster from cyclone and flood, was a grim one in the crowded annals of natural calamities. It was terrible, indeed, in the low-lying, densely populated delta lands at the mouth of the Ganges and Brahmaputra, in East Pakistan, on Friday, November 13, when a cyclone piled up the waters of the Bay of Bengal before its 150 m.p.h. winds and sent them hurtling over towns, villages, and farms. There had been nothing like it since "China's sorrow", the river Hwang-Ho, overflowed in 1887 and was reputed to have drowned 900,000.

Deaths on such a scale in the Eastern world can never be counted accurately, but within a few days of East Pakistan's catastrophe the official count of bodies had reached 55,000. Unofficial estimates rose daily from 100,000 to 200,000, half a million, a million and then over 1½ million. The Pakistan government eventually gave figures of 175,104 confirmed dead and 23,987 missing. Red Cross officials gave their opinion that the toll was higher and suggested 380,000 dead but added that it could be 100,000 more or less than that. With hindsight came the view that two thirds could have been saved with adequate warning and evacuation to the mainland. A meteorological station failed to stress the extent of the menace, and a radio station failed to interrupt its programmes. But after warnings about a cyclone a month earlier, which struck a limited area and killed, a "mere" 300, many people felt they had left their homes for nothing. They would probably not have responded to a new warning even if it had been given.

Death-dealing cyclones have come to the Ganges delta eight times in the past decade. But still over 2 million people pack themselves into under 3,000 square miles of the delta and the surrounding coast, one of the most densely populated regions in the world. The reason why they choose to live in the shadow of death is a simple one—the fertile silt of the delta provides life, in the rice it produces. But for many the paddy-fields became graves. The land is flat, already dyked against the sea. The major islands have some embankment protection. One island which had not, Manapura, lost three quarters of its 22,000 population. As the tidal wave overtopped high points on

At top of page. Map of the site of the worst disaster of the year, the cyclone and tidal wave that overwhelmed islands in the Ganges delta, East Pakistan. Left: picture taken by the weather satellite ITOS-1 on November 12, showing the cyclone a few hours before it struck the spot marked X.

the islands, many people were drowned in their single-storey homes. Eighty per cent of the young children, 100 per cent of the babies, were swept away.

Many days later corpses were still floating alongside the carcases of cattle on Bhola, the largest island, where 1 million people lived. The stench of death rose to nauseate pilots of relief planes above. Where land was visible, some village sites were marked only by the foundations of the huts that had been swept away. Everywhere the rice crop was blackened, fishing boats were destroyed as well as homes, starvation and exposure threatened. Then came reports of epidemics. But after 2 weeks in the area Red Cross officials denied reports of widespread starvation and cholera. To cope with the tragedy was beyond the powers of the Pakistan government, but help came from a score or more of countries—from neighbouring India, distant New Zealand. Helicopters with the Soviet Red Star flew alongside those with the U.S. army insignia. Two thousand British troops were brought by a naval flotilla from Singapore, with essential supplies for everyone in an area of 1,600 square miles. While there were calls for an international disaster agency, the World Bank launched a $180 million reconstruction plan, to include embankments and concrete underground shelters.

International aid also came to Peru when, on May 31, a single shock exacted a death toll probably greater than that from all the previous 42,000 recorded 'quakes and tremors of the decade. It ranked with such major disasters as the Tokyo earthquake of 1923, in which 143,000 died, and that of Messina in 1908, which killed 75,000—although China, again, is believed to have suffered worst, in 1556, with an earthquake which killed 830,000. The Peruvian earthquake was exceptional in its effects even more than in its strength. Its force, recorded at 7·7 on the Richter scale, an energy equivalent to over 100 million tons of T.N.T., although great, has often been exceeded. But it sent tidal waves engulfing coastal towns, shook the adobe walls of buildings into dust, and wrought its most terrible havoc in towns and villages hidden in steep Andean valleys, overshadowed by mountains. Thousands of people were crushed by rocks rolling down from the towering heights, shaken by the earth movement at their foundations. Llanganuco Lake, high in the Andes, burst its dam and swept away the two towns of Caras and Yungay. Another town, Huaras, in the same long mountain valley, the Huaylas corridor, was reported 95 per cent destroyed and to have lost 5,000 of its 80,000 population.

Five thousand were killed in Huaras, and 95 per cent of the town destroyed, by the terrible earthquake in Peru on May 31.

The epicentre of the earthquake lay 200 miles north-west of Lima and 12 miles offshore from Chimbote, a formerly thriving coastal town of 200,000, with a steel mill and a large fishing industry. After the shock, Chimbote lay in ruins with 1,000 people dead or dying, thousands more injured, and all but a handful of survivors homeless. Fourteen Czechoslovak climbers died in the earthquake, buried under a huge rock on the 20,000-ft. Mount Huascaren. The news of their fate was brought by Japanese and New Zealand climbers, on the same mountain, who had escaped unhurt. There were other escape stories, such as that of 250 survivors from the buried town of Huallanca who filed on foot down paths through mountain canyons, threatened all the way by further rock falls. Those rock falls hampered rescue and relief operations by blocking roads. An air lift had to be hurriedly organized on improvised airstrips and helicopter landing patches. Counts of the dead could only be estimates; for fear of disease bodies were burnt as soon as recovered, and orders were given to set fire to areas of demolished buildings because of the threat from the decomposing corpses beneath.

Terror of the Snow

Terrible as they were, these were just two among a series of events which demonstrated again, after the relative quiet of 1969, the power of natural forces to override man's efforts to protect himself. Avalanches in Europe, earthquakes in all the vulnerable parts

Air photo showing the path of the April avalanche that killed 72 in the Roc des Fiz sanatorium near Chamonix, in the French Alps.

of the world, high winds and tornadoes, floods, droughts, and forest fires all asserted the awful power of nature. In Europe it was the tragic overwhelming of a sports hostel and a children's sanatorium by avalanche and landslide in Central France that first brought home man's inability to forecast disasters or to manage them. The avalanche which came down on a hostel in the popular French Alpine resort area of Val d'Isère covered the not particularly broad front of 50–100 yards, yet killed 39 young people. The gay chatter of anticipation of the day's sport ahead, at breakfast time on a morning in February, was hushed by a rumbling sound like that of a railway train. Snow may be a silent menace as it hangs motionless on the mountain side above a village. On the move, however, the sound is terrifying to those who know what is coming. One survivor told of a huge mass of snow bursting through a staircase window of the hostel, carrying him more than 40 yards along a corridor and then out through another window. But many were submerged and suffocated in the breakfast room which they would probably have left five minutes later.

Even worse happened in April when a mixture of snow, earth, and rock overwhelmed three chalets of the Roc des Fiz sanatorium on the d'Assy plateau in the French Alps. Seventy-two people, mostly boy patients in the children's tuberculosis clinic, died in France's

worst mountain tragedy. Only seven people survived, including a nursing sister who was thrown out of her room through a window by the force of the impact and was found with a broken back. The evening before, the boys had gone to bed later than usual after a conjuring show. For the officials in charge of the sanatorium it had been a worrying time since a fall of 2 ft. of snow a week earlier had brought down a small avalanche on the roof of one building, fracturing the walls. Forestry experts had then examined the area, flying round the cone of snow rising 1,500 ft. above the sanatorium. They pronounced it safe, and children who had been evacuated to hospitals lower down the Plateau d'Assy were brought back, to be engulfed three days after their return.

Earlier, in February, 30 people had died when an avalanche roared down a mountain side near Reckingen, in the upper Rhône valley, and on the same day six more were killed at the Alpine ski resort of Lans le Villard—that avalanche was ten times as big as the one which killed over ten times as many in the Val d'Isère. The next day, two were killed at St. Leonhard am Pitztal in a remote Tyrolean valley. Just over a week later, seven Alpine soldiers lost their lives in a snow-slide in the Italian Dolomites. Marcel de Quervain, head of the Davos avalanche institute, explained that the exceptional avalanche record was due to the unusually deep snow on the slopes and continuous warm weather at high altitude. The underlay was not strong enough; sparse snowfalls early in the year were too weak to support the huge amounts which had fallen in February and after.

The worst avalanche had come in northern Persia, where 150 were reported to have been killed in January by a number of slides on the Haraz road to the Caspian coast, 50 miles north-east of Teheran. The snow overwhelmed buses, lorries, and cars. In one bus, all 36 occupants were found frozen to death. A lorry driver told of seeing an entire mountain side collapsing, sweeping with it a bus, two lorries, and a car and rolling them into a ravine to leave no trace—just a level stretch of snow where minutes before there had been a deep cleft.

Floods, Fires, and Drought

The year had begun with harsh weather sweeping across the U.S.A., where nine people were drowned in severe flooding in the Appalachian mountain regions of Tennessee, Virginia, and Kentucky. In January, Portugal suffered its worst floods for many years. In Ceylon, 100 were drowned and a million reported homeless after tropical rains which left rivers full of the swollen carcases of animals. Eight Germans were drowned in February, when a sudden thaw and heavy rain brought the Rhine to its highest level for 15 years. In May the worst floods for over a century hit Rumania, killing 200 people and resulting in an expected loss of 5 per cent of both agricultural and industrial production. One third of the average annual rainfall fell in two days, on land soggy from the April rains that had already lifted the Danube to a record height. In Transylvania, the rivers sometimes rose above the tops of the trees, filling whole valleys and flowing on to swell the Danube still further. It was the worst disaster in the history of the country, apart from war. Houses destroyed or damaged numbered 41,000; 1,000 bridges, 1,000 miles of road, and 100 industrial plants were damaged or destroyed. Ninety thousand families, and cattle by the million, had to be evacuated.

In June, 100 died in floods in south-west Nepal. In Genoa and along the Italian Riviera, heavy rain brought flooding in October. In Genoa itself the floods were caused by the river Bisagno, a partly covered stream running through the city's centre, which brought down mud, rocks, and other debris to form a dam against a concrete gallery through which it flowed. Eventually the pent-up waters burst through the concrete cover to flood the lower levels of the city. Eighteen were killed and hundreds injured. The casualty list would have been higher but for warning cracks in a wall which led to the evacuation of a building housing 14 families and a school just before it collapsed.

In contrast, South Africa had a record drought, after several years of poor rains; and in August, in a drought-stricken area of South Australia, 150 miles north-west of Adelaide, sheep were being sold at 2p each. In Kashmir, the worst drought for 72 years dried up almost all the major rivers and streams. As so

The worst floods for over a century swept Rumania in May. Above is the town of Satu Mare, one of the worst affected places.

often happens in India, however, the ending of that drought was just a change of disaster, for the rains flooded 15 million acres in Gujarat, Assam, North Bihar, West Bengal, Orissa, and Uttar Pradesh, claiming more than 1,000 lives.

Another summer of forest fires in southern France brought charges of arson against alleged pyromaniacs. Whatever their origin, the fires, fanned by the 60 m.p.h. mistral, engulfed tens of thousands of acres, and sent holiday-makers fleeing from camping sites. One particularly violent fire in October resulted in 11 deaths, including those of a mother and her four children, burnt alive while trying to escape from the village of Tanneron, encircled by the flames. In Southern

Vast sheets of flame rose above the Santa Monica hills, California, in immense forest fires in September.

California, the worst bush and timber fires in memory devastated half a million acres in September and October.

Horror of High Winds

The East Pakistan cyclone was exceptional in the toll that it took of human life, but elsewhere hurricanes and typhoons of perhaps equal ferocity exacted their usual tribute. One month before, in the Philippines, 1,109 had been killed and 522,000 rendered homeless by two typhoons within a week, and in November another killed 40 and destroyed the homes of thousands. In September, 85 were killed in Formosa, and when, in August, the first typhoon of the season hit Shikoku, smallest of Japan's four main islands, at least 20 died. On that same August day, across the world, a hurricane battered the French Caribbean island of Martinique for nearly 17 hours, killing 42. Over 12 in. of rain fell in 9 hours. Shortly before, in the same month of August, the south-west of the U.S.A. was pounded by another hurricane, and President Nixon declared the affected territory a major disaster area. From Corpus Christi, Texas, came the official assessment that 32 people had died, and 9,000 houses had been destroyed; damage to property amounted to $233 million and to crops $60 million. At the beginning of the year, cyclone Ada killed at least 11 and caused damage amounting to $A10 million along the Great Barrier Reef and the central coastal resorts of Queensland.

Before the August hurricane, Texas had already had more than its usual quota of terror from the "twisters" or tornadoes which sweep up from the south each spring. One of the most violent and prolonged ever to hit the state killed 23 in Lubbock on May 11, cutting an 8-mile-long path of destruction through this important cotton-marketing centre. A month earlier, 24 had died when a series of tornadoes had swept through Texas from New Mexico to Oklahoma. The greatest loss of life from a tornado, however, came in September in Venice, from one of the rare European tornadoes. This lifted a ferry boat out of the water, hurled it back upside down, drowning 27, and then went on to kill 12 more people in an international camping site where caravans were left in the trees, and a thirteenth on an island where an entire pine wood was uprooted. Europe had had another tornado in August which ravaged the coast of south-west France, killing 9 and injuring 29.

Even in Britain, it was not an uneventful year in the matter of weather. There were blizzards in March, when 688 Kentish miners were trapped for a while below ground, after power

One of the most violent tornadoes ever to strike Texas left this path of destruction in the town of Lubbock on May 11. Ten thousand people were made homeless.

cables had been cut. A thunderstorm in August flooded roads, the Underground, and five theatres in London; the heaviest rain since 1927 flooded Belfast a few days later, and on the 20th flooding in England and Scotland was widespread. In the same month torrential rain fell in Belgium, in Austria, in Germany, where the Oberammergau Passion play hall was flooded, in Switzerland, and in Czechoslovakia. Warning was given to England that disaster even on the East Pakistan scale might not be impossible there. Professor Andrew Schofield, of Manchester University, pointed out that over 1 million people live and work in London below the height of the present flood defences. The chances of a catastrophic flood occurring through a combination of high tide and a storm surge are increasing steadily as south-eastern England sinks and dredging for giant tankers in the Thames allows an easier flow.

Man-Made Earthquakes?

Speculation was renewed that man might be playing a part in causing earthquakes. The possibility was first put forward seriously when a study showed an increased number of tremors after the building of an artificial lake in the U.S.A. in the 1930s. In the 1960s tremors occurred after waste water was injected into a 12,000-ft. well in the Rockies and ceased when the well was closed. The argument is that extra strain can trigger off the release of pent-up forces in fractured rocks. The obvious question is whether nuclear explosions do the same. Professor C. Emiliani of Miami University and some of his colleagues reported during 1970 that increased seismic activity had occurred as much as 500 miles away from underground nuclear tests at Nevada. The idea was supported by the studies of Canadian scientists, but denied by other American teams. The subject was reopened when it was realized that three major earthquakes had followed nuclear tests during the year. The disaster in Peru was preceded by a French test. A series of equally powerful earthquakes in Turkey in March followed an American test, and another bad earthquake in Persia in July followed another French test.

An estimated 3,000 people were killed in the series of Turkish earthquakes that occurred during the Easter week-end, centred on the town of Gediz, 150 miles south of Istanbul. Half the houses in Gediz collapsed completely, and fires started by the destruction of a power station engulfed people trapped in the wreckage of their homes. Bodies were still being pulled out of the rubble when violent new shocks brought more buildings crashing down. A score of near-by villages were wrecked, and altogether about 90,000 were reported homeless in an area of 150,000 population. The Persian earthquake occurred in the remote Khurasan province in the north, where 10,000 had died 2 years before. This time the centre was in a sparsely populated area, near the village of Marave Tappeh, close to the Russian border. The death toll, although only a fraction of that of the 1968 disaster, still came to 175. Many of the victims were women and children. The shock came at dawn, and men praying in the courtyards of mosques rushed home to find their families buried in the remains of houses. The large Soviet city of Ashkhabad, over the frontier, was shaken, but there were no reports of casualties.

An earthquake centred in the U.S.S.R., in the central Asian republic of Kirghizia, left more than 30,000 homeless in June. One in India, in March, killed 24. Even Britain, well outside the normal earthquake zones, had tremors which earned headlines, when on August 9 the north shook for 4 seconds. Incidentally, the last and only recorded earthquake fatality in Britain was in 1580, when an apprentice was killed by a falling brick.

Moon-Made Weather?

Whatever part man plays in triggering off earthquakes, scientific support came during the year for the old belief that the Moon affects the weather. A study of thunderstorms in the eastern and central Great Plains, carried out by Dr. M. DeVoe Lethbridge of Pennsylvania State University, showed that a peak regularly occurs 2 days after full moon. It might be, he suggested, that the Moon is interfering with the Earth's magnetic tail, which is caused by interaction between the Earth's magnetic field and the solar wind. British meteorologists, although prepared to admit that this argument might apply to areas with extreme climates, commented that the effect was hardly likely to be noticeable enough to affect forecasting the British weather, which is more profoundly influenced by the Atlantic than by the Moon.

Thousands were killed by earthquakes in Turkey and Persia in 1970. Left: an old man surrounded by the ruins of his home in Khurasan, Persia. Right: fires followed the quake at Gediz, Turkey, where 3,000 were killed at Easter.

Wild Life

JOHN CLEGG, Hon. F.L.S.

IN A YEAR when the conservation of the European environment was front-page news, it was inevitable that birds and their habitats should receive much attention. Not only are birds often useful indicators of what is happening to the environment, but in most countries they have an emotional and aesthetic appeal that provokes a quick public reaction to unfavourable changes in their distribution or populations.

It became clear that some major unfavourable change had taken place in the seas around Great Britain's west coasts, when almost half of the guillemots and over one quarter of the razorbills did not return in the spring of 1970 to breed in the normally vast sea-bird colonies on the cliffs surrounding the Irish Sea. Repeated counts in the course of "Operation Seafarer" (a census of British sea birds carried out by a team of volunteers at half the colonies) indicated a loss of about 50,000 breeding guillemots and 14,000 razorbills. This was partly expected, for 15,000 birds, mostly guillemots and razorbills, were found dead around the Irish Sea in the autumn of 1969, and 22,000 were washed up around Britain's coasts in the first three months of 1970. Many are known to have been killed by oil pollution, but the cause of the death of the majority is not known for certain, although it seems that some other serious form of pollution was responsible. The puffin, another member of the auk family, is also decreasing at an alarming rate, and one is led to wonder whether man is not now driving all these attractive auks to their ultimate extermination, as he did the giant of the family, the great auk, in the early part of the last century.

Bird Slaughter in Italy and France

Concern for birds is less widespread in some other countries. In Italy, it has been estimated, about ten million birds, mostly small songbirds, are captured for food every year by netting and in other ways. Italian conservation organizations have tried hard to stop the practice, and at the beginning of 1969 a law totally banning the capture of small birds was passed. The satisfaction with which this law was greeted by bird-lovers was short-lived, however, for in the autumn of the same year the government approved an amendment permitting some 3,000 "stations" throughout Italy to catch small birds, provided they are left alive in cages or sold to be used as decoy birds in the trapping of other species. Coming into force in January 1970, this amendment aroused a storm of protest, not only in Italy but through-

in Conservation Year

out Europe; the Italian government bowed to the storm and reimposed the ban on the netting of small birds.

France is another country with a bad record in bird conservation. Every year vast numbers of birds have been slaughtered on migration in both spring and autumn at the Gironde and the *landes*. Efforts by the International Council for Bird Preservation, and especially by the French section, have been unavailing. In the autumn of 1969, the French section of I.C.B.P. invited representatives of other countries to visit the areas concerned, at the time of the shooting of turtle doves and other migratory species, and a good deal of publicity was aroused. As a direct result, in 1970 the French prime minister and the secretary of state for agriculture took a strong stand in spite of pressure, and even demonstrations, from the shooting factions, and imposed a ban on shooting from May 1.

Preserving Birds of Prey

On the credit side, French conservationists have successfully campaigned for the total protection of all owls, vultures, eagles, harriers, and the osprey, and hope shortly to have full protection for all birds of prey. It is also intended to reintroduce the Griffon vulture in the Massif Central. Apart from a few remaining in the Pyrenees, these fine birds have disappeared as a breeding species in France.

The decline of birds of prey in all countries has coincided with a consuming desire of many people to keep them in captivity, not only in zoos but as private pets. Unfortunately, they fare badly in captivity unless under expert care. It was good news, therefore, to bird-lovers when the British government on July 1 imposed regulations which make it necessary to have a licence to import birds of prey into the United Kingdom. Licences will be issued only to those who have good facilities and the experience to care for the birds adequately. The regulations provide a problem for customs officers, who can hardly be expected to be able to identify the 405 species—271 diurnal raptores and 134 owls—that could be imported. To help them, the I.C.B.P. provided lists of local ornithologists to whom customs officers at seaports and airports can turn for help.

London Pride

We are so accustomed to hearing of changes in environmental conditions adversely affecting birds that a report by members of the London Natural History Society in April came as a pleasant surprise. In the third season of a five-year survey of the distribution and breeding of birds within 20 miles of St. Paul's Cathedral, they found that, encouraged by the cleaner air of widespread smokeless zones, birds that are unfamiliar except in the greenest suburbs are returning to central London.

Grey wagtails are breeding in Whitechapel, and kestrels in the docks, Notting Hill, and Finsbury Square, and a pied flycatcher nested under Holborn Viaduct. Since insects thrive in the cleaner air, tree creepers, spotted flycatchers, and house martins are increasing.

A new miniature railway gives visitors to Whipsnade a view of the breeding herd of rare white rhinoceroses sent to the London Zoo from Natal in 1970.

The "spotted cat" tribe, threatened by the fashion for fur coats in leopard, ocelot, cheetah, and jaguar (as shown by models at right), were, it was hoped, reprieved in 1970 through the actions of wild-life societies and some repentant furriers. The leopard in its natural state (left) may be left in peace for three years.

The black redstart, which made a spectacular colonization of bomb sites after the war, has been driven out of central areas by rebuilding, but continues to nest on gas works and power stations in outer London.

Fate of the Spotted Cats

The modern interest in wild life, although it is to be welcomed on humanitarian grounds, undoubtedly has its disadvantages for some species. An immense international traffic in animals now exists. Figures published in 1970 of animal imports into the U.S.A. alone included such staggering figures as 1,393,970 reptiles, ranging from boa constrictors to chameleons; 339,489 amphibians, mostly frogs; 571,663 wild birds (excluding canaries and parrots); and 116,341 mammals, of which 99,668 were primates.

It was cheering to learn, however, that the number of "spotted cat" skins—leopard, ocelot, cheetah, and jaguar—imported into the U.S.A. showed a decrease compared with previous years. Concern is still expressed about the survival of these members of the cat family, and Prince Bernhard of the Netherlands personally wrote to a number of heads of states in which the animals live, to point out the precarious situation of the spotted cats. "The only way to save the leopard and other spotted cats", he wrote, "is either to prohibit completely the importation of these skins or at least make the permissible quota so small that resale of such a quantity of skins becomes impractical."

Some furriers imposed their own ban. Natan, a very important *maison de haute couture* in Brussels, agreed to renounce the sale of articles made from spotted cat skins, and also from crocodile and marine turtles. In July, members of the furriers' council of New York agreed that they will "no longer cut, fashion, or fabricate skins of the endangered spotted cats". On August 4 there was more welcome news when the International Fur Trade Federation announced that they were prepared to impose a voluntary ban on trade in giant otter, La Plata otter, snow leopard, clouded leopard, and tiger, and a temporary ban for three years on cheetahs and leopards. Conservationists have been concerned for years about the decrease of tigers. It is believed that only about 2,500 still exist in the whole of the Indian subcontinent. In August, it was announced in New Delhi that 12 Indian states had imposed a moratorium of at least five years on the hunting of tigers. It is expected that the remaining states will follow suit.

Strangely enough the Asiatic lion, of which the total population is only 177 animals, all living in a single location—the Gir Forest—is not considered to be in as serious danger of extinction as are tigers. For the lions the impact of tourism has been advantageous, and the wardens of their forest sanctuary go to great lengths to ensure that visitors have ample opportunities of seeing many lions and photographing them at prepared baits.

Safari Parks and Zoos

In Great Britain too, lions—in this case African lions—have become tourist attractions in recent years at various "safari parks", where the idea of the traditional zoo has been turned inside out, the humans being in boxes (their family cars) and the animals loose. Free-ranging lions were introduced on the Marquess of Bath's estate at Longleat in 1966, and the imagination of the public was instantly captured. A smaller venture followed in 1968 at Lord Gretton's estate at Stapleford, near Melton Mowbray in Leicestershire. In 1970 three more large safari parks were opened—at Windsor, Woburn, and Blair Drummond in Scotland—and a smaller reserve with 22 lions was opened at Benvarden, Northern Ireland.

Some 150 lions now roam freely in British parkland, and more than 9 million people are estimated to have passed through these reserves and similar ones abroad. The vast number of visitors to the parks—up to 6,000 cars a day at peak periods at the larger safari parks—raises considerable problems, particularly the "bunching" together of the cars and the consequent discomfort of the passengers, who feel the need to open windows, which is strictly against regulations. In such conditions in August a small girl was badly mauled by a lioness at Woburn when it attacked the car in which she was a passenger, and put its head and paws through an open window.

The safari parks have revived the old controversy of whether animals should be used merely to amuse human beings. The London Zoo expressed itself strongly on this point in its annual report: "The day is long past when animals should be held in captivity solely because they provide a source of amused curiosity to the visiting public or of profit to the owners. The problem is urgent because of the very rapid and uncontrolled proliferation of zoos which is now occurring."

The modern concept of a zoo is a place where research on animals is a main concern, and where rare or endangered species can be bred. To this end, a breeding herd of 20 white rhinoceroses from two game reserves in Natal were sent to Whipsnade, the London Zoo's "out station", where an enclosure of 30 acres was set aside for them. In the Natal parks, stocks of this formerly rare animal have built up to over 1,000, and the Parks Board decided

Giant tortoise of Hood Island in the Galapagos Islands. The salvation of these rare creatures was assured by the creation of breeding centres. *Photo, Eric Hosking*

that it would be a wise measure to establish breeding groups in other parts of the world. The London Zoological Society was designated as the agent for distribution in Europe.

Tortoise and Turtle

On the other side of the world, attempts were being made by similar artificial breeding programmes to save the giant tortoises of the Galapagos Islands from extinction. Each of the larger islands of the Galapagos had its own sub-species of giant tortoise. Today 10 sub-species are known to survive, but two are in serious danger of extinction—one of them, on the island called Duncan, because black rats, introduced by man, eat the young. The Charles Darwin Research Station in the Galapagos successfully reared young tortoises in captivity, and in 1970 returned to Duncan 29 four-year-olds, which are large enough to defend themselves against the rats. A new and larger tortoise-breeding centre started operations during the year.

The marine relatives of the tortoises, the turtles, are seriously threatened, especially the green turtle, from which turtle soup is made.

Roaring welcome for car-borne visitors to the new "safari park" at Windsor, Berks. This was one of the four new wild-life parks opened in the United Kingdom in 1970.

However, the picture is decidedly more encouraging in Queensland, including the Great Barrier Reef area, where turtles and their eggs are fully protected at all times, except for the use of aborigines. A survey by Dr. Robert Bustard showed that the breeding female populations of the green, flatback, and loggerhead turtles stand at about 75,000, with the green turtle predominating. Dr. Bustard recommended that the more important nesting grounds, which are mainly on small islands, should be declared national parks to give the turtles an even better chance of survival.

Conservation in Australia

The adequacy of national parks and nature reserves generally in Australia came under review in a wide-ranging inquiry that started in 1970. A parliamentary select committee was appointed to inquire into and report on wildlife conservation. In addition to national parks, the committee is to investigate the effects of pollution and the widespread use of pesticides on wildlife populations; the effect on the kangaroo population of the trade in meat and hides; the need for international and inter-State agreement for the effective conservation of migratory animals; the threat to wild life by the large numbers of domestic animals gone wild, particularly in Northern Australia; and the need for a Federal wildlife conservation authority. The Australian Conservation Foundation urged that special measures be taken to conserve the sub-alpine zones of the mountains of south-eastern Australia, and suggested that the planning of the natural resources of the region—grazing, water supply, and public recreation, as well as wildlife conservation—should be the responsibility of some authority in each State, as has already been done for the Snowy Mountains in New South Wales.

Two new national parks were approved by the New South Wales government in 1970. One of 20,500 acres in rugged country in the Weddin Mountains near Grenfell provides an open forest range 13 miles long, and is rich in wild life, including kangaroos, emus, parrots, ibis, egrets, and herons. The other comprises 36,900 acres in the Myall Lake area, north of Port Stephens, and offers great recreational potentialities for water sport, including surfing on the beaches. A small area of the beaches will still be open to zircon-miners, however, to the disappointment of conservationists. These two new parks bring the total area of national parks in New South Wales to about 350,000 acres. In March 1970 a National Parks and Wildlife Foundation was formed in New South Wales, and in six weeks it collected sufficient funds to hand $A580,000 to the State government to assist measures of fauna-conservation. Two of the 20 projects listed by the Foundation are a wild life reserve in western New South Wales and a game reserve in the Riverina; preservation of the red kangaroo was also given high priority.

Australian conservationists were deeply concerned about threats to the Great Barrier Reef, both from its natural enemy (the crown of thorns starfish, which consumes coral at an alarming rate) and from human exploitation (chiefly drilling for oil). A new marine science institute was set up at Townsville, Queensland, to research into ways of preserving the Reef, and a public inquiry into the matter was started. All the 26 companies licensed by the Queensland government to drill for oil were ordered to suspend operations during the inquiry.

At the Australian Museum, Sydney, a National Photographic Index of Australian birds was started. This, it is hoped, will ultimately comprise 5,000 outstanding colour photographs of the 700 or so kinds of Australian birds. A duplicate set will be housed in the National Library, Canberra.

No Shortage of Funds

The two organizations chiefly concerned on an international level to conserve the world's wild life are the International Union for the Conservation of Nature (I.U.C.N.), based at Morges, Switzerland; and the World Wildlife Fund (W.W.F.), which has organized national appeals in a number of countries. In European Conservation Year, both enjoyed a brighter financial outlook. In April, it was announced that the Ford Foundation had given $650,000 to finance the ambitious programme put forward by I.U.C.N. at its general assembly in New Delhi in November 1969. In January, when the International Trustees of W.W.F. asked the European national appeals of Switzerland, the Netherlands, Germany, Austria, Belgium, Italy, France, Spain, and Britain, to raise 25,000,000 Swiss francs (about £2,500,000), the British national appeal immediately took up the challenge and offered to raise £1,000,000. A donation of £100,000 was made by the Ernest Kleinwort charitable trust; another British donor, this time anonymous, promised £250,000 to an endowment fund set up to provide a regular income to meet the costs of the international office; and later in the year another anonymous British donor promised £50,000, if a similar sum could be raised by World Wildlife supporters in Britain. With such generosity, it seems certain that the targets of both I.U.C.N. and W.W.F. will be achieved, and the future conservation of the world's wild life made more secure.

Farmers Up in Arms

PETER BELL

of *British Farmer and Stockbreeder*

THE AGRICULTURAL year revealed the extra-ordinary way in which surplus can swing over to shortage, and just how suddenly drought or pestilence can change a scene of plenty into one of scarcity. The years immediately before 1970 saw the big grain-producing countries of the world embarrassed by their bursting silos. As the year ended the picture was sadly different. In the U.S.A. the maize crop was hit by blight—a virulent form of the old southern corn-leaf fungus which American farmers fought more than a century ago. By the end of the year it looked as though the American crop would be down by some 1,000 million bushels, while the department of agriculture's stock-pile amounted to only 610 million bushels. The ripples from this disaster spread out to affect the prices (and availability) of beef, pork, poultry, dairy products, and, of course, other cereals such as wheat.

Poor yields did not end with maize. Almost all the main cereal-growing areas of the world recorded reduced yields. In Argentina there were gloomy forecasts of a 4-million-ton cut in the wheat crop due to reduced sowings as a result of drought. Wheat output in Australia had been dropping anyway—by intent and through a quota system aimed at balancing supply to demand. In 1970 drought seemed likely to result in an end to the stored Australian surpluses of 200–250 million bushels. Australia has been losing wheat markets, notably in India and Pakistan which are rapidly becoming self-sufficient, thanks to the use of high-yielding Mexican wheat. Mainland China has been taking as much as half Australia's wheat exports, but this market is neither settled nor predictable. New grain markets were being sought in Japan and Argentina. Sales of Australian dairy products, however, rose significantly throughout Asia during the year. Japan was the major market, and in the 1969–70 season bought some 10,600 tons of cheese, 10,000 tons of casein, and 3,000 tons of milk powder from Australia.

In Europe, the Common Market wheat crop was down by about 5 per cent to around 30 million tons. France, for example, sowed 10 million acres less; and most of Europe had very little rain in the important months of May, June, and July. This was also the case in Britain, and although a bigger-than-average sowing of winter wheat came away well and yielded adequately, later-sown crops, especially barley, suffered badly from the drought. Barley yields were down to 5 cwt. an acre in places. (An average yield is 30 cwt. plus.) Thus, despite the fact that the acreage under cereals in England and Wales was a trifle up on the previous year, early-season estimates of actual tonnages harvested in 1970 indicated a marked

One of the disasters that struck agriculture during 1970 was the southern corn-leaf blight, a fungus disease of maize, which reduced the American crop by a thousand million bushels. The resultant shortage put up the price of feed and thereby those of meat and dairy products, as well as the prices of other cereals.

The increased costs of feeding stuffs and all the other necessities of farming bore hard on farmers who could not increase their prices or their subsidies to protect themselves against inflation. A wave of public demonstrations swept many agricultural communities. Above: the scene in Maidstone, Kent, on a Saturday in January when a procession of tractors caused traffic chaos. Below: a farmers' protest march in Melbourne, Australia, in March. Top: representatives of many European farming communities, converging upon the Common Market headquarters in Brussels in June, were dispersed by riot police.

shortfall on 1969. For this reason feeding-stuffs became scarce and expensive in the autumn, and the situation was aggravated by the world shortage. There was a correspondingly low straw yield, and although the hay harvest was of good quality it was extremely thin because of lack of rain at the right time.

Poverty on the Farm

1970 was a year of uncertainty and bitterness for many Australian farmers, faced with tight markets and plummeting prices. Angry demonstrations took place—notably those at Melbourne on March 23 and at Perth on March 31. During February the little town of Jerilderie had its biggest shock since the Kelly gang robbed the bank in 1879. Boomerang Way, Jerilderie, was thronged with angry agriculturists waving slogans such as "Farmers Demand Just Prices" and "Rural Poverty Below the Basic Wage". The March 23 Melbourne "demo" brought over 8,000 furious farmers to the city roaring for "rural justice". After a mile-long "march against want" the farmers handed over black-bound copies of a "farmers' manifesto" to parliament.

The farmers of the world generally have incomes substantially below the various national averages—a fact which has caused a great deal of resentment in recent years. In Great Britain, protests built up to a climax in 1970 as a result of the cereal set-backs, which hit the already struggling British farmers hard. To understand their deep sense of frustration one must remember the events that took place in the autumn of 1969, when there were widespread anti-government demonstrations—parades of tractors and the like. Farmers complained that while the government had come out firmly in favour of an expansion of agriculture to save imports, they had done nothing practical to help.

You don't get expansion simply by talking about it. Capital is needed to step up production, and the most satisfactory way of raising it is that a man should get enough for his products to enable him to plough a bit back. Farmers cannot simply raise the price of their products, for most agricultural commodity prices are fixed at the annual price review in March.

That was the trouble: the government stuck at exhortation and did not raise prices sufficiently. Farmers were furious, and the leaders of the National Farmers' Union found it hard to keep ahead of their more militant members. Nevertheless they tried, and at the end of 1969 the Union had officially come out with a demand for an income lift from about £500 million to £650 million. Thus farmers waited eagerly for the 1970 price review, in which they hoped this demand would be met. The early months of 1970 were spent in ramming their case home to Cledwyn Hughes, the Labour minister of agriculture. At the beginning of January, for instance, he was put through the hoop in Devon, when the N.F.U. county chairman introduced him to a farmer audience with the words: "I never remember a time when so many farmers were so angry at the same time." There was a rumpus of a rather different kind as a sequel to the N.F.U.'s annual general meeting in January. The Union's president, Sir Gwilym Williams, did not quite make a good enough showing to ensure his re-election and failed to get the 80 per cent majority that a sitting president needs to keep his seat. His place was taken by Henry Plumb—young, tough, and the kind of man the industry seemed to need. Inevitably and immediately Plumb found himself in the midst of price review negotiations. He was launched into this annual piece of horse-trading by the biggest rally of farmers ever to descend on London: some 8,000 came from all over England and Wales, and the scene outside the ministry's Whitehall offices had to be seen to be believed.

When the review determinations were announced they were hard to quantify, but they were undoubtedly short of the N.F.U. target. The minister, the N.F.U., the farmers themselves, and a wide range of pundits all arrived at different answers. At all events the N.F.U. Council flatly rejected the determinations. An immediate demand was made to have the review referred to the prices and incomes board, and for the whole matter of the review mechanisms to be examined and brought up to date. The militants were persuaded to row in with the Union, and farmers settled down to get their spring corn sown and the land made ready for another year of "seed time and harvest". It was late spring, and crops were slow to come away.

Conservatives and the Common Market

The return of a Conservative government at the general election in June 1970 put a different complexion on the agricultural scene. The Conservatives were committed to ushering in a new method of agricultural support—levies on imports—thus bringing the U.K. into line with Common Market practice. But the Conservative election manifesto had also come out unequivocally in favour of British agriculture as an import-saver. Pressure was kept up on the new minister, James Prior, an East Anglian farmer M.P. Indeed pressure was

British agriculture is the most highly mechanized in the world, and in order to take full advantage of their machinery British farmers have been uprooting the traditional hedgerows to create miniature prairies. As a result, many birds and small mammals have been made homeless. Top: hedge-removal in practice in Hertfordshire. Bottom: a modern "prairie" in Bedfordshire, devoid of the hedges that formerly divided it into fields. Above: a compromise, also in Bedfordshire, by which, although the hedges have been uprooted, a few trees have been left to relieve the monotony.
Pictures by "British Farmer"

increased as inflation, which earlier in 1970 had been proceeding at a brisk canter, began to break into a gallop.

Inflation hits farmers more than most: they find themselves squeezed between the upper millstone of falling returns and the nether of rapidly rising costs. Talk of expansion thus became a bad joke. All they asked as a preliminary was enough cash to keep going. It was at this time that the national and world grain shortage pushed the cost of feed to unprecedented heights.

As feed and money became short, the risk of a meat and milk shortage loomed. Accordingly in October the minister announced increases in the guaranteed farm prices totalling about £54 million in normal price review terms. Mr. Plumb gave a qualified welcome to the announcement. The chairman of the militant breakaway Farmers' Federation declared that the increases were only about half what was needed, but in general farmers greeted the news with relief.

A few weeks later the new chancellor of the exchequer in his "mini budget" announced the government's intention of introducing a levy on imports of beef, lamb, and some dairy products. A 3-year transition period from the existing price guarantee system was mentioned. With the introduction of these tariff duties and the abolition of what is in effect a subsidy to consumers, the price of food in the shops can be expected to rise.

The imports levy scheme is related to the U.K.'s application to join the Common Market. During the year negotiations were going on in Brussels which could have a momentous effect on British farming—not to mention the economies of New Zealand and the sugar-producing islands of the West Indies. The cost of joining the Community could be impossibly high for a country like Britain which imports so much of its food. A government white paper, published in February 1970, suggested that Britain might have to contribute as much as £650 million to the Community budget, while the total cost of entry might range from £100 million to £1,100 million.

Britain was not the only country applying for entry. There were three others, all with different problems and viewpoints. Ireland, a country with an economy based on agriculture, wanted to get in quickly on the farm front, but wished to be allowed rather longer on the industrial side, where it is only just gearing up. Denmark, wanting to find all the markets she can as quickly as possible, could not sign on the dotted line quickly enough. Norway wanted to join a big political outfit, but was

anxious that her fishing industry should be safeguarded. Britain was prepared to have a 3-year transition for industry, but asked for the longest possible run-in for agriculture.

New Zealand and Australia made their views crystal clear. Both wanted assurances about their access to their traditional British market. New Zealand's case is particularly strong, as her exports to Britain of dairy products and of lamb have been for many years the keystone of her economy. Take them away, and New Zealand could be hit for six. For better or worse, the outcome of the negotiations should be known during the first half of 1971. In the meantime the farmers' unions of Britain and Australasia can be relied upon to exert all possible pressure to get a reasonable deal for their members.

Farmers and Conservation

The year 1970 was designated European Conservation Year. A variety of big conferences were held, and it became clear that agriculture had a decisive part to play. Happily, in Britain at least, farmers are awakening to their responsibilities towards the country's wild life. The N.F.U. are particularly active in this field. Hedgerows are a centre of controversy. Farmers are accused of demolishing them at a frightening rate, to the detriment of wild life and the appearance of the countryside. All sorts of figures were brought out, the highest being 14,000 miles supposedly ripped up in a year. The ministry of agriculture maintained that the rate was only 1,000 miles a year, and an inquiry was launched to obtain the true facts. One thing had already emerged as the year ended: farmers and conservationists have broadly the same interest at heart—the good of the countryside.

During 1970 steps were taken to curb the indiscriminate use of chemical sprays, notably of persistent chemicals used for the destruction of pests. (But land still gets taken for motorways and urban developments at the rate of about 50,000 acres a year in Britain, a process which sterilizes land even more surely than the most vicious chemical.) In January 1970, it was announced that the pesticide DDT and others of the same chemical group were to be progressivly banned for most agricultural uses in Australia.

Late in the year, the report of the veterinary surgeons who had been investigating the application of the 1969 livestock welfare codes announced their findings. Farmers had reason to be pleased, for the report revealed little to cause disquiet and much that was reassuring. Intensive farm practices are certainly here to stay.

The Arts

WARS OF WORDS

HUMPHREY BROCKHOLST

De Gaulle unexpectedly unleashed *Mémoires d'Espoir* on October 7, generating a furore eclipsed only by his death.

Tнe мost unexpected publishing event of 1970 was the sudden appearance—with an impact compared by one critic to that of a 75-ton meteorite—of *Mémoires d'Espoir: Le Renouveau* (*Memoirs of Hope: Springtime*), by General Charles de Gaulle. Some 250,000 copies of this, the first of three volumes of the general's post-war reminiscences, had been printed and distributed to booksellers with absolute secrecy, while the world erroneously expected the memoirs to appear on what would have been the ex-president's 80th birthday in November. Commentators attributed the unexpected publication as a deliberate gesture of malice to steal thunder and headlines from President Pompidou, who was visiting Moscow at the time. To add insult to this alleged injury the book hardly mentioned Pompidou, despite the fact that he was de Gaulle's principal lieutenant during the years covered by the book. This Gallic *cause célèbre* was abruptly extinguished by the General's death, but proved an apt highlight to a year that bristled and seethed with controversy.

The Mushroom and the Cross

The year 1970 saw the publication of several books by less august authors, each of which was at the eye of an individual storm. One has only to glance at "blurbs" and book advertisements to see the value publishers attach to the word "controversial". Not only is it guaranteed to catch the browser's wandering eye, but an actual clash of opinion can, with luck, provide fodder for the ever-grinding jaws of the mass media—and when that happens a few acrimonious sparks can light a blaze of instant free publicity.

March 1970 saw the publication of a work launched with just such a blaze: this was *The Mushroom and the Cross* by John Allegro, until April 1, 1970, lecturer in Old Testament and Intertestamental Studies at Manchester University, and an acknowledged authority on the Dead Sea scrolls. His book, alleging that the gospels were coded messages written by a mushroom-worshipping drug cult, was bound to be provocative and its first appearance, serialized in the *Sunday Mirror* complete with screaming headlines, smacked of manufactured controversy. With the hook thus baited, pundits, academics, and, of course, clerics bounded in to denounce, thus unwittingly lending their shoulders to the publicity bandwagon. *The Times* had sharp exchanges in its correspondence columns in which 15 distinguished dons dismissed the book as "fantasy", to be in their turn dismissed by the author as

Mary Wilson triumphed in September, shortly after her husband Harold's election setback, when her first volume of poems sold out in a matter of days rather than weeks—despite the arched eyebrows of highbrows.

"a coterie of scholars getting together to smear a book".

PQ 17

A battle that ended less happily for author and publisher was the £40,000 libel suit that greeted the publication of *The Destruction of Convoy PQ 17* by David Irving. One of the highest sums ever awarded in a British libel action, it was hailed by Irving as proof that

the offending book's fly-leaf "blurb" for scathing comment. An appeal was entered.

Portnoy in Australia

The censor's blue pencil scratched itself indelibly on the Australian literary scene during 1970. February saw the appearance of *Australia's Censorship Crisis*, edited by Geoffrey Dutton and Max Harris. This tome boldly claimed to be making "cultural history", and

Among novelists who brought forth during 1970 were (left to right): the nubile colleen of Putney, Edna O'Brien, with *A Pagan Place*; the aspersive Iris Murdoch, with *A Fairly Honourable Defeat*; Eric Segal, the American whose "five-Kleenex weeper", *Love Story*, sold a million copies and was hailed as heralding a return to romance; Gunter Grass, the German master of comic surrealism, who published *Local Anaesthetic*; and Pat McGrath, a literary stripling of 15, author of *Green Leaves of Nottingham*.

"the establishment" was out to get him for his collaboration with Rolf Hochhuth, the German dramatist who wrote *The Soldiers*—the play that asserted that Winston Churchill engineered the assassination of his Polish ally, General Sikorski.

The 17-day *PQ 17* libel case—which took place during February—concerned the "scatter" signal sent to Captain John Egerton Broome commanding the naval escort of the convoy PQ 17 on its way to Russia during the summer of 1942. The Admiralty—acting on intelligence reports indicating that the German battle fleet, including the mighty *Tirpitz*, was about to put to sea—ordered Broome's six destroyers to leave the convoy and join a British fleet preparing to meet the enemy. In the event, the German fleet remained in harbour, while the unguarded PQ 17 was attacked by U-boats and enemy aircraft: 24 of the convoys's ships were sunk.

Captain Broome maintained that Irving's book not only blamed him personally for the fatal decision to leave PQ 17 unguarded, but also asserted that in doing so he disobeyed orders. The jury decided that the book was defamatory and untrue: they awarded £15,000 compensation and £25,000 punitive damages against David Irving and his publishers Cassell and Co. In his summing-up the judge referred to the commercial interest that publishers have in controversy, singling out

indeed did so—if only by printing lurid extracts from some of the many novels banned in Australia. Prophetically, one of these was *Portnoy's Complaint*, the "comic sex novel" that had enjoyed a vast success in the U.S.A. and Great Britain during 1969 (and also a measure of success in Australia, where some 800 duplicates of smuggled copies had, by the summer of 1970, circulated illegally).

The law did not pounce on Messrs. Dutton and Harris, despite their trailing their coats so provocatively under its nose. But later in the year, when Penguin Books printed 75,000 copies of *Portnoy* in Australia, thus dodging the customs officers, the authorities swooped. On August 28, when news of the forthcoming publishing event was announced, three States—Queensland, Victoria, and New South Wales—immediately warned that legal action would be taken against anyone selling or publishing the book. Penguin (Australia) replied: "We are prepared to be prosecuted . . . it could easily cost us 10 or 15 thousand dollars: but we are prepared to do this." Next day, about 2,000 retailers in all the State capitals, apart from Perth, received stocks of the book, and brisk sales were reported.

Only one State, South Australia, announced that it would allow the sale of *Portnoy*. On September 2 vice-squad detectives seized 819 copies of the offending novel in raids on three bookshops in Sydney, N.S.W., and warned

William and Charles

I T WAS THE YEAR of the centenary of Dickens's death (June 9, 1870) and the bicentenary of Wordsworth's birth (April 7, 1770). The citizens of Grasmere and Broadstairs, Cockermouth and Portsmouth, Carlisle and the Old Kent Road, and divers burghers besides, bestirred themselves. The Post Office smartly brought out commemorative stamps. The pens of distinguished hacks and the pencils of obscure nonentities were greatly agitated. Throughout the year of grace 1970 Dickensiana and (less) Wordsworthiana flew from the presses. Dickens the adulterer was atomized, also Dickens the hypnotist, the reformist, the etceterist. Angus Wilson paused awhile from "stinging the middle class to death" and climbed aboard the bandwagon (*The World of Charles Dickens*), but J. B. Priestley was there before him (*Dickens and His World*). More scholarly offerings were *The Inimitable Dickens* by A. E. Dyson, and *Dickens the Novelist* by the redoubtable F. R. and Q. D. Leavis.

Descendants of the two great men were sought out and interviewed. The six Dickens great-grandsons celebrated, as they do each year, with lunch at Pickwick's favourite inn, The George and Vulture. The Dickens Fellowship gave ear to memorial lectures. On June 4 Angus Wilson (again), in his *persona* as Professor of English Literature at the University of East Anglia, gave forth to the Fellowship. Professor Sylvere Monod flew from France and did likewise. Angus Wilson (yet again) lectured the television masses who had already been warmed up with illustrated essays analysing the subtle links between Dickens the man and Dickens the artist.

Wordsworth fared less blatantly. A small bust was unveiled in a quiet ceremony at Cockermouth, his birthplace, and on a biting April day (spring was more than a little late in 1970) a procession of children in overcoats carried daffodils (imported from the Scilly Isles because the local ones had not yet appeared) through the streets. Lectures, exhibitions, and the like were given at Carlisle, Grasmere, Hawkshead, Kendal, Keswick, Ambleside, and Whitehaven, and his only play, *The Borderers*, performed. More effusive was the *Sunday Times* colour magazine, which celebrated the great pantheist's affair with Annette Vallon between an advertisement for kitchenware and another for (of course) the complete works of Dickens.

The Post Office celebrated the two major literary anniversaries of 1970 with philatelic homage. The nation licked the backs of Dickensian characters Pickwick, Micawber, Copperfield, and Twist; while Wordsworth, once Distributor of Stamps for Westmorland, was remembered with postal pastoral, a view of his beloved Grasmere.

booksellers not to sell the offending novel. In the State of Victoria, prosecution of the publishers went ahead, and on November 9 a magistrate ruled that, although *Portnoy's Complaint* had literary merit, it was obscene. Penguin Books were fined $A100 with $A435 costs. Stocks of the book in Victoria were not destroyed, as notice of appeal was given.

Papillon

A publishing sensation in France that rocked bookshops throughout the world also concerned a work which generated heated controversy. *Papillon*—autobiography of ex-convict and self-styled escapee extraordinary, Henri Charrière—had by May sold 800,000 copies in France alone. The book had also spawned two rival literary cottage industries in France—one dedicated to supporting and exploiting the claims of Charrière, and the other to denouncing him as a liar. *Papillon* tells how the 25-year-old Charrière (who had earned the soubriquet Papillon because of the butterfly tattooed on his chest and the delicacy of his touch while opening safes) was accused of shooting a pimp in Montmartre in 1931, and despite his protestations of innocence, condemned to transportation and forced labour for life. His story was cynically received by the anti-Papillon school, notably by Georges Menager, author of · *Les Quatre Verités de Papillon* (*Le Livre que Papillon a voulu interdire*).

Henri Charrière, the light-fingered ex-convict late of Devil's Island, whose autobiography *Papillon* inspired a sceptical chorus in France.

According to his own account, as soon as Charrière arrived at the brutal penal settlement of Devil's Island, French Guiana, he set about escaping, with a break from the prison hospital: he covered 1,000 miles before he was caught. His last, and successful, attempt took place in 1941, when he and another convict, buoyed up with sacks of coconuts, leapt into the sea and were carried by tide and current over 20 miles to the mainland—whence he trekked to Venezuela.

Solzhenitsyn and Khrushchev

The most sinister literary battle of 1970 began on October 8, when it was announced in Stockholm that the dissident Russian writer Alexander Solzhenitsyn (whose works are banned in Russia) had been awarded the Nobel prize for literature. By awarding Solzhenitsyn the prize the Swedish Academy knew that it risked causing a showdown between the Soviet regime and the 51-year-old author, for everyone remembered the fate of the late Boris Pasternak, who had been forced to reject the Nobel prize awarded to him in 1958.

While Pasternak's *Dr. Zhivago* aired only a subtle, almost ambiguous dissent, Solzhenitsyn's works are unequivocal. The most famous of them are *One Day in the Life of Ivan Denisovich*, *Cancer Ward*, and *The First Circle*. Party hacks were quick to react, and soon after the Stockholm announcement the Soviet Writers' Union—which had expelled Solzhenitsyn from its ranks in 1969—published an attack on the Swedish Academy, entitled "An Unseemly Game". On October 16 the Soviet Press agency Novosti released the first direct personal attack on the author, declaring him "a man with morbid self-importance, who easily gave way to the flattery of people who are not too choosy about the means when the fight against the Soviet system is concerned".

This attack was eerily reminiscent of the virulent hounding that Pasternak had received in 1958, and speculation as to whether or not Solzhenitsyn would ever arrive in Stockholm to receive his award from the King of Sweden continued until November 27 when the author told the Swedish Academy that he would not be able to go to Stockholm on December 10, as he had hoped, to receive the award. He explained his decision in a letter which declared: "The hostile attitude towards my prize shown in the national press and, as before, the baiting of my books, the dismissal from jobs and the expulsion from institutes for reading them, compelled me to suppose that my trip to Stockholm would be used to cut me off from my native land by simply barring my return home." He also feared that "celebrations of

The Best Best-Seller

THE COMPLETE New English Bible, including the Old Testament and the Apocrypha, was officially published on Monday, March 16, 1970, and no less than a million copies were sold on that day alone. In 1947 a joint committee of representatives of the participating Churches and Bible societies was set up, charged with the appointment of members for three translation panels for the Old Testament, the New Testament, and the Apocrypha. In March 1961, the new translation of the New Testament was published, the total sales of which had exceeded 7 million by the beginning of 1970.

Translation of the Old Testament was a far more formidable task than that of the New Testament. Old Testament Hebrew is a much more obscure language than New Testament Greek, with many words which are used only once. The early translators could often only guess what a word meant, whereas the translators of the new version had recourse to the Dead Sea scrolls as well as inscribed tablets and pottery discovered by modern archaeologists.

Because of these studies the new version contains many changes from the Authorized Version published in 1611. Radical Christians, however, regarded the perpetuation of "Thou" in addressing God as irredeemably old-fashioned, while traditionalists condemned the committee-wrought "plain man's" English as dull and uninspired in many places. In the complete New English Bible, opportunity was taken to make a few changes in the 1961 version of the New Testament. In general, the new Bible enjoyed a favourable reception among the faithful, and there is no doubt that it will remain the world's best-seller for years to come.

On September 29 another full new translation of the Bible was published in the U.S.A. The New American Bible is a Roman Catholic Bible intended to replace the Douai version which has been the standard translation in Catholic churches for 220 years. The product of 25 years' labour by 51 scholars, including, latterly, four Protestants, the new Bible was sponsored by the American Bishops' Committee of the Confraternity of Christian Doctrine. Most of the translation of the Old Testament had already been issued since 1948 under the name of the Confraternity Edition. The New American Bible, unlike the New English, abandons the use of "Thou" in addressing the deity.

a festive character would be exhausting for me as one whose manner of life and character has not prepared for such things".

Another Russian who found himself at the eye of a literary storm during 1970 was former premier Nikita Khrushchev, whose alleged memoirs were published in serial form in several Western publications during October and November. He was summoned from his sickbed to Moscow and forced to sign a statement, published on November 16, in which he declared that *Khrushchev's Reminiscences* were a "fabrication". I did not give anyone—*Time* magazine or any foreign publishers—any memoirs or materials with the character of memoirs," the statement said. "I did not turn over such materials to the Soviet publishing houses either." The Western publishers concerned pointed out that this merely amounted to a denial that he had personally transmitted any memoirs, and claimed that the *Reminiscences* were "an authentic record of Mr. Khrushchev's words".

The Sunday Times—part of Lord Thomson's publishing empire, which had an interest in the "memoirs" since they were serialized in *The Times*—spelt out this vague claim in detail. Khrushchev, it stated, "is known on good authority to have dictated extensive notes . . . [and also to have] kept open house for relatives and friends . . . there were books, manuscripts, diaries, notes, and tapes lying around for all to see and hear. Any one of the visitors could have helped himself. . . . This is the most likely way some of the material now forming part of *Khrushchev's Reminiscences* may have reached the West." The Russian authorities claimed that the controversial memoirs were merely a fabrication by British and American intelligence services.

New Books in Britain 1970

Fiction. Eric Ambler, *The Intercom Conspiracy*; A. Anatoli (Kuznetsov—the Russian writer who escaped to England in 1969), *Babi Yar*; H. E. Bates, *A Little of What You Fancy*; Saul Bellow, *Mr. Sammler's Planet*; Ray Bradbury, *I Sing the Body Electric*; John Braine, *Stay with Me Till Morning*; Richard Brautigan, *Trout Fishing in America/In Watermelon Sugar*; Anthony Burgess, *M.F.*; Agatha Christie (80 years old in 1970), *Passenger to Frankfurt*; Diane Cilento (Mrs. Sean Connery), *Hybrid*; Leonard Cohen, *Beautiful Losers*; Hunter Davies, *The Rise and Fall of Jake Sullivan*; Len Deighton, *Bomber*; R. F. Delderfield, *God Is an Englishman*; Monica Dickens, *The Listeners*; Lawrence Durrell, *Nunquam*; George MacDonald Fraser, *Royal Flash*; Paul Gallico, *Matilda*; Erle Stanley Gardner, *The Case of the Phantom Fortune*; Stella Gibbons, *The Woods in Winter*; Richard Gordon, *Doctor on the Boil*; Winston Graham, *Angell, Pearl, and Little God*; Günter Grass, *Local Anaesthetic*; Guareschi (posthumous), *Don Camillo Meets Hell's Angels*; Ernest Hemingway (posthumous), *Islands in the Stream*; Alexander Kent, *Enemy in Sight*; Alistair Maclean, *Caravan to Vaccares*; Colin MacInnes, *Three Years to Play*; Robin Maugham, *The Wrong People*; Iris Murdoch, *A Fairly Honourable Defeat*; Bill Naughton, *Alfie Darling*; Edna O'Brien, *A Pagan Place*; Mary Renault, *Fire from Heaven*; Harold Robbins, *The Inheritors*; Erich Segal, *Love Story*; Alan Sillitoe, *A Start in Life*; Dodie Smith, *A Tale of Two Families*; C. P. Snow, *Last Things* (the last of the 11-volume sequence *Strangers and Brothers*); Muriel Spark, *The Driver's Seat*; John Wain, *A Winter in the Hills*; Alec Waugh, *A Spy in the Family*; Patrick White, *The Vivisector*; Colin Wilson, *The God of the Labyrinth*; P. G. Wodehouse, *The Girl in Blue*.

Autobiographies. Harold Acton, *More Memories of an Aesthete*; Christian Barnard, *One Life*; Billy Cotton (posthumous), *I Did it My Way*; Geoffrey Grigson, *Notes from an Odd Country*; Otto Hahn (posthumous), *My Life*; A. P. Herbert (80 in 1970), *A.P.H., His Life and Times*; Julian Huxley, *Memoirs*; Cecil King, *With Malice Towards None*; Erik Link-

later, *Fanfare for a Tin Hat*; Sir Compton Mackenzie, *My Life and Times: Octave Nine*; Sir Robert Menzies, *The Measure of the Years*; Nicolas Monsarrat, *Life is a Four-Letter Word: Part 2—Breaking Out*; Bobby Moore, *World Cup Captain*; Margaret Powell, *The Treasure Upstairs*; Lord Francis-Williams, *Nothing So Strange*; Godfrey Winn, *The Positive Hour*.

Biographies. *Cocteau*, Francis Steegmuller; *Brendan Behan*, Ulick O'Connor; *Zelda Fitzgerald*, Nancy Mitford; *Frederick the Great*, Nancy Mitford; *Horatia Nelson*, Winifred Gerin; *Enoch Powell—Tory Tribune*, Andrew Roth; *Sir Walter Scott: The Great Unknown*, Edgar Johnson; *Eamon de Valera*, Lord Longford.

History. Correlli Barnett, *Britain and Her Army*; Max Beloff, *Imperial Sunset: Vol. I, Britain's Liberal Empire, 1897–1921*; Robert Conquest, *The Nation Killers*; Otto von Habsburg, *Charles V*; Sir Basil Liddell Hart (posthumous), *History of the Second World War*; Erik Linklater, *The Royal House of Scotland*; Robert Rhodes, *Churchill: A Study in Failure 1900–1939*; Peter Townsend, *Duel of Eagles* (Battle of Britain); Sir Llewellyn Woodward, *British Foreign Policy in the Second World War* (five vols.).

Poetry. Dannie Abse, *Selected Poems*; George Mackay Brown, *Fishermen with Ploughs*; Robert Graves, *Poems 1968–70*; Hugh MacDiarmid, *Selected Poems*; Ezra Pound, *Drafts and Fragments of Cantos CX to CXVII*; Tom Scott (ed.), *The Penguin Book of Scottish Verse*; Mary Wilson, *Selected Poems*.

General. Sean Bourke, *The Springing of George Blake*; *Cartier-Bresson's France*; Anthony Grey, *Hostage in Peking*; Thor Heyerdahl, *The Ra Expeditions*; Bernard Moitessier, *Sailing to the Reefs*; Richard Neville, *Play Power*; C. Northcote Parkinson, *The Life and Times of Horatio Hornblower*; *Shell Guide to England*; Benjamin Spock, *Decent and Indecent*; Cliff Tait, *Flight of the Kiwi* (account of Tait's 1969 solo round-the-world bid in smallest ever aircraft to attempt such a flight); Nicholas Tomalin and Ron Hall, *The Strange Voyage of Donald Crowhurst*; Arnold Toynbee, *Cities on the Move*.

Five charming little bears, William, Andrew, Charles, Robert, and John, sit down to breakfast at the beginning of another adventurous day. *The Bears Who Stayed Indoors*, written and illustrated by Susanna Gretz, is full of that special humour which delights younger readers.
Ernest Benn

New Books for Younger Readers ELIZABETH HOGARTH

AMONG THE FIRST reactions to children's books in 1970 was a feeling of sympathy for parents who wish to buy books for their children to encourage them to build up a library of their own. On the whole, prices were undeniably high. This was, no doubt, unavoidable as costs of paper and production continued to rise, but it seemed exorbitant for a small child's book containing under 200 words and with only about 10 illustrations to cost something between 60p and £1, and several such books were published. Another criticism of books for children under the age of 6 is that many of the illustrations are far too impressionistic and, although they have artistic merit, may bewilder many children who cannot recognize the animals, people, and objects portrayed.

This said, it would be churlish and unfair not to add that the year produced an abundance and variety of books for all ages at which no such criticism could be levelled.

For the Very Young

The Young Puffin Book of Verse, compiled by B. Iveson and illustrated by G. Fiammenghi, will give endless pleasure, for the poems are simple enough for a child to read aloud and learn, and there is a good index of first lines and authors. Alison Uttley again delighted her readers with eight stories in *Lavender Shoes*, and her love of the countryside and the small creatures that live there was as clearly shown as in her earlier books. *The Fantastic Story of King Brioche the First* by Anne Jenny, illustrated by Jocelyne Pache, translated from the French; *Aladdin and his Wonderful Lamp* and *The Sleeping Beauty*, both retold and illustrated by Charles Mozley; *The Children of Hamble House* by W. d'Enno, illustrated by M. Gorde; *The Truck on the Train* by Janet Burroway, illustrated by John Vernon Lord; and *Angelo*, written and illustrated by Quentin Blake, all had great appeal. Tibor Gergely's *Great Big Book of Bedtime Stories*, an excellent collection of tales and poems, old and new, contains dozens of coloured pictures and is ideal for reading aloud. The youngest author of 1970 was Janet Aitchison, whose *The Pirates' Tale* was written when she was

5 years old; she dealt happily with death and disaster, and Jill McDonald added colourful illustrations with panache.

Fairy Stories

One of the year's most beautiful books was *The Golden Bird* by Edith Brill, which grew out of stories told to her by her Polish father. Jan Pienkowski, whose early childhood was spent in Poland, interpreted the story with silhouettes of great originality and with exciting use of colour, brilliantly capturing the unreality of the fairy world. This was one book of which the high price was wholly justified. Another fine production was *Sir Orfeo*, the retelling by Anthea Davies of a medieval English poem, illustrated by Errol Le Cain in the manner of an illuminated manuscript, perfectly in keeping with the mystery and romance of the story. The editor and re-teller of *South American Fairy Tales*, J. Meehan, chose his tales from many parts of South America; translated into English for the first time, the stories have a freshness, humour, and liveliness typical of the people among whom they originated, while J. Praders's illustrations show an authenticity which adds to the interest. *Fairy Tales from Japan* by Miroslav Novak was a marvellously varied collection·of 26 stories, its many exotic illustrations contributing to their enchantment.

Non-Fiction in Great Variety

In the bicentenary year of Cook's great voyages, *Captain Cook* by Bernard Brett vividly related his adventures at sea, with many details of contemporary life on board ship. The author's pictures, many in fine colour, beautifully illustrate his text, and a clear, well-drawn map shows the three voyages Cook made between 1768 and 1779. This is a fascinating, informative, and altogether very attractive book. We encountered Cook again in *They Sailed from Plymouth* by Jacynth Hope-Simpson, who told absorbing stories of seafaring men who, from Tudor times to the present day, have set sail from Plymouth.

In *The Story of Handwriting* Alfred Fairbank traced the beginnings of writing in Sumer and Egypt through the invention of the alphabet to modern times and the revival of italic writing. The book is packed with information, clearly and concisely expressed, with many good illustrations. R. J. Unstead's *Castles* traced the history of the British castle from the Iron Age hill fort, Maiden Castle in Dorset, to the Queen's house at Balmoral with its battlements and turrets. Splendidly illustrated with drawings, photographs and old prints, it contains a chapter on what to look for on visiting a castle, as well as a good glossary. Alan Sorell superbly illustrated M. Drower's *Nubia: A Drowning Land* with drawings made during the international rescue operation before the completion of the Aswan High Dam. The author assisted at the excavation and recording of one of the sites, and the book is a lasting record of a vanished region.

The Story of Communication by Ludvik Soucek traced communication from its most primitive forms to the technical marvels of the present day. The varied, colourful, and often amusing illustrations are a feature of the book. *Maps and Map Reading* by R. B. Matkin, with its many diagrams, dealt with maps in general and for the walker in particular, making it of especial interest to all young lovers of the countryside. Boys enjoyed *The Sea Dreamers* by Basil Heatter, *Robin Around the World* by Robin Knox-Johnston, and the *Puffin Book of Football*, an informative history of the game. *Anne, Portrait of a Princess* by Judith Campbell, an informal picture of the popular young princess, her life, pastimes, and tastes, profusely illustrated with photographs, some never before published, fascinated teenage girls. They also enjoyed the sensitively written study of the early life of George Eliot, *Towards a High Attic*, by Elfrida Vipont.

Horse-lovers welcomed *Horses and Their Owners*, an illustrated anthology, compiled by Josephine Pullein-Thompson, who drew on world literature over the past 2,500 years to present a picture of the part the horse has played in man's life. They enjoyed, too, *Parade of Horses* by Vian Smith, an interesting collection of anecdotes containing many personal reminiscences. Sadly, this was the last book by this popular author, for he died in December 1969.

F. M. Kelly wrote an interesting account of the cells of the human body, *The Mighty Human Cell*; although the illustrations are not up to the high standard of the text, a good glossary makes this a useful informative book. Two other worth-while books for those interested in science were *Beginnings and Blunders* by Lancelot Hogben, the first of four volumes on the beginnings of science, and *Medicine* by Alfred Wurz, which outlined the history of medicine in simple terms.

Fiction for All Tastes

From the many excellent novels for the young it is possible to select only a few for individual mention because their originality and fine writing will linger in the memory long after they have been returned to the shelf, and to list some others for the teenager's library list. *Where the Lilies Bloom* by Vera and Bill Cleaver was an enchanting story about children in the Appalachian region of America, which, when it was earlier published in the U.S.A., was chosen as one of the year's best novels for children. *The Daybreakers* by Jane Curry was a very unusual and exciting story of a lost civilization, the relationship between time past and present, and how some children became involved in its mysteries. Set in 15th-century England, Violet Bibby's *The Mirrored Shield* sensitively related a young boy's struggle against the supersition that because he is left-handed he is "witch's breed". André Norton, acknowledged master of children's science-fiction, wrote another gripping and imaginative story, *Star Gate*. Rosemary Harris in *The Shadow on the Sun*, a sequel to her prizewinning *The Moon on the Cloud*, continued the story of Reuben, animal-trainer and musician, with all the ingredients of narrative, humour, and a feeling for history.

Library List for Young Readers

The Lark and the Laurel by Barbara Willard, set in the Sussex weald in the 15th century (for children aged 12+); *The Drummer Boy* by Leon Garfield, a sensitive story of an idealistic boy (10+); *Sky Carnival* by William F. Hallstead, exciting and amusing adventures of American aerial stuntmen in the First World War (10+); *Come Back Peter* by Joan Woodbury, a story of the journey of a white boy and an aboriginal boy through the terrible heat of a waterless country (10+); *The Speaking Drums of Ashanti* by Martin Ballard, based on historical fact (10+); *That Summer Long Ago* by Lora Hennessy, a First World War story set in the Hebrides (12+); *The Sea Islanders* by Joyce West, adventure on an island off New Zealand (10+); *The Player's Boy* by Antonia Forest, set in Elizabethan England, with exciting plot and excellent dialogue (12+); *A Kind of Secret Weapon* by Elliott Arnold, a small boy's adventures with resistance groups in Nazi-occupied Denmark (11+); *Jim Grey of Moonbah* by Reginald Ottley, a moving and exciting story of a teenage country boy from the Snowy Mountains (12+); *The Boy on the Dam* by W. A. Baudouy, translated from the French, a vivid picture of a giant engineering feat (11+); *The Forgetful Robot* by Paul W. Fairman, good science-fiction (11+); *The White Cockade* by Alexander Cordell, fast-moving adventure at the time of the 1798 rebellion in Ireland (11+); *Farm Beneath the Sea* by Mary Patchett, gripping and credible story about fish farming beneath the Great Barrier Reef (10+).

A dragon wields his club to prove his strength to a watching shepherd. This is one of the many delightful illustrations by Krystyna Turska in *Dragons*, edited by Roger Lancelyn Green. This excellent collection contains authors ranging from Sir Thomas Malory and Edmund Spenser to G. K. Chesterton and L. P. Hartley.
Hamish Hamilton

THE WORLD OF MUSIC IN
Beethoven's Year

BARRIE HALL

WHEN THE YEAR 1970 was first sighted from afar, and it was realized that with it would come the bicentenary of the birth of Beethoven, concert promoters all over the world began to scratch their heads, wondering how on earth, in this particular year, they could pay *more* homage to the world's most popular composer. Well might those heads be scratched, for Beethoven, though his own life had ground to a halt in poverty and wretchedness, has paid the rent for thousands since his death. Performers, impresarios, publishers, writers, and record manufacturers all owe more to Beethoven than to any other composer, even Tchaikovsky. The problem, then, was how to celebrate his bicentenary when his music is constantly performed.

Needless to say, music organizations everywhere contributed towards this anniversary. Celebrations ranged from a concentrated 10-day festival in the small Swiss city of Braunwald to the cycle of his nine symphonies worked into the season's concerts by most of the world's major symphony orchestras. In 1970, as perhaps in no other year, a traveller might have found it musically repetitive to tour the festivals. Not only would he have encountered the same Beethoven works; in some cases he might even have heard them performed by the same soloists or orchestras. Had he chosen Oslo instead of Aix-en-Provence, or Lisbon instead of Montreux, it would have made no difference: in Bergen, Florence, Amsterdam,

Tanglewood, U.S.A., Munich, or London, the great composer was being honoured.

Beethoven was born in Bonn, on the Rhine. He lived, worked, and died in Vienna, on the Danube. Naturally one would expect these two cities to extend themselves, and this they certainly did. During a three-part international festival in May, September, and December, Bonn brought together a massive collection of world talent. The city invited no less than a dozen master-pianists to play the piano sonatas, including Germany's Wilhelm Kempff, Jörg Demus, Bruno Leonard Gelber, and Friedrich Gulda; Russia's Emil Gilels; Italy's Arturo Benedetti Michelangeli; Hungary's Geza Anda and Andor Foldes (now an American citizen); Chile's Claudio Arrau; and France's Philippe Entremont. Symphonic music was played by the Berlin Philharmonic under von Karajan; the Vienna Philharmonic under Karl Böhm; Amsterdam's Concertgebouworkest under Eugen Jochum; and London's New Philharmonia under 85-year-old Otto Klemperer. These orchestras could also be found at other times playing Beethoven in cities as far apart as Lucerne and Tokyo. Bonn also had Dietrich Fischer-Dieskau singing Beethoven's songs, and two performances of both the opera *Fidelio* and the great *Missa Solemnis*. This wealth of music was

---

At top of page: Beethoven's only ballet, *The Creatures of Prometheus*, choreographed by Sir Frederick Ashton, was performed by the Royal Ballet in London, Bonn, and Vienna.

accompanied by a big exhibition, which subsequently went on tour. It contained instruments, scores, first editions, letters, paintings, etc., all associated with Beethoven.

London's Royal Ballet was invited to dance Sir Frederick Ashton's new *Creatures of Prometheus*—Beethoven's only ballet—first in Bonn and then in Vienna. Vienna had another exhibition, called "The Glowing Flame"; and also produced the most passionate *Fidelio* heard anywhere, played at unrelenting pace, and with evil and good portrayed deepest black and whitest white. Leonard Bernstein conducted this performance, which showed what a great opera it really is. Many countries also took the opportunity to perform the earlier version of Beethoven's only opera, known as *Leonore*: these included Austrian Radio and the BBC in England.

Vienna's Beethoven Society planned to perform all Beethoven's chamber music between March 26 (the day he was born) and December 15 (the day he died). There were recitals in Viennese parks and squares, and sonatas were played in front of the various houses where he lived. The big cycle of his string quartets was a frequent choice with which to celebrate: Aix-en-Provence, for example, engaged the Italian, Borodin, and Juilliard Quartets to perform them. Most musical centres presented at least one big work: the *Missa Solemnis* in Bergen, Turku, Perugia, Leipzig, Rome, and

The Beethoven bicentenary was commemorated on May 23 in St. Peter's, Rome, with a concert that included an impressive performance of his *Missa Solemnis*. Among the audience was the Pope (at head of aisle, right centre).

many more cities; the *Choral Symphony* almost everywhere. Zürich also gave Beethoven's rare cantata *The Mount of Olives*, while the hybrid *Choral Fantasia* (a kind of piano concerto en route to becoming the *Choral Symphony*) turned up in several places.

Possibly one of the most interesting contributions to the bicentenary was an appendix by Dr. Edward Larkin to Martin Cooper's book on the composer's *Last Decade*. In it, the doctor painstakingly reconstructs Beethoven's entire medical history, deducing from his research that the unfortunate composer had bone forming in his ears all his life. This would have given him unbearable head noises, and explains why he was often irritable and short-tempered (he once threw a plate of stew over a waitress). It was this complaint that eventually made him stone deaf. Dr. Larkin also laid to rest some long-standing myths: that Beethoven's later works were in some way mystical and religious (simply because he could not hear them); that he had syphilis; that he was a homosexual. Not true, on the evidence—and that refutation did Beethoven real service on his anniversary.

Bailiffs in the Balcony

Meanwhile, behind the festive exterior of the bicentenary, it became clear during 1970 that all was not well with some major orchestras, particularly in America. Suddenly a number of them looked like becoming bankrupt. Indeed, the Cleveland Symphony nearly went out of existence. To add to their difficulties, their prestigious conductor George Szell died, their manager resigned, and the players went on strike, whereupon other orchestras tried to tempt the best to desert. One observer predicted that, within the next few years several of the top American orchestras could disappear. Their money problem is basically simple and is known in the Stock Exchange as "futures", where dealers buy and sell corn that has not yet been sown. American orchestras have no government subsidy and the huge gap between concert takings and total expenses is made up from private and business grants with which most orchestras have built up huge trust funds. When one of them makes a gramophone record, it receives no money at the time from the recording company, but contracts to receive royalties on every record sold, for ever and ever. The musicians, however, have to be paid immediately. So the orchestra's management dips into its trust fund to pay their very high recording fees, knowing that it will all come back some time in the future when the record starts to sell and that eventually there will be a handsome profit.

The opera star of the year was the American coloured soprano Grace Bumbry. She was a seductive Salome in Richard Strauss's opera at Covent Garden, London (left), where her Dance of the Seven Veils was a sensation. In Rome, with Richard Tucker as Don Jose (right), she created another furore as Carmen in a controversial version of Bizet's opera.

The system breaks down, of course, if for some reason records suddenly fail to sell. That is apparently exactly what was happening during 1970. An orchestra like the Cleveland which makes records all the time has laid out millions of dollars from its fund in players' fees and now, unexpectedly, there is little prospect of this cash ever being recovered from royalties. Several American orchestras appear to have been in this same sinking boat together during 1970, and were worried about prospects for the future.

What happens in America has a habit of happening elsewhere shortly afterwards—which raises the uncomfortable question: *why* were record sales falling off during the year? There may be many causes, from the advent of tape-recorders and cassettes to a lack of spare cash for luxuries. Perhaps, too, there are those who, having bought the nine Beethoven Symphonies recorded by Klemperer, find it unnecessary to buy them all again, recorded by Karajan, and then by George Szell, and so on. Records keep their playing qualities much longer nowadays, and once one has a decent recording of some work, it is likely to satisfy one for many years.

Arts Council's Report

Great Britain was trying during the year to put its musical house in order before any disasters could overtake its institutions. The Arts Council Report on Opera and Ballet was followed by another on Orchestras. The Opera report spoke sensibly of developing London's Covent Garden when the market moves elsewhere. (The opera house is completely surrounded by vegetables at present.) It was also recommended that money should be given for the Royal Opera to tour the provinces more often; that new opera houses should be built in England (probably in Manchester), in Wales, and in Scotland; and that a committee should look into ways and means of keeping seat prices pegged to a reasonable level. The

Orchestra report fared less well—in fact, it was generally felt to be a flop. Indeed, in a preface the Arts Council's chairman, Lord Goodman, disassociated the Council from two of the major recommendations—(1) that instead of the present four London orchestras there should be only two; and (2) that there should be equal pay for provincial players. Meanwhile the secretary of the Musicians' Union took a page in the report to disagree with several points. It was opined in musical circles that members of the reporting committee had been too long out of touch with the practical realities of Britain's music.

In an attempt to salvage something from an effort that may not be made again for a long time, Lord Goodman called all the committee

Sadler's Wells Opera's *Valkyrie* was a first step towards a complete performance in English of Wagner's *Ring of the Nibelungs*. Rita Hunter sang Brunnhilde and Norman Bailey Wotan.

members together in November 1970, to hold a seminar on the report and perhaps to think again. There are certainly things wrong with British music, but the report did not suggest how to put them right. Four orchestras (five if the BBC Symphony is included) are not too many for a city the size of London. Tokyo has six. The report's implication that London orchestras cannot afford sufficient rehearsal time, and that their standards suffer as a result, was strongly resented.

Still on the thorny theme of music's money, the Russian ministry of culture put up the fees for its artists appearing overseas during 1970, which appears to have priced out of the British market soloists like David Oistrakh and Leonid Kogan, and conductors like Evgeny Svetlanov. The trouble is that much higher fees than Britain can afford are commonly paid in America, Europe, and Japan. British employers (mostly orchestral managements) may be forced to take a stand and forgo Oistrakh.

John Lill, joint winner of the 1970 Tchaikovsky piano competition

But there are others who can play violin concertos. In Moscow, John Lill jointly won the Tchaikovsky contest, the second British pianist to succeed in it. Emil Gilels called him "a master, with a lofty world of emotions and an impeccable technique". That triumph solved financial problems for John Lill who was instantly in demand all over the world. His parents once scraped to buy his first piano and to pay for his lessons.

Opera from London to Sydney

London is the only place in the world (apart from Bayreuth) where the opera season begins with two complete performances of Wagner's four-opera *Ring of the Nibelungs* cycle, and in 1970 Georg Solti conducted it for the last time before going to the Chicago Symphony. In 1971 it is to be conducted by Edward Downes; in 1972 there will be no performance; in 1973 a new production will begin with two of the

operas; and by 1974 there will be a completely new *Ring*. Solti took the Royal Opera to Berlin while Lorin Maazel and the Berlin Opera were at Expo 70 in Japan. Berlin praised British singers in German opera, and called Solti unique among the world's opera chiefs. But Richard Rodney Bennett's *Victory*, written for Covent Garden and moderately praised in England, was attacked in Berlin by a hostile press as intellectually dull and musically barren, a mixture of Debussy, Puccini, and Menotti. This came as a shock, for Bennett is highly regarded in Britain.

Karajan's rival *Ring of the Nibelungs* at Salzburg was completed at Easter with *Götterdämmerung*, a performance distinguished by the utmost beauty of sound, lacking tenderness perhaps, but not easily to be forgotten. Meanwhile, London's Sadler's Wells Opera, at the Coliseum Theatre, took the first step towards a complete version in English by staging *Valkyrie* as a follow-up to their remarkably successful *Mastersingers*. Sir Michael Tippett's third opera, *The Knot Garden*, a Peter Hall–Colin Davis production at Covent Garden in December, was acclaimed his best, and consolidated his recent re-assessment as perhaps England's greatest living composer.

In New York the poor old Metropolitan Opera stayed firmly and unprecedentedly shut by trade union disputes during the 1969–70 season until New Year's Eve, whereupon, as 1970 began, Australia's Joan Sutherland immediately became the toast of the town for her performance in Bellini's *Norma*. At the City Opera that glittering coloratura Beverley Sills, in *Lucia* and *The Daughter of the Regiment*, threatened to rival Sutherland as the season's darling.

In England, Benjamin Britten achieved the impossible, by rebuilding his acoustically ideal concert hall at Snape Maltings, Aldeburgh: phoenix-like it arose from the ashes of the fire that burned it out in 1969. Even with that huge problem on his hands, he still found time to write a new opera, *Owen Wingrave*, especially for BBC television. He was also seen in Australia for the first time, directing performances of his three *Church Parables*. Karlheinz Stockhausen also visited Australia, complete with all his electronic gadgetry. In Sydney and Melbourne the ABC's John Hopkins conducted promenade concerts before packed houses. He included Peter Sculthorpe's new *Love 200*, named after the planet Venus and the bicentenary of Captain Cook's arrival on Australia's east coast. Sydney lost Her Majesty's Theatre by fire in July 1970—a great blow, as the dramatic new Opera House was still far from finished.

REVIEW OF ARCHITECTURE

BARBARA AULD, B.A.(Arch.), A.R.I.B.A.

University of East Anglia. The student residences at this new English university, which is situated on a former golf course outside Norwich, Norfolk, show a marriage between building and landscape, both in the form of the blocks and in their lay-out along the contours of the site. The buildings lie against the slope of a hillside overlooking the river Yare, their stepped-back profiles looking like ancient Babylonian ziggurats. In the student residences (right) the study bedrooms, which are higher in the front part of the rooms than the rear, slot into each other. Staircases between these rooms run progressively up the slope, giving access to a long footpath running at a constant level round the hill. This links all the buildings together—and provides plenty of exercise for young legs. The corner rooms on each floor under the gargoyles are used as breakfast rooms. Rainwater carried by the gargoyles cascades down the steps of the "pyramid".

The buildings were constructed from pre-cast concrete sections to a height of six or seven storeys. They house two thirds of the total number of students at East Anglia. In the photograph at the top of the page, showing the library, with lecture theatres on the left, one of the staircases is seen at the left.

Architects: Denys Lasdun & Partners

New Secondary School, Pimlico, London. Designed for 1,725 pupils—boys and girls between the ages of 11 and 18—this new school (above) has been built on a rather restricted site, yet it is only four storeys high. The principal circulation level is on the upper ground floor, and from a gallery round the main concourse on this level stairs lead to groups of teaching rooms on the second floor. The assembly hall has a sunken arena floor which can be used for drama and music. Roof glazing has been used to give adequate light to the many deep rooms. It has two thicknesses of glass with expanded polystyrene between, and blinds control the amount of sunlight admitted. The whole structure is in reinforced concrete, with the external surfaces ribbed either horizontally or vertically.

Designed under the direction of Sir Hubert Bennett, F.R.I.B.A., F.S.I.A., architect, and Michael Powell, B.A. (Cantab.), A.R.I.B.A., A.A.Dip., education architect, Department of Architecture and Civic Design, for the Inner London Education Authority. Photo, John Laing & Son Ltd.

Office Block in Vancouver. This twin-towered office building in the heart of the business area of Vancouver, British Columbia, Canada, is the headquarters of MacMillan Bloedel Ltd., a large forest products company. The twin towers are linked at each floor, and the interior is column-free. The building is of reinforced concrete with sandblasted exterior surfaces, and the windows have solar grey glass.

Architects: Erickson/Massey and Francis Donaldson

Protestant Church at Sion, Switzerland. The shapes and planes of this small church were designed to harmonize with an ancient Catholic chapel adjoining it. The building fits tightly on to a narrow site, with one long wall against the main road. To avoid noise, this wall has no openings in it to the church itself, which is on the first floor; on the ground floor are situated classrooms, library, and air-raid shelters. Inside, five curved rows of seats for 150 people face the pulpit. Extra seating for 220 people is grouped on a slightly higher level, for use at special services.

Architect: Pierre Schmid. Photo, Oswald Ruppen

166

Royal Commonwealth Swimming Pool, Edinburgh. In designing this splendid pool for the Commonwealth Games at Edinburgh, the architects set out to obviate the main objections to large indoor swimming baths, such as noise and glare. To avoid glare from direct sunlight on the surface of the water, which makes it impossible to see underwater swimmers, the large hall housing the main Olympic-standard pool is enclosed by groups of smaller rooms on all sides and at various levels. Most of these surrounding rooms are glazed both to the outside and to the pool hall, so providing a form of double glazing. Acoustically absorbent materials, principally on the ceilings, prevent unpleasantly high noise levels when many people are using the baths. Three separate pools are provided, one for swimming, one for diving, and one for teaching and for small children; and there are seats for 2,000 spectators.

Architects: Robert Matthew, Johnson-Marshall & Partners

World Trade Centre in Amsterdam. Located as it is in the heart of the Western European industrial areas, and visited every year by more than a million businessmen, Amsterdam is a natural site for a World Trade Centre, due to be opened in 1971. A model of the building is shown below. The Centre will house a full range of national and foreign business firms engaged in international marketing, as well as consulates, public and private trade promotion agencies and the commercial offices of foreign nations. It is built round two spacious plazas, with multi-storey office buildings, reception and information centres on the North Plaza, where sheltered galleries house foreign and national government offices, chambers of commerce, international banks, and other service organizations. A hotel, conference rooms, and apartments are on the South Plaza, with shops and service organizations in the galleries. The basement can take 3,800 cars, and a railway station and bus terminal give direct access to the Centre via escalators and lifts. The most up-to-date communication system ever devised for commercial use is being installed, with direct telephone and closed-circuit television connections to aid long-distance conferences. A complex clover-leaf-type roadway scheme will make the Centre readily approachable from all directions.

Photo, Ad Van Bennekom, Amsterdam

New Town of Beersheba, Israel. A splendid new town is being built round the old biblical city of Beersheba on the edge of the Negev desert. The master plan for the town, which was prepared for the Israeli ministry of housing, won the second R. S. Reynolds Memorial Award for Community Architecture. This award is given by the Reynolds aluminium firm and administered by the American Institute of Architects. The photo at left shows one of the tall apartment buildings designed by G. Gamerman and M. Lofenfeld, which are to be sited where high density housing is appropriate. The projecting rooms are cantilevered from a central core to give some shade to the rooms below—a valuable feature in a situation of scorching heat.

The town centre building (below), designed by R. Carmi and Associates, has an open-air gallery along the middle. It contains shops and offices on the ground and first floors, and housing on the upper floors, and can be extended in length as needed. The Reynolds award jury described it as "a dynamic building of linear design". The old town centre built before the First World War, now retained temporarily as a commercial and entertainment centre, will be reconstructed and co-ordinated with the new. It is, however, intended to preserve its oriental character as far as possible.

Beersheba, lying 45 miles south-west of Jerusalem, was in ancient times at the southern extremity of the land of the Israelites, and Dan was at the northern extremity. Hence the biblical phrase "from Dan to Beersheba". The name Beersheba, meaning "the well of the oath", was bestowed by either Abraham or Isaac.

Architects: M. Rosner; R. Reifer and M. Macrae. Engineer: M. Laor. Photos, The British Aluminium Co.

New Office Block in London. The 27-storey Commercial Union Assurance Company's tower in Leadenhall Street (above) faces a paved piazza which forms an underground podium to the building and houses the staff restaurant. The core of the building is a reinforced concrete structure containing lifts, staircases, and service rooms. From this, steel frames are cantilevered to support trusses and girders from which, in turn, steel hangers support the floors.

Architects: Gollins Melvin Ward and Partners

Computer Centre in New York. A multi-storey operations centre (above) to house mainly computers and business machines has been built by the banking firm of Manufacturers Hanover Trust Company on a site overlooking the harbour on the East river-side of New York. The outside walls are faced with a hard burnt red-brown brick, the cheapest material for narrow window openings. The computers and machines are housed on all the main floors except the three lowest and seven at the top, in large rooms with widely spaced slit windows. The small administrative staff, on the first floor, have larger windows. In the top seven floors the slit windows are spaced at closer intervals, so that they are adaptable for either people or machines.

Architects: Carson, Lundin & Shaw

BOAC Passenger Terminal, Kennedy Airport. The only terminal owned and built by a non-American airline at Kennedy Airport, New York, this striking building was opened in September 1970. Arrivals complete their formalities on the ground floor, and departing passengers go by way of the first floor which is reached by a ramped road. A mezzanine floor contains first-class lounges, VIP room, bar, restaurant, and offices. The inward slope of the glass walls in the main areas reduces sun glare and reflections, and the steel roof over the main concourse cantilevers 60 ft. over the glass sides. Built on a very wet, sandy site, the concrete building is supported on 6,000 timber piles, like telegraph posts, between 30 and 50 ft. long.

Architects: Gollins Melvin Ward and Partners. Consulting Engineers: Ammann and Whitney, New York

New Resort in France. The apartment blocks (above) at La Grande Motte, one of six tourist towns planned by the French government on the Languedoc–Roussillon coast, face a newly created yachting harbour. Looking white or grey according to the sunlight, many of them are pyramidal on two or more sides, so that the balconies do not overshadow each other. Their enclosing shapes make curved or triangular patterns on the façades. To make this development possible in a wild, almost deserted stretch of country bordering the Camargue, where communications were hitherto interrupted by many brackish inland seas, fresh water had to be brought to the area and a network of roads and motorways built.

In the centre of the town (below) many of the little shops, bars, and restaurants are in arcades at ground level under the apartment blocks. Landscaping is being carefully planned, and many shrubs and flowers have been planted. Even fully grown trees have been transplanted to give immediate shade.

Architect in charge and town planner: Jean Balladur.
Photos, French Government Tourist Office
(Ministère Français de l'Équipement)

University of Hull Library. The west building which forms the major part of a new extension to the Brynmor Jones Library at Hull University (top) has five upper floors of reading area which are lit with double-glazed windows tilted at an angle of 60 degrees with the horizontal. The angle reduces the amount of direct sunlight and heat through the glass, while providing good natural light for reading. These five upper floors are faced with grey vitreous-enamelled steel cladding, and the five lower floors of the ten-storey concrete-framed building have a dark brown glazed-tile finish. This new building, together with an extension and alterations to the old library, brings the library's total capacity to 1,000,000 books and 1,650 places for study, which will ultimately serve about 6,000 students. The small illustration immediately above shows students in a typical reading area in the new building. The tilted windows are clearly shown in this photograph.

The University of Hull is not entirely one of Britain's "new" universities. It was incorporated as the University College of Hull in 1927 and opened in 1928, being raised to the status of a full university with a royal charter in 1954. Another distinctive architectural addition to it in 1970 was the Gulbenkian Centre, a drama studio with a central acting area, which can be changed in less than half an hour from theatre-in-the-round to apron-stage or proscenium-arch theatre by repositioning the seats. *Library Architects: Castle Park Dean Hook*

WELCOMING THE MIDI

BETTY HALE
Editor of *Fabulous* and *Rave*

A dress that combined all the 1970 trends—see-through lace, fringes, midi-maxi length, and the inevitable poncho.

THE SILHOUETTE for 1970 was tall, lean, and waisted. The year began with the maxi coat, belted and with revers, in plain wool or small tweeds in scarlet, clear yellow, brown, grey, or black. But plenty of mini-length coats, and some midi, were worn, with boots which came at least to just below the knee, fitted closely to the leg. Headgear consisted of pinhead caps—knitted or crocheted—or loose monk-style hoods trimmed with fur. Beneath the coats, mini skirts were still worn.

Throughout the year, the hem was the point of interest. In the U.K. the mini remained a firm favourite. But there were midis, more and more of them, for the girl who was prepared to commit herself to the business of buying new boots (summer and winter weights) and bar shoes or granny lace-ups to go with the new skirt length. The waist, too, had to be emphasized. In some cases it meant wearing a special waspie corselet.

A-line with Variations

Midi (and maxi) skirts were always A-line, but there was plenty of variation both in styling and fabric. Midis were cut with an inverted pleat at the front or button-through from waist to hem, with a contrasting broad band at the hem, with fringing, with Spanish-style flounces, with a single frill at the hem, with bands of stitching or leather trim, or with fur. All were nipped in at the waist, sometimes on a band or with rows of shirred elastic. Some were cut in several panels for a tailored fit at the waist and over the hips. Wide belts were usually worn, and big and important-looking buckles were a feature.

Tops to go with the midi varied from prim Victorian-miss blouses in lawns and voiles with long puffed sleeves and high necks to skinny ribbed sweaters, belted longer sweaters, shirts, and long waistcoats. Midi dresses were often in simple shirt-waist style with collar or more plunged neckline, and always belted. With the midi the bosom returned. The softly rounded champagne-glass shape was the ideal, and the bra, which had had a brief banishment the previous year, came back. As hems came down so, gradually, did necklines. Chokers, like great-grandma once wore, returned, made from velvet, suede, leather, or metal.

Trouser Suits and Crochet Clothes

For those who could not decide which skirt length to buy there were trousers, which were more in evidence than in any previous year. With slightly flared legs, they were styled for all occasions, although they were still banned in a few top-flight hotels and the more genteel business houses. For casual wear, trousers were in printed cord (stars, flowers, fake snake), cotton, velvet (especially panne velvet and crushed velvet), suede, leather, jersey, knitteds, and silk. Trouser suits were not the conventional jacketed suit; mostly the tops were tunic style, to be belted either at waist or hips, with short or long sleeves, and thigh or midi length. Sometimes buttoned-to-the-waist waistcoats of midi length were worn with matching trousers and sweater.

Knitted and crocheted clothes featured more prominently in 1970 than ever before. Knitted non-fastening coats and midi skirts had matched horizontal bands of ribbing at the hems, to go with ribbed skinny sweaters. Thick cabled coats and waistcoats went over plain knitted trousers with fluted legs. There were Aran patterned sweaters and trouser suits (made with side buttoning tunic), and there was Fair Isle. Long midi button-through cardigans went over something else or were worn by themselves with nothing beneath except perhaps a scarf at the neck. Knitted dresses in both mini and midi lengths and even knitted top-coats were worn.

Jacquard-knit geometric jerseys were a scene on their own. The patterns were gay and colourful diamonds, leaves, and strictly non-representational squiggles. They were made into coat-dresses worn with matching trousers, knickerbocker and waistcoat suits, midi skirt and jerkin suits, as well as into mini, midi, and maxi length dresses. With such "busy" patterns, designs were simple, usually with zipper fastenings, self belts, and no extra trim.

Tee Shirts and Gypsy Blouses

For summer time there were elongated Tee shirts which became mini dresses, mostly the "fun" kind with printed or appliquéd Disney characters on them; there were even maxi Tee shirts, to the ankle, in cotton or Tricel jersey, in all-over prints on a white ground. The infinite variety of fashion included midi printed cotton skirts and dresses, Bermuda shorts, floaty dresses with enormously wide sleeves, short-sleeved dresses with long fringes, cotton trousers and matching brief tops with fringing over the bare midriff and on the trouser legs, lace-up dresses made of calico, and wraparound sarong skirts. Swimsuits were brief—nothing more than small shapes of fabric

The bare midriff was a ruling style.

Popular throughout the year was the poncho-and-trousers outfit.

linked with metal or plastic rings at the sides and front. Some had a high polo-necked front, cut-away sides, and an exaggerated plunge back. Bikinis were cut on minimal lines. It was a very bare look, but there were plenty of beach cover-ups in the form of sleeveless towelling jackets and simple beach dresses.

Early in summer we saw the gypsy look—predominantly midi length—which was almost a fancy dress with a strong peasant flavour. Full, gaily printed, or checked gingham skirts, often flounced and frilled flamenco style, were teamed with Hungarian-type blouses and a bandeau at the waist. Wooden beads were worn at the neck, with loopy earrings, bangles, and a scarf tied round the head. Gypsy dresses of patchwork, or with polka dots (usually large sized) and with braid trimming, were made in garish colours.

Reptiles and Ponchos

Another trend was fake snake. Reptile prints included smocked mini dresses made from printed "snake" wool mixture in beige and brown; a lace-up tunic in "snake"; printed shiny "mock croc" in red, green, or brown made into a midi belted raincoat; "snake"-printed knee-length boots; and belted, revered jackets in soft imitation snake. Soft fabrics printed with "python" were produced for dresses and blouses. Reptile trim (usually made from anything *but* reptile) appeared on coats, jackets, and dresses. Reptile shoes came in all colours, including purple, green, yellow, and natural, and so did handbags, belts, and watch straps.

New for 1970 was the poncho. Ideal for every occasion, it appeared in Jacquards,

The reptile look: simulated alligator leather and toning patent leather in tunic and trousers.

Autumn trouser suit in acrilan and wool marl, over skinny rib sweater.

Shiny raincoat in soft crushed Vistram.

Warm for winter: tweed cape and skirt, with woollen jersey.

knitteds, tweeds, towellings, and plain jerseys. It came in all colours, and with polo neck and fringed edges. In towelling it slipped over a bikini; in other fabrics it was worn with skirts, trousers, shorts, or dresses.

Autumn and Winter Styles

The autumn collections made a feature of knickerbocker suits with pouched or accordion-pleated knickers brought into a band below the knee. There were also midi culotte suits. Both lined up with the midi-length skirt, and were worn either with boots or with "total look" (same colour as outfit) tights. Tights also became patterned, with a simple design running up the side or textured all over.

For winter, coats were predominantly midi, with the hem anywhere below mid-calf, but there were also full maxis. Fake leather and fake fur (usually curled) featured a great deal. Soft crushed Vistram in white, black, brown, navy, and red was made into raincoats cut on princess lines, with twin-buckle fastening, butterfly revers, and small peplum with parallel lines of stitching for extra detail. Jacquard was there, too, usually belted and with fur trimming. Most coats had emphasis at the hem, which would perhaps be bound with a wide band of leather and rows and rows of stitching, or trimmed with fur or cut wool. Fake furs were mainly in black, white, or brown, made in fairly skimpy belted styles and often teamed with wool or "leather" trimming on collar, sleeves, shoulders, fronts, pockets, or hem. Some had hoods attached. Big, bold, and flowing capes were very much in fashion—midi or maxi length or anything in between—in tweeds, or in the season's most fashionable colours, purple, burgundy, and plum.

Revolution in Footwear

Convention in shoes was swept away early in the year, and in came a range of very colourful clumpy shoes, different from any that had gone before. They had really thick heels, and some were of an exaggerated wedge shape. Soles were mostly platform style, some as much as an inch thick. "Carmen Miranda flavoured" sandals with high wedge heels and platform soles, made in gay red, purple, yellow, and natural "mock croc", were back twice as large as life. Apart from the soles and heels, vamps were pronounced and so was trimming. Clean white piping was particularly used. Toes were very round.

As the year progressed, the exaggerated clumpiness began to wane as the granny look began to grow, and was replaced by slightly higher heels with more shape and fined-off toe. There were lots of lace-ups (lacing of all kinds was a fashion note all through 1970), also bar shoes of pure granny design, made in glossy calf, in aubergines, deep plums, and burgundies. Some boots took on a granny look, too, being either buttoned or laced and just below the calf or mid-calf length. There were also heavier boots above and just below the knee, made from printed "python" and "cobra", wet-look leather, and laced-up-the-leg leathers and suedes.

Casual Clothes for Young Men

Unisex gear was still a fashion story. Perhaps the biggest part of it was Tee shirts. Seen

Above: "mock croc" shoes with massive, clumpy heels.

Below: eye-catching shirts in printed python and lace-up styles.

Above: casual battledress suit in Harris tweed, with breast pockets and suede "wear" patches on the elbows.

Left: midi for men, in a jersey coat trimmed with fur fabric, with shiny "gun" patches on the shoulders.

everywhere were Mr. Freedom Tee shirts with prints of Walt Disney or Enid Blyton characters on them. Tie-and-dye vests were another craze for both sexes. They were bought ready to wear, or one could buy a white three-button vest, tie it in a knot, and throw it into a dye bath: when it came out and was dried it bore a tie-dye pattern. For girls, a vest was often a mini dress. For men, a vest top was usually worn with velvet, cord, or satin slacks or with pantaloons (trousers tucked into boots).

The informal look for young men reached a peak, and it was quite acceptable for them to go to work in an office in a very casual jacket. The extra casual trend began in April and reached its summit in early autumn. The few high-fashion suits were unconventional in design but sometimes very conservative in cloth. There was, for instance, a Harris tweed suit with waist-length battledress jacket, chest pockets, cuffed sleeves, and leather patches on the elbows. More unconventional in cloth was the Jacquard suit, with waistcoat and trousers made of this geometrically patterned jersey. The waistcoat either came to almost fingertip length or was full midi.

The shirt suit was a long belted shirt worn over trousers; this could become a jacket, with nothing underneath and no tie. The safari suit was another variation, with hip-length lace-up jacket with four button-down pockets, buttoned cuffs, and trousers styled to be worn inside knee-length boots. In the earlier part of the year there was a slight disappearance of the button, and lacing had a season in laced

shirts, laced belts, and even laced trouser legs. Leather-trimmed Shetland sweaters had lace-up neck and cuffs; Tricel jersey figure-hugging tunic shirts had collar and self-lacing neck; and there were even some lace-up suede shirts to be seen.

The suit, in a very casual style, was re-introduced for summer in pure silk-satin with butterfly revers, edge-to-edge zippered jacket, and matching trousers. The colours were white and beige for sunny days; these were also worn for evening, with a crew-necked sweater and lots of jewellery. The lounge shirt, also introduced for evenings, was made in grandiloquent printed Lurex and cut on shirt lines to midi length to be worn Russian-style over trousers tucked into boots.

Narrow Shirts and Long Coats

Shirts were tapered as before, and some new designs had a military flavour, with high necks and regimental-type side buttoning; they were made in soft crepe in salmon, grey, blue, red, and black. In this very casual year men wore scarves at neck and waist. Ties, when worn, were wide and brilliant.

The young man's silhouette, like the girl's, was long and lean. Trousers were tight at the top, and went straight from there. Any flare was from the calf, and not from the knee as previously. Top-coats were long, whatever the fabric. Some were made in heavy jersey trimmed with fur fabric on the cuffs and along collar, hem, and fronts, plus leather patches on the shoulders. Some were in cotton jersey heavily trimmed with mock Mongolian lamb on pockets, hem, cuffs, collar, and revers. This exactly mirrored the fake furs on the female fashion scene. Colours were sober—petrol, dark green, dark brown, and purple.

Men's shoes were mostly in pull-on moccasin style, often in wet-look leathers or "patent", in black and dark colours. Toes were round. They began by being clumpy, with gilt buckles and instep trim, but became more tailored by the end of the year.

The last word on unisex fashion was said by these notices on the conveniences at the Young Vic Theatre, opened in 1970 near the more staid and respectable Old Vic in Waterloo Road, London.

The Changing Role of Art

CHARLES SPENCER
Editor of *Art and Artists*

From the Tate Gallery exhibition in October 1970 of the work of Julio Gonzalez, pioneer of welded metal sculpture: an iron *Harlequin,* dated 1927–29.

THE QUESTION OF the part that art has to play in modern society, and the plight of the individual artist, were much debated subjects in the art world in 1970. In their book *Art in Britain 1969–70,* Edward Lucie-Smith and Patricia White referred to the current "period of transition for the institutions which support modern art". They suggest that commercial galleries are struggling to survive, and that "contemporary art is moving steadily out of the private into the public sector". "What is the place of the arts", they ask, "in the kind of society which we now have?" and answer, "What its relevance is remains in doubt."

Jean Gimpel in his book *The Cult of Art* made some radical suggestions: "It is surely time today for us to revise our traditional classifications of the arts." Instead of painting and sculpture, he insists, photography, cinema, and television are the appropriate art forms for modern life. He further adds: "The notion of usefulness must be reintroduced into the arts. . . . The arts should have a social content, should contribute to the betterment of society and of relationships between people . . . They should be monopolized neither by a single man, nor by a single social class, nor by a single ideology." A number of exhibitions carried the discussion further—*Art and Technology* at the Los Angeles Museum (and later at Expo 70 in Japan), *Kunst und Industrie* at the Munich Modern Art Museum, *Plastic as Plastic* at the Museum of Contemporary Crafts, New York, *Art and Technology* at the University of Surrey, *Manufactured Art* at the Camden Art

Centre, London, and the Arts Council's *International Multiples Exhibition.*

It has taken a long time to question the importance of the artist's "touch" or of the uniqueness of the art object. In the ancient past art could function and be admired without "signature", even if the object was "manufactured" and widely disseminated. In modern times William Morris, the Bauhaus, de Stijl, and the Constructivists pioneered a more utilitarian role for the artist, who has always been fascinated by new techniques. With the advent of the machine and mass production, artists were given new stimuli—both in terms of imagery and in the new materials provided. The exhibition of the Spanish sculptor Gonzales at the Tate Gallery in October 1970 showed the work of a pioneer in metal welding; he taught Picasso and influenced artists like David Smith and Anthony Caro. After his experiments the distance from the atelier to the factory floor was in the process of being eliminated.

Art in the Factory

Nowadays it is not uncommon for a sculptor to draw or design a form and pass it to a skilled craftsman or a factory for completion. This also allows him to work on a monumental scale that no single artist could tackle. These considerations led the American industrial designer Don Lippincott to found Lippincott Inc. in Connecticut, U.S.A., some years ago. Artists such as Claes Oldenburg, Ellsworthy Kelly, Robert Morris, and Barnett

An example of co-operation between artist and industry, Brian Wall's *Thornaby*, in the new town centre at Thornaby-on-Tees, was fabricated in the works of Head Wrightson & Co. Ltd., of Yarm, Yorkshire.

Newman have used Lippincott to create monumental public works. In Britain, although no similar full-time factory for sculpture exists, a number of artists have sought industrial aid. The largest modern sculpture on a public site in England—Brian Wall's *Thornaby* for the new town centre at Thornaby-on-Tees—was fabricated by a local firm, Head, Wrightson (Teesdale), Ltd. Firms like Pilkington's, the glass manufacturers, have a long tradition of co-operation with artists, as have

I.C.I. whose plastic division inspired the Continuum Group which in 1970 held enterprising exhibitions in London.

The argument for this kind of co-operation between art and industry was well put by Gyorgy Kepes, head of Advanced Visual Studies at the Massachusetts Institute of Technology, on the occasion of an exhibition called *Explorations* in April–May 1970—"I've felt for a long time that the artist has become almost a displaced person in this life, and that art is more than just esoteric comments on the world, or just an emotional striptease . . . I always dreamed of a place where artists could go whose aspirations go beyond this personal elegy, and face reality through interaction with urban planners, scientists, sociologists, and with life, and also learn new potential tools—technological, scientific tools which are in scale with the new dimensions of the task. . . ."

Perhaps the most interesting area in which the artist and the technologist meet is that of "multiples". This is the new term for mass-produced copies of works of art put on sale to the public at reasonable prices. The touring exhibition of multiples organized by the Arts Council and seen at the Whitechapel Art Gallery in November was the first international survey seen in London. In 1969 the Ikon Gallery in Birmingham held a useful pilot show, and in 1970 both the Scottish and Welsh Arts Councils actively promoted discussion of the subject. The Scottish Council's exhibitions in Glasgow and Edinburgh were on the lines of supermarkets, where customers could buy their multiples and pay at a cash register. The idea is to establish the multiple as an unlimited commodity rather than a precious art object. The London exhibition expressed no particular philosophy on the subject; it in-

"Multiples" is the name given to mass-produced copies of new works by living artists, who design them for the purpose. Thus art is brought within the financial reach of ordinary people. The two "multiples" shown below are: (left) *Twins*, by Brian Yale, made of steel stove-enamelled black; and (right) a miniature caryatid, *Mini-Maria*, in polished metal, by Berrocal, published by Multicetera, Geneva.

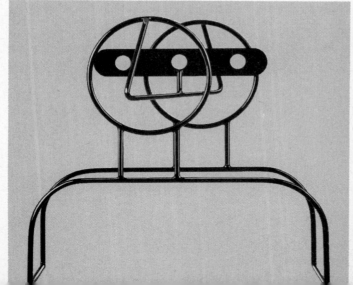

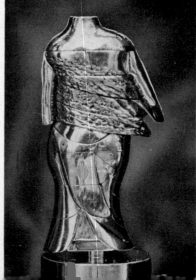

Royal Portraits of the Year

The year saw a number of royal portraits unveiled to the critical gaze of the public. Annigoni's second portrait of the Queen (above), put on show in the National Portrait Gallery, London, on February 25, excited special interest. Many of her subjects disliked the severity of the Queen's expression and the general austerity of the picture. Annigoni himself was quoted as saying: "It is 16 years since I last painted your Queen . . . The whole atmosphere and the whole inspiration have changed. I have painted her as a person alone: if you like, as a monarch who takes her responsibilities very seriously."

There was nothing controversial about the first official portrait of Princess Anne, by Bernard Hailstone, which was on show in London during September. The painting was commissioned by the 14th/20th King's Hussars, of which the Princess is colonel-in-chief. The artist described his sitter as "a first-class subject, relaxed and composed".

Facing page 176

Bryan Organ's expressionist portrait of Princess Margaret—unveiled on her 40th birthday, August 21, 1970—was the most controversial royal portrait of the year, exciting a chorus of horror from traditionalists. The Princess, however, who had chosen the artist herself, expressed her approval of the portrait—which was commissioned by Lincoln's Inn.

Traditionalists were reassured by Alex Strathearn's cheerfully conventional portrait of Prince Charles on show in London during the month of September. The artist is seen here looking at his picture, which was commissioned by Qantas, the Australian airline, and destined for Timbertop, the country annexe of Geelong Grammar School which the Prince attended in Australia.

cluded objects, prints, photographs, and other art statements in serial form, in limited and unlimited editions. The idea was to state the problem; the discussion that followed was of the greatest interest. It will be seen whether, as some believe, the multiple movement will establish the long-hoped-for ideal of a democratic art form, or whether, as others fear, mass-production will only lead to a cheapening of art and the destruction of its special prophetic, spiritual qualities.

Round the Shows and Exhibitions

1970 was a year of Biennales—São Paulo, Tokyo, Medellin, and, the "daddy" of them all, Venice. Apart from disseminating information about international art developments and focusing public attention on contemporary work, the Biennales in recent years have provided dissatisfied or puzzled artists, and political activists, with the opportunity for protest. The public demonstrations which attended the 1968 Venice Biennale were sufficiently serious to prejudice its continuance, and had the effect of cancelling financial awards, as well as bringing into being, in addition to the national exhibitions, some form of central display reflecting current experiments.

The first Biennale of the year, at São Paulo, Brazil (September 1969–January 1970), appeared to presage a year of violence. It was used by many international artists to register their disapproval of the Brazilian regime—although, in fact, the exhibition is privately financed and organized. Protests were ostensibly directed at state censorship in Brazil, which caused some countries and artists to withdraw. The critic Robert Kennedy, writing in *Art and Artists*, compared Dubuffet's belief in the local and specific subversiveness of art with those "who elected to paint anti-Vietnam pictures which they chose not to show in São Paulo in order not to influence a policy over which they can exert no control".

In terms of art, few critics found much to praise at São Paulo. It was generally agreed that the most noteworthy sections were from England, Canada, Germany, Japan, and Switzerland, and the major prizes went to Anthony Caro, the English sculptor, Ernst Fuchs (Austria), Ramirez (Colombia), Bonevardi (Argentina), Robert Murray (Canada), Swierzy (Poland), Kolar (Czechoslovakia), and Herbert Distel (Switzerland).

The Coltejer Biennale in Medellin, Colombia (May–June 1970), was almost negated by a revolution, but in the end took place. This again is a private enterprise, founded in 1968 by the Coltejer Textile Company, and devoted to art in the Americas—plus Spain and Portu-

One of the most successful works at the Coltejer Biennale at Medellin, Colombia, was Le Parc's fun fair, which poked satirical fun at the activities of commercial art.

gal, for historical and cultural reasons. The exhibition is held not in the capital Bogotá, but in the charming commercial centre of Medellin. It is mainly an event for the townsfolk, but gradually more and more foreign visitors are attracted. This year the jury (Professor Argan of Italy, the English critic Lawrence Alloway, who lives in New York, and Señor Vincente Cerni from Spain) seemed to prefer the clever "op" and kinetic art which South American artists specialize in, and the principal awards went to Tomasella (Argentina), Salazar (Venezuela), and Brizzi (Argentina).

Since the country was in the throes of a political storm when the exhibition opened, and the whole South American continent is known for social ferment, the lack of active protest at Medellin was surprising. There were a few protest-works—such as a metal sculpture of the letters S.O.S. and a painting of heads and hands behind bars—but little more direct than that. More effective were the informal works, such as Le Parc's fun fair, which satirized commercial art activity. The most explicit protest was a hand-written notice in the entrance hall of the exhibition referring to the decision of "the people of Latin America . . . suffering such misery, oppression, torture, etc.", to "fight the oligarchies and dictators and North American imperialism". Exhibitors and the public were invited to sign in sympathy with the cause, and some of them did. It was all as peaceful as a Sunday morning in Hyde Park.

The Venice Biennale

Venice 1970 did not even arouse written protest. In every sense—artistic, social, political—it was a very dull affair. The decision not to award any further monetary prizes was welcomed by most artists and critics. (No doubt, some dealers had their regrets, since these bi-annual distinctions greatly helped to raise the international ratings of their artists. But it was the excitement and anxiety over jury decisions which in former years gave the vernissage-days at Venice their special febrile quality. Fewer artists and dealers bothered to come to Venice in 1970, and there was a marked decrease in the number of cocktail parties at which international art gossip was formerly retailed. In addition to the national offerings, the Italian authorities produced, as promised, a major central display entitled *A Proposition for an Experimental Exhibition*. But

oil paintings, and at other extremes the rather boring print-workshop at the American pavilion and the example of "total environment" arranged by the French. A few artists emerged as personally impressive—Michael Snow (Canada), Arakawa (Japan), Jagoda Buic, the brilliant Yugoslav maker of tapestries, Villalba (Spain), Cruz-Diez (Venezuela). Two pavilions received special attention—the Dutch display of the Centre of Cubic Construction, basically the work of two artists, Slothouber and Graatsma; and in the Polish the separate exhibitions of Joszef Szajna, inspired by personal experience in German concentration camps, and a show of icon-like banners and religious symbols by Wladyslaw Hasior.

The Venice Biennale, having dropped its customary monetary awards to prize-winning artists, was less exciting in 1970 than formerly. Two of the works exhibited that won fairly general recognition were (left) an extraordinary construction by the Norwegian sculptor Arnold Haukeland; and (right) a statuesque group by the Spanish artist Villalba.

since this was not ready during the four or five press days, and only emerged weeks after the opening (in June 1970), it is impossible to comment on its effect. It does, however, indicate that in future an effort will be made to turn the Venice Biennale into a thematic exhibition on the lines of the four-yearly Kassel Documenta.

But in 1970 it remained a collection of national pavilions. This not unattractive basis will continue, in some form, in the years to come, but even here changes are bound to occur. The dominant impression in 1970 was one of transition: on the one hand, the British pavilion doggedly devoted to one artist —Richard Smith—in a traditional display of

The Manaichi Biennale in Tokyo (May–July) is financed by a Japanese newspaper group. This year a distinguished Japanese art critic, Yuseke Nakahara, was invited to make a private choice of 40 artists—including a number from abroad, such as Kounellis, Christo, Serra, Hacke, and the English sculptor Flanagan. His theme was *Between Man and Matter*. The other major collective exhibition of the year was the Pittsburgh International, founded in 1896, a year after the Venice Biennale. This, too, decided to abandon its award system, and instead of attempting a complete international survey, with national selection committees, the exhibition, which opened in October 1970, concentrated on 90 chosen

Richard Smith, a British artist who was well represented at Venice, made this attractive work in brushed aluminium, *Envelop No. 1*. Each side is 16 inches long.
Richard Feigen Galleries, New York

Russians Lissitsky, Malevitch, and Gabo, as well as Moholy-Nagy, Bornik, and Berlewi. At the Palazzo Reale, Milan, *Sixty Years of de Chirico's Painting* paid tribute to the 80-year-old artist, one of the seminal figures of Surrealism. Another pioneer, the French painter Francis Picabia (1879–1953), was remembered in a superbly mounted show at the Solomon R. Guggenheim Museum, New York, in September.

Among many other exhibitions one of the strangest was Andy Warhol's *Raiding the Icebox*, at Rice University, Houston, Texas, arranged from discarded works of art found in museum basements. Equally bizarre was an exhibition at the Chicago Museum of Contemporary Arts for which artists from all parts of the world designed works by telephone, leaving members of the staff to have them executed by intermediaries.

Explorations of the past were headed by the superb Gainsborough exhibition at the Queen's Gallery at Buckingham Palace. Rodin was well displayed at the Hayward Gallery, and other French artists, such as Carrière (Marlborough Gallery), Bourdelle (Grosvenor Gallery), and the Symbolists (Piccadilly Gallery), were given public airing. An unusual survey of 20th-century British art resulted from an exhibition of *Narrative Art* at the Camden Art Centre, in which some remarkable canvases from the Imperial War Museum attracted attention. American artists given

artists. The choice was made entirely by L. A. Arkus, director of the Carnegie Institute, which finances and houses the exhibition. Each artist was represented by a group of his works, not by one only as in previous years; and in addition to this selected number there were also works by 12 living "masters" including Picasso, Miro, Gabo, Ernst, Tobey, Albers, and Henry Moore. The other British artists shown at Pittsburgh were Francis Bacon, John Hoyland, Richard Smith, Bridget Riley, Reg Butler, Eduardo Paolozzi, and Gwyther Irwin.

Other Important Shows

At Strasbourg the Council of Europe held from May to September another of its important historical surveys, *L'Art en Europe—1925*. Two hundred artists were included, representing significant movements—Expressionism, Constructivism, the Bauhaus, de Stijl, and, above all, Surrealism. The early years of the century are constantly being re-assessed. Enterprising London galleries arranged scholarly enquiries into two remarkable movements; the d'Offay Couper Gallery illustrated the English abstract movement before the First World War, centred upon Wyndham Lewis and the Vorticists; and the Annely Juda Fine Art, throwing its net wider, held an exhibition entitled *The Non-Objective World*, which included such remarkable artists as the

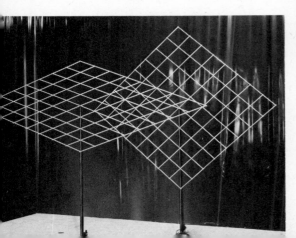

Two contrasting exhibitions at the Hayward Gallery, London, during 1970 were devoted respectively to kinetic art and early Celtic art. No still photograph can do justice to kinetic art, the essence of which is movement, but the interesting construction at least of *Grilles déformables* by François Morellet can be appreciated (left). Above is a detail of the Gundestrup cauldron, from the National Museum in Copenhagen, an example of early Celtic art remarkably like some "modern" work.
Courtesy of the Arts Council of Great Britain

major shows in London included Frank Stella (Hayward Gallery) and Oldenburg (Tate Gallery). In October, the Hayward Gallery mounted two fascinating and contrasting shows, *Kinetics* and *Early Celtic Art*, the latter transferred from the Edinburgh Festival. Two major print events were the Kelpra Studio exhibition at the Hayward Gallery, relating the success of the British silk-screen print renaissance; and the Second British Print Biennale at Bradford, an important event which deserves metropolitan exposure.

Major Paris exhibitions during the year were devoted to Matisse, Gonzales (later seen in London), Viera da Silva, Giacometti, Max Bill, the English engraver William Hayter, Gargallo, Dubuffet, and César. Modern German art, of which little has been seen in England, was given a boost at the Edinburgh Festival in a survey of art from Düsseldorf, arranged by the Richard Demarco Gallery, in which the work and personality of Josef Beuys made a startling impression. A similar gesture to non-commercial art forms was made by the Arts Council of Great Britain who enterprisingly took over the former tea-house in Hyde Park and opened it as the Serpentine Gallery for young artists.

Modern art suffered three major losses during the year. Mark Rothko, the American painter, died on February 25, shortly after his gift to the Tate Gallery of nine large paintings, originally intended for a New York restaurant. He and Barnett Newman, who died on July 4, were two of the leading figures in the great American Abstract-Expressionist group which represented perhaps the most important development in modern American art. In May,

Henri Hayden, the Polish-born French painter, died in Paris; a gifted early Cubist, he later developed a lyrical style in landscapes and still-lifes of intense colour.

Erotic Art

A much discussed theme was the perennial problem of the degree of eroticism, or even pornography, permissible in art. Sexual matters have been portrayed in both public and private art since the beginning of time, and we are clearly living through one of those permissive eras which alternate with puritan restrictiveness. At the Institute of Contemporary Art in London, the 89-year-old Picasso showed nearly 350 engravings on sexual themes, a subject long popular with this famous artist. In old age he regards such preoccupations with detachment and humour. A number of younger British artists handled the theme with unusual frankness; Allen Jones, at Tooth's Gallery and in a publication of his source material; David Hockney, in a charming retrospective at the Whitechapel Art Gallery; and, with his own brand of elegant delicacy, Richard Hamilton in his Tate Gallery exhibition, which incidentally was probably the most impressive exhibition by a British artist during the year.

The most notorious contribution was John Lennon's lithographs shown at the London Arts Gallery, illustrating intimacies between the Beatle and his wife Yoko Ono. These lithographs were commissioned by an American publisher and later shown in the U.S.A. In London, the police raid on the gallery and the temporary banning of the works had the predictable result that the show was a sell-out.

The first full retrospective exhibition of the work of Richard Hamilton, pioneer of "pop" art, opened at the Tate Gallery, London, in March. Everything Hamilton had made since 1956, date of his first "pop" collage, was included. Three varied examples are shown below. Left, a visitor studying *I'm Dreaming of a White Christmas*, a "Screenprint" of Bing Crosby. Centre, a light-hearted construction from a plastic denture and an electric toothbrush, entitled *The Critic Laughs*, first created in 1968. Right, *Cosmetic Study* (1969), a multiform work of collage and mixed media, slightly more than 3 ft. high and 2 ft. wide.

The Performing Arts

THEATRE

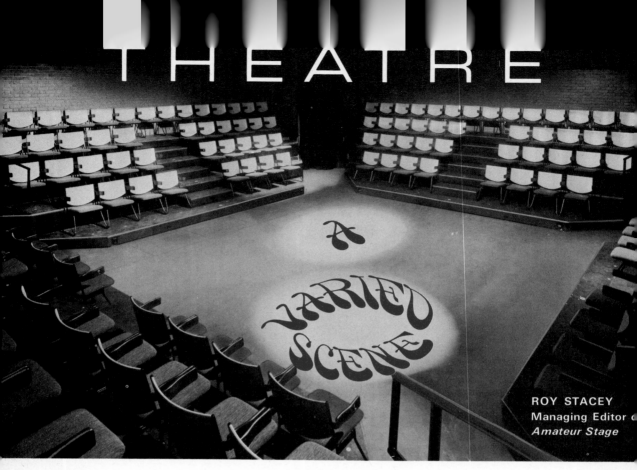

A VARIED SCENE

ROY STACEY
Managing Editor of
Amateur Stage

Ever since the Second World War the arts in Great Britain have been receiving increasing financial support from government funds—to such a degree that the Arts Council can justifiably claim that without this help probably not a single one of the 50 provincial repertory theatres would be alive today. A change of government, such as occurred in June 1970, is therefore a matter of some anxiety to all organizers and practitioners of the arts. Fortunately, the principle of public subsidy is supported by all political parties, although there are differences of approach and emphasis. Lord Eccles, the successor to Jennie Lee as minister with special responsibility for the arts, gave clear evidence in his speech to the Conservative party conference of the new government's full commitment to the arts. He stressed the vital role of the newly formed regional arts associations, whose income comes about equally from the central exchequer and the local authority funds, with private sources "a very poor third". He also hinted at the possibility that the present administration might be able to make some modest tax concessions.

Although help for the arts has grown considerably, there is still a long way to go. In a report of a survey undertaken by the Institute of Municipal Entertainment it was shown that the situation is very uneven throughout the country. The average rate equivalent spent on entertainment by English local authorities is still well under $\frac{1}{2}$p—compared with the expenditure permitted by the Local Government Act, 1948, of a $2\frac{1}{2}$p rate. Moreover, this figure covers all "entertainment" (including Bingo!); the theatre receives less than £1 million a year from local authorities, which spend £45 million on public libraries. Also published during the year was a report of the Arts Council theatre enquiry. This stated that the plight of the commercial (privately operated non-subsidized) theatre in the provinces is desperate. In the last 40 years the number of provincial theatres and music halls has declined from 130 to about 30, and the remainder will disappear within the next few years unless immediate salvage action is taken. The report recommended

At top of page: the Cockpit Youth Arts Centre theatre, designed for the Inner London Education Authority under the direction of Sir Hubert Bennett, F.R.I.B.A., F.S.I.A., architect, and Michael Powell, B.A. (Cantab.), A.R.I.B.A., A.A. Dipl., education architect, in the department of architecture and civic design.
By courtesy of the Greater London Council

the establishment of a theatre investment fund, and a circuit of at least a dozen refurbished major theatres, forming a new "No. 1" touring circuit. There are, however, differences of opinion about the wisdom of bolstering up a touring system, which many contend is outdated and uneconomic.

Theatre for the Young

Central London, where there are some 40 commercial theatres, remains the Mecca of the theatrical arts. The London theatres, and the arts generally, are being increasingly viewed as a powerful attraction and an important factor in the tourist industry. All London theatres remain open throughout the year, in marked contrast to those in many other capital cities.

In 1970 the most significant development in the London theatre was the special efforts made to cater for younger audiences. Most notable was the opening of the Young Vic, in a rapidly erected temporary building a few yards along the road from its illustrious parent, the Old Vic. Using National Theatre players, under the direction of Frank Dunlop, the Young Vic aims to provide, at very reasonable prices, quality productions aimed primarily at audiences up to 25 years of age (although the more mature are not excluded). So far, with the exception of *Stomp*, an American student multi-media rock musical, the repertoire has comprised classics, ancient and modern, presented with a modern outlook— *The Pranks of Scapin* (from Molière), *Oedipus, The Soldier's Tale* by Stravinsky, *The Taming of the Shrew*, *The Duchess of Malfi*, *Waiting for Godot*, the Wakefield Nativity Plays—also two for younger children, *The King Stag* and *Timesneeze*.

The Royal Shakespeare Company took over the Roundhouse for a six-week festival by Theatregoround, a small group within the R.S.C. which has been taking a taste of theatre to any organization which invited it, in the hope of building up future audiences. The season included a five-hour Shakespeare history cycle, *When Thou Art King*, *Arden of Faversham*, *King John*, and *Dr. Faustus*; studio presentations of three Shakespeare plays in the current Stratford repertoire; "work demos", talks, and discussions—from 11 a.m. to nearly midnight. At the same time the Royal Court was running a three-week festival of new work, appropriately called "Come Together". To accommodate the wide range of new and experimental work put on by "fringe" groups, and to provide the genuine community atmosphere of its title, the theatre was stripped of its normal seating.

Another important event was the opening of London's first purpose-built youth arts centre and theatre-in-the-round, the Cockpit, built by the Inner London Education Authority for under £100,000. The I.L.E.A. now has two main theatre centres—the Cockpit as a more experimental workshop for all the arts, and the renamed Curtain (formerly Toynbee) where amateur groups, both adult and youth, can receive training and mount productions in a well-equipped proscenium theatre. Still awaited is the Shaw Theatre, the new home for Michael Croft's National Youth Theatre, which is being built in a new development by Camden borough council: originally scheduled for the autumn of 1970, it is now expected to be ready early in 1971.

Both the new provincial theatres opened during the year—at Leeds and Newcastle—although fully professional theatres, were provided with university co-operation. Indeed, one of the conditions imposed upon the Leeds architect was that the building should be readily convertible in 10 years' time into a

The first production at the Young Vic opened on September 10, 1970. It was *Scapino,* **a musical version of Molière's 300-year-old comedy** *Les Fourberies de Scapin.* **Former pop singer Jim Dale (centre) both composed the score and played the title role.**

university sports hall. This was no easy brief, but in the event a 750-seater theatre was built for £150,000, which is extremely cheap for these days.

Permissiveness on Stage

The new liberty enjoyed by the theatre since the abolition in 1968 of the censorship of plays by the Lord Chamberlain still made press headlines in 1970. Generally the new-found freedom was used with responsibility, and only occasionally was it abused for private gain. After providing the venue for Arnold Wesker's play *The Friends* for a short run, the Roundhouse (which was to have been the base for his ill-fated Centre 42) gave a new twist to the term "try-out" theatre. Kenneth Tynan's revue of "elegant erotica", *Oh! Calcutta!* (produced in New York the year before), was considered too risky to take straight into the West End; but when, despite some protests, it was apparent that the Director of Public Prosecutions did not intend to take action against it, the management moved it into Central London, to the Royalty Theatre. The latter had already proved itself a suitable home for this type of show. A disastrous all-male revue, *Birds of a Feather* (Danny la Rue at the Palace showed how camp should be done), was followed by *The Bed*, the most blatant exhibition of full frontal nudity yet seen on the London stage. In the programme, strip-club king Paul Raymond told the critics that he bore no malice for their icy reception of his previous venture *Pyjama Tops* (which was still running at the Whitehall), for he "is catering for the public first and the arty, aesthetic viewpoint a long way behind".

Council of Love was another example of the greater freedom—less in physical exposure, although including a Borgia orgy, than in

blasphemy (ridiculing and impersonating the deity). The play did not last long at the Criterion. The emphasis laid by the popular press on any sensational elements often completely distorts a play's real intent; this happened to Ronald Millar's sensitive reworking of the medieval love story of *Abelard and Heloise*, in which there was a brief, darkened nude love scene. No doubt the publicity gave a fillip to the Wyndham's box office, but one wonders how many people went expecting something quite different and came away feeling cheated. Surprisingly, another equally legitimate use of nudity, in a Pinter play, *The Basement*, went unremarked by the press.

Back to Entertainment

The resurgence of the *"derrière-garde"*—the move away from the more extreme forms of alienation and non-communication—continued in 1970, but the public became more discriminating in its rejection of the more trashy offerings. William Douglas Home had another light-comedy success with *The Jockey Club Stakes*, which leant rather heavily on the expertise of Alastair Sim and his two "old boy" steward-accomplices of the Jockey Club, Robert Coote and Geoffrey Sumner. Another familiar name to reappear was Terence Rattigan, with an extended version of an earlier TV play about Nelson and Lady Hamilton, *A Bequest to the Nation*, a moderately successful, though far from vintage Rattigan. The author was also represented by a revival of *The Win-*

The spectacular musical *The Great Waltz*, based on Johann Strauss's life and melodies, brought new life to Drury Lane, London, from July onwards. This is the "Blue Danube" finale.

slow Boy, with Kenneth More. Another expert craftsman, Robert Bolt, scored an immense success with his new treatment of the familiar story of Elizabeth and Mary, *Vivat! Vivat Regina!* (transferred from Chichester after breaking all records there in the summer), in which Eileen Atkins revealed her full stature.

Among the newer playwrights' work, Alan Ayckbourn's comedy *How the Other Half Loves* was rather disappointing after the witty *Relatively Speaking*, but Robert Morley's outrageous hamming gave it a successful run. A delightful comedy by Jack Pulman, *The Happy Apple*, had the original comic idea of a Cockney secretary (Pauline Collins) proving the perfect median response to all marketing research—a goldmine to an advertising agency—but it ran out of steam before the end. Peter Shaffer's twin brother Anthony made a brilliant West End debut with *Sleuth*, an ingenious suspense thriller which at the same time succeeded in sending up the conventional thriller with its stereotyped characters. More conventional, but with an intriguing final twist, was Terence Feely's *Who Killed Santa Claus?*, decorated by Honor Blackman.

A comedy-thriller *A Woman Named Anne*, by Henry Cecil, set itself the difficult task of sustaining the drama of the courtroom without that vital suspense ingredient, murder. It was about an apparently drab divorce case; however, another clever twist and Moira Lister's charm gave it a reasonable run. David Mercer has hitherto been more successful in films and

TV than on the stage. With *After Haggerty* (Royal Shakespeare Company) and *Flint*, an outrageous play about an ageing, lusting renegade priest, he was rather more successful, but both suffered from being too uneven and episodic to hold the interest throughout. Hopes that *Poor Horace* would emulate its predecessor from Bristol, *Conduct Unbecoming*, proved unfounded, although this semi-documentary about the life of a Dartmouth naval cadet deserved a better fate. Peter Shaffer's *Battle of Shrivings* offered too verbose and intellectual a debate, and even the presence of Sir John Gielgud failed to save it.

Musicals and Multi-Plays

New musicals were scarce. The sentimental nostalgia and opulent settings of *The Great Waltz* with the lilting Strauss music admirably sung will fill Drury Lane for a long time to come. *1776*, an ambitious attempt at an original musical treatment of the American Declaration of Independence, had a fair run, but understandably failed to repeat its outstanding New York success. *Sing a Rude Song*, after playing to packed houses at Greenwich, failed to catch the West End public's fancy; it was a rather disappointing treatment of the Marie Lloyd story. A British counter-attack to *Hair*, called *Lie Down I Think I Love You*, despite all the trappings of multi-media presentation, amplified pop music, and the zest of its youthful cast, proved unoriginal and imitative.

In the past, shorter plays forming a composite bill have rarely proved popular. Perhaps taste is changing, for three enjoyed more than expected success in 1970—the Pinter double bill of *The Basement* and *The Tea Party*; John Mortimer's *Come As You Are*, a quartet of cameos of middle-aged sex in London; and Michael Frayn's first effort in London, *The Two*

Another London success was *Sleuth*, a thriller by Anthony Shaffer, twin brother of Peter Shaffer, one of the leading British playwrights. It starred Paul Rogers (right).

In *The Two of Us* (above) by Michael Frayn, Richard Briers and Lynn Redgrave played eleven parts between them in four playlets. *The Philanthropist*, a comedy by Christopher Hampton, starred Alec McCowen and Jane Asher (below).

of Us, in which Richard Briers and Lynn Redgrave played eleven parts between them.

The Classics

London can usually offer a selection of well-staged star-studded revivals: in 1970, Goldsmith's *She Stoops to Conquer*, Maugham's *Lady Frederick*, Noël Coward's *Blithe Spirit*, and Ibsen's *Wild Duck* proved the most successful. Of course, the perennial Shaw was also represented—by *Widowers' Houses* (Nottingham and Royal Court) and *The Apple Cart* and *Saint Joan* (Mermaid).

The National Theatre more than doubled its audience potential by taking over the Cambridge Theatre for some months, and enhanced its enviable reputation with Webster's *The White Devil*, a Simon Gray adaptation of Dostoevsky's *The Idiot*, *The Merchant of Venice*, *Hedda Gabler*, *The Beaux' Stratagem*, and *Cyrano*.

Unhappily the illness of director Sir Laurence Olivier caused radical changes in the company's programme. The Royal Shakespeare Company were again more successful with revivals (*The Revenger's Tragedy*, *London Assurance*, *The Winter's Tale*) than in finding new plays (*Tiny Alice* by Albee, *The Plebeians* by Grass, and *After Haggerty*). But the Royal Court had an outstanding year, transferring to the West End David Storey's *The Contractor* and *Home* (starring Gielgud and Richardson), *Three Months Gone* by Donald Howarth, and *The Philanthropist* by Christopher Hampton, the Court's "resident playwright".

Theatre in Australia

The event of the year in the Australian theatre was the Adelaide Festival of Arts, directed by Sir Robert Helpmann. Highlights among visiting companies were the R.S.C. in the controversial *The Winter's Tale* and the more sedate *Twelfth Night*, and the English Opera Group with Benjamin Britten and Peter Pears. The best local dramatic offering was Genet's *The Maids* at the adventurous semi-professional Theatre 62. The Sheridan Theatre mounted the only completely indigenous work, *Pacific Rape*, which was appropriate in concept during the Cook bicentenary year, but resembled a lecture rather than drama.

Australian writers received an airing by Jane Street Theatre, Sydney. Greatest success was *The Legend of King O'Malley*, a collaboration of a number of theatre people on the staff of the National Institute of Dramatic Art, based on the story of an American layabout adventurer of the turn of the century, and dealing with satire and hilarity with a slice of Australian history. A more ambitious undertaking was the re-enactment of the landing of Captain Cook at Botany Bay, part of the official celebrations witnessed by the Queen and the royal family.

Another new professional repertory company was established—the Queensland Theatre, Brisbane, directed by Alan Edwards. Its first full professional production was a new Australian musical, *A Rum Do*, based on the conflict between the notorious Rum Corps and Governor MacQuarie, a performance of which was also attended by the Queen, Prince Philip, and Princess Anne. The Melbourne Theatre Company steadily consolidated its position as the leading Australian company; by comparison Sydney's Old Tote seemed in the doldrums. Sir Tyrone Guthrie was injecting his revitalizing know-how into Australian theatre, and it is hoped that it will spread through the continent. Certainly, theatre building is accelerating—particularly in Brisbane, where three new theatres opened during the year.

Dancing into the New Decade

PETER WILLIAMS

Editor of *Dance and Dancers*

NO DECADE IN Britain's ballet history ever started with such a clear change in direction as the 1970s. The first months of the year showed that the consolidation and re-alignment recommended in the Arts Council's Opera and Ballet enquiry of 1969 were to become effective more quickly than anyone had imagined. The first sign of this came from the top—from the Royal Ballet. Long before Sir Frederick Ashton retired as artistic director in July 1970, and Kenneth MacMillan and John Field jointly took over from him, plans for a complete reorganization were announced.

Since the scheme did not take effect until the autumn of 1970, it is impossible to say how successful it will eventually turn out to be. Nevertheless, enough of the plan was in effect as the year ended for commentators to be able to assert that the Royal Ballet was moving in the only way that a company of its size and importance could move in the future. Under the new scheme the Royal Opera Ballet ceased to exist as a separate unit, and the Royal Ballet's Covent Garden and touring company were amalgamated. In operas which require dancing, Royal Ballet dancers will appear.

With all Royal Ballet activity based on London, the one company can now use all the talents, of dancers and repertory, that were previously dispersed between two companies. The new plan is more economically practical, since the cost of touring a large company incessantly through the regions has become astronomically expensive. The Royal Ballet has not ceased to tour the regions, but the main company, with full-length classics and larger works, will appear only in those regional cities which have theatres large enough to show such works properly. At the same time,

a group of about 25 dancers will tour the smaller regional stages in a more contemporary repertory needing smaller casts.

Royal Ballet's New Creations

With so much change ahead the Royal Ballet did not mount many new creations during the 1969–70 season, but those that it did—Rudi van Dantzig's *The Ropes of Time* and Ashton's *Lament of the Waves*—showed awareness of new forms. Curiously enough, in the years that Nureyev has been a permanent guest artist with the Royal Ballet no work has been created specially for him, but only for his partnership with Margot Fonteyn. The Dutch choreographer Rudi van Dantzig (also artistic director of the Dutch National Ballet) put this right. *The Ropes of Time*, with an electronic score by Jan Boerman and design by Toer van Schayk, is about the lonely struggle of man or artist to find his identity through the relentlessness of passing years. It is an abstract work in which the Traveller (Nureyev) becomes involved with Death (Monica Mason), Life (Diana Vere), and a large *corps de ballet* representing elements which encourage or hinder man's progress. It provided a magnificent role for Nureyev, who danced non-stop during the work's half-hour length.

Ashton's *Lament of the Waves* was virtually an extended *pas de deux* for two young dancers: Marilyn Trounson and Carl Myers. Following

At top of page: Rudolf Nureyev as the Traveller, with (left) Diana Vere as Life and (right) Monica Mason as Death, in *The Ropes of Time*, a work created for Nureyev by Rudi van Dantzig, which had its premiere at Covent Garden on March 2, 1970.

the implications of the music—Gérard Masson's tone poem *Dans le Deuil des Vagues 11* —Ashton gave his theme as "Two young lovers are drowned". Using a more contemporary dance vocabulary than in any of his previous works, Ashton again proved what a master he is of poetic movement.

Tribute to Sir Fred

The Royal Ballet's last performance in its old form at Covent Garden was a tribute to Sir Frederick Ashton. Devised by Michael Somes and John Hart, retiring assistant directors, with help from Leslie Edwards and a commentary written by William Chappell, the performance consisted of 37 extracts covering 40 years of Sir Frederick's creativity. The entire programme, compèred by Sir Robert Helpmann, was rehearsed in complete secrecy so that the recipient of the tribute would not know what was to happen (even the audience were not handed the programme until after the performance). The whole panorama of Ashton's many-sided genius was revealed in superb performances, beautifully arranged and presented by all the Covent Garden company—with Fonteyn appearing in no less than five different roles, and Nureyev in three. This occasion, probably one of the most exciting and moving in the Royal Ballet's history, showed how great has been Ashton's contribution not only to British ballet but to the whole international dance scene of the 20th century.

New Works by the "Little Royal"

In the last year of the Royal Ballet's touring section, the company managed to mount four new works and one distinguished revival. Geoffrey Cauley created *Symphonie Pastorale*, based on a story by André Gide to Martinu music, as well as adapting his *Lazarus* (origin-

ally created for the Royal Ballet Choreographic Group) for a larger stage. Neither work totally fulfilled the promise of this Royal Ballet dancer's early work, although the former provided a splendid opportunity for Alfreda Thorogood to show her dramatic ability. Another Royal Ballet dancer, David Drew, fared better with his *From Waking Sleep* which, although slightly obscure in theme (based on Buddhist philosophy), showed an intelligent awareness of choreographic construction in the relationship between a young man (Nicholas Johnson), his "awakening self" (Margaret Barbieri), and a *corps de ballet* of followers.

The other creation, the last one for the Royal Ballet's touring company, was Ashton's *Creatures of Prometheus*. This work was given in Bonn as part of the Beethoven bicentenary celebrations, and was not seen in Great Britain until the autumn (see page 161).

The distinguished revival was Ninette de Valois' *Job* which, though one of the first important British works to be created in the early 1930s, came up as fresh as when it was first given. The reason for this may well lie in the fact that, with the greater understanding of contemporary forms, the work is more in tune with today than it was with those pre-war years. It also has the benefit of Vaughan Williams's magnificent score; there is no doubt that ballets survive longest when they have music as fine as this still is.

Festival Ballet Successes

The London Festival Ballet will continue to tour the full-length classics throughout the British regions and abroad. With a certain

foresight, the company not only added a new production of *Coppélia* (revised by Jack Carter and designed by Peter Farmer) to its existing classics, but also mounted a full-length version of the Minkus *Don Quixote* (revised by Witold Borkowski in a more elaborate version of the interpretation he did some years ago for Ballet Rambert) during the company's London Coliseum season. As a splendid vehicle for Galina Samtsova, and André Prokovsky, *Don Quixote* still needs more revision and tightening-up, but it should eventually prove a valuable addition to the company's repertory.

In over 20 years of existence, Festival Ballet has mainly shown works that were created for other companies. A break came during 1970 when Ronald Hynd was commissioned to mount a work for the company's Barcelona season. This, *Dvorak Variations*, was a near-plotless work to Dvorak's *Symphonic Variations*, in which Hynd carried a most ingenious flow of movement through the various changes of mood in the 27 musical variations on a Czech folk theme. With this work Festival Ballet have created one of the most successful British abstract works since Ashton's *Symphonic Variations* for the Royal Ballet in 1946. They also produced one of the best revivals of Fokine's *Scheherazade* seen in Britain since the early years of the Diaghilev ballet.

Young Companies of the North

Promotion of regional ballet companies was one of the many developments for the arts in Britain encouraged by Jennie Lee (minister for the arts until the election of June 1970), and a metamorphosis by which the former Western Theatre Ballet became the Scottish Theatre

Ballet, based in Glasgow, was one fruit of her efforts. Another was the formation of Laverne Meyer's Northern Dance Theatre based in Manchester. Both new companies were seen in London during the summer of 1970.

Scottish Theatre Ballet is still directed by Peter Darrell, who is also responsible for choreographing the majority of new works. One of its first productions under its new title was an ambitious full-length ballet by Darrell based on Madame de Villeneuve's story *Beauty and the Beast*. The work was slightly uneven, but its best moments were very good indeed. It also had a very fine score by Thea Musgrave, one of the very few full-length ballet scores to be commissioned in Britain. This ballet together with Darrell's most recent creation, *Herodias*, were shown in London during their Sadler's Wells season. *Herodias* uses the human voice, declaiming Mallarmé's *Herodiade* poem over Hindemith's score of the same name. An interesting way of relating the biblical story— of Herod, Salome, and the beheading of John the Baptist—it nevertheless suffered from a lack of cohesion between its various elements. There was, however, no doubt about the excellence of Peter Docherty's imaginative and powerful designing. During 1970, Scottish Theatre Ballet had yet to relate its distinguished past repertory and achievements to its new surroundings, but doubtless this will happen soon.

Northern Dance Theatre, although only a year old, was already showing during 1970 that it has a firm conception of its place in the balletic scheme. Laverne Meyer did not attempt anything too ambitious or beyond the capabilities of his 10 dancers. The company is lucky to have two excellent young dancers in John Fletcher and Carol Barrett, who receive very capable support from the other eight. Of the

works shown in London at The Place, Meyer's *Brahms Sonata* and a revival of Frank Staff's *Peter and the Wolf* were outstanding.

Ballet Rambert Caters for Youth

The companies already mentioned are classically based, but the greatest ballet progress of the year was seen in the contemporary field. Ballet Rambert, although still mixing classical and contemporary techniques, is now moving more towards the latter. The great success of its London seasons proves that this direction is attracting the younger audience. In fact a new addition to the company's work, Bertram Batell's *Sideshow*, is directed towards children, although it was enjoyed equally by adults. This charming series of short works, mainly created by members of the company and designed by Peter Cazalet, was given with a great sense of fun, and enjoyed such success that it might have overshadowed the more serious work of the company had the latter not reached so tremendously high a standard. As the first major British company to produce a programme for junior audiences Ballet Rambert was building up its future adult audience.

Its adult repertoire now contains a new work from Norman Morrice, *Blind Sight*, to an impressive jazz score by Bob Downes. Another work from dancer Christopher Bruce, *Living Space*, for himself and Sandra Craig to words by Robert Cockburn, exploited the relation between movement and spoken word in a duet about a couple's intimate relationship which made effective theatre. Two couples in rather more obscure relationship were seen in John Chesworth's *Four According*, but this puzzling work was well danced and looked impressive in Cazalet's setting. The only non-company member to mount a work for Ballet Rambert during 1970 was Anna Sokolow, who revived her *Opus '65*. When created in New York in 1965, this work must have had great impact since it concerns youthful protest and unrest. In 1970 this seemed a rather hackneyed theme, although the dancing revealed how well integrated the company has become.

Cohan at The Place

The other major company in this category, Robert Cohan's London Contemporary Dance Theatre, has gone from strength to strength in its few years of existence. In the beginning it was a group of young dancers surrounding three stars of the Martha Graham company: Noemi Lapzeson, William Louther, and Robert Cohan (now its artistic director). The year proved once again that Robert Cohan has developed an exceptionally fine modern dance company, the repertory of which has been enriched by a number of new works. Outstanding in a year of great activity, including numerous workshop performances for young creators, was Cohan's *Cell*. Highly dramatic, this work—concerning fear of the unknown felt by a group of people in a confined space—was a smash hit, and was also given on BBC television.

Another interesting development has been the use of music by the modern British composer Peter Maxwell Davies. His *Vesalii Icones*—in which William Louther as solo dancer and choreographer interprets the Stations of the

A pose for the two couples in John Chesworth's puzzling work for Ballet Rambert, *Four According*, to music by Bacewitz, with design by Peter Cazalet.

Ballet Rambert; photo, Anthony Crickmay

The London Contemporary Dance Theatre produced *Cell*, a study in claustrophobic fear by Robert Cohan. These dancers are Noemi Lapzeson and William Louther.

London Contemporary Dance Theatre; photo, Elaine Bowman

Cross as seen through the anatomical engravings of the 16th-century artist Andreas Vesalius—is one of the most remarkable dance works of our time. Together with many other creations all wonderfully danced, these works have made The Place, off Euston Road, London, a power house of *avant garde* dance theatre in Europe.

On the educational level, Ballet for All continued its invaluable work by taking a demonstration ballet to places where larger companies cannot go. Not only is this educating the public with a new kind of theatre presentation, but it is also building up appreciation in the audiences of the future. Its most important creation during 1970 was to celebrate the centenary of the creation of *Coppélia* in a full-evening programme giving the history of the ballet and showing how it has changed through years of developing technique and attitude—from the first Paris Opéra performance through its revision in Russia to present-day Britain.

Stream of Visitors

The work of all these companies has restored Britain to its former status of world capital of the dance, and this was emphasized in 1970 by the number of foreign companies which came to London in a constant stream. In addition to smaller modern groups at The Place, Sadler's Wells received the Dutch National Ballet (with Nureyev as guest), Antonio Gades and his Spanish Ballet, the Polish State Ballet, the Polish Mime Theatre, the Paul Taylor Dance Company from America, the Kathakali Dance Company from India, and several others.

Sir Robert Helpmann as the eccentric Don, and Ray Powell as Sancho Panza, in Nureyev's production of *Don Quixote* by the Australian Ballet at the 1970 Adelaide Festival.
Australian Ballet; photo, Athol Smith & John Cato, Melbourne

American Ballet Theatre came to Covent Garden for a season, and the Leningrad State Kirov Ballet gave a six-week season at Festival Hall. Each of these companies had something to offer British ballet which will help to influence its dancing in the Seventies.

Ballet in Australia

The principal ballet attraction of the 1970 Adelaide Festival was undoubtedly Rudolf Nureyev's production of *Don Quixote*, in which he danced the principal male role, Basilio. Lucette Aldous was Kitri, and Sir Robert Helpmann played the title role of the Don. Basing the production on the one he knew when he was a member of the Kirov Ballet in Leningrad, Nureyev slightly changed the old Petipa classic so that it made a great deal more sense. To do this he altered the order of the scenes and also of the Minkus music (orchestrated by the Royal Ballet's musical director, John Lanchbery) so that there was a steady flow not only to the story but also to the way in which the dances emerge naturally from the situations in it. Although the greatest impact came from the three principals, the dancers of the Australian Ballet must share equally in this triumphant success.

It was easier to see the qualities of the company in programmes of shorter works. In a revival of Ashton's *Les Patineurs*, reproduced by Peggy van Praagh, Alan Alder gave a good account of himself as the twirling Blue Skater. In a revival of Balanchine's *Serenade*, a great test for any company, the dancers showed how well they had been trained to take on any kind of classical choreography; particularly good were Elaine Fifield, a former Royal Ballet dancer, and the promising young Australian Marilyn Rowe. In a rather different kind of work, Helpmann's *Hamlet*, the company gave impressive dramatic backing to Nureyev's moving performance in the title role, with young Josephine Jason as Ophelia.

Everything on display in Adelaide showed that in its eight-year life the Australian Ballet has built up a varied repertory which it can show with honour in any country in the world. Not only has it all the major classics in its repertoire, but also works by Anthony Tudor (*Pillar of Fire*), John Butler (*Threshold*), and Igor Moiseyev (*The Last Vision*), and others choreographed by Balanchine, Ashton, and Cranko. Australia is developing its own native choreographers, following the example of Helpmann, whose *Sun Music* is a popular addition to the Australian Ballet's programme. The company proved, during 1970, that they will be welcome guests on their next foreign tours—to America in 1971 and Europe in 1972.

Broadcasting in Britain

M. J. BRYDEN

Ian McKellen made his highly individual mark on television drama during 1970, with interpretations of such tortured introverts as Lawrence of Arabia and Richard II. Lawrence, attended by the faithful Hamed (David Spencer), appeared in BBC 1's October production of Terence Rattigan's *Ross*, while Shakespeare's tragedy was screened by BBC 2 in July.

PREDICTABLY THE furore that greeted the 1969 publication of the BBC's plans for the new decade, *Broadcasting in the Seventies*, continued unabated into 1970. The first two months of the new year saw a spate of letters in *The Times* criticizing the BBC's proposals for radio. Singled out for special comment was the plan to "unmix" programmes on all four radio channels. It had long been an axiom of public service broadcasting—endorsed by Reithian edict—that programmes on the same network should be planned in such a way as to lead the listener from one programme to others of a different type and quality. In other words, the BBC assumed an educational role, setting itself the task of expanding the listener's experience by stealthily introducing him to matters and forms that he might never have selected for himself.

The letters to *The Times* came from members of the High Table of King's College, Cambridge (including E. M. Forster); a mysterious and anonymous "well-known broadcaster"; and, above all, 134 London-based BBC programme planners and producers and 63 of their regional colleagues—all of whom breached staff regulations by criticizing the Corporation in public. The BBC rebels pointed out that virtually all serious musical broadcasts would be diverted to Radio 3 (the old Third Programme), thus rendering Radio 4 (the erstwhile Home Service) an all-speech service, apart from one Sunday night concert. Their letter stressed the importance they attached to the concept of mixed planning.

Replying to the rebels Charles Curran, BBC director general, questioned the sacrosanct nature of mixed programming by claiming:

Opposite: Among comic combinations appearing on British screens during the year were (left to right) the irrepressible Eric Morecambe and long-suffering Ernie Wise; Steptoe and Son (Wilfrid Brambell and Harry H. Corbett) whose winter series was allegedly their last; and the melancholy Peter Cook and the musical Dudley Moore.
Above: Situation comedy as served by Dad's Army (left) remained a family favourite, with (left to right) Pte. Walker (James Beck), Pte. Godfrey (Arnold Ridley), L/Cpl. Jones (Clive Dunn), Capt. Mainwaring (Arthur Lowe), and Pte. Frazer (John Laurie). Laughs were elicited from more sophisticated jaws by the surreal antics of Monty Python's Flying Circus (right), with (left to right) Graham Chapman, Eric Idle, John Cleese, Terry Jones, and Michael Palin.

"This theory depends on the assumption that people are prone to stay with a single network, whatever it offers. All our investigations show that this is true of television, but not radio. Most radio listeners either switch off or look for another programme. The radio audience is not captive."

"Newsak"

The most significant result of the April "unmixing" turned out to be an obsession with current affairs on Radio 4. Those listeners who defied BBC statisticians and remained "captive" to the only intelligible day-time service—eschewing the non-stop barrage of pop and light music on Radio 1 and 2—found themselves caught in the works of an insatiable news machine. A series of five news magazine programmes hogged the wavelength from dawn to closedown. Although punctuated by the odd talk, serial, play, panel game, and "straight" news bulletins and parliamentary reports, these five—*Today, World at One, P.M., News Desk,* and *World Tonight*—provided the regular programme pattern for the new Radio 4.

Thus the mainstream of middlebrow British culture was polluted by an unremitting flood of news, gathered, packaged, and relentlessly communicated by programmes deadeningly indistinguishable in tone and content. Indeed, since there is no Parkinson's Law of News—the genuine commodity does not always proliferate to fill the time allotted to reporting it—not only were the five repetitive in style but the same taped interviews and stories were apt to crop up again and again. This *newsak* pervaded the medium waveband during 1970, exuding

an unwholesome mixture of irreverence and portentousness after the manner of the chirpy archetype, William Hardcastle's *World at One.*

Modern moralists, eager to gauge the effect of the mass media on the luckless mass, often maintain that the constant juxtaposition of fact and fiction blurs the distinction between the two. Whatever the truth of this assertion, there can be no doubt that the Radio 4 style of magazine newsmongering—in which the grave and the whimsical are juxtaposed and the various items are apt to be interspersed with sudden bursts of frantic melody—can have a trivializing effect on the communication of serious affairs. An even greater tendency towards the unreal is caused by the format's need to cling to a theme in order to give each offering form and force. Slick packaging of news tends inevitably to overemphasize and distort, and the listening public is left with the disturbing impression that the significance of an event lies in its value as a commodity to be exploited by the media.

"Loaded" Reporting

Politicians are always quick to protest at any hint of "loaded" reporting on the air, but 1970 brought accusations of misrepresentation from non-political quarters, notably from Lord Stokes—complaining about an alleged anti-British bias in BBC programmes concerning the motor industry—and John Boulting, who complained publicly about the glib sacrifice of accuracy and objectivity for dramatic effect in an ATV documentary about the film industry. He had agreed to be interviewed for this programme on the understanding that it was to be a serious, responsible, and accurate

BBC 2 "classic" serials of 1970 included adaptations of Charlotte Bronte's *Villette* (above), starring Judy Parfitt and Peter Jeffrey, and Trollope's *The Way We Live Now* (below), with (left to right) Rachel Gurney, Irene Prador, and Colin Blakely.

Above: John Nolan (left) and John Bennett in a scene from BBC 2's serial adaptation of George Eliot's *Daniel Deronda*. Below: Alison Fiske and Michael Bryant in an episode from *The Roads to Freedom*, by Jean-Paul Sartre (BBC 2).

examination of the subject. The October showing of the programme, *The Celluloid Village of Dreams*, inspired the following from Mr. Boulting: "Masquerading as an objective truth, it was, in fact, a village idiot's view of a centre of industry. . . . Surely this sort of programme raises an issue of increasing urgency. Can it be said to be in the public's interest that an individual, or a group of individuals, controlling a vital communications medium should be permitted to use arbitrarily, and without the knowledge and agreement of those participating in the programme, excerpts of appearances before the camera in order to convey an impression which may emerge as a complete distortion of the truth?"

October saw another example of loaded reporting, this time on Radio 4's *World at One*. It was a harrowing interview with the unfortunate wife of an invalid husband with nine children to support. The report purported to show how the rise in National Health prescription charges threatened in Anthony Barber's "mini budget" would affect this particular family, and implied that its members would be forced to go without medicine as a result of the chancellor's swingeing measures. The reporter inferred, moreover, that the children had already had to go without medicines as a result of the previous administration's prescription charges. After this heart-rending report was over it fell to link-man William Hardcastle to announce what all reasonably informed people must have known: that children and certain classes of the chronically sick are exempt from prescription charges anyway.

Angry Asians

It was this sort of broadcasting that gave rise to repeated calls from politicians and others for a Broadcasting Council, similar to the Press Council but with sharper teeth. Happily these suggestions went unheeded, but the danger remained that shoddy newsmongering could lead not merely to the sapping of public confidence in the veracity of radio and television journalism—as had happened in the U.S.A.—but to the advent of some form of subtle political censorship.

The sort of encroachment upon the freedom of broadcasters that can result from a political reaction to what is believed to be loaded reporting was illustrated by the Indian government's response to the showing on BBC 2 of an excellent travel series, *Louis Malle's India*. On August 7, the Indian high commissioner wrote to the BBC to say that the Malle series was "repugnant to good taste and a distortion of a great country", and asked for the series to be stopped. The BBC refused, and on August 27 was forced to close its New Delhi office, while Ronald Robson, its South Asia correspondent, was sent packing. The BBC had made it clear that M. Malle's programmes were highly personal and no more than a series of subjective film essays, while the Indian government had, allegedly, not seen the films and had acted on complaints received from Indian journalists in London. Moreover, French television had previously shown the series without giving offence.

On the same day as the BBC New Delhi office was closed Indian customs officials entered a Calcutta hotel and seized unexposed film from a Thames Television team operating in the city for the *This Week* programme. This somewhat hysterical and arbitrary Indian reaction to Western, particularly British, documentary film makers had its roots in a genuine belief, held by most educated Indians, that the image of India in the West had been constantly distorted by a tendency for film makers to dwell on slums, plagues, disasters, and starvation.

Commercial Break

The advent of a Conservative administration in June, armed with a pledge to introduce commercial radio, focused attention on the BBC's costly experiment with local radio and the fate of the 40 proposed BBC local radio stations—eight of which were already broadcasting and 12 more scheduled to start soon. Matters were clarified by an announcement from Christopher Chataway, the new minister of posts and telecommunications, that plans for a commercial radio network were to go ahead and that a government white paper outlining the scheme would be published early in 1971. On August 6, Chataway revealed that Britain is to have a mixed system of both commercial and public service local stations. The first 20 of the proposed 40 BBC stations would be retained; thus the launching of the 12 new ones (Birmingham, Blackburn, Bristol, Chatham, Derby, Hull, London, Manchester, Middlesbrough, Newcastle, Oxford, and Southampton) was not held up, and the first, Bristol, duly began broadcasting on September 4, followed by Radios London, Manchester, Birmingham, Medway (Chatham), Teesside (Middlesbrough), and Solent (Southampton), by the end of the year.

A groundswell of groans from all involved in the 15 British commercial television companies echoed dimly down the year, intensified by sudden bursts of wailing and the gnashing of executive dentures as individual TV moguls bemoaned the meagre profits of an industry that had once boasted it had a "licence to print money". Since the reshuffling of contracts in

1968 the ITV companies had faced, without flinching, a constant rattle of critical fire over their cynical failure to honour their lofty pre-contract pledges. Less easy to brush aside was the exchequer levy on their advertising revenues that bit deep into profits at a time of rising production expenses and the astronomical cost of conversion to colour. So grim were the financial prospects, particularly for the small companies, that when a two-year extension of contracts until 1976 (when the Television Act ends) was announced in January 1970, the news was faced by the companies in a spirit of resignation rather than rejoicing.

Frank Finlay and Gemma Jones in the best of BBC 1's "Play for Today" series, *The Lie*, by Ingmar Bergman—screened throughout Europe as a "Biggest Theatre in the World" production.

On March 16 the government threw a considerable sop to the companies by cutting the levy by some £6 million a year and altering the levy's sliding scale so that small companies making less than £2 million a year were exempt. This timely tax relief brought about an immediate battle between the companies and the TV employees' trade union over how the cash should be spent. The employees demanded an end to economy cuts (which included the cutting of 90-minute plays to 60 minutes and the closure of small news studios such as that of Grampian in Edinburgh), but the companies remained adamant that programme budgets could not be increased.

The Association of Cinematograph, Television, and Allied Technicians were still seething from this rebuff when it was announced—during their annual conference in April—that the new director general of the ITA was to be a certain Brian Young—a name unknown to the assembled delegates. Their tempers were scarcely mollified by the information that the new ITA boss was an erstwhile headmaster of Charterhouse and a director of the Nuffield Foundation, and his appointment was greeted with heavy irony. Despite mutinous murmuring concerning his lack of broadcasting experience, the ex-pedagogue succeeded the retiring Sir Robert Fraser in October.

Meanwhile the plight of the 10 small regional companies continued desperate despite the March levy cut. To add insult to injury, the five network companies were failing to give the small companies their share of the national network, and considerable friction was generated between the "big five" and the "tiny ten". This was highlighted in July by the "big five's" boycott of Channel TV's 45-minute colour documentary *The Bitter Years*, made to mark a solemn event—the 25th anniversary of the liberation of the Channel Islands from German occupation—designed for the whole network.

Another small company, Border TV—based on Carlisle and covering much of southern Scotland and Northumberland as well as Cumberland, Westmorland, and the Isle of Man—announced on August 25 that it had been forced to drop its plans for colour. National network programmes will, of course, be transmitted in colour when it becomes available in the area in late 1971. Prevailing economic pressures combined with technical problems associated with the introduction of UHF led to the first British TV merger—announced on August 20—when Yorkshire (one of the "big five") and Tyne-Tees formed a joint holding company. They continued to operate as separate companies despite the merger, as the licences had been granted to the individual companies and not to the new parent.

These events occurred during a year in which the Prices and Incomes Board were busily examining the whole economic structure of ITV. On October 29, 1970, they issued a shock report recommending a reduction in the number of companies and an ITA "early warning sys-tem" for those companies considered to be performing unsatisfactorily. The PIB also expressed doubts on "the joint viability" of the two London contractors (Thames and London Weekend) sharing the week between them. To rub salt into these wounds, no recommendation for the abolition of the levy was forthcoming, despite vocal campaigning by ITV. It was thus hardly surprising that the report was attacked, derided, and refuted by the companies. Nevertheless, it is bound to be consulted when current contracts end.

Broadcasting in Australia

August 12, 1970, saw an angry meeting of some 400 Australian television actors, writers, producers, and technicians protesting that British and American programmes were swamping Australian screens. Meeting in Sydney, the TV workers urged the Federal government to consider creating an organization to sell Australian programmes overseas, and also to enforce the Broadcasting and Television Act's section 114, which requests the employment of Australian artists, writers, musicians, and technicians in local television. These resolutions were put to the meeting by officers of the various Australian unions and guilds catering for those creatively involved in television. A joint statement issued by this combination declared: "The Australian television industry is staging a massive fight for more time on Australian networks." The statement went on to criticize the way the Australian Broadcasting Control board made up the overall 50 per cent Australian content required by law, which was, it claimed, "composed of cheap day-time programmes, football, news broadcasts, quiz shows, amateur talent, boxing, and wrestling".

While this row rumbled a number of technical breakthroughs marked the Australian year. On February 20 Australia received its first live television relay from Britain via a new $A4 million satellite communications earth station built at Ceduna, a little port on South Australia's coast. A joint production by the ABC and the BBC marked the opening of Ceduna, Australia's fourth satellite earth station. The British contribution—a 15-minute news programme—was transmitted from London to Goonhilly, Cornwall, and then beamed to an Intelsat III satellite in orbit 22,300 miles over the Indian Ocean. The satellite received the Goonhilly signals, amplified them, and retransmitted them to the 97-ft. disc-shaped antenna at Ceduna, where guests at the reception enjoyed the programme in colour. The rest of the Australian viewing public had to be content with black and white.

David Frost (right) appeared perplexed as one of his L.W.T. chat-shows was reduced to chaos by a horde of "yippies" led by Jerry Rubin (extreme left, standing) in November.

BOB DAWBARN

End of an Era in Pop?

The death on September 18, 1970, of Jimi Hendrix robbed the pop scene of a creative genius.

THE DECADE of popular music which produced the Beatles and the Rolling Stones will probably go down in history as the "Super Sixties". The next ten years may well become known as the "Confused Seventies", if we can judge it by the way both pop and jazz seemed to splinter into a dozen different directions during 1970.

There was still a little "teenybopper pop", aimed at the younger teenagers, although this was a market that continued to shrink throughout the year. There were more attempts, by the more intellectual pop musicians, to come closer to jazz at one end of the spectrum and to the classics at the other. But, generally speaking, the only real growth area in popular music seemed to be in what was loosely termed "Progressive Pop". This was the rock-based pop—aggressive, often complex music—aimed largely at the student population.

Importance of the College Circuit

It was, in fact, the universities and colleges which kept the groups in work throughout 1970. As the more successful musicians priced themselves out of the clubs and there was a decline in concert audiences, the colleges became more and more dominant as a rich source of work. The college circuit continued to produce its own set of heroes, with some curious results. Probably the most successful group in Great Britain throughout the year was Led Zeppelin. They could demand £1,500 or more for a single appearance at a university, and to the pop student population they were the biggest thing since the Beatles. Like so many British groups over the past two or three years, Led Zeppelin had first found acceptance in the U.S.A. before acquiring a reputation in their native country.

The Finances of Festivals

Various economic squeezes probably had much to do with the decline in popularity of pop as a whole. Record sales were down, and most of the festivals were financial disasters. Following the huge success of the 1969 Isle of Wight Festival, when Bob Dylan topped the bill, innumerable promoters—large and small, some experienced and some utterly new to music promotion—announced festivals ranging from three- and four-day events with fantastically expensive bills to one-day affairs on the local football pitch. Almost without exception they failed to draw the expected public. One reason was a lack of genuine big-name attractions. The same few names appeared over and over again around the country; Ginger Baker's Airforce, for example, seemed as necessary for a festival as hot-dog stands and rain.

Even the 1970 Isle of Wight Festival itself was reported to have lost vast sums of money, although early estimates of the extent of the disaster seem to have been rather wildly overstated. Part of the Isle of Wight Festival's problems stemmed from the fact that the promoters had not realized that a near-by hillside would allow many thousands to hear and see what went on without paying the entrance fee. Partly, too, they had to face an influx of "anarchists" and others, mostly from outside Britain, who broke down fences and demanded that the festival should be free for all.

Departures from the Scene

The greatest loss to pop music during the year was surely the death of Jimi Hendrix, an erratic genius who had exercised enormous influence on the course of pop music over the past five years. He was the first successfully to translate the old, original blues into the electronic terms of today's pop. Undoubtedly a brilliant musician, he inspired thousands of guitarists to search for new sounds and new ways of expressing old chord sequences.

The death of Hendrix was followed by that of another significant performer, Janis Joplin. Despite her habit of using on stage language

Led Zeppelin ousted the Beatles from their position as top group, in both the British and the international sections of the 1970 *Melody Maker* poll. Left to right: John Bonham, Robert Plant, singer Sandy Denny, and Jimmy Page. Robert was also voted best British male singer, and Sandy best British girl singer.

which would have shocked the average docker, she had genuine talent as a singer, and was the first of the white girl singers to show that "soul" was not necessarily a prerogative of negroes. Al Wilson, the quiet bass-guitarist with Canned Heat, was another whose death left pop music the poorer.

Beatles and Stones

In another sense, perhaps the greatest loss to pop was the death not of an individual but of a group—the greatest group of them all. The Beatles, it seems certain, will never appear in public as a unit again, and it remains doubtful if they will even get together again for recording purposes.

They had survived a long time for a group— seven years—and the break-up had been seen

"Soul" singer Janis Joplin, who died at the age of 27 on October 4, 1970, in Hollywood.

for some time to be inevitable. John Lennon and Paul McCartney, the guiding geniuses of the Beatles, had been growing farther and farther apart, both musically and intellectually. John became an espouser of "causes" while Paul, once the most gregarious of the foursome, preferred the privacy of married life. Ringo had long since ceased to worry about the music business, beyond making an occasional record of nostalgic ballads. George Harrison, like John and Paul, wanted to go his own way. It is possible that the break-up may have beneficial consequences. Certainly John and Paul, in particular, have such strong and individual musical personalities that they are bound to come up with something new and worth while from time to time.

The Rolling Stones, as always, continued to cause controversy although making little music. Mick Jagger concentrated chiefly on his new career as a film actor—a career which promised to be as controversial as his old one when he was cast as the Australian folk-hero the outlaw Ned Kelly.

Splitting Groups

Another fine group which decided to call it a day while at the height of their corporate powers was the Nice. Their leader and organist Keith Emmerson re-emerged during the year with two new colleagues as Emmerson, Lake and Palmer, otherwise billed as 'ELP. After several years of hard struggle round the club circuit, the Taste, from Ireland, also decided to split, just when they had broken through to become one of the big hits at the festivals

Another big star who did the unexpected was Eric Clapton, for long idolized as Britain's best pop guitarist, and a writer of pop history as a member of the Cream. While most of the big names of British pop priced themselves out of the range of the clubs, Eric first went on tour as a member of the backing group for the American duo Delaney and Bonnie. He then formed his own rock group under the title of Derek and the Dominoes, with which he played many of the country's smaller clubs. His former Cream colleague, drummer Ginger Baker, somehow managed to keep together a bunch of individual stars under the name of Airforce, a unit of varying size but constant excitement which, as already indicated, was on show at most of the year's festivals.

Perhaps the oddest phenomenon of the year was the mixing of pop music with the occult. Groups like Black Sabbath and Black Widow produced stage acts which were nearer to meetings of a witches' coven in the forest than to the old type of group presentation. Needless to say, this gimmick soon began to wear rather thin as more and more groups jumped on to the bandwagon.

Emergence of Jazz-Rock

Deep Purple, under the guidance of organist Jon Lord, were among those groups which moved towards classical music, and presented various original works in combination with large orchestras. Others, like Ginger Baker and the experimental Soft Machine, moved closer to the more avant-garde forms of jazz. In fact, so many pop groups were using a high degree of improvisation it became almost impossible to tell where pop ended and jazz started.

The move was two-way. A number of authentic jazzmen turned towards pop and produced what came to be known as "jazz-rock". Among them were Lifetime, which comprised Miles Davis's former drummer Tony Wilson, jazz organist Larry Young, and the brilliant British guitarist John McLaughlin who had also worked with Davis in New York. Some historians even claimed that Davis himself was now leading a rock group, but the attribution seemed somewhat doubtful when judged by his recordings and by his appearance at the Isle of Wight Festival.

Miles Davis, acknowledged a king among jazz trumpeters, appeared at the 1970 Isle of Wight Festival.
Melody Maker photo

Two more jazzmen, tenor saxist Dick Morrissey and guitarist Terry Smith, after years of scratching a meagre living in the jazz clubs, found success with their "jazz-rock" group If, both in Great Britain and in the U.S.A. It will be surprising if more jazzmen do not follow their example. The British jazz scene offers few opportunities to earn a living. Ronnie Scott's remains the only internationally famous club operating in London, and even this largely depends on visiting American stars to make it an economic proposition.

Jazz Finds a Third Force

One of the problems has been the splitting of jazz itself. Formerly there were traditional jazz and modern jazz. Now there is also avant-garde jazz which, while appealing to younger listeners, has difficulty in finding sympathetic promoters. Many of the best of the British avant-garde musicians have had to find much of their work on the Continent. Some, indeed, have gone to live there permanently. Others, like Tony Oxley, Howard Riley, Mike Westbrook, and Graham Collier, struggle on in Britain. Oddly enough, their record sales are quite good, although their opportunities for personal appearances remain few and far apart.

On the traditional jazz scene the older names remained the biggest draws—Alex Welch, Chris Barber, Ken Colyer, Acker Bilk among them. One of the happiest sights of the year was the appearance of Louis Armstrong on stage in London for a charity concert, after his long illness. Louis, who celebrated his 70th birthday on July 4, blew only a few choruses on trumpet, but sang nine songs and proved that his personality was as powerful as ever.

Jazz Expo, the week of concerts which has become a major event in the London jazz calendar, justified its lack of imagination in sticking to old, established names by drawing full houses almost every night to hear such performers as Dave Brubeck, the Modern Jazz Quartet, and Oscar Petersen.

Altogether, 1970 was a strange, indefinable year in pop music and jazz. Perhaps it was merely a pause before some new and wonderful pop craze breaks upon us and carries us tapping our feet through the rest of the Seventies.

RECORDS THAT TOPPED THE HIT PARADE IN 1970

Song	Artist	Weeks
Two Little Boys	Rolf Harris	4 weeks
Reflections of my Life	Marmalade	1 week
Love Grows	Edison Lighthouse	3 weeks
I Want You Back	Jackson 5	1 week
Wand'rin' Star	Lee Marvin	3 weeks
Bridge over Troubled Water	Simon and Garfunkel	4 weeks
Spirit in the Sky	Norman Greenbaum	4 weeks
Back Home	England World Cup Squad	1 week
Yellow River	Christie	3 weeks
In the Summertime	Mungo Jerry	4 weeks
All Right Now	Free	3 weeks
The Wonder of You	Elvis Presley	5 weeks
Tears of a Clown	Smokey Robinson and the Miracles	2 weeks
Band of Gold	Freda Payne	5 weeks
Black Night	Deep Purple	1 week
Woodstock	Matthews Southern Comfort	3 weeks
Indian Reservation	Don Fardon	1 week
I Hear You Knocking	Dave Edmunds	2 weeks
When I'm Dead and Gone	McGuinness Flint	2 weeks

The young, rebellious, off-beat mood of the cinema in 1970 is reflected in these scenes from films of the year. Left: the forces of law and order clash with radical university students in *The Strawberry Statement*. Right: a hilarious moment in the black comedy, *M*A*S*H*, set in a mobile army hospital in the Korean War. In the facing page are (left) Glenda Jackson and Jennie Linden in the highly praised screen version of D. H. Lawrence's novel, *Women in Love*; and the young French-Canadian actress Genevieve Bujold who played Anne Boleyn opposite Richard Burton as Henry VIII in *Anne of the Thousand Days*.

Youth Calls the Tune in the

Above: one of the quieter scenes in Antonioni's puzzling and revolutionary film, *Zabriskie Point*, shot in California without a script, and the Italian director's first film since *Blow-Up*. Below: *John and Mary* meet when Dustin Hoffman interrupts a conversation at Mia Farrow's table.

TYPICAL OF THE SHIFT that the film studios made during 1970 was a publicity slogan about the latest campus-revolution film: "Today's generation lay it on the line!" The back-office moguls, plagued by rising costs and falling receipts, fastened on to the fact that the hard core of cinema audiences is made up of the under-35 age group. As a result there was a marked decrease in the number of star-orientated romances and epics that have for so long been the screen's staple fare. The studios put out several completely nonconformist and even revolutionary films intended to appeal to young people in revolt against the standards of contemporary society. Every major company produced its off-beat "minority", "protest" film in the hope of making a killing.

The film above all that brought about this reappraisal was *Easy Rider*. Made for about £200,000, it attracted capacity audiences all over America and western Europe, and is expected to bring a total profit of £6 million. It was a lyrical, beautifully photographed film, which showed how the American dream has gone sour. Two drug-running hippies motorcycle across the United States, their humanity and tolerance contrasting with the ignorance and brutality of the small-town southern American. Another film distinguished for its fine camera-work and for its gentle gaiety was *Butch Cassidy and the Sundance Kid*. Again two

Cinema

K. E. LOWTHER

friends, this time bank robbers, travel the U.S.A. swapping wisecracks. "What happened to the old bank? It was beautiful," says Butch, sympathetically played by Paul Newman, as he finds it firmly bolted and shuttered. The film shared with *Easy Rider* and the earlier *Bonnie and Clyde* a climax of extreme violence and a tendency to glamorize the drop-outs from society.

Even more directly aimed at the young market was the film of the 1969 Woodstock pop festival, *Woodstock*, "3 days of peace, music . . . and love". Edited down from 120 hours of film, it used split-screen techniques and stereo, but to the non-aficionado it was ultimately exhausting. At least it did not patronize the young, unlike *The Strawberry Statement*, which, in attempting to portray the radical revolutionary mood in some of America's universities, too often lapsed into commercial cliché. Similarly compromising ultimately was *The Buttercup Chain*, in which four young people come together in a swinging permissive foursome, but two of them (first cousins born of twin mothers!) marry to legalize a prospective baby. Student protest received fairly sympa-

thetic treatment in *Getting Straight*, with Elliott Gould as an experienced radical who cannot avoid participating in the campus revolution.

From M*A*S*H to Flesh

One of the most ecstatically and perhaps extravagantly praised films of the year was *M*A*S*H*, directed by Robert Altman. It fully exemplified the new irreverent approach to some of the sacred cows of society. A hilarious, blasphemous black comedy set in a mobile army surgical hospital during the Korean War, it was regarded as anti-war, but was rather anti-army. The officers refuse to behave other than as civilians; their life outside the incredibly gory hospital wards is devoted principally to "making" the nurses. There are many very funny throw-away lines and the humour is engagingly zany. But in general the film was perhaps slightly overrated, and it was fortunate to win the first prize at the Cannes film festival.

Catch 22, from Joseph Heller's brilliant bestseller, took a similar attitude to the army, but was less successful. Mike Nichols, director of the enormously successful *The Graduate*, spent 15 million dollars on a film that has some very funny scenes and some fine individual performances, but is in general sprawling and uncontrolled. It tried to appeal to everyone: indeed, a spokesman for the distributors said, "It carries a message that appeals to everyone and particularly the 18 to 25 year olds."

Perhaps the most serious of all the "protest" films was *Medium Cool*, a work of high integrity made on a very small budget by Haskell Wexler. Shot in Chicago at the time of the Democratic party convention riots, it questions the role of the mass media by showing a cameraman's conscience stirred by the injustices he photographs.

One of the most discussed and highly praised films of the year was Ken Russell's *Women in Love*. It was described as being a film about D. H. Lawrence's novel rather than of it, but it had many memorable and superbly photographed moments. The frank love-making scenes, and the nude wrestling match by firelight between Birkin (played by Alan Bates) and Crick (played by Oliver Reed), pushed farther back the bounds of permissiveness.

A rather fatuous attempt was made to arrest this process in February. Three minutes before the end of a showing of *Flesh*, made by the best known "underground" film-maker Andy Warhol, a small army of police raided the Open Space Theatre in London, seized the film, the projector, and the screen, and took names and addresses. After some days it was decided that no further action should be taken, and showings of the film were resumed. Several M.P.s protested at this action against a film of which John Trevelyan, secretary of the Board of British Film Censors, had said he could see "no objection to its being shown to specialized audiences . . . under club conditions". The Open Space is a club. Another film by Warhol, *Lonesome Cowboys*, was a spoof Western. All the cowboys were homosexual, continually worrying about clothes and hairstyles, while the sheriff wore a black bikini. In December Mr. Trevelyan resigned. He said he was tired of the cinematic emphasis on sex and hoped more family films would be made.

New Film Categories

From July 1, the Board of British Film Censors applied new categories to films. The old X (over 16), A (under 16 if accompanied by an adult), and U (universal) were scrapped and replaced by X, AA, A, and U. Films with an X certificate may be seen only by those over 18. Films with an AA certificate are for the over-14s. The A certificate is purely advisory, suggesting that a film is more suitable for the over-14s. The U category is unchanged. A result of the raising of the X-film age limit is that the Board will be able to grant an X certificate for some films that would previously have been banned or cut. The new arrangement brings Great Britain into line with most other European countries.

The Greater London Council opposed the introduction of the new categories. It was the first to grant a certificate to Joseph Strick's film of Henry Miller's notorious *Tropic of Cancer*. As with the director's previous film, *Ulysses*, the Board of British Film Censors refused to give their imprimatur to what many regard as a tedious farrago of nudity and four-letter words. But Cinecenta in London at once booked it for all their four cinemas.

The European Directors

Most of the leading European film-makers produced notable films during the year. The most widely shown was Antonioni's *Zabriskie Point*. This vision of America with a revolutionary hero pitted against it had a mixed reception. It was certainly not as popular as *Blow Up*, but visually it was perhaps Antonioni's most beautiful film. It gained notoriety for its scene of mass love-making in a canyon. But it was a serious indictment of materialist society, contrasting it with the idealism of young love. As in so many recent films, the hero dies a violent death at the hands of the police.

Luchino Visconti's contribution, *The Damned*, was set in the last days of the Weimar republic in Germany. It was a flamboyant film that dissected the emotional lives of the members of a German munitions dynasty. Although suffering from overstatement, it vividly portrayed the corruption and decadence of the period with its parade of homosexuality, transvestism, and brutality. Dirk Bogarde starred in the film, as he does, along with Silvana Mangano, in Visconti's *Death in Venice*.

Pier Pasolini's highly symbolic *Pigsty* portrayed a German industrialist's son who had, literally, a passion for pigs. The animals he loved finally tore him apart and ate him. Interwoven with this theme as a kind of counterpoint was the story of a band of cannibalistic robbers.

Federico Fellini's version of Petronius's *Satyricon* (written about A.D. 60) gave a keyhole view of imperial Rome. The film had great visual power, presenting haunting images as

Encolpius and his friend Ascyltus made their way from brothel to Trimalchio's feast, from galley to the Minotaur's pit. It was typical if not vintage Fellini.

Robert Bresson's first film in colour, *A Gentle Creature* (Une Femme Douce), was, like all his work, technically faultless. But many found it austere and chilly. It began with the suicide of a young wife, and then followed the husband's anguished reconstruction of their courtship, marriage, and quarrels.

The Gloss of Hollywood

In spite of its new-found concentration on youth, Hollywood's image has not changed beyond recognition. The year saw some excellent "entertainment" films made with the inimitable gloss and professionalism of the California dream city. It was a thin year for musicals. But the Lerner and Loewe musical *Paint Your Wagon* was sharp and funny; Lee Marvin and Clint Eastwood starred in it. *Bob and Carol and Ted and Alice* was a good example of the witty, mildly satirical type of film. It concerned itself with the impact of the permissive society and free love on two middle-aged bourgeois couples with hippy aspirations. John Mortimer wrote the brilliant script for *John and Mary*, a sensitive film that starred Dustin Hoffman and Mia Farrow; it showed a single day in the lives of two vulnerable but knowledgeable young New Yorkers. *The Boys in the Band* has been described as Oscar Wilde in drag; this Broadway play translated well on to the screen. Billy Wilder's *The Private Life of Sherlock Holmes* annoyed Holmes devotees, but was often witty and even moving.

It was not a vintage year for thrillers. Alfred Hitchcock's *Topaz*, set during the 1962 Cuban missile crisis, was not up to the master's best. It was rather rambling, although it did have sequences of true Hitchcock brilliance, as when the camera prowled about while a woman stared into the eyes of the man who was about to kill her. The latest James Bond film, *On Her Majesty's Service*, lacked tension—and gadgetry. George Lazenby, the new Bond, did not have Sean Connery's charisma, but the ski chase was brilliantly photographed. Probably the best thriller of the year was *The Sicilian Clan* by the French director Henri Verneuil, starring Jean Gabin and Alain Delon as a family gang leader and a Corsican outsider. The film handled well the deteriorating relations between the two as they planned and executed a daring jewel robbery.

Hollywood gave us a number of strong dramas, as usual well acted. *They Shoot Horses, Don't They?* was a harrowing film about one of the marathon dance contests held during the depression era. Jane Fonda played the tough and ruthless Gloria. Elia Kazan directed the film version of his own novel, *The Arrangement*, in which Kirk Douglas gave a memorable portrayal of a man disintegrating under pressures from the outside world and from within himself. *Tell Them Willie Boy is Here* was an austere film about an Indian rejected by both his own people and the whites. Implacably pursued by a sheriff, he and his girl friend flee to the wilderness to preserve their love—and die. *Watermelon Man* had an unusual theme. A white man wakes up one day to find himself black. As a white man, he was a rather unsympathetic, slightly anti-negro commuter. The results of his colour change are brilliantly and logically worked out by director Melvin van Peebles, himself blind. MGM staked its future on *Ryan's Daughter*, a 3-hour film set in Ireland. Critics gave it a cool reception.

War Films Soldiered On

Even after 25 years, there was no sign of an end to the flood of war films. 1970 was an

Left to right in this and the facing page: Dirk Bogarde and Ingrid Thulin in Luchino Visconti's film of decadence in pre-Hitler Germany, *The Damned*; Lee Marvin in his first "singing" role in *Paint Your Wagon*; Mick Jagger of the Rolling Stones as the Australian outlaw hero of *Ned Kelly*; and Sir Alec Guinness's brilliant portrayal of King Charles I in *Cromwell*.

average year. George C. Scott gave a towering performance as the war-obsessed crusader General Patton in *Patton: Lust for Glory*. Patton dwarfed all the other characters including Montgomery, who was caricatured as a peacock by Michael Bates. In Stanley Kramer's *The Secret of Santa Vittoria* Anthony Quinn played his usual wild and heroic resistance fighter, this time hiding bottles of wine from the Germans. *Kelly's Heroes* was the mixture as before; this time a group of G.I.s penetrated behind the German lines to rob a bank of a vast quantity of bullion.

Director Robert Aldrich and a strong cast including Michael Caine made an exciting film of *Too Late the Hero*, the story of an attempt to knock out a radio transmitter in a Japanese army camp. But the war epic of the year was undoubtedly *Tora! Tora! Tora!* Directed by Richard Fleischer at a cost of 25 million dollars, it described the events leading up to the Japanese attack on Pearl Harbor in 1941, and culminated in a brilliant reconstruction of the actual raid. The film was made in an unusual way. One half was shot in Japan with Japanese director, actors, and crew. The other half Fleischer directed in America and Hawaii. He then intercut the two sides of the story. The result was considerably more absorbing than the average war film.

The year was mercifully short of historical epics. *Anne of the Thousand Days* gave us $2\frac{1}{2}$ hours of quarrelling and lusting between Anne Boleyn and Henry VIII played by Richard Burton. *Cromwell*, directed by Ken Hughes, was a much better film. Richard Harris presented Cromwell as a heroic figure, and Alec Guinness was convincing as Charles I, complete with stammer and Scottish accent. The battle scenes were impressive.

The Screen in Britain

Shakespeare did not do too well in 1970. An American production of *Julius Caesar* was badly cast, apart from John Gielgud as Caesar. Tony Richardson's *Hamlet* was interesting because of Nicol Williamson's proletarian Hamlet and Marianne Faithfull's delicate Ophelia. But the film betrayed its stage origins. British films, in fact, had a moderate year. Christopher Miles's *The Virgin and the Gypsy* caught the sensuality of Lawrence's short story very well and deserved the praise it received. *The Magic Christian* was a smoothly made satire on British capitalist society, starring Peter Sellers, Ringo Starr, Spike Milligan, and the usual British character actors. Many of them reappeared in Richard Lester's *The Bed Sitting Room*, a scarcely recognizable adaptation of the extremely funny stage play by Milligan and John Antrobus. In

Entertaining Mr. Sloane, which followed Joe Orton's play fairly faithfully, Peter McEnery exactly caught Sloane's faunlike quality. Inevitably three new *Carry On* films delighted packed audiences: they were *Carry on Again, Doctor, Carry On Up the Jungle*, and *Carry On Loving*. The titles were self-explanatory and the jokes a little bluer, and they made a lot of money. Mick Jagger fulfilled all expectations by failing to carry off the role of the outlaw hero in *Ned Kelly*. Tony Richardson caught the feeling of the Australian outback impressively in an otherwise disappointing film.

An independent film that was taken off the shelf at the insistence of many critics was the charming *Kes*. Kenneth Loach shot this story of a boy and his pet kestrel on location in Barnsley. After a considerable interval it received its première in Doncaster. The distributors were worried about the northern accents used by all the actors, but after another three months' delay it opened in the West End and eventually got a limited release.

As Christmas approached, Mr. Trevelyan got his wish and U films appeared in time for family holiday visits to the cinema. Best of all was *Scrooge*, a musical version of Dickens's *Christmas Carol* with Albert Finney as the miser and Kenneth More, Edith Evans, and Alec Guinness in other leading parts. *The Song of Norway*, a film version of a popular stage musical presenting a fictional story of Edvard Grieg, the Norwegian composer, was a rather lifeless but, of course, tuneful film, with among others, Harry Secombe (in the unlikely part of Norway's great poet and dramatist Björnson). The first effort at direction by the British comic actor Lionel Jeffries—a film version of E. Nesbit's classic, *The Railway Children*—was a well-timed Christmas attraction and an immediate success.

David Bradley and his kestrel in the Yorkshire film *Kes*.

and Haston to subsist on porridge for some days before reaching the summit. There they arrived, suitably offhand and laconic, on June 2. Some indication of the activity in the Himalayas during 1970 (following the relaxation of restrictions by Pakistan and Nepal) was given by footprints already implanted on Annapurna's crest by the combined Nepalese and British Army expedition, led by Captain Henry Day, that had followed Herzog's route and arrived at the summit two weeks before. The south-face success was tempered by tragedy. Ian Clough was killed by a falling 1,000-ton pillar of ice only days before the climbers left the mountain. He was buried at the base camp in full view of the south face.

Daredevil Descents

Japanese climbers were especially prominent among the Himalayan peaks during 1970. A team from the Japan Alpine club tackled Everest by the unclimbed south-west face. Despite their efforts this face remained unclimbed, but the expedition did succeed in climbing the mountain by the conventional route. One effort by the Japanese Everest team symbolized the enormous strides into the "impossible" that adventurers have taken since the days of Hillary and Tenzing—this was Yuichiro Miura's daredevil attempt to ski down the mountain. He began with an easy 30-second glide down the south col in good alpine conditions. After waiting for gale-force winds to lull, he launched himself—at 25,918 ft. above sea level—on what must be the most dangerous ski-run ever. Within five seconds he had reached a speed of 100 m.p.h. down a 40-degree slope which narrowed into a rock-flanked gully buffeted by howling winds. It was at this point that he lost a ski and continued—his brake parachute hopelessly inadequate—weaving on one foot across corrugated ice studded with jagged rocks, headlong towards a crevasse. Travelling so fast that he was unable to steer or stop, the demon skier would have certainly crashed to his death had he not collided with a rock at 23,600 ft. and rolled and tumbled semi-conscious but unhurt until he skidded miraculously to a halt at the brink of the abyss. In a few desperate minutes Yuichiro Miura covered just under two miles!

It took Swiss skiing teacher Silvain Saudan 2½ hours to ski down Mount Eiger on March 9, 1970. He made this risky descent from the summit of the north-west face down to Kleine Scheidegg. At times he approached 80 m.p.h. down angles of descent between 40 and 50 degrees. A fall while speeding down such slopes would have spelt certain death. Fired by his success, Saudan packed his bags for North

An astonishing mountaineering feat was achieved in 1970 by Mitch Michaud (right), who became the first man to climb the tallest peak in each of the 50 States of the U.S.A. in one calendar year. He is seen here after descending from his last peak, Mount Hood, Oregon, on December 4.

America—where more summits awaited him. Other mountaineering achievements of 1970 included the August conquest of the highest unscaled peak in the Arctic, the 10,700-ft. Mikkelsen's Fjeld, Greenland, by a four-man British team which braved drifting pack ice and a polar-bear attack; a September ascent of the Eiger by the hitherto unclimbed north pillar route by three Scots; and the second winter ascent of the north face of the Eiger *direttissima* by a Swiss team in January.

Nordic Navigators

In 1969 the famous Norwegian explorer Thor Heyerdahl had been thwarted in his bid to demonstrate that the ancient Egyptians could have crossed from North Africa to South America by bullrush rafts, when his papyrus reed boat *Ra* sunk 625 miles off Barbados. The *Kon Tiki* veteran and his crew were rescued by an escorting vessel, and plans were immediately laid for a repeat performance. Thus it was that on July 12, 1970, *Ra II* arrived in Bridgetown, Barbados, to a tumultuous reception. Bearded, barefoot, and bare-chested, Heyerdahl clambered ashore on to a red carpet where he knelt before a scarlet-gowned

Two more U.S. climbers, Dean Caldwell (left) and Warren Harding, spent a month (Oct. 19–Nov. 18) climbing the hitherto unconquered east face of the granite mountain El Capitan in Yosemite National Park.

The longest known raft journey—7,000 miles—was completed on Nov. 6, 1970, when *La Balsa*, made of a dozen balsa logs lashed together, reached the coast of Queensland, Australia, 161 days after leaving Guayaquil, Ecuador, on May 29. The crew (right), who aimed to prove that early voyagers from South America could have reached Australia, were (left to right) Norman Tetrault (Canada), Vitale Alzar (Spain), Gabriel Garces (Chile), and Marcel Modena (France). The design on their sail was by Salvador Dali.

dignitary to receive the honour of Knight Commander of the Grand Cross of the Knights of Malta. The voyage had taken the eight-man, multi-racial crew 57 days from Safi, Morocco. For over a month the square-rigged raft was submerged at the stern and her crew had to stand on the small poop deck.

Another Scandinavian, the Dane Hans Tholstrup, performed a feat involving somewhat more horsepower when he circumnavigated Australia in his powerboat *Tom Thumb*. He set out on May 11. After bouncing from wave to wave trailing a sheen of spray for 9,000 miles, the 25-year-old mariner steered his 17-ft. 80-h.p. outboard-powered runabout back into Sydney harbour on July 26 and observed to reporters that his complete ignorance of navigation and lack of navigational aids had presented no problems. "I just kept Australia on my left," he remarked with Viking simplicity. Tholstrup's severest test was the Great Australian Bight, which he took three days to cross.

But tragedy struck another lone sailor in Australian waters, when in March canoeist Alf Altmann, of Warrnambool, drowned on the last lap of his attempted 160-mile Bass Strait crossing in a home-made kayak. Heavy seas swamped his 15-ft. craft off the south-eastern tip of Victoria. The body of the drowned adventurer was found off Snake Island, only nine miles from his mainland destination, Port Albert.

By Boat and Balloon

Alf Altmann's widow described her luckless husband as "an incurable romantic"—a description that could apply to all those individuals who, often recklessly but always courageously, pit their strength and wits against the sea. One incurable romantic who lived to tell his tale in 1970 was 51-year-old house-painter Sidney Genders, a Buddhist from Sutton Coldfield who became the first man to row the Atlantic westwards from Britain. Genders's 6,000 miles of remigation

Left: Hans Tholstrup (Denmark) entering Sydney harbour after circumnavigating Australia in his speedboat *Tom Thumb*—9,000 miles in 76 days. Right: 51-year-old Sidney Genders (Great Britain), the first man to row the Atlantic east to west. He left Penzance, Cornwall, on September 11, 1969, and arrived at Miami, Florida, on June 26, 1970, having rowed 6,000 miles.

and contemplation began at Penzance, Cornwall, on September 11, 1969, and took 166 rowing days, with stops at Las Palmas in the Canary Islands and Antigua in the West Indies. He stepped ashore in Miami, Florida, on June 26, 1970—having lost a stone in weight and worn out 13 pairs of gloves and three pairs of oars. His conjugal state had also altered. "When I reached Las Palmas," he remarked bleakly, "I got a letter from my wife's solicitors saying she had divorced me." Long-distance litigation was not the only hazard to hit the oarsman in his 19 ft. 9 in. Portuguese-style dory, *Unicorn*. His plastic water tanks were damaged and he ran out of water 14 days off Antigua, surviving only by catching rainwater. *Unicorn* was also struck by a ship and waterlogged at one point. But the intrepid man from the Midlands bailed out and rowed on. Genders had been severely criticized by profes-

Pride of Thunder Bay plunged 10,000 ft. into the Irish Sea.

sional sailors for embarking on so dangerous a voyage, yet he survived to confound and also to amaze them: for his navigational aids were only a school atlas, a wristwatch, and a sextant.

Other romantics challenged the ocean by air—in an attempt to make the first balloon crossing of the Atlantic. Aboard their 80-ft.-high helium balloon's 12 ft. by 14 ft. gondola, Englishman Malcolm Brighton and Americans Rod and Pamela Anderson took off from East Hampton, Long Island, New York, on September 20. Hit by storms, their balloon *The Free Life* crashed down in heavy seas 500 miles south-east of Newfoundland two days later. There were no survivors. Another balloon

failure—but one with no loss of life—happened on January 26 when two Canadians plunged 10,000 ft. into the freezing waters of the Irish Sea. Their 75 ft.-high hot-air balloon, *Pride of Thunder Bay*, in which they were attempting to cross from Ireland to Wales, had run out of fuel—and hot air. Aeronauts Norman Jones and Ray Munro were saved from watery graves after a passing plane picked up the radio distress call which the pair desperately sent out while undergoing their "controlled drop" to the sea. A bedraggled Jones was plucked from the waves by a rescue craft 10 minutes after crash-landing. But the gallant Munro refused rescue until a ship arrived to take up the £5,000 balloon. After an hour in the sea he was rushed to hospital—victim of severe exposure.

A remarkable record was claimed by 21-year-old Robin Lee Graham in April 1970. He

Twenty-one-year-old Robin Lee Graham became the youngest person ever to travel alone round the world in a sailing boat—a journey that started in 1965 and ended in April 1970.

arrived in California to become the youngest person ever to sail alone round the world—having embarked on this incredible voyage during July 1965. Another American yachtsman, Francis Stokes, sailed solo across the Atlantic during the year. On July 11 his 30-ft. sloop *Crazy Jane* slipped discreetly into Plymouth without so much as a ripple of publicity. His solo voyage had started on June 14 from Barnegat Light, New Jersey, and *Crazy Jane* had averaged 120 miles a day. A month later, on July 18, fellow American Neal McCullum sailed into Plymouth, Mass., after a solo Atlantic crossing in his yacht *Sundance*. He had left Plymouth, Devon, 61 days previously on his lone voyage to commemorate the Pilgrim Fathers' sailing of the same route 350 years before. Other lone sailors of 1970 included James Balley, who sailed a home-made catamaran from Penzance to Block Island, off Rhode Island, U.S.A., arriving on June 19, and Chay Blyth who on October 18 embarked on a solo, east–west circumnavigation of the world against the trade winds in his steel-hulled ketch *British Steel*.

Red Sea Reefs

March 1970 saw the return of the British expedition to the Dahlak archipelago, one of the most mysterious and dangerous regions of the world. The archipelago consists of some 368 coral islets in the Red Sea, 70 miles off Massawa, Ethiopia. The prospective dangers of the expedition, led by Major John Blashford-Snell (of Blue Nile fame), had been described with military brevity before it set off: "The waters around the Dahlak Islands are the home of barracuda, shark, and manta ray. The [expedition] must find out how prevalent these are and in what areas, and also keep an eye open for the deadly stone fish, whose well-camouflaged body can emit poison through its sharp spines." Apart from these zoological hazards the archipelago is reputedly a staging post for Eritrean guerrillas and international smuggling rings. The expedition found tangible evidence of the latter activity: a quarter of a million cigarettes secreted in a mangrove swamp! The explorers successfully completed a survey of the area, blasted out some wells (part of their brief was to report to the Ethiopian government on the economic prospects, if any, of the coral islets), charted the coral reefs, and filmed their teeming and often menacing marine life.

Braving the stinging fire coral, poisonous sea urchins, lethal stonefish, sting-rays, moray eels, barracudas, manta rays, and manifold varieties of shark, expedition divers discovered the wreck of an Italian luxury cruiser *Urania*, sunk in 1936. On land the expedition examined the massive, stone ruin of Dahlak Kebir—augmented with vultures and black kites—and inhabited by a small, macabre human colony of aged blind. Behind this "city of the dead" ancient graveyards were found festooned with cracked tablets carved from black diorite—which is not found in the archipelago. Flocks of flamingo, heron, and plover were recorded eagerly by the expedition's ornithologists, while those rare birds of prey, ospreys, wheeled overhead.

Deepest Dives

Another underwater "first" of 1970 took place on dry land. This was the world record deep "dive" performed by the Royal Navy at the physiological laboratory, Alverstoke. The "dive" began on March 3, when two volunteers from the R.N. scientific service—Peter Sharphouse and John Bevan—entered a pressure-chamber to "dive" to the equivalent of 1,500 ft. (a pressure of 660 lb. per square inch). They remained at that simulated depth for 12 hours. The former dry-dive record, set up by a joint Franco-American effort some months previously, was 1,190 ft. for four minutes. This "dive" had been stopped because instruments indicated changes in the divers' brain activity

which led to the supposition that a "helium barrier" existed at 1,200 ft. below sea level—and this, it was concluded, constituted the greatest depth a man could dive to and survive. Thus the Alverstoke dive was one of great significance to the future of oceanology as well as a sterling example of courage. Altogether, the divers spent $3\frac{1}{2}$ days "below" the formerly dreaded 1,200-ft. mark. Peter Sharphouse celebrated his 21st birthday at a simulated depth of several hundred feet and was given a birthday cake through an air-lock.

An even odder location for a diving feat was found deep under the Mendip Hills of Somerset on January 26, 1970. Here an intrepid team of skin-diving speleologists, including a young woman, Moire Urwin, discovered a 70-ft.-high dry underground cave by swimming, crawling, and squeezing through submerged subterranean tunnels. The cave will be opened to the public via a somewhat easier entrance once a 200-ft. mine-shaft has been sunk from the surface. Another skin-diver, Frenchman Jack Meiyeur, beat the world skin-diving record by diving to a depth of 76 metres off the Japanese coast on September 8, 1970. The previous record was 74 metres, held by an Italian, Anzzio Majorda.

Notwithstanding the Somerset speleologists, the most stunning pot-holing stunt of 1970 was performed by Milutin Veljković, an electrician from Belgrade, who had descended 975 ft. into the Samar cavern in the Svrljig Mountains, Yugoslavia, during June 1969 with the intention of remaining walled-up underground for a whole hydrological year. For 15 months he stayed below in the damp and gloom where the silence was emphasized by the mournful dripping of water and the occasional croaking of frogs. He was linked to the surface only by a field telephone and was solitary save for a dog, a cat, three cocks, seven hens, five ducks, and a drake. His feathered brood, like his luxuriant beard, had prospered by the time he emerged into the autumnal tints of 1970—after a record-breaking 463 days underground. The count was 20 ducks and 32 chickens.

Marathon Swims

The year saw some notable long-distance swimming. On August 6, 21-year-old London journalist Kevin Murphy became the first Briton (and the third man ever) to swim the English Channel both ways non-stop. This 35-hour 10-minute marathon proved merely the first of Murphy's exploits during 1970, for on September 11 he became the second man to succeed in swimming the North Channel of the Irish Sea—one of the most treacherous stretches of water in the world. The 22 miles between Orlock Point, Northern Ireland, and Portpatrick, Scotland, had been vainly attempted over the years by many great long-distance swimmers. Jason Zirganos, the Greek, was killed attempting it in 1959. Only one man had ever succeeded—the amicable, 18-stone giant, Tom Blower—in 1947. Blower's friends attribute his early death at 41 to the rigours of this exacting swim. After waiting anxiously for gale-force winds to abate, Murphy entered the water at Orlock Point, at 11.48 a.m. on September 11. He staggered ashore in Scotland at 11.09 p.m. half paralysed and raving from jellyfish stings.

Another swimming saga, this time performed by a distinctly reluctant novice, occurred when William Honeywill, a passenger aboard the liner *S. A. Vaal* bound from Cape Town to Southampton, ended a night of revelry by tripping over a deck rail and plummeting into the Atlantic. Telling his story later, Honeywill recounted: "I saw the tail end of the ship disappearing into the distance and thought: 'I have fallen overboard: I'd better start swimming.' Then I lost consciousness again. When I came to for the second time the sun was coming up and I found I was doing a gentle breaststroke. My first thought was that it was a beautiful morning. It was a fine, sunny day and the Atlantic was clear blue—I thought that if I was going to drown this would be a beautiful place to die. My first thought when I saw the ship coming back was 'the damn thing is going to miss me'. So I took off my jacket—I had kept all my clothes and shoes on because I did not want to be arrested for indecent exposure—and tried to wave my jacket. Unfortunately I was not as fit as I might have been at that time and dropped the jacket—which had 15s. in it!" He had been in the water $11\frac{1}{2}$ hours and owed his life both to his incredible stamina and the superb navigation of the ship's skipper, Captain Alan Freer, who took the ship back 140 miles along its course to within 80 yards of the man overboard.

Another remarkable rescue took place off Hawaii when the U.S.S. *Niagara* picked up Winfried Heiringhoff, Laurence Kokx, and Julian Ritter from their crippled 42-ft. sloop *Galilee*. They had survived 48 days on a diet of algae and spice soup. More remarkable still was the rescue of four Russian fishermen from an ice floe on which they had spent eight days and nights adrift in the Gulf of Tartary. With only the clothes they stood up in, a few matches, and—appropriately—a copy of a Jack London novel, they jumped from one patch of ice to another as the floe disintegrated. They had been fishing Eskimo-fashion through holes in the pack ice just off the U.S.S.R.'s Far East coast, when they started to drift out to sea. They covered 120 miles before they were picked up, suffering from frostbite and exposure.

There was a heartbreaking end to the year's most gruelling walk. On August 14, David Ryder, the London poliomyelitis victim who had walked from John O' Groats to Land's End in 1969, swinging along on his crutches walked down Broadway, New York, having completed a 3,000-mile walk from coast to coast to raise money for the North American Riding for the Handicapped Association. In fact David collected only 20 cents for every courageous mile—across desert, mountain, and prairie.

1970 had its measure of the more crazy endurance records such as have amused and amazed mankind since 5th-century St. Simeon Stylites sat out 30 years of his life on top of a series of pillars. Left: in July, two young Californians, Steve Cooper (left) and Gary Turpen, seesawed non-stop for 124 hours—a new world record. Right: in June, 14-year-old Hereford boy David Rose broke the 10-year-old world record for non-stop yo-yo with a time of 8 hours 3 minutes.

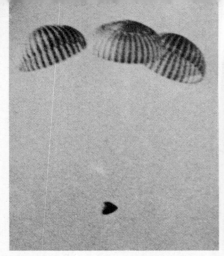

Triumph and Failure in Space

L. J. CARTER, Executive Secretary of the British Interplanetary Society

A "FAILURE" THAT was greeted the world over with more cheers of joy and tears of relief than any triumph would have received was the splash-down by the three American astronauts —James Lovell, Frederick Haise, and John Swigert, the crew of Apollo 13—after their abortive attempt in April at the third landing on the Moon. Their return from the edge of eternity was witnessed on television by some 700 million people, all of whom were certainly concentrating their whole will-power and their prayers for a miracle that would save the lives of the three men. As the world-wide hush of anxiety during the 3 minutes' radio silence that is always imposed by re-entry from space into the Earth's atmosphere was broken by Swigert's laconic "Okay, Joe", there erupted a storm of cheers from the scores of technicians at the Houston ground control centre, echoed by TV viewers in every country. A few seconds later the parachute-borne command module came into view, settling safely on the waters of the Pacific Ocean 600 miles from Samoa, only 5 seconds late and 3 miles from the computed landing point; and the whole world breathed again.

The unlucky-number Apollo 13 had had its troubles from the start. Only 3 days before launch on Saturday, April 11, the nominated command module pilot Thomas K. Mattingly had been withdrawn on suspicion of having contracted german measles, and replaced by Jack Swigert. Then, soon after the giant Saturn 5 rocket left the launch-pad at Cape Kennedy at 8.13 p.m. B.S.T., the centre engines of its S-11 second stage shut down prematurely.

Fortunately, the outer engines and the engine of the S-4B stage were able to fire for a longer period to compensate for this.

"Hey, we've got a problem"

The crew went about their usual tasks in Odyssey, the command module, and Aquarius, the lunar module, getting ready to explore the hilly uplands near the Fra Mauro region of the Moon on Tuesday the 14th, 55 hours 55 minutes after launch and 200,000 miles from Earth, they heard a loud explosion which was followed at once by a drop in the main electrical circuits. Lovell's remark, "Hey, we've got a problem" gave ground controllers the first intimation of trouble, and it soon became clear how serious it was. An explosion in the service module had caused the pressure in one of the two cryogenic (super-cold) oxygen tanks to drop to zero in 8 seconds. These tanks feed the three fuel cells which not only generate Apollo's electric current but also provide oxygen and water. The current from the remaining fuel cell dropped slowly until, 3 days from home, the craft had electricity for only 15 minutes under normal conditions.

Back on Earth, the ground controllers feverishly worked out a new flight-plan to deal with the emergency. It was clear that the mission had to be aborted immediately, and the path of the spacecraft altered so that it would swing round behind the Moon, without landing, and then return to Earth. The lunar module descent engine (intended for landing on the Moon) had to be used for this, with the lunar

Hundreds of millions waited in hopeful suspense for the sight (opposite page, left) of the parachute-borne capsule of Apollo 13, bringing astronauts Lovell, Haise, and Swigert back from the edge of eternity. Their Moon-landing mission in April had been aborted after an explosion had torn a hole in the service module, shown here (opposite page, right) as it was photographed by Lovell when it was jettisoned. The miraculous recovery of the three men was almost entirely due to the brilliant work of the control team at Houston, Texas (right), who planned their every move 200,000 miles away.

module itself used as a "lifeboat" to provide emergency communications, power, guidance, and life support. A "burn" to put Apollo 13 into Moon orbit was made, and the next day another "burn" put it on course for Earth.

Throughout April 15 the flight-plan was adapted from minute to minute, with communications becoming extremely difficult as Apollo 13 developed a slow tumbling motion. The command module had become uninhabitable through lack of heat and oxygen, and the crew crawled into the lunar module. As their oxygen ran low they improvised an air filter out of a space-suit part, a tube, and a strip of cardboard, but while the crippled spacecraft raced back towards Earth, the crew found added difficulty in writing down the new flight plan in the cold, chilly and carbon-dioxide-polluted environment. All their actions were duplicated in simulators on Earth, and their next moves similarly worked out.

"The Skill of Many Men"

On Thursday, the ground controllers decided on their final plans. While recovery ships raced to a revised south Pacific splashdown point, the crew learned that the useless service module had to be jettisoned early in the re-entry sequence; the crew would then transfer into the command module, 70 minutes before re-entry, for the final descent; and the lunar module would be jettisoned. Everything went according to plan. Throughout an ice-cold Thursday night, taking dexedrine pep pills to keep them warm and alert, the men carried out the instructions radioed from Houston. Two further "burns" were made to ensure they would enter the Earth's atmosphere at the correct angle. As the service module was jettisoned the men saw for the first time the extent of the damage; a whole panel had been torn from its side. "It's really a mess," Lovell reported, as he photographed it. As the lunar module was sent off into space, "Farewell, Aquarius," Lovell said, "and we thank you."

After the crew's rapturous reception on the rescue aircraft-carrier *Iwo Jima*, the ship's chaplain said a simple prayer: "O Lord, we joyfully welcome back to Earth astronauts

The brave and fortunate crew of Apollo 13 were met at Honolulu by President Nixon.
Left to right: Haise, Lovell, the President, Swigert.

Lovell, Haise, and Swigert who, by Your grace, their skill, and the skill of many men, survived the dangers encountered in their mission and returned to us safe and whole. We offer our humble thanksgiving for this successful recovery. Amen." He did well to mention "the skill of many men" for, apart from the courage of the crew, the credit for the rescue belongs to the ground control team at Houston, who calculated, revised, adapted, and improvised for 80 hours in a combined operation of unequalled technological skill. "Never have so few owed so much to so many," President Nixon said, as he announced the award to the team of the Congressional Medal of Honour.

Investigations into the cause of the accident began immediately. It seemed that a short-circuit in a wire leading to a fan inside the liquid oxygen tank, used to stir up the oxygen to keep it flowing smoothly into the fuel cells, caused combustion inside the tank, increasing the temperature and pressure, and eventually producing an explosion. The damage stopped just short of the main tanks of the service propulsion system, containing fuels that become highly explosive when mixed; a rupture in these units would have meant the instant

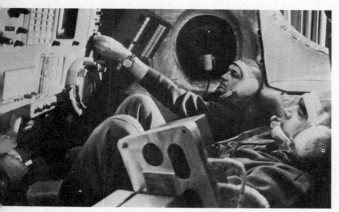

Russian cosmonauts Nikolayev (foreground) and Sevastyanov in Soyuz 9, in which they made the longest ever space-flight.

destruction of Apollo 13. Much, of course, was learnt from the disaster, and modifications are being made to later spacecraft. They include adding a third oxygen tank and a battery in the service module to provide additional power in case all fuel cells are lost. Meanwhile, Apollo 14's flight, planned for December 1970, was postponed.

There was one incidental success from the Apollo 13 flight for, on April 14, the 15-ton spent third stage of the Saturn 5 launch vehicle crashed on to the Moon, as planned, with a force equivalent to $11\frac{1}{2}$ tons of TNT. It hit the Moon 85 miles W.N.W. of the site where the Apollo 12 astronauts had set up their seismometer. Scientists on Earth said that "the Moon rang like a bell". The shock-waves produced by the impact were 20–30 times greater and four times longer than those resulting from the Apollo 12 lunar crash in November 1969.

Russian Successes

By contrast, Russian space science had a remarkably successful season. It started on June 1 with the Earth-orbit launch of Soyuz 9, containing the cosmonauts A. Nikolayev and V. Sevastyanov. The aim was to undertake bio-medical studies of the human system during a long flight, to observe and photograph the Earth's oceans, geology, and geography to see how this could benefit the economy, to study the Earth's atmosphere, snow- and ice-cover to help long-range weather forecasting, and to check the spacecraft itself. A programme to investigate the propagation of radio-waves in the Earth's atmosphere was also carried out. During its flight Soyuz 9 twice altered its orbit to increase its altitude. Many experiments were made to establish the position of the Earth's horizon, using photographic, visual, and spectrographic methods, particularly at

sunrise, as the first rays appeared. Photo-graphs of moonrise and of the Moon near the Earth's horizon were also taken.

The Soyuz 9 command module soft-landed with a final rocket braking and parachute on June 19, near the village of Intumak, about 47 miles west of Karagandar, after a record-breaking flight lasting 424 hours 59 minutes. Both cosmonauts had to be helped from their spacecraft because their bodies felt very heavy. Nikolayev, who lost 82 lb. during the mission, reported that, during the initial phases of the flight, the crew experienced the feeling of blood rushing to their heads. For 2 days after their 18 days in Earth orbit they were virtually immobilized, as the long period of weightless-ness affected their co-ordination; they also took 4–5 days to readjust to normal sleeping habits.

In the autumn two spectacular soft-landings on the Moon were made by spacecraft from Soviet Union. The first was by the 4,163-lb. Luna 16, launched by a Proton-class booster rocket on September 12. It entered orbit around the Moon on September 17, and the orbit was later reduced, enabling Luna 16 to land in the Sea of Fertility on September 20. After drilling about $3\frac{1}{2}$ ounces of samples from the lunar surface, the craft transferred these to a sealed container in its ascent stage, which was then re-launched from the Moon on September 21 and recovered on Earth 3 days later. The descent stage was left on the Moon to continue to transmit temperature and radia-tion data.

The "Moon-Cart"

An even more surprising event took place with the launch of Luna 17 on November 10.

Unmanned spacecraft Luna 16 returned to Earth from the Moon with samples it had drilled from the surface under radio control.

The incredible Russian "Moon-cart", Lunokhod 1, resting on Luna 17 before its first roving mission on the surface.

On reaching the Moon 5 days later, it first entered a circular orbit and then soft-landed on the Sea of Rains on November 17, shortly afterwards revealing an eight-wheeled remote-controlled self-propelled vehicle, Lunokhod 1, which rolled down a ramp from the top of Luna 17 and moved across the lunar surface. Lunokhod 1 carried control gear and radio and TV equipment, besides scientific instruments for collecting and chemically analysing the lunar soil and transmitting findings to Earth. It also included a French-built laser reflector for checking Earth-Moon distances. After travelling about 200 yds. from its landing point, Lunokhod 1 settled down to rest for the fortnight-long lunar night. On "waking" it started again to roam the surface, travelling a total distance of 1,862 yds. before settling down for its second lunar night, at a point 1,483 yds. from its parent spacecraft.

Probes to Venus, Mars, and Mercury

On August 17 the Russians launched a 2,600-lb. probe, Venus 7, on a 4-month mission to the planet Venus. The spacecraft was described as an "improved version", about 1 cwt. heavier than earlier probes. Shortly afterwards they launched Cosmos 359, which was believed to be a second "back-up" Venus probe, but this failed to leave Earth orbit. Throughout its 200 million mile journey Venus 7 functioned normally and transmitted data. It arrived over Venus on December 15, and floated down to the rocky surface on its parachute. After landing, it transmitted for 23 minutes information about the intense heat (475° C) and pressure (about 90 atmospheres). This was the first ever reception of radio signals from a spacecraft actually on the surface of another planet.

Meanwhile, an interesting experiment was being undertaken with the two American Mariner spacecraft which successfully flew by Mars in 1969, and are now orbiting the Sun. The experiment was intended to check Einstein's general theory of relativity, using several hundred radio measurements. Einstein's theory is really a geometrical theory of gravitation, which predicts that the speed of light (186,000 miles per second) should be slower in the gravitational field of the Sun; the same, of course, should be true of radio signals. Today, the performance of the deep-space network has been so greatly improved that tracking can be accomplished to within 100 ft. over a distance of 250 million miles, and time measured to within a millionth of a second or less. Thus time-delays in radio waves passing near the Sun can be measured. The measurements showed that Einstein's predictions were right and that, if there was any doubt, it was about the accuracy of some alternative theories produced by later workers.

Space Satellites

Apart from communications and weather satellites, little information was disclosed about the great majority of satellites launched during the year, for most had military purposes. Russian launchings were dominated by Cosmos satellites—over 60 of them—ostensibly for scientific purposes, but undoubtedly including reconnaissance. Cosmos 373–375 were thought to be part of a plan to intercept and destroy orbital satellites, with Cosmos 373 as the "enemy" satellite and 374 and 375 as interceptors. All were fully manoeuvrable, and weighed more than 1 ton each. Cosmos 374 and 375 were shattered into many individual fragments.

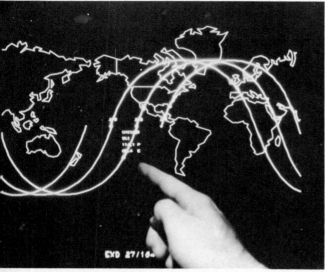

China's first satellite went into Earth orbit on April 24. This screen at an American defence centre recorded its first complete orbit and forecast the paths of its next two.

Both Japan and China successfully launched their first satellites during 1970. On February 11, a Japanese OSUMI satellite was launched from Uchinoura space centre to provide a test payload. Its signals were used as a tracking target until these faded during the 7th orbit, after about 30 hours. Thus, at her fifth attempt, Japan became the fourth nation (after the U.S.S.R., U.S.A., and France) to launch an artificial satellite. China became the fifth member of the club on April 24. Its 380-lb. satellite, China-1, broadcast a revolutionary tune as it orbited 275–1,490 miles above the Earth. The launch was made from a base in Inner Mongolia, about 1,250 miles west of Peking.

European countries outside the U.S.S.R. were sadly unsuccessful in the satellite sphere. On June 12, Europa-1 failed in its third and last attempt to orbit a test satellite from Woomera in Australia. The first and second stages fired successfully, but the nose shroud failed to jettison and the third-stage thrust was depleted by a pressurization fault, thus providing insufficient power to inject the 570-lb. satellite into orbit. The first all-British test satellite using the Black Arrow rocket followed from Woomera on September 2, but failed to reach orbit as the second stage of the launcher rocket cut out prematurely. Failure dogged the French, too, with the launch of the three-stage Diamant B on March 10, intended to orbit a German-built 132-lb. Dial payload, consisting of a technology capsule and a scientific satellite. Although the satellite was successfully placed in orbit, it was so damaged by vibration during launch that its performance was ruined.

Military communications satellites included the 284-lb. Nato-1, launched on March 20, located over the eastern Atlantic Ocean to provide communications between Nato h.q. and sea- and land-based terminals; and the 284-lb. Skynet-2 satellite, launched from Cape Kennedy on August 19 by a Thor-Delta rocket. On April 25 the Russians launched eight Cosmos satellites from a single rocket, presumably to deploy a navigation and communications system. This capped an extremely active month in which 15 payloads were put into space.

The new space centre in French Guiana from which Diamant B (right), carrying a German satellite, was launched in March.

Sport and Games

Compiled and edited by

DON WOOD
former editor of *World Sports*

Review of British Sport in 1970

THOSE WITH LITTLE or no interest in sport found it difficult to turn their backs on everything that happened in the sporting world during 1970. For those who suddenly sit up and take notice when a British competitor captures the headlines, there were some really outstanding world-class successes. But while names like Tony Jacklin and Henry Cooper were yet again dominating the end-of-year polls, the vote for the outstanding British sporting achievement during the year might well have been given to a country, Scotland, for her staging of the IX Commonwealth Games in Edinburgh. For 10 days during July, record crowds, totalling 234,949, watched competition in the nine sports of these traditional "friendly games". The Scottish organization won warm praise from officials and competitors from 42 competing countries and, as new friendships were made during the Games fortnight, Scotland found herself the heart of the sporting Commonwealth.

Superbly though they had planned for the Games and the future with the new £2·2 million Meadowbank sports centre, with its three multi-purpose sports halls and all-weather athletics track, the Scots, alas, could not organize their weather. Rain and strong winds seriously handicapped competitors from warmer climates and ruled out many record possibilities but, despite the conditions, some outstanding stars emerged. The hosts could not have wished for a better start and finish to the track programme than home victories in the 10,000 metres and 5,000 metres from Lachie Stewart and Ian Stewart. Lachie's win in the longest track event had one sad footnote: the popular Australian distance star Ron Clarke ended his top-class career with only yet another silver medal. For all his marks in the record books, front-runner Clarke once again found himself without the finishing kick to beat a rival prepared to play the waiting game. Australia, with 20 of the 33 gold medals at stake in the superb Royal Commonwealth Pool, dominated the swimming and diving, followed by Canada (11 golds). In all, 27 of the 42 competing countries had a place in the final medals table.

This aerial view of the superb new Meadowbank Stadium created at Edinburgh for the Commonwealth Games gives an idea of the splendour of its setting—and also, alas, of the inclemency of the Scottish weather in July 1970.

Happily the Games avoided the threatened boycott by African, Asian, and West Indian countries, but Edinburgh, like much of sport during 1970, found itself thrust under the shadow caused by South Africa's apartheid policy. More sports organizations severed their links with the Republic, and those, like Rugby Union and cricket, that considered it best to retain some contact, paid a heavy price for their policy. The Springbok Rugby Union tourists were hounded by anti-apartheid demonstrators wherever they played in Britain during their 1969–70 tour, and returned home the first team not to have won an international on a full tour of Great Britain. At the same time, demonstrators opened hostilities against the proposed South African cricket tour of the U.K. During one night in January, 12 grounds due to stage Springbok matches were visited. Slogans warned of actions to come, and in one case a hole was dug in the pitch.

Demonstrators Won the Day

In the following month, barbed wire went up at the major grounds, and the tour of 28 games was cut to 12 and restricted to grounds that could be protected from demonstrators. In addition, arrangements were made for each ground to have a portable playing strip available, lest the wicket should be damaged during a match. "Official" cricket seemed determined to retain the tour, although, while polls suggested that public opinion in Britain was also slightly in favour of it, even some of the most avid cricket followers were questioning the wisdom of welcoming the South Africans. They had soundly beaten the Australians at home, and were certainly the most outstanding cricketing side in the world on current form. But many African countries threatened to boycott the Commonwealth Games if the tour went on; one commercial TV company decided not to screen any tour matches; and an (unsuccessful) attempt was made to get British journalists not to report the tourists' games.

The matter came to a head in May, when the various anti-apartheid movements using sport as a weapon scored a double victory within a week. On the 15th the International Olympic Committee, meeting in Amsterdam, agreed by 35 votes to 28 to expel South Africa from the Olympic movement—the first occasion this has happened to a member country (South Africa's invitation to compete in the 1968 Olympic Games in Mexico was withdrawn because of the fear of violence). A week later, on the 22nd, the English Cricket Council, at the request of the Home Secretary, cancelled the summer's cricket tour. In its place, England met a Rest of the World team, but the series, despite the stars involved (including South Africans), failed to arouse great public interest and merely acted as a guide to the England selectors preparing for the 1970–71 Ashes meeting with Australia.

Despite its flagging appeal at the box office, cricket provided more than its fair quota of surprises during the year. South Africa, fresh after a long absence from Test cricket due to the cancellation of the M.C.C.'s 1969 tour, hammered the Australians in the year's only major series. Led by Ali Bacher, a Jewish doctor, South Africa scored her finest Test victory at Durban, when left-hander Graeme Pollock contributed 274 (highest score by a South African) in a total of 622, South Africa's highest total in 170 Tests. At home, Kent celebrated their centenary year with one of the most remarkable victories in the history of the county championship when they took the title after being bottom of the table in July.

New Life in the Ring

Boxing enjoyed a sudden revival with the return to the ring of Cassius Clay, undefeated world heavyweight champion. Looking only slightly the worse for his three-year lay-off, he beat Jerry Quarry (U.S.A.) and Oscar Bonavena (Argentina) to put him in line for a meeting with Joe Frazier, who, in official if not in the boxing public's eye, had taken over as world champion in Clay's absence. Britain's boxing fortunes got a strange boost in September when Scotland's Ken Buchanan, British lightweight champion, journeyed to Puerto Rico and outpointed Panama's Ismael Laguna. The shock win caused a few red faces back home. Before the fight the British Boxing Board, falling into line with the World Boxing Council, had announced that they did not recognize Laguna as world champion because of his failure to defend his title against a nominated challenger. This decision robbed Buchanan of the full credit for being the first British fighter since Ted "Kid" Lewis to win a world title abroad.

One overseas British success in which there was no room for doubt was Tony Jacklin's seven-stroke victory in the U.S. Open golf championship. Only the fourth overseas player to master the Americans on their own fairways, Jacklin's success came less than a

year after his victory in the British Open, and put him among the all-time golfing greats. At the year's end this performance was giving the sportswriters and sports fans some problems in the "sportsman of the year" polls. The honours were shared with the ever-popular Henry Cooper, who regained the European and British heavyweight titles and topped the BBC-TV sports personality poll among viewers. The British Sports Writers Association placed Jacklin top for the second successive year, coupling with his the name of Mary Gordon-Watson, the attractive 22-year-old Dorset farmer's daughter who won the individual title in the toughest of all equestrian contests—the world 3-day event championships. *Daily Express* readers also plumped for Henry Cooper, and expressed their sympathy with Britain's second golden girl of athletics, Lillian Board, who was then lying seriously ill in a German cancer clinic, by voting her sportswoman of the year. Her death on December 26 was the saddest event in 1970 sport, and cast a gloom over the end of what had been a brilliant year.

The World Cup (see page 225), commanding the Soccer spotlight, threw a big strain on the England men, who had just finished a busy European and home Cup and League programme. Leeds United, chasing the golden treble of Football League championship and European and F.A. Cups, ended the season with nothing, after losing a marathon F.A. Cup Final to Chelsea. Feyenoord of Rotterdam dashed the hopes of a British clean sweep in the European Soccer competitions by beating Glasgow Celtic for the European Champions' Cup, after Manchester City and Arsenal had carried off the other two European club competitions.

At the snow-covered Oval in February barbed wire protected the pitch from anti-South Africa cricket tour activities.

TEST MATCH SERIES OF THE 1970 SEASON

SOUTH AFRICA v. AUSTRALIA
South Africa won all four matches

1st TEST: Cape Town, Jan. 22–27
South Africa won by 170 runs
1st inns.: South Africa 382 (A. Bacher 57, G. Pollock 49, E. Barlow 127; A. Mallett 5—126)
Australia 164 (D. Walters 73; P. Pollock 4—20)
2nd inns.: South Africa 232 (G. Pollock 50, M. Proctor 48; A. Connolly 5—47)
Australia 280 (W. Lawry 83, I. Redpath 47 n.o.; Proctor 4—47)

2nd TEST: Durban, Feb. 5–9
South Africa won by an innings and 129 runs
1st inns.: South Africa 622 for 9 dec. (B. Richards 140, G. Pollock 274, H. Lance 61; J. Gleeson 3—160)
Australia 157 (P. Sheahan 62; E. Barlow 3—24)
2nd inns.: Australia (follow-on) 336 (K. Stackpole 71, D. Walters 74. I. Redpath 74 n.o.; M. Proctor 3—62, E. Barlow 3—63)

3rd TEST: Johannesburg, Feb. 19–24
South Africa won by 307 runs
1st inns.: South Africa 279 (B. Richards 65, G. Pollock 52, B. Irvine 79; J. Gleeson 3—61)
Australia 202 (D. Walters 64, A. Sheahan 44; P. Pollock 5—39, P. Proctor 3—48)
2nd inns.: South Africa 408 (E. Barlow 110, G. Pollock 87, Irvine 73; Gleeson 5—125)
Australia 178 (I. Redpath 66; P. Proctor 3—24, T. Goddard 3—27)

4th TEST: Port Elizabeth, March 5–10
South Africa won by 323 runs
1st inns.: South Africa 311 (B. Richards 81, E. Barlow 73; A. Connolly 6—47)
Australia 212 (I. Redpath 55, A. Sheahan 67; P. Proctor 3—30)
2nd inns.: South Africa 470 for 8 dec. (B. Richards 126, A. Bacher 73, B. Irvine 102, D. Lindsay 60; L. Mayne 3—85)
Australia 246 (W. Lawry 43, A. Sheahan 46; P. Proctor 6—73)

ENGLAND v. THE REST OF THE WORLD
Rest of the World won 4; England won 1

1st TEST: Lord's, June 17–22
Rest of the World won by an innings and 80 runs
1st inns.: England 127 (R. Illingworth 63; G. Sobers 6—21)
Rest of the World 546 (Sobers 183, E. Barlow 119, G. Pollock 55, Intikhab Alam 61; A. Ward 4—121)
2nd inns.: England 339 (B. Luckhurst 67, B. D'Oliveira 78, R. Illingworth 94; Intikhab Alam 6—113)

2nd TEST: Nottingham, July 2–7
England won by 8 wickets
1st inns.: Rest of the World 276 (C. Lloyd 114 n.o., B. Richards 64)
England 279 (R. Illingworth 97; E. Barlow 5—66)
2nd inns.: Rest of the World 286 (E. Barlow 142)
England 284 for 2 (B. Luckhurst 113 n.o., K. Fletcher 69 n.o., C. Cowdrey 64)

3rd TEST: Edgbaston, July 16–22
Rest of the World won by 5 wickets
1st inns.: England 294 (B. D'Oliveira 110, A. Greig 55; M. Procter 5—46)
Rest of the World 563 for 9 dec. (R. Kanhai 71, C. Lloyd 101, G. Sobers 80, Procter 62, D. Murray 62)
2nd inns.: England 409 (C. Cowdrey 71, B. D'Oliveira 81, A. Knott 50 n.o.)
Rest of the World 141 for 5

4th TEST: Leeds, July 30–August 4
Rest of the World won by 2 wickets
1st inns.: England 222 (K. Fletcher 89, R. Illingworth 58; E. Barlow 7—64)
Rest of the World 376 for 9 dec. (D. Murray 95, G. Sobers 114, E. Barlow 87)
2nd inns.: England 376 (G. Boycott 64, B. Luckhurst 92, K. Fletcher 63, R. Illingworth 54; E. Barlow 5—78)
Rest of the World 226 for 8 (Intikhab Alam 54, G. Sobers 59)

5th TEST: The Oval, August 13–18
Rest of the World won by 4 wickets
1st inns.: England 294 (C. Cowdrey 73, R. Illingworth 52, A. Knott 51 n.o.)
Rest of the World 355 (G. Pollock 114, G. Sobers 79, M. Procter 51; P. Lever 7—83)
2nd inns.: England 344 (G. Boycott 157, K. Fletcher 63)
Rest of the World 287 for 6 (R. Kanhai 100, C. Lloyd 68)

GILLETTE CUP FINAL
Lord's, September 5, 1970
LANCS bt. SUSSEX by 6 wkts
Lancashire bt. Gloucestershire (by 27 runs); Hampshire (by 5 wkts); Somerset (by 4 wkts)
Sussex bt. Essex (by 4 wkts); Kent (by 47 runs); Surrey (with 2 wickets in hand with scores level after 60 overs)

SHEFFIELD SHIELD
1969–70

	Points
Victoria	48
Western Australia	38
New South Wales	24
South Australia	24
Queensland	38

LEADING AVERAGES

Gary Sobers, West Indies captain who led Nottinghamshire and the Rest of the World team, easily topped the English first-class batting averages with 75·73.

Don Shepherd (Glamorgan) headed the bowling averages with 106 wickets for 19·16 runs each.

COUNTY CHAMPIONSHIP
Final Table

	P	W	L	D	Btg.	Blg.	Pts
Kent (10)	24	9	5	10	70	77	237
Glamorgan (1)	24	9	6	9	48	82	220
Lancashire (15)	24	6	2	16	78	78	216
Yorkshire (13)	24	8	5	11	49	86	215
Surrey (3)	24	6	4	14	60	83	203
Worcestershire (12)	24	7	1	16	46	84	200
Derbyshire (16)	24	7	7	10	51	78	199
Warwickshire (4)	24	7	6	11	53	71	199
Sussex (7)	24	5	7	12	62	87	199
Hampshire (5)	24	4	6	14	69	88	197
Nottinghamshire (8)	24	4	8	12	71	73	184
Essex (6)	24	4	6	14	64	76	180
Somerset (17)	24	5	10	9	40	86	176
Northamptonshire (9)	24	4	6	14	60	74	174
Leicestershire	24	5	6	13	46	77	173
Middlesex (11)	24	5	5	14	47	69	166
Gloucestershire (2)	24	3	8	13	56	80	166

Warwickshire's record includes 5 points in drawn match when scores finished level and they were batting. Figures in brackets indicate 1969 positions.

PLAYER'S SUNDAY LEAGUE
Final Table

	P	W	L	No Rslt	Pts
Lancashire (1)	16	13	2	1	53
Kent (4)	16	12	4	0	48
Derbyshire (15)	16	11	5	0	44
Essex (3)	16	8	5	3	35
Warwickshire (9)	16	8	6	2	34
Worcestershire (11)	16	8	7	1	33
Leicestershire (11)	16	7	7	2	30
Gloucestershire (6)	16	7	7	2	30
Surrey (5)	16	7	7	2	30
Nottinghamshire (13)	16	7	9	0	28
Middlesex (7)	16	6	8	2	26
Hampshire (2)	16	6	10	0	24
Northamptonshire (14)	16	6	10	0	24
Glamorgan (9)	16	5	9	2	22
Somerset (15)	16	5	9	2	22
Yorkshire (7)	16	5	9	2	22
Sussex (7)	16	3	10	3	15

Figures in brackets indicate 1969 positions.

IX COMMONWEALTH GAMES
Edinburgh, Scotland: July 16–25, 1970

For the first time in these Games, athletics and swimming events were contested over the standard metric distances, but official conversions for field events and weight-lifting have been included in the following tables. Times in swimming events, although taken to two decimal points at the Games, have been reduced to one, as accepted by FINA for record purposes. Abbreviations:

Aus—Australia	Gam—Gambia	Ind—India	NZ—New Zealand	STV—St. Vincent
Bar—Barbados	Gha—Ghana	Jam—Jamaica	Nig—Nigeria	Tan—Tanzania
Can—Canada	Guy—Guyana	Ken—Kenya	NI—Northern Ireland	Tri—Trinidad & Tobago
Eng—England	HK—Hong Kong	Mwi—Malawi	Pak—Pakistan	Uga—Uganda
Fij—Fiji	IOM—Isle of Man	Mal—Malaysia	Sco—Scotland	Wal—Wales
			Sin—Singapore	Zam—Zambia

Sports arranged in alphabetical order   w = World record   e = European record

Event	Gold Medal	Silver Medal	Bronze Medal
ATHLETICS			
Men			
100 metres	D. Quarrie (Jam), 10·2 s	L. Miller (Jam), 10·3 s	H. Crawford (Tri), 10·3 s
200 metres	D. Quarrie (Jam), 20·5 s	E. Roberts (Tri), 20·6 s	C. Asati (Ken), 20·7 s
400 metres	C. Asati (Ken), 45 s	R. Wilson (Aus), 45·6 s	S. Tamani (Fij), 45·8 s
800 metres	R. Ouko (Ken), 1 m 46·8 s	B. Cayenne (Tri), 1 m 47·4 s	W. Smart (Can), 1 m 47·4 s
1,500 metres	K. Keino (Ken), 3 m 36·6 s	T. Quax (NZ), 3 m 38·1 s	B. Foster (Eng), 3 m 40·6 s
5,000 metres	I. Stewart (Sco), e 13 m 22·8 s	I. McCafferty (Sco), 13 m 23·4 s	K. Keino (Ken), 13 m 27·6 s
10,000 metres	J. Stewart (Sco), 28 m 11·8 s	R. Clarke (Aus), 28 m 13·6 s	R. Taylor (Eng), 28 m 15·4 s
3,000 m. Steeplechase	A. Manning (Aus), 8 m 26·2 s	B. Jipcho (Ken), 8 m 29·6 s	A. Biwott (Ken), 8 m 30·8 s
110 metres Hurdles	D. Hemery (Eng), 13·6 s	M. Baird (Aus), 13·8 s	G. Murray (Jam), 14 s
400 metres Hurdles	J. Sherwood (Eng), 50 s	W. Koskei (Uga), 50·1 s	C. Jego (Ken), 50·1 s
Marathon	R. Hill (Eng), e 2 h 9 m 28 s	J. Alder (Sco), 2 h 12 m 4s	D. Fairclough (Eng), 2 h 12 m 19 s
20 miles Walk	N. Freeman (Aus), 2 h 33 m 33 s	R. Gardiner (Aus), 2 h 35 m 55 s	W. Sutherland (Sco), 2 h 37 m 24 s
4 × 100 metres Relay	Jamaica, 39·4 s	Ghana, 39·8 s	England, 40 s
4 × 400 metres Relay	Kenya, 3 m 3·6 s	Trinidad & Tobago, 3 m 5·4 s	England, 3 m 5·5 s
High Jump	L. Peckham (Aus), 2·14 m; 7 ft 0 in	J. Hawkins (Can), 2·12 m; 6 ft 11½ in	S. Faye (Gam), 2·1 m; 6 ft 10¾ in
Pole Vault	M. Bull (NI), 5·1 m; 16 ft 8¼ in	A. Kane (Can), 4·9 m; 16 ft 0¾ in	R. Raftis (Can), 4·9 m; 16 ft 0¾ in
Long Jump	L. Davies (Wal), 8·06 m; 26 ft 5¼ in	P. May (Aus), 7·94 m; 26 ft 0½ in	A. Lerwill (Eng), 7·94 m; 26 ft 0½ in
Triple Jump	P. May (Aus), 16·72 m; 54 ft 10 in	M. McGrath (Aus), 16·41 m; 53 ft 10 in	Mohinder Singh (Ind), 15·9 m; 52 ft 1¾ in
Shot Put	D. Steen (Can), 19·21 m; 63 ft 0¼ in	J. Teale (Eng), 18·43 m; 60 ft 5½ in	L. Mills (NZ), 18·4 m; 60 ft 4¼ in
Discus	G. Puce (Can), 59·02 m; 193 ft 7 in	L. Mills (NZ) 57·84 m; 189 ft 9 in	W. Tancred (Eng), 56·68 m; 185 ft 11 in
Hammer	H. Payne (Eng), 67·8 m; 222 ft 5 in	B. Fraser (Eng), 62·9 m; 206 ft 5 in	B. Williams (Eng), 61·58 m; 202 ft
Javelin	D. Travis (Eng), 79·5 m; 260 ft 9 in	J. McSorley (Eng), 76·74 m; 251 ft 9 in	J. FitzSimmons (Eng), 73·2 m; 240 ft 1 in
Decathlon	G. Smith (Aus), 7,492 pts	P. Gabbett (Eng), 7,469 pts	B. King (Eng), 7,201 pts
Women			
100 metres	R. Boyle (Aus), 11·2 s	A. Annum (Gha), 11·3 s	M. Hoffman (Aus), 11·3 s
200 metres	R. Boyle (Aus), 22·7 s	A. Annum (Gha), 22·8 s	M. Critchley (Eng), 23·1 s
400 metres	M. Neufville (Jam), w 51 s	S. Brown (Aus), 53·6 s	J. Ayaa (Uga), 53·7 s
800 metres	R. Stirling (Sco), 2 m 6·2 s	P. Lowe (Eng), 2 m 6·2 s	C. Peasley (Aus), 2 m 6·3 s
1,500 metres	R. Ridley (Eng), 4 m 18·8 s	J. Page (Eng), 4 m 19 s	T. Fynn (Can), 4 m 19·1 s
100 metres Hurdles	P. Kilborn (Aus), 13·2 s	M. Caird (Aus), 13·7 s	C. Bell (Eng), 13·8 s
4 × 100 metres Relay	Australia, 44·1 s	England, 44·2 s	Canada, 44·6 s
High Jump	D. Brill (Can), 1·78 m; 5 ft 10 in	A. Wilson (Eng), 1·7 m; 5 ft 7 in	M. Wallis (Sco), 1·7 m; 5 ft 7 in
Long Jump	S. Sherwood (Eng), 6·73 m; 22 ft 0¼ in	A. Wilson (Eng), 6·5 m; 21 ft 4 in	J. Hendry (Can), 6·28 m; 20 ft 7¼ in
Shot Put	M. Peters (NI), 15·93 m; 52 ft 3 in	B. Poulsen (NZ), 15·87 m; 52 ft 0¾ in	J. Roberts (Aus), 15·32 m; 50 ft 3 in
Discus	R. Payne (Sco), 54·66 m; 178 ft 8 in	J. Roberts (Aus), 51·02 m; 167 ft 5 in	C. Martin (Can), 48·42 mm; 158 ft 10 in
Javelin	P. Rivers (Aus), 52 m; 170 ft 7 in	A. Farquhar (Eng), 50·82 m; 166 ft 8 in	J. Dahlgren (Can), 49·54 m; 162 ft 6 in
Pentathlon	M. Peters (NI), 5,148 pts	A. Wilson (Eng), 5,037 pts	J. Meldrum (Can), 4,736 pts

Rita Ridley (*left*) was first in the women's 1,500 metres, and Marilyn Neufville (*right*) set a new world record in the 400 metres. *Centre:* Ian Stewart (right), gold; I. McCafferty (centre), silver; and Kip Keino, bronze, in the 5,000 metres.

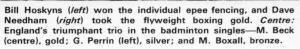

Bill Hoskyns (*left*) won the individual epee fencing, and Dave Needham (*right*) took the flyweight boxing gold. *Centre:* England's triumphant trio in the badminton singles—M. Beck (centre), gold; G. Perrin (left), silver; and M. Boxall, bronze.

Event	Gold Medal	Silver Medal	Bronze Medal
BADMINTON			
Men's Singles	J. Paulson (Can)	P. Whetnall (Eng)	R. Sharp (Eng)
Men's Doubles	Ng Boon Bee & P Gunalan (Mal)	Tan Soon Hooi & Ng Tat Wai (Mal)	J. Paulson & Y. Pare (Can)
Women's Singles	M. Beck (Eng)	G. Perrin (Eng)	M. Boxall (Eng)
Women's Doubles	M. Boxall & S. Whetnall (Eng)	G. Perrin & J. Rickard (Eng)	R. Ang & Teoh Siew Yong (Mal)
Mixed Doubles	D. Talbot & M. Boxall (Eng)	R. Mills & G. Perrin (Eng)	J. Eddy & S. Whetnall (Eng)
BOWLS			
Singles	D. Bryant (Eng), 24 pts	N. Bryce (Zam), 18 pts	R. Fulton (NI), 18 pts
Pairs	N. King & P. Line (Eng), 24 pts	R. MacDonald & H. Robson (NZ), 20 pts	J. Donnelly & S. Thompson (NI), 19 pts
Fours	Hong Kong, 23 pts	Scotland, 18 pts	Northern Ireland, 17 pts
BOXING			
Light-Flyweight	J. Odwori (Uga)	A. Davies (Wal)	M. Abrams (Eng) / P. Butterfield (Aus)
Flyweight	D. Needham (Eng)	L. Rwabogo (Uga)	A. McHugh (Sco) / D. Larmour (NI)
Bantamweight	S. Shittu (Gha)	S. Mbowga (Ken)	C. Atherly (Gha) / S. Ogilvie (Sco)
Featherweight	P. Warninge (Ken)	D. Musoke (Uga)	S. Mir (Pak) / A. Richardson (Eng)
Lightweight	A. Adeyemi (Nig)	J. Gillan (Sco)	M. Mbogwa (Ken) / T. Chionga (Mwi)
Light-Welterweight	M. Muruli (Uga)	D. Davies (Wal)	E. Lawson (Gha) / P. Mulenga (Zam)
Welterweight	E. Ankudey (Gha)	J. Olulu (Ken)	T. Joyce (Sco) / S. Bhonsle (Ind)
Light-Middleweight	T. Imrie (Sco)	J. Luipa (Zam)	P. Doherty (NI) / D. Attan (Ken)
Middleweight	J. Conteh (Eng)	T. Simba (Tan)	R. Murphy (Aus) / S. Kasongo (Zam)
Light-Heavyweight	F. Ayinla (Nig)	O. Wright (Jam)	V. Attivor (Gha) / J. Rafferty (Sco)
Heavyweight	B. Masanda (Uga)	J. McKinty (NI)	L. Stevens (Eng) / J. Meda (Can)
CYCLING			
1,000 metres Sprint	J. Nicholson (Aus)	G. Johnson (Aus)	L. King (Tri)
Tandem Sprint	G. Johnson & R. Jonker (Aus)	B. Harvey & J. Lovell (Can)	J. Hatfield & J. Beswick (Wal)
1,000 metres Time Trial	H. Kent (NZ), 1 m 8·69 s	L. King (Tri), 1 m 10·4 s	J. Lovell (Can), 1 m 10·53 s
4,000 metres Pursuit	I. Hallam (Eng)	D. Clarke (Aus)	B. Stockwell (NZ)
10 miles Scratch	J. Lovell (Can), 20 m 46·7 s	B. Temple (Sco), 20 m 47·6 s	V. Stauble (Tri), 20 m 47·7 s
Road Race	B. Biddle (NZ), 4 h 38 m 58 s	R. Bilney (Aus), 4 h 38 m 58 s	J. Trevorrow (Aus), 4 h 40 m 26 s
FENCING			
Men			
Foil: Individual	M. Breckin (Eng), 4 wins (won barrage 5-3)	B. Paul (Eng), 4 wins	G. Paul (Eng), 3 wins
Team	England	Australia	Canada
Sabre Individual	A. Leckie (Sco), 5 wins	R. Craig (Eng), 4 wins	R. Cohen (Eng), 3 wins
Team	England	Scotland	Australia
Epee: Individual	W. Hoskyns (Eng), 4 wins	L. Wong (Can), 3 wins	P. Jacobs (Eng), 3 wins
Team	England	Scotland	Canada
Women			
Foil: Individual	J. Wardell-Yerburgh (Eng), 4 wins (won barrage 4—0)	M. Exelby (Aus), 4 wins	S. Young (Sco), 3 wins
Team	England	Scotland	Canada

Event		*Gold Medal*	*Silver Medal*	*Bronze Medal*
SWIMMING				
Men				
Free-style	100 metres	M. Wenden (Aus), 53·1 s	G. Rogers (Aus), 54·3 s	W. Devenish (Aus), 54·3 s
	200 metres	M. Wenden (Aus), 1 m 56·7 s	R. Hutton (Can), 1 m 58·4 s	G. Rogers (Aus), 1 m 58·6 s
	400 metres	G. White (Aus), 4 m 8·5 s	R. Hutton (Can), 4 m 8·9 s	G. Brough (Aus), 4 m 12·2 s
	1,500 metres	G. Windeatt (Aus), 16 m 23·8 s	M. Tavasci (Aus), 16 m 34·1 s	M. Treffers (NZ), 16 m 44·7 s
	4×100 metres Relay	Australia, 3 m 36 s	Canada, 3 m 37·6 s	England, 3 m 41·2 s
	4×200 metres Relay	Australia, *w* 7 m 50·8 s	Canada, 8 m 0·7 s	England, 8 m 10·6 s
Back-stroke	100 metres	W. Kennedy (Can), 1 m 1·6 s	M. Richards (Wal), 1 m 1·7 s	E. Fish (Can), 1 m 2 s
	200 metres	M. Richards (Wal), 2 m 14·5 s	R. Terrell (Eng), 2 m 15·5 s	N. Rogers (Aus), 2 m 15·6 s
Breast-stroke	100 metres	W. Mahony (Can), 1 m 9 s	P. Cross (Can), 1 m 9·4 s	P. Jarvie (Aus), 1 m 10 s
	200 metres	W. Mahony (Can), 2 m 30·3 s	P. Jarvie (Aus), 2 m 30·7 s	D. Wilkie (Sco), 2 m 32·9 s
Butterfly	100 metres	B. Macdonald (Can), 58·4 s	T. Arusoo (Can), 59 s	R. Jacks (Can), 59 s
	200 metres	T. Arusoo (Can), 2 m 9 s	M. Woodroffe (Wal), 2 m 9·1 s	J. Findlay (Aus), 2 m 9·4 s
Medley	200 metres	G. Smith (Can), 2 m 13·7 s	K. Campbell (Can), 2 m 16·6 s	M. Woodroffe (Wal), 2 m 16·6 s
	400 metres	G. Smith (Can), 4 m 48·9 s	R. Terrell (Eng), 4 m 49·8 s	J. Findlay (Aus), 4 m 51·9 s
	4×100 metres	Canada, 4 m 1·1 s	Australia, 4 m 4·5 s	Wales, 4 m 8 s
Women				
Free-style	100 metres	A. Coughlan (Can), 1 m 1·2 s	L. Watson (Aus), 1 m 1·4 s	J. Watts (Aus), 1 m 1·8 s
	200 metres	K. Moras (Aus), 2 m 9·8 s	A. Coughlan (Can), 2 m 10·8 s	A. Jackson (IOM), 2 m 13·5 s
	400 metres	K. Moras (Aus), 4 m 27·4 s	D. Langford (Aus), 4 m 31·4 s	R. Risson (Aus), 4 m 39·8 s
	800 metres	K. Moras (Aus), *w* 9 m 2·4 s	H. Gray (Aus), 9 m 27·5 s	R. Risson (Aus), 9 m 37·9 s
	4×100 metres Relay	Australia, 4 m 6·4 s	Canada, 4 m 12·2 s	England, 4 m 14·9 s
Back-stroke	100 metres	L. Watson (Aus), 1 m 7·1 s	D. Cain (Aus), 1 m 7·7 s	D.-M. Gurr (Can), 1 m 8·9 s
	200 metres	L. Watson (Aus), 2 m 22·9 s	D.-M. Gurr (Can), 2 m 24·3 s	D. Cain (Aus), 2 m 26 s
Breast-stoke	100 metres	B. Whitfield (Aus), 1 m 17·4 s	D. Harrison (Eng), 1 m 17·6 s	C. Jarvis (Eng), 1 m 19·8 s
	200 metres	B. Whitfield (Aus), 2 m 44·1 s	D. Harrison (Eng), 2 m 46·2 s	A. Radnage (Eng), 2 m 50·1 s
Butterfly	100 metres	D. Lansley (Eng), 1 m 7·9 s	S. Smith (Can), 1 m 8·2 s	A. Mabb (Aus), 1 m 8·7 s
	200 metres	M. Robinson (Aus), 2 m 24·7 s	J. Comerford (Aus), 2 m 24·9 s	A. Mabb (Aus), 2 m 31·1 s
Medley	200 metres	D. Langford (Aus), 2 m 28·9 s	S. Ratcliffe (Eng), 2 m 29·6 s	D. Rickard (Aus), 2 m 30·8 s
	400 metres	D. Langford (Aus), 5 m 10·7 s	G. Neall (Aus), 5 m 15·8 s	S. Ratcliffe (Eng), 5 m 17·9 s
	4×100 metres	Australia, 4 m 30·7 s	England, 4 m 38·9 s	Canada, 4 m 39·6 s
DIVING				
Men	Highboard	D. Wagstaff (Aus), 485·73 pts	P. Drew (Eng), 429·24 pts	A. Gill (Eng), 421·47 pts
	Springboard	D. Wagstaff (Aus), 557·73 pts	K. Sully (Can), 497·37 pts	R. Friesen (Can), 495·9 pts
Women	Highboard	B. Boys (Can), 361·95 pts	N. Robertson (Can), 350·49 pts	S. Burrow (Eng), 330·63 pts
	Springboard	B. Boys (Can), 432·87 pts	E. Carruthers (Can), 391·20 pts	G. Morley (Aus), 389·04 pts
WEIGHT-LIFTING				
Flyweight		G. Vasil (Aus), 290 kg (639 lb)	A. Ghafoor (Pak), 287·5 kg (633½ lb)	J. McNiven (Sco), 265 kg (584 lb)
Bantamweight		P. McKenzie (Eng), 335 kg (738¼ lb)	A. Phillips (Bar), 317·5 kg (699¾ lb)	C. Tung (Sin), 302·5 kg (666½ lb)
Featherweight		G. Perrin (Eng), 342·5 kg (754¾ lb)	P. Chua (Sin), 340 kg (749¼ lb)	A. Navis (Ind), 335 kg (738½ lb)
Lightweight		G. Newton (Eng), 372·5 kg (821 lb)	I. Owen (Wal), 355 kg (782¼ lb)	B. Cameron (NZ), 355 kg (782¼ lb)
Middleweight		R. Pery (Aus), 412·5 kg (909 lb)	A. Ebert (NZ), 402·5 kg (887 lb)	P. St. Jean (Can), 400 kg (881½ lb)
Light-Heavyweight		N. Ciancio (Aus), 447·5 kg (986¼ lb)	J. Bolton (NZ), 445 kg (980¾ lb)	P. Arthur (Wal), 427·5 kg (942 lb)
Middle-Heavyweight		L. Martin (Eng), 457·5 kg (1008¼ lb)	R. Santavy (Can), 425 kg (936½ lb)	G. Manners (STV), 410 kg (903½ lb)
Heavyweight		R. Prior (Can), 490 kg (1079¾ lb)	D. Hancock (Eng), 470 kg (1035¾ lb)	E. Morris (Can), 470 kg (1035¾ lb)
Super-Heavyweight		R. Rigby (Aus), 500 kg (1102 lb)	T. Perdue (Wal), 500 kg (1102 lb)	G. Anderson (Sco), 432·5 kg (953 lb)
WRESTLING				
Light-Flyweight		Ved Prakash (Ind)	K. Shand (Can)	D. Urquhart (Sco); M. Sadiq (Pak)
Flyweight		Sudhesh Kuhar (Ind)	Mohammad Nazir (Pak)	D. Stitt (Can)
Bantamweight		Sardar Mohammad (Pak)	H. Singerman (Can)	T. Robinson (Eng)
Featherweight		Mohammad Saeed (Pak)	P. Bolger (Can)	Randhawa Singh (Ind)
Lightweight		Udey Chand (Ind)	Mohammad Yagul (Pak)	O. Sorenson (Can)
Welterweight		Mukhtiar Singh (Ind)	A. Wurr (Can)	G. Mackay (NZ)
Middleweight		Harish Chandler Birajir (Ind)	N. Shori (Can)	R. Grinsted (Eng); D. Aspin (NZ)
Light-Heavyweight		Mohammad Faiz (Pak)	Sajjan Singh (Ind)	C. Pilon (Can)
Heavyweight		E. Millard (Can)	Vishwanath Singh (Ind)	Mohammad Riza (Pak)
Heavyweight Plus (over 100 kg)		Ikram Ellahi	Marutimane (Ind)	D. McNamara (Eng)

NATIONAL MEDALS TABLE

	Gold	*Silver*	*Bronze*	*Total*		*Gold*	*Silver*	*Bronze*	*Total*		*Gold*	*Silver*	*Bronze*	*Total*
England	27	25	32	84	Northern Ireland	3	1	5	9	Hong Kong	1	0	0	1
Australia	36	24	22	82	Jamaica	4	2	1	7	Barbados	0	1	0	1
Canada	18	24	24	66	Uganda	3	3	1	7	Tanzania	0	1	0	1
Scotland	6	8	11	25	Ghana	2	3	2	7	Fiji	0	0	1	1
Kenya	5	3	6	14	Trinidad & Tobago	0	4	3	7	Gambia	0	0	1	1
New Zealand ..	2	6	6	14	Zambia	0	2	2	4	Guyana	0	0	1	1
India	5	3	4	12	Malaysia	1	1	1	3	Isle of Man	0	0	1	1
Wales	2	6	4	12	Nigeria	2	0	0	2	Malawi	0	0	1	1
Pakistan	4	3	3	10	Singapore	0	1	1	2	St. Vincent	0	0	1	1

Two competitors at the Commonwealth Games who were robbed of almost certain victory by falls on the track: Sylvia Potts (N.Z.) in the 1,500 metres, and K. D. O'Brien (Australia) in the steeplechase.

After 102 miles, Bruce Biddle (N.Z.) took the cycling road race gold medal from Ray Bilney (Australia) by a whisker, both being given the same time of 4 h 38 m 58 s.

Dr. Ron Hill (England), winner of the marathon.

Mary Peters (N. Ireland), gold medallist in the shot.

Winners of the 110 metres hurdles: D. Hemery (England, centre), gold; M. Baird (Australia, left), silver; G. Murray (Jamaica), bronze.

The finish of the men's 100 metres final. Left to right: E. Stewart (Jamaica); L. Miller (Jamaica), second; G. Daniels (Ghana); H. Crawford (Trinidad and Tobago), third; D. Quarrie (Jamaica), first; G. J. Eddy (Australia); L. Piggott (Scotland); and R. Symonds (Bermuda).

14-year-old Ved Prakash (India), won the light-fly wrestling final.

Married gold medallists: Howard Payne (England), in the hammer, and wife Rosemary (Scotland), in the discus.

First gold of the Games went to G. Vasil (Australia), fly-weight weight-lifter.

Above: President Ordaz opened the World Cup tournament in Mexico City's Aztec Stadium on May 31. Lined up were the Russian and Mexican teams who drew 0–0 in the first match.

Below: Brazilian Pelé, hero of the series, chaired by victorious team-mates.

Left: England lost 3–2 to West Germany on June 14; leapers are England's keeper Bonetti, German forward Müller (13), and Labone.

Right: Brazil's captain Alberto with the World Cup after beating the Italians 4–1 in the final.

IX WORLD CUP 1968–70

Final Tournament in Mexico, May 31–June 21, 1970

BRAZIL PROVED undisputed world Soccer masters by winning the World Cup in Mexico for the third time in 12 years, to gain outright possession of the Jules Rimet trophy. The victory was a triumph for individual flair and attacking play, which many had thought could never succeed in an era of rock-hard defensive systems. There were weaknesses in defence in the Brazilian side, but these were more than offset by the outstanding attacking four-some of Tostao, Pele, Rivelino, and Jairzinho.

The IX World Cup surprised all the experts, who had predicted plenty of rough play and few goals. Happily the refereeing was firm but fair, and not one player was sent off. In all, the 16 teams in the final rounds scored 95 goals in 32 matches, and twice there were seven goals in a game. Brazil's stars notched up 19 in six matches, including a 4–1 victory over Italy in the Final.

The heat rather than the altitude proved the biggest problem for European teams, and the holders, England, persisting with a 4–4–2 line-up, paid the penalty for adopting a system that places a great strain on the two front attackers. England managed only two goals (one from a penalty) in the three group matches against Rumania, Brazil, and Czechoslovakia, but seemed to be coasting towards the semi-finals when leading West Germany by two goals early in the second half in the quarter-final at Leon. Then disaster struck as England seemed prepared only to defend. The West Germans stormed back and equalized, and in extra time Gerd Muller, leading scorer of the tournament, gained revenge

for his country's defeat in the 1966 Final at Wembley. Italy, humbled by the North Koreans four years earlier, regained some of her international soccer prestige by winning an exhausting semi-final 4–3 against West Germany in extra time, only to find no answer to Brazil's brilliant attack in the Final.

There were no North Korean giant-killers this time, although Morocco had a 25-minute spell of glory in a group match by holding a one-goal lead over the Germans. Peru, stunned by the news of the earthquake which had hit their homeland, won much local support with a rousing comeback against Bulgaria, but they too could not stop the Brazilian march to perhaps the most outstanding of three post-war Cup wins.

Whether the 1970 Brazilian side was their greatest is something critics and fans will argue for years to come. Pele, playing in his fourth and probably last World Cup, was the outstanding star on the field, but on the touchline Brazil had another hero—unsung and almost forgotten outside his own country. Less than three months before the Finals were due to be played, Brazil sacked team-manager Joao Saldanha and handed to Mario Jorge Zagalo the task of restoring confidence and form to a squad unsettled by injury and disputes. Using the players left him, Zagalo called for a change of role from some, and succeeded in convincing Pele that he still had an important place in the team. Thus Zagalo completed as manager a hat-trick he had helped start as a playing member of Brazil's winning 1958 and 1962 Cup teams.

GROUP 1
Played at Mexico City

				P	W	D	L	F	A	Pts
Mexico ..	0	Russia ...	0							
Belgium ..	3	El Salvador	0	RUSSIA	3 2 1 0 6 1 5					
Russia ...	4	Belgium ..	1	MEXICO	3 2 1 0 5 0 5					
Mexico ..	4	El Salvador	0	Belgium	3 1 0 2 4 5 2					
El Salvador	0	Russia ...	2	El Salvador	3 0 0 3 0 9 0					
Belgium ..	0	Mexico ..	1	(Russia won toss for first place)						

GROUP 2
Played at Puebla and Toluca

				P	W	D	L	F	A	Pts
Uruguay .	2	Israel	0							
Sweden ..	0	Italy	1	ITALY	3 1 2 0 1 0 4					
Uruguay .	0	Italy	0	URUGUAY	3 1 1 1 2 1 3					
Israel	1	Sweden ..	1	Sweden	3 1 1 1 2 2 3					
Sweden ..	1	Uruguay .	0	Israel	3 0 2 1 1 3 2					
Italy	0	Israel	0							

GROUP 3
Played at Guadalajara

				P	W	D	L	F	A	Pts
England	1	Rumania	0							
Czechoslovakia	1	Brazil	4	BRAZIL	3 3 0 0 8 3 6					
Rumania	2	Czechoslovakia	1	ENGLAND	3 2 0 1 2 1 4					
England	0	Brazil	1	Rumania	3 1 0 2 4 5 2					
Brazil	3	Rumania	2	Czechoslovakia	3 0 0 3 2 7 0					
Czechoslovakia	0	England	1							

GROUP 4
Played at Leon

				P	W	D	L	F	A	Pts
Peru	3	Bulgaria	2							
Morocco	1	W. Germany ..	2	W. GERMANY	3 3 0 0 10 4 6					
Peru	3	Morocco	0	PERU	3 2 0 1 7 5 4					
Bulgaria	2	W. Germany ..	5	Bulgaria	3 0 1 2 5 9 1					
W. Germany ..	3	Peru	1	Morocco	3 0 1 2 2 6 1					
Morocco	1	Bulgaria	1							

The arrangements for the knock-out competition were as follows. Quarter-Finals: Match A—Winner of Group 1 v. Runner-up of Group 2; Match B—Winner of Group 2 v. Runner-up of Group 1; Match C—Winner of Group 3 v. Runner-up of Group 4; Match D—Winner of Group 4 v. Runner-up of Group 3. Semi-Finals: Winner of Match A v. Winner of Match C; Winner of Match B v. Winner of Match D.

QUARTER-FINALS
June 14

BRAZIL .... 4}
Peru .... 2⌡
(Guadalajara)

Russia .... 0}
Uruguay ..:.................. 1⌡
(Mexico City; after extra time)

W. Germany .... 3}
England .... 2⌡
(Leon; after extra time)

Mexico .... 1}
ITALY .... 4⌡
(Toluca)

SEMI-FINALS
June 17

BRAZIL .... 3}
(Guadalajara)

Uruguay .... 1⌡

West Germany .... 3}
(Mexico City; after extra time)

ITALY .... 4⌡

FINAL
June 21
Mexico City

BRAZIL 4
(Felix, Carlos Alberto, Brito, Piazza, Everaldo, Gerson, Clodoaldo, Rivelino, Jairzinho, Tostao, Pele.)

ITALY 1
(Albertosi, Burgnich, Facchetti, Cera, Rosato, Bertini, Domenghini, De Sisti, Mazzola, Riva, Boninsegna. Substitutes—Juliano, Rivera.)

Match for 3rd place (June 20, Mexico City): W. Germany ... 1   Uruguay ... 0

Leading goal-scorers in the Tournament: 10—Muller (W. Germany); 7—Jairzinho (Brazil); 5—Cubillas (Peru); 4—Bishovets (Russia), Pele (Brazil); 3—Rivelino (Brazil), Seeler (W. Germany), Riva (Italy).

EUROPEAN CHAMPIONS' CUP 1969–70

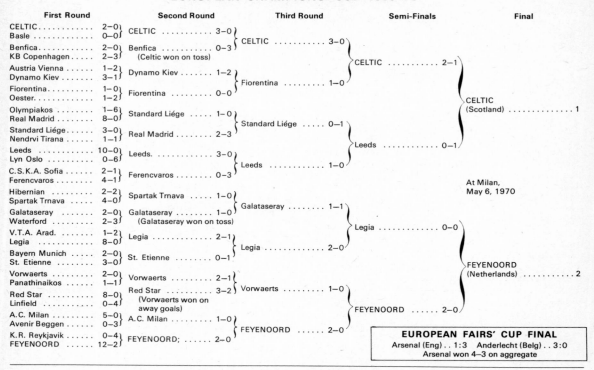

First Round		Second Round		Third Round		Semi-Finals		Final	
CELTIC	2–0	CELTIC	3–0						
Basle	0–0			CELTIC	3–0				
Benfica	2–0	Benfica	0–3						
KB Copenhagen	2–3	(Celtic won on toss)				CELTIC	2–1		
Austria Vienna	1–2	Dynamo Kiev	1–2						
Dynamo Kiev	3–1			Fiorentina	1–0				
Fiorentina	1–0	Fiorentina	0–0						
Oester.	1–2							CELTIC	1
Olympiakos	1–6	Standard Liége	1–0					(Scotland)	
Real Madrid	8–0			Standard Liége	0–1				
Standard Liége	3–0	Real Madrid	2–3						
Nendrvi Tirana	1–1					Leeds	0–1		
Leeds	10–0	Leeds	3–0						
Lyn Oslo	0–6			Leeds	1–0				
C.S.K.A. Sofia	2–1	Ferencvaros	0–3					At Milan,	
Ferencvaros	4–1							May 6, 1970	
Hibernian	2–2	Spartak Trnava	1–0						
Spartak Trnava	4–0			Galataseray	1–1				
Galataseray	2–0	Galataseray	1–0						
Waterford	2–3	(Galataseray won on toss)				Legia	0–0		
V.T.A. Arad.	1–2	Legia	2–1						
Legia	8–0			Legia	2–0				
Bayern Munich	2–0	St. Etienne	0–1						
St. Etienne	3–0							FEYENOORD	2
Vorwaerts	2–0	Vorwaerts	2–1					(Netherlands)	
Panathinaikos	1–1			Vorwaerts	1–0				
Red Star	8–0	Red Star	3–2						
Linfield	0–4	(Vorwaerts won on away goals)				FEYENOORD	2–0		
A.C. Milan	5–0	A.C. Milan	1–0						
Avenir Beggen	0–3			FEYENOORD	2–0				
K.R. Reykjavik	0–4	FEYENOORD;	2–0						
FEYENOORD	12–2								

EUROPEAN FAIRS' CUP FINAL
Arsenal (Eng) . . 1:3   Anderlecht (Belg) . . 3:0
Arsenal won 4–3 on aggregate

EUROPEAN CUP-WINNERS' CUP 1969–70

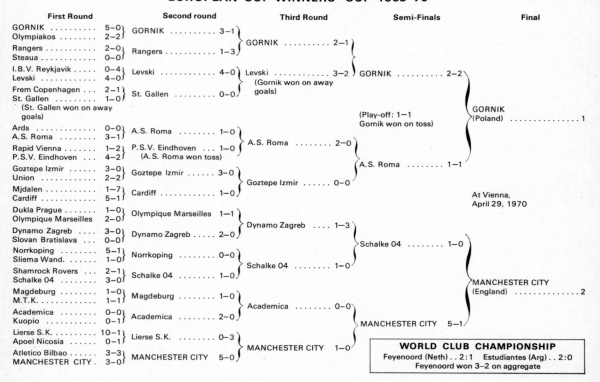

First Round		Second round		Third Round		Semi-Finals		Final	
GORNIK	5–0	GORNIK	3–1						
Olympiakos	2–2			GORNIK	2–1				
Rangers	2–0	Rangers	1–3						
Steaua	0–0					GORNIK	2–2		
I.B.V. Reykjavik	0–4	Levski	4–0						
Levski	4–0			Levski	3–2				
Frem Copenhagen	2–1	St. Gallen	0–0	(Gornik won on away goals)					
St. Gallen	1–0							GORNIK	1
(St. Gallen won on away goals)						(Play-off: 1–1 Gornik won on toss)		(Poland)	
Ards	0–0	A.S. Roma	1–0						
A.S. Roma	3–1			A.S. Roma	2–0				
Rapid Vienna	1–2	P.S.V. Eindhoven	1–0						
P.S.V. Eindhoven	4–2	(A.S. Roma won on toss)				A.S. Roma	1–1		
Goztepe Izmir	3–0	Goztepe Izmir	3–0						
Union	2–2			Goztepe Izmir	0–0				
Mjdalen	1–7	Cardiff	1–0					At Vienna,	
Cardiff	5–1							April 29, 1970	
Dukla Prague	1–0	Olympique Marseilles	1–1						
Olympique Marseilles	2–0			Dynamo Zagreb	1–3				
Dynamo Zagreb	3–0	Dynamo Zagreb	2–0						
Slovan Bratislava	0–0					Schalke 04	1–0		
Norrkoping	5–1	Norrkoping	0–0						
Sliema Wand.	1–0			Schalke 04	1–0				
Shamrock Rovers	2–1	Schalke 04	1–0						
Schalke 04	3–0							MANCHESTER CITY	2
Magdeburg	1–0	Magdeburg	1–0					(England)	
M.T.K.	1–1			Academica	0–0				
Academica	0–0	Academica	2–0						
Kuopio	0–1					MANCHESTER CITY	5–1		
Lierse S.K.	10–1	Lierse S.K.	0–3						
Apoel Nicosia	0–1			MANCHESTER CITY	1–0				
Atletico Bilbao	3–3	MANCHESTER CITY	5–0						
MANCHESTER CITY	3–0								

WORLD CLUB CHAMPIONSHIP
Feyenoord (Neth) . . 2:1   Estudiantes (Arg) . . 2:0
Feyenoord won 3–2 on aggregate

LEAGUE FOOTBALL 1969–70

THE FOOTBALL LEAGUE

Division	Champions	Runners-up	*Relegated Clubs †Re-elected Clubs
One	Everton .... 66 pts	Leeds United .... 57 pts	*Sunderland .... 26 pts *Sheffield Wednesday ... 25 pts
Two	Huddersfield Town .... 60 pts	Blackpool .... 53 pts	*Aston Villa .... 29 pts *Preston North End .... 28 pts
Three	Orient .... 62 pts	Luton Town .... 60 pts	*Bournemouth .... 39 pts *Southport .... 38 pts *Barrow .... 30 pts *Stockport County .... 23 pts
Four	Chesterfield .... 64 pts	Wrexham .... 61 pts 3rd. Swansea Town ..... 60 pts 4th. Port Vale .... 59 pts	†Newport County .... 37 pts †Darlington .... 36 pts †Hartlepool .... 30 pts Bradford, 23 pts, were not re-elected, their place being taken by Cambridge United

SCOTTISH LEAGUE

	Champions	Runners-up	*Relegated Clubs
One	Celtic .... 57 pts	Rangers .... 45 pts	*Raith Rovers .... 21 pts *Partick Thistle .... 17 pts
Two	Falkirk .... 56 pts	Cowdenbeath .... 55 pts	

LEAGUE CUP FINALS

Football League
March 7, 1970 (Wembley):
Manchester City 2   West Bromwich Albion .... 1 (after extra time)

Scottish League
Oct. 25, 1969 (Hampden Park):
Celtic 1   St. Johnstone 0

INTER-LEAGUE MATCHES

Sept. 5, 1969 (Ibrox Park)   Scottish League . 5   Irish League 2
Sept. 10, 1969 (Barnsley)   Football League . 3   League of Ireland 0
March 18, 1970 (Coventry)   Football League . 3   Scottish League . 2

EUROPEAN LEAGUE CHAMPIONS 1970

Albania .... Nenduri Tirana
Austria .... Austria Vienna
Belgium .... Standard Liege
Bulgaria .... Levskiy Spartak
Czechoslovakia .... Slovan Bratislava
Denmark .... KB Copenhagen
East Germany .... Karl Zeiss-Jena
Eire .... Waterford
France .... St. Etienne
Greece .... Panathinaikos, Athens
Hungary .... Ujpest Dosza
Iceland .... KR Reykjavik
Italy .... Cagliari
Luxemburg .... Jeunesse D'esch
Malta .... Floriana
Netherlands .... Ajax Amsterdam
Northern Ireland .... Glentoran
Norway .... Rosenberg
Poland .... Legia, Warsaw
Portugal .... Sporting Lisbon
Rumania .... UT Arad
Spain .... Atletico, Madrid
Switzerland .... Basle
Turkey .... Fenerbache
U.S.S.R. .... Moscow Spartak
West Germany .... Borussia Munchengladbach
Yugoslavia .... Red Star, Belgrade

UNDER-23 INTERNATIONALS

Oct.   1, 1969 (Bristol)   England. 2   Wales 0
Oct. 22, 1969 (Manchester) England 2   U.S.S.R. 0
March 4, 1970 (Sunderland) England 3   Scotland 1
April 8, 1970 (Plymouth)   England 4   Bulgaria 1

AUSTRALIAN SOCCER 1970
Moscow Dynamos' Tour
Feb.–March 1970

Feb. 18 (Perth)	Western Australia ... 0	Dynamos 5
Feb. 22 (Sydney)	N.S.W. 1	Dynamos 2
March 1 (Newcastle)	Northern N.S.W. 1	Dynamos 6
March 2 (Canberra)	Aus. Capital Territory . 0	Dynamos 6
March 4 (Sydney)	N.S.W. 3	Dynamos 3
March 7 (Adelaide)	South Australia 1	Dynamos 3
March 8 (Melbourne)	Victoria 1	Dynamos 7

Manchester City Tour
May 1970

At Perth:	Western Australia ... 1	Manchester City 1
At Adelaide:	South Australia 0	Manchester City 4
At Sydney:	N.S.W. 1	Manchester City 2
At Brisbane:	Queensland 0	Manchester City 3
At Melbourne:	Victoria 0	Manchester City 3
At Newcastle:	Northern N.S.W. 1	Manchester City 4
At Sydney:	N.S.W. 0	Manchester City 4

Major Competitions

New South Wales Federation Premiership . Hakoah Eastern Suburbs
Victorian Federation Premiership .... Juventus
South Australian Federation Premiership .. Adelaide Juventus
Federation of Western Australia Premiership . E.F. Tricolore
A.C.T. Federation Premiership .... Juventus
Northern N.S.W. Federation Premiership .. Adamstown Rosebud
Tasmanian Council Premiership .... Croatia
Queensland Federation Premiership ...... Azzurri

AUSTRALIAN NATIONAL FOOTBALL
Premiership Teams 1970

Victorian Football League .... Carlton
Victorian Football Association .... Prahran
South Australia .... Sturt
Western Australia .... South Fremantle
Tasmania .... Clarence
New South Wales .... Newtown
Queensland .... Sandgate
Canberra .... Ainslie
State Premiers Challenge Match .. Carlton (Vic.) bt. Sturt (Sth. Aus.)

A record crowd for any sporting fixture in Australia—121,696—saw Carlton defeat Collingwood to win the Victorian Football League Premiership at the Melbourne Cricket Ground on September 26, 1970.

F.A. CUP COMPETITION 1969–70

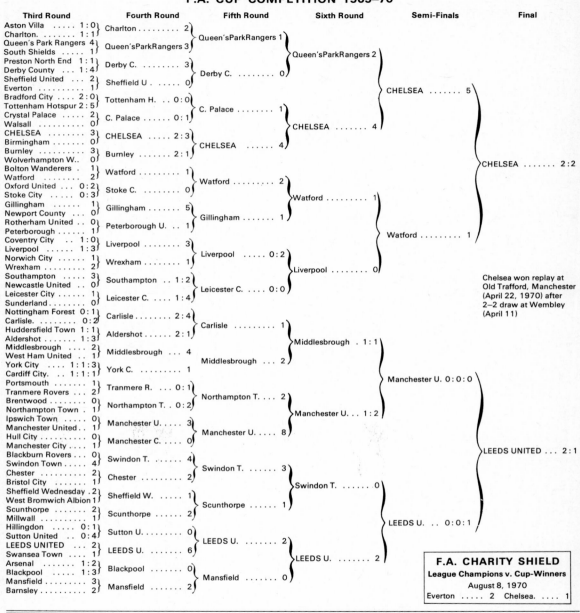

Third Round	Fourth Round	Fifth Round	Sixth Round	Semi-Finals	Final
Aston Villa 1:0	Charlton 2	Queen'sParkRangers 1	Queen'sParkRangers 2	CHELSEA 5	CHELSEA 2:2
Charlton. 1:1	Queen'sParkRangers 3				
Queen's Park Rangers 4					
South Shields 1					
Preston North End 1:1	Derby C. 3	Derby C. 0			
Derby County ... 1:4	Sheffield U. 0				
Sheffield United .. 2					
Everton 1					
Bradford City 2:0	Tottenham H. .. 0:0	C. Palace 1	CHELSEA 4		
Tottenham Hotspur 2:5	C. Palace 0:1				
Crystal Palace 2					
Walsall 0					
CHELSEA 3	CHELSEA 2:3	CHELSEA 4			
Birmingham 0	Burnley 2:1				
Burnley 3					
Wolverhampton W.. 0					
Bolton Wanderers . 1	Watford 1	Watford 2	Watford 1		
Watford 2	Stoke C. 0				
Oxford United ... 0:2					
Stoke City 0:3					
Gillingham 1	Gillingham 5	Gillingham 1			
Newport County ... 0	Peterborough U. .. 1				
Rotherham United .. 0					
Peterborough 1					
Coventry City .. 1:0	Liverpool 3	Liverpool 0:2	Watford 1		
Liverpool 1:3	Wrexham 1				
Norwich City 1					
Wrexham 2					
Southampton 3	Southampton .. 1:2	Leicester C. ... 0:0	Liverpool 0		
Newcastle United .. 0	Leicester C. 1:4				
Leicester City 1					
Sunderland 0					
Nottingham Forest 0:1	Carlisle 2:4	Carlisle 1			
Carlisle. 0:2	Aldershot 2:1				
Huddersfield Town 1:1					
Aldershot 1:3					
Middlesbrough 2	Middlesbrough ... 4	Middlesbrough ... 2	Middlesbrough . 1:1		
West Ham United .. 1	York C. 1				
York City 1:1:3					
Cardiff City. . 1:1:1				Manchester U. 0:0:0	
Portsmouth 1	Tranmere R. ... 0:1	Northampton T. ... 2	Manchester U. ... 1:2		
Tranmere Rovers ... 2	Northampton T. . 0:2				
Brentwood 0					
Northampton Town . 1					
Ipswich Town 0	Manchester U. 3	Manchester U. 8			LEEDS UNITED ... 2:1
Manchester United.. 1	Manchester C. 0				
Hull City 0					
Manchester City ... 1					
Blackburn Rovers .. 0	Swindon T. 4	Swindon T. 3	Swindon T. 0		
Swindon Town 4	Chester 2				
Chester 2					
Bristol City 1					
Sheffield Wednesday .2	Sheffield W. 1	Scunthorpe 1			
West Bromwich Albion 1	Scunthorpe 2				
Scunthorpe 2				LEEDS U. .. 0:0:1	
Millwall 1					
Hillingdon 0:1	Sutton U. 0	LEEDS U. 2	LEEDS U. 2		
Sutton United .. 0:4	LEEDS U. 6				
LEEDS UNITED ... 2					
Swansea Town 1					
Arsenal 1:2	Blackpool 0	Mansfield 0			
Blackpool 1:3	Mansfield 2				
Mansfield 3					
Barnsley 2					

Chelsea won replay at Old Trafford, Manchester (April 22, 1970) after 2–2 draw at Wembley (April 11)

F.A. CHARITY SHIELD
League Champions v. Cup-Winners
August 8, 1970
Everton ..... 2 Chelsea 1

INTERNATIONAL CHAMPIONSHIP 1970
(England, Scotland, N. Ireland, Wales)

April 18 (Belfast)	N. Ireland 0	Scotland 1	
April 18 (Cardiff)	Wales 1	England 1	
April 21 (Wembley)	England 3	N. Ireland 1	
April 22 (Glasgow)	Scotland 0	Wales 0	
April 25 (Swansea)	Wales 1	N. Ireland 0	
April 25 (Glasgow)	Scotland 0	England 0	

	P	W	D	L	F	A	Pts
						Goals	
England	3	1	2	0	4	2	4
Scotland	3	1	2	0	1	0	4
Wales	3	1	2	0	2	1	4
N. Ireland	3	0	0	3	1	5	0

OTHER INTERNATIONALS 1969–70
Not including World Cup matches (see page 225)

1969

Sept. 21 (Dublin)	Rep. of Ireland ... 1	Scotland 1
Nov. 5 (Amsterdam)	Netherlands 0	England 1
Dec. 10 (Wembley)	England 1	Portugal 0

1970

Jan. 14 (Wembley)	England 0	Netherlands 0
Feb. 25 (Brussels)	Belgium 1	England 3
May 20 (Bogota)	Colombia 0	England 4
May 24 (Quito)	Ecuador 0	England 2

SCOTTISH CUP COMPETITION 1969–70

First Round	Second Round	Third Round	Semi-Finals	Final
CELTIC 2	CELTIC 4			
Dunfermline Athletic 1		CELTIC 3		
Dundee United 1	Dundee U. 0			
Ayr United 0			CELTIC 2	
Dumbarton 1	Forfar 0			
Forfar Athletic 2		Rangers 1		
Rangers 3	Rangers 7			CELTIC 1
Hibernians 1				
Albion Rovers 1	Dundee 3			
Dundee 2		Dundee 1		
Airdrieonians 5	Airdrieonians 0			
Hamilton Academicals ... 0			Dundee 1	
East Fife 3	East Fife 0			
Raith Rovers 0		East Fife 0		
Morton 2	Morton 0			
Queen of the South 0				
ABERDEEN 4	ABERDEEN 2			
Clyde 0		ABERDEEN 1		
Arbroath 1	Clydebank 1			
Clydebank 2			ABERDEEN 1	
Falkirk 3	Falkirk 2			
Tarff Rovers 0		Falkirk 0		
St. Mirren 2	St. Mirren 1			ABERDEEN 3
Stirling 0				
Kilmarnock 3	Kilmarnock 2			
Partick Thistle 0		Kilmarnock 1		
Montrose .... 1 : 0	Hearts 0			
Heart of Midlothian .. 1 : 1			Kilmarnock 0	
Motherwell 2	Motherwell 3			
St. Johnstone 1		Motherwell 0		
Stranraer 2	Inverness Caly 1			
Inverness Caly 5				

At Hampden Park, Glasgow, April 11, 1970

AMATEUR FOOTBALL
F.A. AMATEUR CUP FINAL
April 4, 1970, Wembley

ENFIELD 5   DAGENHAM 1

Enfield bt Redhill 3–2; Whitley Bay 4–1 (0–0); Alton Town 5–2; Preswich H. 2–0; Skelmersdale 1–0 in semi-final.

Dagenham bt Hoddesdon 2–1; Barking 3–1 (1–1); Emley 5–0 (0–0); Walton & Hersham 1–0; St. Albans 1–0 (1–1) in semi-final.

AMATEUR INTERNATIONAL CHAMPIONSHIP
(England, Scotland, Ireland, Wales)

Sept. 27, 1969	(Portadown)	Ireland 1	England 4
Nov. 29, 1969	(Cardiff)	Wales 0	England 1
Jan. 10, 1970	(Ballymena)	Ireland 3	Wales 1
Feb. 14, 1970	(Stranraer)	Scotland 3	Ireland 1
Feb. 28, 1970	(Berwick)	Scotland 0	Wales 3
March 20, 1970	(Dulwich)	England 1	Scotland ... 0

	P	W	D	L	F	A	Pts
England	3	3	0	0	6	1	6
Wales	3	1	0	2	4	4	2
Scotland	3	1	0	2	3	5	2
Ireland	3	1	0	2	5	8	2

OTHER AMATEUR INTERNATIONALS

July 20, 1969	(Nassau)	Bahamas 0	England ... 4
July 23, 1969	(Port of Spain)	Trinidad 0	England ... 0
July 26, 1969	(San Fernando)	Trinidad 0	England ... 3
July 29, 1969	(Georgetown)	Guyana 0	England ... 8
July 31, 1969	(Georgetown)	Guyana 0	England ... 8
Aug. 2, 1969	(Willemstad)	Netherlands Antilles 0	England ... 2
Oct. 8, 1969	(Enfield)	England 1	France ... 2
Oct. 22, 1969	(Dulwich)	England 1	Spain 2
Nov. 20, 1969	(Tenerife)	Spain 2	England ... 2
Feb. 2, 1970	(Slough)	England 1	Iceland ... 0
Feb. 28, 1970	(Wycombe)	England 3	Rep. of Ireland 1
May 10, 1970	(Reykjavik)	Iceland 1	England ... 1
May 13, 1970	(Brest)	France 3	England ... 2

IRISH F.A. CUP FINAL
April 4, 1970 (Cliftonville) Linfield 2   Ballymena United 1

SCHOOLS' AND YOUTH FOOTBALL
SCHOOLS INTERNATIONAL TOURNAMENT (VICTORY SHIELD) 1970

Wales 0	Scotland 3
N. Ireland 1	Scotland 2
England 4	N. Ireland 0
England 4	Wales 0
Scotland 2	England 1
Wales 1	N. Ireland 2

Final Placings: 1st, Scotland (6 pts); 2nd, England (4); 3rd, N. Ireland (2); 4th, Wales (0).

OTHER SCHOOLS INTERNATIONALS 1970

March 6	(Sheffield)	England. 11	Rep. of Ireland. . 0
March 11	(Leicester)	England. 1	Scotland 2
March 21	(Wembley)	England 2	Scotland 0
March 28	(Bangor)	Wales 3	England 5
April 4	(Wezep)	Netherlands ... 0	England 0
May 16	(Wembley)	England 3	W. Germany .. 0
May 19	(Sunderland)	England 0	W. Germany .. 0

ENGLISH SCHOOLS TROPHY FINAL

1st leg:	Liverpool 0	East London 0
2nd leg:	East London 0	Liverpool 1

Liverpool won 1–0 on aggregate

F.A. YOUTH CHALLENGE CUP FINAL

1st leg:	Tottenham 1	Coventry 0
2nd leg:	Coventry 1	Tottenham 0
1st Replay:	Tottenham 2	Coventry 2
2nd Replay	Tottenham 1	Coventry 0

INTERNATIONAL YOUTH TOURNAMENT
(Scotland, May 1970)

Final: East Germany 1   Netherlands 1
(East Germany won on toss)

Third Place: Scotland 2   France 0

HOME INTERNATIONAL YOUTH CHAMPIONSHIP 1970

Jan. 31	(Derby)	England 1	Scotland 2
Feb. 7	(Coleraine)	Ireland 2	Wales 1
Feb. 28	(Lurgan)	Ireland 3	England 1
March 14	(Newtown)	Wales 1	Scotland 0
March 21	(Clydebank)	Scotland 3	Ireland 3
April 20	(Reading)	England 0	Wales 0

Final Placings: 1st, Ireland (5 pts); 2nd, Scotland (3); 3rd, Wales (3); 4th, England (1).

RUGBY UNION

INTERNATIONAL CHAMPIONSHIP 1970

Jan.	10	(Murrayfield)	Scotland 9	France 11
Jan.	24	(Paris)	France 8	Ireland 0
Feb.	7	(Cardiff)	Wales 18	Scotland 9
Feb.	14	(Twickenham)	England 9	Ireland 3
Feb.	28	(Dublin)	Ireland 16	Scotland 11
Feb.	28	(Twickenham)	England 13	Wales 17
March	14	(Dublin)	Ireland. 14	Wales 0
March	21	(Murrayfield)	Scotland 14	England 5
April	4	(Cardiff)	Wales 11	France. 6
April	18	(Paris)	France 35	England. 13

	P	W	D	L	F	A	Pts
France	4	3	0	1	60	33	6
Wales	4	3	0	1	46	42	6
Ireland	4	2	0	2	33	28	4
Scotland	4	1	0	3	43	50	2
England	4	1	0	3	40	69	2

Points over F, A columns.

University Match. Oxford . . . . 9 Cambridge 6
County Championship Final. Staffordshire . . 11 Gloucestershire . . 9
Hospitals Cup Final. St. Bartholomew's . . 15 Guy's 0

Schoolboys' Internationals

Feb.	21	(Cardiff)	Wales 8	England 6
March	18	(Twickenham)	England 9	Wales 3
April	10	(Murrayfield)	Scotland 0	Wales 21

S. AFRICAN TOUR OF BRITAIN 1969–70

Dec. 6, 1969	(Murrayfield)	Scotland 6	S. Africa 3
Dec. 20, 1969	(Twickenham)	England 11	S. Africa 8
Jan. 10, 1970	(Dublin)	Ireland 8	S. Africa 8
Jan. 24, 1970	(Cardiff)	Wales 6	S. Africa 6

NEW ZEALAND TOUR OF S. AFRICA 1970

July 25	(Pretoria)	S. Africa 17	New Zealand . . . 6
Aug. 8	(Cape Town)	S. Africa 8	New Zealand . . . 9
Aug. 29	(Port Elizabeth)	S. Africa 14	New Zealand . . . 3
Sept. 12	(Johannesburg)	S. Africa 20	New Zealand . . 17

SCOTTISH TOUR OF AUSTRALIA
May 20–June 6, 1970

At Melbourne	Victoria 0	Scotland 34
At Sydney	New South Wales . 28	Scotland 14
At Bathurst, N.S.W.	N.S.W. Country . . 15	Scotland 18
At Brisbane	Queensland 16	Scotland 13
At Sydney	Sydney 12	Scotland 27
At Sydney	Australia 23	Scotland 3

AUSTRALIAN STATE CAPITAL PREMIERSHIPS

Sydney Premiership . . . . Sydney University
Brisbane Premiership . . . . University of Queensland
Adelaide Premiership . . . . Old Collegians
Perth Premiership . . . . Nedlands

RUGBY LEAGUE

FINAL TABLE 1969–70

	P	W	D	L	F	A	Pts
Leeds	34	30	0	4	674	314	60
Castleford	34	25	1	8	495	298	51
St. Helens	34	23	1	10	702	292	47
Wigan	34	23	0	11	698	420	46
Hull Kingston Rovers	34	22	2	10	566	395	46
Salford	34	22	1	11	572	332	45
Leigh	34	21	3	10	554	325	45
Featherstone Rovers	34	22	1	11	578	385	45
Swinton	34	20	4	10	550	351	44
Widnes	34	21	2	11	473	356	44
Hull	34	20	2	12	420	357	42
Bradford Northern	34	19	0	15	511	404	38
Whitehaven	34	18	2	14	404	450	38
Warrington	34	17	2	15	559	421	36
Huddersfield	34	17	1	16	377	395	35
Halifax	34	16	0	18	395	454	32
Batley	34	15	1	18	388	485	31
Bramley	34	14	1	19	374	498	29
Barrow	34	14	1	19	379	511	29
Rochdale Hornets	34	13	3	18	334	524	29
Wakefield Trinity	34	13	2	19	521	455	28
Dewsbury	34	13	1	20	383	451	27
Hunslet	34	13	1	20	391	574	27
Workington Town	34	12	2	20	416	483	26
Keighley	34	13	0	21	370	555	26
York	34	11	1	22	378	502	23
Doncaster	34	7	0	27	264	564	14
Huyton	34	5	3	26	177	643	13
Oldham	34	6	0	28	343	590	12
Blackpool Borough	34	6	0	28	318	762	12

Top 16 Play-off Final: St. Helens . . . . 24 Leeds 12

INTERNATIONALS

Oct. 18, 1969	(Leeds)	England 40	Wales 23
Oct. 23, 1969	(Salford)	Wales 2	France 8
Oct. 25, 1969	(Wigan)	England 11	France 11
Jan. 25, 1970	(Perpignan)	France 11	Wales 15
Feb. 24, 1970	(Leeds)	England 26	Wales 7
March 15, 1970	(Toulouse)	France 14	England 9

WORLD CUP 1970

Oct. 21 (Wigan)	Australia 47	New Zealand 11
Oct. 24 (Leeds)	Britain 11	Australia 4
Oct. 25 (Hull)	France 15	New Zealand 16
Oct. 28 (Castleford)	Britain 6	France 0
Oct. 31 (Swinton)	Britain 27	New Zealand 17
Nov. 1 (Bradford)	Australia 15	France 17
Final: Nov. 7 (Leeds)	BRITAIN 7	AUSTRALIA 12

CHALLENGE CUP FINAL
May 9, 1970, Wembley

CASTLEFORD 7   WIGAN 2

Castleford bt. Hull 5–0 (1st round), Barrow 12–4 (2nd), Salford 15–0 (3rd), St. Helens 6–3 (semi-final).

Wigan bt. Dewsbury 11–6 (1st round), Oldham 17–4 (2nd), Leigh 6–4 (3rd), Hull Kingston Rovers 19–8 (semi-final).

COUNTY CHAMPIONSHIP

Lancashire 14	Yorkshire 12
Cumberland 10	Lancashire 30
Yorkshire 42	Cumberland 3

Final Placings: 1st, Lancs; 2nd, Yorks; 3rd, Cumberland

Yorkshire Cup Final. Hull . . . . 12 Featherstone 9
Lancashire Cup Final. Swinton . . . . 11 Leigh 2

AUSTRALIAN RUGBY LEAGUE 1970

Sydney Premiership . . . . South Sydney
Brisbane Premiership . . . . Valleys

New South Wales Country Competitions

Newcastle . Western Suburbs	Group 9/20 West Wyalong
Illawarra . Western Suburbs	Group 10 . Oberon
Group 1:	Group 11 . Forbes
Richmond Clarence	Group 12 . Woy Woy
League Grafton	Group 13 . Albury Roos
Bonalbo League Baryulgil	Group 14 . Coonabarabran
Group 2 . . Coffs Harbour	Group 15 . Bourke
Group 3 . . Forster-Tuncurry	Group 16 . Candelo-Bemboka
Group 4 . . Narrabri	Group 17 . Lake Cargelligo
Group 5 . . Armidale	Group 18 . Cudgen
Group 6 . . Campbelltown City	Group 19 . Delegate
Group 7 . . Gerringong	Group 21 . Scone
Group 8/9 . Queanbeyan	Riverina R.L.—Zone 3 Tumut
Kangaroos	

GREAT BRITAIN TOUR OF AUSTRALASIA 1970

June 6 (Brisbane)	Australia 37	Great Britain . . . 15
June 20 (Sydney)	Australia 7	Great Britain . . . 28
July 4 (Sydney)	Australia 17	Great Britain . . . 21
July 11 (Auckland)	New Zealand . . . 15	Great Britain . . . 19
July 18 (Christchurch)	New Zealand . . . 9	Great Britain . . . 23
July 25 (Auckland)	New Zealand . . . 16	Great Britain . . . 33

International Sports Personalities of 1970

G. Agostini (Italy), world motor-cycle racing champion.

Uwe Seeler, W. German soccer captain, played in his last international.

Jack Nicklaus (U.S.A.), Piccadilly world match-play golf champion.

Margaret Court (Austral.) won the 1970 lawn tennis "grand slam".

John Newcombe (Australia) was the Wimbledon men's singles champion in 1970.

Jean Noël Augert (Fr.), ski-ing champion.

At the world ice-dancing championships: left to right Judy Schwomeyer and James Sladky (U.S.A.), silver; Ludmila Pakhomova and Alexander Gorshkov (U.S.S.R.), gold; and Angelika and Erich Buck (W. Germany), bronze.

Nijinsky, wonder racehorse of the year, with Lester Piggot up, seen here after his victory in the Derby.

Sassafras, who beat Nijinsky in the Prix de l'Arc de Triomphe.

Pat Taaffe on Gay Trip romping home in the Grand National.

Eddy Merckx (Belgium), all-conquering cyclist of 1970.

Women's pursuit medallists on the rostrum at the world cycling championships at Leicester: left to right, Raisa Obodovskaya (U.S.S.R.), silver; Tamara Gorkuchina (U.S.S.R.), gold; and Beryl Burton (G.B.), bronze.

SWIMMING

	Metric Distances	**MEN**	Records at Jan. 1, 1971 (y) = set over longer yards course
Event	*World Record*	*European Record*	*British Record*
Free-style			
100 m	51·9 s, M. Spitz (USA), 1970	52·8 s, M. Rousseau (Fr), 1970	53·4 s, R. McGregor, 1967
200 m	1 m 54·3 s, D. Schollander (USA), 1968; M. Spitz (USA), 1969	1 m 55·2 s, H. Fassnacht (W. Ger), 1970	2 m 0·1 s (y), A. Jarvis, 1968
400 m	4 m 2·6 s, G. Larsson (Sweden), 1970	Same as world record	4 m 19·6 s (y), M. Woodroffe, 1969
800 m	8 m 28·8 s, M. Burton (USA), 1969	8 m 41·4 s, H. Fassnacht (W. Ger), 1970	9 m 5·4 s, A. Kimber, 1966; (y), M. Woodroffe, 1969
1,500 m	15 m 57·1 s, J. Kinsella (USA), 1970	16 m 19·9 s, H. Fassnacht (W. Ger), 1970	17 m 13·2 s, A. Kimber, 1966
4 × 100 m	3 m 28·8 s, Los Angeles (D. Frawley, D. Havens, F. Heckl, M. Weston), 1970	3 m 32·3 s, USSR (V. Bure, V. Mazanov, G. Kulikov, L. Ilichev), 1970	3 m 38·3 s (A. Jarvis, K. Bewley, J. Thurley, R. McGregor), 1967
4 × 200 m	7 m 48 s, USA (J. Kinsella, T. McBreen, G. Hall, M. Lambert), 1970	7 m 49·5 s, W. Ger (W. Lampe, O. von Schilling, F. Meeuw, H. Fassnacht), 1970	8 m 5·6 s, GB (M. Woodroffe, M. Bailey, M. Windeatt, R. Terrell), 1970
Back-stroke			
100 m	56·9 s, R. Matthes (E. Ger), 1970	Same as world record	1 m 0·9 s, M. Richards, 1970
200 m	2 m 6·1 s, R. Matthes (E. Ger), 1970	Same as world record	2 m 14·5 s, M. Richards, 1970
Breast-stroke			
100 m	1 m 5·8 s, N. Pankin (USSR), 1969	Same as world record	1 m 9·9 s (y), R. Roberts, 1968
200 m	2 m 23·5 s, B. Job (USA), 1970	2 m 25·4 s, N. Pankin (USSR), 1969	2 m 32·5 s, D. Wilkie, 1970
Butterfly			
100 m	55·6 s, M. Spitz (USA), 1968	57·5 s, H. Lampe (W. Ger), 1970	58·8 s, M. Woodroffe, 1969
200 m	2 m 5 s, G. Hall (USA), 1970	2 m 6·9 s, H. Fassnacht (W. Ger), 1970	2 m 7·8 s, M. Woodroffe, 1969
Medley			
200 m	2 m 9·3 s, G. Larsson (Swed), 1970	Same as world record	2 m 16·6 s, M. Woodroffe, 1970
400 m	4 m 31 s, G. Hall (USA), 1970	4 m 36·2 s, G. Larsson (Swed), 1970	4 m 49·5 s, M. Woodroffe, 1969
4 × 100 m	3 m 54·4 s, E. Ger (R. Matthes, K. Katzur, U. Poser, L. Unger), 1970	Same as world record	4 m 3·9 s, GB (R. Jones, R. Roberts, M. Woodroffe, R. McGregor), 1970

WOMEN

Event	*World Record*	*European Record*	*British Record*
Free-style			
100 m	58·9 s, D. Fraser (Austral), 1964	59·3 s, G. Wetzko (E. Ger), 1970	1 min 5 s, A. Jackson, 1968
200 m	2 m 6·7 s, D. Meyer (USA), 1968	2 m 8·2 s, G. Wetzko (E. Ger), 1970	2 m 13·5 s, A. Jackson, 1970
400 m	4 m 24·3 s, D. Meyer (USA), 1970	4 m 32·9 s, E. Schmisch (E. Ger), 1970	4 m 45·6 s (y), S. Williams, 1967
800 m	9 m 2·4 s, K. Moras (Austral), 1970	9 m 29·1 s, K. Neugebaurer (E. Ger), 1970	9 m 58·4 s, S. Hogg, 1970
1,500 m	17 m 19·9 s, D. Meyer (USA), 1969	18 m 11·6 s, N. Calligaris (It), 1969	Not established
4 × 100 m	4 m 0·8 s, E. Ger (G. Wetzko, I. Komor, E. Sehmisch, C. Schulze), 1970	Same as world record	4 m 9·6 s, GB (L. Allardice, L. Hill, K. Smith, A. Jackson), 1970
Backstroke			
100 m	1 m 5·6 s, K. Muir (SA), 1969	1 m 7·8 s, T. Lekveishvili (USSR), 1970	1 m 8·7 s (y), L. Ludgrove, 1967
200 m	2 m 21·5 s, S. Atwood (USA), 1969	2 m 25·5 s, A. Gyarmati (Hung), 1970	2 m 26·2 s, W. Burrell, 1970
Breast-stroke			
100 m	1 m 14·2 s, C. Ball (USA), 1968	1 m 15·4 s, G. Prosumenschikova (USSR), 1968	1 m 17 s, D. Harrison, 1970
200 m	2 m 38·5 s, C. Ball (USA), 1968	2 m 40·7 s, G. Stepanova (née Prosumenschikova (USSR), 1970	2 m 45·6 s, D. Harrison, 1970
Butterfly			
100 m	1 m 4·1 s, A. Jones (USA), 1970	1 m 4·5 s, A. Kok (Neth), 1965	1 m 7·4 s (y), M. Auton, 1968
200 m	2 m 19·3 s, A. Jones (USA), 1970	2 m 20·2 s, H. Lindner (E. Ger), 1970	2 m 31·6 s (y), D. Lansley, 1970
Medley			
200 m	2 m 23·5 s, C. Kolb (USA), 1968	2 m 27·5 s, M. Grunert (E. Ger), 1969	2 m 29·5 s, S. Ratcliffe, 1970
400 m	5 m 4·7 s, C. Kolb (USA), 1968	5 m 7·9 s, E. Stolze (E. Ger), 1970	5 m 17·9 s, S. Ratcliffe, 1970
4 × 100 m	4 m 27·4 s, USA (S. Atwood, K. Brecht, A. Jones, C. Schilling), 1970	4 m 30·1 s, E. Ger (B. Hofmeister, B. Schuchardt, H. Lindner, G. Wetzko), 1970	4 m 35·9 s, GB (S. Platt, D. Harrison, D. Lansley, A. Jackson), 1970

AUSTRALIAN NATIONAL CHAMPIONS Drummoyne, N.S.W., Feb. 1–March 1, 1970	*Event*		*Men*	*Women*
	Free-style	100 m	M. Wenden, 54 s	L. Watson, 1 m 1·7 s
		200 m	M. Wenden, 1 m 59·4 s	K. Moras, 2 m 9·8 s
		400 m	G. Brough, 4 m 10 s	K. Moras, 4 m 26·3 s
		800 m	M. Tavasci, 8 m 40·1 s	K. Moras, 9 m 1·1 s
		1,500 m	G. Windeatt, 16 m 23·1 s	R. Risson, 17 m 58·5 s
		4 × 100 m	N.S.W., 3 m 38·7 s	N.S.W., 4 m 13·4 s
		4 × 200 m	N.S.W., 8 m 0·5 s	
	Back-stroke	100 m	N. Rogers, 1 m 3·6 s	L. Watson, 1 m 9·2 s
		200 m	N. Rogers, 2 m 17·1 s	L. Watson, 2 m 28·9 s
	Breast-stroke	100 m	Amman Jalmaani (Phil), 1 m 10·7 s	B. Whitfield, 1 m 18·5 s
		200 m	N. Gynther, 2 m 37 s	B. Whitfield, 2 m 48 s
	Butterfly	100 m	N. Rogers, 59·7 s	A. Mabb, 1 m 7·2 s
		200 m	J. Findlay, 2 m 10·2 s	M. Robinson, 2 m 27 s
	Medley	200 m	J. Findlay, 2 m 18 s	D. Rickard, 2 m 31·3 s
		400 m	J. Findlay, 4 m 49·6 s	D. Langford, 5 m 17·8 s
		4 × 100 m	N.S.W., 4 m 11·3 s	Qld, 4 m 41·9 s

EUROPEAN SWIMMING CHAMPIONSHIPS
Barcelona, September 5–12, 1970

* World record   † European record

MEN

Event	Gold Medal	Silver Medal	Bronze Medal
Free-style			
100 m	M. Rousseau (Fr), 52·9 s	R. Matthes (E. Ger), 53·5 s	G. Kulikov (USSR), 53·7 s
200 m	H. Fassnacht (W. Ger), 1 m 55·2 s†	G. Larsson (Swed), 1 m 55·7 s	G. Kulikov (USSR), 1 m 56·6 s
400 m	G. Larsson (Swed), 4 m 2·6 s*	H. Fassnacht (W. Ger), 4 m 3 s	S. Esteva (Sp), 4 m 8·3 s
1,500 m	H. Fassnacht (W. Ger), 16 m 19·9 s†	W. Lampe (W. Ger), 16 m 25·6 s	S. Esteva (Sp), 16 m 35·7 s
4 ×100 m	USSR, 3 m 32·3 s†	W. Germany, 3 m 34·1 s	E. Germany, 3 m 34·6 s
4 ×200 m	W. Germany, 7 m 49·5 s†	USSR, 7 m 52·8 s	E. Germany, 7 m 54·5 s
Back-stroke			
100 m	R. Matthes (E. Ger), 58·9 s	S. Esteva (Sp), 59·9 s	B. Schoutsen (Neth), 1 m
200 m	R. Matthes (E. Ger), 2 m 8·8 s	S. Esteva (Sp), 2 m 9·7 s	V. Werner (E. Ger), 2 m 11·5 s
Breast-stroke			
100 m	N. Pankin (USSR), 1 m 6·8 s	R.-P. Menu (Fr), 1 m 7·8 s	R. Klees (W. Ger), 1 m 8·1 s
200 m	K. Katzur (E. Ger), 2 m 26 s	N. Pankin (USSR), 2 m 26·1 s	W. Kusch (W. Ger), 2 m 28·2 s
Butterfly			
100 m	H. Lampe (W. Ger), 57·5.s†	U. Poser (E. Ger), 57·9 s	V. Nemshilov (USSR), 58 s
200 m	U. Poser (E. Ger), 2 m 8 s	F. Meeuw (W. Ger), 2 m 8·2 s	H. Flockner (E. Ger), 2 m 9·6 s
Medley			
200 m	G. Larsson (Swed), 2 m 9·3 s*	M. Pechmann (E. Ger), 2 m 13·6 s	H. Ljungberg (Swed), 2 m 14·3 s
400 m	G. Larsson (Swed), 4 m 36·2 s†	H. Fassnacht (W. Ger), 4 m 36·9 s	M. Pechmann (E. Ger), 4 m 40·6 s
4 ×100 m	E. Germany, 3 m 54·4 s*	France, 3 m 57·6 s	USSR, 3 m 58 s
DIVING			
Springboard	G. Cagnotto (It), 555·21 pts	K. Dibiasi (It), 534·72 pts	V. Vasin (USSR), 529·8 pts
Highboard	L. Matthes (E. Ger), 454·74 pts	K. Dibiasi (It), 444·18 pts	G. Cagnotto (It), 435·36 pts
WATER POLO	USSR, 10 pts	Hungary, 8 pts	Yugoslavia, 6 pts

WOMEN

Event	Gold Medal	Silver Medal	Bronze Medal
Free-style			
100m	G. Wetzko (E. Ger), 59·6 s	M. Segrt (Yugo), 1 m 0·8 s	A. Jackson (GB), 1 m 0·8 s
200 m	G. Wetzko (E. Ger), 2 m 8·2 s†	M. Segrt (Yugo), 2 m 11 s	Y. Nieber (E. Ger), 2 m 12·8 s
400 m	E. Schmisch (E. Ger), 4 m 32·9 s†	G. Jonsson (Swed), 4 m 36·8 s	K. Tulling (E. Ger), 4 m 38 s
800 m	K. Neugebauer (E. Ger), 9 m 29·1 s†	L. De Boer (Neth), 9 m 35·7 s	N. Calligaris (It), 9 m 38·8 s
4 ×100 m	E. Germany, 4 m 0·8 s*	Hungary, 4 m 2·7 s	Sweden, 4 m 7·4 s
Back-stroke			
100 m	T. Lekveishvili (USSR), 1 m 7·8 s†	A. Gyarmati (Hung), 1 m 7·9 s	C. Buter (Neth), 1 m 8·5 s
200 m	A. Gyarmati (Hung), 2 m 25·5 s†	B. Hofmeister (E. Ger), 2 m 26·6 s	T. Lekveishvili (USSR), 2 m 27·1 s
Breast-stroke			
100 m	G. Stepanova (USSR), 1 m 15·6 s	U. Fromater (W. Ger), 1 m 16·9 s	A. Grebennikova (USSR), 1 m 16·9 s
200 m	G. Stepanova (USSR), 2 m 40·7 s†	A. Grebennikova (USSR), 2 m 43·5 s	D. Harrison (GB), 2 m 45·6 s
Butterfly			
100 m	A. Gyarmati (Hung), 1 m 5 s	H. Lindner (E. Ger), 1 m 5·4 s	E. Koch (W. Ger), 1 m 5·8 s
200 m	H. Lindner (E. Ger), 2 m 20·2 s†	H. Segrt (Yugo), 2 m 24·5 s	E. Stoltze (E. Ger), 2 m 25·6 s
Medley			
200 m	M. Grunert (E. Ger), 2 m 27·6 s	E. Stolze (E. Ger), 2 m 29·3 s	S. Ratcliffe (GB), 2 m 29·8 s
400 m	E. Stolze (E. Ger), 5 m 7·9 s†	B. Schuchardt (E. Ger), 5 m 18·3 s	S. Ratcliffe (GB), 5 m 19·6 s
4 ×100	E. Germany, 4 m 30·1 s	USSR, 4 m 31·3 s	W. Germany, 4 m 33·4 s
DIVING			
Springboard	H. Becker (E. Ger), 420·63 pts	M. Janicke (E. Ger), 407·22 pts	T. Safonova (USSR), 405·6 pts
Highboard	M. Duchkova (Czecho), 336·33 pts	M. Janicke (E. Ger), 329·85 pts	S. Fjedler (E. Ger), 322·26 pts

NATIONAL MEDALS TABLE

	Gold	Silver	Bronze	Total
East Germany ...	16	7	9	32
USSR	6	4	8	18
West Germany ..	4	5	4	13
Sweden	3	2	2	7
Hungary	2	3	0	5
Italy	1	2	2	5
France	1	3	0	4
Czechoslovakia ..	1	0	0	1
Yugoslavia	0	3	1	4
Spain	0	2	2	4
Netherlands	0	1	2	3
Great Britain	0	0	4	4

CHANNEL SWIMMERS, 1970

Date	Direction	Name	Time
July 31	England–France	Mervyn Sharp	15 h 14 m*
July 31	France–England	Raymond Cossum	13 h 41 m
August 4	England–France–England	Kevin Murphy	35 h 10 m
August 9	England–France	Desmond Renford	13 h 9 m*
August 13	England–France	Barry Watson	15 h 14 m
August 13	France–England	Kenneth Brewer	14 h 10 m
August 27	England–France	Desmond Renford	12 h 55 m*
August 30	England–France	Michael Read	12 h 18 m*
September 19	France–England	Michael Paesler	11 h 45 m†
September 20	France–England	Robert Lyle	16 h 35 m
September 20	France–England	Thomas J. Hetzel	14 h 14 m
September 23	France–England	Robert McNae	12 h 38 m

* First leg of double attempt   † Fastest time of the year

Supplied by the Channel Swimming Association

ATHLETICS

Records at Jan. 1, 1971 — **MEN** — Track and Field events

Event	*World Record*	*European Record*	*British Record*
100 m	9·9 s, J. Hines (twice), C. Greene, R. Smith (all USA), 1968	10·0 s, A. Hary (W. Ger), 1960; R. Bambuck (Fr), 1968; V. Sapeya (USSR), 1968; V. Borzov (USSR), 1969; G. Metz (W. Ger), 1970	10·2 s, M. Campbell, 1967
200 m	19·8 s, T. Smith (USA), 1968	20·3 s, P. Clerc (Switz), 1969	20·5 s, P. Radford, 1960
400 m	43·8 s, L. Evans (USA), 1968	44·9 s, C. Kaufmann, 1960, M. Jellinghaus, 1968 (both W. Ger)	45·7 s, A. Metcalfe, 1961; R. Brightwell (twice), 1964
800 m	1 m 44·3 s, P. Snell (NZ), 1963; R. Doubell (Austral), 1968	1 m 44·9 s, F. Kemper, 1966, W. Adams, 1970 (both W. Ger)	1 m 46·3 s, C. Carter, 1966
1,500 m	3 m 33·1 s, J. Ryun (USA), 1967	3 m 34 s, J. Wadoux (Fr), 1970	3 m 39·0 s, I. Stewart, 1969; P. Stewart, 1970
5,000 m	13 m 16·6 s, R. Clarke (Austral), 1966	13 m 22·8 s, I. Stewart (GB), 1970	Same as European record
10,000 m	27 m 39·4 s, R. Clarke (Austral), 1965	28 m 04·4 s, J. Haase (E. Ger), 1968	28 m 6·2 s, D. Bedford, 1970
Steeplechase	8 m 22 s, K. O'Brien (Austral), 1970	8 m 22·2 s, V. Dudin (USSR), 1969	8 m 30·8 s, G. Stevens, 1969
110 m/120 yd hurdles	13·2 s, M. Lauer (W. Ger), 1959; L. Calhoun, 1960, E. McCullouch, 1967, W. Davenport, E. Hall, 1969, T. Hill, 1970 (all USA)	Same as world record (Lauer)	13·6 s, D. Hemery, 1969
400 m hurdles	48·1 s, D. Hemery (GB), 1968	Same as world record	Same as world record
4×100 m relay	38·2 s, USA, 1968	38·4 s, France, 1968	39·3 s, GB, 1968
4×400 m relay	2 m 56·1 s, USA, 1968	3 m 0·5 s, W. Germany, 1968; Poland, 1968	3 m 01·2 s, GB, 1968
High jump	7 ft 5¾ in (2·28 m), V. Brumel (USSR), 1963	Same as world record	6 ft 10 in (2·08 m), G. Miller, 1964
Pole vault	18 ft 0¼ in (5·49 m), C. Papanicolaou (Gr), 1970	Same as world record	16 ft 8¾ in (5·1 m), M. Bull, 1970
Long jump	29 ft 2½ in (8·90 m), R. Beamon (USA), 1968	27 ft 4¾ in (8·35 m), I. Ter-Ovanesian (USSR), 1967; J. Schwarz (W. Ger), 1970	27 ft 0 in (8·23 m), L. Davies, 1968
Triple jump	57 ft 0¾ in (17·39 m), V. Saneyev (USSR), 1968	Same as world record	54 ft 0 in (16·46 m), F. Alsop, 1964
Shot	71 ft 5½ in (21·78 m), R. Matson (USA), 1967	67 ft 8½ in (20·64 m), H.-P. Gies (E. Ger), 1969	64 ft 2 in (19·56 m), A. Rowe, 1961
Discus	224 ft 5 in (68·40 m), J. Silvester (USA), 1968	223 ft 3 in (68·06 m), R. Bruch (Swed), 1969	189 ft 6 in (57·76 m), J. Watts, 1968; W. Tancred, 1969
Hammer	247 ft 7½ in (75·48 m), A. Bondarchuk (USSR), 1969	Same as world record	227 ft 2 in (69·24 m), H. Payne, 1970
Javelin	304 ft 1 in (92·70 m), J. Kinnunen (Fin), 1969	Same as world record	273 ft 9 in (83·44 m), D. Travis, 1970
Decathlon	8,417 pts, W. Toomey (USA), 1969	8,319 pts, K. Bendlin (W. Ger), 1967	7,486 pts, B. King, 1970
Marathon	2 h 8 m 33·6 s, D. Clayton (Austral), 1969	2 h 9 m 28s, R. Hill (GB), 1970	Same as European record

Linear world records set in 1970. 100 yd, 9·1 s (equals), W. McGee (USA); 440 yd hurdles, 48·8 s, R. Mann (USA),

WOMEN

Event	*World Record*	*European Record*	*British Record*
100 m	11·0 s, W. Tyus (USA), 1968; Chi Cheng (For), 1970; R. Meissner (E. Ger), 1970	Same as world record (Meissner)	11·3 s, D. Hyman (twice), 1963; D. James, V. Peat 1968
200 m	22·4 s, Chi Cheng (For), 1970	22·5 s, I. Szewinska (Pol), 1968	23·2 s, D. Hyman, 1963; M. Critchley, 1970
400 m	51·0 s, M. Neufville (Jam), 1970	51·7 s, N. Duclos, C. Besson (both Fr), 1969	52·1 s, L. Board, 1968
800 m	2 m 0·5 s, V. Nikolic (Yugo), 1968	Same as world record	2 m 01·1 s, A. Packer, 1964
1,500 m	4 m 10·7 s, J. Jehlickova (Czecho), 1969	Same as world record	4 m 15·4 s, R. Ridley, 1970
100 m hurdles	12·7 s, K. Balzer (E. Ger), 1970; T. Sukniewicz (Pol), 1970	Same as world record	13·4 s, C. Bell, 1970
4×100 m relay	42·8 s, USA, 1968	43·4 s, Netherlands, 1968; USSR, 1968	43·7 s, GB, 1968
4×400 m relay	3 m 30·8 s, GB, 1969; France, 1969	Same as world record	Same as world record (GB)
High jump	6 ft 3¼ in (1·91 m), I. Balas (Rum), 1961	Same as world record	5 ft 10½ in (1·79 m), L. Hedmark, 1969; B. Inkpen, 1970
Long jump	22 ft 5¼ in (6·84 m), H. Rosendahl (W. Ger), 1970	Same as world record	22 ft 2¼ in (6·76 m), M. Rand, 1964
Shot	67 ft 0¼ in (20·43 m), N. Chizhova (USSR), 1969	Same as world record	53 ft 6¼ in (16·31 m), M. Peters, 1966
Discus	209 ft 10 in (63·96 m), L. Westermann (W. Ger), 1969	Same as world record	190 ft 7 in (55·04 m), R. Payne, 1970
Javelin	204 ft 8½ in (62·40 m), Y. Gorchakova (USSR), 1964	Same as world record	182 ft 5 in (55·60 m), S. Platt, 1968
Pentathlon	5,406 pts, M. Pollak (E. Ger), 1970	Same as world record	5,148 pts, M. Peters, 1970

Linear world records set in 1970. 100 yd, 10·1 s, Chi Cheng (For); 220 yd, 22·6 s, Chi Cheng (For).

BRITISH NATIONAL ATHLETICS LEAGUE Final Placings

Division 1. 1, Thames V.; 2, Birchfield; 3, Cardiff. *Relegated:* Brighton & Hove and Surrey
Division 2. 1, Edinburgh Southern; 2, Sale Harriers (both promoted); 3, Woodford Green, *Relegated:* Polytechnic and Blackheath.
Division 3. 1, Wolverhampton & Bilston; 2, Liverpool (both promoted); 3, Notts.

EUROPEAN CUPS

Men. 1, E. Germany, 102 pts; 2, U.S.S.R., 92·5 pts; 3, W. Germany, 91 pts.
Women. 1, E. Germany, 70 pts; 2, W. Germany, 65 pts; 3, U.S.S.R., 43 pts.

TENNIS

AUSTRALIAN CHAMPIONSHIPS

White City, Sydney, January 1970

Men's Singles. A. Ashe (USA) bt. R. Crealy (Austral), 6–4, 9–7, 6–2.

Women's Singles. Mrs. M. Court (Austral) bt. Miss K. Melville (Austral), 6–3, 6–1.

Men's Doubles. R. Lutz & S. Smith (USA) bt. J. Alexander & P. Dent (Austral), 8–6, 6–3, 6–4.

Women's Doubles. Mrs. J. Dalton & Mrs. M. Court (Austral) bt. Miss K. Krantzcke & Miss K. Melville (Austral), 6–3, 6–1.

SOUTH AFRICAN CHAMPIONSHIPS

Johannesburg, April 1970

Men's Singles. R. Laver (Austral) bt. F. McMillan (SA), 4–6, 6–2, 6–1, 6–2.

Women's Singles. Mrs. M. Court (Austral) bt. Mrs. B. King (USA), 6–4, 1–6, 6–3.

Men's Doubles. R. Hewitt & F. McMillan (SA) bt. C. Drysdale & R; Taylor (GB), 6–3, 6–3, 6–2.

Women's Doubles. Mrs. B. King & Miss R. Casals (USA) bt Miss K. Krantzcke & Miss K. Melville (Austral), 6–2, 6–3.

Mixed Doubles. M. Riessen & Mrs. B. King (USA) bt. F. McMillan & Miss P. Walkden (SA), 7–5, 3–6, 7–5.

ITALIAN CHAMPIONSHIPS

Rome, April 20–27, 1970

Men's Singles. I. Nastase (Rum) bt. J. Kodes (Czecho), 6–3, 1–6, 6–3, 8–6.

Women's Singles. Mrs. B. King (USA) bt. Miss J. Heldman (USA), 6–1, 6–3.

Men's Doubles. L. Tiriac & I. Nastase (Rum) bt. W. Bowrey & O. Davidson (Austral), 0–6, 10–8, 6–3, 6–8, 6–1.

Women's Doubles. Mrs. B. King & Miss R. Casals (USA) bt. Miss V. Wade (GB) & Miss F. Durr (Fr), 6–2, 3–6, 9–7.

FRENCH CHAMPIONSHIPS

Paris, May 25–June 7, 1970

Men's Singles. J. Kodes (Czecho) bt. Z. Franulovic (Yugo), 6–2, 6–4, 6–0.

Women's Singles. Mrs. M. Court (Austral) bt. Miss H. Niessen (W. Ger), 6–2, 6–4.

Men's Doubles. L. Tiriac & I. Nastase (Rum) bt. A. Ashe & C. Pasarell (USA), 6–2, 6–4, 6–3.

Women's Doubles. Mrs. G. Chantreau & Miss F. Durr (Fr) bt. Miss R. Casals & Mrs. B. King (USA), 6–1, 3–6, 6–3.

Mixed Doubles. R. Hewitt (SA) & Mrs. B. King (USA) bt. J.-C. Barclay & Miss F. Durr, (Fr), 3–6, 6–4, 6–2.

WIMBLEDON CHAMPIONSHIPS

London, June 22–July 4, 1970

Men's Singles. J. Newcombe (Austral) bt. K. Rosewall (Austral), 5–7, 6–3, 6–2, 3–6, 6–1.

Women's Singles. Mrs. M. Court (Austral) bt. Mrs. B. King (USA), 14–12, 11–9.

Men's Doubles. J. Newcombe & A. Roche (Austral) bt. K. Rosewall & F. Stolle (Austral), 10–8, 6–3, 6–1.

Women's Doubles. Mrs. B. King & Miss R. Casals (USA) bt. Miss F. Durr (Fr) & Miss V. Wade (GB), 6–2, 6–3.

Mixed Doubles. I. Nastase (Rum) & Miss R. Casals (USA) bt. A. Metreveli & Miss O. Morozova (USSR), 6–3, 4–6, 9–7.

GERMAN CHAMPIONSHIPS

Hamburg, August 11–17, 1970

Men's Singles. T. Okker (Neth) bt. I. Nastase (Rum), 4–6, 6–3, 6–3, 6–4.

Women's Singles. Miss H. Hoesl (W. Ger) bt. Miss H. Niessen (W. Ger), 6–3, 6–3.

Men's Doubles. R. Hewitt & F. McMillan (SA) bt. T. Okker (Neth) & N. Pilic (Yugo), 6–3, 7–5, 6–2.

Women's Doubles. Miss K. Krantzcke & Miss K. Melville (Austral) bt. Miss W. Shaw & Miss V. Wade (GB), 6–0, 6–1.

Mixed Doubles. F. McMillan (SA) & Mrs. J. Dalton (Austral) bt. R. Hewitt (SA) & Miss E. Goolagong (Austral), 6–4, 6–4.

U.S.A. CHAMPIONSHIPS

Forest Hills, New York, Sept. 1–13, 1970

Men's Singles. K. Rosewall (Austral) bt. A. Roche (Austral), 2–6, 6–4, 7–6, 6–3.

Women's Singles. Mrs. M. Court (Austral) bt. Miss R. Casals (USA), 6–2, 2–6, 6–1.

Men's Doubles. P. Barthes (Fr) & N. Pilic (Yugo) bt. R. Emerson & R. Laver (Austral), 6–3, 7–6, 4–6, 7–6.

Women's Doubles. Mrs. M. Court & Mrs. J. Dalton (Austral) bt. Miss R. Casals (USA) & Miss V. Wade (GB), 6–3, 6–4.

Mixed Doubles. M. Riessen (USA) & Mrs M. Court (Austral) bt. D. Ralston (USA) & Miss F. Durr (Fr), 6–3, 6–7, 6–3.

ALL-ENGLAND JUNIOR CHAMPIONSHIPS

Wimbledon, Sept. 1–5, 1970

Boys' Singles. M. Collins (holder) bt. R. Walker, 0–6, 7–5, 6–3.

Girls' Singles. Miss N. Dwyer bt. Miss L. Charles, 6–4, 6–4.

Boys' Doubles. M. Farrell & J. Lloyd bt. K. McCollum & R. Walker, 7–5, 7–5.

Girls' Doubles. Miss L. Charles & Miss C. Colman bt. Miss A. Coe & Miss N. Dwyer, 7–5, 6–2.

DEWAR CUP

British Indoor Championships

Edinburgh. *Men:* T. Gorman (USA). *Women:* Miss S. Walsh (USA).

Stalybridge. *Men:* I. Tiriac (Rum). *Women:* Miss V. Wade (GB).

Aberavon. *Men:* G. Battrick (GB). *Women:* Miss V. Wade (GB).

Torquay. *Men:* V. Zednik (Czecho). *Women:* Mrs. P. Jones (GB).

London. *Men:* J. Alexander (Austral). *Women:* Miss F. Durr (Fr).

FEDERATION CUP

Women's International Team Championship

Freiburg, W. Germany, May 19–24

Semi-Finals

W. Germany bt. U.S.A. (holders) 2–1
Australia bt. Gt. Britain. 3–0

Final

Australia bt. W. Germany. 3–0
Miss K. Krantzcke bt. Miss H. Hoesl, 6–2, 6–3. Mrs. J. Dalton bt. Miss H. Niessen, 4–6, 6–3, 6–3. Miss K. Krantzcke & Mrs. J. Dalton bt. Miss H. Hoesl & Miss H. Niessen, 6–2, 7–5.

WIGHTMAN CUP

Wimbledon, June 12–13, 1970

U.S.A. (holders) bt. Great Britain by 4 matches to 3, and retained the Cup.

Singles. Mrs. B. King (USA) bt. Miss V. Wade (GB), 8–6, 6–4; and bt. Mrs. P. Jones (GB), 6–4, 6–2. Miss V. Wade (GB) bt. Miss N. Richey (USA), 6–3, 6–2. Mrs. P. Jones (GB) bt. Miss N. Richey (USA), 6–2, 6–3. Miss J. Heldman (USA) bt Mrs. J. Williams (GB), 6–3, 6–2.

Doubles. Mrs. P. Jones & Mrs. J. Williams (GB) bt. Mrs. M. Curtis & Miss J. Heldman (USA), 6–3, 6–2. Mrs. B. King & Miss P. Bartkowicz (USA) bt. Miss V. Wade & Miss W. Shaw (GB), 7–5, 3–6, 6–2.

DAVIS CUP

1. **European Zone "A" Final.** Spain bt. Yugoslavia, 4–1.
2. **European Zone "B" Final.** W. Germany bt. U.S.S.R., 3–2.
3. **American Zone Final.** Brazil bt. Canada, 3–2.
4. **Eastern Zone Final.** India bt. Australia, 3–1.
5. **Winner of 1 v. Winner of 3.** Spain bt. Brazil, 4–1.
6. **Winner of 2 v. Winner of 4.** W. Germany bt. India, 5–0.
7. **Winner of 5 v. Winner of 6.** W. Germany bt. Spain, 4–1.
8. **Challenge Round: Winner of 7 v. U.S.A. (holders).** U.S.A. bt. W. Germany, 4–1.

BOXING

PROFESSIONAL CHAMPIONS

Weight	World Champion	European Champion	British Champion
Fly	Chartchai Chionoi (Thailand)	Fernando Aztori (Italy)	John McCluskey
Bantam	Chucho Castillo (Mexico)	Franco Zurlo (Italy)	Alan Rudkin
Feather	Vicente Saldivar (Mexico)	Jose Legra (Spain)	Jimmy Revie
Junior Light	Hiroshi Kobayashi (Japan)		Jimmy Andersen
Light	Ken Buchanan (Great Britain)	Miguel Velazquez (Spain)	Ken Buchanan
Junior Welter	Bruno Arcari (Italy)	Rene Roque (France)	
Welter	Billy Backus (USA)	Ralph Charles (Great Britain)	Ralph Charles
Junior Middle	Carmelo Bossi (Italy)	Jose Hernandez (Spain)	———
Middle	Carlos Monzon (Argentina)	Carlos Duran (Italy)	Bunny Sterling
Light-Heavy	Bob Foster (USA)	Piero del Papa (Italy)	Eddie Avoth
Heavy	Joe Frazier (USA)	Henry Cooper (Great Britain)	Henry Cooper

AMATEUR CHAMPIONS

Weight	Olympic Champion (1968)	European Champion (1969)	Commonwealth Champion (1970)	Great Britain Champion (1970)
Light-Fly	F. Rodriguez (Venezuela)	G. Gedo (Hungary)	J. Odwori (Uganda)	———
Fly	R. Delgado (Mexico)	C. Cluka (Rumania)	D. Needham (England)	D. Needham
Bantam	V. Sokolov (USSR)	A. Dumitrescu (Rumania)	S. Mbogwa (Kenya)	L. Oxley
Feather	A. Roldan (Mexico)	L. Orban (Hungary)	P. Waruinge (Kenya)	D. Polak
Light	R. Harris (USA)	C. Cutov (Rumania)	A. Adeyemi (Nigeria)	N. Cole
Lt.-Welter	J. Kulej (Poland)	V. Frolov (USSR)	M. Muruli (Uganda)	D. Davies
Welter	M. Wolke (E. Germany)	G. Meier (W. Germany)	E. Ankudey (Ghana)	T. Waller
Lt.-Middle	B. Lagutin (USSR)	V. Tregubov (USSR)	T. Imrie (Scotland)	D. Simmonds
Middle	C. Finnegan (GB)	V. Tarrasenkov (USSR)	J. Conteh (England)	J. Conteh
Lt.-Heavy	D. Pozdnik (USSR)	D. Poznyak (USSR)	F. Ayinla (Nigeria)	J. Rafferty
Heavy	G. Foreman (USA)	I. Alexe (Rumania)	B. Masanda (Uganda)	J. Gilmour

MOTOR RACING

World Champion. J. Rindt (Austria, Lotus-Ford)

S. African G.P. J. Brabham (Austral, Brabham-Ford)

Spanish G.P. J. Stewart (GB, March-Ford)

Monaco G.P. Rindt (Lotus-Ford)

Dutch G.P. Rindt (Lotus-Ford)

French G.P. Rindt (Lotus-Ford)

British G.P. Rindt (Lotus-Ford)

German G.P. Rindt (Lotus-Ford)

Italian G.P. C. Regazzoni (Switz, Ferrari)

Canadian G.P. J. Ickx (Belg, Ferrari)

U.S.A. G.P. E. Fittipaldi (Braz, Lotus 72)

Mexican G.P. J. Ickx (Belg, Ferrari)

Le Mans 24-Hour. R. Attwood (GB) and H. Herrmann (W. Ger), Porsche

Indianapolis 500. A. Unser (USA)

MOTOR-CYCLE RACING

World Champions 1970

500 cc. G. Agostini (It, MV-Agusta)

350 cc. G. Agostini (It, MV-Agusta)

250 cc. R. Gould (GB, Yamaha)

125 cc. D. Braun (W. Ger, Suzuki)

50 cc. A. Nieto (Sp, Derbi)

Sidecar. K. Enders (W. Ger, BMW)

Isle of Man TT

500 cc. G. Agostini (It, MV-Agusta)

350 cc. G. Agostini (It, MV-Agusta)

250 cc. K. Carruthers (Austral, Yamaha)

125 cc. D. Braun (W. Ger, Suzuki)

Sidecar. K. Enders (W. Ger, BMW)

SPEEDWAY

World Champion. I. Mauger (NZ)

World Pairs. New Zealand (I. Mauger and R. Moore)

World Team. Sweden (O. Fundin, R. Jansson, A. Nichanek, and S. Sjoesten)

European Champion. I. Mauger (NZ)

British League Champions. Belle Vue, Manchester

CYCLING

World Championships
Leicester, England, August 6–16, 1970

Professional

Sprint. G. Johnson (Austral)

Pursuit. H. Porter (GB)

Motor-Paced. E. Rudolph (W. Ger)

Road race. I. Montsere (Belg)

Amateur

MEN

Sprint. D. Morelon (Fr)

Pursuit. X. Kurmann (Switz)

Team Pursuit. W. Germany

Time-Trial. N. Fredborg (Den)

Team Time-Trial. U.S.S.R.

Tandem. V. Barth, R. Muller (W. Ger)

Motor-Paced. C. Stam (Neth)

Road Race. J. Schmidt (Den)

WOMEN

Sprint. G. Careva (USSR)

Pursuit. T. Garkushina (USSR)

Road Race. A. Konkina (USSR)

Cyclo-Cross Championships

World Prof. E. de Vlaeminck (Belg)

World Amateur. R. Vermeire (Belg)

British Prof. J. Atkins

British Amateur. O. Nagle

European Classic Winners

Tour of France. E. Merckx (Belg)

Tour of Italy. E. Merckx (Belg)

Tour of Britain. J. Mainus (Czecho)

Milan–San Remo. M. Dancelli (It)

Tour of Flanders. E. Leman (Belg)

Paris–Roubaix. E. Merckx (Belg)

Flèche–Wallonne. E. Merckx (Belg)

Liège–Bastogne–Liège. R. de Vlaeminck (Belg)

Bordeaux–Paris. H. van Springel (Belg)

Paris–Tours. J. Tschan (W. Ger)

Tour of Lombardy. F. Bitossi (It)

British National Championships

Professional Sprint. R. Barnett

Amateur Sprint. E. Crutchlow

Women's Sprint. B. Swinnerton

Professional Pursuit. D. Bonner

Amateur Pursuit. I. Hallam

Women's Pursuit. B. Burton

Professional Road Race. L. West

Amateur Road Race. D. Rollinson

Women's Road Race. B. Burton

Tandem. A. Brockhurst & P. Mugglestone

Amateur 10-Mile Track. R. Keeble

British Time-Trial Championships

MEN

25 miles. R. Allsopp, 54 m 39 s

50 miles. D. Whitehouse, 1 h 54 m 16 s

100 miles. A. Creaser, 4 h 2 m 5 s

24 hours. J. Baines, 473·52 miles

WOMEN

25 miles. B. Burton, 59 m 48 s

50 miles. B. Burton, 2 h 1 m 58 s

100 miles. B. Burton, 4 h 19 m 56 s

HORSE RACING

Grand National. Gay Trip (P. Taaffe)

1,000 Guineas. Humble Duty (L. Piggott)

2,000 Guineas. Nijinsky (L. Piggott)

Oaks. Lupe (A. Barclay)

Derby. Nijinsky (L. Piggott)

St. Leger. Nijinsky (L. Piggott)

Champion British Jockey. L. Piggott (162 wins)

Australian

Melbourne Cup. Baghdad Note

Australian Cup. Crewman

Sydney Cup. Arctic Symbol

Brisbane Cup. Cachondeo

Adelaide Cup. Tavel

Perth Cup. Fait Accompli

Hobart Cup. Dark Purple

Caulfield Cup. Beer Street

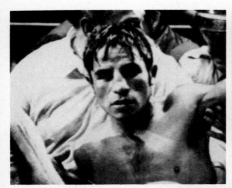

NEW WORLD BOXING CHAMPIONS

All but one of the main world boxing titles changed hands in 1970. Five of the new champions are shown here, after their winning bouts. Top: left, Chucho Castillo (Mexico) took the bantamweight championship from Ruben Olivares in October; right, Vicente Saldivar (Mexico) became featherweight champion by defeating Johnny Famechon in May. Bottom: left, Ken Buchanan (Scotland) defeated the lightweight champion Ismael Laguna in September; centre, Carlos Monzon (Argentina) knocked out Nino Benvenuti to gain the middleweight title in November; right, Joe Frazier (U.S.A.) became the undisputed heavyweight champion by defeating the W.B.A. choice Jimmy Ellis in February.

WRESTLING

	World Championships Edmonton, July 4–11		European Championships E. Berlin, June 7–10	
Weight	Free-style	Greco-Roman	Free-style	Greco-Roman
Light-fly	E. Hayady (Iran)	G. Berceanu (Rum)	T. Gadsheyev (USSR)	G. Berceanu (Rum)
Fly	A. Aalan (Tur)	P. Kirov (Bul)	B. Bejev (Bul)	P. Kirov (Bul)
Bantam	H. Yanagida (Jap)	J. Varga (Hun)	I. Schvov (Bul)	J. Varga (Hun)
Feather	S. Syedabass (Iran)	H. Fujimoto (Jap)	E. Todorov (Bul)	H. Wehling (E. Ger)
Light	A. Mohaved (Iran)	R. Roru (USSR)	I. Jusseinov (Bul)	K. Goefert (E. Ger)
Welter	W. Wells (USA)	V. Igunienov (USSR)	S. Beriashvilli (USSR)	V. Igunienov (USSR)
Middle	Y. Shamuradov (USSR)	A. Nazarenko (USSR)	H. Stottmeister (E. Ger)	A. Nenadic (Yug)
Light-Heavy	G. Stachev (USSR)	V. Resanzov (USSR)	B. Gurevich (USSR)	V. Resanzov (USSR)
Heavy	V. Gulyutkov (USSR)	P. Svensson (Swe)	A. Ayik (Tur)	P. Svensson (Swe)
Super-Heavy	A. Madyed (USSR)	A. Roshin (USSR)	L. Kitov (USSR)	R. Bock (W. Ger)

WEIGHT-LIFTING

Weight	World Champions	European Champions
Fly	S. del Rosario (Phil), 710½ lb. (322·5 kg)	V. Krishishnin (USSR), *749¼ lb. (340 kg)
Bantam	M. Nassiri (Iran), 798¾ lb. (362·5 kg)	I. Foeldi (Hung), *820¾ lb. (372·5 kg)
Feather	J. Benedek (Hung), 843 lb. (382·5 kg)	M. Kuchev (Bulg), 843 lb. (382·5 kg)
Light	Z. Kaczmarek (Pol), 969¾ lb. (440 kg)	J. Bagocs (Hung), 953¼ lb. (432·5 kg)
Middle	V. Kurentsov (USSR), 1,019¼ lb. (462·5 kg)	V. Kurentsov (USSR), 1,025 lb. (465 kg)
Light-Heavy	G. Ivanchenko (USSR), *1,113 lb. (505 kg)	G. Ivanchenko (USSR), 1,074¼ lb. (487·5 kg)
Middle-Heavy	V. Kolotov (USSR), *1,184½ lb. (537·5 kg)	K. Kangasniemi (Fin), 1,168 lb. (530 kg)
Heavy	J. Talts (USSR), *1,245 lb. (565 kg)	J. Talts (USSR), 1,240 lb. (562·5 kg)
Super-Heavy	V. Alexeev (USSR), 1,350 lb. (612·5 kg)	V. Alexeev (USSR), *1,350 lb. (612·5 kg)

* World record total

JUDO

European Championships
E. Berlin, May 22–24, 1970

Weight	Champions
Light	J. Mounier (Fr)
Light-Middle	R. Hendel (E. Ger)
Middle	B. Jacks (GB)
Light-Heavy	V. Pokatyev (USSR)
Heavy	K. Glahn (W. Ger)
Open	K. Hennig (E. Ger)

MODERN PENTATHLON

World Championships

1. P. Kelemen (Hung)
2. A. Balczo (Hung)
3. B. Oniskenko (USSR)

Team: Hungary

British Champion. J. Fox

TABLE TENNIS
European Championships
Moscow, April 1–8, 1970

Men's Singles. H. Alser (Swed) bt. I. Korpa (Yugo), 21–19, 21–18, 21–9.
Women's Singles. Z. Rudnova (USSR) bt. I. Vostova (Czecho), 15–21, 21–11, 11–21, 21–5, 21–17.
Men's Doubles. A. Stipanic & D. Surbek (Yugo) bt. K. Johansson & H. Alser (Swed), 21–16, 17–21, 9–21, 21–19, 21–13.
Women's Doubles. Z. Rudnova & S. Grinberg (USSR) bt. D. Schoeler & A. Simon (W. Ger), 21–15, 21–13, 18–21, 21–7.
Mixed Doubles. S. Gomoskov & Z. Rudnova (USSR) bt. S. Sarkhayan & R. Pogosova (USSR), 21–18, 21–12, 21–15.
Men's Team. Sweden bt. Yugoslavia, 5–4.
Women's Team. U.S.S.R. bt. Czechoslovakia, 3–0.
European League (Final Placings). 1, Sweden; 2, U.S.S.R.; 3, Hungary.

English Open Championships
London, January 26–28, 1970

Men's Singles. S. Kollarovits (Czecho) bt. I. Jonyer (Hung), 18–21, 21–18, 21–18, 19–21, 21–17.
Women's Singles. M. Alexandru (Rum) bt. J. Shirley (GB), 21–15, 21–10, 21–13
Men's Doubles. I. Jonyer & T. Klampar (Hung) bt. Z. Cordas & M. Karakasevic (Yugo), 21–17, 21–17, 21–16.
Women's Doubles. K. Mathews & M. Wright (GB) bt. M. Alexandru & C. Crisan (Rum), 14–21, 21–12, 22–20, 14–21, 21–19.
Mixed Doubles. D. Neale & M. Wright (GB) bt. C. Barnes & K. Mathews (GB), 18–21, 21–13, 21–15, 21–15

English Closed Championships
Eston, Teeside, January 1–3, 1970

Men's Singles. D. Neale bt. C. Barnes, 22–20, 21–16, 21–15.
Women's Singles. M. Wright bt. J. Shirley, 21–14, 21–19, 21–19.
Men's Doubles. A. Hydes & D. Neale bt. C. Barnes & T. Taylor, 21–16, 21–19, 21–18.
Women's Doubles. M. Wright & K. Mathews bt. L. Radford & D. Simpson, 21–12, 22–20, 19–21, 21–16.
Mixed Doubles. D. Neale & M. Wright bt. C. Barnes & K. Mathews, 21–17, 11–21, 21–9, 21–9.

BADMINTON
All-England Championships
Wembley, March 18–21, 1970

Men's Singles. R. Hartono (Indo) bt. S. Pri (Den), 15–7, 15–1.
Women's Singles. E. Takenaka (Jap) bt. E. Nielsen (GB), 11–3, 11–4.
Men's Doubles. T. Bacher & P. Petersen (Den) bt. J. Eddy & R. Powell (GB), 15–11, 15–0.
Women's Doubles. M. Boxall & P. Whetnall (GB) bt. G. Perrin & W. Rickard (GB), 15–6, 8–15, 15–9.
Mixed Doubles. P. Walsoe & P. Molgaard (Den) bt. W. Bochow & I. Latz (W. Ger), 17–14, 15–12.
Thomas Cup (Kuala Lumpur). **Final:** Indonesia 7
Malaysia (holders) 2

SQUASH RACKETS

British Open Championship. J. Barrington (GB)
British Amateur Championship. G. Hunt (Austral)
British Women's Championship. H. McKay (Austral)
Australian Championship. J. Barrington (GB)

AUSTRALIAN BASEBALL
Claxton Shield
Oriole Park, Sydney, September 1970

1. South Australia .. .. .. 12 pts. (won on better average)
2. N.S.W. .. .. .. 12 pts.
3. Victoria .. .. .. 8 pts.
4. Western Australia .. .. 4 pts.
5. Queensland .. .. .. 4 pts.

WATER SKI-ING
European Championships

Men. R. Zucchi (It). **Women.** W. Stahle (Neth).

British Championships

Men. I. Walker. **Women.** G. Brantingham.

ROWING
Henley Royal Regatta
July 1–4, 1970

Grand Challenge Cup. A.S.K. Vorwarts Rostock (E. Ger) bt. G.S.R. Aegir (Neth): ⅓ length (6 m 34 s)
Visitors' Cup. Fitzwilliam College (Cambridge) bt. St. Thomas's Hospital (London): easily (7 m 40 s).
Double Sculls. T. McKibbon & J. Van Blom (Long Beach, USA) bt. P. J. Webb & A. V. Cooke (Nott. and Union): 3½ lengths (7 m 43 s).
Princess Elizabeth Cup. Ridley College, Canada bt. Hampton Grammar School: 2⅓ lengths (7 m 40 s).
Prince Philip Challenge Cup. Renngeme Inschaft Konstanz, Wetzlar (W. Ger) bt. S.G. Dynamo, Potsdam (E. Ger): 3½ lengths (7 m 24 s).
Britannia Cup. London R.C. bt. Bedford R.C.: ⅔-length (7 m 48 s).
Stewards Cup. S.G. Dynamo (Potsdam) bt. London R.C.: 3 lengths (7 m 22 s).
Thames Cup. Leander Club bt. London R.C.: 1¾ lengths (7 m 1 s).
Wyfold Cup. Trident R.C. (S. Africa) bt. Thames Tradesmen: disqualified.
Ladies Plate. G.S.R. Aegir (Neth) bt. University of London: 3¾ lengths (7 m).
Silver Goblets and Nickalls' Cup. H. Schreiber & M. Schmorde (S.G. Dynamo, Berlin) bt. G. Xouris & J. R. Watt (Corio Bay, Australia): easily (8 m 17 s).
Diamond Challenge Sculls. J. Meissner (Mannheimer Ruderverein Amicitia (W. Ger) bt. P. G. R. Delafield (Tideway Scullers Schl.): easily (8 m 18 s).

Men's World Championships
St. Catherines, Canada, September 2–6, 1970

Single Sculls. A. Demiddi (Arg)
Double Sculls. Denmark (Engelbrecht & Secher)
Coxed Pairs. Rumania (Tudor & Ciapura)
Coxed Fours. W. Germany
Coxless Pairs. E. Germany (Klatt & Gorniv)
Coxless Fours. E. Germany
Eights. E. Germany

Women's European Championships
Budapest, September 20–23, 1970

Single Sculls. A. Kuhlke (E. Germany)
Double Sculls. E. Germany (Jaeger & Schmidt)
Coxed Fours. U.S.S.R.
Coxless Fours. Rumania
Eights. E. Germany

Other Events

University Boat Race. Cambridge won by 3½ lengths
Doggett's Coat and Badge. Martin Spencer (26 m 43 s)

Australian

King's Cup, 1970 (Lake Wendouree, Victoria).
1, Victoria; 2, South Australia; 3, Tasmania; 4, New South Wales.

YACHTING
World Champions 1970

Dragon	A. Birch (Den)	Vauriens	R. Meyer (Neth)
Finn	J. Bruder (Braz)	"420"	J. Gilder (Austral)
Fireball	J. Caig (GB)	"505"	L. Marks (GB)
Flying Dutchman	R. Pattison (GB)	5-5	D. Forbes (Austral)
Moths	P. Maes (Belg)	Contender	D. Jobbins (GB)
Soling	S. Wennerstrom (Swed)	Cherub	R. Bowler (NZ)
		Enterprise	R. Hance (GB)
		Thunderbird	T. Parkes (Austral)
Star	W. Buchan (USA)	OK Dinghy	K. Carlsson (Swed)
Tempest	J. Linville (USA)	"470"	Y. Carre (Fr)

European Champions

Dragon. P. Borowski (E. Ger)
Finn. T. Lundqvist (Swed)
Flying Dutchman. R. Pattison (GB)
Moths. M.-C. Faroux (Fr)
Snipe. J. Santos (Port)
Soling. P. Elvstroem (Den)
5-5. J.-M. Leguillou (Fr)

America's Cup (Newport, R.I.). *Intrepid* (USA), holder, bt. *Gretel II* (Austral), 4 races to 1.
Sydney–Hobart Race. First: *Pacha* (R. Crichton-Brown, NSW). First over line: *Buccaneer* (T. E. Clarke, NZ).

HOCKEY
MEN
Home Internationals 1970

Champions: Scotland and Ireland

Wales	1	Ireland	2
Scotland	2	England	1
Ireland	0	Scotland	0
England	2	Wales	0
England	0	Ireland	0
Scotland	0	Wales	0

Other Internationals 1970

Wales	0	Spain	2
England	1	Spain	1
England	1	France	0
Wales	0	Netherlands	1
Czechoslovakia	0	Wales	0
Poland	5	Wales	0
W. Germany	1	Scotland	0
England	0	Wales	1
England	2	Switzerland	0
England	1	Switzerland	0
Czechoslovakia	0	England	2
W. Germany	0	England	1
Denmark	0	England	1
Denmark	0	England	3
Belgium	0	England	2
Netherlands	1	England	0

Men's County Champions Wiltshire.
British Clubs' Champions. Lisnagarvey, N.I.

EUROPEAN CUP
Brussels, Sept. 18–27, 1970

POOL A

	P	W	D	L	F	A	Pts
West Germany	3	2	1	0	8	0	5
Poland	3	1	2	0	2	1	4
Wales	3	0	2	1	3	2	2
Italy	3	0	1	2	0	7	1

POOL B

	P	W	D	L	F	A	Pts
Netherlands	4	3	1	0	8	2	7
England	4	3	0	1	7	3	6
Austria	4	1	1	2	3	5	3
Russia	4	1	1	2	5	9	3
Denmark	4	0	1	3	0	4	1

POOL C

	P	W	D	L	F	A	Pts
France	4	3	1	0	10	1	7
Spain	4	2	2	0	21	2	6
Ireland	4	2	1	1	9	2	5
Czechoslovakia	4	1	0	3	1	9	2
Malta	4	0	0	4	0	26	0

POOL D

	P	W	D	L	F	A	Pts
Belgium	4	4	0	0	12	0	8
Switzerland	4	2	1	1	8	3	5
Finland	4	2	1	1	2	1	5
Scotland	4	1	3	0	1	5	2
Hungary	4	0	0	4	0	8	0

Quarter-Finals

West Germany	1	England	0

(after extra time)

Netherlands	1	Poland	0

(after extra time)

France	2	Switzerland	0
Spain	2	Belgium	1

Semi-Finals

Netherlands	2	Spain	0
West Germany	2	France	1

Final

West Germany	3	Netherlands	1

Final Ranking. 1, West Germany; 2, Netherlands; 3, Spain; 4, France; 5, Belgium; 6, England; 7, Poland; 8, Switzerland; 9, Ireland; 10, Czechoslovakia; 11, Austria; 12, Wales; 13, Italy; 14, U.S.S.R.; 15, Scotland; 16, Finland; 17, Hungary; 18, Denmark; 19, Malta.

GOLF
Professional Champions
Australian Open. G. Player (SA)
Australian P.G.A. B. Devlin (Austral)
British Open. J. Nicklaus (USA)
Canadian Open. K. Zarley (USA)
German Open. J. Garaialde (Fr)
French Open. D. Graham (Austral)
South African Open. T. Horton (GB)
U.S. Open. A. Jacklin (GB)
U.S. Masters. W. Casper (USA)
U.S. P.G.A. D. Stockton (USA)
"Piccadilly" Match-Play. J. Nicklaus (USA)
"Alcan" Golfer of the Year. B. Devlin (Austral)
World Cup. 1, Australia; 2, Argentina; 3, S. Africa
World Series. J. Nicklaus (USA)

Amateur Champions
Australian. P. Bennett (NSW)
British. M. Bonallack
English. D. Marsh
British Boys. I. Gradwell
British Youths. B. Dassu (It)
Eisenhower Trophy (World Team Championship). U.S.A.

Women's Champions
British Open. D. Oxley
British (stroke-play). M. Everard
British Girls. C. Le Feuvre
Home Internationals. England
Curtis Cup. U.S.A. bt. G.B. & Ireland, 11½–6½

CANOEING
World Championships
MEN
Kayak Singles.
   500 m I. Tichenko (USSR)
  1,000 m A. Shaperenko (USSR)
 10,000 m Y. Tsarev (USSR)
   Relay U.S.S.R.
Kayak Pairs.
   500 m Andersson & Peterson (Swed)
  1,000 m Pfaff & Seibold (Aus)
 10,000 m Kaestenko & Kononov (USSR)
Kayak Fours. 1,000 m U.S.S.R.
 10,000 m Norway
Canadian Singles.
  1,000 m T. Tatai (Hung)
 10,000 m T. Wichmann (Hung)
Canadian Pairs.
  1,000 m Covaliov & Patzaichin (Rum)
 10,000 m Maxim & Simionov (Rum)
WOMEN
Kayak Singles. 500 m L. Pinyeva (USSR)
Kayak Pairs. 500 m Breuer & Esser (W. Ger)
Kayak Fours. 500 m U.S.S.R.

SHOOTING
World Championships
Phoenix, Arizona

	Men	Women
English Match	M. Feiss (SA)	D. Perovic (Yugo)
Small-Bore	V. Parkimovich (USSR)	
Free Rifle		
Air Rifle	G. Kustermann (W. Ger)	T. Sherkasova (USSR)
Standard Rifle	J. Writer (USA)	M. Murdoch (USA)
Free Rifle	V. Kornev (USSR)	——
Service Rifle	J. Foster (USA)	——
Free Pistol	H. Vollmar (E. Ger)	——
Air Pistol	K. Marosvari (Hung)	S. Carroll (USA)
Standard Pistol	R. Suleimanov (USSR)	J. Trim (Aus)
Centre-Fire Pistol	R. Carpio (Mex)	N. Stolyrova (USSR)
Rapid-Fire Pistol	G. Liverzani (It)	——
Running Boar	G. Gaard (Swed)	
Olympic Trerich	M. Carrega (Fr)	I. Sidorova (USSR)
Skeet	E. Petrov (USSR)	V. Koshinskaya (USSR)

CHESS
British Champions
Men. R. G. Wade
Women. Mrs. J. Hartston
Men under 21. D. M. Wise
Boys under 18. J. G. Nicholson, J. P. Sommerville, K. J. Wicker (jointly)
Boys under 16. A. J. Mestel, J. Speelman (jointly)
Boys under 14. T. P. Chapman
Girls under 18. A. J. Povall
Girls under 14. S. A. Jackson

Australian Championship
Sydney, January 1970

1, Alfred Flatow (N.S.W.); 2, Terrey Shaw (N.S.W.)

BRIDGE
World Championship. U.S.A.
European Championship. Open: France. Women: Italy
Home International. Scotland
Women's International. England
Crockford's Cup. A. Wolfeld, E. Silverston, C. H. Brenner, M. Dale, C. Hille
Tollemache Cup. Middlesex
Pachabo Cup. London
English Pairs. J. Miezis & S. Zychlinski
Life Masters Pairs. L. Tarlo & C. Rodrigue
"Daily Mail" Schools Cup. Royal G.S., Newcastle upon Tyne

ANGLING
World Championships (Berg)

1, M. van den Eynde (Belg)
2, P. Michiels (Belg), J. Paquet (Belg)

BASKETBALL
World Championships
Belgrade, May 11–24, 1970

1, Yugoslavia; 2, Brazil; 3, U.S.S.R.

European Women's Championships
Rotterdam, Sept. 10–21, 1970

1, U.S.S.R.; 2, France; 3, Yugoslavia

HANDBALL
World Championships
Paris, Feb. 26–March 8, 1970

1, Rumania. 2, E. Germany. 3, Yugoslavia.

VOLLEYBALL
World Championships (Sofia)
Men
1, E. Germany
2, Bulgaria
3, Japan
Women
1, U.S.S.R.
2, Japan
3, N. Korea

SHOW-JUMPING
World Championships 1970

Men's Show-Jumping. D. Broome (GB) on Beethoven
Women's Show-Jumping. J. Lefebvre (Fr) on Rocket

Three-Day Event. Miss M. Gordon-Watson (GB) on Cornishman V.
Team: Gt. Britain   **Dressage:** E. Petusakova (USSR) on Pepel

Royal International Horse Show
Wembley, July 27–Aug. 1, 1970

Horse & Hound Cup. H. Smith on Mattie Brown
Phillips Stakes. R. Howe on Balmain
Moss Bros. Cup. Capt. R. d'Inzeo on Bellevue
Country Life Cup. Miss A. Drummond-Hay on Xanthos
John Player Trophy. Mrs. M. Mould on Stroller
Daily Mail Cup. Capt. R. d'Inzeo on Bellevue
Wembley Stakes. Miss B. Simpson on Australis
Prince of Wales Cup. 1, Gt. Britain; 2, Italy; 3, Canada

Horse of the Year Show
Wembley, Oct. 5–10, 1970

Butlin's Championship. A. Oliver on Sweep III
Phillips Championship. G. Hobbs on Battling Pedulas
Foxhunter Championship. Mrs. P. Graham on Pennywort
Daily Telegraph Cup. Miss A. Drummond-Hay on Xanthos
Dick Turpin Stakes. G. Fletcher on The Whip
Ronson Trophy. A. Oliver on Pitz Palu
Sunday Times Cup. Mrs. A. Dawes on The Maverick
Leading Show-Jumper of Year. Mrs. M. Mould on Stroller.

SKATING

Event	World Championships 1970	European Championships 1970
Men's Figure	T. Wood (USA)	O. Nepala (Czecho)
Women's Figure	G. Seyfert (E. Ger)	G. Seyfert (E. Ger)
Pairs	A. Ulanov & I. Rodnina (USSR)	A. Ulanov & I. Rodnina (USSR)
Dancing	A. Gorshkov & L. Pakhomova (USSR)	A. Gorshkov & L. Pakhomova (USSR)
Speed-Skating		
Men	A. Schenk (Neth)	A. Schenk (Neth)
Women	A. Keulen-Deelstra (Neth)	N. Statkevich (USSR)

WINTER SPORTS
World Championships 1970

ALPINE SKI-ING (Val Gardena)

Event	Men	Women
Slalom	J.-N. Augert (Fr)	I. Lafforgue (Fr)
Giant Slalom	K. Schranz (Austria)	B. Clifford (Can)
Downhill	B. Russi (Switz)	A. Zryd (Switz)
Combined	W. Kidd (USA)	M. Jacot (Fr)

Ski-Jumping. 70 m Jump: G. Napalkov (USSR). 90 m Jump: G. Napalkov (USSR)
Biathlon (Oestersund). Individual: A. Tikhonov (USSR). Team Relay: U.S.S.R.
Bob-Sledding (St. Moritz). Two-Man: W. Germany (H. Floth & P. Bader). Four-Man: Italy (N. de Zordo, R. Zandonella, M. Armano & L. de Paolis)

NORDIC SKI-ING (Vysoke-Tatry)

Men	Women
15 km. L.-G. Aslund (Swed)	**5 km.** G. Kulakova (USSR)
30 km. V. Vedenin (USSR)	**10 km.** A. Olyunina (USSR)
50 km. K. Oikarainen (Fin)	**3 × 5 km.** U.S.S.R.
Combined. L. Rygl (Czecho)	
4 × 10 km. U.S.S.R.	

Snow-Karting (Grindelwald). Men: M. Schratt (W. Ger). Women: M. Hoss (W. Ger)
Tobogganing (Berchtesgaden). Men: J. Fendt (W. Ger). Women: B. Piecha (Pol). Men's Pairs: M. Schmid & E. Walch (Austria)
Curling (Utica, USA). 1, Canada; 2, Scotland; 3, Norway
Ice Hockey (Stockholm). 1, USSR; 2, Sweden; 3, Czechoslovakia

European Championships

Bob-sledding (Cortina). Two-Man: Italy (G. Gaspari & M. Armano). Four-Man: W. Germany

Ski-bob (Livigno). Men: A. Fischbauer (Austria). Women: W. Jost (Austria)

Australian Ski-ing

Thredbo Cup. 1, Max Rieger (Germany)
2, Christian Neureuther (Germany)
3, Larry Poulsen (USA)

Wills International Cup. 1, Carlo Demetz (Italy)
2, Max Rieger (Germany)
3, David Zwilling (Austria)

FENCING

	World Champions	British Champions
Foil	F. Wessel (W. Ger)	W. Hoskyns
Sabre	T. Pezsa (Hung)	D. Acfield
Epee	A. Nikanchikov (USSR)	P. Jacobs
Ladies' Foil	G. Gorokhova (USSR)	J. Wardell-Yerburgh

SNOOKER

World Amateur Championship (Edinburgh). J. Barron (GB) bt. S. Hood (GB), 11–7.
World Professional Championship (Sydney). J. Spencer (GB) bt. W. Simpson (Austral), 42–31.
Australian Professional Match Play Championship (Sydney). E. Charlton (Austral) bt. P. Morgan (Ire), 44–29.
Australian Professional Championship. 1, E. Charlton; 2, W. Simpson; 3, N. Squire; 4, P. Morgan; 5, A. McDonald; 6, R. King; 7, N. Graham.

GYMNASTICS
World Championships
Ljubljana, Oct. 20–22, 1970

Men. 1, E. Kenmotsu (Jap); 2, M. Tsukahara (Jap); 3, A. Nakayama (Jap)
Women. 1, L. Turichyeva (USSR); 2, E. Zuchold (E. Ger); 3, Z. Voronina (USSR)

BRITISH SPORTSMAN AND SPORTSWOMAN OF THE YEAR 1970

Sports Writers' Choice: **Tony Jacklin** and **Mary Gordon-Watson**
Daily Express Poll: **Henry Cooper** and **Lillian Board**
BBC-TV Sports Personality Poll: **Henry Cooper**

which, if implemented, would make Denmark virtually a sleeping partner in Nato. The SDP had been ousted from office following the elections of 1968 and the cementing of a coalition between the Radicals, Liberals, and Conservatives. Its defence proposals were seen as a tactical move in domestic politics meant as bait to persuade the traditionally pacific Radicals to defect from the coalition and join ranks with SDP.

Finland

Finland's elections of March 15–16, 1970, showed a swing to the Right. The result (with previous seats in brackets) was:

Social Democrats	51	(55)
Centre party	37	(49)
Conservatives	37	(26)
Communists	36	(41)
Rural party	18	(1)
Swedish People's party	12	(12)
Liberals	8	(9)
Christian League	1	(0)

Thus the six "bourgeois" parties together wielded a majority of 26 over the Social Democrats and Communists—who, together with the "bourgeois" Centre party, had formed the previous Popular Front government. Eighty per cent of the 3 million electorate voted, including, for the first time, 20-year-olds. The swing from the Left occurred despite murmurings from Moscow warning of "growing reactionary forces" in Finland and timely reminders that she is linked to Russia by a military assistance and friendship pact. Finns needed no reminder of this fact of political life. Russia invaded Finland in 1939 —in the same year that, allied with Germany, she annexed a liberal hunk of Poland. Thus, when in 1940 Hitler turned on his Soviet allies, the Finns found themselves, in effect, fighting the Second World War in alliance with the Germans. German defeat and Russian triumph destined Finland to a post-war posture of eager good-neighbourliness with the Soviet Union, enshrined in the 1948 agreement on friendship, co-operation, and mutual assistance.

The Finnish electorate turned to the Right chiefly because of economic restrictions imposed following devaluation in 1967. The fact that the Finnish Communist party was split down the middle between feuding "moderates" and "hard-liners" also contributed to the government's failure. The results of the election brought one dramatic surprise—the rise of Mr. Veikko Vennamo's Rural party. This party is peculiar in that it has no avowed policy and scorns allegiance to Right or Left, striking out at all sides like a box full of squibs and thus attracting the "protest vote"—particularly that of small farmers.

After the general election, President Kekkonen asked Mr. Rihtniemi, the Conservative leader, to form a coalition. His first attempt to form one embracing all eight parties was foiled by the Communists' refusal to join. His second, to form one without the Communists, was foiled by the refusal by Centre party and Social Democrats to come in without the Communists. The president then asked Mr. Rafel Paasio, Social Democratic leader, to form a broadly based coalition. He failed also, and on May 14 the president announced the formation of a non-partisan caretaker government of experts under Mr. Teuvo Aura, mayor of Helsinki, which lasted until July 14, when a five-party majority coalition was agreed on. This comprised Social Democrats (five portfolios), Centre party (4), Communists (3), Swedish People's party (2), and Liberals (1).

The maverick Jean-Jacques Servan-Schreiber, who flashed, fizzled, and finally flopped across the French political scene.

The new government (headed by Ahti Karjalainen of the Centre party) commands 144 of the 200 seats in the unicameral parliament, but is not expected to last out its 4-year parliamentary mandate.

On July 20 in Moscow Mr. Gromyko, the Soviet foreign minister, and Mr. Leskinen, his Finnish counterpart, signed a protocol prolonging their treaty of friendship, co-operation, and mutual assistance until 1990. The agreement was not due to expire until 1975, and this premature extension was presumably intended to lessen any chance of Finland's relations with Russia being disturbed by the Finnish Right should it be in power by 1975.

President Kekkonen visited the U.S.A. in August to speed up preparations for the proposed European security conference which Finland had been hawking to the West on Russia's behalf for some two years. Helsinki was the venue for the third session of the SALT talks that lasted from November 2 to December 18, and is expected to be the scene of the proposed European security talks during 1971.

France

It was the year in which Jean-Jacques Servan-Schreiber rose like a rocket emitting flashes and sparks, only to fall flat at the feet of the burghers of Bordeaux. He stepped into the limelight at the special congress of the moribund Radical party, February 13–15. Party secretary-general Servan-Schreiber presented a controversial manifesto urging revolutionary reforms, including the abolition of inherited wealth. He was next amongst the headlines when he swooped into Greece by chartered jet and, securing the release of the Communist composer Mikis Theodorakis from prison, bore him triumphantly through the stratosphere to Paris. Next the Nancy by-election brought him chattering like a jay right into the political dovecote. This contest arose when the sitting Gaullist deputy resigned in outrage at his government's decision to allow the new Paris–Strasbourg motorway to by-pass Nancy. Servan-Schreiber saw his chance, and

August 31, 1970, saw this dramatic scene in a suburb of The Hague, Netherlands, when Amboinese separatists armed with guns, daggers, and swords swooped into the Indonesian ambassador's residence, killing a policeman, and held it for 11 hours before surrendering. Their action was planned to coincide with the arrival in The Hague of President Suharto of Indonesia. His visit was, however, postponed and shortened to avoid trouble.

stood as a candidate in the by-election, skilfully exploiting the government's economic neglect of the area and campaigning on a devolution ticket while urging the necessity of a co-ordinated, reforming "third force" in French politics between the Gaullist Right and the Marxist Left. J.-J. S.-S. (as he was now called by the newspapers) trounced the Gaullists and the Communists, taking 55 per cent of the vote in the run-off poll of Sunday June 28 against 25 per cent for the Gaullists and 20 per cent for the Communists.

Despite local pressures peculiar to Nancy, the result was hailed as an event of great national significance and sent many a nervous shudder down the backs of Gaullists who considered the possible emergence of the much vaunted—but previously lifeless—"third force" as heralding a return to the collapsing coalitions of the Fourth Republic. It was thus with considerable apprehension that the government heard in September that the dynamic "French Kennedy" had decided once again to enter the electoral arena at Bordeaux.

Under the constitutional complexities of the Fifth Republic, deputies in the French parliament must resign their seats on taking ministerial office and hand them over to a substitute. July 26 saw the death of the substitute of no less a Gaullist than the prime minister, Jacques Chaban-Delmas, who was thus forced to name a new substitute and stand in a by-election in his Bordeaux constituency. There is also nothing in the French constitution to prevent a deputy from standing as candidate in another constituency. If he wins, he must choose whether to represent his old or his new voters. Thus, on August 27, the opening thunder of the premier's campaign was stolen by the unexpected arrival of the newly elected deputy for Nancy. J.-J. S.-S. succeeded in harassing Chaban-Delmas at a press conference, eventually commandeering the microphone to harangue press and public. Next day saw a stormy meeting of the feuding non-Communist Left—Radicals, Socialists, and the Convention of Republican Institutions—to decide on a single "third force" candidate to oppose the prime minister at Bordeaux. Sterile

wrangling followed for some days until Servan-Schreiber threatened to stand for the city himself. He was turned down, but 15 minutes before the lists closed came the announcement that he would stand as a candidate for Bordeaux—as an independent.

Challenging the Gaullists on Chaban-Delmas's home ground was a somewhat overweening gesture, since the premier had represented Bordeaux since 1946 and had been mayor of the city since 1947. Moreover, the 40,000 Bordelais voters are solidly bourgeois and two thirds of them are over 40. Nevertheless, the dynamic radical's barnstorming campaign went ahead with a £200-an-hour hired executive jet, a team of pretty girls, and much optimism. Early on, J.-J. S.-S. admitted he could not hope to win and lowered his sights to a more reasonable target. He aimed to win 30 per cent of the votes—enough to show "that the politics of tomorrow are neither Gaullism nor Communism, but Reformism". In the event the voters of Bordeaux offered the "French Kennedy" a crushing rebuff on September 20, giving him a mere 16·59 per cent of the vote while Chaban-Delmas amassed a towering majority.

While the antics of Servan-Schreiber served to highlight the disputing disorganization of the "third force", the main French opposition party—the Communists—writhed with internal convulsions during 1970. Theirs was the familiar feud between hard-liners and pro-Dubcek softliners. On February 4 the party's central committee issued a report upholding Soviet leadership of international communism and minimizing the 1968 invasion of Czechoslovakia. This reaffirmation of the French party's place within the Soviet orbit led to the expulsion of M. Roger Garaudy, an active and formerly orthodox Communist intellectual. In July, veteran French Communist Charles Tillon announced on television that he had been excluded from his party cell in Aix-en-Provence.

Meanwhile, Chaban-Delmas's government was planning significant reforms during the year under President Pompidou's guidance. In September wide-ranging tax changes aimed at relieving the self-employed and the low paid, and also P.A.Y.E. measures to meet persistent tax-evasion, were announced. M. Olivier Guichard, minister of education, revealed plans for the reorganization of his ministry as a first step in the ultimate overhaul of the whole archaic —and anarchic—French education system. During April, it had been announced that two of the 21 French regions were to be chosen as guinea-pigs for a regional scheme of administrative and political devolution starting in January 1971. This was the government's first cautious jab at the question of decentralization that had led to the fall of de Gaulle in 1969.

Notwithstanding a spate of trials involving student revolutionaries charged with reconstituting banned extremist organizations, the most militant members of French society during 1970 were the small shopkeepers. Despite Napoleon's disparaging dictum, there are far more shopkeepers in France than in Britain, and in recent years they have been squeezed by fierce competitive forces allied with a hostile government anxious to cut the nation's expensive legion of middlemen. Demonstrations by these militant tradesmen marked the year, particularly the month of March, and talk of a Poujadist revival agitated the lips of pundits.

President Pompidou paid a state visit to the U.S.A. in February at a time when the American public were indignant following the French sale of Mirage jets to Libya, coupled with a refusal to deliver jets previously ordered

The political picture of the year: Chancellor Brandt and Premier Kosygin signing the German–Soviet non-aggression treaty in the Kremlin on August 12, 1970.

by Israel or to return the down-payment on them. Thus there were hostile demonstrations by American Jews when the French president visited Chicago—after which, clearly outraged, he threatened to cut short his visit and return home in a huff. This brought Nixon hot-foot from Washington to mollify him at a banquet in New York.

When the Soviet–German non-aggression pact was signed in August a resounding click was reported heard in the environs of the Quai d'Orsay as the Gaullist nose was put out of joint. The French initially feared that the Germans would replace them as Russia's principal diplomatic and economic partner in western Europe, and also that Western security would be threatened by the treaty. These fears were to some extent allayed by President Pompidou's Russian tour, October 6–13, and by defence minister Debré's visit to Bonn on October 22–23. While in Russia M. Pompidou signed a "protocol agreement" for bilateral political consultations, if possible twice a year at foreign minister level. A joint declaration promised that efforts would be made to expand Franco-Soviet economic co-operation, and that France would receive Soviet help in building a metallurgical complex. It was symbolic of the mysteries of Gaullist foreign policy that on the same day as Pompidou left for Moscow the former premier, M. Couve de Murville, left for his holidays in Peking.

West Germany

It was a hectic year for West German diplomats and a significant one for European historians as Chancellor Willy Brandt pursued his new *Österpolitik*—*rapprochement* with eastern Europe. Brandt had cemented a coalition between his Social Democrats and the small, somewhat ramshackle Free Democrats, following the general election of September 28, 1969, to form a government enjoying a slim 12-man majority over the conservative Christian Democrats. A cornerstone of Brandt's election campaign had been a pledge to attempt to bridge the East–West cold-war chasm, and specifically to attempt to rationalize and relax West German relations with Russia, Poland, and East Germany. In other words it was Brandt's intention to re-

define West Germany's ossified post-war position in Europe—a matter with tremendous economic, strategic, and symbolic implications.

As 1970 began West Germany had still not signed a peace treaty with Russia following the Second World War and, of course, recognized neither East Germany as a sovereign state nor the Oder–Neisse line as Poland's western frontier. To recognize either would be to agree to the permanent division of Germany and the permanent occupation by Poland of huge former German territories. The opposition Christian Democrats were anxious lest Brandt yield significant concessions on these important points, and kept up an uninterrupted chorus of criticism throughout the year. On a broader front, fears were voiced in the West that Brandt might inadvertently compromise vital Western strategic interests. Nevertheless, reactions in London, Paris, and Washington were, if cautious, favourable, for Brandt was manoeuvring within a general movement towards East–West *rapprochement*—despite the Soviet invasion of Czechoslovakia in 1968. The two dominant military powers, Russia and the U.S.A., were anxious for tension to relax in Europe, Russia because she feared war with China and wanted to divert troops from her western to her eastern flank, and America because of the great cost of providing the mainstay of Western defences in Europe. Moreover, Russia and her Warsaw Pact allies need to tap Western, especially German, economic resources and know-how in order to revitalize their sagging economies. Politicians in the West also argued that East–West barriers would be eroded and the monolithic Communist regimes be inevitably modified as a result of Western contacts and rises in Eastern living standards.

It was under this clearing diplomatic sky that the new West German government set about negotiations with Moscow, Warsaw, and East Berlin. The most spectacular reception came from the Russians. Negotiations between West Germany and Russia began in earnest with the arrival of Egon Bahr (state secretary in the federal chancellor's office) in Moscow at the end of January 1970, and proceeded until on June 7 draft proposals for a non-aggression treaty between the two nations were approved by the West German cabinet. On June 12 the German tabloid *Bildzeitung* startled the world by publishing the leaked text of this "secret" draft, known as the "Bahr paper". The disclosure was seen as a Right-wing blow aimed at the government just before elections which took place in three *länder* on June 14. The leaked "Bahr paper" stated that the proposed treaty would not affect existing treaties binding either party, but that West Germany would "acknowledge the inviolability" of present European frontiers. Opposition leaders were quick to point out that this was tantamount to a recognition of East Germany and the Oder–Neisse line.

Formal negotiations on the treaty began on July 27 when Herr Scheel, West German foreign minister (and leader of the Free Democrats) first flew to Moscow. High-level talks continued until August 6, when both sides agreed on the text of a treaty renouncing the use of force. On August 11 Willy Brandt arrived in Moscow and on the next day the non-aggression treaty was signed by Mr. Kosygin, the Soviet prime minister, on behalf of the U.S.S.R. and Herr Brandt for the German Federal Republic. The complete text of the treaty was published by two German papers, while still "secret" and unsigned on August 11. The articles of the treaty are as follows:

Article 1: The Federal Republic of Germany and the Union of Soviet Socialist Republics consider it an important objective of their policies to maintain international peace and achieve *détente*. They affirm their endeavour to further the normalization of the situation in Europe and the development of peaceful relations among all European states. . . .

Article 2: The Federal Republic of Germany and the Union of Soviet Socialist Republics shall in their mutual relations as well as in matters of ensuring European and international security be guided by the purposes and principles embodied in the charter of the United Nations. Accordingly they shall settle their disputes exclusively by peaceful means and undertake to refrain from the threat or use of force, pursuant to Article 2 of the charter of the United Nations. . . .

Article 3: In accordance with the foregoing purposes and principles the Federal Republic of Germany and the Union of Soviet Socialist Republics share the realization that peace can only be maintained in Europe if nobody disturbs the present frontiers. They undertake to respect without restriction the territorial integrity of all states in Europe within their present frontiers. They declare that they have no territorial claims against anybody nor will assert such claims in the future. They regard today and shall in future regard the frontiers of all states in Europe as inviolable such as they are on the date of signature of the present treaty, including the Oder–Neisse line which forms the western frontier of the People's Republic of Poland and the frontier between the Federal Republic of Germany and the German Democratic Republic.

Article 4: The present treaty between the Federal Republic of Germany and the Union of Soviet Socialist Republics shall not affect any bilateral or multilateral treaties or arrangements previously concluded by them.

Article 5: The present treaty is subject to ratification and shall enter into force on the date of exchange of the instruments of ratification, which shall take place in Bonn.

The treaty was attacked by the West German parliamentary opposition, particularly by Franz-Josef Strauss, the Bavarian former finance minister, who denounced it as "a tin opener for a Pandora's box from which a multitude of evils would be released".

A draft treaty intended to usher in normal relations between West Germany and Poland was initialled in Warsaw on November 18, 1970, by Walter Scheel and Stefan Jedrychowski, foreign minister of Poland. The treaty was signed in Warsaw on December 8 by Willy Brandt and the Polish premier. The treaty provides for *de facto* recognition by West Germany of the Oder–Neisse line, and states that neither country has any territorial claim on the other. Thus, the treaty is nothing less than an historic acceptance by Germany of a loss of almost 44,000 square miles of land. On November 20, Willy Brandt broadcast to the nation, saying: "Over 30 years have passed since the Second World War began with the German attack. The Polish people have suffered unspeakable agonies." The chancellor was not exaggerating: one in five Poles—6 million in all—perished during the War. He continued by declaring that the treaty was "a liberating step towards a better Europe—a Europe in which borders no longer divide. That is what the youth of our countries expect, and we no longer want to burden them with the past. Instead, we want to give them a new beginning." In another document the Poles agreed to allow some 100,000 ethnic Germans still in Poland to resettle in West Germany.

West German overtures to East Germany were less well received, although Chancellor Brandt met the East German prime minister, Willi Stoph, twice during the year, thus breaking the diplomatic ice that had remained frozen since the partition. The first East–West German summit was at Erfurt, 32 miles over the Eastern border, where Brandt was given an emotional welcome by crowds of East Germans. At this meeting Willy Brandt listed six principles: 1. Both states have the duty to preserve the unity of the German nation; they are not foreign to one another. 2. The "generally acknowledged principles of international law must apply", including peaceful solution of disputes, respect for territorial integrity, and "the exclusion of all forms of discrimination". 3. There must be no use of force to change the "social structure" on either side. 4. The two governments should strive for "neighbourly co-operation", particularly in technical affairs. 5. The rights and responsibilities of the four powers—America, Great Britain, France, and Russia—in Berlin and Germany as a whole must be respected. 6. There should be support for the efforts of the four powers to reach agreement on improving the situation in and around Berlin.

In reply Stoph stated seven "basic questions": 1. Creation of "normal, equal relations" and renunciation of the Bonn government's claim to be the sole representative of the German people. 2. Non-intervention in each other's foreign relations and final abandonment of the West German objections to other countries' giving diplomatic recognition to East Germany. 3. Renunciation of the use of force between the two states. 4. Application by both for membership of the United Nations. 5. Renunciation by both of "the demand for and possession of nuclear weapons in any form"; renunciation of biological and chemical weapons; and reduction of defence spending by 50 per cent. 6. "Discussions of questions connected with 'the necessary burial of all vestiges of the Second World War'." 7. Settlement of all debts between the two states.

On May 21 discussions between the two men were continued at Kassel, West Germany. They were fruitless, and foundered on the first of Stoph's "questions"—East German insistence on full recognition by Bonn as a condition for any easing of relations between the two Germanys. East German pressure on the Russians was behind the long-drawn-out four-power talks on Berlin which continued throughout the year. The Western three (U.K., U.S.A., and France) aimed to wrest significant concessions from the Communists on West Berlin, including the dismantling of the wall. Although the talks were protracted—and continued beyond the end of 1970—the auguries were favourable, since the Russians knew very well that their treaty with Bonn would not be ratified by the German parliament unless they offered significant concessions over Berlin. Both Scheel and Brandt constantly reiterated that the Soviet–German treaty would not be ratified until the Berlin talks had come to a favourable conclusion.

All this important diplomatic activity took place against a domestic background of uncertainty. Brandt's coalition government owed its slim majority to the small parliamentary presence of the Free Democrats. Thus commentators regarded each local election that occurred during 1970 as a vote of confidence in the Federal government, and the fortunes of the Free Democrats were especially open to analysis. The situation was complicated by the fact that the Free Democratic espousal of the Left was of recent date, and many of that party's supporters—and members—regarded it with disdain. Indeed, on October 8, Right-wing Free Democrats split from the party, thus reducing Brandt's parliamentary majority to six.

Free Democratic fortunes fluctuated in the various *land* elections held during the year. Briefly, the party failed badly in the Saarland, Lower Saxony, and North Rhine-Westphalia during June, but picked up, to the confusion of political prophets, in November in Hesse and Bavaria. In Hesse they captured 10·1 per cent of the poll, while in Bavaria they secured 5·5 per cent (as compared to 5·1 per cent in the previous poll 4 years earlier). Brandt's Social Democrats, however, slumped in Bavaria from 35·8 to 33·3 per cent, while the Bavarian wing of the Christian Democrats, led by Herr Strauss, leapt from 48·1 per cent in 1966 to a thumping 56·4 per cent of the vote. Thus by the end of 1970 both government and opposition claimed the support of the electorate for their diametrically opposite diagnostics of the year of *Österpolitik*.

Gibraltar

It was an uneventful year on the Rock. Following the July 1969 election the Left-wing Integration with Britain party had joined with the Right-wing Isola group in a coalition, leaving Sir Joshua Hassan's Labour party in opposition. Four months after taking office, the new government accepted a general wage rise in accordance with their philosophy of "high wages, high productivity". June 1970 saw another general wage increase. Rocketing prices and rampant inflation marked the year, accompanied by a chorus of demands for price control. As a result of the withdrawal of the 4,700 Spanish workers in 1969, a labour problem loomed. Although 3,000 Moroccans were imported to fill some vacant jobs, a desperate shortage of skilled labour remained. Thus the economic emphasis rested firmly on high productivity, longer working hours (including part-time work), and training schemes. Aid from the U.K. totalling £4 million was announced at the tail end of 1969, and the year saw the start of work on a British-financed development plan. Projects include 750 housing units built on land released by the ministry of defence; medical and recreational facilities; and the provision of a comprehensive secondary school system.

Gibraltar's first national anthem, *Our Rock, Our Home, Our Pride*, was sung by Dorothy Squires at the end of a week-long Gibraltar song festival which began on November 11. During the previous month Spain had once again raised the matter of Gibraltar's status at the U.N.

Iceland

Following the tragic death of the prime minister, Dr. Bjarni Benediktsson, in a fire on July 10, 1970, the president, Krisjan Eldjarn, appointed Johann Hafstein, minister of justice and industry, as interim prime minister until a new government was formed. On October 10, Hafstein formed a new government, remaining as premier. His administration was based, like the previous one, on a coalition between the Independence party and the Social Democrats. Iceland became a member of Efta (European Free Trade Association) on March 1, 1970.

Republic of Ireland

Shortly before 3 a.m. on May 6, 1970, political circles in Dublin were sent spinning with the news that two senior ministers had been sacked for alleged gun-running. In an emergency debate in the Dail the same night, Jack Lynch, the prime minister, announced that he had received reports from security forces of a plot to import arms into the republic, and that the reports involved two members of his government, Neil Blaney, minister for agriculture and fisheries, and Charles Haughey, minister of finance. Mr. Lynch declared that he had twice asked the ministers for their resignations and twice been refused. He continued: "At my request the president has today terminated their appointments." At a meeting of the Fianna Fail (Soldiers of Destiny) parliamentary party held earlier, the two sacked ministers had both expressed their loyalty to the party, while the meeting had given the premier a unanimous vote of confidence. Another development of that eventful day was the announcement that Kevin Boland, minister of local government and social welfare, and Paudge Brennan, parliamentary secretary to the ministry of local government, had resigned at the premier's request. Michael O'Morain, minister of justice, had resigned a week previously.

The events of May 6 were the culmination of a cabinet split that had been detected and discussed by commenta-

October saw one of the more *outré* incidents to illuminate a bizarre year for Ireland when U.S. President Nixon visited Timahoe to inspect alleged ancestors.

tors since the explosion of violence in Ulster during August 1969. The crisis in the North is reputed to have taken the Dublin government by surprise and to have wrought instant division in the cabinet between hard-liners as advocating militant action—even invasion—and moderates claiming that the cause of Irish reunification had nothing to gain from action that might lead to another civil war.

On May 28 the crisis erupted once again with the arrest of Charles Haughey, Neil Blaney, and three others—Captain James Kelly, an Irish Army intelligence officer who had been recently dismissed for alleged gun-running, John Kelly, a Belfast man with a history of IRA activity, and one Luyks, a naturalized ex-Belgian. The five were charged with importing, or attempting to import, arms. The case against Blaney was dismissed at the preliminary hearing on July 2, but the trial of the remaining four began on September 22. The case was interrupted on September 29, when the judge stood down following allegations of bias by defence counsel, and was resumed under a new judge on October 6. The jury gave their verdict on October 23; all the defendants were found not guilty.

Following this verdict the future of Jack Lynch's government was the subject of intense speculation in Dublin and pundits waxed eloquent on the question whether the moderate premier could survive the crisis or be supplanted by the vindicated Haughey and be cast into the wilderness as the O'Neill of the South. Party interest dictated that the matter should be thrashed out immediately by the parliamentary party rather than be allowed to smoulder on until a grass-roots show-down at the party congress in February 1971. On October 28 Lynch tabled a motion of confidence in himself and his government—thus forestalling votes of no confidence already tabled by the opposition—and on November 4 the government won the vote with a majority of 74 to 67. All the Fianna Fail party members, including Blaney, voted for the motion, thus illustrating the legendary party loyalty of Fianna Fail. Kevin Boland formally resigned his seat just before the vote was taken. The crisis flared into the headlines again in early December when the government proposed measures for internment without trial following police investigations into an alleged conspiracy involving political kidnapping, bank robberies, and even organized murder. This announcement was greeted by a storm of protest from the opposition, and a heated debate on December 9 led to the suspension of three Labour T.D.s.

The small Irish Labour party emerged during 1970 as the focal point for Irish opposition to the country's proposed membership of the Common Market. The government were engaged in negotiations with the E.E.C. in Brussels during the year. The Six are reported to believe that there is no serious obstacle to Irish entry provided Britain joins. The Irish banks were closed by a strike for 7 months of the year, from April 30. When they re-opened on November 17, businessmen, publicans, and shopkeepers lodged millions of pounds worth of cheques, many stacked in suitcases, sacks, and boxes. It had been an object lesson in trust, and a few economists speculated whether an absence of currency and banks might not be a blessing in disguise in other countries.

In the autumn the world enjoyed via television and the press an episode of undiluted Irishness. October 3 saw the arrival in the republic (complete with wife and entourage) of Richard Milhous Nixon, president of the United States of America, in pursuit of ancestors with whom to beguile, it was libellously said, the Irish-American vote in the American congressional elections. Diligent research metaphorically unearthed the mouldering remains of a Milhouse family in a Quaker graveyard at Timahoe, co. Kildare, and by an admirable exercise in genealogical logic these slumbering Quakers were declared of the blood that yet coursed through the veins of Nixon. The Quaker graveyard was hastily refurbished for a presidential visit on October 5, and a diplomatic veil was drawn discreetly over assertions that the family had been hounded from Ireland by religious persecution in the early 18th century. A similar veil mantled the memory of the ancestors of Patricia Nixon (née Ryan); they, it was wickedly suggested, had embarked for the U.S.A. after turning Protestant for material rather than metaphysical motives. At all events, Mrs. Nixon visited Ballinrobe, co. Mayo, on October 4, to see the church where her grandparents were married and her grandmother's house, which had been converted into a barn. She also took tea with 70-year-old Miss Katie Naughton, her second cousin. The president and his lady jetted out of Dublin on October 5, having met President De Valera, suffered the exhilaration of a Dublin anti-Vietnam-war demo—during which eggs sailed narrowly near the presidential ear—and attended a banquet given by Mr. Lynch in Dublin Castle.

Italy

A year of crisis in Rome began with a Christian Democrat minority government, headed by Mariano Rumor, trying desperately to form a Centre-Left coalition with the Socialists, Social Democrats, and Republicans. The Socialists proved the initial bar to unity. They had split and left the previous coalition in July 1969 (thus bringing down the government) after violent internal argument over co-operation with the Communists. The parties met fruitlessly during January 1970. Finally, on February 7, Rumor and his cabinet resigned, thus intensifying the crisis, which continued until March 27 when a new four-party Centre-Left coalition under Rumor was formed. The new government lasted only until July 6, when Rumor suddenly resigned again, claiming that quarrelling and intrigue between the coalition partners made his position impossible.

President Saragat immediately began talks with the leaders of the 10 parliamentary parties, as a result of which Giulio Andreotti, chairman of the Christian Democrats parliamentary party, emerged as prime minister designate. Andreotti failed to form a government, and resigned his mandate to do so on July 23. On July 25 another Christian Democrat, an aloof, enigmatic bachelor, Emilio Colombo—whose predilection for dead languages and the higher fiscal mysteries had earned him the soubriquet of "the lay Cardinal"—was nominated by the president as next to attempt to form a government. Again the major obstacle concerned relations with the Communist opposition: the Social Democrats fulminated against the Marxists, while the Socialists were content to co-operate with them, particularly at a local level. The "lay Cardinal", however, surmounted these difficulties and was able to form a government by August 6. His list of ministers was almost identical with that of Rumor's previous coalition. Colombo's government was still in office at the year's end, having survived an October cliff-hanger: the final vote on the controversial divorce bill—which threatened, if thrown out, to lead to a dangerous clash between the two houses of parliament. A private member's bill, it finally passed the Senate—with a majority of 14—on October 9, and the lower house a second time on

Jubilant Italians celebrated the final passing of the divorce act on December 1.

December 1, becoming law on receiving the president's signature and publication in the official gazette.

Chapter V of the Italian constitution, which came into being on December 27, 1947, provided for the division of Italy into 20 partly self-governing regions, thus breaking the highly centralized system of government from Rome that had existed since unification. Of these 20 proposed regions five were to be "special", with a high level of self-government, and 15 were to be "ordinary". Four of the five "specials"—Sicily, Sardinia, Trentino-Alto Adige (South Tyrol), and Val d'Aosta—were swiftly set up, and Friuli-Venezia Giulia was held back until 1963 because of the Trieste dispute. But successive governments ignored the constitution with regard to the other 15, because powerful forces had doubts about the wisdom of regionalism in a country that has only been united for a century.

At last, after parliamentary wrangles and prolonged filibuster, a bill setting up the 15 "ordinary" regional institutions was passed in October 1967. The regions were Piedmont, Lombardy, Venetia (Veneto), Liguria, Emilia-Romagna, Tuscany, Umbria, the Marches, Latium (Lazio), Abruzzo, Molise, Campania, Apulia (Puglia), Basilicata, and Calabria. Each of the 15 was to have a regional council elected by universal franchise, and would, in turn, choose regional presidents and executive boards. The new structure came into effect after the first regional elections on June 7, 1970. The elections strengthened the Centre-Left coalition, the governing parties polling over 58 per cent of the vote.

One result of the advent of regionalism was indignation in the southern city of Reggio Calabria in protest against the government's decision to make another city, Catanzaro, the capital of the new region of Calabria in the toe of Italy. Indignation led to anarchic street violence in mid-July. The police station was razed to the ground, one civilian was killed and several policemen were injured. Spasmodic rioting, burning of cars and property, shootings, and bombings organized by a "committee of agitation" continued for three months and flared up into intensive rioting at the start of October. Over October 12–13 the post office was gutted by rioters, and on October 14 police moved in with bulldozers and other equipment to tear down 30 or 40 barricades. Riots greeted their

intervention, and a policeman was shot. On October 16 the government moved in 3,000 troops to restore order. Some 500 citizens were charged with disorderly behaviour, and 116 were jailed.

The town was calm by October 20, when the constitutional affairs committee of the Italian parliament met to consider Reggio's claim to be capital of its region. Meanwhile, police searched the homes of several members of the "action committee for Reggio as Capital" and took away various papers. All those searched were members of the "neo-fascist" MSI, although Calabrian Christian Democrats are alleged to have played a more important part in the rioting. Violence broke out again on November 13 when students rioted in protest against the committee's delay in coming to a decision.

Norway

On April 21, 1970, the Norwegian foreign minister, John Lyng, announced that he would resign in May to make way for a younger man, and added that he would retire from politics completely. Lyng's resignation set in motion a reshuffle of Conservative ministers in the four-party, non-Socialist coalition, which was announced in Oslo on May 22. Svenn Stray succeeded Lyng as foreign minister. This change and the other changes it initiated—particularly the elevation of the Conservative party chairman, Kåre Willoch, to Stray's old position as leader of the Conservative parliamentary party—tightened the somewhat slack bond between the Conservative leadership and the party organization. May 4 saw the election, at the Liberal party congress, of Helge Seip to his party chairmanship. Seip was minister of labour in the coalition, and his elevation within the Liberal ranks showed a bridging party and leadership similar to that of the Conservatives. Seip, who represents his party's moderate wing, took over from Gunnar Garbo, a leader of the radical wing.

During September the opening session of the Norwegian E.E.C. entry negotiations provoked storms over the question of fishing policies. Briefly, the Six refused to give an undertaking to redraft the E.E.C. fishing policy after Norwegian entry. Norway, of course, catches more fish a year than all the Six combined.

On October 5 a "shock" budget was presented by Ole

253

Myrvoll, minister of finance. Price increases were slapped on tobacco, drink, petrol, car licences, and electricity for industry. Social insurance tax was also increased, and the special tax levied to finance foreign aid was doubled. This budget was designed to restrict personal consumption and give priority to the public sector. The Norwegian T.U.C. called a 15-minute token strike on October 7 as a symbolic protest and a warning to the government that it found the record £1,416m budget unacceptable.

Portugal

On February 20, Dr. Marcello Caetano, the Portuguese premier, was elected president of the central committee of a new political organization, National Popular Action, which replaced the National Union that had been the predominant power in Portugal for 40 years. Meeting at Estoril, the congress of the National Union had voted the new organization into existence during February, thus aligning itself with the progressive liberalization promised by the new administration.

Internal Portuguese politics also showed some signs of welcome liberalization during 1970. On May 7 a political amnesty pardoning offenders against state security was announced to commemorate the anniversary of the birth of Marshal Carmona, a former president. On October 7 far-reaching changes in Portugal's laws on religious freedom were announced by the government. A draft bill was put before parliament banning all forms of religious discrimination and giving individuals the right to opt for and practise the religion of their preference. The bill restated the principle of separation between Church and State. Some 90 per cent of European Portugal's 9 million people are Roman Catholic, but the new bill was not a rebuff to Rome, despite friction between Lisbon and the Vatican over Portugal's policies in her African provinces. Wide-ranging constitutional amendments were unveiled by Dr. Caetano on December 2. These proposed the abolition of press censorship (within certain expansive limits); the protection of the rights of newspapers and journalists; the extension, on reciprocal basis, of Portuguese citizen's rights to Brazilians on Portuguese soil; and autonomy for the overseas provinces.

During the year, much was made by commentators of the choice which they declared faced Dr. Caetano's admin-

istration: Africa or Europe. The old guard, pundits averred, advocated the shunning of close economic and political ties with Europe in favour of concentrating on subduing the rebels and boosting the economy in Portuguese Africa. The new "technocrats" were said to favour European integration at the expense of Africa. Speaking on September 28, the eve of the first meeting between Portugal and the E.E.C. commission on the question of some sort of future association, Dr. Caetano outlined his government's solution to the dilemma when he said: "As far as a customs union is concerned we have much to gain. As far as a political federation is concerned we have all to lose."

Spain

The worst crisis to hit Spain since the civil war disturbed the slumbers and the waking hours of El Caudillo, Francisco Franco, during his 79th year. This stemmed from the "liberation war" in the northern provinces of Guipuzcoa, Biscay, and Vitoria of Alava organized by a group of militant Basque separatists, the E.T.A. (*Eusaka Ta Askatusana*—meaning Basque Nation and Freedom), first formed in 1959 as a Marxist-Leninist offshoot of the Basque Nationalist party. E.T.A. launched a terrorist campaign during 1968 (in response to a mass police round-up of E.T.A. sympathizers) which resulted in the murder of two policemen—one of whom was Inspector Manzanas, head of the security police in San Sebastian —who were killed during August 1968. E.T.A. continued to wage a guerrilla campaign of sabotage, bombing, bank-raids, banditry, and battles with police—until by the end of 1970 four states of emergency had been declared in the Basque provinces, and five guerrillas had been killed and 40 seriously wounded. There were allegedly some 500 full-time guerrillas divided into three-man cells operating in the Basque provinces by late 1970, and also thousands of sympathizers, including priests.

On December 1, 1970, the conflict was brought suddenly before the eyes of the world with the kidnapping of Herr Eugen Beihl, the West German honorary consul in San Sebastian, by E.T.A. guerrillas who held him as a hostage against the fate of 16 Basques scheduled to be tried by a military court in Burgos on December 3. The public prosecutor was demanding death sentences for six

The trial of 16 militant Basque separatists at Burgos, Spain, during December inspired anti-government demonstrations and massive counter-demonstrations in favour of Franco. Here government supporters wave the Falange flag.

of these 16, accused of planning or carrying out the murder of Manzanas. The remaining 10, including two priests, faced charges of banditry, terrorism, and illegal possession of arms.

Beihl's capture was part of a wave of protests, demonstrations, riots, and strikes marking the trial, which resulted in the declaration of a 3-month state of emergency in the province of Guipuzcoa. This decree allowed police to search premises without warrant and to hold suspects indefinitely. Anti-government demonstrations continued throughout the country, notably a 48-hour sit-in by 300 artists and intellectuals (including Joan Miró) at the Benedictine monastery of Monserrat, Barcelona. Meanwhile Spanish embassies abroad were attacked by demonstrators, often led by Basque exiles. These activities inspired counter-demonstrations by pro-government supporters which gathered strength and spread throughout Spain as the crisis continued. Mass rallies pledged loyalty to the regime, denouncing foreign interference and calling for Spanish unity.

Christmas Day saw the release of the captured Beihl, a gesture which E.T.A. hoped would persuade the court to show mercy. On December 28, however, the sentences were announced: the six accused of complicity in Manzanas's murder were sentenced to death by firing squad, three with double death sentences; another nine, including two women and two priests, received sentences of between 12 and 50 years; and the remaining accused, a woman, was acquitted. This news brought fresh waves of protest and demonstrations both in Spain and abroad, and representations from foreign governments urging Franco to commute the death sentences, including an appeal from the Pope, flooded into Madrid. They are unlikely to have influenced the Generalissimo. Nevertheless, Franco reprieved the condemned six on December 30 after an emergency meeting of the council of the realm. The death sentences were commuted to 30 years' imprisonment. Speaking to the nation on television, Franco said that the demonstrations of loyalty and solidarity had given him the authority to be merciful.

The Burgos affair may prove of great significance in Spain. Autumn had seen a symbolic government gesture towards the gradual eclipse of the Falange, the Spanish fascist movement, when Franco banned the wearing of the Falangist blue shirt at celebrations marking the 37th anniversary of the movement on October 29. The fading of Falange influence over recent years had been parallel with the rise in power of Opus Dei, the lay Catholic order of pragmatic technocrats (11 members of the Spanish cabinet during 1970 were understood to be members of the order). The rise of Opus Dei had been watched with dismay by the Falangist faithful, wont to chant at their mass rallies the refrain *Franco si, Opus no!*—a sentiment that echoed down certain echelons of the Spanish military as a cautious shift towards "liberalization" was undertaken by the ascendant technocrats. Thus the aftermath of Burgos may bring about a waning of Opus influence as the Falange reasserts itself—boosted by the pro-Franco mass rallies which it organized during the crisis.

Sweden

Swedes went to the polls on September 20, 1970, in their first general election for a one-chamber parliament. The new system introduced a single chamber of 350 members, 310 of whom are elected from 28 polling districts. The remaining 40 seats are divided between the parties on the basis of the number of seats each would have won if the whole of Sweden had been a single polling district. The reason for this complex system is to ensure that—at least as regards the final 40 seats—each vote cast is of equal value. The election was fought mainly on the increasing cost of living and rising food prices. Between July 1969 and July 1970 the general cost of living in Sweden rose by 7·8 per cent and food prices rose by 10 per cent. In the face of this inflation, and also labour unrest, the election was seen as one of the most unpredictable ever fought in 38 years of Social Democratic rule.

The constitutional changes favoured the small opposition parties, and the prime minister. Olof Palme, had held office for only one year and lacked the widespread popularity across party lines enjoyed by his predecessor and mentor, Tage Erlander, who had retired in 1969 after 23 years as premier. Economic difficulties made the government's position still worse, for Sweden faced a balance of payments problem with a total trade deficit at the beginning of August of 1,457 million crowns (£116·56 million).

However, the non-Socialist opposition—the Conservative, Liberal, and Centre parties—conducted a lack-lustre campaign, appearing more disposed to attack one another than the government, and the electoral fortunes of the Communists seemed to be at a low ebb following the Russian invasion of Czechoslovakia and facing competition from the Communist League, a Maoist splinter group. Interest focused on whether the Communists could muster the 4 per cent of the national poll (or 12 per cent in any one constituency) required, under the new system, for a party to win any seats whatsoever.

In the event, the Communists did better than expected (taking 4·9 per cent of the vote), and with 17 seats held the balance in the new parliament. The final result was: Social Democrats 163; Centre Party 71; Liberals 58; Conservatives 41; Communists 17. The Social Democrats continued in office as a minority government with support from the Communists—with which it could count on a majority of 10. The Communist leader, C. H. Hermannson, declared that his party would never combine with the non-Socialist opposition to overthrow the government. But the Communists are thought likely to expect some consideration in return for this support—for a failure to demonstrate their political independence could lead voters to regard them as merely an auxiliary of the Social Democrats. Left-wing voters might then opt for the Maoist Communist League.

As from October 12, 1970, the prices of all goods and services in Sweden were frozen. This anti-inflation measure is to last until April 1971.

Sweden was one of those nations courting the Common Market during 1970. On November 10, Austria, Switzerland, and Sweden asked the Six in Brussels for trading links with the Market which would in no way undermine their "permanent neutrality". Sweden asked for a customs union which would mean that, in addition to abolishing tariff barriers, she would accept the external tariff of the Six. All three neutral nations said that they wished to opt out of the treaty linking them with the Market in time of war, and could not, therefore, join in common foreign policies.

Switzerland

Over June 6 and 7, 1970, Switzerland's all-male electorate narrowly rejected a proposal to reduce the foreign population of nearly 1 million (over half of them Italians) by one third over the next 4 years. The vote was 654,588 against the proposal, and 557,714 for it. Some 74 per cent of the electorate voted. One worker in three is a foreigner in Switzerland, and an economic crisis would undoubtedly have resulted from an acceptance of the proposal. The fact that almost half the voters were prepared to face this possibility indicates the strength of Swiss feelings on the subject. Foreigners formed 16 per cent of the population during 1970. Under the Swiss system of direct democracy the vote took place following an "initiative" proposing to limit the number of foreigners to 10 per cent in each of the 25 cantons. The initiative came from Herr James Schwarzenbach, an independent member of the federal parliament, who presented a petition with 70,000 signatures.

On June 12 the federal prosecutor's office completed a probe into Switzerland's largest arms scandal by announcing that seven people had been charged for allegedly illegally exporting £9 million worth of arms to South Africa, Israel, Nigeria, Egypt, Saudi Arabia, and the Lebanon. On November 27, three of the seven, all former employees of the Oerlikon arms firm, were jailed by the Swiss supreme court, their sentences ranging from 15 to 18 months. The remaining four were fined and given suspended sentences.

3 The Soviet Union and Eastern Europe

Bulgaria

Todor Zhivkov, the Bulgarian premier and first secretary of the Bulgarian Communist party, proposed a reorganization of co-operative and state farms at a plenary session of the central committee on April 27, 1970. The farms will be made larger and will be known as "agricultural-industrial complexes". Zhivkov is alleged to have sent a letter to President Tito during September proposing a friendship pact and mutual renunciation of territorial claims between Bulgaria and Yugoslavia. During November, however, a Yugoslav delegation returned from Bulgaria dissatisfied: the Bulgarians apparently still cherished claims on Macedonia.

Czechoslovakia

The wholesale purging of the Czech government, party, and legislature of all pro-Dubcek liberals continued unabated in 1970. Alexander Dubcek himself—who had been removed as first secretary of the party on April 17, 1969—was, in effect, in exile as ambassador to Turkey as 1970 began. On January 28 came the announcement that Dubcek had "resigned" from the central committee of the Communist party, and the same day saw a cabinet shuffle that brought Lubomir Strougal, a "hard-liner", to the premiership in place of Olrich Cernik. It also ushered out all remaining "liberals" in favour of "hard-liners".

On February 3, a 10,000-word official document was published in Prague listing "revisionists", both individuals and organizations. Among these were the majority of the Prague Communist party committee, leaders of the journalists' union, and 47 prominent people, including Professor Ota Sik, former deputy premier, and Josef Smrkovsky, former president of the national assembly. The document closed with the advice that all party members should be examined closely before being issued with new party cards. Some 400,000 of the country's 1,400,000 party members were expelled during the year. On February 22, Rude Pravo, the party paper, disclosed that political tests for children seeking admission into high schools were to be reintroduced. The following day Czechoslovak citizenship was revoked from four leading "liberals" in exile, including Professor Sik, and on March 21 it was announced that Dubcek was to be suspended from the party while an investigation into his conduct as first secretary was carried out. He was expelled from the party and deprived of his parliamentary seat on June 26, having returned from Turkey during May.

A mass purge of Czech teachers and artists was also under way. Modest estimates calculated that 900 scholars, teachers, and scientists had been dismissed from academic institutions by the end of the spring. Secondary and primary school teachers were also put through the process of an ideological test, and hundreds of intellectuals suspected or known to have supported the reformist policies of the Dubcek regime were reported to be doing menial work on the land by the end of the year.

East Germany

West Germany's policy of *rapprochement* with the East, launched during 1970 by the federal chancellor, Willy Brandt, was not well received by the German Democratic Republic. Herr Ulbricht, the East German Communist leader, feared that East Germany's hard-won economic boom—which depends to a large extent on confining technocrats within the country's borders—might be jeopardized by a slackening of East-West tension, particularly by the dismantling of the Berlin wall. Thus Ulbricht and his premier, Herr Stoph, waged a protracted diplomatic campaign, in the face of Russian pressure, to frustrate Brandt's efforts. Meetings between Brandt and Stoph were fruitless. East German intransigence was most conspicuous on the question of the future of the divided city of Berlin—still legally run by the victorious Second World War allies, Russia, U.S.A., France, and Britain. In February, the Russians agreed to hold talks in Berlin with the Western powers on such matters as free access by land from West Germany to West Berlin; and in the general climate of East-West *rapprochement* these talks went forward with every hope of success, especially as Berlin was the pivot in the foreign policies of both Russia and West Germany. The latter constantly reiterated that the non-aggression treaty signed with the U.S.S.R. during August would not be ratified unless the four-power talks came to an acceptable conclusion, and the Russians knew that the Nato powers would use the outcome of the four-power talks to gauge Russian sincerity in calling for a *détente* in Europe and a European security conference.

While meetings between the four powers continued through the year the East German government appeared bent on wrecking them. Obstructive action, designated as manoeuvres, on the autobahn leading from West Berlin to West Germany marked the year, and tension mounted in the days before West Germany's Social Democratic party meeting in West Berlin on December 21. Meanwhile West Germany and the Western allies wanted: (1) a guarantee of free access to land routes to West Berlin; (2) an end to discrimination against West Berlin and the inclusion of the city in Bonn's international treaties; (3) recognition from Moscow of West Berlin's legal and economic ties with Bonn; (4) West Berliners to be allowed to visit East Germany all the year round.

Breaking off their talks for Christmas on December 10 the four ambassadors agreed to meet again on January 19, 1971. Simultaneously, Herr Ulbricht tossed a weighty spanner into the diplomatic works when, in a speech to his central committee, he declared that agreement on West Berlin could be reached only on the basis of recognition of East Germany's full sovereign rights.

Hungary

The tenth congress of the Hungarian Communist party was held in late November 1970. On November 23 the party boss, Janos Kadar, speaking in the presence of the Soviet leader Leonid Brezhnev, called for creative freedom and more democracy within the party. His audience comprised 690 Hungarian delegates and 380 guests, including delegations from 32 other Communist parties.

On March 5 legislation easing travel restrictions, and giving the right of appeal to any citizen refused a passport, came into force. Formerly an unsuccessful applicant could neither question nor appeal against a police decision to refuse a passport.

Poland

Bloody riots marked Christmas 1970 and led to the fall of Wladyslaw Gomulka as first secretary of the Polish Communist party and the elevation of Edward Gierek into his place. The "revolution" was sparked by the sudden announcement on December 14 of a drastic 20 per cent rise in food prices. Shipyard workers at the Baltic port of Gdansk responded with a strike, and on December 15 marched to the local party headquarters singing the *Internationale* and gathering on their way hundreds of students, housewives, and others, until a mass of about 20,000 demonstrators mobbed the party h.q., hurling stones and petrol bombs. Police fired on the crowd, and riot flared into savage fighting; the rioters also received the attentions of troops and tanks, and were quelled temporarily. But the fighting and looting continued for a week longer.

Within hours of the outbreak of violence in Gdansk, similar outbursts erupted in the neighbouring towns of Gdynia and Sopot, and spread thence in an angry swathe across the nation, affecting Slupsk, Szczecin, Wroclaw, Poznan, Katowice, Lodz, Cracow, and even Warsaw. The Baltic coast, however, remained the centre of the crisis. The riot-torn ports were sealed off by the authorities, and Soviet warships steamed along the coast. A Russian freighter under construction at Szczecin was scuttled by shipyard workers. As the riots continued, militiamen are alleged to have turned their machine-guns on the demonstrators and charged them with armoured cars. The mob took its revenge: at least ten militiamen were hanged from lamp-posts, and others flung into the sea. As the riots subsided after raging for a week, the total death toll was estimated at over 300.

Behind the riots and the announcement that inspired them loomed economic stagnation and, above all, an archaic agricultural system. Some 80 per cent of Polish agricultural land remains in private hands, while over the heads of the peasants hangs the perpetual threat of collectivization—which, of course, makes them reluctant to invest in modern equipment. To make matters worse, Polish farmers had faced two bad harvests running. Meanwhile, in Warsaw rival factions within the party, armed with their respective quivers of statistics and arsenals of dogma, exchanged nostrums of economic theory, leaving practice to a rigidly orthodox, highly centralized

West German Chancellor Willy Brandt signed a treaty with Poland on December 8, giving *de facto* recognition to the Oder–Neisse line. While in Warsaw, Brandt knelt at the monument to the Jewish insurgents killed by the Nazis during the Ghetto uprising of 1943.

bureaucracy presided over by Gomulka. It was this body that unleashed the unexpected and ill-timed announcement of December 14, freezing wages and shifting prices—up on food and down on consumer goods.

Five leading members of the Politburo were made scapegoats after the riots, including Gomulka, who resigned (because of "ill-health") as first secretary of the party on December 20. The four other axed Poles were President Marian Spychalski; Boleslaw Jaszczuk, an economic specialist deemed the man behind the food increases; Zenon Kliszko, a top ideologist; and Ryszard Strzelecki, in charge of the party organization. At the same time the government adopted a conciliatory stance, and Gomulka's successor, Edward Gierek, appeared on television and declared that the nation's most urgent task was to "ensure peace and the normal process of work and life". Gierek admitted that badly thought-out economic ideas had played a part in the riots.

The new Polish leader, dubbed "dynamic" by all organs of the Western press, received the stamp of Soviet approval when Brezhnev, the Soviet party leader, despatched him a fulsome telegram of congratulations on December 21. Gomulka was not mentioned. Another head to roll was that of the prime minister, Josef Cyrankiewicz, who was replaced by a former schoolteacher and army general, Piotr Jaroscewicz, on December 23. The new premier appointed a cabinet of technocrats, and Gierek announced that the food price increase would be frozen for 2 years. Cyrankiewicz, who had been premier for 21 years, was chosen as Poland's new president on resigning as prime minister, as his name is on the Bonn-Warsaw treaty which had still to be ratified as 1970 ended.

Rumania

The Danube flooded in late May and June 1970, taking over 200 lives and inundating all but two of Rumania's 39 districts. Heavy rains and a sudden thaw in the Carpathian mountains were responsible for the disaster, which destroyed some 284 bridges and one sixth of the country's railway lines, demolished towns, leaving half a million homeless, and washed away most of the topsoil. It will take 4 or 5 years to rebuild the country's economy. Meanwhile, economic weakness could jeopardize President Ceausescu's independent stance within the Soviet bloc. Aid flowed in from over 30 nations—including China and the U.S.A., which gave more than the Russians. Relations between Bucharest and Moscow, which had been cool since the Soviet invasion of Czechoslovakia and Ceausescu's anathematic response to the "Brezhnev doctrine" (by which the U.S.S.R. reserves the right to intervene in the affairs of other Communist countries), sank a few degrees cooler when, in July, the long-delayed signing of a new Soviet–Rumanian friendship treaty took place in Bucharest. Brezhnev cancelled his plans to visit Rumania for the signing at the last moment because of a "catarrhal ailment"—which he went out of his way to prove a "diplomatic ague" by appearing at a football match in Moscow. The Russian premier Aleksei Kosygin was sent instead to Bucharest where he was met by crowds meagre in comparison to those that turned out for President Nixon in 1969. The treaty revises a 1948 pact, and provides that Rumania will help the U.S.S.R. in the event of an armed attack—from the West, according to the Rumanian interpretation, from anywhere (i.e. China) according to the Russians.

Russia

The year of the centenary of Lenin's birth was a critical one for the Soviet Union and an intriguing one for Kremlinologists in the West. While economic difficulties and rumours of impending changes in the leadership marked the year within, the outside world was confronted by an ambivalent Russian posture poised between expansion and conciliation. The year opened with confessions from Brezhnev, the party boss, and various other august quarters, notably *Pravda*, that Russia was in dire economic trouble. Chief among the defects catalogued were inefficient management, wastage of public funds, failure to introduce up-to-date machinery, and lack of labour discipline—designated as "loafing and drunkenness". The shaft of party scrutiny was turned upon the "liberal reforms" introduced during 1965 by the premier, Kosygin, which had decentralized the economic decision-making machinery and handed out more power to individual managers, although the measures had been quietly shelved by Brezhnev soon after their inception. Western commentators claimed to perceive dimly a power struggle within the Kremlin, from which Brezhnev would emerge

all-powerful from the triumvirate that had supplanted Khrushchev (Brezhnev, Kosygin, and President Podgorny). Shadowy substance was lent to this view by the party's failure to agree on a policy for the 1971–75 5-year plan which should be introduced at the 24th party congress —due in March 1970 but postponed, as the wrangling continued, until March 1971.

In foreign affairs, Russia's military and propaganda confrontation with China continued, highlighted by occasional skirmishing but subdued by Sino-Soviet talks which appeared to vacillate between insult-swapping deadlock and courteous deadlock. Danger in the East added impetus to Russia's policy of *rapprochement* with the West, but although a non-aggression pact with West Germany was signed in August, it was not ratified during the year, as Bonn and the Western powers awaited a successful outcome to the four-power talks about Berlin. The SALT talks with the U.S.A. continued in Vienna and Helsinki, but Moscow's earnest pleas for a European security conference were generally greeted with a mixture of suspicion and guarded interest. These peaceful overtures were made against a background of military manoeuvring which gave grave cause for concern to Nato. The Russian naval build-up in the Mediterranean and Indian Ocean continued, matched by a continued cementation of relations with the Arab world, especially Egypt.

All the signs pointed to increasing repression within the U.S.S.R. during 1970. Not only were writers, scientists, and artists warned repeatedly to toe the party line and "ward off the influence of Western thought", but grave concern arose for the fate of Russian Jews. Although some leading members of Soviet Jewry were permitted to emigrate to Israel, most of those wishing to do so were frustrated. A number of arrests of Jews were made, including nine arrested together with two Gentiles for plotting to hijack an aircraft in June. Two of these, Mark Dymshyts and Edward Kuznetsov, were sentenced to death, but on December 31, in the face of world opinion, their sentences were commuted to 15 years' imprisonment.

On June 14, 150 million Soviet citizens dutifully cast their votes for 1,517 candidates for the two chambers of the Supreme Soviet. All the 1,517 were members of, or supported by, the Communist party.

4 The Eastern Mediterranean

Albania

Towards the end of May 1970, General Enver Hoxha, the leader of the Albanian Communist party, made a public appeal for better relations with Yugoslavia. This was reported favourably in the Yugoslav press and behind-the-scenes talks between the two nations are presumed to have started. There was certainly a public Yugoslav response to Hoxha's overture, notably a speech by President Tito on August 7. Tito declared: "We fought shoulder to shoulder in the war against the common enemy. After the war cooperation did not work out too well, but in the present international situation we have much in common and we should come to a better understanding once more." This, of course, was a euphemistic way of saying that both countries were in some degree of danger from a Soviet drive to the Adriatic.

Legislature "elections" were held in Albania on September 20.

Cyprus

President Makarios narrowly escaped assassination on March 8, 1970, when shots riddled the helicopter in which he was taking off from Nicosia. The pilot, although badly wounded, managed to land the aircraft safely and the president-archbishop, unscathed, helped him out and flagged down a passing van in order to send him to hospital. The outlawed National Front, an extremist organization calling for union with Greece, was deemed responsible for the attempted assassination, and on the night of March 15 Polycarpos Georghadjis—a former minister of the interior and Eoka leader who was suspected of being behind the plot—was found shot dead in his car outside Nicosia. Mystery shrouds his demise. On April 15 six Greek Cypriots, including three policemen, allegedly supporters of the deceased Georghadjis, were charged with the Makarios assassination attempt and, on May 24, 30 others—allegedly National Front members—were arrested following discoveries made during a raid on a police station at Limassol.

The first general election since independence in 1960 was held in Cyprus on July 5. (The life of the first parliament had been extended by presidential decree for five years because of the strife between the Greek and Turkish communities.) The house of representatives is supposed to have 50 members, divided 35 to 15 between Greek and Turkish Cypriots, but the latter had eschewed their seats in it since December 1960, and had met in the Turkish quarter of Nicosia as part of the *de facto* "transitional Cypriot administration". The Turks held an election for this body on July 5 also. The results of the election to the 35 Greek seats of the house were as follows: Unified Party (right-of-centre supporters of the president) 15; Akel (Communist) 9; Progressive Front (right-wingers) 7; Democratic Centre Union (left-of-centre) 2; Independents 2. Glafcos Clerides was re-elected president of the house by 26 votes to 2 on July 2.

The U.N. military presence remained on the island throughout the year, to the financial embarrassment of that august organization and reciprocal benefit to the Cypriot economy. Meanwhile, as in previous years, fruitless talks continued between representatives of the two communities on a constitutional settlement of their differences.

Greece

Two important trials marked 1970 in Greece. From March 27 to April 12 the largest trial since the military coup of 1967 took place before the Athens military tribunal. On trial were 34 defendants accused of sedition. Many were also accused of detonating bombs, as a result of which 20 people had been injured. Seven of the accused were acquitted, and the remainder received sentences of between 18 years and 1 year (five of them were suspended sentences). A retired general, George Iordanidis, allegedly the leader of the group, received 8 years. On March 31, 1970, the three publishers, the editor, and the managing editor of the Athenian evening newspaper *Ethnos* appeared before the Athens military court charged with spreading false reports "likely to evoke anxiety among citizens" and engaging in "anti-national propaganda". The charges arose from an interview with Ioannis Zigdis, a former cabinet minister, published by *Ethnos* on March 24. Zigdis (who was also on trial) called for the restoration of democracy in Greece. On April 2, all six were found guilty and received prison sentences ranging from 4 to 5 years, apart from the managing editor who received 13 months' imprisonment.

On April 10 the prime minister, George Papadopoulos, announced the restoration of constitutional safeguards against arbitrary arrest and detention, and promised the release of 350 political exiles by April 21—the third anniversary of the coup. Also abolished were the martial law's provisions suspending *habeas corpus*. The premier declared that the "moribund" martial law would only prohibit anti-government propaganda and the possession or use of radio transmitters and duplicating machines without permit. On August 10 the government announced that some 500 of the 1,096 alleged Communists remaining in detention were to be released under a "new measure of liberalization". Another 290 political prisoners were set free on Christmas Eve. In mid-October Mr. Papadopoulos issued a proclamation announcing elections for a consultative committee on legislation to be held on November 29. This "small parliament", selected rather than elected, consists of 59 members chosen by the premier, 46 of whom were picked from a list of 92 candidates elected by the nation's mayors—who were themselves appointed by the regime—and the executives of labour and professional organizations. The prime minister claimed that the "small parliament" has advantages over more democratic assemblies as it is free "from the conflict of party interests". In December, announcing the release of more detainees, he said that there would be no major political or constitutional changes during 1971.

During October various government statements outlined the conditions that must be met before the regime restores full democracy. Briefly these were: (1) the national income per head must increase from the present £300 to £450 a year; (2) public administration must be streamlined; (3) national income must be distributed more equitably; (4) educational reform must be completed; (5) the Greek mentality should be reformed and the press should be cleansed so that there could be no relapse into political corruption.

Greece was found guilty of torturing prisoners and of denying basic human rights to her citizens by the 15 members of the ministerial committee of the Council of Europe at Strasbourg on April 15, 1970.

Israel

The third anniversary of the six-day war of June 1967 was observed amid mounting military activity, particularly on the Suez front where Soviet-manned missiles menaced Israeli superiority in the air. For 3 years an Arab "war of attrition" had gradually taken its toll of the victors' manpower and morale until, by June 1970, 558 Israeli soldiers and 112 civilians had been killed (compared with 777 soldiers and 26 civilians killed during the six-day war), and during the month of May alone the Israeli death toll was 61. At the same time a massive infusion of Soviet aid and advisers had rebuilt the shattered Egyptian forces, and a host of Palestinian guerrilla groups had been spawned intent on terrorism and sabotage within Israel.

A feature of the early months of 1970 was "deep penetration" flights by Israeli aircraft into Egypt, intent on preventing the establishment of missile sites. Three tragic

An Israeli soldier cautiously raised his helmet to test the 90-day cease-fire on August 7; no shooting came from the Egyptian lines. On November 6 the cease-fire was extended for another 90 days.

incidents roused the interest and concern of the outside world during these months: the Israeli bombing of a scrap-metal plant near Cairo on February 12 when 68 were reported killed and 98 wounded; the Israeli bombing, as a result of misidentification of a school in the village of Bahrel Bakr in the Nile delta on April 8, in which 30 children were reported killed and over 50 injured; and an Arab guerrilla bazooka attack on an Israeli school-bus near the Lebanon frontier on May 22, when eight children and three adults were killed and 21 children injured.

Missiles shipped from Russia during March began to arrive in the Canal zone during July when SAM 2s and 3s began to bite into Israeli aerial supremacy. At the same time Russian pilots were reported to be flying operational missions over Egypt. This significant tilt in the balance of power led to a repetition of Israel's urgent request to Washington for warplanes to redress the balance (25 Phantoms and 100 Skyhawks). The requests remained unfulfilled while the American state department worked on a peace-plan for the area. This appeared on June 25 when Mr. Rogers, the U.S. secretary of state, brought out an American peace initiative. Briefly the Rogers plan (which stemmed from the 1967 U.N. resolution No. 242) called for (1) an immediate 90-day cease-fire; (2) Israeli withdrawal from occupied territories; (3) Arab recognition of Israel's right to exist. Both Arabs and Israelis were subjected to intense pressure from their super-power mentors to accept the American initiative. The cease-fire, as a first step to peace talks on the basis of the Rogers plan, was accepted by the Israeli cabinet on July 31, 1970, and formal acceptance arrived in Washington on August 5. That same day, as Mrs. Golda Meir, the prime minister, announced her government's decision to the Israeli *Knesset* (parliament), the much-mooted government split over the matter was illustrated when, as the premier intoned the word "withdrawal", Menchem Begin, leader of the right-wing Gahal party, rose from his seat on the government benches and paced slowly past her bound for the back benches. Despite this first split in the 3-year-old coalition the government's policy was endorsed by a majority of 66 to 28 (there are 26 members of the Gahal party in the *Knesset*).

Meanwhile, after 19 days in Moscow and an Arab summit in Tripoli, Nasser responded favourably to the American initiative, and the cease-fire (covering 31 miles on either side of the Suez Canal) came into effect on August 7. On August 24 the U.N. mediator, Dr. Gunter Jarring—"the silent Swede"—began talks with the belligerents, but by then Israel had lodged a number of complaints with the U.N. truce supervision organization in the Near East (UNSTO) alleging cease-fire violations by the Egyptians, whom they accused of moving SAM missile batteries into the cease-fire zone. These allegations were confirmed by Washington on September 3. Three days later, after making ten formal complaints, Israel withdrew from the peace talks, and announced that it would not resume them until "such a time as the cease-fire agreement is fully implemented". From then until the year's end Israel politics revolved around whether or not such a time had arrived until, on December 28, Mrs. Meir announced that her government had decided to resume the talks. Meanwhile, in order to maintain the balance of power, the U.S.A. had promised to supply the warplanes that Israel had requested. While both sides strengthened their military position, the actual shooting war over the Suez Canal remained at a stand-still and when the 90 days ended the cease-fire was extended until February 5, 1971.

Turkey

Sulyman Demirel's government was defeated in the national assembly when 41 dissident members of the ruling Justice party joined with the opposition to vote down the budget on February 11, 1970. The voting was 244 to 214. This split in the Justice party had its origins in 1964 when Demirel was elected party leader, defeating Dr. Sadettin Bilgic. Bilgic and some of his right-wing following were included in Demirel's first administration, but the faction was excluded from Demirel's second government, formed after the general elections of October 1969. The dissident Bilgic faction thereafter waged a propaganda war against the premier which culminated in the voting down of the budget.

Following this defeat, Demirel resigned on February 14, but was asked by President Sunay to form a new government by the end of the month. On March 6 Demirel presented an unchanged cabinet to President Sunay, and the "new" government received a 232 to 172 vote of confidence on March 15. Sixteen of "the 38" (dissident Justice party M.P.s) were suspended from the party for a year (including Dr. Bilgic), three resigned, and four voted for the government. Nine opposition members also voted with the government while the remaining dissidents boycotted the session. The government's revised, indeed tougher, budget was subsequently approved by a small majority.

Anti-Demirel feeling continued in the Justice party, however, and other dissident factions emerged within the ranks, engendering a pervasive atmosphere of instability. This was intensified during the spring and summer when extremists from right and left rioted in the streets of major cities and several factories were "occupied". The government responded to this turbulence by tabling bills for the prohibition of political activities in the student union and trade unions; and for the maintenance of greater control at public meetings and demonstrations. Moreover, a labour law amendment act was introduced under which the government would not recognize trade unions that did not represent at least one third of all workers in any one industry. This led to massive riots in Istanbul and Izmir on June 15 and 16. Martial law was declared for a month in both cities.

On August 9 the Turkish government devalued the currency by 66·5 per cent because of a balance of payments problem due to export difficulties. During July, after a year of negotiations, Turkey and the Common Market agreed on the passage to a new stage of Turkey's association agreement with the Six.

Yugoslavia

In an autumn speech at Zagreb, President Tito surprised his audience with the words: "I have been in this post quite long enough, and I would like to have more possibilities to work on some other project." The 78-year-old President went on to outline the creation of a collective presidency made up of representatives of the country's six republics and of major political and industrial organizations. Tito's proposals were an attempt to allay fears that when he goes the country may divide along its long-standing ethnic, religious, and linguistic boundaries into a chaos of regional bickering. The president's ideas were being thrashed out in detail in Belgrade in the last months of 1970.

Tito was active on the international scene during 1970, playing host to Princess Margaret and Lord Snowdon in June and President and Mrs. Nixon in October. He embarked on a long African tour in February 1970, paying official visits to Tanzania, Zambia, Ethiopia, Kenya, Uganda, the Sudan, Egypt, and Libya. He was also prominent at the third summit of the non-aligned nations held at Lusaka, Zambia, September 8–10. He put off an official visit to Rome during December, however, because he objected to the exclusion of Yugoslavia's claims to part of the old Trieste free territory from the proposed talks.

The Yugoslav economy remained a problem during the year. The country faced balance of payments difficulties despite a 5 per cent import tax, and inflation was rising. On November 18, Dr. Nikola Miljanic, one of three vice-presidents of the federal executive council (the government), resigned, allegedly over the economic issue. It is understood that he wanted firmer and sharper measures to stabilize the economy.

5 The Arab World

Algeria
The council of the Algerian revolution met on June 9, 1970, under President Boumédienne and drew up a document listing the regime's achievements in 5 years which was published on the anniversary of the "revolutionary readjustment" of June 19, 1965. The achievements were: (1) the state had been solidly built with the help of the masses; (2) an economic recovery had been effected; (3) economic growth had improved; (4) education had been provided for all children; (5) a new society was in the process of construction.

Belkacem Krim, a former Algerian deputy premier, was found strangled in a hotel in Frankfurt on October 20. During April 1969, Krim had been sentenced to death in his absence by a court in Oran. On November 1, 1970, President Boumédienne remitted the sentences of some 100 political prisoners.

Egypt
President Nasser died of a heart attack on September 28, hours after the ending of the hectic Arab summit meeting during which the Egyptian leader had exerted himself in gruelling and successful efforts to end the civil war in Jordan. His death was greeted with profound sorrow and extravagant manifestations of grief throughout the Arab world, and a crowd estimated at four million mobbed his funeral procession through Cairo on October 1. On October 5 Vice-President Anwar el Sadat, who had taken over as acting president, was unanimously nominated for the presidency by the executive committee of the Arab

Socialist Union, a choice which was approved unanimously by the National Assembly on October 7. On October 15 a national referendum took place, and Sadat was endorsed as president by 90·4 per cent of the electorate (there was no rival candidate). He was sworn in on October 17.

Apart from the shock of Nasser's death and the continuing confrontation with Israel, the most significant political development in Egypt during 1970 was the agreement—taken in Cairo on November 8—by Sadat of Egypt, Nimery of the Sudan, and Kadhafi of Libya to prepare for an eventual federation of their three countries. The agreement outlined a joint triumvirate leadership, a supreme planning committee, and a supreme national security council. (See also under Israel and Syria.)

Gulf States
December 1970 saw a high-powered delegation from Kuwait and Saudi Arabia touring the nine southern Persian Gulf emirates in an attempt to coax their rulers back to the conference table to finalize the federation plans which they had been deliberating, off and on, since February 1968 following the announcement that Britain was going to withdraw from that oil-rich area. This U.K. decision was reaffirmed late in 1970, despite pledges to the contrary, by the new Conservative government.

Talks between the nine rulers had reached deadlock in late 1969 over the issues of (1) the number of seats each state should have in the proposed lower house, and (2) the

An estimated four million Egyptians thronged the route of President Nasser's funeral parade in Cairo on October 1.

A pall of smoke hung over Amman, Jordan, during the September civil war between the army and the Palestinian guerrillas.

site of the federal capital. The "big four" Gulf emirates are Abu Dhabi, Qatar, Dubai, and Bahrain. The power vacuum which the British will leave could be filled by Saudi Arabia, Iran, or Iraq. Each of these nations has various territorial claims in the area, and all were manoeuvring for position during 1970. The only power in the Gulf regarded as neutral was Kuwait, which Iraq was attempting to infiltrate and influence.

A coup in the backward but oil-rich Muscat and Oman occurred on July 23, when Sultan Said bin Timur was deposed by his son, Qabis bin Said. The ousted sultan had set his face firmly against change of any sort, and had ruled in medieval style. Trousers, football, glasses, and eating or conversing in public were forbidden. The new sultan changed the country's name to the Sultanate of Oman and, on August 9, announced a number of reforms and development plans.

Iraq

The Baath party that rules in Iraq and Syria was seriously split by the Jordan civil war of September 17–25, with a civilian wing demanding intervention on behalf of the Palestinian guerrillas and a military wing opposing intervention. Since it was the generals who had the final say in the matter Iraqi troops remained neutral during the fracas—despite the fact that the Iraqi government had assured the guerrillas that its 12,000 troops stationed in Jordan would come to their aid. General Hardan al-Takriti, one of Iraq's two vice-presidents, remained at the Iraqi base in Jordan during the war to see to it that none of his men became involved. He was sacked from all his civil and military posts by the civilian faction led by Sadam Hussein Takriti on October 15. This gesture, amounting to a seizure of power by Sadam Hussein, brought the general flying back to Baghdad from Madrid,

where he was at the time, only to be despatched straightway to Algiers, where he was given asylum. Mass purges followed, and six officers were shot on November 5.

The long-standing war with the Kurds ended on March 11, 1970, and a committee of Arabs and Kurds was set up on March 18 to work out a settlement between the two peoples. This body published a provisional constitution, promulgated on July 16, which declared that Iraq consisted of two peoples, Arabs and Kurds, and that Kurdish and Arabic would be the official languages in the Kurdish region. It had previously been agreed that a Kurd should be vice-president, but on September 11 the government refused the Kurdish nominee.

Jordan

The Jordanian civil war was short, sharp, but not sudden. Long before September, friction between the Fedayeen—the various Palestinian commando groups formed after the Six-Day War to wage irregular guerrilla war with Israel—and the Royal Jordan army had flared into bullet-flying battles. Frequent clashes continued as 1970 advanced, and skirmishing turned to heavy fighting in June. Mediation by other Arab states led to an agreement signed between the belligerents on June 10. This pact proved as substantial as desert sand, for fighting continued and intensified until full-scale war—highlighted by a brief Syrian invasion—erupted on September 17.

The differences between the two camps stemmed partly from ideological and partly from national differences: the king and the army broadly represent the political Right and the interests of the Bedouin, while the guerrillas represent the aspirations of the Left and the ambitions of the multitude of Palestinians who had flooded into the kingdom as refugees from Israeli expansion in 1948 and 1967.

The 9-day fratricidal fighting was bitter and bloody, and large parts of Amman, the capital, and other cities were destroyed. Crowded refugee camps—where guerrilla groups had their headquarters and stored their ammunition—were reduced to rubble by artillery bombardment, and large numbers of civilians were killed. When the fighting subsided and a peace pact was signed, thanks to frantic efforts by Arab statesmen, notably Nasser, the army held sway in Amman and the centre and south of the country. The guerrillas controlled a triangle of territory in the north marked by Jerash, Ramtha, and Irbid—three towns which were each surrounded by government troops.

Political machinations within the army command had led to the showdown. Irritated beyond endurance by constant harassment from fedayeen openly professing revolutionary ideals, army leaders allegedly bearded King Hussein (who had narrowly escaped an assassin's bullet on September 1) and told him bluntly that the time had come for action. On September 16, Hussein, who had formerly attempted to conciliate the factions, yielded to this pressure from his power-base and, sacking his civilian government, appointed a military one under Brigadier Mohammed Daoud—a Palestinian; proclaimed martial law; and appointed Field-Marshal Habes al-Majali c.-in-c. of the forces with full power to restore order.

Daoud resigned on September 24 while in Cairo. He was there leading the Jordanian delegation at peace talks arranged by an Arab summit under Egyptian aegis and involving the good offices of leading Arab statesmen including General Nimery of the Sudan, who led a mission to Amman to meet the king and guerrilla leaders. A 14-point agreement ending the war and ushering a cease-fire was signed in Cairo by King Hussein and Yasser Arafat, the guerrilla leader, before 10 Arab heads of state. Under this agreement, supervised by a committee led by the Tunisian premier, army and guerrillas were bound to withdraw from towns and cities by October 1, 1970. Army officers and guerrilla leaders in northern Jordan signed a cease-fire on that date. On September 26 the king appointed a half-military, half-civilian cabinet under Ahmed Toukan.

Massive relief operations were launched by various international organizations, and Jordan slowly returned to normal during the last months of 1970. The government claimed that 700 people were killed in the fighting and 1,300 wounded, while guerrilla spokesmen declared that 25,000 had been killed or injured during the 9 days of war.

For the hijacking of aircraft in early September by Palestinian guerrillas and the destruction of three of them at "Revolution airfield" near Amman, see pp. 92–93.

Lebanon

Soliman Frangié, minister of national economy, was elected president for a 6-year term, in succession to Charles Helou, by the Lebanese parliament on August 17, 1970. Frangié formed his administration on October 7, appointing Saeb Salam prime minister, and forming a cabinet of non-parliamentarian technocrats.

Lebanon continued to be used by Palestinian guerrillas operating in Israel, and frequent border clashes inspired by their activities marked 1970—notably an Israeli armoured excursion into Lebanese territory against guerrilla strongholds, May 12–13. Lebanese regular troops were involved in this fighting, and six were reported killed.

Libya

Colonels Adam al Hawaz and Moussa Ahmad, erstwhile ministers in the revolutionary government who had been arrested in December 1969, for plotting to kill the Libyan leader Colonel Kadhafi, and 21 of their henchmen, were imprisoned on August 7, 1970, on sentences ranging from 3 to 30 years.

The Italian population of Libya (13,000 strong—Libya was once an Italian colony) suffered a rude shock at the hands of the revolutionary regime on July 21 when Colonel Kadhafi announced the expropriation of all Italian property in Libya. (Land owned by absent Jews was also taken over.)

Morocco

A national referendum held on July 24 approved almost unanimously a revised constitution; an end to the state of emergency that had been in effect since 1965; and a return to parliamentary democracy. A general election for the chamber of representatives proclaimed in the new constitution took place on August 21 and 28. King Hassan had announced on July 30 that the chamber would have 90 M.P.s elected by universal suffrage; 60 selected by electoral colleges of professional groups; and another 90 elected by local councils. After the election of the 240 members, 158 were deemed neutral; 60 were members of the pro-government *Mouvement populaire*; and 22 were of mottled ideological hue.

The main concern in foreign affairs during the year was Morocco's long-standing dispute with Spain over the phosphate-rich Spanish Sahara. The dispute was highlighted during June when anti-Spanish riots took place in the desert territory's capital El-Aaiun. The clash was seen as the start of a new phase in Morocco's campaign to wrest the vast 102,680-sq.-mile territory from Spain.

During 1970 Morocco was active on the diplomatic front, seeking to form an anti-Spanish North African alliance between Morocco, Algeria, and Mauretania—an aim formerly foiled by bitter disputes between these three Arab nations. In May 1970, King Hassan of Morocco and President Boumédienne of Algeria resolved a border dispute concerning the iron-rich oasis of Tindouf, over which they had fought a brief war in 1963: Morocco dropped her claims on the oasis in return for Algerian support in the Spanish Sahara. (During 1958 the Moroccans had sent waves of warriors into the territory.)

Syria

The split in the Syrian ruling Baath party (between military "nationalists" and civilian "progressives") that had been highlighted by crises in 1968 and 1969 widened during September 1970 when a further crisis erupted in the aftermath of the Jordan civil war. Before the outbreak of war in Jordan, General Assad, Syria's defence minister and leader of the military Baath wing, is alleged to have agreed with General Hardan Takriti, then vice-president of Iraq, that neither Syria nor Iraq would intervene in the event of a showdown between the Jordan government and the Palestinian guerrillas. When the fighting began, however, Assad was outvoted by the "progressives" led by General Jadid, and a Syrian tank brigade rolled into Jordan to aid the guerrillas on September 20. Under pressure from the U.S.S.R. and President Nasser of Egypt, who warned of the danger of American intervention (and under even greater pressure from the Jordanian army), these tanks were pulled out of Jordan on September 23.

The humiliating display led to mutual recrimination

within the Syrian government and unrest in the army. As a gesture of protest at this quarrelling, President Atassi resigned on October 16, and an emergency party congress was called in Damascus on October 30 at which the rival wings exchanged invective. A motion calling for Assad's dismissal was forestalled by the general, who led a bloodless military coup on November 18. "Progressive" leaders were arrested and the army took over all radio and TV stations and newspaper offices. Ex-President Atassi was placed under house arrest. Assad appointed Ahmed Khatik president and took over himself as premier on November 18.

On November 26 it was announced that Syria had applied to join the proposed federation of Egypt, Libya, and the Sudan, and had been accepted.

Tunisia

The Tunisian premier, Bahi Ladgham, presided over the committee that supervised the cease-fire of September 27 after the civil war in Jordan, and in his absence President Bourguiba appointed Hedi Nouira acting premier during October. On November 1 it was announced that this appointment was definitive.

Yemen

The civil war between republicans and royalist rebels operating in northern Yemen from bases in Saudi Arabia had flared up after a period of calm during late 1969, and heavy fighting continued into 1970. On February 1 the premier, Mr. Khorshumi, resigned after failing to formulate a budget adequate for both the armed forces and the bribes required to buy the loyalty of the various tribes. On February 5, Muhsin al Aini, a left-winger, was appointed prime minister. A shift in Saudi policy during March resulted in negotiations to end the civil war in Yemen, and an unwritten agreement was concluded whereby the Imam Mohammed al Badr was to remain in exile but leading royalists were to be appointed to the government. Four of the Imam's followers joined the administration on May 23.

6 Africa South of the Sahara

Cameroon

Ahmadou Ahidjo was re-elected unopposed as president of Cameroon on March 28. The parliamentary elections of June 1970 were equally free from suspense, as the Cameroon National Union is the country's only political party.

Chad

The Franco-Chadian campaign against Arab rebels of the northern Toubous tribe near the Libyan border continued during 1970. The number of French troops engaged in Chad during the year was about 1,500. Some 39 of them had been killed in the 2-year war by the end of 1970.

Congo (Brazzaville)

About 30 armed rebels seized Brazzaville radio station on March 23, 1970, announced the "overthrow" of President Ngouabi's left-wing regime, and declared a new one. The rebels did not last long, however, for within hours the president—who in January had transformed the country into a people's republic—personally led loyal troops in a sharp and victorious battle to recapture the station. The rebel leader, an army lieutenant, was killed and his body exhibited to the public.

Congo (Kinshasa)

On June 30, 1970, the 10th anniversary of the Congo's independence was celebrated by the signing of a treaty of friendship between Congo and Belgium. King Baudouin was in Kinshasa for his former territory's celebrations, and his visit marked an end to an era of coolness between the two countries.

Nine million Congolese endorsed the pro-Western policies of General Joseph Mobutu and on November 2 elected him president for a 7-year term, with almost 100 per cent of the votes. The presidential election marked a return to constitutional rule after 5 years of military government.

Dahomey

On May 7, 1970, the tiny West African state of Dahomey ushered in the sixth regime of its ten-year history—a new three-man presidential council headed by Hubert Maga, who thus became the 11th head of state. Under the latest constitution each of the presidential triumvirate—Hubert Maga, Justin Ahomadegbe, and Sourou-Migan Apithy—will take a two-year turn as head of state.

Equatorial Guinea

Frau Irmgard Pleuger, the wife of a Hamburg industrialist, was allegedly being held hostage on the island of Fernando Po as 1970 ended. The Hamburg tabloid *Bild Zeitung* declared that on December 18 President Macias Nguema had demanded a ransom of some £114,000 for her release.

Ethiopia

Emperor Haile Selassie paid a state visit to Rome during November—his first visit to Italy since Mussolini invaded Ethiopia in 1936. The rebellion in the Moslem province of Eritrea intensified during 1970. By December 16, when a state of emergency was declared and military rule imposed in parts of Eritrea, most of Ethiopia's 40,000 troops were fighting insurgents in the province. The rebels, armed with Chinese weapons, are trained by various Arab states and by Al Fateh, the Palestinian guerrilla organization. Eritrea was incorporated into Ethiopia in 1962.

Gambia

A republican constitution approved by the house of representatives in December 1969 was approved by a referendum during April 1970, and came into effect on April 24. Sir Dauda Jawara, the prime minister, became president. The Gambia remains in the Commonwealth.

Ghana

Following the return to civilian, democratic government in 1969, August 28, 1970, saw the election of Edward Akufo-Addo as president of Ghana for a 4-year term. The new head of state, the principal author of the 1969 constitution and formerly chief justice, was elected by a secret ballot of the electoral college, which comprises the 140 members of the national assembly and 24 chiefs. The new

This internal acrimony in Pakistan took place in a year destined to usher in civilian government after years of military, or military-backed, rule. President Yahya Khan —who had rescued the country from chaos in March 1969, and imposed martial law—declared late in 1969 that a general election would be held on October 5, 1970. It was postponed, owing to floods, until December 7, and went ahead on that date, except in nine devastated constituencies in the Ganges delta; there it was delayed "for a few weeks". It was the first free, one-man-one-vote election ever held in Pakistan. Nearly 40 million people voted, including women, and only two parties won substantial support. These were Mr. Zulfikar Ali Bhutto's People's party, which won 94 of the 138 seats in West Pakistan; and Sheikh Mujibur Rahman's Awami League, which won a decisive victory in the East, taking 149 of the 153 seats. The League is also expected to win the nine Ganges delta seats. The Awami League stands for autonomy for the East, but not for secession. Only when all constituencies have polled will the new national assembly be convened to frame—within a time limit of 120 days— a constitution which will replace military with civilian rule.

Persia (Iran)

During 1970 Persia dropped her long-standing claim to Bahrain, the group of islands in the Persian Gulf that had been a British protected territory since 1861. The Labour government's plan for British withdrawal from "east of Suez" by 1972 had given rise to a renewed emphasis on the Persian claim to the territory—which had been under Persian rule until leased to Britain 150 years before. Teheran's territorial ambitions were opposed by the Arab rulers of the islands, by Great Britain, and by various Arab states, notably Saudi Arabia. On May 11 the U.N. security council endorsed a report from a U.N. mission which declared that "the overwhelming majority of the people of Bahrain wish to gain recognition of their identity in a fully independent sovereign state". The security council endorsement was ratified by the Persian *Majlis* (lower house) by 186 to 4 on May 14, and unanimously by the Senate on May 18.

The Awami League, led by Sheikh Mujibur Rahman (centre, with white sleeves and dark jacket), won an overall majority in the Pakistan general election of December 7—the first free one-man-one-vote poll ever held in the country. The elected representatives will meet to frame a new civilian constitution.

The proposed British departure from the Gulf and the prospect of a power vacuum generated much friction between the larger states in the area, particularly between Persia and Iraq, who had fought a number of border skirmishes during 1969 and continued at daggers drawn during 1970. On February 8, the Persian premier, Amir Noveida, announced an increase of almost 50 per cent in defence expenditure—from £228 million in 1969 to £325 million in 1970.

8 South-East Asia and the Far East

Burma

U Nu, the former Burmese premier who exiled himself to Thailand amidst a blaze of publicity in 1969, was reported to have formed during July 1970 a national liberation front of Burmese rebels to overthrow the regime of General Ne Win. The front allegedly had the support of Mon rebels under Nai Shwe Kyin—reported to be in control of Tenasserim state in southern Burma—and the Karen tribe's 20,000-strong army. Burmese Communist rebels were also reported active in the north. General Ne Win is believed to have suffered a heart attack on October 30.

Cambodia

Prince Norodom Sihanouk, who had steered Cambodia deftly down the neutralist path during the turbulent years of fighting in neighbouring Vietnam, left Cambodia for medical treatment in France on January 4, 1970. He did not return. In early March, student demonstrators in Phnom-Penh, protesting against the presence of some 40,000 Viet Cong and North Vietnamese troops in Cambodia—where they operated supply lines, operational headquarters, and billeted themselves in sanctuary all down the South Vietnamese border—stormed the North Vietnamese embassy and also that of the Viet Cong (South Vietnamese Communist) provisional revolutionary government. Cambodians nurse a traditional enmity towards Vietnamese (regardless of ideology), and the attentions of the mob were next turned on the Vietnamese community (some 500,000) within Cambodia. On March 18, the national assembly deposed Prince Sihanouk, who was replaced as head of state by General Cheng Heng.

The ousted prince flew from Paris first to Moscow and next to Peking where, on March 23, he issued a proclamation dissolving General Lon Nol's government and announced the creation of a government of national union, a national liberation army, and a united national front. The leaders of the Cambodian Communist "Red Khmer" rebels announced their support for Sihanouk on

Cambodia became a battlefield in the Indo-China war during the year. Over a million refugees from the countryside crowded into the capital. Phnom-Penh.

March 26, and a royal government in exile was set up in Peking on May 5. The prince, although unpopular in urban areas because of having turned a blind eye on North Vietnamese infiltration still retained a mystical and feudal hold on the loyalties of the peasants. Thus mass demonstrations in rural areas, inspired by Viet Cong elements, supported his action.

Clashes between the Cambodian army and Viet Cong and pro-Sihanouk forces followed, during which several hundred Vietnamese civilians were massacred by Cambodian troops. By mid-April, guerrilla wars were raging along the South Vietnamese border, and in southern provinces west of the Mekong. On July 3, the absent Prince Sihanouk was tried by a military tribunal in Phnom-Penh, accused of allowing Vietnamese Communist troops to ensconce themselves within Cambodia and inciting the populace to "rally to the enemy". He was found guilty and sentenced to death in his absence.

The anti-Communist General Lon Nol appealed to the Americans for military aid and received it. On April 30 it was announced that South Vietnamese and American troops had invaded Cambodia, intent on flushing out North Vietnamese and Viet Cong troops, supplies, and communications networks—a campaign which President Nixon declared would facilitate the slow American withdrawal from Vietnam. A 21-mile limit for penetration into Cambodia was imposed by the President, and the American troops were withdrawn from Cambodia throughout June until the deadline of June 30 (set by Nixon to assuage American protests at the extension of the war in Indo-China) was met.

Whatever the military effect of the invasion on the war in Vietnam was, it did little to ease the position of the Cambodian government. By July the Communists were in control of the northern provinces and most of the southwest, and were active within miles of Phnom-Penh. On October 5 the Cambodian senate and national assembly voted unanimously to abolish the monarchy, and the Khmer Republic came into being on November 1. Some 12,000 South Vietnamese troops were still in Cambodia as the year ended; the population of Phnom-Penh had grown, thanks to refugees, from 500,000 to 2,000,000; and the Cambodian army was losing men at the rate of

a battalion a week. President Nixon's request for £106 million in arms aid to Cambodia was finally granted by the U.S. Congress on December 16.

China

China-watchers in Hong Kong distinguished three main factions wrestling for power in Peking during 1970: (1) generals grouped about Huang Yung-Sheng, the chief-of-staff; (2) government ministers headed by the premier Chou En-lai; and (3) those who backed Chairman Mao when he launched the "cultural revolution" in 1966, including Marshal Lin Piao, political heir to Mao, and Mao's wife, the ex-film star Chiang Ching. The first two factions —standing broadly for order, discipline, and sanity— appear to have gained ground during 1969 and entrenched themselves during 1970. One factor in their favour was the threat of war with Russia, which gave more power to the army and was used as a rallying cry for unity and discipline after the chaos of the cultural revolution. Thus 1970 saw a gradual "return to normality". Elderly professors, frogmarched from their chairs in dunces' caps during 1966–68, began to return to the universities. Another major symptom of normalization was an announcement on October 8 that the Chinese Communist party was to convene the national people's congress "at an appropriate time" to elect a head of state to replace the "arch-revisionist" Liu Shao-chi (disgraced in the cultural revolution) and draft a new constitution.

Talks with the U.S.S.R. over border disputes and the ideological chasm dividing Moscow and Peking continued throughout 1970. By early November it appeared that, as far as ideology was concerned, the pair had agreed to differ without mounting mutal attempts at conversion, and ambassadors were exchanged for the first time for years. Meanwhile, China began to pursue a more outgoing and reasonable foreign policy, a significant feature of which was the resumption, early in 1970, in Warsaw, of talks with the U.S.A. Diplomatic effort was rewarded notably by recognition by Canada and Italy. On November 20 the U.N. general assembly voted for the 20th time on the admission of Communist China to the U.N., and for the first time the motion received a majority vote—which, however, fell short of the two thirds required for the measure to take effect. Thawing of diplomatic ice led to the release of certain British citizens imprisoned for "spying" during the cultural revolution: George Watt in August; Peter Crouch during October; and David Johnston in December.

Hundreds, perhaps thousands, of Tibetans were arrested and interrogated by "people's courts" during the year as part of a massive purge of those suspected of "counter-revolutionary collusion with reactionaries". Mass public executions were also reported.

Fiji

Fiji became an independent state within the Commonwealth on October 10, 1970, after 96 years of British rule. The Prince of Wales and the New Zealand premier attended the celebrations in Suva, the capital.

Indonesia

With the cry "*Hidup Bung Karno*" (Long Live Brother Sukarno) Brigadier General Supardjo, one of the leaders of the abortive Communist coup of 1965, was shot on May 19. He was the ninth coup leader to be executed. The Fates added insult to fatal injury, for Brother Sukarno did not long survive him. President Suharto arrived in

The Hague on September 3 for a 24-hour visit amidst a confusion of diplomatic embarrassment following the armed invasion of the Indonesian ambassador's residence a few days before by 32 young Amboinese in exile, protesting about the Suharto regime's refusal to give independence to Amboinese islands in the archipelago. Nevertheless, the visit symbolized an improvement in relations between Holland and its former colony. On March 17, Indonesia signed a friendship treaty with Malaysia.

An "unborn baby" in the womb of a "19-months-pregnant" woman, which was able to talk, pray, and recite from the Koran, was visited by thousands of miracle-worshipping Indonesians, including president Suharto, his foreign minister, and his minister for religious affairs during the year. Red faces were universal when on November 3 it was exposed by the police as a bundle of towels and a tape recorder.

Japan
Following the ruling Liberal Democratic party's success in the elections of December 27, 1969, Eisaku Sato was re-elected by the house of representatives for a third term as prime minister on January 14, and announced his cabinet on the same day. Japanese parliamentarians were augmented in number by elections in Okinawa and other islands of the Ryuku group on November 15. These were the first elections in Okinawa since the war, and represented the first step in the reversion of the Ryukus from the U.S.A. to Japan under the terms of the U.S.–Japanese agreement signed in 1969.

During July it was announced that early in 1971 Japan will begin a construction programme for 9½ million new flats in the suburbs of the nation's main cities. On July 31 Mr. Sato took personal control of Japan's emergency anti-pollution body—formed to tackle the blankets of smog which could make Japan's cities "gigantic tombstones"—and on August 11 the government decided to introduce a bill making industrial pollution a crime. On December 21 America informed Japan that she will withdraw over two thirds of her forces from Japan during 1971; nine bases will close, and 12,000 troops will be pulled out.

North Korea
Chou En-lai, the Chinese premier, arrived in Pyongyang, the North Korean capital, on April 5. The visit symbolized the closer ties between the two countries in the face of the new "Japanese–American military alliance"—the renewal, in June 1969, of the security treaty between those powers—and also North Korea's stance in the ideological quarrel between China and Russia.

South Korea
As part of President Nixon's "low profile" doctrine for South-East Asia, Washington announced during 1970 that troops were to be withdrawn from East Asian bases in South Korea, Japan, and Taiwan (Formosa). All three governments were considerably disturbed, and South Korea, the most vulnerable, was the most disturbed of the three. About one third of the 64,000 U.S. troops in South Korea were earmarked to be withdrawn during 1971, and in July 1970 Seoul learnt that Washington's plans were "not negotiable". The 550,000-strong South Korean army was still mainly equipped with obsolete arms, while the North Korean army of 446,000 was armed with modern Russian and Chinese weapons. Thus when the American vice-president, Spiro Agnew, arrived in Seoul for talks over August 25–26 President Park demanded

Yukio Mishima, the Japanese novelist, actor, and film director, seized an army h.q. in Tokyo on November 25 with the aid of members of his 80-strong private army and harangued the military from a balcony, hoping to enlist their support for a right-wing *coup d'état*. Greeted with derision, Mishima retired into a general's office and crying *"Tenno heika banzai!"* (Long live the Emperor!) committed *hara kiri* in the classic manner.

$3,000 million over the next 5 years to modernize his forces. The unfortunate Agnew was reported to have looked "grim" as he returned to his hotel from Park's Blue House residence. On August 28 the Pentagon modified its plans and announced that only 10,000 American troops would be withdrawn by June 1971.

Laos
The civil war between Prince Souvanna Phouma's royalist wing of the "neutral government" and the Communist Pathet Lao, led by his half-brother, Prince Souphanouvong, smouldered through 1970, occasionally exploding into the headlines. Royalist troops, stiffened during 1970 with Thais and aided by U.S. aerial support, disputed the Plain of Jars (which divided the areas controlled by the two sides) with the North Vietnamese-backed Pathet Lao in a war that had been almost a ritual since 1962. But in April 1970 the Communists pushed into the Mekong valley and on to the Bolovens plain in southern Laos, thus taking towns previously deemed, by tacit agreement, to fall within the royalists' sphere. This change in the conduct of the war resulted from Communist manoeuvring following the American intervention in Cambodia, with Hanoi blazing new infiltration routes through south Laos into northern Cambodia.

Malaysia
On July 23 it was announced that the Sultan of Kedah, H.H. Abdul Halim Shah Mu'azzam, had been elected by the Malay rulers as supreme head of state (king) of Malaysia for a 5-year term, succeeding the Sultan of Trengganu, H.H. Ismail Nasiruddin Shah. The new king's uncle, Tunku Abdul Rahman, resigned as prime minister on September 21, to be succeeded by Tun Abdul Razak, the director of the national operations council formed after the Chinese–Malay race riots of 1969. Announcing his resignation decision, the Tunku also stated that the Malaysian parliament and state assemblies would be restored in February 1971. The ban on political discussion and the curfew were lifted.

Philippines

The assassination of a congressman, Floro Crisologo, in Vigan during late October sparked off riots and bloody clashes between the private armies and armed bodyguards that do so much to enliven Filipino politics. Crisologo was a loyal henchman of President Marcos, responsible for gaining valuable support for the ruling Nacionalista party in the lawless Northern Luzon provinces. Further murders followed, and among those slain was the gravedigger assigned to dig Crisologo's resting place. The Pope narrowly missed a similar fate on November 27 when an anti-clerical, dagger-brandishing Bolivian surrealist, dressed as a priest, lunged at him at Manila airport during his eastern tour. A karate blow from the President, however, and a flying tackle from an elderly English divine served to save the pontiff.

The Filipino peso was "floated" on February 21, 1970, and eventually settled at 6·2 to the American dollar—a devaluation of 37 per cent. During June, Manila secured a massive restructuring of its overseas debt to Europe and the U.S.A.

Thailand

The Thai premier, Field Marshal Thanom, announced on August 11, his 59th birthday, that he was tired of politics and will not seek another term in office when his present one ends in 1972. The previous month had seen the government squeeze its controversial tax increase bill through the house of representatives. The bill increased some taxes by as much as 100 per cent. On September 3, Bangkok announced that plans had been completed for the withdrawal of some 12,000 Thai troops from South Vietnam, following reports that heavy concentrations of North Vietnamese and other Communist forces were massed in Southern Laos, poised to invade Thailand. By December the Thai government was faced with the possibility of abandoning Nan province to Communist rebels.

Tonga

Tonga, the south Pacific kingdom of 150 islands and 80,000 people that had been a British protected state for 70 years, became independent on June 4, 1970, as a sovereign member of the Commonwealth. A ceremony held in Nukualofa, the capital, was attended by Prince William of Gloucester, representing the Queen, and Keith Holyoake, the New Zealand premier. King Taufa'ahau Tupou IV had requested independence during 1969.

North Vietnam

General Giap, the North Vietnamese military commander, was given considerable logistical problems by the overthrow of the Sihanouk regime in Cambodia during the spring of 1970. The combined South Vietnamese and U.S. offensive along the Cambodian border flushed out the sanctuaries that had played a vital role in Giap's strategy by allowing the Communists to amass arms and men before attacking wherever they wished over the border. Attempts to infiltrate back into areas near the border were repulsed by frequent South Vietnamese offensives.

The single remaining logistic channel to the South in the latter part of 1970 was the Ho Chi Minh trail through Laos, which the Americans were bombing to the tune of 3,500 tons of bombs a day. On December 10, Mme. Nguyen Thi Binh, the North Vietnamese chief negotiator in the Paris peace talks (which continued fruit-

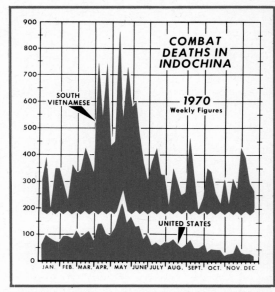

This graph of the numbers of combatants killed during 1970 in the war against Communism in Indo-China shows how the South Vietnamese bore the brunt of allied casualties, and thereby bears witness to the withdrawal of U.S. troops.

lessly throughout the year), announced that Hanoi would consider releasing American prisoners of war if Washington agreed to pull its troops out of Vietnam by June 1971. Hanoi released, at the same time, a list of American prisoners held in North Vietnam. Early in December the U.S. bombed north of the demilitarized zone and, for the first time for 3 years, in the Red River valley north of the 19th parallel, and simultaneously launched an airborne commando raid in a fruitless attempt to rescue American prisoners of war from Son Tay camp near Hanoi. The camp was found empty.

Despite reports that the North Vietnamese were exhausted, over-extended, and demoralized, at the end of 1970 all the signs were that Hanoi was preparing for a big winter and spring offensive in Indo-China.

South Vietnam

President Nixon's "Vietnamization" plan—to withdraw American troops gradually from South Vietnam at the rate of 15,000 a month, while building up the South Vietnamese armed forces—continued during 1970. By May 1, 1971, American troop strength should have dropped to 284,000, and by the end of 1971 the Vietnamese are scheduled to shoulder half the air war. (On January 28, 1970, it was announced that the U.S.A. planned to double the South Vietnamese air force.) As the year ended, Washington announced that no American ground troops were expected to be fighting in Vietnam by the end of 1971.

Predictions that the Communists would lie low pending the U.S. withdrawal were refuted in August when captured documents revealed "Resolution 14" from Hanoi's central office for South Vietnam, which called for "a new high tide of guerrilla warfare". Meanwhile Hanoi was reported to have 13 divisions—300,000 men—as yet uncommitted to the war and only biding a favourable time for invasion. Enemy movements indicated that a major offensive would take place in 1971. The C.I.A. (the American Central Intelligence Agency) were alleged to have estimated that by October 1970 over 30,000 enemy agents had been infiltrated into the South Vietnamese civil service, police, and army. According to a report published in the *New York* *Times* on October 19, the C.I.A. consider that the South Vietnamese government has little chance of survival in the long term because of the scale of this Communist infiltration.

9 Australia and New Zealand

Australia

The year 1970 in Australia presented a confused picture. The economy, buoyant in the early part of the year, sagged sharply in March, and then partially recovered. Queensland suffered one of its worst droughts on record, and by October more than two thirds of the State was badly affected. New South Wales and Western Australia were also stricken by drought until heavy rain in September brought relief, and some flooding. Tasmania was hit by floods. Farmers were forced into such a plight that the government, later in the year, came to their aid. Mining developments continued, but on a quieter scale than during the previous year; and manufacturing made steady growth, adding substantially to the export income.

Elections for the Senate—the Federal upper house—were held on November 21, when about 6½ million voters went to the polls to elect 32 senators. Under the Australian system each of the six States is represented by 10 senators, elected for six years, half of whom retire every 3 years. In the 1970 elections two additional vacancies were caused by death. The campaign preceding the elections was marked by a great amount of acrimony which tended not only to obscure the main political questions, but also to cause a good deal of distaste among voters, who considered the elections unnecessary in any case. Although Australia's participation in the Vietnam war, the depressed state of land industries, inflation, education, and age pensions were freely bandied about during the campaign, they did not emerge as vital issues in the final election result.

The voting showed that while the majority of electors were dissatisfied with the Liberal–Country party government they did not see in the Labor party a satisfactory alternative. Accordingly the minor parties—particularly the Democratic Labor party—polled well. The government obtained about 38 per cent of the votes; the Labor party about 43 per cent; and the Democratic Labor party about 11 per cent. As a result of the elections, in the Senate in 1971 the Liberal–Country party government will hold 26 seats, the Labor party 26, the Democratic Labor party 5, and Independents 3.

Two State elections—in Victoria and South Australia—were held on May 30, 1970. In Victoria, the Liberal party, led by Sir Henry Bolte, was returned for the sixth consecutive term. In the legislative assembly, the Liberals won 42 seats, the Labor party 22, and the Country party 8, and one went to an Independent Labor candidate. The Liberal party also gained control of the legislative council. After 15 years in office Sir Henry Bolte in his campaign emphasized the quality of life which his regime had brought to the State of Victoria, and promised to pursue his existing policies with even greater vigour. His programme, as foreshadowed at the opening of parliament following the elections, included energetic action against pollution, the preservation of natural resources, a decentralized education system, the commencement of Melbourne's underground railway, and the creation of a ministry of social welfare. The Labor party, led by Clyde Holding, fought its campaign on reform in education by the establishment of a board of education which would assess the needs of both State and private schools; measures to combat pollution; housing; consumer protection; and aid to the small farmer.

In South Australia, the Labor party, led by Don Dunstan, decisively defeated the sitting Liberal Country League government, led by Steele Hall, by 27 seats to 20. The government, which depended on the vote of the Speaker for its majority, had been defeated in the house of assembly on a bill to ratify the building of the Dartmouth dam on a Victorian tributary of the Murray instead of the Chowilla dam on the Murray in South Australia. An amendment that both dams should be built simultaneously was supported by the Labor party, and the government fell. Until the Labor party's success in the ensuing election every State in Australia had been controlled by a non-Labor government.

The Federal treasurer, Mr. L. E. Bury, brought down the 1970–71 budget in Canberra on August 18. Its most notable provision was the reduction of income tax by 10 per cent on incomes up to $10,000, and by graduated lesser amounts up to $32,000. Age, invalid, widows', service, and war pensions were increased on a moderate scale, and sickness benefits were improved. The budget provided for a dollar-for-dollar subsidy to sheltered workshops towards the salaries of staff helping the handicapped, and a training fee of $500 for each employee placed in open employment. It also allowed for a two-dollar-for-one subsidy to the capital cost of hostels for disabled people in normal employment but requiring special accommodation. An amount of $30 million was set aside for the assistance of wool-growers, all affected by lower prices and many badly hit by drought. The allocation for education was increased by 25 per cent, and the number of university scholarships increased by 1,000 to 8,500 in 1971.

The treasurer's estimate for expenditure on defence in 1970–71 was $1,137 million, an increase of a little more than 3 per cent; it included the cost of leasing 24 Phantom aircraft from the U.S.A. and provided for a growth in the armed forces of 1,400 men. The performing arts received an allowance of $3,850,000, an increase of 45 per cent on the preceding financial year's, and aboriginal advancement programmes were granted $10,400,000, with emphasis to be placed on housing, health, and education.

Increases in indirect taxes and other charges covered a wide range. Duty on petrol, diesel fuel, and aviation fuel advanced by 3 cents a gallon; sales tax went up from 25 per cent to 27½ per cent; air navigation charges were increased by 10 per cent from January 1971; excise duty of 50 cents a gallon was imposed on Australian grape wine, and customs duty on imported wine was raised by the same amount; company tax was increased by 2½ per cent; the duty on cigarettes, cigars, and manufactured tobacco went up; telephone rentals were increased; postage on letters and postcards was advanced from 5 cents to 6 cents

The Queen and Prince Philip greeted by Maoris and "Captain Cook" at Ship Cove, during New Zealand's bicentenary celebrations.

economic health is vitally dependent upon a satisfactory arrangement, possibly extending well beyond the 5-year transition period which Britain seemed ready to accept for its own industrial and agricultural adjustment. In pursuit of understanding by Europe of what it would mean to New Zealand's economy to be cut off from the British market, the government invited several influential European personalities to see for themselves, including the vice-president of the Common Market Commission, Dr. Mansholt.

In the past 4 years, New Zealand had carried out an intensive diversification programme. 1970 showed a significant growth in trade outside the usual links, and in 4 years exports of manufactures have increased five-fold to well over $NZ100 million. But this is still only about 10 per cent of the more than $1,000 million trade most of which is in meat and dairy produce. Only a very small proportion goes to some 80 countries other than Britain, although North America is becoming a good customer for meat.

Overseas reserves were higher than they had ever been; but towards the end of the year the balance of payments position showed signs of deterioration with a 12-month current account deficit for the first time in $2\frac{1}{2}$ years. In a budgetary effort to contain inflation, a 2 per cent pay-roll tax was introduced against considerable opposition. Later in the year, a "mini-budget" imposed higher taxes to reduce consumer spending, and a 2-month price freeze was imposed to precede controlled rises and parallel curbs on wage demands planned for the first half of 1971.

On the industrial front further progress was made. Steel production from the abundant ironsands began, the $80 million Comalco aluminium smelter at Bluff neared completion, and considerable interest was shown by Japanese industrialists in joint projects for development of timber and mineral resources. Prospecting for minerals and oil was stepped up sharply, and several hundred licences were taken out. Promising finds included sulphide deposits at Kerikeri, Northland, containing platinum, silver, and gold; the grade of platinum ore is said to be higher than that mined in South Africa. The Maui oilfield off the Taranaki coast was shown to be one of the 15 largest in the world. Feasibility studies confirmed that its exploitation for both gas and oil would be commercially viable. The 400-mile natural gas pipeline to the two main cities, Auckland and Wellington, from the Kapuni field was completed.

One of the biggest local issues was whether Lake Manapouri in the South Island should be further enlarged to provide more water for the hydro-electric needs of industry, notably the Bluff aluminium complex. Eventually a public inquiry decided that economic considerations outweighed the preservation of a comparatively small part of the countryside. The first private radio stations were granted licences outside the control of the Broadcasting Corporation, ending the activities of off-shore pirate stations.

With the Americans withdrawing from the war in Vietnam, New Zealand decided upon a reduction in its token force there. Superseding anti-Vietnam war demonstrations was anti-apartheid agitation directed at stopping the All Blacks Rugby team going to South Africa on its winter tour. But as South Africa accepted a mixed Maori and white team the New Zealand Rugby Union saw no reason to cancel the tour. The All Blacks failed to achieve their ambition of winning a test series in South Africa—they won only one of the four tests—but they were unbeaten in all their provincial fixtures.

Ivan Mauger won the world speedway championship for

for the basic rate, and telegrams became dearer. The budget evoked emphatic protest from certain sections of the people. The Australian Council of Trades Unions called a 3-hour national stoppage during the following week, mainly because of the small increase in age, widows', and invalid pensions, and because it considered the new taxation scale unjust. The increase in air navigation charges was sharply criticized by international airlines, who said that Australian charges were already far above the world average, and that the action of the government must result in higher fares. **Bruce W. Pratt**

New Zealand

On the swell of an expanding economy, the year began full of promise; it ended with visible strains, industrial unrest, and government corrective action—and the spectre of the Common Market loomed.

Uncertainty and apprehension about whether adequate special arrangements would be made for New Zealand produce in Britain, should Britain succeed in joining the European Economic Community, kept the Dominion's ministers on the alert at every point in the Brussels negotiations. The deputy prime minister, John Marshall, who holds the trade portfolio, twice went to Europe—first to ensure an identity of approach by the new British Conservative government, and later to put again before ministers of the Common Market countries the problems that an enlarged community including Britain would present for New Zealand.

The end of the year showed a wide gulf between the agreed British position in regard to New Zealand produce —continuing arrangements on the basis of the present large volume of imports of butter, cheese, and lamb, subject to review—and the Common Market stand for phasing out all cheese and half the trade in butter over 5 years. Because no other country can take such a volume of dairy produce as is now sent to Britain, New Zealand's future the third successive year; the famous Melbourne Cup horserace in Australia was won by the New Zealand gelding Baghdad Note; and in the Commonwealth Games in Edinburgh, New Zealand emerged with two gold medals, six silver, and six bronze. In motor racing, a field in which New Zealanders have excelled, tragedy overshadowed success with the death of Bruce McLaren. He died without knowing he had won the coveted Segrave Trophy for the best performance of 1969, when he won every race in the Can-Am challenge cup series. In the same series in 1970, the McLaren image was perpetuated by a McLaren driver, New Zealander Denis Hulme, who secured the trophy by a good margin.

The year was enlivened by a royal visit. The Queen, the Duke of Edinburgh, the Prince of Wales, and Princess Anne toured the country, in connection with the Captain Cook bicentenary celebrations, from March 12 to March 30. Other visitors included the American vice-president Spiro Agnew, and the Canadian prime minister Pierre Trudeau. Sir Keith Holyoake—knighted in June—completed 10 years as prime minister to become the country's second longest serving leader. **W. M. Elliott**

10 North America

Canada

A campaign of bombings and bank-raids that had cost six deaths and 50 woundings in recent years came to a climax in October 1970, when the French Canadian separatists' organization F.L.Q. (*Front de la Libération du Québec*) kidnapped James (Jasper) Cross, senior British trade commissioner in Montreal, and Pierre Laporte, Quebec's minister of labour. Four men arrived at Cross's Montreal home on October 5 claiming to be the bearers of a birthday present. Forcing their way past a frightened maid, they kidnapped the diplomat at gun-point and bundled him into a taxi. For his release the F.L.Q. demanded a ransom of $500,000 in gold, the release of 23 jailed terrorists, and safe passage to Cuba or Algeria. When the Canadian government refused to meet these demands, terrorists kidnapped their second victim, Laporte (a leading member of Quebec's new Liberal government). The politician—a French-Canadian who, like Canadian premier Pierre Elliot Trudeau, was a committed Federalist—was snatched from his garden on October 10. His abductors issued an abrupt ultimatum to the authorities: Laporte would be executed unless their demands were met.

Negotiations by the Quebec premier Robert Bourassa led nowhere, and Trudeau had to act. He made it clear that, although the government was willing to negotiate over the release of their captives, he would not be black-mailed into granting anything approaching the terrorists' demands. He called out thousands of troops to guard VIPs and patrol major cities, and on October 16 invoked the emergency powers of the War Measures Act that had been put into force only twice before, during the two world wars. On the same date a cabinet proclamation declared: "Insurrection, real or apprehended, exists." Trudeau and his ministers are believed to have been acting on information alleging that the F.L.Q. was planning selective assassinations of leading politicians. In the 12 months before the kidnappings over 2,000 lb. of dynamite had been stolen in Quebec province—enough to furnish fuel for terrorist threats to have a "blow up" in Montreal. The F.L.Q. was thought to have about 2,000 active members operating in 22 separate "cells".

After invoking the War Measures Act, which suspends a large part of the Canadian Bill of Rights for up to 6 months and empowers police and troops to search and arrest without warrant, Trudeau appeared on television to explain his decision to the nation. "If a democratic society is to continue to exist," he said, "it must be able to root out the cancer of an armed, revolutionary movement that is bent on destroying the very basis of our freedom."

The F.L.Q. response to Trudeau's measures was brutal and swift. On October 18, an anonymous telephone call directed the authorities to a message secreted in a dustbin. It read: "In the face of the arrogance of the federal government, we have decided to move into action." With the note was a marked map which led the police to a parked taxi in the Montreal suburb of St. Hubert. In the taxi's boot police found Laporte's corpse. He had been strangled by the thin gold chain of a crucifix that he wore round his neck. The fate of James Cross remained a mystery. But the government was still prepared to negotiate for his release, and the Concordia Bridge, spanning two islands in the St. Lawrence river in Montreal, was temporarily declared Cuban territory where the abductors could claim sanctuary before being flown to Havana.

Meanwhile, under the emergency measures, police and troops swooped on suspected members of the outlawed F.L.Q. Over 300 were arrested, including the radical Montreal lawyer, Robert Lemieux, who had been acting as

A soldier on guard outside the Canadian parliament, Ottawa, during the October crisis inspired by F.L.Q. terrorists.

the organization's unofficial spokesman. After Laporte's murder, activities were intensified and some 10,000 police made over 2,000 raids but uncovered no clue to Cross's whereabouts or the identity of the murderers. The search continued through November until "information received" led the authorities to a house in Rosemont, Montreal, which was surrounded by police and troops early on December 3. Cross emerged from the house after 15 hours' negotiations, during which armed police and 1,000 troops with fixed bayonets patrolled the area. A cavalcade of police cars and motor-cycles escorted the diplomat and two terrorists—identified as Jacques Lanctot and Marc Carbonneau, both of whom were being sought by the authorities in connection with the kidnapping—to an "exchange" spot on St. Helen's Island in the St. Lawrence, site of Expo 67. There they were met by officials from the Cuban embassy in Ottawa who had come to Montreal at the request of the government. Cuba had worked closely with the Canadians in the affair and had agreed to give asylum to the kidnappers and various of their relatives. These were taken by helicopter and Canadian military aircraft to Havana. Cross remained on the island until word came that the terrorists had landed in Cuba, and was then released and flown to England.

The main political implication of the affair—apart from the harassing of the F.L.Q. by police and the distinct lack of sympathy the extremists generated for their cause—was that Pierre Trudeau emerged from it, despite Laporte's death, with his reputation enhanced and his popularity strengthened. The flagging Trudeau image of the "swinging" bachelor of liberal persuasion was refurbished by his surprising display of toughness. Trudeau's style during the crisis is best illustrated by his reply to those Canadians who opposed his assumption of emergency powers: "There are a lot of bleeding hearts around who just don't like to see people with helmets and guns. All I can say is go and bleed!"

United States of America

Within the U.S.A. the year was dominated by the mid-term Congressional elections of November 3. At stake were 35 senate seats (one third of the chamber), the 435 seats in the house of representatives, and 33 of the 50 State governorships. Since his inauguration on January 20, 1969, Richard Nixon and his Republican government had faced Democratic majorities in both houses of Congress—a frustrating fact that had wrought much vexation in the White House. Twice the President's supreme court nominees had been rejected by the senate, which had also waxed obdurate over the president's anti-ballistic missile system, been enraged by the invasion of Cambodia, and demanded a firm withdrawal date for American troops in Indo-China. The Republicans, however, controlled 32 of the 50 State governorships, including nine of the ten most populous states. The governorships are of considerable significance to the parties during presidential campaigns as they carry immense patronage and fund-raising potential. Moreover, they assumed particular importance during the 1970 elections, as congressional district lines are to be redrawn by 1972 and each State governor will have a voice in where the pencil goes, thus influencing national politics for many years ahead.

Thus during 1970 the president devoted much time and acumen—and the vice-president almost all his reserves of both—to an election strategy that they hoped would ensure an infusion of Republicans into Congress and pave the way to victory in the presidential campaign of 1972.

The Republican assault was concentrated on the senate, where Nixon aimed to win control of the vital committees that steer legislation. He was encouraged by the fact that 25 Democratic seats in the senate were to be disputed, some of which were warmed by "Goldwater babies"—Democratic senators from traditionally Republican areas who owed their election to President Johnson's landslide victory over Goldwater in 1964. The Republicans had to increase their membership of the senate by seven to enjoy parity (and also control, since the vice-president wields a casting vote in the senate). They required an extra 29 seats to capture control of the lower house. But this was an almost impossible target: not only is the Republican a minority party—the Democrats being traditionally associated with labour—but historically the party represented in the White House rarely prospers in mid-term polls.

While Nixon's election strategy was to capture the senate, his ideological tactics were advanced on a broad front. They consisted of exploiting what he diagnosed as a conservative shift within the nation, caused by reaction to student unrest, rising crime, permissiveness, and the bomb-and-bullet outrages by the new revolutionaries. The administration sought to identify itself with the aspirations and misgivings of the middle-of-the-road, non-demonstrating, short-haired, patriotic "silent majority". This ideological appeal across party lines implied that the Democrats were somehow aligned with the forces of anarchy and sedition. Whether the electorate would swallow this somewhat glib association was questionable. Nevertheless the Democrats were impressed enough by Republican law-and-order invective to take up the chorus themselves. It is no coincidence that two draconian anti-crime bills sailed through the senate with hardly a murmur from leading liberal Democrats shortly before the elections.

Vice-President Spiro Agnew proved the ideological and rhetorical spearhead of the Republican campaign as he stumped the country constantly reiterating the theme he himself defined early in the campaign: "One issue dominates this election: will the radical-liberalism that controls the senate of the United States prevail in the nation? Or will America be led into the future by the moderates, centrists, and conservatives who stand behind the president of the United States?"

The importance Nixon attached to the elections was illustrated by the energy with which he entered the partisan fray himself, thus throwing his personal prestige into the battle and elevating it into both the hardest-fought mid-term election in memory and a vote of confidence in his administration. He declared that the elections were "probably the most important and decisive in the 190-year history of this country". In the month before polling Nixon visited some 23 States and plugged away relentlessly at the law-and-order issue, blaming Congress, particularly the senate, for throwing out tough legislation and blocking the appointment of strong judges. It was time, he declared, for "the great silent majority" to stand up and be counted. An unvarying accompaniment to Nixon's theme were the jeers and catcalls of demonstrators which served the president with an anarchic foil. These came to a climax at San Jose, California, on October 29, when the president's car was surrounded by some 900 anti-war demonstrators, and pelted with eggs and stones.

The Nixon-Agnew line was backed by an expensive Republican publicity campaign; the party is said to have spent over £10 million on advertising alone. In contrast, the Democrats laboured leaderless and in financial straits. They campaigned mainly on the economic record of the government, arguing that inflation and unemployment were rampant and recession round the corner. They also maintained that the Nixon-Agnew law-and-order duet polarized opinion, divided rather than reconciled the people, and therefore encouraged rather than discouraged violence and anarchy. No Democrat said this more eloquently than Senator Edmund Muskie of Maine, who was selected by his party to give an eve-of-poll nation-wide television broadcast. Speaking from an armchair the man from Maine declared: "There are those who seek to turn our common distress to partisan advantages, not by offering better solutions but with empty threat and malicious slander."

In the event, the elections ended in a draw, with the run of the play favouring the Democrats. The results can be tabulated thus:

Senate		Reps.	Dems.	Others
New Senate	.....	44	54	2
Old Senate	.....	43	57	0

Republicans won 4 Democratic seats;
Democrats won 2 Republican seats

House		Reps.	Dems.
New House	.....	181	254
Old House	.....	189	246

Republicans won 9 Democratic seats;
Democrats won 17 Republican seats.
Net change: Democrats gain 8.

Governors		Reps.	Dems.
New	.....	21	29
Old	.....	32	18

The Democrats lost some of their lead in the senate (where they still retained a majority and continue to control steering committees), but increased their seats in the house of representatives and captured many important State governorships. Nixon could claim the negative success of keeping losses below what a president's party usually loses in a mid-term election. He also claimed to have won an ideological "working majority" in the senate, from which four of his strongest critics were ousted.

In Massachusetts Edward Kennedy was re-elected to a second term in the Senate with 63 per cent of the vote, thus emerging triumphantly from the clouds that had swathed his political persona since the Mary Jo Kopechne episode in 1969. His success put him once again in the running, together with Muskie and Humphrey, for the Democratic nomination for president in 1972.

The Vietnam war continued to be America's prime external problem. At first, Nixon appeared to have neutralized it as a domestic issue with the planned withdrawal that he announced in 1969 and subsequent troop reductions. The war, however, leapt once again into the forefront of the nation's consciousness on April 30 when Nixon announced that American and South Vietnamese forces had launched an offensive against North Vietnamese troops and depots in Cambodia. The president explained that the introduction of military activity into Cambodia did not constitute a "new Vietnam" but was to hasten the "Vietnamization programme" and the disengagement of American troops by destroying enemy supply routes. Nevertheless, the invasion was greeted by protests and demonstrations throughout America. Staunch opposition came from the senate, which questioned the president's

In May, Manhattan "hardhats"—construction workers—counter-demonstrated in support of America's war effort in Indo-China.

power under the constitution to wage war in Indo-China without a formal declaration of war.

Student anti-war demonstrations burst out afresh. It was during one of these, at Kent State University, Ohio, that nervous National Guardsmen replied to a volley of stones and abuse by opening fire on demonstrators. Four students were killed. The incident stunned America and shook the government. It inspired waves of demonstrations and counter-demonstrations—notably one organized in Manhattan by "pro-war" "hardhats" (helmeted construction workers) who attacked student demonstrators in Wall Street.

Together with the war, the "peace" talks in Paris continued throughout 1970. In July it was announced that David Bruce, former U.S. ambassador in London, was to be the new leader of the American delegation. He arrived in Paris to take up his duties on August 3. On October 4, during Nixon's brief sojourn in Ireland, Bruce was summoned to receive new instructions to get the deadlocked discussions going, and 3 days later the president spelt out his new proposals in a television address to the nation. They were briefly as follows: (1) a standstill cease-fire throughout Indo-China; (2) an international conference on Vietnam, Laos, and Cambodia on the lines of the Geneva conferences on Indo-China; (3) negotiations on a time-table for withdrawal of all U.S. forces; (4) a political settlement allowing all South Vietnamese to "determine for themselves the kind of government they want"; (5) talks on prisoner-of-war exchange. But this initiative was promptly dismissed as propaganda by the North Vietnamese.

Agnew and Nixon both set out on extensive foreign tours during the year in order to try to reassure allies that "lowering America's profile"—a constant Nixon theme that was echoed once again in a foreign-policy statement on February 18, 1970—would not mean they were to be thrown to the wolves. In August, Agnew travelled 30,000 miles, visiting South Korea, Formosa, Thailand, and South Vietnam. From September 27 to October 5, Nixon visited Italy (to show the flag in the Mediterranean, consult Nato allies, and emphasize America's commitment to regional defence of the alliance's southern flank), Yugoslavia, Spain, the U.K., and the Republic of Ireland.

Nixon's budget, presented in January 1970, slashed deep into federal expenditure. Defence cuts alone will reduce service manpower from some 3½ million to 1,700,000 by mid-1971. Anti-inflationary measures so swelled the unemployment figures that during the last weeks of 1970 the president and his economic lieutenants, busy on the budget to be presented during January 1971, were racking their brains for measures to enliven the economy. Unemployment was then running at 5·6 per cent, considerably above the 3·4 per cent level which is regarded as full employment in America, allowing for job turnover.

See also under Austria, Cambodia, Republic of Ireland, and South Vietnam.

11 Latin America and the Caribbean

Argentina

The discord that had rumbled through the upper echelons of the Argentine armed forces since the military coup of 1966 came to a head in 1970. The 1966 coup—which ousted the civilian president, Dr. Arturo Illia—gave power first to a provisional junta and then to one man: General Juan Carlos Ongania, who became president on June 29, 1966. Two factors strained the loyalty of senior officers: first, Ongania's aloof obsession with economics (which had brought fiscal stability) and the pervading feeling that the nation had a slide-rule government at a time when it was seething with social unrest; and secondly, the president's refusal to discuss the possibility of elections. Matters were brought to a head with the kidnapping of the former provisional president, Pedro Aramburu, allegedly by left-wing extremists. Voices were raised accusing the government of complicity in the crime—allegations that were echoed in the influential Buenos Aires daily *La Razon*. Aramburu's body was found on July 17 following the arrest of four people in connection with the kidnapping on July 10. A pro-Peronist group claimed responsibility for the "execution".

On June 8 the commander-in-chief of the army, General Alejandro Lanusse, issued a statement demanding more power for the armed services, and declaring that the military were no longer prepared to give President Ongania "a blank cheque" of authority. This was, in effect, the start of another military coup. Ongania held out for 8 hours before relinquishing his power to the commanders of the army and air force, and 10 days later, on June 18, Brig.-Gen. Roberto Marcelo Levingston was sworn in as president of Argentina. The 50-year-old Levingston, former military attaché in Washington, immediately broadcast a promise to observe the constitution and the charter of the Argentine revolution. (This charter is a supra-constitutional document adopted after the 1966 coup, which contains the guidelines for revolutionary reform and empowers the military chiefs to appoint and remove presidents.) The new president's cabinet reflected a "liberal" flavour in social and constitutional matters, but the choice of Carlos Moyano Llerena as minister of economy and labour suggested that the new regime would continue with Ongania's economic policies. On June 20, Levingston published a 160-point document promising to establish "an efficient and stable democracy" under a representative republican and federal government, and assuring individual freedom and fundamental rights. No mention was made, however, of future elections, despite the fact that Ongania had been ousted for failing to set a time limit on military rule.

On October 1 another presidential speech declared that parliamentary democracy was still 4 or 5 years away, and that the ban on political parties was irreversible. The government, Levingston declared, was working on schemes for the formation of new political groups. This speech lent support to the opinion that the government wants two large political groups to emerge: liberal conservatives on the one hand and nationalist Peronists and Populists on the other.

Bolivia

The leftward-leaning military-backed regime headed by General Alfredo Ovando Candia, which had taken power in September 1969, veered to the right under pressure from conservative elements within the military, and fell during October 1970. The Ovando regime had nationalized American oil interests on taking power, under the political aegis of the dynamic oil minister, Quiroga Santa Cruz—who was thus identified with the administration's left-wing pretensions. His sacking in mid-1970, thanks to right-wing pressures within the army, led to violent riots, renewed guerrilla activity, and a split both in the government and in the armed services, which widened into a chasm on October 3 when 123 right-wing rebel officers in La Paz—led by the c.-in-c. of the army, General Rogelio Miranda—launched a short-lived bloodless coup. The rebels, after setting up a three-man junta, held truce talks with Ovando arranged in secret by the papal nuncio. These led to the despatch of the president hot-foot for the Argentine embassy in La Paz where he sought, relinquishing the cares of office, and was granted, asylum. The junta and its supporters ensconced in Miraflores barracks, La Paz, were then strafed by the Bolivian air force in the shape of three World War II Mustang-type fighters as a prelude to a more down-to-earth exchange of bullets. From this a left-winger, General Juan Jose Torres, emerged on October 7 to proclaim himself the new "revolutionary president" of Bolivia. Torres, an Indian, had been dismissed from the post of army chief of staff by ex-President Ovando in July 1970.

On July 19 two West German mining engineers were kidnapped by Bolivian guerrillas. They were released after the government had agreed to free 10 political prisoners. Regis Debray, the French Marxist who was sentenced to 30 years' jail for his part in Che Guevara's guerrilla campaign in 1967, was released by the new regime on December 23, 1970.

Brazil

A virulent "anti-communist" campaign waged by President Emilio Garrastazu Medici's military-backed government in response to left-wing terrorism led to allegations of police torture in Brazil during 1970. Several guerrilla organizations operate in Brazil's main cities, raiding banks, planting bombs, and, of course, kidnapping foreign diplomats. These various organizations received the attentions of "Operation Bandeiranles" run by an operational centre for internal defence in Rio under General Sarmento. On August 3 it was announced in Geneva that the Brazilian government had banned the international commission of jurists from sending a team of investigators to Brazil to inquire into widespread allegations that political prisoners were being tortured by police. The Pope condemned police torture in Brazil on October 21.

The military-backed government continued to wrestle successfully with the economy. Figures released in April 1970 showed a healthy balance-of-payments surplus for 1969 and an inflation rate of a mere 20 per cent—virtually static by Brazilian standards—compared with the alleged 140 per cent pre-1964-revolution norm. The president's pledge to raise the living standards of Brazil's underfed masses was given a practical impetus during 1970 with legislation which set up a programme for "social integration". This programme—which was published in time for the Independence Day celebrations on September 7—is based on a participation fund financed by all private employers and state-owned companies in the form of turnover tax and a percentage of each firm's income tax. The fund is expected to reach £500 million by 1974. Every employee in Brazil, apart from civil servants, is to be issued with a savings book which will record a "capital nest-egg" accruing in proportion to his salary and years of service. Interest can be withdrawn each year, but recipients can touch the capital only on marriage, retirement, serious illness, or to buy a house. The savings go to the family on death. Elections were held for Brazil's carefully controlled congress on November 15 as a first step towards "a return to democratic normality". They led, not unexpectedly, to a crushing victory for the pro-government National Renewal Alliance.

On March 11, 1970, the Japanese consul-general in São Paulo was kidnapped by guerrillas. He was later released after the government agreed to free five political prisoners, who were flown to Mexico. On March 29 and April 5 unsuccessful kidnapping attempts on Russian and American diplomats respectively took place. On December 10 the Swiss ambassador Giovanni Bucher was kidnapped and one of his security guards killed. A massive hunt for Bucher and his captors was launched, involving 2,500 police and six tanks, but he was still held by guerrillas—who were negotiating with the government—as 1970 ended.

Chile

The presidential election of September 4, 1970, resulted in a victory for the candidate of the "Marxist left", Dr. Salvador Allende Gossens. Three aspirants to the presidency contested the election—Dr. Allende, Senor Alessandri (the son of a president and an ex-president himself) who claimed no party but had liberal and conservative backing, and Senor Tomic, former ambassador to the U.S.A. and the champion of the Christian Democrats. The results of the election were as follows:

Allende	1,075,616 votes	(36·3 per cent)
Alessandri	1,036,278	(34·9 per cent)
Tomic	824,849	(27·8 per cent)

Six people were killed and some 200 wounded during the election campaign in clashes inspired by the Revolutionary Movement of the Left.

Under the Chilean constitution a successful presidential candidate must receive an absolute majority in the general election, and if no candidate has such a majority an extraordinary joint session of congress (both houses) meets to decide between the leading contestants. Out of a total of 200 deputies a mere 81 could have been expected to support Dr. Allende and the "Marxist left", which comprised a coalition of left-wing parties including the Action Movement for Popular Unity, Independent Popular Action, the Communists, Allende's own Socialist party, and the Radical party. Senor Alessandri announced that he would accept the support of congress to assume the presidency in order to block Allende, and then, as soon as he was elected, he would resign, thus causing a new presidential election. Meanwhile Allende had publicly declared his willingness to maintain democracy and freedom of speech, and guaranteed that executive, legislative, and judicial institutions would retain their independence and that education would continue non-ideological. These assurances led the Christian Democrats to support Allende at the congress vote of October 24, and also to an announcement from Alessandri that he was withdrawing his candidacy. In the event Allende obtained 153 votes and Alessandri 35 in spite of his withdrawal.

Following Chile's September presidential election, Salvador Allende became the first freely elected Marxist head of state in Latin America.

General Rene Schneider, c.-in-c. of the armed forces, was shot and fatally wounded on October 22 in Santiago following his repeated announcements that the army would not intervene in the political crisis whoever was elected president. His three alleged assassins were later arrested, together with others supposedly involved in the plot. They were revealed as right-wing extremists.

Dr. Allende was sworn in as president on November 3, and formed the first Marxist government on the Latin American mainland.

Colombia

The presidential election of April 19 was remarkable for the candidacy of ex-General Gustavo Rojas Pinilla, the dictator who ruled the country from 1953 to 1957 and was still, at 70, a charismatic demagogue. Since his overthrow in May 1957 a National Front of Liberals and Conservatives had run the country, putting up coalition presidential candidates every 4 years. A split in their ranks, however, led Rojas to enter the presidential lists, posing as the saviour of the nation and the "enemy of the oligarchy", and promising far-reaching economic reforms and grandiose schemes for irrigation from snow. When the election results came out it first appeared that he had won, with a majority of 21,000 over the coalition candidate Misael Pastrana. Later it was announced that Pastrana had won by some 50,000 votes—mainly from expatriates in the U.S.A. Rojas accused the government of fraud and threatened to call a general strike and a guerrilla war. Riots ensued, and President Lleras declared a state of emergency under which Rojas was put under house arrest. A commission, set up to recount the votes, confirmed the result.

Costa Rica

On February 1, 1970, elections took place for a new president in Costa Rica. Jose Figueres Ferrer, of the National Liberation party, won the contest with 294,266 votes to the 221,152 cast for Mario Echandi Jimenez of the National Unification party.

Dominican Republic

Dr. Joaquin Balaguer, of the Reformist party, was re-elected president of the Dominican Republic on May 16. Some 45 people were killed in violent clashes during the campaign, which was not contested by the Dominican Revolutionary party led by former president Juan Bosch.

Ecuador

President Jose Velasco Ibarra assumed dictatorial powers on June 22, 1970, with army approval, after proposed fiscal reforms had been rejected by congress and the supreme court. Leftist leaders were rounded up and

Ecuadorian President
Jose Velasco Ibarra
assumed dictatorial powers
during June.

paratroopers occupied the universities. The 77-year-old president announced that he will step down in 1972 when his constitutional term expires. General Cesar Rohn Sandoval, Ecuador's air force commander, was briefly kidnapped in October, but soon released.

El Salvador

The ruling National Conciliation party won a resounding victory in the general election of March 8, 1970, increasing its number of seats in the legislative assembly from 27 to 36, while the opposition Christian Democrats' parliamentary party was reduced from 19 to 15. Of 1½ million voters only 42 per cent went to the polls. Allegations of fraud and sharp practice were tossed about by both parties. Occasional skirmishings over the border with Honduras continued during 1970, following the famous "football war" of 1969.

Guatemala

A presidential election took place in Guatemala on March 1 after a campaign marked by many acts of terrorism from extreme left- and right-wing groups. Three candidates stood in the election. Colonel Carlos Arana Osorio represented the extreme right-wing National Liberation Movement; a former commander (1966–67) of the Zacapa Brigade which successfully crushed left-wing guerrilla groups operating in the Sierra de las Minas and Zacapa province, he campaigned on an anti-communist law-and-order ticket and was regarded as the hot favourite. Mario Fuentes Pierruccini, finance minister, was the candidate put up by the centre Revolutionary party, which held a

majority in the newly elected congress. Gorge Caballeros, professor of economics at the university of Guatemala, was the hope of the Christian Democrats. None of the candidates received the necessary overall majority, the votes being cast as follows: Osorio 234,625, Pierruccini 194,798, Caballeros 116,865. Under the constitution, congress had the task of choosing the new president; it voted on March 21 for Colonel Osorio, who received 37 votes against 17 for Pierruccini. The new president took office on July 1, 1970.

Illegal Communist and revolutionary groups had been barred from putting up candidates—hence much of the pre-election violence, which included the kidnapping by urban guerrillas of the foreign minister Alberto Fuentes Mohr on February 27. He was held captive for 30 hours, and released in exchange for the release of a student arrested some days earlier in connection with an attempted assassination.

A spate of political murders and kidnappings marked the first months of 1970. During January, Isidoro Zario, a newspaperman, and Colonel Oscar Giron Perrone, a right-wing officer, were killed. On March 11, Jose Bernabe Linares, former chief of the secret police, was gunned down in the street. On March 6, Sean M. Holly, a secretary in the American embassy, was kidnapped in Guatemala City; he was released unharmed on March 8 in exchange for four jailed *guerrilleros*. On March 31, the West German ambassador, Count Karl-Maria von Spreti, was kidnapped in Guatemala City by guerrillas who demanded the release of 17 left-wing political prisoners. The demand was refused, as was their later demand for the liberation of 24 political prisoners and $700,000 ransom. On April 5 the ambassador's dead body was found in a hut 10 miles north of Guatemala City. He had been shot through the head.

On November 14 a mystery "invasion armada" was sighted, attacked, and presumably sent packing, off the Guatemalan coast. Air Force planes strafed at least 15 flagless boats after they had refused to identify themselves. Some were less than a mile from the Pacific coast with the "evident intention of disembarking". A state of emergency was declared.

Guyana

Guyana became a "co-operative republic" within the Commonwealth at midnight on February 22, 1970, amid nation-wide rejoicing. The date commemorates an 18th-century slave revolt. Forbes Burnham, the prime minister, said that the change to republican status was not merely an emotional break with the British monarchy "under whose seal the charters to the owners of slave ships were issued", but also marked symbolically "Guyana's determination to depend on Guyana for Guyana's progress in the world". A marble statue of Queen Victoria was removed from the law courts in Georgetown to the Promenade Gardens as a further symbolic gesture. Guyana's first president, Arthur Chung, was sworn in on March 23, 1970.

The long-standing Venezuelan claim to about five-eighths of Guyana continued to irk the government during 1970. A number of frontier incursions by Venezuelan troops in February involved machine-gun and mortar fire. But on June 18 Forbes Burnham announced that a protocol signed between Guyana and Venezuela in Trinidad had agreed (1) that Venezuela would not assert any claim to the Essequibo region (57,000 square miles); and (2) Guyana would not claim any Venezuelan territory

On her visit to Canberra, the Queen was present at the official opening of the 450-ft water jet in Lake Burley Griffin (left), which is the Australian government's memorial to the Cook bicentenary; and accepted the British government's gift of a carillon (right) to commemorate the 50th anniversary of Canberra's foundation in 1913.

was mounting excitement as the climax day— April 29—drew near. People came from hundreds of miles away to see the visiting ships, the floodlit buildings, the decorations, and the pageantry. The day itself dawned fine and sunny, much as it did for Cook and his party, and from early morning the road to Kurnell— the site of Cook's landing and of its re-enactment—was crowded with officials, pressmen, photographers, technicians, participants, and visitors. Because of the difficulty of access to Kurnell, the re-enactment was primarily a television show, seen by many hundreds of thousands of viewers. They saw "Captain Cook" and his party (in the presence of the Queen, the Duke of Edinburgh, and Princess Anne) leave the *Endeavour* and make for the shore in a longboat and a pinnace, the surprise and ineffective resistance of the aborigines, the stepping ashore of Isaac Smith—reputedly the first white man to land on the east coast of Australia—followed by James Cook, Joseph Banks (carried ashore), Daniel Solander, and others, and finally the planting of the flag by the leader of the expedition.

The Botany Bay ceremonies completed, there was a general rush from Kurnell and from television sets for good positions around Port Jackson from which to view the harbour carnival promised for the same evening. Long before nightfall the heights of Vaucluse, Rose Bay, Mosman, Cremorne, and other harbourside suburbs, the tall buildings of King's Cross, Elizabeth Bay, and the city itself, and the harbour bridge were packed with expectant sightseers. By the time the carnival started, the streets were so crowded that it was almost impossible to move. It was a night of gaiety,

excitement, milling crowds, floodlit craft of all kinds, with soaring fireworks lighting up the whole scene—a dramatic finale to the most important day of the celebrations.

Other Celebrations

While Sydney, with its spectacular activities, was attracting most of the attention, country centres, too, were remembering Cook. Re-enactments of his landing took place in many places, distance from the coast and absence of ocean being no deterrents. For instance, the people of the Leeton district, nearly 300 miles from the sea, used the waters of the Murrumbidgee river for Botany Bay, and its banks for the planting of the flag. Other country centres situated on rivers held similar ceremonies. The historic village of Wollombi remembered Cook in a different way. Instead of a portrayal of his first landing, a pageant of pioneers was held. The celebrations included a service at the beautiful local church, at which the names of the men who sailed with Cook in the *Endeavour* were read out—an unusual tribute to those 18th-century seamen who, no doubt, thought their names would soon be forgotten. Later in the same day, trees were planted by children in memory of the men who died on the voyage.

Of the 11 landings on Australian soil made by Cook, 10 were on what is now Queensland, and that State held many functions to commemorate his progress along its coast. At Round Hill Head—the site of his first Queensland landing—at Rockhampton, Whitsunday island, Townsville, Cairns, and Cooktown appropriate activities took place. Finally, on August 22, at lonely Possession Island off the northernmost point of Queensland, where on

At Cooktown, North Queensland, the Queen was greeted in characteristic fashion by aboriginal adults and children. The ferocious leap (above) by a Murray Island tribal chief was part of the war dance of the Torres Strait islanders with which she was entertained. More peaceful was the welcome provided by flag-waving schoolboys (below) on the same occasion.

the same date in 1770 Cook proclaimed possession of the whole of the eastern coast of the continent in the name of George III, the last ceremony directly linked with his Australian voyage was held.

Visits by Sovereign and Pope

The visit of the Queen, the Duke of Edinburgh, the Prince of Wales, and Princess Anne was an outstanding success, and their presence added lustre and distinction to the celebrations. They arrived in Sydney by air from New Zealand on March 30 and—with the exception of Prince Charles who returned to England earlier—they left on May 3. During their tour they visited New South Wales, Tasmania, Victoria, Queensland, and Canberra, travelling partly by air and partly in the royal yacht *Britannia*. In a series of celebrations, inspections, receptions, entertainments, football matches, lunches, dinners, and meetings, they

came into contact with Australians in many walks of life. Wherever they went, they were greeted with warmth and affection, and their visit did much to strengthen the position of the monarchy in Australia.

The announcement that Pope Paul would visit Sydney in the bicentenary year was greeted with enthusiasm by the majority of Australians. That all religious denominations were overlooking their differences in the celebrations was shown by an Inter-faith Service held in Temple Emmanuel, Sydney, in April at which members of the Roman Catholic, Anglican, and other major Protestant Churches as well as Jews joined in thanksgiving.

His Holiness arrived at Sydney by air on November 30 and was greeted by the Governor-General, Sir Paul Hasluck, the Prime Minister, Mr. Gorton, and other leading citizens. During his four days' stay in Sydney he visited many Roman Catholic institutions. A vast crowd gathered at Randwick racecourse on the evening of December 1 for the celebration of the bicentenary commemorative Mass in his presence, and a large number of young people were present at the same place for a similar ceremony on December 2. In the evening of the same day His Holiness attended an ecumenical service in Sydney's Town Hall, organized jointly by the Roman Catholic Church and the Australian Council of Churches. The service was shadowed to some extent by the refusal of the Anglican Archbishop of Sydney and certain other churchmen to take part, but their absence did little to mar the spirit of unity that prevailed.

No summary of the bicentenary celebrations would be complete without some mention of the people for whom Cook's arrival ultimately brought loss of their land and near-extinction of their race. For the most part, the aborigines treated the anniversary of his Botany Bay landing as a day of mourning, and while its re-enactment was taking place, representatives of various tribes, on the other side of the Bay, cast wreaths on the water as a plea for justice, for land rights, and for equality for the aboriginal people.

In her speech on that day, the Queen included the following words: "I believe we need to remind ourselves from time to time that we are also architects of the future and that we carry today a great responsibility for the generations who will be living here two hundred years from now." If these words are truly heeded by all Australians, perhaps at the next national commemoration of the great Yorkshire seaman all bitterness caused by the coming of the Europeans will have been forgotten.

Alphabetical Guide to 1970

NAMES IN THE NEWS

FACT DIGEST

INDEX

Names in the News 1970

Alexi, Patriarch (1877–1970). This venerable churchman, who died on April 17, 1970, was not only Patriarch of Moscow and All the Russias—to give him his full title—but was also a remarkable link with the past. Born Sergei Vladimirovich Simansky 93 years ago, he was consecrated a bishop four years before the Russian revolution of 1917. Thus his own life as a bishop spanned the great gulf between the Czarist regime and the Bolshevik revolution, and covered the reigns of Lenin, Stalin, and their successors. Himself of aristocratic lineage, he lived to accommodate himself to religious leadership within an avowedly atheistic state based on the rule of the proletariat. In his first diocese, Novgorod, he had to face the full blast of Communist anti-religious zeal, and suffered exile for his stand for the Church. Later, with most of the Church, he achieved an accommodation on the basis of declaring a desire to be a faithful member of the Orthodox Church but also a loyal citizen of Russia. He became Metropolitan of Leningrad, living in a simplicity which was in marked contrast both with his predecessors and with the style of his own family in the past. It was during the siege of the city in the Second World War that he won the admiration and affection of his fellow-citizens, and the recognition of the government, by refusing the offer of being escorted from the city. Certainly the degree to which the Orthodox Church sustained the spirit of the beleaguered city and Russia as a whole led to a "new deal" from Stalin under which it became possible for the Patriarchate of Moscow to be reinstated.

Eight months after this happened the Patriarch (Sergei) died and Alexi succeeded in 1945. Although already 67, he was to preside over the Church for a quarter of a century. Controversy is bound to attend consideration of his rule. It saw great growth in the life of the Church, and its openness to the world (symbolized by the aged Patriarch's journeys to the Second Vatican Council and in 1964 to Lambeth, calling at Athens and Geneva *en route*). But it also saw almost complete accommodation to Soviet ideas, and the willingness of the Patriarch to be the advocate of the peace policies of the U.S.S.R.

Anders, Wladyslaw (1892–1970). General Wladyslaw Anders, the Polish patriot and soldier whose name is synonymous with his country's heroic but tragic struggle against the brutal embrace of Russian and German arms, died in exile in London on May 12, 1970. It was General Anders who led 100,000 Polish ex-prisoners out of Russian bondage, through Persia, to join the British in the Middle East and fight alongside them through Italy to the storming of Monte Cassino in May 1944. It was in that monastery—now rebuilt and tranquil—that the general was buried with military honours.

Anders was born in 1892 and educated at the university of Riga—then part of Imperial Russia—and at a Russian military staff college. From 1914 to 1917 he was chief staff officer of a division of the Russian Imperial army before joining the First Polish Corps. During the Russo-Polish war of 1919–20, he commanded the 15th Polish Lancers. The German invasion of Poland in September 1939 found him commanding the Independent Cavalry Brigade—soon fighting both the Nazis and the Red Army which invaded from the east. Wounded in battle and captured by the Russians, Anders joined tens of thousands of his countrymen as prisoners in Russia until Hitler's sudden attack on his Russian ally led to the Polish-Soviet agreement of July 1941, and his release. Anders became commander of a Polish army comprised of P.O.W.s and Poles deported into Russian labour camps. Despite their debilitated condition and the vast march they undertook—hundreds died on the way—he led this ragged, 100,000 strong crusade into Persia, where an army of 75,000 was organized.

It was in harness with the British Eighth Army in Italy that the Polish II Corps, under Anders, won immortal fame at the battle of Monte Cassino. A week after the first infantry assault upon the monastery, after bloody carnage, the Poles stormed the battlements and hoisted the Union Jack and the Polish flag above the ruins. After Cassino, Anders's men turned to the Adriatic coast, completing their campaign with the capture of Bologna. With the end of the war and Poland firmly in the hands of her Russian "liberators", he settled in London where, hounded by vindictive Communists, he looked after the interests of the 100,000 Polish ex-soldiers in Britain and wrote *An Army In Exile*.

Aylward, Gladys (1902–1970). This remarkable little Englishwoman, unswervingly dedicated to her work in China as a missionary and protector of orphaned children for 40 years, died of pneumonia in Tai Pei, Taiwan (Formosa), at the beginning of January 1970. Born in Edmonton, North London, the daughter of a postman, she became a parlourmaid when she left school at the age of 14. Always religious, she became more and more interested in missionary work, and in her early twenties, determined to go to China, took a course at the China Inland Mission. To her intense disappointment the Mission refused to send her, partly because her lack of education convinced the principal that she would be unable to learn Chinese. Miss Aylward did not allow this to deter her and, after more domestic service, on October 18, 1930, used all her savings to buy a railway ticket to the port of Tientsin in North China. Quite alone, with only ninepence in cash and a traveller's cheque for £2, she travelled rough over the Trans-Siberian railway.

Gladys Aylward, the "Small Woman".

Once in Tientsin, she persuaded the head of the Anglo-Chinese college to help her, and was sent to join Mrs. Jeannie Lawson, then 74 years old, at her remote missionary post at Yangcheng in Southern Shansi. Here she learnt the local dialect and began to understand and love the people, many of whose customs shocked and upset her. She found the practice of binding Chinese girls' feet particularly distressing and it was her influence with the local mandarin that helped to ban the custom. She soon won the people's affection and, because of her lack of inches—she was only 5 ft. tall—they called her the "Small Woman", a name by which she was known in China for the rest of her life. After the death of Mrs. Lawson Miss Aylward continued to run the mission and, in 1938, during the Sino-Japanese war, she had her most remarkable adventure. Alone she led a long column of nearly 100 Chinese children on foot from the danger of the advancing Japanese armies. Somehow, week after week, she urged them on, over mountains, across the Yellow River, without money or equipment and with very little food, to eventual safety in the ancient city of Fufeng. This incredible journey was re-enacted in the film *The Inn of the Sixth Happiness*, starring Ingrid Bergman. It brought to Gladys Aylward a world-wide fame which she received with characteristic incredulity and modesty.

After further years in Nationalist China she returned to England for a time, giving lectures throughout the country. But her heart was in China and she returned to the Taiwan children's home which bears her name, where at the time of her death, she was in charge of 40 children all under the age of five. Her funeral, on January 24, was attended by over a thousand people. The "Small Woman" will not be forgotten.

Balchin, Nigel Marlin (1908–1970). This famous British novelist, author of *The Small Back Room* and *Mine Own Executioner*, died on May 17, 1970, at the age of 61. He was born in Wiltshire on December 3, 1908, and educated at Dauntsey's School and Peterhouse College, Cambridge, where he was an exhibitioner in natural science. Although Balchin rose to fame and fortune as a writer, he was also a distinguished industrial psychologist, dividing his time between writing and scientific research. During the Second World War he worked in the personnel section of the War Office and was later deputy scientific adviser to the Army Council, with the rank of brigadier. The literary fruit of his industrial experience was harvested not only in his novels but in two satires on industrial efficiency, *How to run a Bassoon Factory* and *Business for Pleasure*, both published under the pseudonym Mark Spade.

As a novelist Balchin pictured the rootless, seedy ambience of post-war England,

Nigel Balchin, British novelist.

combining his power of evoking atmosphere with a tight, fast-moving narrative technique. For seven years in the 1950s he was in Hollywood as a scriptwriter where he worked, among other films, on *Cleopatra*—the costly epic that nearly bankrupted 20th Century-Fox. Some of his novels were adapted into plays or films. and he wrote some plays himself: *Miserable Sinners* and *The Leader of the House* were the most successful. Among his novels were *The Small Back Room* (1943), *Mine Own Executioner* (1945), *The Borgia Testament* (1948), *A Sort of Traitors* (1949), *Sundry Creditors* (1953), *The Fall of the Sparrow* (1955), *Seen Dimly Before Dawn* (1962), and *In the Absence of Mrs. Petersen* (1966).

Barber, Anthony Perrinott Lysberg (born 1920). Anthony Barber, as chairman of the Conservative party organization during the British election campaign, must receive a considerable part of the credit for that party's surprising victory in June 1970. He remained in the public eye after the general election—first as chancellor of the Duchy of Lancaster with responsibility for negotiating Britain's possible entry into the E.E.C., and then, following the death of Iain Macleod, as chancellor of the exchequer. Barber was born in Yorkshire on July 4, 1920, and went to Retford grammar school. At the outbreak of the Second World War he held a commission in the Territorial Army, and in 1939 went to France. After being evacuated from Dunkirk he was seconded into the R.A.F. as a Spitfire pilot. In 1942 he was captured by the Germans, and while a prisoner studied law and took a first-class degree. He was also mentioned in despatches for attempted escapes in Germany and Poland. After the war he went to Oriel College, Oxford, where he graduated in "modern greats" (politics, philosophy, and economics). He was called to the bar in 1948 and thereafter practised as a barrister.

Barber was narrowly defeated when he stood as a parliamentary candidate for his home town, Doncaster, in 1950, but won the seat in 1951 and represented Doncaster for the next 13 years. After various minor offices, he became in 1958 parliamentary private secretary to the prime minister, Harold Macmillan, and accompanied him on visits to Moscow, Washington, and other capitals. By 1963 Anthony Barber was minister of health and a member of the Cabinet, but in the Conservative defeat in 1964 he lost Doncaster. In 1965 he re-entered the House after a by-election as member for Altrincham and Sale. In 1950 Anthony Barber married Miss Jean Asquith, who was a Conservative candidate in the 1950 general election; they have two teenage daughters.

Bateman, Henry Mayo (1887–1970). Henry Bateman, who died on the Maltese Island of Gozo on February 12, 1970, five days before his 83rd birthday, was one of the best-loved of all British cartoonists from the time his first drawings were published in 1906, and during the 1930s was pos

**Anthony Barber,
Conservative chancellor.**

sibly the best-known artist in Great Britain. Born at Sutton Forest, New South Wales, he was brought to England during his childhood and was educated at Forest Hill House in London. He studied drawing and painting in the Westminster and New Cross art schools, and at the age of 19 began to fulfil his childhood ambition "to draw and make people laugh". His most famous cartoons were a series of military scenes with titles like "The Guardsman Who Dropped It", "The Man Who Smoked Before the Loyal Toast", and "The Second Lieutenant Who Took the C.O.'s Savoury" —all depicting social gaffes and their effect on spectators.

H. M. Bateman's work was not confined to humorous drawings, for all his life he retained an interest in oil and water-colour, and he achieved a fair reputation as a landscape painter. A keen angler, he often visited Dartmoor to fish, and he eventually settled in Devon. Trout-fishing was always his favourite relaxation, and in 1960 he published *The Evening Rise: Fifty Years of Fly Fishing*. One of his ambitions was to see the foundation of a National Gallery of Humorous Art, and he put forward this idea to the Royal Society of Arts in 1949; although it was received with enthusiasm, work on the project came to nothing, largely through lack of suitable premises.

Benediktsson, Bjarni (1908–1970). Dr. Benediktsson, prime minister of Iceland, died tragically when fire engulfed his summer house at Thingvalla, near Reykjavik, early on the morning of July 10, 1970. His wife, Sigrigur Bjoernsdattir, and his four-year-old grandson, Benedikt Willmundarsson, were also killed.

Dr. Benediksson had been the Icelandic premier since 1963. Born in 1908, and educated at universities in Iceland and Berlin, he became a professor of law at the age of 24. Entering politics in 1940, he was first elected mayor of Reykjavik for the Independence party—and re-elected in 1942 and 1945. He was successively Icelandic delegate to the U.N., minister of foreign affairs, minister of justice, and minister of justice and education. The Independence party lost the general election of 1956, and Dr. Benediktsson was then chief editor of the newspaper *Morgunbladid* until 1959, when he became president (Speaker) of the Althing (Icelandic parliament) and, later, minister of justice and industries, and premier from September to December 1963, as a head of a coalition between the Independence party and the Social Democrats. As foreign minister, Dr. Benediktsson was responsible for Iceland's decision to join Nato.

Board, Lillian (1948–1970). Death overtook this charming and courageous British athlete shortly after her 22nd birthday, which she spent at Dr. Issels's Ringberg clinic in Bavaria undergoing treatment for inoperable cancer. No more popular personality in British athletics had captivated reporters, television audiences, and track spectators; her passing on December 26 at a Munich hospital after an operation cast a nation-wide gloom over the

Lillian Board, who died at 22.

Christmas festivities. Twin daughter of a tunnel bricklayer, she was born on December 13, 1948, in Durban, S. Africa, and brought to England by her Lancashire-born parents in 1950. The family settled in West London, where Lillian first showed promise in school athletics, winning the English schools junior long jump at $14\frac{1}{2}$. With the encouragement and coaching of her father she devoted herself to athletics and in 1966 was selected to represent England in the 440 yards at the Commonwealth Games in Jamaica. In the following year she won a remarkable 440 yards at Los Angeles in a U.S.A versus Commonwealth meeting, beating the world record holder Judy Pollock of Australia. This victory made her a favourite for the Mexico City Olympic Games 400 metres, although her best pre-Olympic performances in 1968 were in the 800 metres. In Mexico, she was beaten into second place by 0·07 sec. by an unknown French girl, Colette Besson.

Lillian now turned to the 800 metres, and took the European championship in

that distance at Athens in September 1969; in the 4×400 metres relay as anchor girl for the British team she met Colette Besson again in the last leg and beat her on a photo finish, contributing to a world record for the event. She took part in the southern women's championships in May 1970, and on June 13 shared in a world record 4×800 metres set by the British team at the new Meadowbank stadium in Edinburgh where she hoped to achieve new triumphs in the Commonwealth Games. But she ran her last race on June 20, coming third in the women's A.A.A. championships 800 metres. By now she was suffering great pain and had to withdraw from the Edinburgh Games.

Soon afterwards she entered hospital, and on October 8 an exploratory operation at St. Mark's Hospital, London, revealed an inoperable cancer. A few weeks later, BBC-TV broadcast a programme about the remarkable treatment of "terminal" cancer at Dr. Issels's Bavarian clinic, and her family decided to take this last chance. She entered the clinic on November 7, and on December 21 was transferred to the Munich University clinic for an operation— her third—to relieve an intestinal blockage. On Christmas Eve she fell into a coma from which she did not recover. Voted "athlete of the year" in 1967 and 1969, she was "sportswoman of the year" in 1968 and (in the *Daily Express* poll) in 1970, and was made M.B.E. in 1970.

Borrelli, Mario (born 1922). Known throughout the world as "the Saint of Naples", Mario Borrelli left the priesthood in 1970. Twenty years earlier, as a 27-year-old priest he had been given permission by the Archbishop of Naples temporarily to exchange his cassock for the rags of a street boy and to live among the *scugnizzi*, the ragged urchins of the slums of Naples. For more than a year this tenth son of a Naples metalworker lived the life of the urchins, begging and sorting through piles of garbage by day and sleeping on pavements by night. Gradually the urchins came to accept him as a friend. Together they made the derelict church of San Gennaro into the first *Casa dello Scugnizzo* (House of the Urchin). Others followed, in which many hundreds of orphaned and unwanted children have received food, education, and affection.

At first, this work of rehabilitation was supported almost entirely by the efforts of the urchins themselves, who sold rags and scrap iron to raise funds. Later Borrelli's work became almost as well known as that of Danilo Dolci in Sicily. As his fame grew, so donations flowed in from many countries. But he always shied away from suggestions that he should expand his work into a world movement. There was more than enough to do in Naples, including the building of an engineering school and many other facilities. Borrelli not only loved but also respected his urchins. He said of them: "A child's soul is like a bank. Whatever you put in you get back 10 years later with interest." Borrelli left the

priesthood because he found "too many strings attached to it". He took a 6-month course at the London School of Economics to help him in the organization of his ever-expanding work. He was quoted as saying, "I want to get the poor organized—and that means protests."

Brabham, Jack (born 1926). Although the news had leaked out prematurely, it was officially announced after the last GP of the season that Jack Brabham was to retire after 23 years in motor racing. Son of a greengrocer in Sydney, Australia, John Arthur Brabham came to Britain in 1954 with an introduction to Charles Cooper, who was then building rear-engined 500 c.c. racing cars. Brabham had already made a name for himself in Australia, driving in and winning hill climbs and races. He started driving for the Cooper works team, first in Formula 2 and then Formula 1 cars. His Grand Prix career began in 1957 with a 2-litre Cooper-Climax at the Monaco GP. He then joined forces with Ron Tauranac and formed

Jack Brabham retired from racing.

Motor Racing Developments, which produced the series of Brabham Formula 1 racing cars. But his first successes were with the Cooper team for 5 years, during which he won the world championship twice in succession, in 1959 and 1960. His championship in 1960 was achieved with five GP victories.

In the early 1960s Brabhams were always fast, but they seemed to be dogged by bad luck until the 1966 season, when Brabham became world champion for the third time, and was awarded the O.B.E. In the following year the Brabham team, with Denis Hulme driving, again won the championship. In 1968 he teamed with Stirling Moss for Aston Martin and won the Nürburgring 1,000 km. race. In the 1970 championship he scored 25 points and was equal fifth with Jackie Stewart. He retired while still a leading contender in Grand Prix racing, thrice world champion.

Bremner, Billy (born 1943). Leeds United waited a long time for their first-ever

**Billy Bremner,
"Footballer of the Year".**

Football League championship win in the 1968–69 season, and if manager Don Revie was the master-mind behind the success off the field, the fiery Scot Billy Bremner was the tactician who put Revie's plans into operation on the field as captain. Bremner, "Footballer of the Year" in 1970, owes much to Revie's influence. The Scot joined Leeds straight from school in Stirling as an inside forward, but it was a switch to wing-half that established him in the Leeds first team, which won promotion to Division One in 1963–64. Having climbed out of Division Two, Leeds —and Bremner—were determined to stay, and it was during this period that Bremner's temperament often got him into trouble with referees. The vital turning-point in his career came when Revie appointed Bremner captain, for under his determined leadership Leeds proved one of the most professional sides in the country, as they captured the Football League Cup (1968), European Fairs' Cup (1968) and League championship with a record 67 points. The award of the "Footballer of the Year" title in 1970 was some consolation for the disppointments of the 1969–1970 season when the task of chasing the treble of European Champions' Cup and the domestic League and Cup proved too much for Leeds; even Bremner's tireless prompting could not spare them the disappointment of finishing the season without a major honour.

Brittain, Vera (died 1970). Author, journalist, and lecturer, Vera Brittain died on March 29, 1970. She was born towards the end of the 1800s at Newcastle-under-Lyme, Staffordshire, the daughter of a businessman. She was educated at St. Monica's School, Kingswood, Surrey, and gained an exhibition at Somerville College, Oxford, in 1914. A year later she volunteered as a V.A.D., and spent the next four years nursing in military hospitals in London, France, and Malta. Her experiences during this period left an indelible mark for, apart from first-hand knowledge of the brutality of war, she suffered per-

sonal tragedies, when the man she expected to marry, and her only brother and his two greatest friends, were all killed. She became an ardent fighter for peace, a keen supporter of the League of Nations, and a proclaimed feminist. At Somerville she met Winifred Holtby, the Yorkshire-woman who was later to write *South Riding*, and they formed a friendship which lasted until Winifred died. When they left Somerville they shared rooms in Doughty Street, Bloomsbury, and devoted themselves to building up their careers. A vivid description of this period is to be found in Vera Brittain's *Testament of Friendship*, which tells the story of Winifred Holtby's life and works.

Vera Brittain's early novels, *The Dark Tide* and *Not Without Honour*, won little acclaim. It was the outspoken autobiographical *Testament of Youth* (1933) that won her wide praise, although its frankness shocked some readers. In 1925 she married George Catlin, at the time professor of politics at Cornell University, and made the first of her seven lecture tours in the U.S.A. and Canada. Although she published in all 29 books, it seems that lecturing appealed to her more. The third book in her autobiographical trilogy, *Testament of Experience*, was published in 1957, and her last book, *Radclyffe Hall: A Case of Obscenity*, in 1968. She had a son and a daughter; the daughter is Mrs. Shirley Williams, who entered Parliament in 1964 as a Labour M.P. and was minister of state at the Home Office in the last Labour government.

Brüning, Heinrich (1885–1970). Chancellor of Germany in the early 1930s, a devout Catholic who nearly took up the religious life, and a politician quite without charisma, Heinrich Brüning died on March 30, 1970. A victim of political intrigues, he was first encouraged and later rejected by the ageing President Hindenburg. It is possible that, given more time, his policies would have saved Germany from the holocause of Nazism and the Second World War, but in general he lacked the ability to control events and, if anything, hastened Hitler's rise to power.

Brüning was born in Münster. He studied political science at various universities, including a period at the London School of Economics. After gaining the Iron Cross (first class) in the First World War, he became Prussian minister for social welfare. In 1924 he entered the Reichstag as a member of the Catholic Centre party, and after five years was elected its parliamentary leader in a coalition with the Social Democrats. The coalition broke down, and President Hindenburg was persuaded by his *eminence grise* General von Schleicher to appoint Brüning as chancellor, the youngest man ever to hold that office. Brüning resorted to severe measures to cure Germany's financial ills, increasing taxes and reducing both unemployment benefit and the pay of public officials. He forced his programme through by presidential decree, ignoring the cries of

"hunger chancellor". When the Reichstag demanded the withdrawal of his fiscal decrees, he dissolved it, and with it parliamentary government in Germany. For in the new Reichstag the National Socialists increased their seats from 12 to 107. Brüning had paved the way for Hitler's imminent triumph.

In 1932 Brüning acted virtually as Hindenburg's election agent as the old man defeated Hitler on the second ballot. But the president blamed Brüning for having to rely on the support of the working class for his success. He was even persuaded that Brüning had sold out to the Bolsheviks. On May 30, 1932, Brüning was dismissed and was succeeded by von Papen, who made way for the Nazis in 1933. Brüning left Germany in 1934. He lectured at Oxford for two years, was a professor at the Harvard Graduate School of Business Administration 1939–52, and then returned to Germany as professor of political science at Cologne University.

Bruxner, Sir Michael Frederick (1882–1970). Few names in the New South Wales State parliament were as respected as that of former Country party leader Sir Michael Bruxner, known affectionately to his friends and associates as "the Colonel". Sir Michael, who died in Sydney on March 28, 1970, at the age of 88, had a political career spanning 42 years, and was a life-long fighter for the interests and welfare of farmers and rural districts.

Bruxner was born on March 25, 1882, at his father's cattle property on the Clarence River in northern New South Wales. He was educated at the Armidale School and Sydney University. He became a stock and station agent at Tenterfield, N.S.W., but when war broke out in 1914 he decided to volunteer, and was attached to the 6th Light Horse Brigade with the rank of captain. During the next four years he was to see active service at Gallipoli, where he was severely wounded, and in Egypt, Palestine, and Syria. He was promoted to lieutenant-colonel, and was awarded the D.S.O. in 1918. Returning to civilian life, he planned to settle down as a grazier. However, he was asked to stand as a candidate for the Progressive party, and was elected to the New South Wales State parliament in 1920. In 1922 he led a "breakaway" group which was later to form the nucleus of the N.S.W. Country party. He was minister for local government from 1927 to 1930, and deputy premier and minister for transport from 1932 to 1941. From 1932 until 1957 he was leader of the Country party; he retired from politics in 1962. Sir Michael was created K.B.E. in 1962. In the same year the Bruxner Highway, running from Ballina to Boggabilla in northern New South Wales, was named in his honour.

Courage, Piers (1942–1970). Near the East Tunnel at Zandvoort, Holland, the de Tomaso car driven by Piers Courage in the Dutch GP on June 21 left the track, rolled over and caught fire, killing its driver, son of the wealthy Courage brewery family. Piers Courage's racing career started in 1962 with a Lotus 7 as a hobby, while he was studying accountancy. He graduated to a Merlyn sports-racing car, and finally gave up studies and joined his friend Jonathan Williams driving Lotus 22s in the 1964 season. The following year he was invited to join the team of Brabham Formula 3 Lotuses, and in company with another friend, Charles Lucas, he won the premier Grovewood award. After another season with Formula 3 Lotuses, he joined BRM for the Tasman series. In 1967 he drove in the Monaco GP, but returned to the Tasman series in 1968, finished every race, and won the final round at Longford, Tasmania. Also in 1968, he finished fourth in the Italian GP and sixth in the French. In the 1969 Tasman series, once again with Frank Williams, he finished third, using a Brabham BT24, and in GP racing with a Brabham BT26 he was second at Monaco and in the U.S. GP. Until the accident in June, prospects with the de Tomaso looked good. His widow was the former Lady Sarah Curzon, daughter of the late Earl Howe; and he had two sons.

Piers Courage,
killed on the racing track.

Cushing, Richard, Cardinal (1895–1970). Cardinal Cushing, Roman Catholic archbishop of Boston, U.S.A., from 1944 until September 1970, when his resignation was accepted by the Pope for reasons of ill-health and old age, died on Nov. 2. Born in south Boston in 1895, the son of Patrick, an immigrant Irish blacksmith, and Mary Dahill Cushing, he was the third of five children. He attended Boston high school and Boston college before entering St. John's seminary, where his studies were briefly interrupted by service in the army cut short by asthma, a complaint which was to plague him all through his life. Ordained in 1921, he worked for a time as a parish priest. He was later appointed assistant in the diocesan office of the Society for the Propagation of the Faith, of which he became director in 1928. In 1939 he became auxiliary bishop of Boston, succeeding Cardinal Spellman, and in 1944 archbishop, the youngest in

Cardinal-Archbishop Cushing.

the Roman Catholic Church. In 1958 Pope John, who like Cushing was a man of the people, made him a cardinal.

It was while he was a young priest that his fund-raising work brought him into contact with Joseph Kennedy, with whom he formed a close friendship, later to be extended to the whole Kennedy family. He supported John F. Kennedy during his presidential campaign, said a prayer at his inauguration as president, and officiated at his funeral. A gregarious man with a great sense of humour, Cushing enjoyed public gatherings, at which he sometimes danced the jig and tried to play the guitar —"very badly" on his own admission. He was a powerful preacher whose conservative streak, combined with his many liberal views, often involved him in controversy. Before his resignation was finally accepted by the Pope, Cardinal Cushing had made several attempts to leave his diocese in order to go to Peru to work with the hundred priests in the Society of St. James, a missionary order he founded and financed. Possessor of many honorary degrees, he was truly, as one citation read: "A Prince of his church, ever mindful of the needs of the least of his flock."

Daladier, Edouard (1884–1970). Daladier, prime minister of France at the time of Munich and at the outbreak of the Second World War, died in Paris on October 10, 1970. He was born at Carpentras, near Avignon, on June 18, 1884, the son of a baker. His education progressed, as one scholarship followed another, from the local lycée via Lyons and the École Normale to the Sorbonne. At the outbreak of the First World War, Daladier was lecturing in history at the Lycée Condorcet in Paris. He entered the ranks of the French army and fought at Verdun. His war record was distinguished: he was mentioned three times in despatches and awarded the Legion of Honour. In 1919 he was elected mayor of Carpentras, and next year was returned to the chamber of deputies as Radical-Socialist member for the department of Vaucluse.

Daladier cultivated brevity in his speeches and conversation, a quirk that earned him notoriety and a reputation for

ruggedness of character. The victory of the *Cartel des Gauches*, in 1924, brought him into the government as minister of the colonies. He became prime minister first in January–October 1933, and again at the beginning of 1934. Daladier vigorously pursued a policy of European conciliation, but events were running against him both at home and abroad. His second administration was brought down by riots, but he continued in and out of government as minister of national defence. He became prime minister once more in April 1938, in time for the Munich agreement, and thus shared with Neville Chamberlain the mantle of appeasement. Daladier, however, did not deceive himself that he had gained "peace with honour" at the expense of Czechoslovakia, and was surprised when, arriving back in France after the Munich meeting with Hitler, he was greeted by wildly cheering crowds at Le Bourget. On the outbreak of war Daladier remained in office and formed a new war cabinet. Although he lacked the drive and popularity needed for war-time leadership, he made optimistic speeches while presiding over a cabinet wracked by intrigue.

Edouard Daladier,
French premier of the 30s.

He resigned in March 1940, and was minister of war and minister of foreign affairs before the fall of France in June.

Following the surrender, Daladier was arrested by the Vichy regime and spent the remainder of the war in prisons. He was released from an Alpine prison camp in May 1945. He resumed his political career in the Fourth Republic, but never again held ministerial rank. In November 1957, he was president of the Radical party, but the following year resigned all political offices, including the mayoralty of Avignon. Thereafter he lived quietly in Paris until his death.

Dash, Jack (born 1907). The financial acumen of this Communist trade unionist, who had taken an active part in every major post-war dock strike, led him to early retirement in 1970—it was, he said, only a matter of common sense, after totting up benefits in ready cash and

Jack Dash, dockers' strike-leader.

pension. At once he began training for his retirement job—to be a guide with the British Tourist Authority—which will give him an opportunity to expound his London knowledge, spiced with humour and working-class philosophy. As a witty yet thoughtful speaker he was already much in demand outside dockland trade-unionist meetings. His score as a lecturer, up to his retirement, included 53 universities, five grammar schools, three British Institute of Management meetings, six rotary clubs, five Round Table groups, and one church. His lively autobiography, *Good Morning, Brothers*, earned serialization in the "capitalist press" and he began writing short stories.

Born near the Elephant and Castle, in South London, the son of a stage-hand and a professional actress disowned by her middle-class family, he experienced barefoot poverty as a child. Leaving school at 14, his main talent an ability to draw, he fell victim to the unemployment of the 1920s and saw, in the 1926 General Strike, "scenes of class hatred and class solidarity that are deeply embedded in my memory". He joined the regular army, but returned to unemployment—in one spell he was enticed into boxing at the Blackfriars Ring—and became converted to Marxism through the National Unemployed Workers Movement. His entry into active trade-unionism came as a hod-carrier on a building site, and he organized his first strike in 1938. Serving in the fire service during the London blitz, he later volunteered and trained as a commando.

After the war he became a docker and chairman of the London Port Workers Liaison Committee, which probably exerted more influence in the docks than any official trade-union group. On his retirement he spoke of his pride in helping dockers to better recognition of their importance. All the strikes he had led had been worth while, he said, except the inter-union struggle in 1955 between the Transport and General Workers and the Stevedores' Unions.

Davison, Frank Dalby (1893–1970). The name of Frank Dalby Davison is probably most widely known because of his novel *Man-Shy*, a story of men and cattle. It was

first produced in book form in 1931, and won the Australian Literature Society medal for that year. Since then it has been published in more than 20 editions, both in Australia and overseas, including, in 1949, an English edition with the title *Red Heifer*. Davison was born in the Melbourne suburb of Glenferrie on June 23, 1893, and educated at Caulfield state school near by. As a youth he worked in the Victorian countryside, first on a cattle property in Gippsland and then on orchards nearer Melbourne. When he was 15 he moved with his parents to the U.S.A., where he became a printer's compositor. On the outbreak of the First World War, Davison sailed for England to enlist, serving first in the cavalry and later in the infantry, and attaining the rank of lieutenant. After the war he married in England, returned to Australia, and became a soldier-settler in Queensland. His venture on the land was not successful, and after four years he joined his father's real estate business in Sydney.

The father, a man of literary interests, established a magazine called, at first, *The Australian* and, later, *Australia*, and two of the son's stories—*Man-Shy* and *Forever Morning*—appeared in it serially. Like *Man-Shy*, *Forever Morning* appeared in book form in 1931. Other of Frank Dalby Davison's works include *The Wells of Beersheba* (1933), *Children of the Dark People* (1936), *The Woman at the Mill* (short stories, 1940), *Dusty* (1946), and *The Road to Yesterday* (1964). His most ambitious work, *The White Thorntree*, appeared in 1968. Davison died on May 24, 1970.

De Gaulle. See Gaulle.

Dixon, Reginald (born 1907). Reginald Dixon, the maestro of the electronic keyboard, whose flying fingers for 40 years caressed and pounded the Blackpool Tower ballroom theatre organ to entrance the ears of generations of holiday-makers and delight nation-wide radio audiences, retired on March 29, 1970. A capacity 4,000-strong audience packed the Tower

**Reginald Dixon,
the Blackpool organist.**

ballroom for his farewell concert. Dixon was born in Sheffield in 1907, first giving public notice of his talents by winning a gold medal for piano playing at a music festival in his native county. Fired by this boyhood success, while yet a stripling of 15 he assumed the responsibilities of church organist before becoming a cinema organist in Chesterfield. In 1930 he started his long and famous association with the Blackpool Tower, symbolized by his signature tune, *I Do Like To Be Beside the Seaside*. When winter cleared the Blackpool sands of recumbent Lancastrians, donkeys, and sandcastles, Dixon was wont to decamp inland to tour the Moss Empire and Stoll Theatre circuits with a specially built electronic organ. With a thousand tunes etched upon his memory, and the personality to lead his listeners into rousing choruses, Reginald Dixon was the epitome of seaside England—as institutional as McGill postcards or lettered rock. He even proposed to his wife in the Tower balcony, seat 33, backed by the inspiring flounce of the Wurlitzer.

Dobell, Sir William (1899–1970). The news that this famous artist had been found dead in his Wangi home, near Newcastle, N.S.W., caused wide regret throughout Australia. He died from natural causes, apparently on the day preceding the discovery—May 13, 1970. Bill Dobell, as he was generally called in his own country, was recognized as a painter of world stature. He won the Archibald prize for portraiture three times—in 1943, 1948, and 1959—as well as the Wynne prize for Australian landscape in 1948. Other honours included the Society of Artists' medal in 1960 and the Britannica Australia award in 1965. On four occasions portraits by him were used for the cover of *Time* magazine.

William Dobell was born at Newcastle, N.S.W., on September 24, 1899, and educated at Cooks Hill public school near that city. He studied art in Sydney under Julian Ashton, and in 1929 won the Society of Artists' travelling scholarship. Transferring to London, he studied at the Slade School, and received some tuition from Sir William Orpen. He gained further knowledge of art while travelling on the Continent, and in 1933 exhibited at the Royal Academy. In 1939 he returned to Australia, and during the Second World War he worked first as a camouflage artist and later as the official war artist to the Civil Construction Corps.

Dobell's first Archibald award, in 1943, for the portrait of fellow artist Joshua Smith, caused an uproar in local art circles and was responsible for the first legal action of its kind in the history of Australian law. On the grounds that the picture was not a portrait but a caricature, two other artists sought an injunction to prevent the trustees of the National Art Gallery of New South Wales from making the award. The case was heard in the supreme court of New South Wales and the verdict was given in favour of the trustees. The accompanying bitter dissension gave great distress to the sensitive Dobell and, although the case helped to establish his fame, he withdrew from the acclaim of Sydney to the quiet backwater of Wangi on Lake Macquarie, where he painted until his death. In later years his pictures were in great demand, and a retrospective exhibition of his works at the National Art Gallery of New South Wales in 1964 was insured for $1½ million. Dobell was awarded the O.B.E. in 1965 and created K.B.E. in 1966. Shortly after his death it was announced that an art foundation, to be known as the Sir William Dobell Foundation, would be established from his estate.

Dodd, Rev. Charles Harold (born 1884). This internationally famous New Testament scholar saw his long labour in directing the production of the *New English Bible* brought to full fruition in the course of 1970 when the Old Testament and Apocrypha were published. He had already retired from his divinity chair at Cambridge when he began the work in 1949; he confessed that he never envisaged being in full work on it when it was completed in his 87th year. Oxford's gift to him of a second honorary doctorate in the summer of 1970 made him the first to receive this recognition.

Dr. Dodd was born in 1884 at Wrexham, North Wales. He studied at Oxford, and trained for the Congregational ministry at Mansfield College there. His only pastorate was at Warwick. For 15 years he taught in his old college, and then spent five years at Manchester. In 1935 came the great distinction of being the first Nonconformist since the 17th century to be appointed to a chair of divinity at Cambridge. When he retired he shouldered the main burden of directing the preparation of the first fully new translation of the Bible that the British Churches had ever sponsored; in later years he shared the work with a joint director.

Dr. Dodd's writings on New Testament themes have won world-wide recognition, but his work for the *New English Bible*, done when most men have fully retired, was perhaps his greatest contribution to biblical scholarship. At the service of thanksgiving for the completion of the *New English Bible*, despite his advanced years his small figure was sturdily erect as he walked in procession in Westminster Abbey, and his voice rang out clearly as he presented the first copy to the Archbishop of Canterbury.

Dos Passos, John (1896–1970). This American author of wayward genius, best known for his trilogy of novels, *U.S.A.*, died in Baltimore aged 74 on September 28, 1970. He was born in Chicago on January 14, 1896, the son of John Randolph Dos Passos, a successful lawyer, politician, and financier of mixed Portuguese and Quaker colonial stock. He was brought up by his mother mainly in Europe, and was at school in England for a short while before going to Choate school in 1907 and Harvard in 1912. He graduated

cum laude in 1916. At Harvard he contributed, like E. E. Cummings, to *Eight Harvard Poets* (1917) and on graduating, also like Cummings, joined the Norton Harjes ambulance corps in France in 1917. He remained in Europe for some years after the war working as a journalist, and his first novel, *One Man's Initiation*, was published in London in 1920. His second, *Three Soldiers*, one of the finest to come out of the First World War, is marked by relentless pessimism—and, more significantly in view of his later work, by an atmosphere of grievance. This bitter thread runs through all Dos Passos's writing: his protagonists are always outfaced by towering odds in a world where the sensitive man is inevitably trampled underfoot.

It was with *Manhattan Transfer* (1924) that Dos Passos first began to exploit impressionism as well as naturalism to reflect the frenetic, broken rhythms of New York life. This work was the forerunner of *U.S.A.*, a confused trilogy comprising *The 42nd Parallel* (1930), *1919* (1932), and *The Big Money* (1936), which covers the period 1900 to 1930 and carries the interwoven accounts of various lives. Interspersed are staccato "biographies" of famous figures—Ford, Valentino, and others—and scrap-book collections of headlines and snatches of popular song. Powerful though *U.S.A.* undoubtedly is, it is not a complete success: its "modernism" is ostentatious and its objectivity too rigid. A strong radical streak ran through Dos Passos's pre-war writing. From the 1940s on, however, he became increasingly conservative both in ideology and technique, and his second trilogy, *District of Columbia* (1952), reflects this change. Besides novels, Dos Passos also wrote poetry, publishing *A Pushcart at the Kerb* (1922); several plays including *The Garbage Man*, which was produced in 1925; volumes of history, travel, biography, and criticism, and essays on the art and culture of Spain.

Dowding, Hugh Caswall Tremenheere Dowding, 1st Baron (1882–1970). Air

Lord Dowding, leader of "the Few".

Chief Marshal Lord Dowding, the aloof and enigmatic chief of Fighter Command during the Battle of Britain, of whom it has been observed "never in history has a commander won so signal a victory and been so little thanked by his country," died at his Kent home on February 15, 1970. "Stuffy" Dowding was born on April 4, 1882, the son of a preparatory-school headmaster. He was educated at Winchester and the Royal Military Academy, Woolwich, where he failed to qualify as a sapper and was gazetted to the Royal Garrison Artillery. After service in Gibraltar, Colombo, and Hong Kong, he was transferred to the Mountain Artillery and spent six years in India. It was at the Staff College, Camberley, 1912–13, that he was first convinced of the importance of aviation in the future of warfare, qualified for a pilot's certificate, and went on a short course with the new Central Flying School.

From the outbreak of war in 1914, Dowding was involved in aerial combat. He served first with No. 6 Squadron in Belgium, then at the R.F.C. headquarters in France, and then with No. 9 (Wireless) Squadron, which he commanded until it was disbanded in 1915. In 1916 he served as commander of the Ninth Wing at the Somme directly under Trenchard, with whom he was not always in agreement on tactical matters. This led to his losing his command and he returned for the remainder of the war to England, where he rose to be brigadier-general and was awarded the C.M.G.

Dowding was not given a commission in the R.A.F. when it was created in 1918 but was merely granted a temporary attachment that later became permanent. From 1930 to 1936 he was on the Air Council, successively responsible for supply, research, and research and development. Here his work on the application of radar to air defence was of paramount importance. In 1936 he was appointed Air Officer Commanding-in-Chief, Fighter Command, a post he held for four years. He stood firm when the government toyed with the idea, in May 1940, of sending a considerable part of Fighter Command to France to encourage the French; thanks to his intransigence they were spared involvement in a battle that was already lost.

It was in the tremendous struggle to control the skies over England that Dowding's "Few" won the victory that scotched Hitler's invasion plans. The Luftwaffe's undoing was wrought in aerial dog-fights that marked the summer of 1940, culminating in a battle over London on September 15. Dowding disagreed with his chiefs on a number of tactical issues towards the end of the Battle of Britain, and he was relieved of his command in November 1940, retiring from the service in 1942. The following year he received a barony.

In retirement Dowding developed an interest in spiritualism and was the author of many books and articles on the occult. His titles include *Many Mansions*, *Lychgate*, and *The Dark Star*.

James Fisher, British ornithologist.

Fisher, James (1912–1970). This well-known ornithologist and broadcaster was killed in a motor accident on September 25, 1970. He was born on September 3, 1912, the son of the headmaster of Oundle school, and educated at Eton (King's scholar) and Magdalen College, Oxford, where he graduated with first-class honours in zoology. An associate of Sir Julian Huxley while assistant curator of the Zoological Society of London (1936–39), he became the guiding light of a group of naturalists studying the Atlantic gannet. Fisher became an expert on this species, publishing papers and articles on the bird, and later turned to the study of the distribution of the fulmar petrel, travelling extensively in northern waters.

As an officer of the British Trust for Ornithology, James Fisher was a pioneer in the data-processing of bird studies. During the war he studied the economic effects of the rook on agriculture, writing a controversial report which was attacked by some stringent critics and which, while often quoted, was never published. After the war Fisher worked as a writer and publisher and became famous as a radio and television broadcaster with such programmes as *Nature Parliament*, *Birds in Britain*, and *World Zoos*. His books include *Birds as Animals* (1939); *Watching Birds* (1940); *The Birds of Britain* (1942); *Bird Recognition* (1947–55); *The Fulmar* (1952); *Birds of the Field* (1952); *Adventure of the Sea* (1956); *The Shell Nature Lover's Atlas* (1966); *The Shell Bird Book* (1967); *Zoos of the World* (1967).

Forster, Edward Morgan (1879–1970). E. M. Forster, who died on June 7, 1970, was an author whose output was remarkably small—five novels, 36 short stories, a biography, two volumes of collected essays, and sundry other pieces—but whose influence on literature and thought was enormous. Born of middle-class parents on January 1, 1879, he was educated at Tonbridge School, which he detested, and at King's College, Cambridge, which he loved. When he left the university, having a private income sufficient for his needs, he travelled round Europe, settling in Italy at the beginning of the century. His first novel *Where Angels Fear To Tread* was published in 1905, a work of great maturity and subtlety of writing in which he drew on his experience of Italian life. These experiences also formed the background of *a Room With a View* (1908). In *The Longest Journey* (1907) the earlier parts are auto-biographical, and reveal the emotions that school and university aroused in him. The personal relationships which play a great part in the book, as they do in all his novels, are presented with quiet irony and restraint. The interplay between two types of character, the conventional and the emotional, was shown even more strongly in *Howard's End*, published in 1910.

In 1911 Forster visited India for the first time, leaving for Egypt in 1914, where he remained until the armistice, doing civilian war work and making some witty and perceptive contributions to the *Egyptian Mail*. After his return to England and a

E. M. Forster, whose high literary reputation was based on a tiny output.

short period as literary editor of the *Daily Herald*, he returned to India in 1921. His experiences there led to his most famous and important work, *A Passage to India*, published in 1924. In this serious, mordant, often poetic work the tragic incompatibility of East and West is shown with great insight. It was widely acclaimed in the U.K. and in America, and was awarded the Femina Vie Heureuse and the James Tait Black memorial prizes. It was to be his last novel. Among his later works were *Aspects of the Novel* (1927), his first work of criticism; *Abinger Harvest* (1936), in which he showed his gifts as an essay writer; and the libretto for Benjamin Britten's opera *Billy Budd* (1950). He will be remembered, too, for his many broadcast talks and lectures.

He spent the last 17 years of his life in his beloved Cambridge after being made an honorary fellow of King's, and devoted himself to the life of the college, and to music, which had always played an important part in his life. Diffident in manner, somewhat unkempt in appearance, though

frequently named as the greatest living British novelist he remained virtually unknown to the outside world. Honours came late in his life. He was made a Companion of Honour in 1953, and appointed a member of the Order of Merit on his 90th birthday. The manuscript of a sixth novel, *Maurice*, which he had written in 1913 but did not wish to have published until after his death, was found among his effects.

Forte, Sir Charles (born 1908). 1970 was an eventful year for Sir Charles Forte. He was given a knighthood in the birthday honours in June, having added a substantial province to his catering empire in May with a merger of Forte (Holdings) Ltd. with Trust House Hotels. The joint concern, with £113 million worth of assets, is probably the largest of its kind in the world; Forte is its deputy chairman until 1972, when he will become chairman. He was born on November 26, 1908, near Rome, of farming stock. His father brought him to Scotland at the age of five, and he was educated at Alloa academy and St. Joseph's College, Dumfries, and then went to Rome to perfect his Italian before joining his father's catering business. To widen his experience he later worked with other relatives in the southern resorts of Bournemouth, Weymouth, and Weston-super-Mare. By the time he was 21 he was managing a large catering concern in Weymouth. When he was 26, having saved £2,000 he selected London's West End to set up his first establishment. By the time the Second World War began he had nine separate establishments in the centre of London. Expansion got under way again in 1945 with the purchase of Rainbow Corner, just off Piccadilly Circus, and 4 years later he bought the Criterion, in the Circus, for £800,000. By 1951 his organization was so soundly based and efficiently operated that he won the catering contract for the whole of the Festival of Britain.

The next move was into the realms of London's top-class restaurants when, in 1954, he acquired the Café Royal in Regent Street. Thus by the mid-1960s the Forte organization was broadly based in

Sir Charles Forte, king of caterers.

both the catering and hotel fields—with 11 hotels across the country. The catering operation had been steadily extended by taking over such groups as Fuller's and Kardomah, Terry's of York (famous for fine chocolates for 200 years), and Ring and Brumer. Having built up one of the largest catering and hotel organizations in Britain, Forte turned his attentions overseas. Joint operations with BOAC include hotels in Paris, Guyana, Jamaica, Hong Kong, and Cyprus. He has also extensive interests in Sardinia, Bermuda, and Florida.

Charles Forte has varied responsibilities and interests outside his business. He is president of the Italian chamber of commerce in the U.K.; consul general in London for the state of San Marino; president of the National Sporting Club; chairman in 1970 of the Prince Albert and Alexandra Children's schools. He is a keen opera and concert-goer and has a penetrating knowledge of art—he was amongst the first to recognize the talent of L.S. Lowry—and he has encouraged art exhibitions in his West End premises. He married in 1943, and has one son and five daughters.

Lord Francis-Williams, writer and broadcaster.

Francis-Williams, Baron (1903–1970). Lord Francis-Williams, the avuncular Labour peer, writer, television personality, journalist, and one-time editor of the *Daily Herald*, died at his home in Surrey on June 5, 1970. His death occurred just as his much-praised autobiography, *Nothing So Strange*, appeared in the bookshops. Edward Francis Williams was born at St. Martins, Shropshire, on March 10, 1903. Educated at the Queen Elizabeth Grammar School, Middleton, he worked for a number of local newspapers before embarking, with a colleague, on a jaunt with horse-drawn caravan round rural England. Running out of funds, the pair sold their assets—the horse—and the youthful Williams headed for Fleet Street. Here he was soon attracting attention as city editor of the *Daily Herald*, a post he owed to a whim of Lord Southwood. In 1936 he became editor of the paper, a post he held for four years with great success. In 1941 he became controller of news and censor-

ship at the Ministry of Information, where he remained until the end of the war. In was made C.B.E. in 1945. After the war he was for two years Attlee's P.R.O. at 10 Downing Street. In 1951–52 he was a governor of the B.B.C.; in 1956 he took over as editor of the short-lived Socialist weekly *Forward*.

Williams's books include *Democracy's Last Battle* (1941), *Tomorrow's Politics* (1942), *Press, Parliament, and People* (1946), *The Triple Challenge, the Future of Socialist Britain* (1946). He also wrote a life of Ernest Bevin, and histories of the Labour Party and trade unionism. *A Prime Minister Remembers* (1961) is one of his better books, drawing directly on his close association with Attlee. For the last 20 years of his life Francis Williams was known to the public chiefly through his many television appearances. He was created a life peer in 1962.

Frazier, Joe (born 1944). The showbusiness world of professional boxing breathed a sigh of relief when Frazier, the seventh son of a family of 13 from Beaufort, South Carolina, stopped Jimmy Ellis at Madison Square Garden, New York, in February 1970 to become undisputed heavyweight champion of the world. For more than a year the richest prize in sport had lacked an official owner. As one ruling body after another withdrew their recognition from Muhammad Ali (Cassius Clay) following his refusal to serve in the U.S. army, the scramble for the vacant title began. Frazier, unbeaten as a professional after winning the U.S.A.'s only boxing gold medal at the 1964 Tokyo Olympic Games, always looked the most formidable of the many challengers, but it was not until his defeat of Ellis in his 25th professional fight that he was accepted as the best—apart from perhaps Clay himself. A rugged fighter, Frazier has been called the "Black Marciano" and "Smokin' Joe" after the infamous hurricane. He moves forward all the time, throwing a damaging left hook perfected first in Philadelphia, where he worked in a slaughter house before being spotted by Yancey Durham, now his boxing manager, in a local gymnasium. After his Olympic success—as a late replacement in the U.S. team—a syndicate of backers launched their protégé on his professional career at a time when boxing was in desperate need of young heavyweight talent.

Gaillard, Felix (1919–1970). This former French premier, whose nonchalant brilliance and amused detachment made him the dandy of French politics in the years immediately before de Gaulle's return to power, was drowned in a yachting accident on July 12, 1970. Gaillard was born in Paris on November 5, 1919, the son of a company director. As a student, he won every conceivable academic distinction, becoming a doctor of law by the age of 20, and coming out first in the competition for the *inspection des finances*. During the war he fought in the Resistance, and afterwards he became assistant to

Jean Monnet, father of the Common Market idea. In 1946 Gaillard entered the political arena himself when he became mayor of Barbezieux and a year later, aged 27, deputy for Charent, which he represented until his death. He was undersecretary for economic affairs from 1946 to 1947, and 10 years later was appointed minister of finance and economics. Later in 1957 he became prime minister, thus reaching the peak of a dazzling career at the age of 38—the youngest French premier under the Third and Fourth Republics.

His government, the last of the Fourth Republic, lasted for 6 months, falling in April 1958 over the bombing by the French air force of a Tunisian village used as a base by Algerian rebels. De Gaulle's return to power in May marked the end of Gaillard's active career. Thereafter he worked within the Radical-Socialist party, seeking to unite the non-Communist left and the centre under Gaston Deferre, mayor of Marseilles. A liberal with conservative instincts, he disliked Servan-Schreiber's revolutionary leadership of the party.

Gardner, Erle Stanley (1889–1970). A former lawyer who became one of the world's best-selling authors of detective stories, Erle Stanley Gardner died in Temecula, California, on March 11, 1970, aged 80. He was born in 1889 at Malden, Massachusetts, the son of a mining engineer who moved with his family through the Klondyke to northern California. Gardner studied law, was admitted to the Californian bar in 1911, worked in commerce between 1916 and 1918, and then opened an office in Ventura, California. To augment his income he began, in 1920, to write fiction for pulp magazines, as well as articles on hunting, fishing, and archery, his favourite hobby. It was in 1933 that he drew on his experience of the American courts and the first of the Perry Mason books, *The Case of the Velvet Claws*, was published. Scores of Perry Mason books followed in which the formula of legal twists leading to a court-room climax with

Erle Stanley Gardner, creator of Perry Mason.

General de Gaulle's death on November 9 "left France a widow", as President Pompidou said. *Left:* the General on his famous walk up the Champs-Élysées on the day of the liberation of Paris in 1944. *Right:* as president and father-figure of France, at the microphone addressing his people.

the acquittal of the accused through Mason's unmasking of the true criminal seldom varied. The lawyer, his secretary Della Street, and the private detective Paul Drake became some of the best-known figures in detective fiction, and reached an even larger public when adapted for a television series.

When his books brought him financial security Gardner gave up his law practice and devoted much of his enormous physical energy to photography, archaeology, travel, and entertaining. He continued to write prodigiously, often producing six books a year with the help of seven full-time secretaries who transcribed from his tape-recorded dictation. He wrote 15 travel and exploration books and, under the pseudonym of A. A. Fair, 29 "non-Mason" crime novels. By the mid-1960s his books were selling in 30 languages and dialects, sometimes at the rate of 20,000 copies a day, and by the end of 1969 his 140 books had sold a total of 170 million copies in the U.S.A. and Canada alone. Always concerned with the protection of the innocent, in 1948 he founded the Court of Last Resort, a private organization to aid prisoners he believed to have been unjustly treated by the courts. When his first wife, whom he had married in 1912, died in 1968, Gardner married one of his secretaries who had worked for him since 1930, and on whom Della Street was modelled.

Gaulle, Charles André Joseph Marie de (1890–1970). General Charles de Gaulle, the haughty embodiment of French pride, twice the saviour of his country and the founder of the Fifth Republic, died suddenly from an aneurysm while playing patience at his country home at Colombey-les-Deux-Églises on November 9, 1970. He would have been 80 on November 22. When the news was flashed belatedly around the world tributes flooded in. President Pompidou, his protégé and successor, announced the news to the nation with the words: "General de Gaulle is dead. France has become a widow. In 1940 de Gaulle saved our

honour. In 1944 he led us to the liberation and to victory. In 1958 he saved us from civil war. To the France of today he gave her institutions, her independence, her position in the world."

De Gaulle was born on November 22, 1890, at Lille, the second of three sons of Henri de Gaulle, a philosophy professor at a Jesuit college in Paris. He was educated at private schools and at the St. Cyr military academy where he was known by the soubriquet "Asparagus". He was commissioned a second lieutenant in 1911 and joined the 33rd Infantry under Pétain, then a colonel. De Gaulle was conspicuous for his courage as a company commander during the First World War, in which he was thrice wounded and eventually captured near Verdun in 1916. After failing in five escape bids, frustrated by his towering height, he was interned in a disciplinary camp, where he began work on his first book, an analysis of the division between the German military and their civilian chiefs.

De Gaulle married Yvonne Vendroux in 1921, and from 1922 he was a professor at the military staff college, the École de Guerre, before becoming aide-de-camp to Marshal Pétain. He disagreed with France's purely defensive strategy based on the Maginot line, publishing *Vers l'Armée de Métier*, in which he argued the case in favour of armoured divisions. His ideas were vindicated when the German armour outflanked the Maginot line and swept into France in 1940. De Gaulle had brief command of the Fourth Armoured Division during the Battle of France, before being appointed under-secretary for national defence in Paul Reynaud's government. As the battle drew to its disastrous finish and the new Pétain government decided to surrender, de Gaulle escaped by R.A.F. plane to England.

On the day following that on which Marshal Pétain announced that the French government was seeking an armistice, de Gaulle broadcast to the people of France from London. "Has the last word been said?" he demanded to know. "Is our defeat final and irremediable? To those

questions, I answer no! Whatever happens the flame of French resistance must not and shall not die." He later became known in France as the "Man of June 18". Ten days later the British government formally recognized him as the leader of the Free French. In this capacity he rallied those Frenchmen who had escaped to England after France's collapse, and also most of France's overseas territories, to the symbol of the fighting Free French—the cross of Lorraine. In August 1940 de Gaulle ensconced himself at Duala in the Cameroons and from there mobilized the Free French troops in the rest of Africa. Throughout the war his relations with the leaders of his "Anglo-Saxon" allies—particularly Roosevelt—were stormy. He was proud, imperious, and quick to respond to any Allied slight to the French government in exile.

Following the Anglo-American landings in North Africa, de Gaulle fought a vigorous political campaign against Churchill and Roosevelt to gain power in Algiers, finally wresting authority from General Giraud, to whom the Allies had handed French civil and military command in North Africa. Churchill invited de Gaulle to England in time for the Allied landings in Normandy. While in London on this occasion, he quarrelled bitterly with both Churchill and Eisenhower, and on arrival in France, several days after D-Day, he established his own civilian administration at Bayeux, thus thwarting the British control commission. Churchill said of de Gaulle: "Of all the crosses I have had to bear, the cross of Lorraine was the heaviest." As General Leclerc's division approached Paris in August 1944 de Gaulle went to France again, arriving in Paris at the moment of its liberation. His famous walk along the Champs-Élysées among cheering Parisians, and while German snipers were still firing from the roof-tops, will never be forgotten.

Victory brought French elections for a constituent assembly in the autumn of 1945, and de Gaulle was asked to form a government. After a few weeks in office he saw that he could not maintain authority over feuding factions without assuming almost dictatorial powers. He therefore summoned his ministers to a meeting on January 20, 1946, at which he arrived in full uniform to declare: ''You have espoused the quarrels of your various parties. I disapprove. . . . therefore I must withdraw!'' He then strode imperiously from the room. The following year he re-entered the political arena as leader of his own party, *Rassemblement du Peuple Français* (RPF), which failed to bring him to power. He again retired to Colombey-les-Deux-Églises, where he remained until the Algerian crisis of 1958 threatened civil war.

On May 13, 1958, the army joined French settlers in Algeria in revolt. They defied Paris and appealed to de Gaulle to form a government. Two days later he declared himself ''ready to assume the powers of the Republic''. Alarmed by the threat of civil war, the politicians agreed that de Gaulle should take over—the National Assembly invested him with autocratic power for 6 months and gave him authority to reform the constitution. This he did, and the new constitution was overwhelmingly approved by the people of France and Algeria on September 28. His power and popularity were confirmed by general elections for the new national assembly, and in December de Gaulle was elected first president of the Fifth Republic. While empowered with the right to rule by decree, de Gaulle had revolutionized laws affecting every branch of French life. As president, remaining deeply suspicious of the ''Anglo-Saxons'' he worked for the restoration of France's ''grandeur'', and gave her an independent nuclear capability.

On the Algerian question, once he had satisfied himself that Algerian independence was inevitable, he shocked his followers by announcing Algeria's right to self-determination. This precipitated rioting, bombings, and assassinations organized by the O.A.S. (secret army organization). In early 1961 an Algerian referendum was held which resulted in a three-to-one majority for self-determination, and a military coup was scotched only by the assumption of emergency powers. In September 1961 the president and Mme. de Gaulle narrowly escaped assassination by the O.A.S., and in August 1962, a month after Algeria had become independent, another assassination attempt was made by O.A.S. gunmen.

As a post-war statesman, de Gaulle was dominated by a vision of a ''Europe of fatherlands'' stretching from the Atlantic to the Urals and enjoying economic unity while each state preserved its individual sovereignty. With this policy in mind he moved to end the long-standing enmity between Germany and France and fought what he considered the threat of Anglo-Saxon domination. Britain's aspirations to join the Common Market were seen by the General as ''the American hand in the British glove'', and he vetoed British applications in 1963 and 1967. Early in 1964 he restored relations with Com-

munist China and toured Mexico and the French West Indies. Later that year he toured 10 South American nations.

He ran for a second term as president in late 1965 and was elected, but only after failure to gain a clear majority in the first ballot forced him to fight a second round. During his second term in office the General went to Canada for Expo '67 and he caused a diplomatic furore when he made his famous controversial speech in Quebec, ending with the words: ''Vive le Québec! Vive le Québec libre!'' Canadian premier Lester Pearson immediately announced in Ottawa that the General's apparent endorsement of the Quebec separatists was unacceptable to the people and government of Canada, and the president abandoned his tour and flew home.

In May 1968 the General had to hasten home again from a state visit—this time from Rumania to a France in chaotic convulsions as students rioted and workers took over factories. The shaken president, having first assured himself of the army's support, rallied the nation with the cry: ''I shall not withdraw. I have a mandate from the people.'' A million pro-government supporters marched down the Champs-Élysées to demonstrate on his behalf. The following year he ill-advisedly and unnecessarily elevated a referendum on reform of the Senate and of regional government into a vote of confidence in himself, and was defeated. Thus, on April 28, 1969, he sent the following terse message to Paris from Colombey-les-Deux-Églises: ''I am ceasing to exercise my functions as president of the republic. This decision takes effect at noon today.'' During the ensuing elections, which returned his protégé Pompidou to the presidency, he studiously absented himself on a holiday in Ireland. He returned to live the last year of his life in seclusion at his beloved Colombey-les-Deux-Églises. Following his wishes, expressed very clearly in a document written in 1952, his funeral was simple and private, attended by his widow, his son and his wife, and his daughter and her husband. His remains were laid in a family grave beside those of his handicapped daughter Anne, who had died at the age of 20. At the same moment, the mighty ones of the earth—kings, presidents, and prime ministers—gathered in Notre Dame, Paris, at a memorial service in honour of the last of the great leaders of the Second World War.

De Gaulle's published works include: *La Discorde chez l'Ennemi*; *Le Fil de l'Épée*; *Vers l'Armée de Métier*; *La France et son Armée*; *Discours et Messages*; *Mémoires de Guerre*; *Mémoires d'Espoir* (1st vol.).

Genée, Dame Adeline (1878–1970). One of the greatest dancers of her day, and a tireless worker for British ballet, Dame Adeline Genée died on April 23, 1970. Born at Hinnerup, near Aarhus, Denmark, on January 6, 1878, the surviving twin daughter of Peter Jensen, and christened Anina, from the age of four she showed

a love of dancing which was encouraged by her father's brother, a ballet-master and dancer, whose professional name of Genée she was to take. He also changed her christian name to Adeline, after the famous singer, Adeline Patti. After training in her uncle's ballet school, she made her début in Christiania (now Oslo) when she was ten and became *première danseuse* in Stettin in 1893. In 1897 she appeared at the Empire Theatre, Leicester Square, London, with a six-week contract which was to last for ten years. In pre-Diaghilev England, ballet was a virtuoso music-hall act and little more. In 1902 she danced at the Royal Theatre, Copenhagen, in 1905 appeared at a command performance before Edward VII and Queen Alexandra (the first dancer ever to be given this honour), and in 1907 made her first tour of the U.S.A. Her marriage in 1910 to a businessman, Frank Isitt, brought her great happiness until his death in 1939.

After further tours in the U.S.A. and Australia, and appearances in London, her official retirement from dancing came in 1914, although she performed several times until 1917, and last appeared in June 1932 when she danced with Anton Dolin at a charity performance. In 1920 she became the first president of the newly founded Association of Teachers of Operatic Dancing, which in 1936 became the Royal Academy of Dancing. She was created D.B.E. in 1950. She maintained her interest in ballet to the end of her life, only resigning her presidency of the Royal Academy of Dancing when she was 80. On the day of her death the audience of the Adeline Genée Theatre, East Grinstead, which was opened in 1967, paid silent tribute to this great dancer and supporter of all causes which advanced the professional interest of young dancers.

Graham, Martha (born 1893). America's finest dancer and the greatest innovator in ''free'' dance since Isadora Duncan, the founder of the Martha Graham school of contemporary dance retired in October 1970 fifty years after her first appearance on the stage. During this time she created

Martha Graham retired from the stage.

dramatic and abstract ballets that in form and style represented a complete break from the conventions of classical ballet. Though tiny and fragile, she portrayed with startling ferocity repressions, violence, and frustration inherent in characters such as Phaedra, Jocasta, and Clytemnestra. In the ballets she created she used music, décor, choreography, and sometimes the spoken word to lay bare the unconscious motives and conflicts that determine action. She preferred to use original music, commissioning works from Aaron Copland, Norman Dello Joio, William Schumann, and others. At one time she became fascinated by the American pioneer spirit and produced the joyous *Appalachian Spring* (1944), but more typical in its introspection is her masterpiece *Clytemnestra* (1958), created at a time when she was deeply interested in Greek myths.

Martha Graham was born in Pittsburg. She entered the school of Ruth St Denis and Ted Shawn in 1916, dancing with them until 1923. After two years on Broadway in *Greenwich Village Follies* she devoted herself to transforming the face of modern ballet as dancer, choreographer, and teacher. In 1930 Léonide Massine and Leopold Stokowski chose her to dance the lead in the New York premiere of Stravinsky's *Rite of Spring*. The same year she founded the Dance Repertory Theatre in New York. In 1932 she became the first dancer to receive a Guggenheim fellowship. She took companies on tours to more than 40 countries throughout the world. She choreographed about 150 solo and ensemble productions, including three films, *A Dancer's World* (1957), *Appalachian Spring* (1958), and *Night Journey* (1960). Among her finest stage ballets are *Punch and Judy* (1941), *Deaths and Entrances* (1943), *Dark Meadow* (1946), *Errand into the Maze* (1947), and *Episodes* (1959). In all her work she used the dancers as vehicles of intense emotion. She has said: "I want to make people feel intensely alive; I'd rather have them against me than indifferent."

Gunther, John (1901–1970). This American author and journalist, whose bestselling "Inside" books were translated into over 90 languages, died in New York on May 29. Born in Chicago, Gunther graduated from the city's university before joining the Chicago *Daily News* as a reporter in 1922. In 1924 he was transferred to the paper's London staff, the first of the journeys that were to take him more miles and to more countries than any other journalist of his time. His first "Inside" book, *Inside Europe*, published in 1936, was an overnight success. Revised and republished many times, it was issued in a dozen languages and sold a million copies. In 1939 *Inside Asia*, which dealt with the whole continent except for Siberia, appeared and was similarly acclaimed. Then came the Second World War and Gunther worked as a war correspondent, taking part in the invasion of Sicily and Italy in 1943. After the war he

John Gunther, the "Inside" author.

returned to his travels, undeterred by increasingly weakened eyesight, and his "Inside" books examined life in Africa, Russia, South America, and Latin America with a lively, enquiring mind. He readily admitted to the charge that his books were superficial, but said that "they're fun to write, and people like them." This was certainly true, for by 1969 more than 3½ million copies had been sold. He had the great gift of bringing distant places to life, of simplifying ideas, and, through his interviews, of making the world's contemporary leaders into real people rather than just names to his countless readers. Among his other books are *Behind the Iron Curtain*; *Roosevelt in Retrospect* (his personal favourite); *Eisenhower, the Man and the Symbol*; *The Riddle of MacArthur*; *Alexander the Great*; and *Julius Caesar*.

Hall, Henry (born 1899). Famous for three decades for broadcast programmes introduced by his signature tune *Here's to the Next Time* and the words "Hello, everyone, this *is* Henry Hall speaking," the band leader Henry Hall retired from broadcasting on April 27, 1970. He ended

Henry Hall gave up broadcasting.

his last broadcast by saying "Goodbye, for this is the end of a very long time in broadcasting." In fact, he joined the BBC in 1932, succeeding Jack Payne as leader of the BBC Dance Orchestra. At 33 he was already an experienced band leader. As a boy he played the cornet with the Salvation Army, and he became secretary to its music department in 1914. In 1922 he was appointed resident pianist at the Midland Hotel, Manchester, after making a great impression as deputy pianist. By the time he joined the BBC, he was in charge of 32 orchestras playing at hotels run by the London, Midland, and Scottish Railway, and was broadcasting regularly from Manchester and Gleneagles.

Henry Hall conducted the BBC Dance Orchestra in the first broadcast from the new Broadcasting House on March 15, 1932. He soon added to the original 14 members of the orchestra, particularly by expanding the brass section. His guest nights began in 1934 and attracted enormous audiences; some were rebroadcast in the U.S.A. and Canada. His quiet, urbane manner was well suited to the tuneful, rather sentimental melodies that formed the basis of his repertoire, although he always tried to introduce new ideas and to extend the scope of his programmes with his own "Hall marks."

Henry Hall left the BBC in 1937 to freelance. But after the Second World War he once more entertained audiences on both radio and television with his inimitable brand of melodies old and new. He was made C.B.E. in June 1970.

Hallstrom, Sir Edward (1886–1970). The name of Sir Edward Hallstrom, who died in Sydney on February 27, 1970, will always be remembered in association with Sydney's Taronga Park Zoo, which had been the chief interest in the busy life of this millionaire Australian philanthropist. Sir Edward, who built a fortune from the manufacture of household refrigerators, spent thousands of dollars on animals and rare birds for the Zoo, making it one of the best known in the world. He also gave generously to many other causes, among them medical research projects and the establishment of an experimental sheep-breeding station in the highlands of New Guinea. Born at Coonamble, N.S.W., on September 25, 1886, Edward John Lees Hallstrom was the son of an English migrant, and the eighth of nine children. Leaving school at 13, he got his first job in a furniture factory and was in charge of it by the age of 18. At 21 he had his own factory in Sydney, making first ice-chests, then cabinets for refrigerators, and finally cheap units to go inside the cabinets. Taking out his own patents, he built up a big business, which grew even larger with the boom in refrigerator sales following the Second World War.

As a small boy Hallstrom was already an animal and bird lover and a regular visitor to Sydney's zoo; as an adult he was to become its greatest benefactor, and in one year (1947) donated to Taronga Park more than 1,500 birds and animals. He said: "I was determined to make Taronga Park one of the finest zoos in the world, and I did that.'' Chairman of the Taronga Park Trust from 1948 to 1959, he was knighted in 1952, and in 1963 was elected an honorary fellow of the Zoological Society of London.

Harada, Mashahiko (born 1943). ''Fighting'' Harada's announcement of his retirement in 1970 ended a career which had heralded the arrival of Japanese fighters as a major force in the lighter weights of professional boxing. Harada made boxing history on October 10, 1962, when he became the youngest-ever undisputed world champion. He knocked out the Siamese holder Pone Kingpetch in the 11th round of their flyweight title fight in Tokyo to cause one of the biggest-ever boxing upsets. Because of his age and lack of experience, Harada had been given little chance and, indeed, he enjoyed only a short flyweight reign, losing to Kingpetch in their Bangkok return match just three months after his Tokyo triumph. Increasing weight then forced Harada into the bantamweight division, and he won the world title from Brazil's Eder Jofre on May 18, 1965. Ironically, the tables were turned on the one-time boy prodigy when Harada finally lost his world bantamweight title to the little-known 20-year-old Australian aborigine Lionel Rose in February 1968. Born on April 5, 1943, Harada was the son of a tree surgeon.

Harben, Philip (1906–1970). Known to millions of viewers in Britain for many years as the television cook, the bearded affable Philip Harben died on April 27, 1970. With his racy style and cheerful personality, he made cooking appear a delightful pleasure rather than a solemn ritual. In his striped butcher's apron he became one of the first great television personalities as, with a twinkle in his eye, he gave remarkably clear descriptions and demonstrations of how to prepare both simple and classic dishes. He took neither cooking nor himself too seriously, although he did really care about the quality of food, and in private life he was a legend to his friends for the magnificent meals he prepared for them.

Harben was the son of Hubert Harben and actress Mary Jerrold. He joined his mother's profession as a stage manager, but soon left the theatre to become a fashion photographer. In 1939 he took up a position as supervisor of BOAC's test kitchen. Four years later he was appointed managing director of Quality Inns' canteen department. He became the BBC's television cook in 1946, and was soon drawing vast audiences. Later he moved to commercial television. In 1959 he gave up television work altogether, and started a successful business as a manufacturer of coated non-stick hollowware. Philip Harben wrote several books on cookery, including *Entertaining at Home*, *Traditional Dishes of Britain*, *Cooking with Harben*, and *The Tools of Cooking*.

Edward Heath, Britain's new P.M.

Heath, Edward Richard George (born 1916). Following the election of June 18, 1970, Edward Heath—leader of the victorious Conservatives—became prime minister of the United Kingdom. He was born at the seaside resort of Broadstairs, Kent, on July 9, 1916, the son of a local builder, and was educated at Chatham House School, Ramsgate, and Balliol College, Oxford, where he read philosophy, politics, and economics, and won an organ scholarship. While an undergraduate he hitch-hiked across Europe, and toured the U.S.A. as a member of the University debating team. He was president of the Oxford Union. In 1939 he enlisted in the Royal Artillery and fought in north-west Europe. He was awarded the M.B.E. (military), was mentioned in despatches, and reached the rank of lieutenant-colonel. After the war Edward Heath worked as a civil servant in the ministry of civil aviation, resigning in 1947 to enter politics. In the general election of 1950 he won the marginal seat of Bexley from Labour, and he has represented that constituency ever since.

Edward Heath was one of the nine Conservative M.P.s who wrote the book *One Nation—a Tory Approach to Social Problems* which greatly influenced Conservative thinking on social and industrial affairs. In 1951 he was appointed assistant whip, and following the Conservative victory in that year became a government whip. By 1955 he was parliamentary secretary to the treasury, chief whip, and a privy councillor. He was minister of labour from 1959 to 1960, and lord privy seal and spokesman in the Commons on foreign affairs from 1960 to 1963. It was during the latter period that he conducted negotiations with the heads of the E.E.C. (Common Market) on the question of Britain's entry. Although the negotiations failed, Heath was acclaimed for his handling of them. It was the detailed haggling during these negotiations over import charges for every conceivable product—including Australian kangaroo meat—that earned him the soubriquet ''Grocer'' Heath. His efforts in Europe were recognized by the

award of the Charlemagne prize—given each year for the ''most notable achievement in the service of international understanding and co-operation in Europe''. Winston Churchill is the only other Englishman to have received this award. In October 1963, Heath was appointed secretary of state for industry, trade, and regional development, and next year he became responsible for economic affairs in the Douglas-Home administration. On Sir Alec's resignation in July 1965, Edward Heath was elected leader of the Conservative party, the first to be chosen under the new system of voting by the parliamentary party.

A bachelor with a somewhat ''square'' if dependable appearance and a ''plummy'' manner, Heath lacks the wit and subtlety of his arch-rival, Harold Wilson, and consistently trailed far behind him in public opinion polls assessing the personal popularity of the pair. But his lack-lustre image received a fillip in December 1969 when he sailed his yacht *Morningcloud* to victory in the 630-mile Sydney–Hobart yacht race. He has a home in his native Broadstairs and a flat in the Albany, enjoys travel, sailing, and sea fishing, and is also an accomplished musician on organ, piano, and conductor's rostrum.

Hendrix, Jimi (1945?–1970). This singing and guitar-playing star whose anarchic violence on stage made him a phenomenon even in the frenzied world of ''pop'', died in London of a drug overdose on September 18, 1970. He was born in Seattle, Washington, of mixed African, Mexican, and Cherokee ancestry, on, by his own account, November 27, 1945, although some place his birth date a few years earlier. Abandoning school early, he hitch-hiked around the southern states before turning up in New York, where he worked in vaudeville and joined the Isley Brothers as a backing guitarist. As a guitarist he toured America, backing various singers, including Little Richard, and in 1966 he formed his own band in Greenwich Village. Here he was discovered by Chas Chandler, former bass guitarist with the Animals, who persuaded him to cross the Atlantic to England. In London, the Jimi Hendrix Experience was formed and the singer quickly found fame and fortune. He was known for the wildness of his performances and appearance; his music, which throbbed with electric energy, was rooted deep in the negro Blues tradition and also owed much to Bob Dylan and the electronic techniques of amplification and feedback. Returning to the U.S.A., he was banned from a tour by the action of the outraged Daughters of the American Revolution, who considered his act obscene. In Hendrix's world this was the final seal of success, and during 1968 he was acclaimed one of the world's most popular rock stars. The following year he spent in seclusion working on new musical ideas at home. Early 1970 saw the birth of his new trio, the Band of Gipsies, which appeared at the Isle of Wight ''pop'' festival during August. The

Gipsies, however, did not come up to his expectations, and his last public statement said that he planned to form a new, big band. Behind his stage façade, Hendrix was a shy and amiable man, totally involved with his music. He was subject, however, to fits of depression, relieved by the drugs which ended his life.

Huddleston, Rt. Rev. Trevor (born 1913). During 1970 Bishop Trevor Huddleston made a strong impact on the British scene as one of the most vigorous opponents of the South African cricket tour (which was cancelled) and a fierce critic of the new Conservative government's proposal to resume the sale of arms to South Africa. He follows the tradition of many English rebels in being born and bred right in the "Establishment". He was born in 1913, the son of a knight, and educated at Lancing and Christ Church, Oxford. He trained for the Anglican priesthood at Wells, and was professed as a member of the Community of the Resurrection in 1943. His posting in that year to the Community's work in South Africa was in fact to determine his future career. In the Bantu townships of Sophiatown and Orlando he became aware of the effect of apartheid, and in 1956 gave expression to his passionate convictions in a book, *Naught For Your Comfort*, which was to bring him instant fame. In the same year Aberdeen honoured him with its D.D., but his own community (amid some criticism) recalled him to be guardian of novices at the mother house in Yorkshire. After a short period as prior of the London house he was elected Bishop of Masasi, in Tanzania, in 1960. He served in that impoverished diocese until 1968, and his convictions about the urgency of world development became as strong as his hatred of racism. In 1969 he became Bishop of Stepney, and made his home in London's East End in the Commercial Road. His controversial positions and power of ready, incisive speech, allied to a gaunt face and magnetic eyes, made him an ideal performer on television, and although his ministry has been for so short a time in Britain he has become one of the best-known religious leaders.

Bishop Trevor Huddleston.

**Ray Illingworth,
England's new cricket captain.**

Illingworth, Raymond (born 1932). While playing his 20th season of first-class cricket, this slow off-spin bowler and sturdily driving middle-order batsman was chosen to lead England on the tour of Australia beginning in autumn 1970. He had been appointed team captain originally as deputy to the injured Colin Cowdrey in 1969, when the defeated visitors were West Indies, against whom he scored a century, and New Zealand; then in nine innings against the Rest of the World he only twice failed to reach 43, and never looked like being deposed. It was a late fruition of talent, for the earliest of Illingworth's 41 test matches was in 1958 against New Zealand, where five years later he became the third native of Pudsey to go in first for England. His tour of West Indies in 1959–60 was unspectacular, though selection for it gained from *Wisden* a place among the "five cricketers of the year". A new radiation of authority seemed to arrive with a change of county allegiance; for after the 1968 season Yorkshire, unwilling to grant a three-year contract, let him depart. Leicestershire were repaid for installing him as captain when he headed their averages for both batting and bowling. Illingworth's noteworthy performances include the following: in six seasons he achieved the double of 1,000 runs and 100 wickets; he finished second in the national bowling averages for 1956; hit 100 for the Players off the Gentlemen in 1959; and captured 15 wickets in a match at Swansea in 1960. His day of days was September 7, 1967, when at Harrogate he claimed 14 victims in an afternoon (7 for 58 and 7 for 6) to bring Yorkshire victory that clinched another championship. The son of a joiner, Illingworth went to school at Farsley and first learned his profession with local cricket teams.

Jenkins, Clive (born 1926). *Bon viveur*, wit, newspaper columnist, and leader of the fastest-growing trade union in Great Britain, white-collar revolutionary Clive Jenkins is seldom out of the headlines.

In March 1970 he was prominent in opposition to the plan to form a privately owned "second line" airline in rivalry with the nationalized BEA and BOAC, and caused a fluttering in the dovecotes of the publishing world when he invited publishing executives to join his Association of Scientific, Technical and Managerial Staffs. Jenkins thrives under criticism, but receives very little from his members. Under his guidance the association's membership has grown from 22,000 in 1961 to nearly 200,000 in 1970. A railway worker's son, he is one of the four highest-paid union leaders in the country.

David Clive Jenkins was born on May 2, 1926, in Port Talbot, Glamorganshire. He was educated at local schools and attended evening classes at Swansea Technical College. In 1940 he started work in a metallurgical factory, becoming a shift supervisor after two years and in charge of the laboratory after three. His trade-union career began in 1946 when he was appointed branch secretary and area treasurer of the Association of Scientific Workers. In 1947 he became divisional officer of the Association of Supervisory Staffs Executives and Technicians (ASSET). In 1961 he became its joint

**Clive Jenkins,
white-collar trade unionist.**

general secretary, at 34 the youngest man ever to reach such a position. From 1967 to 1968 he was chairman of the National Joint Council for Civil Air Transport. In 1968 his union became the Association of Scientific, Technical and Managerial Staffs. Jenkins has shown himself a brilliant negotiator, with a razor-sharp mind and typical Welsh eloquence. He is a great phrase-maker: in 1968 he declared "the Prices and Incomes policy is as irrelevant as the blush on a dead man's cheek."

Jenkins enjoys the luxuries success has brought—his motor-launch moored at the bottom of his garden, his bespoke suits, his elegant office. His attitude to life is summed up by his favourite phrase: "It's all a lot of fun really, isn't it?" In September 1970 he accepted a commission from Thames TV to do television *reportage* from North Vietnam.

Johnston, George (1912–1970). For many years of his life Australian novelist George Johnston, who died in Sydney on July 22, 1970, had been an expatriate; yet his greatest strength as a writer lay in his ability to interpret Australia and aspects of the Australian experience. This strength was first fully realized in his most successful novel, *My Brother Jack,* published in 1964. Following its publication, Johnston and his wife, writer Charmian Clift, returned with their family to live in Australia. However, their presence on the local literary scene was to be tragically brief: Charmian Clift died in July 1969, and her husband, who had been in ill-health for some time, a year later.

The son of a tramways employee, George Johnston was born in Melbourne on July 20, 1912, and grew up in the Caulfield district of that city. He was educated at state schools, took a job as a printer's assistant, and attended night classes at the National Gallery of Art. Later he became a journalist, and during the Second World War established an international reputation with his dispatches from battle zones for American magazines and Australian newspapers. His first success as a novelist came in 1948, when *High Valley,* written in collaboration with his wife, won first prize in a literary competition conducted by the *Sydney Morning Herald. The Big Chariot,* also written with his wife, was published in 1953, and in 1954, having spent a period in London, Johnston decided to give up a well-paid newspaper position to live in Greece and write creatively for a living. The Johnstons lived on the island of Hydra for ten years, during which George published *The Sponge Divers* (1955), *The Darkness Outside* (1959), *Closer to the Sun* (1960), and *The Far Road* (1962).

On his return to Australia, *My Brother Jack,* in which the author recreated his youth in the Melbourne of the 1920s and 1930s, was adapted as a serial for television. A sequel to *My Brother Jack,* entitled *Clean Straw for Nothing,* was published in 1969, and both novels won the Miles Franklin Award, given annually for an outstanding Australian novel.

Joseph, Maxwell (born 1914). With Grand Metropolitan Hotels' successful £33 million bid for Mecca in late June 1970—a few weeks after taking over Berni Inns—Maxwell Joseph, the financier and hotel tycoon, snatched the "Mr. Biggest" mantle that had briefly adorned the shoulders of his arch-rival, Sir Charles Forte, in the booming world of British catering. After the Mecca deal, Joseph's "Grand Met" controlled a commercial empire with a market capitalization of £135 million, assets of £100 million, and pre-tax profits of £16 million.

As a youth Maxwell Joseph trained in estate agency, starting with a firm in Hampstead which dealt in the selling of small hotels. This gave him an invaluable insight into the property business that was to boom so profitably after the war, and a particular knowledge of hotels. On leaving

the army in 1945 (having attained the rank of lance-corporal in the Royal Engineers) Joseph bought his first hotel, in London's Bayswater, and then made his first big "killing" when he bought and renovated a bomb-damaged hotel off Wigmore Street, London. When he acquired this ruin in the late 1940s it contained a mere six rooms and one bathroom, and cost him £25,000; by 1970 it was worth £600,000. The rising tycoon firmly established himself with his successful tender for the Washington Hotel, Mayfair, built for tourists visiting the Festival of Britain, 1951.

There followed the Green Park, the May Fair, Gordon Hotels, and a £1 million take-over of the Mount Royal. This huge deal brought Joseph into the City, and it was natural that from that time onwards he should begin to branch out beyond the hotel business—particularly into the world of investment companies and merchant banking which, in 1970, formed an important part of the web of companies he controlled. Joseph's domain, however, remains predominantly a catering empire, including, besides those mentioned, the Chef and Brewer chain, the Express Dairy, the Old Kentucky Restaurants, and Crockford's gaming club.

Kearton, Christopher Frank Kearton, Baron (born 1911). One of the most prominent of the new breed of businessmen on whom Britain depends for success in the technological age, a scientist-cum-salesman-cum-administrator, Frank Kearton, chairman of Courtauld's, received a life peerage in 1970. As a scientist he is a Fellow of the Royal Society who worked on the "Manhattan" atomic bomb project during the war. As a businessman he came to the fore in 1961 when he was instrumental in fighting off a £200 million bid from I.C.I. for Courtauld's, of which he was then deputy chairman. As an administrator he was called in as first chairman of the Industrial Reorganization Corporation, the government-backed body set up in 1966 to promote rationalization by, in particular, regrouping industries into larger units.

Born on February 17, 1911, Kearton went from Hanley high school to St John's College, Oxford, where he gained a first-class degree in natural science. He joined I.C.I., working in research and technical development on a number of products. After his war-time spell as a co-ordinator of atomic energy development, he joined Courtauld's in 1946, as the head of its chemical engineering research section. In 1952 he was taken on to the board, and his career became set in the cut and thrust of business. As well as fighting off bids from others, he has fought through Courtauld's own take-overs, expanding the firm to a £400 million giant. He personally negotiated contracts valued at £40 million for the erection of man-made fibre plants in the Soviet Union, Poland, Yugoslavia, and China. At one time he reckoned to travel 100,000 miles a year in search of new

Lord Kearton, chairman of Courtauld's.

business. His commitments also include chairmanship of the Electricity Supply Research Council, part-time membership of the U.K. Atomic Energy Authority, and membership of the National Economic Development Council (Neddy), the council of the Confederation of British Industry, and the advisory council on technology. He was knighted in 1966.

Kerensky, Alexander Fyodorovitch (1881–1970). Liberal revolutionary, brilliant orator, and frustrated idealist, Alexander Kerensky died on June 11, 1970, in New York. One of the early leaders in the Russian revolution of 1917, when Tsar Nicholas II abdicated he became a member of the first provisional government and eventually rose to be prime minister, but he found it impossible to impose his moderate approach in the red-hot revolutionary climate of Russia. He was overthrown by the Bolsheviks and compelled to live the remainder of his life in exile.

Kerensky was born in the Volga city of Simbirsk (now Ulyanovsk). His father was the headmaster of the local high school, which Kerensky attended before going to Petrograd (Leningrad) University to study law. There he became convinced of the need for a peaceful revolution in Russia. He went to Paris for a while and then settled in Moscow, where he made his reputation as a crusading barrister. He lost no opportunity of attacking the arbitrary government of the Tsar and was happy to defend those accused of political offences. He was elected to the Duma, the Russian parliament, in 1912, and joined a small group of moderate revolutionary socialists.

After the Tsar's abdication in March 1917, Kerensky accepted the post of minister of justice in the liberal provisional government formed by Prince Lvov. He was a powerful figure, being the only Socialist and vice-president of the militant Petrograd Soviet. Kerensky at once ordered the release of all political prisoners and exiles; a general amnesty followed, and the death penalty was abolished. In May, Kerensky succeeded Guchkov as minister of war.

He was anxious that Russia should remain in the war on the Allied side, but the army's morale was at rock-bottom. An offensive in July proved a complete failure, and the government fell. Kerensky took over the premiership from Prince Lvov. In September General Kornilov, the commander-in-chief, attempted a *coup d'état*. His troops refused to follow him and the attempt failed ludicrously. Week by week the influence of the revolutionary Bolsheviks was growing. Kerensky had no military support and could only await the inevitable. This came in the night of November 6–7, when Red Guards occupied strategic buildings throughout Petrograd. Kerensky escaped just before they seized the Winter Palace. After some months in hiding he left Russia in a British destroyer. He lived briefly in several European countries before settling in Paris, where he edited an emigré Russian journal *Dni* (Days). In 1940 he went to the U.S.A. where he lectured and wrote his memoirs.

Knight, Dame Laura (1877–1970). This distinguished artist. best known to her paintings of circus and fairground life and backstage scenes at the ballet, died on July 8, 1970, aged 92. The daughter of Charles Johnson, she was born at Long Eaton, Derbyshire, and brought up in Nottingham, where her mother was an art teacher. Even as a small child she shared her mother's ambition that she should become a painter, and although in her early years she experienced real poverty and many difficulties she never wavered in her determination. After her mother's death Laura took over her classes in an artists' colony at Staithes, near Whitby, and it was here that she met her future husband, Harold Knight, whom she married in 1903. The young couple went to live among a colony of painters at Newlyn, Cornwall, and from here Laura Knight began to contribute regularly to the Royal Academy. Her first major success was "The Daughters of the Sun", a picture of girls bathing from the rocks in Mount's Bay. Other paintings included portraits of local people, and landscapes of the Land's End area.

After the First World War Laura Knight began to paint pictures of circus life, spending many hours at Olympia and the Royal Agricultural Hall, Islington. She loved the circus and its people, and for a time gave up her studio to travel with them, sharing every aspect of their nomadic life. Later she became equally fascinated by gypsies, and lived and travelled with them, painting their portraits and scenes of their day-to-day activities. During the Second World War, factories and munition works captured her interest and imagination; her pictures of men and women at work vividly captured the mood and urgency of the times, and will, like her circus and gypsy paintings, surely interest social historians in years to come.

From the day in 1927 when she was elected A.R.A. Laura Knight received many honours. She was created D.B.E. in 1929, and in 1936, the same year that

her memoirs, *Oil Paint and Grease Paint* were published, she was elected R.A., the first woman since Angelica Kauffmann in 1768 to receive this honour. When her husband became an R.A. a year later they were the first married couple in history to be Royal Academicians at one and the same time. After he died in 1961 she continued to live in their old home at St. John's Wood, London, and to exhibit regularly at the Royal Academy.

Lange, Halvard Manthey (1902–1970). Halvard Lange, the Norwegian statesman and a founding father of the NATO alliance, died in Oslo on May 19, 1970. He was born on September 16, 1902, the son of the distinguished pacifist, historian, and politician, Christian Lange, who won the Nobel Peace Prize in 1921. His father's travels led to an international education for Halvard. He attended schools in Belgium and Italy, the University of Geneva, and the London School of Economics before graduating at Oslo University in 1929. On graduation he immersed himself in the affairs of the Norwegian Labour party, becoming, in 1938, rector of the Norwegian trade union college. The German invasion of 1940 found Lange actively involved in the Norwegian resistance. In August 1940 he was captured and kept naked in a cell for four months, after which—his spirit unbroken and confession unsigned—he was released. In 1942 he was again arrested and was sent to the concentration camp at Sachsenhausen, where he became the leader and champion of the Norwegian prisoners and embarked, with Gerhardsen—the future Prime Minister of Norway—on drawing up a post-war programme for the Labour party.

Shortly after the war Lange became foreign minister. To begin with, he followed the neutralist policies of his predecessor Trygve Lie, but the onset of the Cold War made such a stance impossible to one of Lange's unequivocal nature. The final prods to his thinking were the Communist coup in Czechoslovakia in 1948, and the breakdown of plans for a Nordic defensive union. Thus, under his influence, Norway linked herself with the other NATO powers in 1949. He had been out of office since the Norwegian Labour party's defeat in 1965, but remained a member of the Norwegian parliament. He spent his last years engaged in political research and advocating Norwegian entry into the Common Market.

Lee, Gypsy Rose (1914–1970). The queen of burlesque, the stripper who quoted from Huxley and Spinoza and disapproved of nudity, Gypsy Rose Lee died on April 26, 1970. She regarded stripping as an art form. She always retained enough clothes to satisfy the authorities, remembering the advice of an early mentor, Tessie the Tassel-Twirler: "You gotta leave 'em hungry for more. You don't dump the whole roast on the platter." Born in Seattle Rose Louise Hovick, Gypsy was

**Gypsy Rose Lee,
doyenne of strippers.**

only four years old when she joined her formidable mother and her sister June on the vaudeville circuit. Her mother gave her much earthy advice, such as "Do unto others before they do you". At 17, Gypsy was a star at Minsky's Republic Theatre in New York. She soon reached the top of the tree with the Ziegfeld Follies. She also appeared in a number of films, and starred as the Bible-thumping gospeller Aimee Semple McPherson. She retired from stripping in 1937 when at the height of her fame. She wrote several thrillers, with titles such as *G-String Murders* and *Mother Finds a Body*. Her entertaining autobiography *Gypsy* was made into a Broadway musical and a film. An intelligent woman and the possessor of a strong sense of humour, she was the most respectable of strippers. When interviewed in 1969 about trends in the modern theatre, she remarked: "The way things are now, the men and women on the stage are nude, the musicians are nude, the members of the audience are nude, there is no one with any clothes on but the police."

Liddell Hart, Sir Basil Henry (1895–1970). Sir Basil Liddell Hart, the military critic and historian whose revolutionary ideas concerning mechanized warfare, published between the wars, were mastered by the Germans before they penetrated the minds of his compatriots, died on January 29, 1970, at the age of 74. He was born on October 31, 1895, the son of Rev. Bramly Hart, and educated at St. Paul's School and Corpus Christi College, Cambridge, where he was reading history when the First World War broke out. He was commissioned in the King's Own Yorkshire Light Infantry in 1914, and fought at Ypres and on the Somme. His experience of these mass infantry battles and their tremendous slaughter exercised a potent influence on his tactical thinking —and he was one of the earliest and most trenchant advocates of surprise, mobility, and the avoidance of vast and costly confrontations. While recovering from wounds in 1916 he wrote a book analysing the Somme offensive which contained his evolution of a battle drill system which was adopted by the War Office after the war, then abandoned, and readopted in 1940. With the end of the First World War, aged 24, Liddell Hart was asked to re-draft the infantry training manual and he first published in it the "expanding torrent" method of attack—ironically the blueprint for the German *blitzkrieg* of 1940. In 1924 he joined the Royal Tank Corps, but, owing to his wounds, was found unfit for general service and put on half pay, retiring from the army in 1927.

As a civilian he supported himself by writing on military matters, bringing out a number of books and serving as military correspondent first of the *Daily Telegraph* and then of *The Times*, from the columns of which he conducted a partially successful campaign for a single co-ordinated defence ministry and ceaselessly advocated mechanization of the army. In 1937 he became personal adviser to Hore-Belisha, then secretary of state for war, and was thus in a position to urge his recommendations on the War Office. The combined efforts of Liddell Hart and Hore-Belisha failed to push their reforms through, however, and the waspish tactician withdrew from the partnership in 1938 to carry on the fight from his old territory, *The Times*. He disagreed, however, with his paper's policy over the British government's guarantee to Poland—which he dismissed as absurd and dangerous—and resigned in 1939. From 1941 until the end of the war he wrote war commentaries for the *Daily Mail*. After the conflict he worked as the most distinguished British military historian. His last book, a monumental history of the Second World War, was finished in 1969 and he was working on the proofs at the time of his death.

Sir Basil was knighted in 1966. Among his 30 books are *Paris, or the Future of War* (1925), *The Strategy of Indirect Approach* (1929), *A History of the World War, 1914–18*, biographies of Scipio, Sherman, Foch, and T. E. Lawrence, *The Tanks* (1959), *Memoirs*, Vols. I and II (1965), *History of the Second World War* (1970).

Lockhart, Sir Robert Bruce (1887–1970). The diplomat and writer Robert Hamilton Bruce Lockhart died on February 27, 1970, at the age of 82. He was born on September 2, 1887, and educated at Fettes where he distinguished himself as a Rugby player. After preliminary training in France and Germany he passed a competitive examination into the Foreign Office and went as vice-consul to Moscow. Here he played Soccer for the famous *Motozovsti* and became acting consul-general on the illness of his chief. Diplomatic relations were broken off at the outbreak of the revolution, but in 1918 the "boy ambassador" was sent to St. Petersburg and Moscow as head of a special mission to the Soviet government. While Lockhart's graphic dispatches were appreciated in Whitehall, the British decision to send

troops into Russia was viewed less than warmly by the Bolsheviks and the British mission was somewhat coolly received. Lockhart himself was flung into jail, where he languished a few weeks before being exchanged for Litvinov, the Soviet representative in London whom the British smartly arrested as a hostage on hearing of their agent's misfortune. Although Lockhart had advised against military intervention, his involvement in the affair made him something of a *bête noir* in Soviet mythology and he was condemned to death in his absence.

In 1920 Bruce Lockhart went to Prague as commercial secretary and thus began an interest in Czechoslovakia which lasted the rest of his life. In 1922 he resigned from the Foreign Office but remained in Central Europe as a banker until 1928. In that year he was taken under the wing of Lord Beaverbrook, and he was on the staff of the *Evening Standard* until 1937. Meanwhile he published *Memoirs of a British Agent* (1932), an account of his adventures in Russia. This was followed by *Retreat from Glory* (1934), describing his life in Czechoslovakia, and *Return to Malaya* (1936), an account of his youthful experience as a rubber planter in 1908.

In 1940 Lockhart was appointed British representative to the Czechoslovak government in exile, working in close association with Jan Masaryk, whom he had known for 20 years. In 1941 he became deputy under-secretary of state in the Foreign Office, directing the Political Warfare Executive. After the war he worked almost exclusively as a writer, bringing out such works as *Jan Masaryk* (1951), *My Europe* (1952), *Your England* (1955), *Friends, Foes, and Foreigners* (1957), and *Ace of Spades* (1968). Sir Bruce was created K.C.M.G. in 1943.

McLaren, Bruce (1938–1970). Although only 32, Bruce McLaren had raced in Grand Prix events for nearly 12 years when the Can-Am car he was testing at Goodwood on June 2, 1970, veered off the Lavant straight at 170 m.p.h. and he was killed when it struck an observer's hut.

Bruce McLaren crashed to his death.

Born in Auckland, New Zealand, he contracted Perthe's disease, which resulted in deformation of the hip and a subsequent slight limp that many wrongly attributed to a racing accident. As a child he spent two years (from 9 to 11) in hospital. His father was a garage owner and a leading motor cyclist in New Zealand; he gave Bruce his first car at the age of 15, and the young McLaren was soon a familiar figure in hill climbs and racing. After success in an ex-Brabham 1750 c.c. Cooper-Climax, he finally gave up his engineering studies at Auckland University, and came to Britain in 1957 to drive a works Formula 2 car. He finished second in the Formula 2 championship that year and fifth in 1958. The following year he became a full member of the Cooper racing team and won the United States GP, his first GP victory. By 1965, when Brabham left Cooper's, McLaren was their leading driver. In 1963 he had formed Bruce McLaren Motor Racing Ltd., and in 1967 won the Can-Am championship with one of his own cars. He won the 1967 Le Mans 24-hour race with Chris Amon, in 1968 won the Race of Champions and the Belgian GP, and in 1970 was second in the Spanish GP. McLaren Racing and the associated construction firm, the Lambretta-Trojan Group, became British motor sport's major dollar-earner. In 1968 Bruce McLaren was awarded the Ferodo trophy in acknowledgment of his work on the construction and development of Can-Am winning cars.

Macleod, Iain Norman (1913–1970). Scarcely had the Conservative government settled into office following their victory in the British elections of June 1970 when they were robbed of one of their most formidable leaders, Iain Macleod, the newly appointed chancellor of the exchequer, who died suddenly of a heart attack on July 20, 1970, following an appendicitis operation. Iain Macleod was one of the "One Nation" group of Conservative theorists who, under the leadership of R. A. Butler, set out soon after the war to reshape Conservative thinking and policies and create a party of broad and popular appeal in line with the Tory philosophy of Disraeli and Lord Randolph Churchill. Endowed with a powerful gift of rhetoric, vituperative in debate, and subtle in strategem, Macleod was the toughest member of the new Cabinet and probably the most principled. Fierce in his loyalties and dangerous to his enemies, he was reputed to have been one of the few M.P.s who ever defeated Aneurin Bevan in debate. With a quixotic and passionate temperament was combined an impressive mind and exceptional memory. He played bridge for England at the age of 22.

As chancellor, Macleod had set himself the task of completely reforming the system of taxation under which Britain has suffered since the war. It was thus at the outset of what should have been the culmination of his career that he died: a fate made the more tragic by the fact that he had groomed himself rigorously for this

**Iain Macleod,
"brain" of the Conservatives.**

**Sir Robert Matthew,
British master-architect.**

the method of selection of party leader, for which office he supported the claims of his mentor, R. A. Butler. Meanwhile, Macleod took over the editorial chair of the *Spectator*, in which he remained until 1965. Following the Labour victory in 1964, he became the Opposition spokesman on steel and, later, the "shadow" chancellor. Iain Macleod married in 1941 and had a son and a daughter. His publications included *Bridge is an Easy Game* (1952) and *Neville Chamberlain* (1961).

Masham of Ilton, Baroness (born 1935). When Lady Masham was made a baroness in the 1970 New Years Honours she became, at 34, Britain's youngest life peeress. This remarkable woman was born in 1935, the younger daughter of Sir Ronald Sinclair, 8th Baron Sinclair of Dunbeath, Scotland, and was christened Susan Lilian Primrose. In 1958 she had a bad riding accident which left her permanently paralysed from the waist down. She spent nine months at the National Spinal Unit at Stoke Mandeville, Bucks, where she says being among other people in the same position as herself made her see that life in a wheelchair "wasn't the end of everything." At the time of her accident she was unofficially engaged to David Cunliffe-Lister, Lord Masham, and they married in December 1959. Since then she has led a full and active life, both in her home and outside it. The couple adopted two children, both when they were five weeks old, and Lady Masham looked after them when they were babies. Because her Yorkshire home is designed with sliding doors and has no stairs, and everything in the kitchen has been placed at a level that she can reach from her chair, Lady Masham does most of the housework and cooking herself.

Much of her time is devoted to the cause of the disabled. She is president of the Yorkshire Association for the Disabled, the Leeds Spastic Society, and the North Riding Red Cross, as well as serving on the disablement advisory committee of the Ministry of Social Security, and acting as treasurer of a Borstal camp in the North Riding. When she took her seat in the

House of Lords in April she made a moving contribution to the debate on the Chronically Sick and Disabled Persons Bill. Lady Masham still finds time for sporting activities, for she has competed in the paraplegic games in several countries, and rides with the aid of a special saddle.

Matthew, Sir Robert Hogg (born 1906). Robert Matthew, who received the Royal Gold Medal for Architecture for 1970, was born in Edinburgh in December 1906, the eldest son of John F. Matthew, well known for his work on the Scottish National War Memorial. He was educated at Melville College, Edinburgh, and studied architecture at the city's College of Art, becoming an Associate of the R.I.B.A. in 1931, and a Soane medallist and an Arthur Cates prizeman in 1932. After a two-year period of post-graduate research work on housing and planning, including the study of modern housing developments in Europe, he joined the department of health for Scotland in 1936, becoming chief architect and planning officer in 1945. In the following year he was appointed chief architect of the London County Council and remained in this post until 1953. During this period the Royal Festival Hall was built for the 1951 Festival of Britain, and the famous Roehampton housing estate was created.

In 1953 Robert Matthew was appointed professor of architecture at Edinburgh University, and also set up his own private architectural practice. Examples of his work include the Commonwealth Institute in London, the new universities of York, Bath, Stirling, and Ulster, and the Royal Commonwealth Swimming Pool in Edinburgh, constructed for the 1970 Commonwealth Games. Sir Robert was president of the International Union of Architects from 1961 to 1965, and was knighted in 1962. Since 1965 he has been president of the Commonwealth Association of Architects, whose work is concerned with furthering architectural education in the under-developed countries of Asia and Africa.

task during the years in Opposition. Nevertheless, Macleod will be remembered—first as a highly successful minister of labour, 1955–59, and secondly for his work as colonial secretary from 1959 to 1961. It was largely due to him that British Africa achieved independence almost entirely without bloodshed. His years at the colonial office earned him the implacable hostility of the Conservative right wing over the future of Rhodesia and Nyasaland. In the teeth of this opposition and also that of Sir Roy Welensky of Rhodesia, Macleod doggedly pursued the principle of majority rule. This led to the break-up of the Federation of Rhodesia and Nyasaland, the creation of the black African states of Zambia and Malawi, and, less directly, to the unilateral secession of Rhodesia.

Iain Macleod was born on November 11, 1913, at Skipton, Yorkshire, the eldest son of a doctor, and educated at Fettes, Gonville and Caius College, Cambridge, and the Inner Temple. He was badly hurt in France in 1940 when a German armoured car crashed into a road block he had set up and dislodged a tree-trunk on top of him; he suffered pain from this back injury for the rest of his life. Promoted deputy assistant quarter-master-general and a major in the 50th (Northumbrian) division, he landed in France on D-Day and afterwards served in Normandy. After the war he contested the Western Isles unsuccessfully in the 1945 elections and in the same year joined R. A. Butler's team at the Conservative research department as an expert on the social services. In 1950 he won Enfield West, the seat he held for the rest of his life. Only two years later he was appointed minister of health, after which he was successively minister of labour, colonial secretary, and chancellor of the Duchy of Lancaster and leader of the house of commons, 1961–63. He was chairman of the Conservative party, 1961–1963, and joint chairman in 1963. When ill-health forced Macmillan to retire in 1963 Macleod refused to serve under Sir Alec Douglas-Home, being affronted by

Lady Masham received a life peerage.

Maudling, Reginald (born 1917). Reginald Maudling, Conservative chancellor of the exchequer from 1962 to 1964, was appointed Home Secretary in the Conservative government formed by Edward Heath in June 1970. Maudling was born on March 7, 1917, and educated at Merchant Taylors' school and Merton College, Oxford, where he took a first in "Greats". He volunteered for the R.A.F. on the outbreak of war in 1939, but poor eyesight meant that he was not accepted until after he had been called to the bar in 1940. In 1941 he transferred from R.A.F. Intelligence to become private secretary to the secretary of state for air, Sir Archibald Sinclair. At the end of the war he entered politics proper when he stood unsuccessfully in the 1945 elections. He was one of the first recruits to R. A. Butler's research department, where he specialized in economics, acting as personal adviser to Sir Winston Churchill on economic matters. In 1950 he was elected M.P. for Barnet, the constituency he has represented ever since. His rise through a succession of posts was rapid: minister of supply, 1955–57; paymaster-general in Macmillan's first government, with the task of co-ordinating negotiations for Britain's participation in the proposed European Free Trade Area; president of the board of trade, 1959–61; secretary of state for the colonies, 1961–1962, with the problems of Kenyan independence and the break-up of the Central African Federation; and then chancellor of the exchequer. His burly figure and cheerful, seemingly somewhat naive manner belie an extremely keen mind; he was a significant contender for the party leadership in the first election for that office in 1965, and is its deputy leader under Edward Heath.

Mauriac, François (1885–1970). In August 1970 when doctors at a Paris hospital knew that one of their patients was dying it was thought fitting and proper to move him to his home, and it was there, on September 1, that François Mauriac, revered author, died, aged 84, his family around him. Mauriac was born

**François Mauriac,
French man of letters.**

in Bordeaux on October 11, 1885, and remained deeply attached to that city all his life, using it as the setting for his many novels of French provincial life. Although he wrote plays, essays, religious works, and poems, he was above all a great novelist, publishing 23 novels during his long life, the majority of them between 1921 and 1941. Mauriac was a devout Roman Catholic with liberal views, and all his novels deal with some aspect of evil and its problems: lust, hatred, possessiveness, greed, and envy, all shown in the environment of the French provincial middle-class family. *Le Baiser au Lépreux* (A Kiss from the Leper), published in 1922, written with economy of style, bitter satire, and sensitivity, was the first of his novels to be hailed as a masterpiece. His earlier published work, two short autobiographical tales, two volumes of poems, and two novels, published in 1913 and 1914, had attracted little notice. Between 1922 and 1933 he wrote six further novels. It was after the publication of *Le Mystére Frontenac* in 1933 that Mauriac was elected to the French Academy, the first of many honours he was to receive. The major recognition came in 1952 when he was awarded the Nobel prize for literature. After the 1930s he turned away from fiction, publishing only *La Parisienne* in 1941, *Le Sagouin* in 1951, and *L'Agneau* in 1954, and turned to journalism. For the last 30 years of his life he wrote weekly, highly controversial articles for the French press, on politics, literature, and life in general. In 1966 he published his biography of General de Gaulle, which, like many of his novels, was translated into English. Only towards the end of his life, when he was living quietly in Malaga, did he return to his first love and wrote *Un Adolescent d'Autrefois* (An Adolescent of Former Years), published in 1969. Always a champion of the poor and the oppressed, Mauriac strongly defended the Republicans during the Spanish Civil War, was an active member of the French Resistance in the Second World War, and in the 1950s denounced French policy in North Africa. One of his last acts was to sign a letter proposing the award of the 1970 Nobel literature prize to Alexander Solzhenitsyn, the Russian author whose works are banned by the Soviet government, who in October was given the prize.

Montefiore, Rt. Rev. Hugh (born 1920). Canon Hugh Montefiore, the controversial cleric who once sent shock-waves echoing down Anglican cloisters by remarking that Christ might have been a homosexual, was appointed Suffragan Bishop of Kingston in January 1970. This appointment marked the final fading of the gaiters-and-croquet image of the episcopalian upper echelons treasured by secular sentimentalists. Hugh Montefiore was born a Jew on May 12, 1920, and educated at Rugby School, where he became a convert to Christianity, and St. John's College, Oxford. During the Second World War he served as a captain in the Royal Artillery and, on leaving the army, trained for the ministry at Westcott

Canon Montefiore was made a bishop.

House, Cambridge. He was ordained deacon in 1949 and priest the following year. He was curate at St. George, Jesmond, Newcastle upon Tyne, from 1949 to 1951; chaplain and then vice-principal of Westcott House, Cambridge, from 1951 to 1954; dean of Caius College, Cambridge, from 1954 to 1963; and from 1963 to 1970 vicar of Great St. Mary's, Cambridge. His publications include *Awkward Questions on Christian Love* (1964), *Commentary on the Epistle to the Hebrews* (1964), and *Truth to Tell* (1966).

Morris, Rev. Colin (born 1930). Colin Morris spent 1970 strangely dividing his time between being minister of Methodism's historic shrine, Wesley's Chapel, City Road, London (where John Wesley lies buried), and flying to Zambia to act as special adviser to his friend Pres. Kenneth Kaunda. The impact on Britain of his two hard-hitting and brilliantly pamphleteering books, *Include Me Out* and *Unyoung, Uncoloured, Unpoor*, was enhanced by his appearances on television and at public meetings. He comes of working-class parentage in Bolton, Lancashire, where he was born in 1930. Being a Marine commando and studying at Oxford offered a mixed preparation for the Methodist ministry. When he was 26 he went out to the Copper Belt of what was then Northern Rhodesia, and rapidly built up a strong white congregation in Chingola. He only gradually moved to the vehement convictions which he now holds on the rights of African nationalism. His gift for controversial and polemic utterance, matched by a remarkable power of phrase-making of the sort that catches the headlines, made him at first a famous, and later (among most of the white community) a notorious, character. He first achieved wide prominence in southern Africa by a sermon vehemently castigating the municipal authorities for their neglect of the African community—a sermon delivered to the mayor and corporation attending in state. When independence came to Northern Rhodesia as Zambia he gave his full support to Kenneth Kaunda, and he has remained a remarkably powerful figure in Zambia, being elected in 1965 president of the United Church in Zambia.

Murdoch, Sir Walter (1874–1970). A greatly loved author, essayist, and philosopher, Sir Walter Murdoch died in South Perth, Western Australia, on July 30, 1970. A son of Scotland, born at Pitsligo in Aberdeenshire on September 17, 1874, he was taken to Australia when ten years of age. He was educated at Scotch College, Melbourne, and then at Melbourne University. After experience as a schoolteacher and as a leader-writer for the Melbourne *Argus*, he was lecturer in English at the University of Melbourne from 1904 to 1911. In 1912 he became the first professor of English at the University of Western Australia. He retired from his chair in 1939, and from 1943 to 1947 was chancellor of the University of Western Australia. Throughout his adult life he was a prolific writer, and in his later years became widely known for his weekly essays published over a long period in newspapers throughout Australia. His writing was scholarly but simple, optimistic, kindly, and warm. His humour, although often penetrating, was always tolerant. He was created C.B.E. in 1939 and K.C.M.G. in 1964. A short time before his death the government of Western Australia announced that the State's second university would be named Murdoch University in his honour. Sir Walter's published works include *The Making of Australia* (1915), *The Life of Alfred Deakin* (1922), *Speaking Personally* (1930), *Saturday Mornings* (1931), *Moreover* (1952), and *The Spur of the Moment* (1939). He was the editor of *The Oxford Book of Australasian Verse* (1918).

Nasser, Gamal Abdel (1918–1970). The president of the United Arab Republic and hero of the Arab world died of a heart attack on September 28, 1970, a few hours after one of his most successful actions—the composing of the differences between King Hussein of Jordan and the Palestinian guerrillas and the ending of the short Jordanian civil war.

Gamal Nasser was born on January 15, 1918, in a suburb of Alexandria, the son of a junior postal official and the grandson of a peasant. He was educated at a secondary school and a military academy in Cairo where, according to his autobiography *Egypt's Liberation*, he occupied his time as a student revolutionary demonstrating against the British military presence in Egypt and plotting the assassination of public figures. In 1940 he was commissioned as a second lieutenant and stationed in the Sudan. By the time of the Palestinian war of 1948 he was a major; he distinguished himself in the fighting against Israel, being wounded at Faluja. Egyptian defeat led to bitter discontent within the army, and it was at this time that Nasser and his fellow military conspirators founded the Free Officers' Committee which planned the coup of July 23, 1952. This was a bloodless revolution: the

British-backed King Farouk abdicated and left Egypt, and General Mohammed Neguib was ushered into power. The general—a mere figure-head—was later ushered out again when the man behind the coup, Colonel Nasser, became first prime minister and military governor of Egypt in 1954, and then president under a new constitution approved by plebiscite in 1956.

The year 1956 also saw Egypt's nationalization of the Suez Canal in retaliation for the West's withdrawal of offers of aid to build the projected Aswan high dam. By the end of that year Nasser possessed the canal and had outfaced an Anglo-French invasion—stopped by American threats to bankrupt the two nations—and a co-ordinated Israeli attack. This triumph established Nasser as a hero of anti-imperialism and laid the foundations for Soviet influence in Egypt. In 1958 Syria and Egypt united briefly to form the United Arab Republic under Nasser's leadership, but

Pres. Nasser's death shook the Arab world.

the union lasted only until 1961 when the discontented Syrians broke away (although Egypt retained the high-sounding name of the U.A.R.). In 1967 Egypt suffered her most humiliating defeat in the six-day war with Israel—a conflict that was largely caused by Nasser's sabre-rattling but for which the Egyptians at least did not hold him to blame.

Nasser was the first Egyptian ruler of an independent Egypt since the days of the Pharaohs. Although his efforts to alleviate the poverty of the Egyptian masses were restrained by war, vast military expenditure, and a corrupt bureaucracy, he did achieve a great deal for the welfare of his country. His most notable domestic legacies were sweeping land reforms and the creation of the Aswan high dam, built with Russian money and engineers. Despite heavy technical and financial reliance on Moscow, and the gradual increase of Russian power in Egypt (particularly after the 1967 defeat), Nasser was basically an anti-Communist and persecuted Egyptian Marxists with a vigour almost equal to his

handling of the right-wing Moslem Brotherhood. He preserved a messianic charisma even in defeat and after death. After Israel's lightning victory in the six-day war he resigned the presidency only to be swept back into office the next day on a vast wave of spontaneous popular feeling. The news of his death was likewise heard distractedly by Arabs everywhere, and incredible scenes of mass mourning marked his funeral in Cairo.

Niles, Rev. Daniel T. (1908–1970). Daniel Niles, who died at Vellore, South India, on July 17, 1970, was perhaps the most widely known of all Asian church leaders; at the time of his death he was the Asian president of the World Council of Churches, to which office he had been elected at the assembly at Uppsala in 1968. He had preached the opening sermon there, taking the place of the recently assassinated Martin Luther King. Twenty years before, at the age of 40, he had been chosen from all the preachers of the world to perform the same office as the World Council of Churches was constituted at Amsterdam. By any reckoning he was a supremely great preacher, illuminating the Bible with rare gifts of scholarship, oriental imagination, and passionate eloquence. His command of English was superb.

Daniel Niles (known all the world over among Christians as "D.T.") was born in 1908 into a fourth-generation Christian family in Ceylon. He became a Methodist minister after training in Bangalore and at London University. He served his church in Ceylon both as principal of a school at Jaffna and as a superintendent of one of its districts. He remained a convinced Methodist and a devoted son of the church in his own country, but his rare gifts and his own passion for Christian unity and evangelism led him to be more and more called upon for world-wide service. He served the World's Y.M.C.A. in Geneva, and was the first Asian chairman of the World Student Christian Federation. From its inauguration he was deeply involved in the life of the World Council of Churches, serving for a time as secretary of its evangelism department. He played a considerable part in the formation of the East Asia Christian Conference, and became its first general secretary, holding the office from 1965 to 1968, when he was elected chairman. His deepest interest was in evangelism—perhaps most of all among students, over whose minds his oratory and intense convictions had great power.

O'Hara, John Henry (1905–1970). This American author of short stories, novels, librettos, and film scripts, died in Princeton on April 11, 1970. He was born in Pottsville, Pennsylvania, the eldest of eight children of a local doctor. His father's early death prevented John from proceeding to university; he turned instead to the succession of menial trades that seems to be the hall-mark of American writers, becoming in turn a ship's steward, railway clerk, steel-mill labourer, and gas-meter reader.

John O'Hara, American novelist.

Turning to journalism, he ran the gamut from film critic to football editor with traditional verve and attack. The year 1934 saw O'Hara crouched over his typewriter in a cheap room in an inexpensive quarter of New York, thrashing out the opening chapters of his first novel, *Appointment in Samarra*. The book was a resounding success, and its author became famous overnight. Many of O'Hara's books achieved fame as films. Among these were *Pal Joey*, published in 1940, *Butterfield 8* (1935), and *A Rage to Live* (1949). In 1956 he won the National Book Award for *Ten North Frederick*, and in 1969 he published his last collection of short stories, *Lovey Childs*. O'Hara excelled as a short-story writer and was a master of dialogue. An astringent realism and keen observation of middle America marks his work, much of which is set in the fictitious town of Gibbsville, Pennsylvania.

Ortiz, Manuel (1917–1970). One of the most active post-war boxing champions died on May 31 at the age of 54 in Balboa, Panama. Born in Corona, California, some 12 miles from the Mexican border, the 5 ft. 4 in. Ortiz spent most of his early life working on a 500-acre farm which he was later able to buy from his earnings in the ring. Son of Mexican parents, Ortiz was the first of Mexican blood to win a world title. This was in 1942 and, except for a brief spell in 1947, when he lost and re-gained the title from Harold Dade, he warded off 20 bantamweight challengers before the problems of years and weight finally took their toll. Ortiz always considered himself lucky to have enjoyed such a long, busy career. In his youth he was gored by a bull, and throughout his career a six-inch scar on his neck was a permanent reminder of the accident. Ortiz began his professional career in 1938, and finally lost his title to South African Vic Toweel in Johannesburg in May 1950.

Palme, Olof (born 1927). Olof Palme completed his first year as prime minister of Sweden on October 1, 1970—a year in which the press dubbed him "trendier

than Trudeau", an inevitable if unenviable tag for one who, at 42, was the youngest premier in the West. Palme was born on January 30, 1927, in Stockholm. His father, managing director of an insurance company, died when his son was a child of six and Olof's mother—a scion of the Baltic gentry—was left to bring up her family alone. The youthful Palme distinguished himself at school, despite poor health, passing his final examinations at the early age of 17, and particularly excelling in languages. He served in the cavalry during his compulsory military service, reaching the rank of lieutenant. As a youth, he became strongly attracted to the policies of the Social Democratic party and especially to the work and thought of Ernst Wigforss, then minister of finance. He joined the party in 1949.

Extensive travel played a part in the development of Palme's character: he spent a year at Kenyon College, Ohio, U.S.A., in 1948—where he took a B.A.—and then hitch-hiked across the U.S.A. for four months; on another journey he visited India, Ceylon, Burma, Thailand, Singapore, and Indonesia. He graduated in law from the University of Stockholm in 1951, and the following year he was elected president of the Swedish Union of Students and became prominent enough in student politics to attract the eye of the prime minister, Tage Erlander, who made him his secretary in 1954. For the next 15 years Palme occupied the position of protégé, confidant, and, at last, successor to Erlander. He first entered the Swedish Riksdag in 1957, and in 1963 he entered the government as minister without portfolio. As minister of communications, which he became in 1965, he officiated over the 1967 change from left-hand to right-hand traffic in Sweden. Later that year he became minister of education.

Palme had by this time already identified himself with the body of Swedish opinion opposed to the American involvement in the Vietnam war, and in 1968 he marched alongside a North Vietnamese ambassador in an anti-war demonstration in Stockholm. This earned him sharp criticism from his political opponents in Sweden, and was received somewhat coolly in Washington. Olof Palme married in 1955 and has three young sons. His recreations include tennis and cross-country running.

Pele (born 1946). Brazilian soccer saw many changes in the 12 years that separated its first and third successes in the World Cup, but the name of Pele brilliantly reigned supreme throughout all changes in team formations and in team managers. From the time the "Black Pearl" first displayed his uncanny ball control, high-speed dribbling, and explosive shooting as a 17-year-old in Brazil's 1958 World Cup-winning team his name has been synonymous with soccer. Injury kept him out of all but two of the matches in the successful defence of the Cup in Chile four years later, and when he and Brazil limped sadly out of the 1966 campaign in England after some

Olof Palme, prime minister of Sweden.

rough handling in the group games, it looked as if fans might have seen the last of the Pele magic in international soccer. Retirement talk was soon forgotten, however, and soccer's most closely marked player emerged as one of the leading artists of Brazil's 1970 World Cup victory in Mexico which earned his country the trophy outright. Scorer of over 1,000 goals for his country and the Santos club, Pele's name has frequently been linked with moves to European clubs. But when a possible transfer fee is requested the answer is usually so prohibitive that his admirers joyfully make it another excuse to fête their idol.

All Brazil waited on tenterhooks as Edson Arantes do Nascimento approached his much-heralded 1,000th goal late in 1969. It came finally from a penalty in a club game, and Rio de Janeiro will never forget it. A special set of stamps was issued to mark the occasion, a plaque was unveiled, and the hero, who reputedly earns £80,000 a year, was presented with a golden soccer ball weighing 4 lb. The mayor of São Paulo once summed up his countrymen's feelings about their hero when he said: "Pele is part of our national heritage, and as such is not for sale. He cannot be given away, lent, or sold. Pele belongs to us." It is little wonder that Santos somehow find the money to keep him in their line-up.

Pepper, Harry S. (1891–1970). This popular broadcaster, composer, and songwriter, known to his many friends as "Pep", died in an Uxbridge hospital on June 26, 1970, aged 79. He will be remembered for his great contribution to radio variety, particularly during and immediately after the Second World War, when nearly all the major programmes carried his name as producer. He broke away from the stereotyped methods of earlier radio programmes in all his shows, which included "Monday Night at Eight", containing "Puzzle Corner", the first broadcast quiz; "Garrison Theatre", which introduced Jack Warner to radio audiences; "Band Wagon", which starred Arthur Askey and

Richard Murdoch, and introduced many catch-phrases into the language; and "Hi Gang", with Bebe Daniels, Ben Lyon, and Vic Oliver.

Harry Pepper was born into the world of entertainment, for his father was the owner and producer of a seaside concert party "The White Coons". When Harry was still in his teens, he acted as pianist, box-office clerk, programme-seller, composer, and general handyman to the company. In the 1920s he joined the "Co-Optimists" concert party as a pianist. In the early 1930s he began working for the BBC, composing songs and playing piano duets with Doris Arnold, whom he later married; she died in October 1969. In 1932 Pepper joined the BBC as a variety producer, and in 1945 was made senior producer of the variety department. He it was who first had the idea of presenting a minstrel show—the "Kentucky Minstrels"—which was the forerunner of television's "Black and White Minstrel Show". Pepper wrote the music and lyrics for many well-known songs, including "Carry Me Back to Green Pastures", and the lyrics for many others, including "Hear My Song, Violetta". He retired from the BBC in 1951.

Pipinelis, Panayotis (1899–1970). The foreign minister of Greece and her one-time prime minister died in Athens on July 19, 1970, aged 71. Pipinelis, a noted royalist, was the only distinguished civilian politician to accept office under the military regime which seized power in April 1967. His arrival on the scene was fortunate, for it was largely due to his efforts and acumen that war between Greece and Turkey over Cyprus was averted in November of that year. He was born at the Athenian port of Piraeus on March 21, 1899, and studied law and political science at the universities of Zürich and Freiburg. He entered the Greek diplomatic service in 1922 and served as ambassador in Sofia, Budapest, Warsaw, and Brussels. After the German invasion, he followed the Greek government into exile in 1941 and was appointed ambassador to Moscow and then, in 1943, ambassador to the free governments of Poland and Belgium in London. From 1947 to 1950 he was permanent under-secretary of state for foreign affairs. In 1950 he entered the government as foreign minister under Alexandros Papagos of the Ralli party. He later became an influential member of the National Radical Union formed to succeed the Ralli. He was prime minister for three months in the summer of 1963 when the former premier resigned over a proposed visit of King Paul and Queen Frederika to London.

Pipinelis's aims in the military government were first to engineer the return of King Constantine from self-exile—in which he failed—and secondly to improve Greece's relations with her Balkan neighbours, especially Turkey—in which he succeeded. He was instrumental in obtaining from the military a timetable for the abolition of several emergency measures—

Panayotis Pipinelis, Greek statesman.

which he hoped would save Greece from being suspended from the Council of Europe. The reforms, however, did not include a return to parliamentary democracy, and he only forestalled expulsion by walking out of the Council's meeting in December 1969 and announcing Greece's voluntary withdrawal.

Price, Nancy (1880–1970). Nancy Price, who died on March 31, 1970, was a distinguished actress and producer who will also be remembered for her devotion to animals and birds, and for her knowledge of the English countryside. She was born at Kinver, Worcestershire, on February 3, 1880, and at the age of 12 ran away from school to attend an audition for a Shakespeare play given by Frank Benson at the Theatre Royal, Birmingham. In September 1899, at the end of the school term, she joined his company, and she made her London début at the Lyceum in the following year. Her first major role was as Olivia in *Twelfth Night* at the same theatre. In a career which spanned half a century, she played over 442 parts in 100 plays, and also produced 87 plays. Among her most

Nancy Price, veteran British actress.

notable roles was the 100-year-old matriarch, Adeline, in *Whiteoaks* by Mazo de la Roche which, produced at the Little Theatre in 1936, ran for two years. She was always especially fond of parrots and her favourite, "Boney", appeared with her in the play. Asthma forced her to give up acting in 1956.

In 1930 Nancy Price founded the People's Theatre Organization, of which she was an honorary director, and in 1950 she was made C.B.E. for her services to the stage. She wrote over 20 books, including *Bright Pinions* (on parrots), *In Praise of Trees*, *The Heart of a Vagabond*, and an autobiography, *Into the Hour Glass*. At the age of 79 she published her fifth book on birds. She married an actor, Charles Maude, in 1907, and after he died in 1943, continued to live in their cottage on the Sussex Downs above Worthing with her many pets.

Rawicz, Maryan (1899–1970). This member of the famous Rawicz and Landauer piano partnership died in London on January 30, 1970. It was in Austria in 1930 that the two men, both professional pianists, first met. Landauer heard Rawicz whistling a tune which he had been trying to identify since hearing it broadcast from a foreign station some time previously. Rawicz told him that it was one of Smetana's polkas, and the two men sat down at a piano and played the tune together. They were so pleased with the joint effect of their individual styles that this chance meeting led to their decision to form a partnership. A year of practising and studying followed before they began to play in Continental cabarets. One of the first to suggest that they should go to London was the Duke of Windsor, then Prince of Wales. Such was their success in Great Britain that they decided to stay in the country, and became naturalized British subjects. The technical secret of their success was the incredible degree of synchronization they achieved; all their music was played in their own arrangements. They made countless broadcasts and recordings, as well as giving numerous concert performances, always sitting back-to-back at their grand pianos.

Remarque, Erich Maria (1898–1970). This German-born author who attained lasting and world-wide fame for his novel about the First World War, *All Quiet on the Western Front*, died after a long illness in Locarno, Switzerland, on September 25 at the age of 72. He was born in Osnabrück, Germany, on June 22, 1898, the son of a clerk. After leaving school he attended a Catholic seminary to train as a teacher but, when he was 18, entered the army and, like the hero of his most famous novel, served in the ranks on the Western Front, where he was seriously wounded. After his discharge from the army he did casual work and, while employed as a sub-editor on a Munich newspaper, decided to write his memoirs in an attempt to purge himself of the memories of his war experiences, which still caused him to

Erich Remarque
(*All Quiet on the Western Front*).

**Geoffrey Rippon,
Britain's "Mr. Europe".**

suffer deep and persistent depression. *All Quiet on the Western Front* (*Im Westen Nichts Neues*) was published in Germany in 1929, and within a year sales had risen to a million copies. Its success was due partly, no doubt, to the widespread disillusionment of the times, but chiefly because its realistic, impassioned, poetic writing so vividly expressed the plight of the conscripted soldier, and the brutality and futility of war. Although translated into many languages—the English and American editions equalled the German sales in their first year—it was banned in Austria, Italy, and Russia on the grounds that it was likely to demoralize troops, and when Hitler came to power in Germany it was among the books publicly burnt in Berlin in 1933. In 1930 an excellent Hollywood film version of the book, starring Lew Ayres and Louis Wolheim, appeared and became a classic. Until some of the scenes were cut, this, too, was banned in both Germany and Austria.

After these successes and the large financial rewards Remarque obtained from them, he settled on Lake Maggiore, where he wrote a sequel *The Road Back* in 1931, and in 1937 *Three Comrades*, neither of which received the acclaim of his first book, although both were made into films. In 1938 the Nazis deprived him of his German citizenship, and in 1939 he went to the U.S.A., becoming an American citizen in 1947. He was to write seven more novels, the last, *The Night in Lisbon*, in 1964, most of them with a background of the Nazi regime and the horrors it inflicted. His first marriage, in 1926, to a German woman, was dissolved in 1931, and in 1957, after a long engagement, he married Paulette Goddard, the film actress. They went to live at his villa at Ticino on Lake Maggiore, where Remarque, a quiet reserved man, was able to lead a sheltered life away from the publicity he hated.

Rindt, Jochen (1942–1970). When Jackie Ickx failed to win the United States GP, he could not—even if he won the Mexican GP —amass sufficient points to beat the total accumulated by Jochen Rindt in 1970. As a result, Rindt, who was killed when his car left the road in practice for the Italian GP on September 5, became the first posthumous world champion racing driver. Jochen was born in Germany of Austrian parents. He started racing with a Simca saloon, then used a works-tuned Alfa Romeo, but his name became known first when, driving his own Brabham in 1964, he won the international Formula 2 race at Crystal Palace, beating Graham Hill. After that victory Rob Walker offered him a Formula 1 drive in the Austrian GP, which was followed by a three-year contract with Cooper, racing the Cooper-Maserati. He had a season with Brabham in 1968; however, the Repco engine gave a lot of trouble, and the season brought him only two third places. For the 1969 season he teamed up with Lotus, and soon became a dominant force in Grand Prix racing, eventually winning the United States GP in October 1969. Lotus had a little trouble at the beginning of the 1970 season, but once it was overcome Lotus and Rindt proved almost unbeatable. His five 1970 Grand Prix victories were the Monte Carlo, Dutch, French, British, and German. Rindt's driving was noted for a wild and spectacular style which the spectators loved. But he himself was very safety-conscious, and was strongly opposed to the high-mounted wings on GP cars, which were banned after a wing failure caused him to have a serious accident at Barcelona in 1969. He lived at Geneva, and left a widow and a two-year-old daughter.

Rippon, Aubrey Geoffrey Frederick (born 1924). Geoffrey Rippon was appointed "Mr. Europe"—chancellor of the Duchy of Lancaster with responsibility for negotiating Britain's possible entry into the Common Market—following Iain Macleod's death in August 1970, which took Anthony Barber to the exchequer within days of his opening the negotiations. Born on May 28, 1924, and educated at King's College, Taunton, and Brasenose College, Oxford, Rippon was called to the bar in 1948 and became a Q.C. in 1964. He has wide

Jochen Rindt, posthumous champion driver.

business experience and is a former chairman of Holland Hannen and Cubitts, the construction company. Having stood unsuccessfully as parliamentary candidate for Shoreditch and Finsbury in 1950 and 1951, he was elected to the Surbiton borough council in 1945, became an alderman in 1949, and was mayor of Surbiton, 1951–52, at the age of 26. He represented Chelsea on the London county council in 1952 and became leader of the opposition in the L.C.C., 1957–61. He first entered parliament for Norwich South in 1955, and he was parliamentary secretary to the ministers of housing and local government, defence, aviation, and housing and local government before becoming minister of public building and works from 1962 to 1964. He joined the Cabinet in 1963.

Rippon was defeated at Norwich in the 1964 general election, but re-entered parliament when he won Hexham in 1966. From 1966 to 1968 he was Opposition spokesman on housing, land, and local government, and from 1968 to 1970 on defence. In the new Conservative government formed in June 1970, he was first appointed minister of technology, and then chancellor of the Duchy of Lancaster. He has travelled widely, and is chairman of the British section of the European league for economic co-operation and joint president of the British section of the council of European municipalities.

Rothschild, Nathaniel Mayer Victor Rothschild, 3rd Baron (born 1910). The prime minister surprised most people when he picked the mercurial Lord Rothschild to head 10 Downing Street's new central policy review staff, a kind of Brains Trust or management consultancy. The baron's friends forecast fireworks, prophesying bitter clashes between him and the civil service establishment. Rothschild's brief is to pronounce on the practicability of measures put forward by the various ministers of the crown. His appointment was compared with Churchill's appointment of Beaverbrook to the ministry of aircraft production. It was an adventurous

**Lord Rothschild,
"brains truster"-in-chief.**

choice and probably a shrewd one, for Lord Rothschild is an eminent scientist and an experienced administrator, and has formidable powers of analysis. In the Second World War he won the George Medal for his bravery in dismantling enemy explosive devices. Although he is an extremely rich man, most of his political friends have been on the left wing.

Rothschild was born on October 31, 1910. He was educated at Harrow and Trinity College, Cambridge, gaining Ph.D. and Sc.D. degrees. From 1935 to 1939 he was a fellow of Trinity. During the Second World War he was in military intelligence. After the war he was appointed director of BOAC (1946–48). He was chairman of the agricultural research council for 10 years, and has sat on several important advisory bodies for varying periods, including the BBC general advisory council, the council for scientific policy, and the central advisory council for science and technology. In 1963 the giant Royal Dutch-Shell group appointed him chairman of research, and two years later he became its research co-ordinator. He holds honorary degrees awarded by his own college and by institutions in Barbados and Israel. He has written a number of scientific papers, the most important being *Fertilization: a Classification of Living Animals*. Of his family the *Sunday Times* remarked: "Of his six brilliant children, one runs a bank, another a kindergarten, a third was the youngest scholar to be admitted in recent times to Oxford, and a fourth is shaping up to be a champion motor-cycle racer."

Russell, Bertrand Arthur William Russell, 3rd Earl (1872–1970). Bertrand Russell, the mathematical logician, philosopher, essayist, and political agitator, died at his home in Plas Penrhyn, North Wales, on February 2, 1970. The philosopher's innumerable years have been elegantly chronicled by his own pen. Indeed in 1948 he even published his own obituary. "In his youth", went this deft parody of *The Times*, "he did work of importance in

mathematical logic, but his eccentric attitude toward the First World War revealed a lack of balanced judgment which increasingly infected his later writings. His life, for all its waywardness, had a certain anachronistic consistency, reminiscent of the aristocratic rebels of the early 19th century. His principles were curious, but such as they were they governed his actions. In private life he showed none of the acerbity which marred his writings but was a genial conversationalist, not devoid of human sympathy."

Bertrand Russell was born at Ravenscroft, Monmouthshire, on May 18, 1872, the youngest child of Viscount Amberley and the former Katherine Stanley, daughter of Baron Stanley of Alderley. Lord John Russell, the Whig politician associated with the passage of the Reform Bill of 1832, who served twice as prime minister, was his grandfather. The family was one of manifold eccentricity: an uncle had taken to Catholicism with such devotion that he became a bishop, another had become a Muslim and undertaken the pilgrimage to Mecca, and a third had assumed the belligerent stance of militant agnosticism. Both his parents were freethinkers, and his mother embraced the feminist cause and also her eldest son's tutor, thus doubly shocking the ranks of Victorian matrons. Lady Amberley died when Bertrand was an infant of two, and her husband followed a year later, leaving the guardianship of his two sons to the aforementioned tutor and another—men whose steadfast atheism recommended them to the peer. Lord John Russell, however, disputed this arrangement at law, and won the guardianship of his grandsons. When the statesman died in 1878, Bertrand was brought up by Lady Russell, a pronounced puritan. Under the stern aegis of this dowager he was introduced to geometry. "At the age of 11 I began Euclid with my brother as my tutor," his autobiography records. "This was one of the greatest events of my life, as dazzling as first love. I had not imagined there was anything so delicious in the world. From that moment until Whitehead and I finished *Principia Mathematica*, when I was 38, mathematics was my chief interest and my chief source of happiness."

At 18 Russell entered Trinity College, Cambridge, as a scholar where he shone among a bright sprinkling of intellectual supernovae which included John Maynard Keynes, Lytton Strachey, G. Lowes Dickinson, and Alfred North Whitehead. In 1894 Russell took a first class in the Moral Science tripos with exceptional distinction. During the same year he embarked on the first of his four matrimonial contracts, marrying Alys Pearsall Smith, an attractive American Quaker five years his senior. One afternoon in 1901 while bicycling, the philosopher suddenly realized that he no longer loved her—nevertheless this first marriage lasted until 1921. In that year he married his second wife, Dora Winifred Black; in 1936 his third, Patricia Helen Spence; and in 1952 his fourth, Edith Finch, who survives him.

Russell and his first wife travelled to Germany and later to the U.S.A., where he lectured on non-Euclidean geometry. It was in 1900, while attending a congress of philosophy in Paris, that Russell met Giuseppe Peano, the Italian pioneer of symbolic logic. "For years", he wrote of this meeting, "I had been endeavouring to analyse the fundamental notions of mathematics. Suddenly in the space of a few weeks I discovered what appeared to be definite answers to the problems which had baffled me for years." That October Russell began *The Principles of Mathematics*, dashing off 200,000 words in three months. With its publication in 1902, he plunged into *Principia Mathematica* in collaboration with Whitehead. This is the work on which his reputation as a philosopher rests, and which has exercised a potent—and arid—influence upon 20th-century English and American philosophy. The collaborators worked on the book from 1900 to 1910, publishing it in three volumes in 1910, 1912, and 1913. The work enshrines Russell's Theory of Descriptions, which postulates that a man, concept, or object can only be considered to exist in terms of its exact description. The linguistic school, which stems from this basic law, and which owes its foundation to Russell's pupil, Wittgenstein, rejects the traditional function of philosophy as a treasury of wisdom, ethical law, and metaphysical conjecture and sees it merely as a test of the truth of statements. The strain of writing *Principia Mathematica* was so great that Russell affirmed that his intellect never quite recovered from it: "I have been ever since definitely less capable of dealing with difficult abstractions than I was before." Indeed its publication marked a new phase in his career—one for which most members of the public remember him—the phase of political action and public polemics. It was the First World War that worked this change: "I underwent a process of rejuvenation because of the war," he recorded in his autobiography. "It shook me out of my prejudices and made me think afresh on a number of

Bertrand Russell died, aged 97.

fundamental questions." As a pacifist he delivered a series of speeches and wrote *War—The Offspring of Fear, Principles of Social Recognition*, and *Justice in Wartime*. This stance earned him six months in a comfortable cell in Brixton Prison.

After the war he visited Russia, met Lenin, Trotsky, and Gorky, and recorded his impressions of, and unflattering reflections on, the revolution in *The Practice and Theory of Bolshevism* (1920). During the 1920s—and his second marriage—Russell founded an experimental progressive school, the Beacon Hill School, which had a vast influence on the growth of schools of a similar type in Britain and the U.S.A. In 1933—two years after he had become the third Earl Russell—his second wife informed him that she was expecting her third child and that he was not the father. He divorced her. In 1938 Russell began a long visit to the U.S.A. where he lectured at the universities of Chicago, Los Angeles, Harvard, and, in 1940, the City College of New York. His appointment to a chair in the last of these led to a storm of protest and eventually a State Supreme Court Justice ruled that he was unfit to sit in it on the grounds that he was an alien and an advocate of sexual immorality. "It would be," said the judge, "a chair of indecency."

During the years 1940–44 Russell remained in the U.S.A. working on his monumental *History of Western Philosophy*, which proved a popular work and the mainstay of his income in the years to come. He returned to England in 1944, and for some time after the war basked in official approval as a mellowed rebel and Grand Old Man, frequently appearing on the BBC's Brains Trust programme. This image was augmented by the Order of Merit (1949) and the Nobel Prize for Literature (1950). In 1948 he showed himself surprisingly athletic when, at the age of 86, he was a passenger in an aircraft that crashed into a Norwegian fiord: the philosopher abandoned the wreck and swam, swathed in an overcoat, until picked up by a lifeboat. Asked whether or not he had thought of mysticism and logic while immersed, he replied "No, I thought the water was cold."

The respectable image was shattered when Lord Russell became a leading light in the Campaign for Nuclear Disarmament, which he helped to found in 1958, and in the Committee of 100 "for civil disobedience against nuclear warfare", taking part in many demonstrations and sit-downs. His activities of this nature led to a seven-day return visit to Brixton in 1961. An anti-American bias to his polemics was a pronounced feature of his last years. Among many projects undertaken by his "Peace Foundation" was the "trial" of the U.S.A. for war crimes in Vietnam by certain intellectuals assembled in Stockholm. Throughout these years Russell was engaged on his autobiography, a polished, yet richly quirkish work that belied much that was shrill and unbalanced about his public utterances. The last volume of this book was published in 1969.

"Don" Ryder,
tycoon of paper and papers.

Ryder, Sydney Thomas (born 1916). "Don" Ryder, the ex-journalist chairman and chief executive of the giant paper and packaging company, Reed Group Limited, became one of the most powerful industrialists in Europe when, on March 24, 1970, it was announced—after weeks of negotiations—that Reed had won control of the massive International Publishing Corporation, publishers of the *Daily Mirror*, *The People*, and the largest range of women's magazines and trade and technical journals in the United Kingdom. Ryder was born in Ealing, London, on September 16, 1916, and educated locally. He embarked on his journalistic career as a member of the City editorial staff of the *Morning Post*, which was later consumed by the *Daily Telegraph*, and then moved to the *Stock Exchange Gazette*. During the Second World War he served in the army, working on the development of guided rockets and reaching the rank of colonel. After the war he returned to the *Stock Exchange Gazette*, but did not stay long before moving to the *Financial Times*, where he started an investment advice service. In 1950, on the retirement of the editor of the *Stock Exchange Gazette*, he returned once again to that journal, this time to fill the editorial chair. The paper had a circulation of just over 1,000 when Ryder took it over; by 1954 he had increased it to above the 40,000 mark. By the time the company owning the *Gazette* was taken over by what was to become the I.P.C., Ryder was already on the board, and thus in a position to meet the eye of the noted press tycoon Cecil King, who in 1959 took him to Canada on a tour of paper manufacturers and soon afterwards set him the task of reorganizing the Kelly-Iliffe section of I.P.C., the profit of which he doubled within three years.

In 1963 Don Ryder joined Reed, and a month later became managing director with the simple brief: "Save Reed." This he did by initiating a dramatic programme of diversification of which the I.P.C. deal is the most spectacular facet. Other

acquisitions have included Wall Paper Manufacturers, Spicer's, Polycell, Alex Cowan, and Field Sons & Co. Ltd. Ryder has earned the reputation of being one of the most marketing-minded men in top management and also an iconoclast and visionary in the vital field of management training.

Salazar, Antonio de Oliveira (1899–1970). Dr. Antonio Salazar, the enigmatic ascetic who for 40 years steered Portugal along the narrow path of the "five values"—God, country, authority, family, and work—died on July 27, 1970. For two years—since September 1968 when he suffered a massive brain haemorrhage—he had lived as an invalid, but no one had dared to inform him that he was no longer prime minister. Under Salazar's aloof paternalism Portugal eschewed the instability of liberal democracy, the godless materialism of Bolshevism, and the pagan fanaticism of fascism. The price was a stifling rigidity enforced by an unobtrusive but omnipresent secret police, and increasing isolation, particularly since the outbreak of guerrilla wars of liberation in Portuguese Africa.

Dr. Salazar was born of peasant stock on April 28, 1889, at Vimieiro, near Comba Dão, in Upper Beira. As a boy of 11 he entered the seminary of Vizeu and remained there eight years, taking minor orders before deciding that he did not have a vocation for the Church. At 21 he entered Coimbra University, where he was awarded his doctorate in 1917 and became an economics don. These were times of political turmoil in Portugal. The monarchy had been overthrown and chaos reigned under the aegis of liberal politicians. Salazar issued numerous pamphlets outlining his plans for Portuguese salvation and, when, in May 1926 came another revolution, a military coup, by then a professor and a disillusioned ex-M.P. he was summoned to Lisbon to iron out anarchy as minister of finance. He resigned within a week, saying that he could not bring order out of chaos without absolute power over other ministries. This he received two years later, on April 27, 1928.

No one can deny that Salazar succeeded in his initial brief: he did lead Portugal from strife to security and bring about stability and fiscal order. His success enabled him to formalize his position as dictator by becoming premier in 1932 and drafting a constitution for the *Estado Novo* (new state). This charter, approved by plebiscite in 1933, made Portugal a "unitary and corporative state", with a corporative assembly. In practice there was only one party, Salazar's, in the assembly and, in any case, the executive was not responsible to it. While prime minister Salazar held many other portfolios, serving from time to time as finance, foreign, and colonial minister. By decree he started a form of social security, and outlawed strikes. He strongly supported Franco during the Spanish Civil War, and created a youth movement along Hitlerian lines, but remained neutral during the Second

World War, renting bases in the Azores to Britain and the U.S.A. Declining the presidency of Portugal, Salazar remained prime minister until 1968—a record run of absolute power. He never married, and his private life was a model of frugality and virtue.

Schacht, Hjalmar Horace Greeley (1877–1970). Brilliant financier and banker, principal engineer of Germany's economic recovery between the wars, and reluctant member of the Nazi party, Hjalmar Schacht died on June 4, 1970. After the Second World War he was tried as a war criminal at Nuremberg on the grounds that he had made possible Hitler's vast rearmament programme. He was acquitted at Nuremberg and by German "denazification" courts.

Schacht was born near the border with Denmark. His father was a naturalized American—hence his first names. Horace Greeley was the man who gave the advice "Go west, young man". Hjalmar went to several universities and travelled extensively. He began a career in banking at the age of 26, and in 1914 was appointed a banking administrator in occupied Belgium. In 1923 he was given special responsibility for restoring the German currency, which was hopelessly inflated. He immediately stopped the printing of paper money and introduced a new currency called the Rentenmark, giving it the same value as the old gold Reichsmark of pre-war days. Schacht's policy was completely successful, and he was appointed president of the Reichsbank. He resigned this post in 1929 and began a campaign against payment of further war reparations and against the government's economic policy in general.

Schacht became a supporter of the Nazi party and approved Hitler's appointment as chancellor in 1933. Resuming his post as president of the Reichsbank and becoming minister of economics, he manipulated Germany's economy with the utmost brilliance. He financed a huge programme of rearmament and public works and succeeded in reducing the number of unemployed. But in 1935 and 1936 he several times warned Hitler of looming economic dangers. He resigned as minister of economics in 1937. In 1939 he again urged Hitler to reduce armament expenditure. Hitler, furious, dismissed him from his Reichsbank post, and Schacht retired from public life. In 1944 he was arrested after the conspiracy against Hitler's life, and he was kept in a concentration camp for the rest of the duration of the war.

After his acquittal at Nuremberg, a German "people's court" at Stuttgart sentenced Schacht to eight years' detention in a labour camp, under the "denazification" laws. But on appeal he was released. Later he founded his own bank at Düsseldorf. He acted as special consultant at various times to Iran, Syria, Egypt, and Indonesia. His resilience is shown by the title of his autobiography, *My First 76 Years*.

Servan-Schreiber, Jean-Jacques (born 1924). J.-J. S.-S., as he became known to millions of Frenchmen during 1970, had his claim to be the "French Kennedy" dashed in the Bordeaux by-election of September 20. As secretary-general of the small Radical party, although newly elected to the French parliament as deputy for Nancy he decided to challenge the government by standing against the prime minister, M. Chaban-Delmas, who (by dint of constitutional complexity) was forced to fight a by-election at Bordeaux. The traditionally phlegmatic voters of that city, however, turned down the barnstorming radical, who received a scant 16·59 per cent of the vote in the first ballot. *La farce Bordelaise* did no good to French parliamentary democracy or to the image of J.-J. S.-S., who had looked like becoming the most interesting personality of post-Gaulle France.

Servan-Schreiber was born on February 13, 1924, the son of the founder of the financial and economic daily *Les Échos*, and was educated at the École Polytechnique, Paris. He escaped from France during the occupation and joined the Free French air force as a fighter pilot, winning the Croix de la Valeur Militaire. After the war he followed his father's footsteps into journalism and was diplomatic editor of *Le Monde* from 1948 to 1951. In 1953 he was co-founder of *L'Express*, an organ of the reformist left. During the mid-1950s he was closely associated with Pierre Mendès-France, supporting his efforts to win full control of the Radical party. From 1963 to 1965 he was active in support of Gaston Deferre in his unsuccessful campaign to form a confederation of the non-Communist left and the Christian Democrats. He backed Alain Poher in the 1969 presidential election. Politically, therefore, he seemed to be a champion of lost causes. In other fields, however, his good sense prevailed. He achieved worldwide fame, for instance, with his book *The American Challenge* (*Le Défi américain*), in which he argued that European unity, under social democratic governments, was the only way Europe could stave off an American economic and technological take-over. It was thanks to Servan-Schreiber also that the Greek composer Mikis Theodorakis was enabled to leave Greece, where he had been kept a political prisoner.

Sheridan, Clare Consuelo (1885–1970). Clare Sheridan, the sculptor, writer, traveller, and cousin of Winston Churchill, died on May 31, 1970, at the age of 84. Hers was a life of talent, zest, fame, and misfortune. Born Clare Frewen on September 9, 1885, she was the daughter of Moreton Frewen and Clara Jerome, sister to Lady Randolph Churchill. It was this famous aunt who launched Clare into London society, where as an ornament of the *beau monde*, she was selected as a friend for Princess Margaret of Connaught, becoming her confidante. In 1910 she married Wilfred Sheridan, great-great-grandson of the playwright Richard Brinsley Sheridan.

The marriage ended tragically in 1915 when Sheridan was killed in action in France, leaving Clare with an infant son and daughter. She had already suffered one bereavement: a third child had died in babyhood. It was while attempting to carve an angel for the child's grave that she discovered her gift for sculpture.

Her talent allied to her position in society proved a potent mixture for success. Within four years she was an established sculptor, holding exhibitions and receiving commissions for busts from such august patrons as Asquith, Lord Birkenhead, and, of course, Winston Churchill. In 1920 she was invited to revolutionary Russia to do portraits of Lenin and Trotsky. By now renowned throughout Europe and America, she was approached by the *New York Times* for an account of her adventures among the Bolsheviks, and was thus launched on her career as a journalist. As a newspaperwoman she covered the Irish civil war and the Turco-Greek war. She also interviewed Ataturk, Mussolini, and King Boris of Bulgaria.

While reporting and sculpting she found time to write travel books and an autobiography, *Nuda Veritas* (1927), which enjoyed a vast success. Among her other books are *A Turkish Kaleidoscope* (1926), *Arab Interlude* (1936, describing her house and family life at Biskra on the edge of the Sahara), and *Redskin Interlude* (1938, which was inspired by a six-month stay on a Red Indian reservation). The early death of her son in 1937 turned her to spiritualism and, later, Catholicism. For the last 20 years of her life she lived quietly gardening in Sussex and Algeria. Her final volume of autobiography, *To The Four Winds*, was published in 1954.

Shinwell, Emanuel, Baron (born 1884). After more than 40 years on the benches of the House of Commons, "Manny" Shinwell in 1970 moved "upstairs" to exercise his belligerent charm as a life peer in the House of Lords. He had decided not to stand for re-election as an M.P., and his elevation in the honours list following the dissolution of Parliament

"Manny" Shinwell became a lord.

was welcomed on all sides. For though Shinwell never shrank from furious combat with the Tories, whom he had fought all his life, and with some of his own colleagues, he left few lasting scars. He was born on October 18, 1884, in the shadow of Spitalfields market in London. It was a time of economic depression and his father was compelled to go north in search of work to feed his 13 children. Eventually Manny joined him in Glasgow. At the age of 12 he began work as an errand boy. He read avidly and soon acquired an interest in socialism. In 1906 he was elected to the Glasgow Trades Council. He was a militant member of the Scottish Independent Labour party and in 1911 began 20 years of work for the Seamen's Union. In 1921 during a general strike on Clydeside he was accused of incitement to riot and served a five-month prison sentence.

A year later the "wild man of the Clyde" was given a delirious send-off on his way to the House of Commons as Labour M.P. for Linlithgow. He was soon appointed parliamentary secretary to the Department of Mines. Defeated in 1924, Shinwell returned to parliament in 1928 and became financial secretary to the War Office. Later he returned to the Department of Mines. After a second defeat in 1931 he swept back with an annihilating victory over his own old leader Ramsay MacDonald at Seaham Harbour.

Although he greatly admired Winston Churchill, he refused to join the coalition government during the Second World War. On Labour's landslide victory in 1945 Attlee appointed him minister of fuel and power with responsibility for nationalizing the mines and a seat in the cabinet. His position became impossible after the serious fuel crisis of 1947 and a notorious speech in which he seemed to suggest that the middle class was worth no more than a "tinker's curse". He was moved to the War Office, losing his seat in the cabinet. He quickly struck up a cordial relationship with Montgomery, then Chief of General Staff, and at their first meeting it was agreed that Shinwell should address the field-marshal as "Monty". In fact Shinwell was greatly missed when he was promoted to the Ministry of Defence in 1950 and returned to the cabinet. He was now M.P. for Easington.

With the defeat of Labour in 1951 Shinwell's ministerial career came to an end, but he remained extremely influential in the party. He perhaps mellowed slightly as an elder statesman, but he was never "tamed" and he was always quick to denounce policies with which he disagreed, particularly Britain's proposed entry into the Common Market. From 1964 to 1967 he was chairman of the parliamentary Labour party.

Simon, André Louis (1877–1970). André Simon, the portly epicure, founder of the Wine and Food Society, and prolific writer on gastronomy, died in London on September 5, aged 93. He was born in Paris on February 28, 1877, into a family of

André Simon, gastronomist to the world.

unshakable royalist and papal principles. Thus when he failed his *Bachot* and had to resort to journalism, he was found a job on a royalist Catholic magazine. A friend of his father's, the Marquis de Polignac, later secured him a position that was to change his life—with the great champagne house of Pommery. Simon married an English bride in 1900 and was sent shortly afterwards by Pommery to England, where his knowledge of wines won him both fame and fortune. With A. J. A. Symons he founded the Wine and Food Society in 1933, and after Symons's death in 1941 he continued as president of the society, which now has branches all over the world.

Although André Simon lived in England almost from the turn of the century, he remained a Frenchman both in nationality and accent. He served in the French army in the 1914–1918 War, winning the Medaille Militaire. A prolific writer on all subjects gastronomic, he was an acknowledged authority on wines. In 1960 he was called as an expert witness in the second of the "Spanish champagne" law cases and replied, when asked about his qualifications, "I am full of my subject." He remained full not only of wine but of energy until the end of his long life and was approaching 90 when he toured the vineyards of Australia, South Africa, and the U.S.A. Simon was an *officier* of the Legion of Honour and was created an honorary C.B.E. in 1965. His manifold publications include *History of the Champagne Trade in England* (1905); *Wine and Spirits—the Connoisseur's Textbook* (1919); *Bottlescrew Days* (1926); *The Art of Good Living* (1929); *A Concise Encyclopaedia of Gastronomy,* 9 vols. (1939–46); *The Gourmet's Weekend Book* (1952); *By Request: an Autobiography* (1956); *The Wines, Vineyards, and Vignerons of Australia* (1967).

Slim, Field Marshal Viscount William Joseph (1891-1970). Lord Slim, the revered "Uncle Bill" of the 14th Army in Burma during the Second World War, died on December 14, 1970, aged 79.

Slim's field marshal's baton was buried deep in his knapsack when he joined the army as a ranker at the outbreak of the First World War. Nothing in his background suggested that he was destined for high military command. He was born on August 6, 1891, and educated at King Edward's School, Birmingham. On leaving he was variously a junior clerk, a schoolmaster, and an engineer. In 1914 he was a N.C.O. in the Territorials and later that year he was commissioned into the Royal Warwickshire Regiment, seeing active service in Gallipoli, France, and Mesopotamia. He was twice wounded and was awarded the M.C. Serving for the latter part of the war in India, he transferred to the Indian Army in 1919, joining the 6th Gurkha Rifles. By 1933 he was a substantive major. He taught at Camberley from 1934 to 1937 with the rank of lieutenant-colonel.

At the outbreak of the Second World War, Slim was sent to the Sudan where, now a major-general, he commanded the 10th Indian Brigade in the first offensive against the Italians. He was wounded at the start of 1941, and shortly after recovering was given command of the 10th Indian Division which saw service in the Near East. He was awarded the D.S.O. in 1941. In March 1942 he was given command of the First Burma Corps during their jungle retreat to India, and in 1943 assumed command of the 14th Army in Burma, inspiring both British and Indian troops in what was one of the most dispiriting theatres of the war. He prevented a Japanese invasion of India by defeating offensives first in the Arakan, then in Assam with battles around Imphal and Kohima. After the Japanese fell back across the Chindwin during the 1944 monsoon, he went on the offensive to recapture Mandalay and Rangoon. In 1945 Slim was appointed c.-in-c. of Allied land forces in S.E. Asia, but in 1946 he returned to England to head the Imperial Defence College. While serving as Chief of the Imperial General Staff from 1948 to 1952 he was promoted field-marshal in 1949. On September 3, 1952, he was

F.M. Viscount Slim—"Slim of Burma".

appointed governor-general of Australia on the recommendation of Mr. Menzies, in the face of strong criticism from those who disapproved of what was a departure from the previous policy of recommending an Australian for this office. Once again, however, Slim's personality triumphed, and his term in Australia was extended until 1960.

A large, bluff character with an air of solidity and determination and above all the ability to inspire his soldiers, Lord Slim was a skilful commander and a master of logistics in difficult terrain. His book *Defeat into Victory*, an account of the Burma campaign, was published in 1956. He was created K.C.B. in 1944, G.C.M.G. in 1952, G.C.V.O. in 1954, and K.G. and Viscount in 1960. He served as governor and constable of Windsor Castle from 1964 until June 1970.

Smith, Maggie (born 1934). Red-haired, pale-skinned, slender Maggie Smith, hailed as the most stylish actress of her generation, found 1970 a year of triumph. The award of the C.B.E. in March was followed the next month by an Oscar for the best performance by an actress, for her memorable portrayal of the eccentric schoolmistress in *The Prime of Miss Jean Brodie*. This was by no means her first award. In 1962 she had received the *Evening Standard* award for the best actress of the year, and in 1963 a similar award from the Variety Club of Great Britain. Maggie Smith was born at Ilford on December 28, 1934. She was educated at the Oxford high school for girls and later studied at the Oxford Playhouse school. She made her first appearance in June 1952, playing Viola in *Twelfth Night*, and in 1957 made her first London hit as the principal comedienne (opposite Kenneth Williams) in the successful review *Share My Lettuce*. She played leading roles with the Old Vic for two years, including Lady Plyant in *The Double Dealers*, Celia in *As You Like It*, and Mistress Ford in *The Merry Wives of Windsor*. Her recent triumphs have been with the National Theatre, as Desdemona

Maggie Smith won Oscar and C.B.E.

to Olivier's Othello, Hedda Gabler, and in great comedy parts such as Mrs Sullen in *The Beaux' Stratagem*. Among her films are *The Pumpkin Eaters* and *Oh, What a Lovely War!* She is an all-round actress, but has certainly given most delight with her comedy performances. Her voice used to sound rather strangled; she says that it was not until a dentist broke her jaw that it became the versatile instrument it is today. She uses every part of her body, particularly her arms, to achieve her effects, and one of her greatest assets is a quiet, secret smile that hints at a mockery born of knowledge acquired by intuition rather than experience. It has been said of her that to capture a laugh she "enters into a conspiracy with her audience and together they give a mad world a whirl". She is married to Robert Stephens, the National Theatre actor.

Spock, Benjamin (born 1903). Guide and mentor to millions of mothers throughout the world and ardent advocate of non-violence, the legendary Doctor Spock has become a controversial figure in the U.S.A. Some regard him as a humanist crying in the wilderness, others as a muddle-headed dupe of the left wing. A convinced opponent of America's involvement in Vietnam, he has led demonstrations and been convicted in the courts.

Benjamin Spock was born on May 2, 1903, at New Haven, Connecticut. He was educated at Yale and at the Columbia University college of physicians and surgeons. For 15 years he specialized in pediatrics at Cornell Medical College, New York Hospital, and the New York City health department. He served in the U.S. navy and then returned to pediatric practice, organizing a teaching programme in child psychiatry and development at Pittsburgh University medical school. In 1955 he was appointed professor of child development at Western Reserve University, specializing in the application of psycho-analytical principles in the treatment of children. He published several books on child care. His *Baby and Child Care* became a fantastic best seller throughout the world. He advocated that parents should bring up children "democratically".

During the 1960s Spock became more and more concerned about the morality of America's actions in Vietnam. In 1967 he became director of the Committee for a Sane Nuclear Policy. He took part in several non-violent demonstrations. In April 1967, he and Martin Luther King led 100,000 people to the U.N. building in New York. In December he was arrested along with Conor Cruise O'Brien and Allen Ginsberg during a demonstration outside the armed forces induction centre in New York. He was charged with conspiring to counsel, aid, and abet young men to refuse to serve in the armed forces. A sentence of from ten to two years' imprisonment was later reversed by a court of appeal. In November 1969, he was among the leaders of the "march against death" in Washington. He expresses his motives

Dr. Benjamin Spock, mothers' guide and defender of the young.

thus: "I've spent my life studying and advising how to bring up children to be well-adjusted and happy. Now I see the futility of such efforts if these children are to be incinerated in an imbecilic war or if when grown they find life disillusioning."

Street, Lady Jessie (1889–1970). Australia has had few fighters for women's rights as redoubtable as Lady Jessie Street, who died in Sydney on July 2, 1970. She was not only an eloquent advocate but also a firm believer in action—often unconventional. At various times she worked in a New York home for prostitutes, campaigned with Emily Pankhurst for votes for women, and during the Second World War was employed in a steel factory.

The eldest daughter of C. A. G. Lillingston, Jessie Mary Grey was born in 1889 at Chota Nagpur, India, and was taken to Australia when seven years of age. She graduated at the University of Sydney in 1911, and in the same year attended the conference of the International Council of Women in Rome. She was a foundation member of the League of Nations Union in Sydney, and in 1930 and again in 1938 attended the League of Nations at Geneva. Joining the Australian Labour party, she contested, and nearly won, the strongly Liberal Wentworth seat at the Federal elections of 1943. In 1945 she was a member of the Australian delegation to the United Nations conference at San Francisco and she became a member of the U.N. economic and social committee.

Jessie Street was elected president of the Australian Russian Society in 1946, and visited Russia on two occasions in the early 1950s. For a time she worked in Paris as the United Nations correspondent for *Labour News*, but her divided loyalties between the Communist party and the Labour party forced her to resign from the latter. In 1966 she published her autobiography with the title *Truth or Repose*. She was the wife of Sir Kenneth Street, lieutenant-governor of New South Wales, whom she married in 1916.

Strougal, Lubomir (born 1924). A profound Communist party shake-up in Czechoslovakia in January 1970, which swept away the last remnants of the Dubcek era, brought Dr. Lubomir Strougal to the premiership, in succession to Oldrich Cernik, who had been appointed at the height of the Dubcek reform campaign in April 1968. Dr Strougal, a tough-minded former minister for the interior, is regarded as a hard-liner who believes that his country's fate hinges on good relations with Moscow. As head of the Communist party's Czech bureau he had carried out a purge of the liberal, reformist elements in the regional party apparatus within weeks of the downfall of Dubcek. He is regarded as the complete technocrat, and little is known of his private life. Yet, despite his steady climb towards the top, his appointment came as something of a surprise to Western observers, who had begun thinking that his star was in the descendant because of the rarity of his public appearances in the previous weeks.

Born on April 24, 1924, in Veseli nad Luzniki, near the Austrian border, Strougal graduated with a law degree in 1948 and at once began work with the Communist party. Soon he was first secretary of his home district, and in 1958 he joined the party's central committee. His talent for organization won him quick promotion. In the same year he was appointed minister of agriculture, and in 1961 became minister for the interior, holding the post for four years before returning to the party apparatus. After Dubcek became first secretary in 1968 Strougal was made deputy premier, but he avoided too close an association with the reformists, warning of the danger of antagonizing the Soviet Union. After the entry of Soviet troops in August 1968, he was one of the men entrusted with the task of restoring the party to its former position. In June 1969, the party praesidum made him the second most powerful man in the country by naming him deputy to the party leader, Dr. Gustav Husak. With his appointment as premier he took responsibility for his country's economic progress, the main problem facing the Czech government.

Lubomir Strougal, Czechoslovak premier.

**Herbert Strudwick,
the great wicket-keeper.**

Strudwick, Herbert (1880–1970). This cricket professional of a vanished age, who died in the night of February 13–14, 1970, a few weeks after his 90th birthday had been celebrated, could claim two records —one probably unique, the other certainly so. He was associated with the same county club, Surrey, for 60 years, having joined the playing staff in 1898 and continuing as scorer until 1958; while as the most respected and popular wicket-keeper of the period, he captured 1,468 victims, easily the most to fall to anybody, by either catching or stumping—not to mention those whom his quickness helped to run out. During 1903–27 he was regularly on duty for Surrey behind the stumps, and from 1911 was selected for 28 Test matches against Australia and South Africa, then the only opponents of England. He toured the former country three times, the latter twice; his final test was at the Oval in 1926, when England regained the "Ashes". Not a graduate of either the acrobatic or the vociferous school, Strudwick depended on sheer concentration and precision, being equally effective whether standing back or crouched over the stumps. One admirer described him as a "merry brown gnome." Gnarled hands and misshapen fingers contributed to this effect, besides reminding his successors of the frequent injuries he had suffered through flimsier gloves than they are used to wearing. But he would have chosen no other career than the craft in which he was supreme.

Sukarno, Achmad (1901–1970). Dr. Sukarno, the first president of the Indonesian Republic, died on June 21, 1970. He epitomized the charismatic leader of an underdeveloped nation in the immediate post-colonial era. Profligate and bombastic, he loaded his country with international debts while at the same time holding it together by the strength and fire of his personality. He was born in Surabaya in 1901, the son of a teacher of Javanese aristocratic background; his mother was of Balinese descent. Sukarno

graduated as an engineer at the Bandung technical institute in 1926, and seemed destined for a promising career in the Dutch service. He was attracted, however, to the nationalist movement in India and the teachings of Gandhi, and joined those whose ambition it was to free Indonesia from Dutch rule. As a schoolboy he had been involved in a Javanese youth movement, and had been inspired by the leader of the first Indonesian mass political movement. Having founded a National party in 1927, Sukarno was jailed by the Dutch in 1929 and 1937. He was in prison when the Japanese overran the Netherlands East Indies and on his agreement to work for them he was released in 1942. Sukarno subsequently led various political organizations sponsored by the Japanese authorities, and formed in 1945 a preparatory committee for Indonesian independence. On August 16, 1945, he and his colleague Mohammad Hatta were kidnapped by young revolutionaries who persuaded them to proclaim independence the following day. Thus Sukarno became the first president of the republic of Indonesia on August 17.

After Japan surrendered to the Allies, his revolutionary government resisted Dutch reoccupation. Fighting continued for three years, during which time Sukarno symbolized Indonesia's struggle and the ideal of national unity. His power rested on his personal magnetism and on his ability to balance Indonesia's opposing political forces. Finally, on December 27, 1949, the Dutch government granted Indonesia independence. President Sukarno's domestic policies followed a radical socialist nationalism. Internationally he was an advocate of "positive neutralism" and a leading representative of what he was pleased to call the "new emerging forces of the post-imperial era". One failing of Sukarno as a leader was his need to have external enemies. First, it was the Dutch. Then came the struggle over West Irian, which was finally handed over as a result of American mediation and the sanction of the U.N. in 1962, despite the feelings of its native Papuans. Next it was the British and a ramshackle, expen-

Ex-President Sukarno of Indonesia.

sive, and unsuccessful "confrontation" with Malaysia. Another failing was his personal extravagance which practically bankrupted Indonesia. In March 1966, a dissident army group launched a coup that forced Sukarno to give up much of his authority. He was not immediately removed as president, but finally surrendered all his powers to General Suharto at the end of February 1967.

Theodorakis, Mikis (born 1926). Popular composer, left-wing politician, and a leading opponent of the military regime in Greece, Theodorakis arrived in Paris from Athens on April 13, 1970. The French politician Jean-Jacques Servan-Schreiber had secured his release from detention after almost three years of imprisonment and house arrest. Theodorakis left behind his wife and children, but they succeeded in joining him later. He announced his determination to continue to fight for the downfall of the Greek government, and reaffirmed his adherence to the Communist party.

Theodorakis won world-wide fame for the music he wrote for the film *Zorba the Greek*, "Zorba's Dance" being particularly popular. But Theodorakis is basically a serious composer. As well as other film scores and more than 200 popular songs, he has written ten symphonic pieces, two oratorios, three ballets, and a folk opera. Much of his music has an underlying political content and commitment. A convinced Communist, as a boy he fought with the resistance against the German occupation troops, and during the Greek civil war he was detained as a political prisoner. On his release he went into exile in Paris, where he composed his first *bouzouki* songs. He returned to Greece to become a Marxist member of the assembly.

When the army officers carried out their *coup d'état* on April 21, 1967, Theodorakis went into hiding. He was arrested in August and, convicted on three counts of insulting or resisting the authorities, was sentenced to eight months' imprisonment on each count. The sentence was reduced on appeal, and he was eventually released under an amnesty after five months. In August 1968, he was exiled to the village of Zatouna in the Arcadian mountains. There he was kept under house arrest, followed everywhere by guards. His health began to deteriorate until the authorities moved him to a military hospital near Athens. Thanks partly to the pressure of world opinion, the Greek government released him unconditionally. While in Zatouna Theodorakis composed six cycles of songs dedicated, he says, "to all men who believe in man, who believe in life, in justice, in democracy and in freedom".

Thurso, Archibald Henry Macdonald Sinclair, 1st Viscount (1890–1970). Better known as Sir Archibald Sinclair, leader of the parliamentary Liberal party for ten years and minister for air during the Second World War, Lord Thurso died on June 15,

Mikis Theodorakis, Greek composer.

1970. Under his leadership the small band of Liberals had a remarkably powerful influence in the House of Commons. He joined Winston Churchill in his opposition to Chamberlain's appeasement policy during the 1930s. Lord Beaverbrook said he was the best minister for air "in our experience". He was not a brilliant debater in the House, but was an influential figure in cabinet discussions.

Sinclair was born on October 22, 1890. His parents both died while he was still a child, a tragedy that might explain his reserved manner. He inherited large estates in Caithness. Educated at Eton and Sandhurst, he entered the army in 1910 and served in France during the First World War. For a time he was adjutant of the battalion of the Royal Scots Fusiliers which Winston Churchill commanded. They struck up a lasting friendship, and after the war Sinclair served Churchill first as personal military secretary at the War Office and then as his private secretary at the Colonial Office. In 1922 he was elected to the House of Commons as Liberal M.P. for Caithness and Sutherland. In 1930 Lloyd George made him chief Liberal whip. The following year Sinclair accepted Ramsay MacDonald's invitation to become secretary of state for Scotland in his first "National" government. Along with other Liberal and Labour members he resigned in 1932 when the government adopted a general tariff.

After the general election of 1935 Sinclair became leader of the parliamentary Liberal party. He vigorously criticized the foreign policy of Baldwin and Chamberlain, and attacked the policy of appeasement towards Japan, Mussolini, and Hitler, allying his party with Churchill. When Churchill formed his coalition government in 1940 Sinclair became secretary of state for air, a post in which he drove himself to the utmost. Sinclair was defeated at the 1945 general election by 60 votes, and at the 1950 election by 269 votes. He was created a viscount in 1952.

Timoshenko, Semyon Konstantinovich (1895–1970). The death of Marshal

Timoshenko, the veteran Russian general known as "the bald eagle of the steppes", was announced in Moscow on March 31, 1970. He was born of peasant stock in the village of Furmanka, Bessarabia, in 1895, and on leaving the village school was employed as a barrel-maker before his conscription into the Imperial Russian army in 1915. Following the revolution and the Bolshevik seizure of power in November 1917, he was first a platoon-commander, and then commander of a southern partisan detachment that burgeoned swiftly into the First Revolutionary Cavalry Guards Regiment, which joined up with the 10th Red Army under Voroshilov. Timoshenko commanded a cavalry brigade throughout the siege of Tsaritsyn and later joined Budyenny and Voroshilov in the élite First Cavalry Army. His success in the fighting against Denikin during 1919 earned him the command of a division, with which he was active during the 1920 Soviet-Polish war.

Advancing from one high command to another, Timoshenko survived Stalin's military purge of 1937 (thanks to his association with Voroshilov) to become, in 1940, people's commissar (minister) of defence. He was prominent in the Soviet occupation of Poland in 1939, and the attack on Finland in 1941, during which he supervised the storming of the Mannerheim Line, an exploit for which he was honoured with the title Hero of the Soviet Union.

Timoshenko and his mentor, Voroshilov, both bear a share of responsibility for the Russian lack of preparedness when Hitler attacked the Soviet Union in June 1941. At the start of the invasion he was commander-in-chief of the Russian forces on the Western Front until Stalin himself took over as defence commissar. In the autumn of 1941 he was posted to the South-western Front, and in 1943 to the North-west. Although he is credited with the halting of the Nazi drive on Moscow and the successful counter-attack of November 1941, in which the Russians recaptured Rostov, Timoshenko's audacious plan for a major Russian attack on Kharkov in the spring of 1942 failed, leaving a gaping hole in the Soviet South-western Front—which led to Stalingrad and the Caucasus. This marked the end of Timoshenko's career as a commander in the field. He retired from the active list in 1960.

Wilson, Rt. Rev. John Leonard (1897–1970). The former Bishop of Birmingham, who died on August 18, 1970, was one of the most widely known church leaders on the British scene. He derived his fame not from any great theological or ecclesiastical achievement, but from the fearless courage with which he withstood floggings and torture from the Japanese. This was his lot during the Second World War, but he was no stranger to war in earlier life. He was born on November 23, 1897, the son of a vicar in County Durham, and as soon as he attained military age he volunteered during the First World War, serving with the Durham Light Infantry. His experience during the two wars fitted him for the role by which he was known to the millions who yearly watched on television his burly figure, complete with a noble Edwardian beard and solemnly vested in cope and mitre, conduct the short service at the Festival of Remembrance at the Royal Albert Hall, London.

It was during his war-time experience as a young man that he found his vocation to the ministry. He trained at Queen's College and Wycliffe Hall, Oxford, and was ordained in 1924. The next few years brought very varied experiences—a curacy at Coventry Cathedral, a year as head of the C.M.S. boys' school at Cairo, and then eight years in parishes in his native Northeast.

Three years as Dean and Archdeacon of Hong Kong were followed in 1941 by the appointment by which he was to attain a costly fame. He became Bishop of Singapore only a few months before it surrendered to the Japanese. His wife reached Australia; the Bishop stayed with his clergy and people. When imprisonment in the notorious Changi jail came it was to lead to appalling suffering in which the Bishop showed great bravery, and an amazing spirit of forgiveness to his captors despite their brutality towards him. After the war he baptized and confirmed a group of Japanese soldiers that included some of his jailers. He was created C.M.G. in 1946.

Again he became a Dean—of Manchester—for a short while, before he was

Bishop Wilson of Birmingham.

appointed to an episcopal see in 1953. He had the hard task of following the late Bishop Barnes as Bishop of Birmingham. Barnes had been an extreme modernist with very imperfect sympathies towards men with other convictions. The new Bishop was also a man of firm modernist convictions; but he was not primarily an intellectual, he was rich in human sympathy, and he had the virile attractiveness of a man who had "confessed the faith" through terrible suffering. He retired in 1969 from a diocese happily reunited in spirit under his leadership, but the grim

years in Changi jail had exacted their toll from even his vigorous frame, and he died after but brief enjoyment of retirement.

Young, Brian Walter Mark (born 1922). A ripple of controversy greeted the announcement, on April 17, 1970, that Brian Young, an ex-headmaster of Charterhouse, was to take over as director general of the Independent Television Authority in October. Brian Young was born in Ceylon, the elder son of Sir Mark Young, a former colonial governor. He was educated at Eton, where he was a King's scholar. He was in the R.N.V.R. during the Second World War, serving in destroyers with the Home, Mediterranean, and East Indies fleets. In 1945 he entered King's College, Cambridge, where he took first-class honours in both parts of the Classical tripos and won half-blues for athletics and Eton fives. He also sang, acted, and played the clarinet. After leaving Cambridge he returned to Eton as a master for five years before becoming headmaster of Charterhouse at the early age of 29. He was appointed director of the Nuffield Foundation in 1964. Young served on the Central Advisory Council for Education which produced the Crowther report, and on the Central Religious Advisory Committee which advises both ITV and the BBC. At the time of his appointment he was a member of the U.K. National Commission of UNESCO, of the Health Education Council, and of the governing board of the Centre for Educational Development Overseas.

OBITUARY

Well-known men and women who died during 1970, and whose biographies are not given under "Names in the News" in the foregoing pages, include:

ROYALTY AND HEADS OF STATE
Gen. Lazaro Cardenas, president of Mexico 1934–40, aged 75, on Oct. 20.
Lt.-Gen. H. H. the Maharaja of Jaipur,, aged 58, on June 24.
Marquis of Milford Haven, aged 50, on April 14.
Ex-King Peter of Yugoslavia, aged 47, on Nov. 5.
Nikolai Shvernik, president of U.S.S.R. 1946–53, aged 82, on Dec. 26.
Yusef bin Ishak, first president of Singapore, aged 60, on Nov. 23.

ART
Barnett Newman, U.S. artist, aged 65, on July 9.
H. E. Popham, British authority on Old Masters drawings, aged 81, on Dec. 8.
Nina Ricci, French fashion designer, aged 87, on Nov. 29.
Mark Rothko, U.S. artist, aged 66, on Feb. 25.
Francis R. Yerbery, founder of the Building Centre, London, aged 84, on July 7.

ENTERTAINMENT
Ed Begley, U.S. actor, aged 69, on April 28.
Neville Blond, chairman of English Stage Co. Ltd., aged 74, on Aug. 5.
Billie Burke, U.S. actress, aged 84, on May 17.
John Paddy Carstairs, British film director, aged 60, on Dec. 12.
Mary Clare, British actress, aged 78, on Aug. 29.
V. C. Clinton-Baddeley, British actor and author, aged 70, on Aug. 6.
Preston Foster, U.S. actor, aged 69, on July 15.
Fernand Gravey, French actor, aged 64, on Nov. 3.
Jimmy Hanley, British actor, aged 51, on Jan. 13.
Hy Hazell, British actress, aged 47, on May 10.
Edward Everett Horton, U.S. actor, aged 83, on Sept. 29.
George Inns, creator of BBC-TV's *Black and White Minstrel Show*, aged 58, on July 21.

Janis Joplin, U.S. singer, aged 27, on Oct. 5.
Malcolm Keen, British actor, aged 82, on Jan. 30.
Harold Lang, British actor, aged 44, on Nov. 16.
Harry Leon, British songwriter, aged 68, on Feb. 18.
Chester Morris, U.S. film actor, aged 69, on Sept. 11.
Conrad Nagel, U.S. film actor, aged 72, on Feb. 24.
Elizabeth Pollock, British actress, aged 71, on Jan. 6.
Roy Rich, former head of BBC sound entertainment, aged 57, on March 24.
Charles Ruggles, U.S. comedian, aged 84, on Dec. 23.
Tom Sloan, former BBC-TV light entertainment chief, aged 50, on May 13.
Naunton Wayne, British actor, aged 69, on Nov. 17.
Alan Wilkie, actor-manager, aged 91, on Jan. 6.
Patrick Wymark, British actor, aged 44, on Oct. 20.

EXPLORATION AND ADVENTURE

Col. Pavel Belyaev, Russian astronaut, aged 44, on Jan. 10.

Ian Clough, British mountaineer, killed in fall on Annapurna, aged 33, on May 30.

Rear-Admiral Donald B. MacMillan, U.S. Navy, last surviving member of Robert Peary's 1908–09 expedition to the North Pole, aged 95, on Sept. 9.

Dr. Tom Patey, British mountaineer, killed in climbing accident in Scotland, aged 38, on May 25.

LAW

Paul Bennet, V.C., M.C., British magistrate, aged 77, on April 4.

Det.-Chief. Supt. "Tommy" Butler, M.B.E., co-ordinator of hunt for Great Train Robbers, aged 57, on April 20.

Sir Laurence Dunne, former chief metropolitan magistrate of London, aged 76, on June 30.

Lord Mitchison, Q.C., aged 79, on Feb. 14.

Judge Waddy, Q.C. (Dorothy Knight Dix), aged 60, on Jan. 8.

LITERATURE

Ralph Arnold, British author and publisher, aged 63, on Sept. 23.

Jean Giono, French novelist, aged 75, on Oct. 8.

Jack Jones, Welsh author and playwright, aged 85, on May 7.

Frances Parkinson Keyes, U.S. authoress, aged 84, on July 3.

Sir Allen Lane, British publisher, originator of Penguin Books, aged 67, on July 7.

Alasdair Alpin MacGregor, British author, poet, and journalist, aged 71, on April 15.

Jane Oliver (Mrs. Helen Rees), British authoress, aged 66, on May 4.

Charles Olson, U.S. poet, aged 60, on Jan. 10.

Pierre Mac Orlan, French novelist, aged 88, on June 28.

Gale Pedrick, British journalist and broadcaster, aged 64, on Feb. 22.

Nelly Sacks, German winner of 1966 Nobel literature prize, aged 79, on May 2.

Dr. Enid Starkie, British authority on French literature, on April 22.

D. E. Stevenson, British authoress, aged 78, on Dec. 11.

Elsa Triolet, French poetess, aged 74, on June 15.

Giuseppe Ungaretti, Italian poet, aged 82.

MILITARY

Air Chief Marshal Sir Norman H. Bottomley, aged 79, on Aug. 13.

Sir Michael Le Fanu, Admiral of the Fleet, aged 57, on Nov. 28.

Gen. Pierre Koenig, former commander of Free French Forces, aged 71, on Sept. 3.

Lt.-Col. Frederick Gerard Peake (Peake Pasha), founder of the Arab Legion, aged 84, on March 30.

Air Chief Marshal Sir Richard Peirse, aged 77, on Aug. 5.

Col. Roscoe Turner, U.S. airman, aged 74, on June 24.

MUSIC

Sir John Barbirolli, conductor of the Hallé Orchestra, aged 70, on July 29.

Roberto Gerhard, Spanish-born composer, aged 73, on Jan. 5.

Ray Henderson, U.S. composer, aged 74, on Dec. 31.

Cyril Scott, British composer, aged 91, on Dec. 31.

George Szell, Hungarian-born U.S. conductor, aged 73, on July 31.

Kerstin Thorborg, Swedish opera singer, aged 73, on April 15.

POLITICS

Baron Adolph Bentinck, Dutch diplomat, aged 64, on March 7.

Lord Bowles, former British Labour M.P., aged 68, on Dec. 29.

Bessie Braddock, British Labour M.P., aged 71, on Nov. 13.

René Capitant, former French Minister of Justice, aged 68, on May 23.

Madame Marie Chaban-Delmas, wife of prime minister of France, as result of car accident, on Aug. 12.

Sir Thomas Cook, British Conservative M.P., aged 68, on Aug. 12.

Roger Gresham Cooke, British Conservative M.P., aged 63, on Feb. 22.

Charles Corbin, French diplomat, aged 88, on Sept. 25.

Stanley Evans, British Labour M.P., aged 72, on June 25.

Capt. Henrique Galvao, Portuguese rebel who seized the liner *Santa Monica* in 1961, in Brazil, aged 74, on June 25.

George Magoffi Humphrey, former secretary of U.S. treasury, aged 79, on Jan. 20.

Sir Herbert Hyland, oldest member of State parliament of Victoria, Australia, aged 86, on March 18.

Abdullah Khalil, former prime minister of Sudan, on Aug. 23.

Lord Latham, former leader of London County Council, aged 82, on March 31.

Sir Firoz Khan Noon, former prime minister of Pakistan, aged 77, on Dec. 9.

Sir Tom O'Brien, British trade union leader, aged 69, on May 5.

Sir David Owen, British U.N. official, aged 65, on June 29.

André Philip, former French minister, aged 68, on July 6.

Henri Queuille, three times premier of France, aged 86, on June 15.

Adam Rapacki, former foreign minister of Poland, aged 60, on Oct. 10.

Walter Reuther, president of U.S. United Auto Workers Union, killed with wife in plane crash, aged 62, on May 9.

Dr. Paul Schmitt, aide and interpreter to Adolf Hitler, aged 71, on April 22.

Mrs. Caroline Thorpe, wife of British Liberal leader Jeremy Thorpe, in car crash, aged 32, on June 29.

Constantine Tsaldaris, former prime minister of Greece, aged 86, on Nov. 15.

RELIGION

Rev. Geoffrey Beaumont, composer of Folk Mass and hymn tunes, aged 67, on Aug. 24.

Dr. H. C. Montgomery Campbell, former Bishop of London, aged 83, on Dec. 26.

Dr. Cecil Roth, Jewish scholar and author, aged 71, on June 21.

SCIENCE

Professor Max Born, nuclear physicist, aged 87, on Jan. 5.

Prof. George Ingle Finch, Australian-born scientist and mountaineer, aged 82, on Nov. 23.

Dr. F. A. Freeth, British industrial scientist, aged 86, on July 15.

Prof. Morris Ginsberg, British sociologist, aged 81, on Aug. 31.

Prof. Edward Armand Guggenheim, British authority on thermodynamics, aged 68, on Aug. 9.

Lord Jackson of Burnley, British scientist and engineer, aged 65, on Feb. 17.

Dr. Hans Kronberger, British nuclear physicist, aged 50, on Sept. 29.

A. I. Mikoyan, Russian designer of MiG aircraft, aged 65, on Dec. 9.

Dr. Geoffrey Vevers, former superintendent of Regent's Park and Whipsnade Zoos, aged 80, on Jan. 9.

Prof. Otto Warburg, German bio-chemist, Nobel prize-winner, aged 86, on Aug. 1.

SPORT

Richard Bergmann, table-tennis player, six times British champion, aged 51, on April 5.

Martin Brain, British racing driver, killed in crash at Silverstone, aged 37, on May 25.

Sid Buller, British cricket umpire, aged 60, on Aug. 6.

Leandro Faggin, Italian cycling champion, aged 37, on Dec. 6.

Ted (Kid) Lewis, British world welterweight boxing champion, aged 75, on Oct. 20.

Harold Stirling Vanderbilt, originator of contract bridge and racing yachtsman, aged 85, on July 4.

Hugh Wardell-Yerburgh, British Olympic oarsman, in road accident, aged 31, on Jan. 28.

OTHERS

Elyesa Bazna, the spy "Cicero", in Munich, aged 66, on Dec. 25.

Marie Houle Dionne, one of Canada's famous quintuplets, found dead in her Montreal flat on Feb. 28.

Thelma, Lady Furness, aged 65, on Jan. 29.

Jack Mills, driver of train in 1963 Great Train Robbery, aged 64, on Feb. 4.

Prof. Donald J. Robertson, prof. of industrial relations at Glasgow University, aged 43, on Aug. 22.

Mrs. Ada Roe, Great Britain's oldest inhabitant, aged 111 years and 339 days, on Jan. 11.

Sir Peter Runge, chairman of British National Export Council, aged 61, on Aug. 19.

Lord Strathalmond, former chairman of British Petroleum Co. Ltd., aged 81, on April 1.

Fact Digest

In this "little encyclopedia" of the year will be found several hundred short articles on topics of importance that came into prominence during 1970 but are not considered in detail in the other main sections of the Year Book. The items are arranged in alphabetical order throughout.

Aberdeen, Scotland. Mullard, the British electronics firm, announced in April 1970 that it is to build a £1 million factory in Aberdeen to produce memory stacks and complete memories for computers. Construction of the main 230,000 sq. ft. factory on a 15-acre site—formerly a railway marshalling yard—at Kittybrewster will start during the first half of 1971. The work, which will be carried out in four stages, is due for completion in 1975. The factory will eventually give employment to over 1,000 people, the majority of them women.

Aborigines. Under legislation to be introduced in the Victoria parliament, aborigines will be granted unconditional land rights. This is the first such government move in Australia. When it was announced in April 1970 it was stated that the aborigines will get full legal title to the land they now live on at Lake Tyers in East Gippsland, and at Framlingham near Warrnambool in the south-west of the State, involving over 4,500 acres of land. Eighty aborigines live at Lake Tyers, and 65 at Framlingham.

At a September meeting of aborigines in Melbourne the constitution of a newly formed National Tribal Council, which will allow only full or part-blooded aborigines and Torres Strait islanders to hold executive positions, was approved. Non-aborigines can be admitted only as affiliate members without voting rights. The Council, set up to promote the interests of aborigines and Torres Strait islanders, and to preserve their culture, has the backing of the World Council of Churches.

Plans to establish a large cattle project in northern Australia, and a town to serve it, were announced by the Methodist Overseas Mission in October. The project will be developed on the mainland near Milingimbi Island, about 350 miles E. of Darwin. The town, to cost about $A2 million, will house about 500 people and will help to reduce the aboriginal population on Milingimbi, where there is a shortage of water.

The Queensland minister for aboriginal affairs said on April 23, 1970, that the Queensland government was to buy $A110,000 worth of shares in the mining company, Comalco Ltd., to hold in trust for the State's aboriginals and islanders.

Announcing in December that financial assistance is to be provided for the setting up of a legal aid service in Sydney for aborigines, the minister for aboriginal affairs said that the service, the first of its kind in Australia, would be directed by a council of 15 volunteers, including aborigines. He said that aborigines are frequently at a greater disadvantage than Europeans under the legal system, and that the new legal service would help them with their particular problems. If it proves successful it will be extended throughout the country.

Information given in August by a research team working in the outback areas of Australia showed that in a remote part of N.S.W. near the town of Bourke nine aboriginal babies are being born every year for every 100 of the total population, compared with one baby a year for every 100 of the white Australian community.

Archaeology. Aboriginal paintings found in 1970 in a cave about 60 miles E. of Wodonga, Victoria, are believed to be unique. The paintings, hand silhouettes about twice life size and painted on the rock wall in faded red ochre, are of emu and other bird footprints, stylized human figures, and spear-heads. The curator of anthropology of the National Museum of Victoria said that the hand silhouettes were unique because, unlike previous discoveries, they are not a stencil type of painting. The site is the fourth to be found in the north-east of Victoria.

The New South Wales government introduced measures in April 1970 which will protect aboriginal relics and archaeological sites, the N.S.W. National Parks and Wild Life Service having control of areas where the search for new evidence of the aboriginal way of life might be made. The new laws make it an offence to disturb, destroy, or knowingly deface any such relics, or to excavate them without a permit. The State government now has the power to declare as aboriginal areas any sites of archaeological significance or Crown land, and, with the owner's consent, is empowered to declare as a protected aboriginal area any private property where relics are found. Anyone finding sites or relics is required to inform the director of the National Parks and Wild Life Service within three months, unless they have grounds for believing that the service is already aware of them. This legislation follows similar measures introduced in Queensland and South Australia, and the same steps will also be taken in Western Australia.

Abortion. The U.K. Registrar-General's statistical review, published on Aug. 12, 1970, showed that the total number of abortions carried out in the first eight months after the Abortion Act became law in April 1968 was 22,332. Classified by the woman's own occupation or, if she was married, that of her husband, the figures showed that the professional class, including doctors, architects, and civil engineers, had the lowest number (645), while women in the skilled working class, including weavers, tailors, and secretaries, had the highest number (8,167). The second highest figure (6,939) was in the "unclassified" group, which includes students, unemployed, members of the Forces, and those who did not state their own or their husband's occupation. In the unskilled group, which includes dock labourers and kitchen hands, there were 735. Nearly half the total of all abortions were performed on unmarried women, and 1,945 on the widowed, divorced, or separated. The largest number of single women who had abortions was in the 20–24 age group, and largest number of married women were in the 30–34 age group. Other figures showed that the total number of legal abortions performed in 1969 was 54,013, of which 1,232 were on girls under 16. In 1970 the rate increased to nearly 75,000 a year (about 1,600 a year on girls under 16).

Denmark. On March 18, 1970, a law legalizing abortion for women under the age of 18 who are able to show that they lack the money, time, or maturity to care for a baby was passed in the Danish parliament by 100 votes to 20.

Australia. South Australia became the first State to legalize abortion when its Abortion Reform Bill became law on Jan. 7, 1970. Abortions, which can be legally performed at 71 hospitals throughout the State, will require the approval of two doctors, except when an emergency occurs in a remote area. They can be legally granted where continued pregnancy would involve the woman in greater risk to her life, or greater danger of physical or mental damage, than if it were terminated, and also when there is a substantial risk of the child being born with serious mental or physical handicap.

Accidents. *Road.* U.K. Ministry of Transport figures issued on April 15, 1970, showed that 7,383 people died on the roads in 1969, compared with 6,810 in 1968, and 7,319 in 1967. The total number of casualties in 1969 was 353,194, compared with 349,208 in 1968, and 369,978 in 1967. Serious injuries in 1969 totalled 90,715, compared with 88,563 in 1968, and 93,757 in 1967, and the number of slight injuries rose by less than a half per cent on the 1968 figure to 255,096. In 1968 the fatal and serious casualties during the hours between 10 p.m. and 4 a.m. number 18,985, compared with 22,895 in 1967, but in 1969 the number rose to 20,667. Traffic was estimated to have increased by 2 per cent in 1969, compared with the previous year. In the first 8 months of 1970 the number of deaths from road accidents was 2·9 per cent higher than in the same period of 1969, and the number of serious injuries 2·6 per cent higher.

The 1969 annual report of the Royal Society for the Prevention of Accidents, published in October 1970, pointed out the number of children included in these figures. Deaths numbered 870, seriously injured 15,387, slightly injured 46,399, giving a total of 62,656 casualties, a reduction of about 2 per cent on the 1968 figures.

Railways. The chief inspecting officer of British railways, in his annual report published in December, said that the number of accidents caused by malicious acts had more than doubled in 6 years, and in 1969 represented 11 per cent of all train accidents. There were 164 incidents of this type in 1969, including one in which the driver of a train was killed by a 12-in. boulder dropped by youths on to the cab of his passenger express near Durham. During the year 105 trains ran into obstacles on the line; five were derailed, and 13 were set on fire as the result of acts of hooliganism. The total number of train accidents rose from 1·63 per million train miles in 1968 to 1·83 in 1969, and goods train derailments, the biggest single category of accidents, increased by 179 per cent over the 1968 figure. Provisional figures for 1970, however, showed a 15 per cent decrease on 1969. The report added that rail travel in Great Britain was "very safe indeed", with only one passenger death in every 1,580 million passenger train miles compared with one in every 1 million road passenger miles during the 1960s.

Industrial. The U.K. 1970 annual report on the Offices, Shops, and Railway Premises Act, published in October, stated that the total number of accidents occurring at work in 1969 was 19,018, and that 20 white-collar workers were killed.

Mining. The *Coal News* reported in June 1970 that the National Coal Board's "all-action" safety drive at the pits had led to 33 fewer deaths in 1969, and 116 fewer serious injuries than in 1968. During the year up to March 1970, 82 pitmen were killed (73 underground and nine on the surface), which represents a rate of 0·12 for every 100,000 manshifts worked. Another 672 were seriously injured, 589 of them underground and 83 on the surface (a rate of 1·01). The 1969–70 safety competition won £12,000 worth of prize money for accident-free pitmen.

Australia. Figures given at the beginning of November showed that, on a population basis, Australia had the worst road toll in the world, with 287 deaths per million of the population, compared with 268 per million in the U.S.A., and 740 deaths for each million vehicles, compared with the U.S.A.'s 533. Australia and Canada have the second highest total of motor vehicles per head of the population, Australia having one car for every 3·4 people, compared with the U.S.A.'s 2·4. Road accidents represented a national disaster, causing an annual economic loss to the country estimated at $A400 million, the Royal Australian College of Physicians stated at a meeting in Brisbane in May 1970. The doctors said that road accidents formed "the most urgent medical problem facing the Australian community. If a similar rate of death were the result of an epidemic, the nation would mobilize all its resources in defence." The College decided to call on the Federal and State governments to set up a road safety authority to support a research programme into the prevention of road accidents and serious injury.

According to information given by the Victorian Chamber of Manufacturers in June 1970 Australia's 300,000 industrial accidents cost the country between $A700 million and $A1,000 million a year. The accident frequency rate of 35 disabling injuries per million man-hours worked was stated to be one of the worst among modern industrial nations. The accident frequency rate in the U.S.A. was 7·35, only 20 per cent of Australia's. Other figures given in June showed that total working time lost through industrial accidents was about 700,000 man-weeks a year, and that compensation claims resulting from these accidents amounted to more than $A100 million.

U.S.A. Figures given by the National Safety Council in March 1970 showed that accidents in the United States in 1969 killed 116,000 people, and injured a further 10·8 million, 400,000 of this number being permanently impaired to some degree. Deaths due to motor accidents rose to 56,400, compared with 55,200 in 1968. Accidents were the main cause of death for people between the ages of one and 37, and remained the fourth overall cause of death, exceeded only by heart disease, cancer, and strokes. The Council's statistics also showed that in the 10 years ending in 1969 there was a 26 per cent rise in the number of accidental deaths, and that over 1 million people lost their lives as a result of accidents in that period.

Children. A 3-month propaganda campaign in the U.K. to save children from accidents in or around the home was launched on April 7, 1970, by the Royal Society for the Prevention of Accidents. In 1967, the last year for which figures are available, 713 children under the age of 4, and 104 between 5 and 14, died from accidents in the home in England and Wales, and a total of 41,970 children under the age of 14, including 31,020 under the age of 4, were treated in hospital. It was stated that the number of small children admitted for alcohol poisoning had risen threefold in 3 years, and that admissions for poisoning from gases and noxious foodstuffs had doubled in 5 years. The major reason for hospital admissions remained aspirin poisoning; half of the cases were due, not to accident, but to overdoses given by parents or doctors.

Adelaide Festival. The sixth Adelaide Festival of Arts was opened by the Governor-General of Australia, Sir Paul Hasluck, on March 7, 1970. The festival, which was extended from its previous two weeks to three, drew an audience at least one third larger than in 1968. The programme included opera by the English Opera Group, and the Intimate Opera Group; ballet by the Australian Ballet with Rudolf Nureyev and Robert Helpmann as guest artists; and orchestral music by the Warsaw Philharmonic Orchestra, the South Australian Symphony Orchestra, the

Accidents. The Japanese Toyota car company built this shrine at Tateshina for the repose of the souls of all those who have died in accidents involving cars of their manufacture.

Bartok String Quartet, and the Adelaide University Wind Quintet. Other music was provided by Nelli Shkolnikova, the famous Russian violinist, and by Peter Pears, who gave song recitals accompanied by Benjamin Britten. The Royal Shakespeare Company presented Judi Dench and Donald Sinden in *The Winter's Tale* and *Twelfth Night*; and the South Australian Theatre Company gave a performance of Chekov's *The Seagull*. Other plays seen at the Festival included *Saved* by Edward Bond, and the première of *Ourselves in Amber* by a South Australian playwright, Ken West. *The Best and Worst of Times*, in which some of the best-known characters from the works of Charles Dickens were presented in a series of monologues linked by narration, was a special attraction staged in commemoration of the centenary of the author's death. There were three loan art collections: one of recent British paintings, one of the works of Leonard French, and the third a "Portrait of Mexico". This last collection included over 200 pieces of sculpture, pottery, and artifacts extending in age from the pre-Columbian period to the present day. Writers' week—a week of discussions, seminars, lectures, recitals, and poetry readings by Australian and overseas writers—included guests Anthony Burgess, Edna O'Brien, and Edward Albee.

AG-61. This is the name of a device which is now being provided free by the Soviet Union health service to people who have been rendered speechless by an operation on or injury to the larynx. The device, which enables them to speak again, is, in effect, an artificial larynx about 6 in. long, weighing about 10 oz. It runs off a 5-volt battery which can be recharged daily from the mains. It will, if necessary, be replaced every 3 years.

Air Passengers (Australia). Figures given by the Minister for Civil Aviation on Jan. 23, 1970, showed that Australia's domestic airlines carried 5·9 million passengers on scheduled services in Australia and Papua–New Guinea in 1969—an increase of 12·7 per cent over 1968. Of the total, 5·6 million travelled on Australian services, and 308,000 with airlines in Papua–New Guinea. Freight carried by the domestic airlines (104,490 tons) increased by 10·9 per cent over 1968, and mail (11,504 tons) rose by 7·3 per cent. Hours flown by the airlines totalled 289,723, an increase of 4·4 per cent.

Airports. The report of a survey carried out by the directorate of civil engineering development of the U.K. ministry of public building and works into the relative advantages of offshore aerodromes, including airports that could be towed to different sites, over land-based sites was published on Feb. 24, 1970. The report concluded that floating airports in coastal waters were not only technically feasible, but had many advantages over land-based sites. Five types of fully floating platforms were

considered in the survey: the "gasholder" type, which could be raised above the waves; a platform supported on pontoons or large floats; a platform supported on hollow concrete box sections filled with expanded polystyrene, post-tensioned together to form a continuous structure (see p. 66); a platform supported on submerged floats with adjustable buoyancy; and a large continuous steel box construction. The ministry favoured the "gasholder" type, which consists of a platform with deep sidewalls all round which could be raised above sea level by maintaining a cushion of controlled pressure underneath, so reducing the magnitude of stresses from waves and swell.

The report also said that, although offshore airports on reclaimed land would be more expensive than land-based sites, they had several advantages. These included the facts that air traffic patterns over land near large cities is complex and congested; that many major cities are near the sea; that aircraft noise would be dispersed over the water; that land near large cities is increasingly difficult to find and very expensive, and the securing of planning approval difficult; and that aircraft fuelling systems from large tankers would be easier to operate. Their disadvantages would be the facts that they would be less stable; maintenance costs would be greater; skidding conditions would be caused by damp runway surfaces; and salt water would increase the contamination of aircraft. It would also be necessary to develop new methods of landing systems and approach lighting to cater for the rise and fall of the tides. Overall, however, the report found that floating airports offered advantages in deep water over fixed construction, largely because they could be orientated to suit wind conditions, and because the whole airport could be resited if necessary.

It was announced in July that reports by British pilots of inadequate landing and navigational equipment at nine European airports which could endanger flights at peak periods or in poor weather conditions were being investigated by the British Airline Pilots' Association. The nine were Turnhouse (Edinburgh, Scotland), Malaga and Alicante (Spain), Faro (Portugal), Catania (Sicily), Innsbruck (Austria), Gibraltar, Rhodes, and Ibiza.

Albert Medal. It was announced on April 1, 1970, that this medal for gallantry in saving life at sea or on land had been awarded posthumously to First Officer Geoffrey Clifford Bye, of Boolaroo, near Newcastle, New South Wales. First Officer Bye made several attempts to save the chief engineer during a fire on a merchant ship, the *Frisia*, in Rabaul harbour in New Britain in May 1968, but both men were killed. A crew member of the ship, Robert Siliko, of Nissan Island in the trerritory of Papua–New Guinea, was awarded the George Medal for risking his life to save his cabin mates during the fire.

Alcoholism. Two alarming reports on alcoholism in the U.K. were published in

1970. The first, "The Alcoholism Explosion", published on Jan. 19 by the National Council of Alcoholism, said that alcoholism was believed to be costing the U.K. £250 million a year. It stated that there were 175,000 chronic alcoholics in the country, and at least another 225,000 "problem drinkers" who, unless they receive help, could become alcoholics. Every Monday a quarter of a million men stay away from work because they have hangovers. The second report, published on July 29 by the medical council on alcoholism, stated that the disease is now Great Britain's third major health hazard, following closely behind heart disease and cancer. Its estimate of the number of alcoholics was higher—300,000—but it put the cost to the economy at a lower figure—£100 million a year. The latter report suggested that the government should devote one tenth of a penny in the pound of the £1,500 million collected in tax from the liquor trade to finance treatment and research. A survey had shown that the total number of beds available in Great Britain in special alcoholic units was only 407, for the 200,000 potential patients who needed hospital treatment.

Aldeburgh Festival. On June 5, 1970, the Queen reopened the Aldeburgh Festival concert hall and opera house, the Maltings, at Snape, Suffolk, burned down on June 7, 1969, and now substantially rebuilt. The concert hall appeared exactly as it did before the fire, but during the restoration work sprinklers were installed in the roof's structure as an additional safeguard against fire. As the rest of the buildings adjacent to the hall—at present used for industrial purposes—become free, it is planned to develop an arts centre with a music library, an art gallery, artists' studios, permanent exhibition space, scenery workshops, and rehearsal rooms. It is also planned to extend the Festival from its present three-week season in June to an artistic festival lasting from spring until late autumn. By May 1970 over £60,000 had been raised towards the initial cost of rebuilding the concert hall, estimated at £112,000, and a foundation was set up with the aim of raising over £250,000 by 1980 to expand the Festival.

Aldergrove, N. Ireland. It was announced in September that £1,500,000 is to be spent on developing this airport, which will be taken over by the Northern Ireland government on April 1, 1971. The main runway, in its extended and re-shaped form, will be 9,100 ft. long, and the new Airports Authority plans to have it completed by the middle of 1972. While the runway is closed for the work, the second runway will be brought up to a high standard to cope with traffic. Aldergrove, which in 1969 handled 1,029,000 passengers, is the sixth busiest airport in the U.K. Passenger traffic has more than doubled since 1960, when the number handled was 428,000, and air freight rose from 6,742 metric tons in 1960 to over 22,000 metric tons in 1969.

Alma Ata, Kazakhstan, U.S.S.R. It was reported in May 1970 that a thermal lake with water at 158°F had been discovered about two miles beneath Alma Ata, the capital of the Kazakhstan Republic. Water from what was described as this "inexhaustible national boiler" is to be used in the houses of the city's 700,000 population, saving about 1,000 tons of coal a day. Experts have estimated that eight wells should be sufficient to extract the water.

Alumina. American Metal Climax announced in May 1970 that it plans to build one of the largest alumina plants in the world to process the huge bauxite reserves in the Kimberley region of Western Australia. One of Metal Climax's subsidiary companies, Amax Bauxite Corporation, is to spend $A330 million on the construction of the complex near Port Warrender. Initially the plant will produce 1,200,000 long tons of alumina a year, but provision will be made to double the output at a later date. Construction is scheduled to begin early in 1971, and alumina production should be under way late in 1973 or early in 1974.

Aluminium. The formation of a new organization, the European Primary Aluminium Association, to represent the interests of European primary aluminium producers, was announced on Jan. 27, 1970. With headquarters in Düsseldorf, West Germany, the Association has 14 founder members from 10 European countries, representing 45 aluminium reduction plants with a total annual capacity of 1·95 million tons. Great Britain is represented by Alcan and British Aluminium.

The leader of the Greater London Council, opening three houses at Lewisham on May 6, 1970, launched a pioneer scheme in the use of aluminium for housing. The three-bedroom houses, built for the Aluminium Federation in conjunction with the Council, form part of a larger scheme designed to reduce maintenance costs for local authorities. Each of the houses incorporates two thirds of a ton of aluminium, including such items as weatherboard facing, roofing, window frames, light switches, and door handles.

Amphetamine. An experiment at Ipswich, Suffolk, during 1969 to reduce addiction to this stimulant drug was described at a May 1970 British Medical Association meeting. The weekly number of tablets dispensed in this town of 120,000, it was said, had been reduced from 7,000– 10,000 in 1968 to about 100 by May 1970. All 55 general practitioners in the town and an equal number of local hospital doctors had agreed to stop prescribing the drug. The experiment began in 1968 with the creation of a committee on which chemists, teachers, probation and children's department representatives, and police all served. At first, amphetamine prescriptions were reduced, and then at the beginning of the winter of 1969, the decision to stop them altogether was

Amphibious Vehicles. This two-engined "aerosleigh", built by young technicians at an institute in Perm, U.S.S.R., will run over snow, land, and water. It has retractable wheels.

taken. The *British Medical Journal* commended the doctors, seeing their action as a small but important step which, if followed elsewhere in the country, could lead to a real advance in the control of drug-taking.

Anoka, Minnesota, U.S.A. In a conservation experiment to stop soil erosion along the banks of the Rum River near Anoka, more than 2,500 old tyres have been anchored to the bank. In the spring of 1970 students and scouts, who had been helping with the project, planted a willow tree in each tyre. The tyres will be hidden as the trees grow and the soil accumulates.

Antiques. In the United Kingdom, from Jan. 26, 1970, individual licences are needed for the export of archaeological material over 100 years old, regardless of its value. Before that date licences were required only if the material was valued at over £2,000. A new open general licence also came into operation from Jan. 26. This permits the export of any antique (article over 100 years old) to any destination other than Rhodesia, provided that it is valued at less than £2,000, that it is not a coin, a document, or a diamond or any article mounted or set with diamonds, and that it has not been recovered from British soil (unless it was uncovered or discovered less than 100 years before the date of export). An individual licence is still necessary for the export of antiques excluded from the open general licence, and for articles more than 100 years old and worth more than £2,000.

Appian Way, Rome. A £16,600,000 plan to turn the Appian Way into a public park was outlined in February 1970 in a bill, supported by members of three political parties, to be presented to the Italian parliament. The plan, to be implemented over a period of 10 years, calls for the development of about 6,250 acres extending along a 6-mile stretch of the famous road as it starts out from the city wall on its way to Brindisi, 275 miles S.E. This road was the supply link that enabled the Roman armies to conquer southern Italy.

Architecture Awards. In February 1970 the U.K. Civic Trust announced the winners of its 1969 competition for architectural design; there was a record number of 940 entries (200 more than in 1968) from 103 of the 110 county boroughs. The awards are divided into three groups: A, for schemes in areas of architectural interest or natural beauty; B, for new buildings in other areas; and C, for landscaping schemes which contribute to good surroundings. Good design awards numbered 54, and there were 144 commendations for buildings or landscaping schemes in county boroughs. Norwich, Norfolk, gained the maximum of one award in each of the three groups. Fourteen others won two apiece: these were Aberdeen, Birmingham, Bolton, Brighton, Bristol, Cardiff, Edinburgh, Leeds, Newcastle, Nottingham, Oxford, Sheffield, Swansea, and York. Twenty-six university schemes received awards or were commended, about 13 per cent of the total. Other awards were given for the development of a stretch of urban canal side in Kingston Row and James Brindley Walk, Birmingham; for the closing of a busy shopping street in Norwich to all but pedestrians; for Boot's, the chemists, new headquarters in Nottingham; and for children's playgrounds in Oldham and Blackburn.

Both the Royal Institute of British Architects and the Concrete Society announced their annual awards on July 1, 1970. The R.I.B.A. received a record number of 370 entries, compared with 150 in 1968, and 11 buildings in the regions were selected as outstanding examples of current architecture. These were:

Yorkshire: Brynmor Jones Library, University of Hull (Castle Park, Dean, Hook) (see p. 170).

North-west: Pall Mall Court Offices, Manchester (Brett and Pollen, associated with A. A. Brotherton and Partners).

West Midlands: Houses for visiting mathematicians, Warwick University (Howell, Killick, Partridge, and Amis).

East Midlands: Tupton Hall comprehensive school, Derby County Council (George Grey and Partners, associated with D. S. Davies, county architect).

New Arrivals at the Zoos in 1970

Left: This male baby elephant is only 8 hours old. He was born to his 18-year-old mother at Expo 70, at Osaka, Japan, where she and 15 others had been brought from Thailand. Centre: twin bear cubs with their mother at Berne, Switzerland, zoo, where they were born in March. Right: a rare sight at the London zoo was this baby rhinoceros on her first outing with her mother in February.

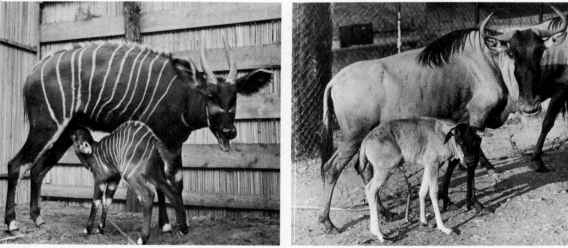

Left: a very uncommon resident at any zoo is the bongo, a member of the deer family found in East Africa. This mother and her calf were photographed at Nairobi airport, just before their take-off for the zoo at Bàsle, Switzerland. Right: another East African antelope is the brindled gnu, a much more common species. This 3-day-old calf, with its mother at the London zoo, was born in September.

This 7-year-old cheetah at Whipsnade produced her third set of cubs in February. Three sets is a world record for a captive cheetah.

Eastern: History Faculty, Cambridge University (James Stirling).

South-West: Police Training Centre, Taunton (B. C. Adams, Somerset county architect).

South-East: Thorndike Theatre, Leatherhead (Roderick Ham).

Southern: Three courtyard houses in Haddenham, Bucks (Peter J. Aldington).

London: Phase I of Lillington Street housing for 2,000 people, Westminster Council (Darbourne and Darke).

Scotland: Royal Commonwealth Swimming Pool, Edinburgh (Robert Matthew, Johnson-Marshall and Partners, associated with A. Steele, city architect) (see p. 167).

N. Ireland: Queen's University Science Library, Belfast (Twist and Whitley).

There were no awards for the North or for Wales.

The Concrete Society received 130 entries, compared with 79 in 1969. The prime award went to the new headquarters and college buildings at the Royal Military Academy, Sandhurst (Gollins, Melvin, Ward and Partners). Certificates of commendation were awarded to the Combination Room, Downing College, Cambridge (Howell, Killick, Partridge, and Amis), and to Kingshold Estate, King Edwards Road, Hackney, London, E.9 (Yorke Rosenberg Marsdall). Buildings receiving honourable mentions were Doncaster police headquarters and law courts, Yorkshire (Frederick Gibberd and Partners, in association with L. J. Tucker, Doncaster Borough Architect); Doncaster Racecourse Grandstand (Howard V. Lobb and Partners); Drax Power Station main chimney, Drax, Yorkshire (Clifford, Tee, and Gale); Longannet Generating Station chimney, Alloa, Clackmannanshire (Robert Matthew, Johnson-Marshall and Partners); St. James's Park Cake House, London, S.W.1 (directorate of special architectural services in the ministry of public building and works); Scammonden Bridge, near Huddersfield, Yorkshire (J. A. Gaffney); and Western Bank Bridge, Sheffield, Yorkshire (Ove Arup and Partners).

The 1970 Royal Gold Medal for Architecture given by the Queen on the recommendation of the council of the Royal Institute of British Architects—the highest honour for architecture in Britain—was awarded in February to Sir Robert Matthew. Sir Robert was architect to London County Council from 1946 to 1953, since when he has been professor of architecture at London University.

Armed Forces. The U.K. defence secretary announced on Nov. 25 that all servicemen who join the forces before the age of 17½ on long-term engagements are to be allowed to change to a 3-year engagement. This measure, which follows the recommendation of the Donaldson committee on boy entrants and young servicemen, will come into effect in April 1971.

Army (British). It was announced on Dec. 17 that separate home army commands for the South, North, and West, as

Architecture Awards. One of the new buildings at the Royal Military Academy, Sandhurst, that won the highest award of the Concrete Society in 1970.   *Photo, Richard Einzig*

well as one functional command, are to be abolished. They will be replaced from April 1, 1972, by a single command, called United Kingdom Land Forces, which will have its headquarters at Wilton, near Salisbury.

Art Awards (Australia). Awards announced during 1970 were as follows: the 1969 $A1,900 Archibald prize for portraiture to Ray Crooke, for his painting of his neighbour, George Johnston, the author; the $A400 Wynne prize to John Olsen for *Chasing Bird*; the Sir John Sulman prize for a subject painting to Louis James; the $A2,000 Australian-TAA national art prize to John Olsen for *Wimmera—Lake Hindmarsh* (the second prize of $A500 to Louis James for *Spy Hole*, and the third prize of $A350 to John Firth-Smith; a special award of $A50 to the aboriginal artist, Yirawala, of Darwin, for a bark painting, *Hunters of the Dream Time*); the International Co-operation art award for 1970 to Arthur Boyd; the $A7,000 First Leasing prize to Asher Bilu for *Woven Echo, 47 Quartet*, and *Noosphere Towards Omega* (the $A1,500 second prize to Brett Whiteley, and equal third prizes of $A750 each to Jan Senbergs and Alan Leach-Jones); the Blake prize for religious art jointly to Eric Smith and David Kemp; the Darcy Morris memorial prize to Rodney Milgate for his painting *Charity*; and the $A5,000 Transfield prize to Bill Clements for *Reading for August 6th*, a paper and string work described as "a visual poem on the tragedy of Hiroshima".

Arthritis. A comprehensive report to the Arthritis and Rheumatism Council by the director of its epidemiological investigations field unit in May 1970 stated that in Great Britain arthritis causes the loss of 35 million working days by men each year at a cost of £190 million. (If women are included, 63 million days a year are lost.) On average, 1,699 working days are lost per 1,000 men employed, but the rate

varies greatly between areas. In the North 2,723 days are lost per 1,000 men employed, and in Wales 2,529 days. In the South-East the comparable figure is 1,136. Facilities for treating the disease are weakest in those areas where the incapacity is the greatest, for Wales has the poorest facilities, followed by the South-West, North-West, Yorkshire, and the North. The report states that nearly 30,000 people are registered as disabled by arthritis.

Art Sales. The sale of the year was without question that of the Velasquez portrait of his servant Juan de Pereja. Before the sale at Christie's, London, on Nov. 27, experts had predicted that the painting might fetch £1,000,000; in the event, the price was £2,310,000, a world record for any painting sold at auction. The previous world record was £821,425, paid in 1961 in New York for a Rembrandt. The Velasquez was sold by Lord Radnor, principally to settle death duties, and bought by Alec Wildenstein of New York.

Other record prices at art sales in 1970 included the following: $1,300,000 (£541,660) for Van Gogh's *Le Cyprès et l'Arbre en Fleurs* on Feb. 26 at a New York auction (the previous record price for a Van Gogh was £183,750, paid in 1966 for his *Portrait of Madame Ravoux*); £220,000 for *A Cheetah with Two Indians* by George Stubbs, at Sotheby's on March 18 (the highest price ever paid at auction for a British work of art: the purchaser was the Manchester City Art Gallery); £31,250 for *Big Painting No. 6* by Roy Lichtenstein on Nov. 19 at Sotheby's (record for a work by a living American artist); £16,746 for *The Harbour at Cannes* by Sir Winston Churchill on May 13 at the Parke-Bernet Galleries, New York (previous highest price for a Churchill painting was £16,389 for *Menaggio, Lake Como* in 1965); £16,000 for L. S. Lowry's *Good Friday, Daisy Nook*, on July 8 at Sotheby's (more than double

Art Sales. The world record price for any painting sold at auction (£2,310,000) was paid in 1970 for Velasquez's portrait of his servant Juan de Pareja (left). The largest sum ever paid for a British work of art (£220,000) was given for George Stubbs's *A Cheetah with Two Indians*.

the previous highest price for a Lowry); £30,000 for a still life dated 1630 by the little-known French artist Louise Moillon on Nov. 25 at Sotheby's; £35,000 for a Rembrandt drawing of an old man on Nov. 26 at Sotheby's; £13,200 for a crayon drawing, *The Sick Child*, by Edvard Münch on Dec. 3 at Sotheby's; £26,000 for *Study for Portrait VIII* (1953) by Francis Bacon on Dec. 9 at Sotheby's (record price for a work by a living British artist); and at Sotheby's, in half an hour on Oct. 14, £1,107,500 for 15 Impressionist and post-Impressionist paintings, including £180,000 for Cézanne's *La Maison et l'Arbre*, £140,000 for Toulouse-Lautrec's *La Poudreuse*, £72,000 for *Vase de Fleurs avec Branches de Pommier en Fleur* by Odilon Redon (1840–1916), £80,000 for Dérain's *Pool of London*, £105,000 for Matisse's *Interieur à la Fillette*, and £82,000 for Picasso's pastel *Fillette au Chien*.

A painting by Van Gogh which was bought in a London junk shop for £45 in 1968 was auctioned at Sotheby's Parke-Bernet sale on Oct. 29 for £45,833. X-ray photographs revealed that the painting, the view of a cottage with a peasant woman, had another painting, of a team of oxen pulling a plough, beneath it.

Australia. On Sept. 16 and 17 the largest and most important collection of Australian paintings was auctioned in Sydney by Christie's of London. The 254 works, which included five by Dobell, eleven by Blackman, two by Drysdale, three by Fairweather, three by Godfrey Miller, eight by Friend, six by Hans Heyson, seven by Streeton, five by Tom Robert, and nine by Conder, fetched a total of $A405,000. A record price of $A30,000 was paid for Sir Russell Drysdale's *Emus in Landscape*, while Dobell's *Wangi Boy* fetched $A20,000, a tiny sketch portrait by the 19th-century artist, Charles Conder, $A6,000, and Tom Robert's *Mountain Muster* $A15,000.

Art Thefts. Major thefts of works of art in 1970 included: a 13th-century painting on wood, 14 in. by 14 in., *Virgin and Child with Two Angels*, worth almost £10,000, from the National Gallery, London, on Feb. 16 (a typewritten label saying "Temporarily removed" was put in its place); 20 paintings, 15 of them by Frederick William Watts, the Victorian landscape painter, valued at an estimated £150,000, from the St. Paul's Churchyard, London, office of Slater Walker Securities, Ltd., investment bankers, at the beginning of July (recovered by the police on July 21); 17 Impressionist paintings, together worth about £700,000, from a Paris apartment of the niece of Gustave Caillebotte, including Renoir's *Little Girls at the Piano* (valued at £225,000), six other Renoirs, three Pissaros, two Sisleys, two Monets, a Manet, a Corot, and a Gustave Caillebotte, during the first week-end in August (these were found intact on Nov. 17 in a disused Paris Métro station); £200,000 worth of silver and paintings from a London flat, at the end of August (paintings included a Peter Breughel, a Van de Meulen, a Corot, and a Cranach); and eight paintings, including several by Picasso, worth in all £125,000 from a New York apartment in October.

Asbestos. It was announced in Sydney, N.S.W., on April 30, 1970, that an asbestos mill to cost $A14 million is to be built near Barraba in northern New South Wales, 343 miles N.W. of Sydney. It will be located on the site of huge deposits of 27 million tons of asbestos, which will be mined by the open-cast method. The mill is due to come into production late in 1971. Production has been estimated at 100,000 short tons a year.

Athens. On April 10, 1970, a new 240,000-ton dry dock went into operation at Hellenic Shipyards, Athens. One of the seven biggest in Europe, the dock is 1,100 ft long and 176 ft. wide, and has a free draught of 30 ft.

Atlanta, Georgia. The world's largest sculpture—of Robert E. Lee, "Stonewall" Jackson, and Jefferson Davis—carved into Stone Mountain near Atlanta, was completed in 1970 and commemorated in this U.S. stamp.

Atlanta, Georgia, U.S.A. The world's largest sculpture, showing the Southern leaders in the American Civil War mounted on horseback, was dedicated by Vice-President Spiro Agnew on May 9, 1970. The gigantic carving is 138 ft. high; each of the figures—of Gen. Robert E. Lee, Gen. "Stonewall" Jackson, and Pres. Jefferson Davis—is 90 ft. from head to toe. The whole is carved on a granite hill, 680 ft. high, called Stone Mountain, which lies 16 miles E. at Atlanta. The plans for the sculpture were first made over 50 years ago, following an idea put forward by the United Daughters of the Confederacy, a patriotic society of Southern ladies. The project was finally officially taken up by the Georgia legislature, and the sculptor, Walter K. Hancock, was appointed. Work on the enormous undertaking began in 1958 and, with the help of high-intensity-gas cutting torches, was completed in 1970.

Berne, Switzerland. The new administration building of the Universal Postal Union in the capital of Switzerland was completed in 1970 and opened in May.

Auctions. Both Sotheby's and Christie's announced record turnovers on July 31 at the end of the summer season. Sotheby's had done business worth £45,211,484, compared with £40,347,341 in 1969; and Christie's £19,999,956, compared with £15,239,661. The totals included sales in the auctioneers' salerooms in New York, Geneva, Florence, Tokyo, and other places.

Australian of the Year. Sir Norman Martin, chairman of the Australia Day Council, announced in Melbourne on Jan. 13, 1970, that the Australian of the Year award for 1969 had been given to Lord Casey, the former Governor-General of Australia. The award is for the Australian citizen who has brought the greatest honour to the nation during the year.

Autism. Great Britain's first all-age fully residential school for autistic children was opened at Slinford, Sussex, in September. The large building, formerly a convalescent home, was converted by the voluntary National Society for Autistic Children.

Automobile Association. Work on the £4½ million buildings on the outskirts of Basingstoke, Hants, which will be the new national administrative headquarters of the Automobile Association, began during 1970. The buildings will consist of a 220-ft.-high, 80-ft.-square, 19-storey tower block, with a two- and three-storey podium at its base, including a three-deck car park with space for 750 cars. When completed in 1973, the premises will house 1,600 staff.

Balloons. It was reported in October that a meteorological research balloon launched at Christchurch, New Zealand, in 1969 had set world records by rising to 48,000 ft. and circling the Antarctic about 50

times in 448 days. The previous record of 441 days in the air was set by a balloon launched earlier by the same organization, GHOST (Global Horizontal Sounding Technique), a joint U.S.-N.Z. programme for launching 10,000 constant-level data-transmitting balloons in the Southern Hemisphere.

Bankruptcy. The U.K. board of trade stated on Oct. 9, 1970, that bankruptcy orders and administration orders rose to 4,369 in 1969 compared with 3,926 in 1968. Estimated liabilities also rose, from £17,728,053 in 1968 to £19,308,485 in 1969; but the average estimated deficiency fell from £3,324 in 1968 to £2,888 in 1969. There were 3,233 trading failures during 1969, the principal groups affected being the construction industry (957 failures), retailers (857), restaurants, cafés, public houses, and clubs (236), and farming (197). The 1,136 non-trading bankruptcies included 208 of directors and promoters of limited companies.

Banks. On Feb. 20, 1970, for the first time the "big four" London clearing banks, together with the National and Commercial Banking group, revealed their true profits and hidden reserves. The five joint stock banks together earned £228 million before tax in 1969. Barclay's made £64·9 million, Lloyds £44·6 million (before an exceptional credit of £2·8 million), Midland £36·4 million, and National Westminster £63·7 million. National Commercial gave its 1968–69 profits as £18·4 million.

Belfast. The N. Ireland capital's new 570-bed central hospital, which will cost about £7 million, will be the largest air-conditioned building in Ireland. It was announced in June that the third and final stage contract for the construction of the hospital had gone to tender, that the first phase of the contract would be finished by 1974, and that the hospital was due for completion in 1977. The project is N. Ireland's

first major public building to be metrically designed and constructed. A special feature will be a roof-top centre for patients and staff, and the design of a 14-storey tower will incorporate solar-resistant shields on its exterior to augment the air-conditioning system by minimizing the effect of the sun's rays. When completed the hospital will have a staff of nearly 2,000.

A contract worth £1,200,000 was awarded in May 1970 by Belfast corporation to John Laing Ltd for the redevelopment of the notorious Shankhill Road area. The scheme includes 265 homes, shops, a meeting hall, old people's flats, and a replacement site for an old people's club.

Berne, Switzerland. The new administration building of the Universal Postal Union, which took two years to build and cost 14 million Swiss francs, was inaugurated here on May 23, 1970. The building has a seven-floor office section, and a four-floor section where conferences can be held. All 60 U.P.U. member countries provided furniture for the building.

Betting Shops. Figures given in January 1970 showed that in June 1969 the number of licensed betting offices in Great Britain had fallen to 15,490 compared with 15,782 in 1968. Bookmakers' permits decreased from 11,069 in 1968 to 10,723 in 1969, and there were 46 betting agency permits compared with 54 in 1968.

Binney Medal. The 1969 Binney memorial awards for acts of bravery in support of law and order, instituted to commemorate Capt. Ralph Binney, R.N., who was killed in a single-handed attempt to prevent the escape of smash-and-grab thieves in the City of London on Dec. 8, 1944, were presented to 16 recipients by the Lord Mayor of London on Dec. 3, 1970. The Binney memorial medal for bravery was given to George Pinkney, aged 61, a former bus conductor, of Forest Gate, London, and to Victor Gell, aged 26, a carpenter, of East Ham, London. In October 1969 Mr. Pinkney jumped off the platform of his moving bus in Upton Park to help two men being coshed with iron bars by seven or eight men, and was himself coshed and shot in both feet. Mr. Gell fought and chased three men armed with coshes and a gun, and foiled their attempt to rob Lloyd's Bank at South Woodford, Essex. Fourteen people received certificates of merit.

Birds. According to P. B. S. Lissaman and Carl A. Schollenberger of the Californian Institute of Technology, birds fly in formation not for reasons of security, but to improve their aerodynamic efficiency. The two scientists, who published the results of their research and calculations in June 1970, stated that a group of 25 birds has a range 71 per cent longer than that of a lone bird. The ''V'' formation provides optimum efficiency. Just beyond the wingtips of a bird in flight there is an upcurrent of air which helps the birds on either side. In a line-abreast formation the birds in the centre are supported by the upcurrent from those around them, but in a ''V'' formation the drag is evenly distributed, so that even the leading bird benefits. The scientists calculated that the more birds there are in a flight formation the more power is saved, but beyond 12 birds the amount of extra power saved is inconsiderable, so that a flight of 12 birds is almost as efficient as one of 25. The calculations also revealed that it does not matter whether or not the birds flap their wings in synchronism.

Spain. In an attempt to increase Spain's declining bird population the Spanish government has ordered the erection of 300,000 nesting boxes in suitable trees. It was announced in March 1970 that a third had already been placed in 100,000 trees in 14 provinces throughout the country. Señor Pedro Ceballas, in charge of ''Operation Birdnest'', said that the decrease in bird population had been caused partly by man's activities in forests, which had robbed the birds of their natural sanctuary, and partly by the widespread destruction of insect food by insecticides. He said that the 15,000 nesting boxes in parks in Madrid were attracting many birds.

Birmingham. The president of the U.K. board of trade announced on July 13, 1970, that Great Britain's new national exhibition centre will be in Birmingham. The 367-acre site, on farmland at Elmdon, is near Birmingham's airport and has motorway links and main-line rail connections.

Details of a £5 million scheme to build a leisure centre in a single 11-storey building at Smallbrook, Ringway, were announced on March 23. The building will contain a 765-seat theatre, two 915-seat cinemas, a ''technocentre'' with conference facilities, a computer centre, a planetarium, TV studios, several restaurants, a

night club, a public house, offices, undercover shopping, and basement parking. Work on the centre should be completed by 1972.

Blair Drummond House, near Stirling. Scotland's first safari park was opened here on May 15, 1970. The £250,000 venture is a joint enterprise involving Jimmy Chipperfield, Keir and Cawdor Estates, and Sir John Muir of Blair Drummond. The park extends over a 100-acre estate; visitors can use either their own cars or a special bus to visit the enclosures, which house 30 lions, 10 giraffes, 100 baboons, eland, seals, and chimpanzees. Later the number of animals will be increased and will include a Bengal tiger, Shetland ponies, and a selection of young animals in a Pets' Corner. There is a shallow pond on which visitors can travel by motorized craft to visit Chimpanzee Island. Game wardens equipped with walkie-talkie radio patrol the area.

Blind Persons. This electronic device enables the blind to read ordinary print. A scanner held in the right hand sends signals to the device, which translates them into Braille-like characters felt by the fingers of the left.

Blind Persons. An electronic device developed by the Stanford Research Institute, U.S.A., which enables blind people to read ordinary print, was demonstrated in February 1970. A scanner, guided by the reader's right hand, transmits the shapes of printed letters into the device, which translates them into Braille-like touch signals, felt with the fingers of the left hand.

Braille books for the blind are extremely bulky because the raised dots have to be punched on very thick paper. A Braille memory and reading device developed at the Argonne National Laboratory, Illinois, U.S.A., reduces a blind person's reading

''Blowpipe.'' A British one-man ground-to-air guided missile fired from the shoulder. The system weighs only 40 lb.

material to as little as one five-hundredth part of the usual bulk. The information is first recorded on magnetic tape; this is ''read'' by a magnetic head that controls plungers which push up Braille dots on plastic tape. When the blind person has read these with his fingertips, the plastic tape passes between rollers which smooth out the characters, leaving the tape ready to be imprinted again.

''Blowpipe.'' This is the name of a portable supersonic guided weapon designed for use by one man against an airborne target. The entire system—missile, launcher, and aiming unit—weighs only 40 lb. and can be made ready for action within seconds. After being launched, the missile is guided to its target by radio commands generated by the movement of a thumb button by the operator. ''Blowpipe'', which has been produced by Short's missile systems division, will come into full production in 1971.

Bournemouth, Hants. The town's catering and entertainments committee announced on Jan. 9, 1970, that a £10 million conference and entertainment centre is to be built on the sea front during the next five years. The conference centre will be the largest in Europe; the entertainments centre will include a 5,000-seat theatre; and there will also be a nursery where parents can leave their children while doing their shopping. Sir Hugh Casson, the architect, has produced outline drawings for the development, and architects all over the world have been invited to submit ideas for individual buildings within the centre. The £10 million required will be raised by private enterprise either in the U.K. or abroad.

Brain. In an experiment at the Yale, U.S.A., school of medicine in September 1970 direct two-way communication by radio was established between the brain of a chimpanzee and a computer. "Brain waves" were transmitted by implanted electrodes to a computer programmed to recognize certain wave characteristics; the computer then sent back signals to another part of the animal's brain, which turned off the original "brain waves"—a process known as negative feedback. The demonstration suggests a means of treating—or, at least, controlling—mental disorders in human beings. The transmitter-receiver, no larger than a matchbox, is fastened on top of the head of the animal, which is thus free to move about, not being attached by wires to any stationary apparatus.

Branfield, R.R.S. The new Royal Research Ship *Branfield*, named after the man who first charted part of the Antarctic mainland 150 years ago, was launched at Leith, Scotland, in September 1970, and went into service in November as a relief ship for the British Antarctic stations. The largest ship of its kind to be built in the U.K. for 60 years, *Branfield* cost £1¾ million; with a helicopter deck and a specially designed hull and stern for ice-breaking, she can accommodate 36 crew and 62 passengers, and has three cargo holds, and laboratories for marine biology. She carries fuel oil in bulk which can be piped ashore instead of landed in barrels. A replacement for R.R.S. *Shackleton*, she will be in Antarctic waters each year from October to May.

Brecon Beacons National Park. The secretary of state for Wales re-opened over 32 miles of the Brecon and Abergavenny canal on Oct. 16, 1970. It was decided in 1968 that the canal should be restored, and the £28,000 cost was shared between Monmouth and Breconshire county councils. Bordered by the Brecon Beacons and the Black Mountains, the canal is the only comparatively long stretch of restored waterway to pass through a national park.

Bretton, Northants. The new garden township of Bretton, near Peterborough, is the first of four such townships proposed for expanding the city's population from 88,000 to 188,000 by 1985. A £2 million scheme, under which one boiler-house will supply hot water and central heating for shops, schools, offices and 3,500–5,500 homes, was announced in December. Householders will pay an average of £1·02 a week for central heating and hot water. Natural gas will be used as the fuel for the heating system, in order to reduce atmospheric pollution to a minimum.

Bridlington, Yorks. A scheme designed to attract yachtsmen to Bridlington Bay was announced in January 1970. A new £2 million outer harbour, 1½ miles wide and protected by a long outer arm, and a yacht basin with space for 1,000 yachts, form part of the development plan. The basin would also have space for 100 fishing boats.

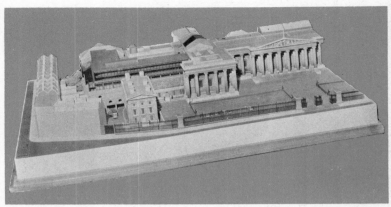

British Museum. Model of the extension (left) to be built in 1972–74. It will contain new galleries, restaurants, and offices, and an educational complex, and will cost £1¼ million.

British Museum. Designs of a five-storey extension to the British Museum were put on exhibition at the museum on Oct. 12, 1970, in order to give the public an opportunity to make their reactions known to the ministry of public building and works. The new wing, incorporating restaurants, galleries for temporary exhibitions, and offices, will be built on a partly vacant site on the south-west side of the museum. An educational complex will be provided close to a children's restaurant. Building, which will cost £1¼ million, will begin in January 1972 and be completed by the end of 1974.

On April 7 the U.K. secretary of state for education and science announced that the British Museum library will be re-housed on the Bloomsbury site first proposed in 1944. The site was approved at that time by the Conservative minister, Sir David (later Lord) Eccles, but the decision was reversed by the Labour minister, Patrick Gordon Walker, in 1967. The announcement that the original plan was to go ahead expressed the hope that both the Museum library and the National Reference Library of Science and Invention would be housed on a somewhat smaller site than that originally envisaged, so as to allow more housing in the development, and thus meet an objection on the grounds of housing need made by the Camden borough council in 1966.

British Standard Time. On Dec. 2, in the House of Commons, a motion to approve the retention of British Standard Time was defeated by 366 to 81 on a free vote. The decision means that clocks in the U.K. will go back one hour to Greenwich Mean Time on Oct. 31, 1971, giving an extra hour of daylight on winter mornings. Summer "daylight-saving" time, with clocks being put forward one hour, will be restored in 1972, giving an extra hour of daylight in the evenings for 7 months of the year. The decision was welcomed by building firms, farmers, and Post Office workers. A spokesman for the latter said that since B.S.T. was introduced in 1967 on an experimental basis there had been

a 50 per cent increase in early morning accidents to postmen.

Brussels, Belgium. Work on the £240 million world trade centre here which began in December 1969 continued throughout 1970. The centre will consist of a group of eight 300-ft. towers, each with 28 storeys, housing about 2,000 offices with a total floor area of about 300,000 sq. yds. Eventually 25,000 people will be employed in the centre, and 50,000 will visit it each day. The towers will rise from a huge three-storey platform; escalators and moving sidewalks will give access to the platform, and express lifts will operate inside each tower. Rooftop helicopter pads will be installed on some of the towers to connect the centre with trade centres at Liège and Antwerp, and with Brussels airport and other centres. A multi-lane motorway will be built to run through the centre of the city and beneath the platform, where underground parking for at least 5,000 cars will be provided. There will also be underground showroom facilities, and the platform itself will have a shopping centre, a convention hall to seat 3,000 people, and display showrooms for permanent or temporary trade exhibitions. A key factor will be an information office which will be equipped with the most up-to-date communications machinery capable of providing continuous, up-to-the-minute information from world business and financial centres.

The world trade centre will form part of the redevelopment of a 135-acre area in Central Brussels, where dilapidated buildings are due for demolition. The city planners intend to build a new "city within a city" here, called the "Manhattan suburb". It will include two hotels with a total of 1,700 rooms, and blocks of flats to house the diplomats, executives, and officials who are expected to work at the trade centre.

Building Safeguards. U.K. regulations providing new safeguards against the progressive collapse of tall buildings came into force on April 1, 1970. They apply to all buildings of five or more storeys, including the basement, to all types of building, and to all forms of construction. The chief requirement is the provision of "alternative paths" to carry the load if part of a structural member is removed or becomes unserviceable.

Business Education. The Australian minister of education and science told parliament in August that the government had accepted the recommendations of a committee of enquiry that a National School of Business Administration should be set up in the University of New South Wales. Post-graduate awards for courses relating to industry, commerce, and government will be introduced, and one hundred of them will be available in 1971. Full-time courses of up to 2 years will lead to a master's degree in such fields as applied science, engineering, education, business and hospital administration, architecture, and economics.

Bustard. The great bustard, one of Europe's rarest birds, is to be reintroduced into Great Britain as a breeding bird by Christopher Marler, the owner of a private zoo at Weston Underwood, Bucks. He said in December that he had imported two male and four female birds from Portugal during the summer, and would release them on a leased 10-acre site on Salisbury Plain in the spring of 1971. It is hoped that they will eventually be able to leave their protected site and nest in the surrounding countryside. A Great Bustard Trust has been formed to run the project, which is expected to cost about £10,000. Great bustards used to flourish on the chalk downs in the south of England, as well as in East Anglia and Yorkshire, but were made extinct by hunters about 150 years ago, and have since been only rare migrants in Great Britain. Officially classed as a game bird, the male weighs between 24 and 35 lb. and stands about 40 in. high; the female is much smaller. Because of their great weight, they fly only when in great danger, usually relying on their strong legs to make their escape. They have vivid black and white plumage. Their favourite food consists of mice and grasshoppers.

C

Cambridge. Work on the re-building of part of Cambridge near the ancient market square began at the end of 1970. The 5-year scheme, costing over £2½ million, includes a new façade for one of the city's best known and most attractive streets, Petty Cury. The plan also provides for a boutique-style shopping complex, with a new library building, offices, and restaurant.

Canberra. On April 26, 1970, the Queen accepted on behalf of the city the British government's gift of a 53-bell carillon housed in a tower on Aspen Island in the centre of Lake Burley Griffin. Costing $A500,000, the carillon was given to Canberra in 1963 in commemoration of the golden jubilee of the founding of the national capital of Australia. The 53 bells have a range of four and a half octaves, and the largest, with a weight of 123 cwt. and diameter of 7 ft. 2 in., is the biggest and deepest-toned bell in Australia.

A new 100-acre Botanic Garden, devoted exclusively to Australian native plants, was opened in October by the Prime Minister of Australia. On the eastern slopes of Black Mountain, near the city's central business area, the garden will be extended by a further 100 acres in about five years' time.

The Australian National University at Canberra is to build a centre for the performing arts, and it was announced in February 1970 that an Australian businessman had given $A100,000 towards its cost. There will be a workshop centre surrounded by studios for painting, sculpture, and design, and exhibition galleries. The whole project will cost $A500,000.

Cancer. Figures published by the U.K. Registrar-General on March 17, 1970, showed that for 1965, the year covered by the report, cancer was more common in the South-East than anywhere else in England and Wales, and least frequent in the Sheffield area. Since 1962 new cases of cancer have been registered voluntarily, and in the first four years cases rose from 283 to 311 in every 100,000 men, and from 257 to 288 in every 100,000 women. The known increases in lung cancer in women, and the known decreases in cancer of the mouth and stomach, were confirmed; the figures also showed that cancer of the pancreas was probably increasing. The report also gave some comparative Scandinavian figures, which, although not all for the same year, showed that while Finland has a very low incidence of breast cancer, it has a high incidence of cancer of the lip and stomach. In Denmark, England, Scotland, and Wales more men than women have cancer of the liver, while in Finland, Norway, and Sweden the reverse is true. Cancer of the prostate is nearly twice as common in Norway and Sweden as in Scotland, while tumours of the nose and larynx are more common in Finland and Britain than in Norway, Sweden, and Denmark.

Treatment. Clinical trials to test the general retarding effect on cancer of the drug, bis-dioxo-piperazine, or ICRF 159, were carried out on patients in London, Glasgow, Manchester, Paris, and Vienna during 1970. It had already been found that the drug, first synthesized in the laboratories of the Imperial Cancer Research Fund in London in 1966, when given to mice with a single primary tumour not only reduces the rate of the tumour's growth but also prevents its spread to other parts of the body. Dr. Kurt Hellman, head of the Fund's cancer chemotherapy department, said in November, when information about ICRF 159 was announced, that it appeared to work by preventing the release of malignant cells from the blood vessels of the primary tumour. Although it had already secured partial remissions and some complete remissions in people suffering from leukaemia, he added, a great deal of research was still needed to discover if it is as effective in the treatment of secondary cancer in human beings as it is in mice.

Great interest was aroused at the beginning of November by a BBC-TV programme on the work of Dr. Josef Issels at his Ringberg clinic at Rottach-Egern, a village in the Bavarian Alps. Treating only "terminal" cases that had been given up by other doctors, he claimed a remission rate of 16–18 per cent. His methods include the removal of all focuses of infection such as tonsils and decayed teeth, diet, exercise, psychotherapy, the induction of an extremely high temperature, and the administration of a secret immunizing serum. His most distinguished patient in 1970 was the British athlete Lillian Board, who at 21 had developed inoperable intestinal cancer. His treatment, however, failed to alleviate her condition, and she died on Dec. 26, after seven weeks at the clinic.

Cannes Film Festival. During the two-week Cannes festival in May 1970 over 400 films were shown. The grand prize for the best motion picture of 1970 went to *M*A*S*H*, directed by Robert Altman, with Donald Sutherland, Elliot Gould, and Sally Kellerman as the principal players. Other awards were:

Best director—John Boorman (G.B.), for *Leo the Last.*

Best film by a new director—*Hoa-Binh*, directed by Raoul Coutard.

Best actor—Marcello Mastroianni, for his performance in the Italian film *A Drama of Jealousy.*

Best actress—Ottavia Piccoli, for her performance in the Italian film *Metello.*

Grand Jury prize—the Italian film *Investigation of a Citizen above Suspicion.*

Special Jury prize—shared equally between the Hungarian film *The Falcons* and the U.S. film *The Strawberry Statement.*

Capital Punishment. The death penalty is to remain in the Northern Territory of Australia. On Sept. 10 the Territory's legislative council voted on a bill which would have abolished it. The voting stood at eight on either side, after three elected members had crossed the floor to vote with the government official members, and the bill was lost on the casting vote of the Speaker.

Cardiff, Wales. The tallest building in the Welsh capital, a 270-ft.-high tower block of offices was opened on April 7, 1970. The 25 storeys are linked on two sides with a three-storey podium providing parking space for 234 cars. The tower has a central service core containing lavatories, staircases, and five large high-speed lifts, serving all floors up to the 23rd. The office space surrounding this core is fully air-conditioned.

Car Ownership. Figures given by the U.K. ministry of transport in October 1970 showed that the number of driving licences rose from 10,800,000 in 1959 to 17,138,000 in 1969. Car ownership figures are available only from 1961, but since that date 2,200,000 more house-holds have acquired a car—or the regular use of one—and the total in 1969 was 18,800,000. The average annual mileage for motorists in Great Britain increased only from 7,600 in 1959 to 8,200 in 1969.

Spain. Statistics issued in April 1970 showed that the number of car licences issued in 1968 was 1,633,937, com-pared with 290,510 in 1960, and that in 1968 377,767 new cars were regis-tered, compared with 50,254 in 1960. At the end of 1969 there were 640,000 commercial vehicles on Spain's roads; while in 1960 only 147,365 new ones were registered, this figure had increased to 592,351 in 1968. In 1969, $2\frac{1}{2}$ per cent fewer commercial vehicles were regis-tered, 10,000 less, than in 1967. The number of tractors registered in 1968 was 32,160 compared with 20,844 in 1962.

New Zealand. On Dec. 31, 1969, New Zealand had more than 850,000 regis-tered motor-cars in a population just over 2,800,000—or one car to every three people. There were also more than 170,000 trucks and other heavy vehicles.

Car Park. In Denver, Colorado, U.S.A., on a plot of ground barely large enough for two full-sized cars, an 84-ft.-high steel tower has been constructed on which cars are parked vertically in two rows. A hy-draulic system powered by an electric motor turns a compression chain in a con-tinuous rectangular path about fixed points at the top and bottom of the tower.

Car Park. On an area small enough to take only two cars on the ground, 22 can be parked in this 84-ft. tower at Denver, Colorado.

Census. Details of the decennial U.K. census to be taken on April 25, 1971, were given when the census order was laid before parliament on Jan. 28, 1970. It will cost about £10 million in England and Wales, and £1$\frac{1}{2}$ million in Scotland, and a record number of 114,000 field workers will be employed to collect the completed form from each household. For the first time the census will give the map reference of every occupied dwelling in the country. Five of the total of about 25 questions on the eight-page form will be new. Two will be on immigration: one asking for the year of entry into the U.K. of all people not born in the country, and the other for the countries of birth of each person's parents, regardless of where the person himself was born. The other three new questions ask for the dates of the

birth of children; information about higher education qualifications, extended to cover ''A'' level and comparable examinations; and, on employment, what job a person held one year and five years before the date of the census.

Further information about the questions to be asked was given in August. For the first time a sample of the population will be questioned on their income. But in order to reduce unnecessary form-filling some reduction in the number of questions will be made: individual subjects gained at ''A'' level need not be stated; in a question on fertility, married women need not state the sex of their children; a question on the duration of a person's daily journey to work and another on second jobs are to be omitted; and it will not be necessary to mention kitchens and non-flush lavatories in answering questions on the size and amenities of the household.

It is expected that the results of the census will be fully processed and pub-lished by the middle of 1973, nine months earlier than usual. All information will be transferred to punched cards, which will be fed into computers at the census office in Southampton.

Charlemagne Prize. This prize awarded annually by the city of Aachen for the most notable work in the cause of European co-operation was given in 1970 to François Seydoux, who had just retired after many years as French ambassador in Bonn. M. Seydoux is the 17th recipient of the award, and the fourth Frenchman. The two Englishmen who have received the award are Sir Winston Churchill, in 1955, and Edward Heath, in 1963.

Chicago, Illinois, U.S.A. A spokesman for Standard Oil Co. (Indiana) announced in January 1970 that the company would build Chicago's tallest building. It will have 80 storeys, but at 1,136 ft., will be 29 ft. taller than the 100-storey John Hancock Centre, already under construction in the city. The only taller buildings in the U.S.A. (both in New York) will be the 1,250-ft.-

Chicago. The world-famous 105-year-old Union stockyards, where animals awaited slaughter for canning, will be closed on February 1, 1971.

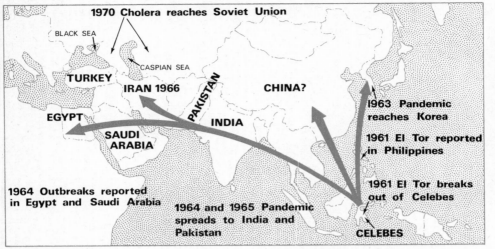

1970 Cholera reaches Soviet Union

BLACK SEA

CASPIAN SEA

TURKEY

IRAN 1966

PAKISTAN

CHINA?

EGYPT

INDIA

SAUDI ARABIA

1963 Pandemic reaches Korea

1961 El Tor reported in Philippines

1961 El Tor breaks out of Celebes

1964 Outbreaks reported in Egypt and Saudi Arabia

1964 and 1965 Pandemic spreads to India and Pakistan

CELEBES

Cholera. This map shows how the El Tor variant of the disease spread from the Celebes Islands in Indonesia, affecting 25 countries in 9 years (1961–70). In 1970 it reached the Middle East, European Turkey, and southern Russia and the Crimea, and for the first time occurred in West Africa.

tall Empire State Building, and the 1,350-ft.-tall twin towers of the World Trade Centre, still under construction. Standard Oil's claim did not stand for long, for in July the chairman of Sears Roebuck and Co., the world's largest retail (mail order) firm, announced that its new central headquarters, Sears Tower, in Chicago would be the largest private building in the world, and also the world's tallest building. To be constructed on a site bounded by Wacker Drive, Jackson Boulevard, and Adams and Franklin Streets, the 109-storey structure will be 1,450 ft. tall. Its floor space will total 4·4 million sq. ft., with actual commercial and office space occupying 3·7 million sq. ft. There will be 102 high-speed lifts, including 14 double-deck units, and 16 escalators will serve the lower floors and the so-called "sky lobbies". Sears Tower, which will cost over $100 million, is due for completion in 1974.

Children in Care. A White Paper giving statistics of the number of children in the care of local authorities and voluntary organizations in England and Wales in the year ending March 1970 was published on Dec. 30. The total number was 78,274, or 5·8 per thousand of the population under 18, compared with 6·1 per thousand in 1966. The cost to local authorities for their maintenance was £45,991,485 in 1969–70, of which £1,266,368 was met by parents' contributions. The average weekly cost of keeping each child was £8·90 compared with £8·08 in 1968–69. The cost of maintaining children varied greatly according to the type of accommodation: the weekly cost for each child in local authority homes averaged £17·33; in local authority hostels £15·81; in voluntary homes £9·77; and in boarding out £3·56.

A report on the work of the U.K. children's department in 1967–69, published by the Home Office on Oct. 30, 1970, showed that the number of children in the care of local authorities and voluntary

organizations in England and Wales fell from 79,996 in 1966 to 78,396 in 1969, a decrease from 6·1 to 5·9 per thousand of the estimated population under the age of 18. The number of children in the care of local authorities rose from 69,157 (March 31, 1966) to 70,188 (March 31, 1969), the highest recorded since the passing of the Children Act in 1948. This increase was, however, more than offset by a fall in the number of children in the care of voluntary organizations—from 10,839 in 1966 to 8,208 in 1969.

Cholera. A sudden spread of the El Tor variety of this disease, which has its endemic form in Indonesia, into the Middle East, Africa, and Europe alarmed health authorities in the late summer and autumn of 1970. On August 6 the Russian authorities ordered nation-wide health precautions to constrain an outbreak in Astrakhan, a port on the Volga near the Caspian Sea, and by Aug. 10 travel restrictions and measures to fight the disease throughout the southern regions of the country had been imposed. Black Sea resorts, and a number of other cities from Odessa to Baku, were closed to everyone except travellers on business, patients going for medical treatment, and local residents returning home. All tourists, whether they had had inoculations against the disease or not, were turned away. River trips down the Volga were reported to have been cancelled, and swimming in the rivers was forbidden. On Sept. 2 it was stated that the epidemic had been "virtually eliminated", but some deaths had occurred. It was confirmed that the disease had spread from Astrakhan to the Black Sea ports of Odessa and Kerch.

Meanwhile, it became known that much more serious outbreaks had occurred in the Middle East, and on Aug. 20 Italy issued new cholera controls on arrivals into the country from Russia, Lebanon, Libya, and Syria, while Yugoslavia tightened up her health regulations, and Turkey launched a nation-wide immunization campaign. The

next day Libya began a programme to inoculate the entire population of 2 million following an outbreak of the disease: 17 cases had been reported in Tripoli, and there were several unconfirmed cases in Benghazi. In Israel doctors began the inoculation of Jordanian Arabs who wanted to cross into Jordan from the occupied area; in Malta travellers from N. African countries were forbidden entry unless they had inoculation certificates; and in Morocco travellers from Libya, Egypt, Jordan, and Lebanon were required to have these certificates. On the same day Australia announced strengthened quarantine precautions and the Federal minister of health said that new regulations required air travellers from Russia and Nepal to have a valid international certificate of vaccination against cholera.

On Aug. 23 confirmed cases were reported in the Jerusalem area, and suspected cases in a refugee camp in Jericho. By the 26th Lebanon, Libya, and Egypt were declared cholera areas, and cases were reported from the Persian Gulf states of Dubai and Oman; by then the number of cases in Israel was 14. The following day, delegates from Egypt, Jordan, Iraq, Lebanon, Syria, and Saudi Arabia held an emergency meeting in Damascus to discuss methods of preventing the spread of the disease. On Sept. 1 the World Health Organization announced that at least 2,000 cases had occurred in Guinea, West Africa, with over 60 deaths. This was the first time that the disease had been known south of the Sahara. On the same day the first death from the disease in Israel was reported.

No further spread of the disease was reported during the rest of September, but in October it reached epidemic proportions in Turkey. One of the worst affected cities was Istanbul, where the entire population of 2,800,000 were inoculated. On the 19th a total of 936 sufferers were known to be in hospital, and the official number of the dead was 30 (press reports put it as high as 150). The next day Bulgaria,

Iraq, and Syria closed their frontiers with Turkey, and a wide security zone was established along the Turkish border with Greece, where the population was ordered to have immediate inoculation. The official number of deaths in Turkey by Oct. 23 was 47. On Oct. 26 the W.H.O. reported that three cases in Czechoslovakia had been notified. The disease continued to spread: on Dec. 27 the Palestine Liberation Organization stated that 138 cases had been reported among Arab inhabitants of the Gaza strip, and on the 29th four confirmed cases (three of them fatal) were reported from Nigeria, the first cases to occur in that country.

Chronically Sick and Disabled Persons Act. This U.K. act of parliament came into force on Aug. 29, 1970. It requires local authorities to keep registers of chronically sick and disabled people, whether or not they have applied for assistance, and make certain types of information available to them. It is mandatory for local authorities to provide such things as sheltered workshop employment, and to adapt council flats or houses to suit the disabled or provide financial assistance towards alterations. Access for the disabled to toilet facilities and other public buildings should be improved and clearly indicated. More specialized motor vehicles are to be provided for the disabled, particularly for haemophiliacs, and more facilities for young chronically sick patients, so that they are not accommodated in geriatric wards of hospitals. More attention must be given to the educational needs of autistic children, and those both deaf and blind. Certain types of slow-moving invalid carriages are to be allowed on footpaths, and children should be permitted to use them; and special parking concessions for the disabled must be given. Financial assistance should be given towards the cost of radio and television licences. Disabled persons are to be allowed representation on all local authority and other committees dealing with their problems.

Churchill Memorials. On June 2, 1970, the Hon. Mrs. Christopher Soames, Sir Winston Churchill's youngest daughter, visited the Royal Military Academy at Sandhurst to name the new assembly hall "Churchill Hall" after her late father. The new building, which seats 1,200, is equipped with the latest visual aids.

On April 28, 1970, the Winston Churchill Memorial Trust, reporting on its first five years, disclosed that it had been sending more than 80 British men and women abroad each year to study and explore a chosen field of activity. The Trust was launched in 1965 after a public appeal had raised £2,907,380; the income is now sufficient to meet running costs and to cover grants ranging from £1,000 to £2,000. Grants made in the first five years totalled £466,370, and covered 63 categories of activity, ranging from fishing methods in Canada to mechanization in the Pennsylvania coalfields.

Church Membership. Statistics showing the declining membership of the Church of England, especially in London, were given by the Bishop of London, Dr. Robert Stopford, in July 1970. Out of every 1,000 babies born in England only 511 are now baptized in the Church; the diocese of London, with only 312 babies out of every 1,000, has the lowest figure. Although the population of England had grown from 35 million in 1920 to 44,500,000 in 1968, confirmations fell from 199,000 in 1920 to 125,000 in 1968; London's figures show a drop of over 600 a year between 1965 (9,000) and 1968 (6,500). The number of Easter communicants, regarded as a test of Church membership, showed a national figure in 1968 of only 59 out of every 1,000 of the population aged 15 and over; London's figures were only 30 out of every 1,000, and Birmingham's only 28. The diocese of London, with a population of 3,107,160, has only 119,645 on the Church electoral rolls, and a communicant total of only 93,185.

According to a survey of 172 Congregational churches out of a total of about 2,000 in the U.K., published in September 1970, 60 per cent of worshippers are over 45 years old. Only 40 per cent of churchgoers who completed questionnaires are interested in church societies and organizations. The survey also showed that, of money given to causes apart from support of the local church, 54 per cent went to Congregational missions, 32 per cent to Christian Aid, and 11 per cent to Oxfam. The great majority give less than 10s a year.

Figures given in the annual report of the Baptist Union of Great Britain and Ireland, published in April 1970, showed that overall membership of the Baptist churches

decreased by 5,970 to 274,871 in 1969, and the number of churches fell by 11 to 3,264. In England, membership fell by 3,607 to 176,222, and in Wales and Monmouthshire by 2,589 to 74,681. In Scotland, however, membership rose by 65 to 16,716, and in Ireland by 161 to 6,922. Baptisms during 1969 numbered 5,102, compared with 5,923 in 1968.

Church of England. A new system of government in the Church of England came into operation during 1970, with the election of the General Synod and its first meeting in London on Nov. 4. The democratic process of synodical government is as follows. The parishes elect representatives to a deanery synod, who in turn elect a diocesan synod in each of the 43 dioceses in the Church. Members of the deanery synods also elect representatives to the General Synod, which is the central legislative and deliberative body of the Church, replacing the Church Assembly. The General Synod comprises three houses: the house of bishops, consisting of the 43 diocesan bishops; the house of clergy, with a maximum of 258 members; and the house of laity, with a maximum of 261 members. The house of clergy includes, besides the proctors elected by the diocesan clergy, 15 representatives of the deans and provosts, one archdeacon for each diocese, six university proctors, and representatives of the religious communities, the Channel Islands, and the chaplains of the Forces. The house of laity includes six ex-officio members, two representatives of the religious communities, and up to five co-opted members. Members of the diocesan synods serve for 3 years, and those of the General Synod for 5 years. It is claimed that, under the new synodical organization, the laity will

Church of England. The Queen presided over the ceremoney of inauguration of the General Synod at Westminster Abbey on November 4.

play a far greater part in Church government than ever before, and the local parishes will no longer feel isolated from the governing body.

It was agreed by the General Synod at its first meeting that the order of deaconesses should in future have the right to read the services of morning and evening prayer, including the epistle and gospel; to instruct and preach; and to distribute the holy sacrament. It was also agreed that, where the goodwill of the persons responsible can be obtained, a deaconess may officiate at a funeral service, and that she may also publish banns of marriage at both morning and evening prayer. These developments are seen as a further step towards the possible ordination of women into the priesthood.

With the coming into force of the Divorce Reform Act on Jan. 1, 1971, the Church of England accepts irretrievable breakdown of a marriage as a ground for divorce. This was announced in a statement of guidance to clergy at the beginning of December by the Archbishops of Canterbury and York, who also, however, declared that the Church remains utterly opposed to any concept of ''divorce by whim or fancy''.

The report of the Archbishops' commission on church and state was published on December 10. Although recommending that matters affecting worship and doctrine should be taken out of the jurisdiction of parliament and decided by the General Synod, and that the appointment of bishops should be in the power of the Church alone and not of the prime minister and the crown, the majority did not favour disestablishment. It stressed, however, that establishment is a major obstacle to union with other churches. Other recommendations were that, like bishops of the Church of England, leaders of other Churches should have seats in the House of Lords, and that clergymen should be allowed to stand as candidates for election to the house of commons, although not necessarily as representatives of a political party. In relation to the powers of the General Synod, the commission stated that no changes should be made by it unless approved by a two-thirds majority in each of its three houses.

Church Unity. A document ''Ecumenism in Higher Education'', issued on May 15, 1970, and forming the second part of an ''ecumenical directory'' compiled by the Vatican to provide guidance for Roman Catholics in closer relations with other churches, proposed collaboration in educational projects. The proposals included the sharing of teachers and facilities with non-Catholic universities and colleges; institutions for ecumenical study; special courses in ecumenism for seminarians; and a general ecumenical direction in ordinary courses in philosophy and theology. The first part of the directory, issued in 1967, contained instructions for joint prayers and services, study commissions, and other activities.

Australia. The third and final report on the proposed basis of union between the Congregational, Methodist, and Presbyterian churches of Australia was published in 1970; it was the work of a 21-member joint commission on Church union set up in 1957. Its first report contained no controversial matter, but its second, published in 1964, aroused opposition by its proposals to institute a system of bishops and for a concordat with the Church of South India. (The latter, formed in 1947, is a union of Anglican, Congregational, Methodist, and Presbyterian churches, with bishops.) In the third report, both these proposals were dropped. It suggested four ''ranks'' of officers in the Uniting Church of Australia (ministers, elders or leaders, deaconesses, and lay preachers) and four levels of government—assembly (national council), synod (regional council), presbytery (district council), elders' or leaders' meeting (local congregation). The assembly, which would be responsible for doctrine, worship, church government, missionary work, theological training, and the reception of ministers of other communions, would have to obtain the agreement of the other councils on important matters. The report will be studied by the three churches for two years, and a vote will be taken in 1972. If the Uniting Church is set up, it will have over 2 million members and will be third in size among Australian churches, after the Anglican and R.C. Churches.

Cigarettes. A new filter tip for cigarettes, developed by Australia's Commonwealth Industrial Research Organization, was announced in November. The filter, which is made from wool, offers 50 per cent filtration efficiency compared with the approximate 35 per cent provided by cellulose acetate. The tar-like constituents of cigarette smoke were permanently bound to wool, whereas the tar in normal filters could be extracted with a solvent. In practical tests smokers had found that the wool filter gave the cigarette a milder taste. The chief of the textile division of the C.I.R.O., who gave this information, said the wool filters were more expensive,

Clocks. This silver-mounted ebony bracket clock made by Thomas Tompion fetched the record auction price of £26,000 in November.

but it had been estimated that the amount of wool filter material that could be used annually would total 20 million lb.

Cinema-going. Figures given in January 1970 showed that in Spain the cinema remained the most popular public entertainment during 1968. The returns for the 5 per cent entertainment surcharge, put on all box-office takings in aid of child welfare, totalled just over £3 million, out of which the cinema contributed nearly £1,500,000; sports meetings £300,000; and the theatre £250,000. In the first quarter of 1969 there were nearly 96 million paying cinema customers, roughly equivalent to attendance by every man, woman, and child once a month. During this period American films earned about £3½ million, Spanish films £2½ million, and British films just over £1 million.

Figures given by the Italian national film distributors' association in November showed that from July 1969 to the end of August 1970 Italian cinemas registered

Clyde, River. Work on the new Erskine Bridge at Old Kilpatrick reached its final stages in the summer of 1970. With a main span of 985 ft., its length with approaches will be about 1,400 yds.

box-office receipts of 43·2 thousand million lire (compared with 42 thousand million in the same period of 1968–69), related to the screening of 587 films. During the past few years, the Italian public has demonstrated a preference for satire offering ironic account of many of the aspects of modern society, but only those films with real artistic merit succeeded in attracting the public's attention.

Clocks. At Sotheby's, London, on Nov. 16 a silver-mounted clock, made by Thomas Tompion at the beginning of the 18th century, was sold for £26,000, a record auction price. The clock is 9 in. high, has a veneered ebony case and richly engraved mounts, and was sold in its original plain oak travelling case lined with green silk and velvet. The previous record auction price for a Tompion clock was £15,500, paid at Sotheby's in 1968.

per cent of the total). Europe began to be a significant buyer towards the end of 1969, and in the year 1969–70 exports to Europe amounted to approximately 900,000 tons, all from New South Wales. New South Wales continued to be the main exporting State, but Queensland's shipments showed a marked increase. The total output of the two States in 1969–70 was 44 million tons.

Coins and Coin-collecting. Progress towards the introduction of decimal currency continued during 1970 in several Commonwealth countries. In Great Britain, the demonetization of the half-crown took place on Jan. 1; in August the Decimal Currency Board announced that of an estimated 410 million half-crowns in circulation, 404 million had been returned to the Royal Mint. This withdrawal rate of over 98 per cent compared favourably

cents, 25 cents, and 50 cents. On the obverse they have the same portrait of Queen Elizabeth II by Arnold Machin, R.A., as that used on British decimal coins. Their reverse designs depict a wild hog (1 cent), an angel-fish (5 cents), Bermuda lilies (10 cents), a long-tail bird (25 cents), and the coat-of-arms of Bermuda (50 cents). New banknotes show local views. For coin-collectors there were specially minted silver dollars and gold 20-dollar pieces.

The royal visit to Australasia was commemorated by the issue of special coins in Australia, New Zealand, the Cook Islands, and Western Samoa. The Australian issue was a twelve-sided cupro-nickel 50 cents, with the Queen's portrait on the obverse and that of Captain Cook, with a map of his voyage of exploration along Australia's east coast in 1770, on the reverse. The New Zealand coin, a

Coins and Medals. Upper row, left to right: reverses of Bermuda 5 cents, with angel fish; Malagasy Republic 20 francs (F.A.O. plan coin), with zebu; Iraq 250 fils, celebrating Agrarian Reform Day (Sept. 30, 1970); and Isle of Man crown piece, with Manx cat. Lower row, left to right: souvenir medals showing Mozart as a boy and Charles Dickens, and both sides of the gold medal presented by the British government to Massachusetts to commemorate the 350th anniversary of the sailing of the *Mayflower* and the landing of the Pilgrim Fathers in 1620.

Clyde, River. At the beginning of June 1970 work on the new Erskine Bridge over the River Clyde at Old Kilpatrick was approaching its final stages. Part of Scotland's trunk road system, it will be linked (with the Glasgow–Greenock trunk road (A8), and the Glasgow–Inverness trunk road (A 82) near Old Kilpatrick. The bridge, which has a main span of 985 ft., is a joint project by the Renfrewshire and Dunbartonshire county councils.

Coal. It was reported at the beginning of October 1970 that test drilling carried out by the National Coal Board at Creswell colliery in north Nottinghamshire had revealed new seams about 2,400 ft. down, which were expected to yield at least an extra 8–9 million tons of coal. The coal, which was said to be in "excellent working thickness", should guarantee about another 10 years of life for the colliery.

Australia. Australian exports of black coal in 1969 rose by 30 per cent to a record of 15,900,000 tons. Japan was the biggest buyer, taking 15 million tons (97

with the rate of 55 per cent achieved when half-crowns were withdrawn in New Zealand during the introduction of decimal coinage there in 1967. The only noticeable effect of the disappearance of the British half-crowns was the increase in sixpences and florins or new 10p coins in giving change. The sixpence (equalling 2½ new pence), which the Decimal Currency Board had intended should be demonetized as soon as possible after Feb. 15, 1971, was granted a reprieve; in April, the chancellor of the exchequer announced that in response to public pressure, sixpences will remain legal tender at least until February 1973.

Bermuda introduced its decimal currency on Feb. 6, 1970, and took the opportunity to issue the first complete series of its own coins to replace the British coins previously in circulation. The basis of the new decimal currency is a Bermudian dollar valued at 8s 4d sterling (equal to the American dollar), and the new coins are in the same sizes and denominations as American coins, 1 cent, 5 cents, 10

cupro-nickel dollar, had a view of Mount Cook with its Maori name, Aorangi, below it. Portraits of Captain Cook also formed the reverse designs of the Cook Islands cupro-nickel dollar and the Western Samoa cupro-nickel 1 tala coin, both designed by a New Zealand artist, James Berry. Other commemorative coins issued in the British Commonwealth during 1970 included a cupro-nickel dollar to mark Guyana's Republic Day on Feb. 23, a Canadian dollar in nickel to mark the centenary of Manitoba's membership of the Canadian Federation, and two coins, 1 and 2 pa'anga, with which Tonga commemorated its independence and full membership of the Commonwealth. In the Gambia a new cupro-nickel coin in an unusual denomination, 8 shillings, had an attractive picture of a yawning hippopotamus on the reverse.

The U.N. Food and Agriculture Organization continued the development of its coin plan, which invites member countries to issue special coins to emphasize the importance of increasing the world's food supplies. Iraq, the Malagasy Republic, Rwanda, and Tunisia were among the countries which joined the Plan during 1970.

Other notable commemorative issues included a Japanese 100-yen coin to mark Expo 70, a Czechoslovak 25-korun coin to mark the 50th anniversary of the Slovak national theatre at Bratislava, an Israeli 10-lirot silver coin for the 22nd independence day, and a Russian 1-rouble coin with a portrait of Lenin to mark the centenary of his birth.

A noticeable feature of coin-collecting in 1970 was a marked recession in the prices being asked for many ordinary British coins issued during the last 20 or 30 years. Speculators who had hoarded large quantities of modern British, Canadian, and American coins to re-sell at inflated prices began to find during 1970 that demand was steadily decreasing, as collectors turned to other branches of numismatics. The trend led to an increased interest in banknotes, in medals and decorations, and in commemorative medallions. Since governments have not yet adopted the policy of issuing commemorative banknotes in the same way as they issue coins and postage stamps for special occasions, it was such items as the notes of early 19th-century provincial banks, the German inflation banknotes of 1921–23, and the British Treasury notes of 1914–28 that began to enjoy popularity and a rapid rise in value. Among medals and decorations, the world record price for a British gallantry award was realized at Sotheby's sale-rooms in London on Sept. 30, when £2,100 was paid for the George Cross earned by Lieut. Robert Davies, Royal Engineers, for saving St. Paul's Cathedral from destruction by an unexploded bomb dropped by a German aircraft in September 1940. Another exceptionally high price, £1,700, was paid at the same sale for ten medals, including a Victoria Cross, awarded to a Seaforth Highlander, Drum-major W. Ritchie. A larger group of fourteen medals, also including a Victoria Cross earned by an Indian Army officer, Captain Ishar Singh, realized £2,000 at a Sotheby sale on June 24.   **C. W. HILL**

Cologne, W. Germany. On Nov. 24 the cornerstone of Europe's highest apartment building was laid on the bank of the Rhine near Cologne. The 46-storey building, which will be 454 ft. high, will contain restaurants, nurseries, a swimming pool, and 353 flats. It was designed by the Cologne architect Henrik Busch.

Commonwealth Games. It was announced in July 1970 that the 1974 Commonwealth Games will be held in Christchurch, New Zealand. They were last held in New Zealand—in Auckland—in 1950.

Continental Shelf (Australia). The Australian minister for national development announced in March 1970 that his department is to conduct a survey to deter-

mine the depth of Australia's continental shelf. The department will produce a series of bathymetric maps (contour maps of the sea-bed), indicating water depth, on a scale of about 4 miles to the inch, and make a geophysical survey of the area by the end of 1972. The survey and mapping will cost $A18 million, and the geophysical investigation an additional $A3 million.

An act to protect the resources of Australia's continental shelf, called the Continental Shelf Living Natural Resources Act, came in force on April 15, 1970. It established controlled areas in Victoria for oysters and abalones; in Tasmania for bêches-de-mer, bell shells, razor fish, abalones, and green snail; in the Northern Territory and the Ashmore and Cartier Islands for sponges, bêches-de-mer, and all sedentary molluscs; and in Queensland for corals, sea urchins, bêches-de-mer, and all kinds of sedentary molluscs. The effect of control is that the commercial taking of any sedentary organisms will require a federal licence. Penalties for infringement of the act comprise fines of up to $A1,000, with forfeiture of the ship and catch.

Cooby Creek, Queensland, Australia. It was announced in June 1970 that the satellite tracking station here was being dismantled for return to the U.S.A. The station was established in 1966 under an agreement between the U.S.A. and Australia as part of a tracking network for America's National Aeronautics and Space Administration. Cooby Creek completed its final assignment in the 1969 satellite programme, and after that was used for Australian communications experiments.

Countryside Awards. The winners of these awards, made under a scheme approved by the Duke of Edinburgh as president of the "Countryside in 1970" series of conferences, were announced in August. The scheme was open to any project completed since 1965 which had produced an improvement in, or contributed to, the understanding of the English countryside. It attracted 472 entries, of which 100 gained awards. Projects included the reclamation of derelict land, setting up nature reserves, nature trails, country parks, field study centres, road landscaping, clearing footpaths, restoring canals and windmills, and tree planting. The conversion of a derelict lighthouse to a bird observatory north of Portland Bill won one of the awards, and another was given for the conversion of a rubbish tip and a pond into a nature reserve at Lowgate, Gosberton, near Spalding, Lincs. Durham county council received an award for reclamation of pit heaps to agriculture and forestry at Roddymoor, Crook, and Willington; Northumberland county council for reclamation at three collieries; South Kesteven rural district council for restoring the village well, roofing the village stocks, and clearing and mowing the overgrown village green at Witham-on-the-Hill, Lincs; and the con-

servation centre of the Wildfowlers' Association for restoring the 200-year-old duck decoy at Brill, Bucks, and for constructing a conservation centre.

Other awards included one for keeping four Hertfordshire commons in the Ashridge area free from litter and rubbish; another for clearing and restoring stretches of the Kennet and Avon canal; and another to J. C. Wilkinson, of Barley, Herts, for a history of his village entitled *Two Ears of Barley.*

Countryside Commission. The Commission announced its first major country-park grant to a private development on Dec. 22. The £25,000 grant was made to Lytton Enterprises Ltd. for the development of the 15th-century Knebworth House and park near Stevenage, Herts. The money will help to provide an access road from the A1 at Stevenage, picnic areas, nature trails and footpaths, an adventure playground, and other facilities.

Cranes. Information about a floating crane with the largest ever lifting capacity, the Kiryu, was given in February 1970. Made by the Hakodate Dock Co. of Japan for the Yorigami Construction Co., Kobe, the vessel's deck carries two cranes which together can lift up to 2,000 tons; singly, either crane can hoist up to 1,000 tons. The inclination angle of the cranes' booms can be reduced to 30 degrees, allowing the vessel to pass below bridges and overhead power cables. The cranes are remotely controlled from a central position. The Kiryu's first job will be the construction of the Kobe Ohashi bridge linking Kobe port and the Port Island, an artificial island under construction in Kobe harbour. The giant crane is then expected to be used in large-scale bridge and port developments, including the mammoth bridge linking Honshu and Shikoku, and a comprehensive development programme planned for Osaka bay.

Cranfield. On May 8, 1970, the famous college of aeronautics at Cranfield, Beds, was formally inaugurated as the Cranfield Institute of Technology, following the granting of a royal charter in December 1969, which gave the institute powers to award higher degrees. The first chancellor of the institute is Lord Kings Norton, chairman of the air registration board, and a member of the council on National Academic Awards.

Crime. A report by the chief inspector of constabulary, published on June 24, 1970, stated that in England and Wales, excluding the Metropolitan area, there were 1,167,207 indictable offences in 1969, an increase of 6·1 per cent over 1968. Crimes of violence against the person rose by 17 per cent, from 26,196 in 1968 to 30,688 in 1969. Complaints against the police in England and Wales increased from 6,357 in 1968 to 7,351 in 1969, and of this number 902 were referred to the director of public prosecutions. Only

72 resulted in convictions, and 63 of these were for breaches of traffic acts and regulations. The number of murders known to the police in England and Wales fell from 148 in 1968 to 125 in 1969.

London. Crime in the Metropolitan Police area increased in 1969 by 7·5 per cent over 1968. Indictable offences in 1969 totalled 321,431, compared with 298,867 in 1968. Woundings and assaults rose by 28·7 per cent to 6,820; robbery and assaults with intent to rob by 17·1 per cent to 2,236; frauds by 22·9 per cent to 16,149; handling stolen goods by 22·3 per cent to 6,378; burglary by forcible entry by 11·2 per cent to 24,590; and thefts by shoplifting by 51·1 per cent to 12,879. There were 51 cases of murder, 77 of attempted murder and threats to murder, and 35 cases of manslaughter and infanticide: all these showed a decrease on the 1968 figures. Arrests for indictable offences increased from 61,184 in 1968 to 75,127 in 1969, and the clear-up rate of all indictable offences rose from 24·7 per cent in 1968 to 26·8 per cent in 1969.

In the Metropolitan Police area, 9·4 per cent of young people arrested were under the age of 14, and 25 per cent were aged 16; 35·8 per cent of arrested persons aged 20 years had previous records. In the 10–13 age group arrests in 1969 rose by 60·7 per cent to a total of 7,763; in the 14–16 age group by 28·2 per cent to 12,119; and in the 17–20 age group by 20·3 per cent to 15,961. Altogether 35,843 people under the age of 21 were arrested, 30·1 per cent more than in 1968. Complaints against the police in the Metropolitan area totalled 3,296 in 1969, compared with 2,924 in 1968; the 253 substantiated mainly concerned allegations about the attitude of police officers to the public.

In the first six months of 1970 indictable offences in London were fewer than in the same period in 1969, but crimes of violence increased. Robberies rose by 11·8 per cent, and overall crimes of violence increased by 6·2 per cent. For robberies 641 people were arrested, and 381 cases solved; of the latter 145 were committed by criminals under the age of 17. The number of burglaries fell slightly (from 39,227 in 1969 to 38,588 in 1970), but fraud cases rose from 8,014 in 1969 to 8,978 in 1970 (12 per cent). Thefts of motor vehicles rose by 4 per cent, but the unauthorized taking and driving away of vehicles fell by 6 per cent, and thefts from cars decreased by nearly 11 per cent.

Figures given by London Transport in April 1970 showed that in 1969 crimes of violence and robbery on London's tubes and buses rose by 6·3 per cent over the 1968 figure. There were 55 cases of robbery, compared with 15 in 1968; 251 cases of indictable assault, compared with 147; 98 cases of indecent assault, compared with 69; 71 cases of common assault, compared with 60; and assaults against London Transport staff were 116, compared with 97. The total number of crimes was 591, over 200 more than in 1968.

Scotland. Figures given at the end of 1970 showed that the number of murders in Scotland fell from 31 in 1969 to 23 in 1970, the lowest figure for 6 years. The number of deaths by violence also fell; there were 43 in 1970, compared with 72 in 1969, and 73 in 1968.

Armed Robbery. A U.K. home office report on the use of firearms by criminals was published in November. Covering offences committed in 1967 and 1968, it stated that in the 2 years there were more than 4,800 indictable firearms offences, 60 per cent of which involved stealing or misappropriation. Firearms were used or presented in 792 crimes in 1967, and in 878 crimes in 1968. In half the cases in which the weapon was fired someone was injured; a total of 89 people were killed. Five out of six robberies involving the use of pistols, revolvers, shot-guns, and sawn-off shot-guns were successful, but the success rate was lower when air-guns or imitation weapons were used. Air guns were the most common weapons (39 per cent of offences), followed by shot-guns (23 per cent), and revolvers and pistols (21 per cent). About 20 per cent of such offences in England and Wales were committed in London, equivalent to 11·7 offences per million population, compared with 10 per million for the rest of England and Wales. In London a gun was either used or drawn in 1,670 cases, about 12 times more often than in the rest of the country. Armed robberies in England and Wales included raids on 20 post offices and nine banks in 1967, and on 51 post offices and 37 banks in 1968.

Australia. A criminologist at the University of Queensland said in August 1970 that crime in Australia is increasing by 14 per cent a year. Queensland, where one person in 12 will meet a violent death ranging from murder to car accidents, is the most violent of all Australian States. The murder rate there is 1·61 per 100,000 population, compared with 1·56 in New South Wales, 1·22 in Victoria, and an average of 1·3 in other States. The rates for all violent crimes—murder, rape, robbery, and assault—per 100,000 population are: Queensland 46·4; Victoria 33.45; Western Australia 31·2; New South Wales 31·1; Tasmania 23·4; and South Australia 14·05.

Also during August a police spokesman from Victoria said that there had been a 63 per cent increase in major crime in the State over the past 9 years. The biggest increase was in robberies with violence, which increased by 175 per cent. In 1969 homicide cases rose to 114, compared with 96 in 1968; assault and grievous bodily harm cases to 4,576, compared with 3,922; robberies with violence to 664, compared with 483; breaking into premises to 29,901, compared with 28,818; and offences involving motor vehicles to 10,702, compared with 10,185. Offences not included on the index of major crimes rose from 17,709 in 1968 to 22.824 in 1969.

Canada. Figures given in August 1970

showed that Canada's rate of violent crime against individuals in 1969 rose by 5 per cent over 1968. There were 85,248 crimes involving violence against the person, compared with 79,162 in 1968. Actual cases reported by the police included 341 murders, 216 attempted murders, and 44 manslaughters.

Spain. In October 1970 the ministry of justice in Madrid issued figures which showed that organized crime in 1969 was 15 per cent lower than in 1968, and crimes against property, including theft, were 18 per cent lower. There was, however, a 6 per cent rise in the number of murders, and a 9 per cent rise in cases of assault. The number of convictions for offences of a political nature also increased; a total of 242 people were sentenced on political charges by the public order tribunals, and 114 acquitted. Acquittals were more than twice the 1968 figure. The number of drug offences increased, but half those arrested were foreigners; most of these offences involved the transport or sale of marijuana, and most of the offenders were classified as unskilled workers or adults without any fixed trade or profession. A fifth of the drug offenders were students.

U.S.A. Figures given by the F.B.I. on Aug. 12, 1970, showed that Americans had been more than twice as likely to be the victim of a serious crime in 1969 as in 1960. The volume of serious crime during those 9 years rose by 148 per cent, while the population increased by only 13 per cent. In 1969 there were 14,590 murders—one every 36 minutes—representing a rate of 7·2 per 100,000 people, compared with 6·8 in 1968; 86 per cent of murders were solved by the police. Serious crime in 1969 included 655,000 cases of violent crime and 4,334,000 crimes against property. The rate for the former was 324 victims for every 100,000 of population, and for the latter 1,147 offences for every 100,000 of population. Of the 197,000 robberies committed in 1969, 55 per cent were street robberies; the average loss was $280. Throughout the country, police forces solved only 20 per cent of 5 million serious crimes in 1969 (4 per cent fewer than in 1968); 19 per cent of burglaries, 18 per cent of larcenies and car thefts, and 29 per cent of robberies were solved.

Nevertheless, these figures, high as they are, represented a decline in the increase rate of serious crime in the U.S.A.; at 11 per cent they were the lowest increase since 1965; the increase in 1968 had been 17 per cent. The use of firearms in assaults in 1969 increased by only 12 per cent, compared with 24 per cent in 1968. Cities with a population of 250,000 and over reported a 9 per cent rise in crime in 1969, compared with 18 per cent in 1968; the suburban rate was 1 per cent higher but the rural rate 1 per cent lower. In 1969 the Western states reported a 12 per cent increase, compared with 18 per cent in 1968; the South 11 per cent, compared with 16 per cent; and the North East 7 per cent, compared with 21 per cent.

Only the North Central states reported a higher rate—15 per cent, compared with 13 per cent in 1968.

The U.S. attorney general on Dec. 22 stated that crime in the first 9 months of 1970 rose by 10 per cent, with the largest increase in the suburbs. Violent crimes rose by 10 per cent: robbery by 15 per cent, murder by 9 per cent, aggravated assault by 7 per cent, rape by 2 per cent. Property crimes also increased by 10 per cent: larceny by 14 per cent, burglary by 9 per cent, and car thefts by 6 per cent. Armed robbery offences, which comprised about two thirds of all robbery crimes, increased by 18 per cent, and aggravated assaults committed with a firearm rose by 10 per cent.

Criminal Injuries Compensation Board. This U.K. body was set up in 1964 to assess state compensation to the victims of violent crime. Figures given by the board on Feb. 10, 1970, showed that in 1969 over 5,500 victims of violent crimes received a total of £1,988,000 in compensation, compared with the 1968 total of £1,610,689. The highest award (£21,157) went to a 25-year-old man, who was repeatedly struck on the head with a hammer, receiving a fractured skull and brain damage. A salesman who was attacked with an axe and robbed was awarded £11,928, and a woman of 60 who was shot in the face by a gunman aiming at someone else was paid £12,000. Nearly 1,000 claims were disallowed by the Board.

Crockford's. This famous London gaming club, which took its name from William Crockford (1775–1844) who in 1827 owned a gambling house in St. James's Street, closed on March 31, 1970, following the court of appeal's upholding of the Gaming Board's earlier decision to refuse the club's two joint managing directors permission to apply for a gaming licence. The club was later bought by Maxwell Joseph, and another application for a licence was made.

Cruft's Dog Show. The supreme champion at the 1970 show, held on Feb. 6 and 7 at Olympia, was a 2½-year-old white-coated Pyrenean mountain dog, Bergerie Knur. Entries were a record 8,398 (compared with 7,786 in 1969), and it was estimated that there were twice the number of overseas buyers for the best dogs.

Cublington, Bucks. In its preliminary report, published on Dec. 18, the Roskill Commission recommended that the third London airport should be built at Cublington, and that the first runway should be in use by 1980. This choice was made by six of the Commission's members, the seventh, Prof. Colin Buchanan, the transport expert, urging the selection of Foulness. He said that the choice of an inland site for an airport would be an ''environmental disaster''. The other members defended their choice by saying that there

was, in fact, no ''ideal'' site for the airport but Cublington would be the least disadvantageous of the four suggested sites (Cublington, Nuthampstead, Thurleigh, and Foulness). The announcement set up an enormous wave of protest from rural preservation societies, farmers, local authorities, over 60 M.P.s—who signed a motion opposing the choice of any inland site and ''strongly advocating'' the selection of Foulness—and, not least, residents of the villages of north Buckinghamshire, whose announced intention was ''to fight to the death''. The government, which has the final word on the siting of the third airport, will not make its decision known until after the publication of the Roskill Commission's full report early in 1971.

Cumbernauld, Scotland. Work on the first stage of a £25,000 scheme to develop a 700-acre country park south of this new town began during the summer of 1970. This first stage involved the building of a £15,000 nature centre in the outbuildings of the old Palacerigg farm, which will provide displays, lectures, and audio-visual aids, as well as show animals living in open enclosures. Next, work will start on recreating a habitat for the wild animals of the area, which include roe deer, badgers, stoats, weasels, and hares. The area will also include a golf course, picnic-sites, and chalets, the whole scheme being intended to increase the town's amenities and provide another attraction for tourists.

Cruft's Dog Show. The 1970 supreme champion, a 2½-year-old Pyrenean mountain dog.

d

Darwin, Northern Territory, Australia. The port of Darwin is to be redeveloped at a cost of $A19 million. New plans include a new general cargo berth, with transit and storage sheds estimated to cost about $A4½ million; a small ship facility and access road in Frances bay, estimated to cost $A4 million; and a new bulk port to cost about $A10½ million. The redevelopment will greatly increase ship facilities in the harbour, provision being made for about 130 vessels of up to 100,000 tons.

Davis Cup. At a meeting in London on March 23, 1970, a committee of delegates from Great Britain, France, U.S.A., Australia, Russia, Uruguay, and Malaysia voted by five votes to two to expel South Africa from the 1970 Davis Cup tennis competition. The meeting was called by the U.S.A. after the South African government had refused to give the coloured American player, Arthur Ashe, a visa to play in the South African championships.

Deafness. A new system of teaching deaf children to communicate, known as ''cued speech'', was demonstrated in London on Aug. 25, 1970. Already in extensive use in America and Australia, the system supplements lip movements and sounds with ''cues'' shown by different positions of the hands. Eight hand shapes identify groups of consonants not readily shown by the lips, like ''k'' and ''g'', while four hand positions show vowel groups. A high rate of success is claimed for the method.

Deaths. According to the U.K. Registrar-General's 1968 statistical review, published on July 15, 1970, 76 per cent of all male deaths in 1968 occurred in the 60-and-over age group, but 78 per cent of female deaths occurred at over the age of 65. While deaths in the 20–34 age group fell to their lowest recorded level, those of children in the 1–4 age range, and for adults over 45, rose slightly. The main causes of death were circulatory diseases (37 per cent), cancer (20 per cent), respiratory diseases (15 per cent, a rise of 3 per cent over 1967), and impairment of the blood vessels in the brain (12 per cent). Cancer of the windpipe, bronchus, and lungs killed 23,903 people (an increase of 393 over 1967), while breast and cervical cancer fatalities fell slightly. Stomach cancer accounted for 32 per cent of cancer deaths among men, and 37 per cent among women. The influenza epidemic in the winter of 1968 raised the number of deaths from this disease to 4,652, the highest figure since 1961. During 1968, in which for the second successive year the infant mortality rate of 18·3 per thousand was the lowest recorded, only three children died from typhoid fever, and two from paratyphoid, while poliomyelitis and diphtheria did not claim a single victim.

A national atlas of disease mortality in Great Britain, compiled by Professor G. Melvyn Howe of Strathclyde University for the years 1954–63, was published in March 1970. It showed that those living south-east of a line from the Severn to the Wash have a higher expectation of life than those living north of it. Salford is revealed as the unhealthiest town in Britain; the healthiest is Bournemouth, where a man is likely to reach the age of 75. For a man living in Salford the risk of dying is one and a half times as great as for a man living in Bournemouth, while for women living in Burnley the risk of death is over 50 per cent higher than in Bournemouth. The suicide rate in the London boroughs of Hampstead, Chelsea, and Kensington is three times the national average. Male cancer victims are most numerous in London, Shoreditch and Deptford being the worst affected boroughs. Other facts revealed by the atlas were that bronchitis was the third highest cause of death during the years under survey, with South-East Lancashire and Merseyside the worst areas for men, and Greater London and the West Midland the worst for women; that Hertfordshire had a relatively high number of deaths from pneumonia; and that alcoholic deaths were particularly high in Scotland. Professor Howe listed Birkenhead, Blackburn, Bradford, Dewsbury, Halifax, Liverpool, Oldham, Rochdale, Stockport, and Warrington as the places with the highest rate of early death, and London, Kent, Middlesex, and Surrey as those with the lowest.

Decimal Currency. A £1¼ million publicity campaign in preparation for the introduction of decimal currency in the U.K. on February 15, 1971, was begun on Dec. 30, 1970. Advertising by poster, in the press, and on television was both intensive and extensive; a postal strike prevented the full issue from Jan. 4, 1971, to every household (20 million of them) of a booklet, *Your Guide to Decimal Money,* which included two "pull-out" copies of an £sd to £p conversion table for shoppers. Advertisements were illustrated with pictures of the new coins and their "old" equivalents, and many examples of conversion were given. The difficulties expected during the transition period of a maximum of 18 months, when both old and new coins would be legal tender, were officially minimized, as it was expected that, within even the first week, the new coins would become more common in use than the old ones. The banking and accounting (or "whole penny") conversion table was explained, and instructions given for the writing of decimal amounts on cheques and bills. A cheering and confident message from Lord Fiske, chairman of the Decimal Currency Board, prefaced the booklet, which concluded with a decimal quiz dealing chiefly with the giving of change. At a press conference on Dec. 29 Lord Fiske stated that nearly

4,000 million decimal coins had been produced (excluding the 5p, 10p, and 50p coins already in circulation); 3,400 million were decimal "coppers" (½p, 1p, and 2p coins), of which 62, with a value of nearly 80p, had been produced per head of the population. Lord Fiske also showed two piles of coins to illustrate the weight-saving of the new coinage: the first was a pile of old pennies worth a total of £5 and weighing 25 lb., the second a pile of new "coppers" worth the same amount but weighing only 4 lb.

All banks closed on Thursday and Friday, Feb. 11 and 12, to prepare for the changeover, and all post offices that were not strike-bound closed on Friday, Feb. 12, until D-Day.

Defence. *United Kingdom.* The Labour government's White Paper on defence published on Feb. 19, 1970, forecast that expenditure in 1970–71 would be £2,280 million, plus the cost (£90 million) of the increase in Forces pay that was announced on Feb. 25. The estimate represented about 5½ per cent of the gross national product, and 9½ per cent of all government expenditure. Withdrawal of British forces from east of Suez and the concentration of defence effort in the NATO area were confirmed. For the navy, orders for two new types of frigate were mentioned, and details were given of the design of a cruiser that would become the replacement for aircraft carriers. Savings through collaboration with other European countries in weapon design and production would be made by the multi-role combat aircraft (MRCA) and the Anglo-French Jaguar aircraft, Martel guided missile, and Gazelle helicopter. A new field gun was being developed in conjunction with West Germany. The new structure for forces pay introduced the principle of a "military salary", commensurate with civilian salaries, from which servicemen pay for their meals, accommodation, and some clothing, which were previously free. Married and unmarried men receive the same pay for the same job, and equal pay for women was promised for 1975.

The new Conservative government's defence plans were published in a White Paper on Oct. 28, 1970. The chief reversal of the Labour government's policy was the retention of British forces east of Suez, in Malaysia and Singapore, but not in the Persian Gulf. The additional cost of this was estimated at only between £5 million and £10 million a year. The defence of Malaysia and Singapore would be part of a five-power Commonwealth arrangement, the five powers being Great Britain, Australia, New Zealand, Malaysia, and Singapore. Britain will contribute a small fleet of five frigates or destroyers, a battalion group including an air platoon and artillery battery, some Nimrod long-range reconnaissance aircraft, and some helicopters. The troops stationed in Singapore will number over 2,000. Other plans in the White Paper included the retention of the aircraft carrier *Ark Royal;* the provision of the French anti-ship surface-launched

guided missile system called Exocet; the halting as far as possible of the run-down of major army units, retention of the brigade of Gurkhas, and expansion of the Territorial and Army Volunteer Reserve; and continuance of the MRCA and Jaguar aircraft agreements, with the replacement of the trainer version of the Jaguar by a cheaper aircraft. The estimated defence cost in 1971–72 was £2,327 million, falling to £2,270 million in 1972–73, and rising again to £2,290 million in 1973–74 and £2,300 million in 1974–75.

Australia. The Australian defence minister announced on March 10, 1970, that Australia will buy two more British-built *Oberon* class submarines, making up a fleet of six; 10 American Skyhawk strike aircraft; and 137 helicopters. These purchases form part of a \$A165 million (£76·9 million) defence programme, which also provides for a naval communications station at Darwin, Northern Territory; strengthened radar defences; a logistic cargo ship; and a detailed design for a light patrol destroyer. In view of Australia's part in the defence of Malaysia and Singapore it is necessary for her military capacity to be highly mobile and capable of rapid deployment in neighbouring regions.

Delaware, River, U.S.A. The world's longest cantilever road bridge was begun in the autumn of 1970, to replace the ferry that crosses the Delaware from Bridgeport, New Jersey, to Chester, Pa.

Delaware, River. Sinking the foundations in Sept. of the largest cantilever road bridge.

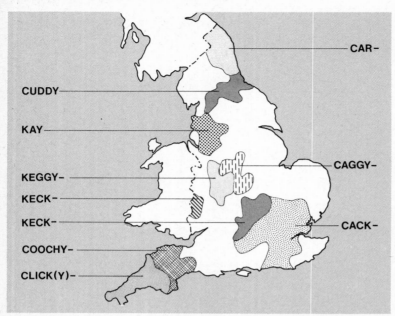

CAR-

CUDDY

KAY

CAGGY-

KEGGY-

KECK-

KECK-

CACK-

COOCHY-

CLICK(Y)-

Dialect. Map showing the geographical distribution of the ten chief variants out of the 88 different words for "left-handed" that are used in England.

With a width of 60 ft., permitting five lanes of traffic, the bridge will have a main span of 1,644 ft. The cost will be $U.S.85 million. The only longer cantilever bridges —at Quebec and across the Forth—are railway bridges.

Desalination. A method of removing the salt from sea water, previously used only in small-scale operations, was suggested in plans to build a large desalination plant at Ipswich, Suffolk, described in June 1970. The commonest method in use— "flash" distillation—requires a vast amount of power; the new method, called the secondary refrigerant process, would need much less. Sea water is mixed with a liquid hydrocarbon freezing agent, e.g. butane, which by taking heat from the water turns it into (a) ice crystals and (b) a brine slurry of unwanted salts and solids. The ice crystals are washed out and melted into fresh water.

Earlier in the year, an American firm had given information about a new method of removing salt from sea or brackish water by means of a chemical solvent. The substance is a secret polymer only a trace of which remains in the water after the salt is extracted. The company said that the solvent is made of easily available chemicals, and can be produced for less than 50 U.S. cents per pound.

Detergents. A February 1970 issue of the *British Medical Journal* carried a report by the department of dermatology at Hallamshire hospital, Sheffield, on the effects of the use of the new "biological" detergents. Clinical evidence showed that these detergents may be capable of inducing a more aggressive type of skin damage than other

detergents, possibly because the protein-splitting action of the enzymes on the keratin layer of the skin enhances the effect of other injurious influences. Observations of 13 women suffering from dermatitis indicated that when eczema follows the use of the "biological" detergents it may be particularly severe.

Dialect (English). Research over 25 years into English regional dialects has provided material for a linguistic atlas that would contain at least 2,000 maps, according to Prof. H. Orton of Leeds University, who has directed the project. Field work in 313 locations by investigators who questioned people over 60 years old who had lived in the same district all their lives lasted from 1950 to 1961. As an example of dialectal variation Prof. Orton quoted to the British Association on Sept. 7, 1970, the 88 different words for "left-handed" that had been unearthed. They are: back-handed, ballock-handed, bang-hand, bang-handed, bawky-handed, buck-fisted, cack-handed, cacky, caggy, caggy-fisted, caggy-handed, cam-handed, car-handed, car-pawed, cat-handed, cawk-fisted, cawk-handed, cawky, cawky-handed, click, clicky, clicky-handed, cob-handed, cock-handed, coochy-gammy, coochy-handed, coochy-pawed, cow-handed, cowey-handed, cowly-handed, cow-pawed, cuddy-handed, cunny-handed, doll-pawed, dollock-handed, dolly-pawed, gallock-handed, gally-handed, gammy-fisted, gammy-handed, gammy-palmed, gawk-handed, gawky-handed, gawp-handed, gibble-fisted, golly-handed, kay-fist, kay-fisted, kay-neive, kay-neived, (s)kay-pawed, keck-fisted, keck-handed, kecky-fisted, kecky-handed, keg-handed, keg-pawed, keggy, kittagh-hand, kittaghy,

left-caggy, left-cooch, left-cooched, left-hand, left-handed, left-keg, left-kegged, left-keggy, left-kelly, left-plug, marl-borough-handed, north-handed, scoochy, scram-handed, scrammy-handed, scroochy, scrummy-handed, skiffle-handed, skiffy, skiffy-handed, skivvy-handed, south-pawed, squiffy, quippy, squivver-handed, watted, watty, watty-handed.

Diamonds. The Nassak diamond, one of the world's largest and most famous gems, was sold for £208,000 at an auction at the Parke-Bernet Galleries in New York on April 16, 1970. The stone was stolen from a Hindu statue in a temple at Nassak, India, and fell into British hands in 1818. Its price was just exceeded by that given for the largest flawless diamond ever offered for sale by Christie's, which fetched £209,523 at a jewel auction held in Geneva on Nov. 18. The unmounted emerald-cut diamond, of 46·05 carats, was found in Africa, and cut in the summer of 1969. That Geneva jewel auction raised a total of £1,477,890, a world record; the previous record for a one-day jewellery sale was £1,331,295, also set by Christie's, in Geneva in April 1969.·

Among the winners of 30 awards in the 1970 Diamonds-International competition, sponsored by De Beers Consolidated Mines to promote good jewellery design, were four young British students. One of them, Susan Barfield, was the first student to win an award 2 years running, and another, Linda Gay, aged 18, was the youngest winner. The record number of entries comprised 2,351 designs from 793 designers. Switzerland came top of the prize-winning list with seven awards, then Japan with six, Germany with five, Great Britain with four, the U.S.A. with three, and Austria, Bermuda, and Brazil with one each. An American and a Japanese designer each won two awards.

Diesel Engine. A new type of ship's diesel engine with no crankshaft was revealed in February 1970 to be under development by Burmeister and Wain, the Danish shipbuilders and marine engineers. After two years of secret development construction of a prototype has begun. The new engine, which is considerably smaller than the conventional diesel, could revolutionize marine propulsion at up to 40,000 shaft-horse-power, if it can be successfully produced.

Divorce. A report by the U.K. Registrar General published on March 3, 1970, stated that the number of decrees made absolute in 1968 reached 46,000, the highest since 1947. The Catholic news agency Kathpress reported in May 1970 that the number of divorces in Austria had increased by 25 per cent since 1961. Vienna leads the Austrian divorce record with 2·7 divorces for every 1,000 inhabitants.

Italy. The long battle for the institution of divorce in Italy was won on Oct. 9, when the senate passed the historic divorce bill, leaving only minor amend-

Council of Industrial Design Awards 1970

Photographs by courtesy of the Council of Industrial Design and of the respective designers and manufacturers

The Duke of Edinburgh's prize for elegant design was won in 1970 by Patrick Rylands for his range of toys (right) for Trendon Ltd. At rear are two constructional toys in which the parts slot or lock together; in the foreground are a fish, a bird, a gyrosphere, and a set of "little men".

The "Opella 500" series of plastic taps above was designed and made by IMI Developments Ltd., a subsidiary of Imperial Metal Industries Ltd., Birmingham. A non-rising spindle is said to give washers a life of 20 years. The entirely new microscope below, designed and made by Dr. John McArthur, Landbeach, Cambridge, although only 4 in. by 2½ in., gives magnifications up to 1,500 times. Entering at the top, light passes through the specimen and then through any of three slide-in objective lenses; it is then reflected 90° along the base and again 90° to the eyepiece.

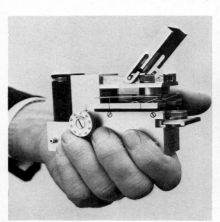

Designed by Henry Kewley and P. R. Kilbey for Kewlox (1969) Ltd., this range of do-it-yourself storage units is supplied in kits of metal uprights and hardboard doors, shelves, panels, etc., which slot together or fit into grooves.

The "Boss" Mark III. range of forklift trucks, designed and made by Lancer Boss Ltd., Leighton Buzzard, comprises a series with capacities from 4,000 lb. to over 80,000 lb. Features of the design are the low profile and the forward and off-centre driving position.

Doncaster, Yorkshire. Two new buildings in this industrial city received special commendation in the 1970 awards of the Concrete Society. They were: left, the racecourse grandstand, designed by Howard V. Lobb and Partners; and right, the new police headquarters and law courts, designed by Frederick Gibberd and Partners in association with the Doncaster borough architect, L. J. Tucker, A.R.I.B.A.

ments to be acted on by the chamber of deputies. The senate vote was 164 in favour of the legislation, and 150 against. On Dec. 1, after an all-night sitting, the chamber of deputies adopted the amendments, and the bill became law. This action overrode objections by Italy's largest party, the Christian Democrats, and defied the bitter opposition of the Roman Catholic Church.

It is expected that between 1 and $1\frac{1}{2}$ million Italians will seek divorce under the new law. Its main clause permits divorce after 5 years' separation. Other grounds are if a partner is jailed for more than 15 years, or is convicted of immorality within the family; if the marriage has not been consummated; or if one partner is a foreigner and has already obtained a divorce or remarried abroad.

Australia. Commonwealth government statistics given in June 1970 showed that one in five of N.S.W.'s marriages end in divorce, compared with one in seven in Victoria, one in eight in Queensland, and about one in nine in Tasmania. In 1969 there were 10,930 divorces in Australia, an increase of 199 (or about 6 per cent) over 1968. In N.S.W., however, divorces, totalling 5,123, increased by almost 50 per cent in the past 5 years. About 63 per cent of these divorces were granted on the petition of the wife; 2,254 petitions were granted on the grounds of desertion, and 1,237 for adultery.

Dockyards. Plans to modernize the Royal Navy dockyards of Devonport and Portsmouth were announced by the ministry of defence in May 1970. The Devonport plan will be completed by the end of the 1970s at a cost of about £43½ million, and the Portsmouth plan early in the 1980s at a cost of £33 million. The Portsmouth plan includes the provision of a covered dock complex to refit the new Type 42 destroyers, the re-siting of a number of

major dockyard installations, and new berthing facilities to replace small basins dating from the 18th century.

Dolls. A rare French Bisque doll, dating from about 1875, was sold at Christie's on May 27, 1970, for a record auction price of 900 guineas. The doll's blond ringleted head swivels, and has two faces, one wide awake and the other sleeping.

Dover, Kent. In the summer of 1970 archaeologists found here remains of the long-sought-for Roman fort of Dubris. Excavations were carried out at four main sites on the west side of the town. At one of them a 50-ft. section of defensive stone wall 8 ft. thick, built on chalk blocks, was found, and at another a short length of masonry and the foundation trench of a further long piece of wall. The fort wall was fronted by a wide defensive ditch over 30 ft. wide and more than 10 ft. deep. Traces of huts were also unearthed, as well as domestic rubbish, pottery, and coins. The new discovery made it possible to trace the south side of the fort for nearly 400 ft. and the west side for about 200 ft. and, taking into account other masonry found many years ago, leads experts to believe that the original fort was rectangular, enclosing between 3 and 6 acres. Before this discovery, Dubris was known only from a Roman list, the *Notitia Dignitatum,* which recorded a garrison on the site. Tiles stamped "CLBR" found on various sites have convinced archaeologists that the fort buildings formed part of *Classis Britannica,* the major naval base of the Roman fleet in Britain.

Drama Awards. The New York League of Theatres "Tony" awards for 1969 were announced in April 1970. The show *Applause* was named the best musical, and Lauren Bacall the best musical actress for her part in it; it also won Ronald Field

the awards for direction and choreography. Other awards included:

Best dramatic play—*Borstal Boy.*
Best dramatic actress—Tammy Grimes, for her role in *Private Lives.*
Best supporting actress—Blythe Danner, for her role in *Butterflies Are Free.*
Best dramatic actor—Fritz Weaver, for his role in *Child's Play.*
Best supporting actor—Ken Howard, for his role in *Child's Play.*
Best actor in a musical—Cleavon Little, for his role in *Purlie.*
Best supporting actor in a musical—Rene Auberjonois, for his role in *Coco.*
Best supporting actress in a musical—Melba Moore, for her role in *Purlie.*
Best director—Joseph Hardy, for his direction of *Child's Play.*
Best scenic and lighting design—Jo Mielziner, for *Child's Play.*

Cecil Beaton received his fourth "Tony" for the costumes he designed for the musical *Coco,* and special awards went to Sir Noël Coward, Alfred Lunt and Lynn Fontanne, and Barbra Streisand.

Driving Licences. Changes in provisions for U.K. driving licences and tests came into force on June 1, 1970. Because many learner drivers need more than 6 months to reach test standard, provisional licences are now issued for a year, and the cost of both provisional and full licences has been increased to £1. There is now no limit to the number of provisional licences obtainable before a driving test (previously limited to seven). Restrictions on epileptics now state that they must have been free from attacks for at least three years, or have a three-year history of attacks only during sleep. Full licences allow holders to drive groups of vehicles not covered by their licence, as if under a provisional licence.

Driving Tests. The U.K. minister of transport announced on Sept. 2 that the driving test fee will be raised from £1·75 to £3·25 in 1971. The increase has been made necessary by rising costs in running the driving test organization; the drop in demand for tests—1,710,000 in 1968–69, compared with 2,100,000 in 1967–68—had caused a deficit of £3,280,000.

Dropmore Papers. This is the name of a large collection of historical correspondence and other papers covering the entire career of Lord Grenville (1759–1834), the British foreign secretary who played a major role during the period of the Napoleonic wars. It takes its name from Dropmore, his Buckinghamshire home. The bulk of the collection consists of 335 portfolios of loose papers, and some 150 bound volumes. They include over 500 letters of George III, and about 270 of William Pitt the Younger. It was announced in March 1970 that the British Museum had purchased the papers with the aid of a generous contribution from the Pilgrim Trust.

Drug Offences. The U.K. home office stated in September 1970 that convictions for drug offences, mostly involving cannabis, rose by 43 per cent in 1969, but heroin addiction dropped to less than 500 cases. There were 6,095 convictions for offences involving drugs controlled by the Dangerous Drugs Act 1965, such as heroin, cocaine, opium, and cannabis; 4,683 involved cannabis, compared with 3,071 in 1968. Fines ranged from £1 to £450, and prison sentences from 1 day to 10 years. The convictions resulted from 6,815 prosecutions, compared with 4,836 in 1968. There were also 3,762 convictions for offences involving drugs controlled under the Drugs (Prevention of Misuse) Act 1964, which includes amphetamines and hallucinogens such as L.S.D., compared with 2,957 in 1968. The figures also showed that on Dec. 31, 1969, there were 1,466 registered addicts, including 499 addicted to heroin or heroin combined with another drug. During 1968, 2,240 people were known to have been addicted to heroin or heroin combined with another drug.

Australia. The head of the central crime intelligence bureau of the Commonwealth police gave figures to the Senate select committee on drug-trafficking and abuse at the end of January 1970 which showed that the number of drug offenders charged in 1969 was in New South Wales 87 per cent higher, and in Victoria 67 per cent higher, than in 1968. Other figures, based on statistical samples, showed that 47 per cent of drug offenders throughout Australia in 1969 were born outside the country; 72 per cent were under 30 years old; 66 per cent were semi-skilled or unskilled workers, and about 8 per cent were students; in 39 per cent of cases involving drug abuse, marijuana or its derivatives were used; and 10 per cent of marijuana users moved on to other drugs. The average age of all offenders was 26·8 years, the average age of the Australian population being 30·9 years. In figures showing the nationality of offenders, slightly more than 53 per cent were born in Australia, 6·9 in New Zealand, 12·5 in Great Britain, 9·4 in China, and 4·8 in the U.S.A. Male offenders outnumbered females by over three to one.

John Gorton, the Australian prime minister, speaking at the official opening of a training seminar on drugs organized by the Federal Bureau of Narcotics on Sept. 6, emphasized the frightening growth in the number of Australians charged with drug offences. In 1968 the number aged between 14 and 34 was less than 300; in 1969 it was 700. Australia's narcotics squad had been trebled since it was formed in 1968, and it is proposed to increase the number again. It is also intended to set up a body to control drug trafficking with the countries of South-East Asia and the Pacific.

U.S.A. It was reported in December that deaths related to narcotics addiction in New York City exceeded 1,000 for the second successive year. The final total was expected to be about 1,100, compared with 1,031 in 1969. Half the victims were under 23 years of age; the youngest was 13. About 90 per cent of the deaths were caused by heroin, and the rest were due to violence arising from drug addiction.

Duxford, Cambridgeshire. It was announced in May 1970 that the disused former R.A.F. fighter base here will be converted into a 550-acre regional sports centre, including a restaurant and a caravan site. The disused runways will become circuits for auto-cross and land-yacht racing, and there will be facilities for go-karting, golf, parachute jumping, and other sports.

Earth Probe. The Australian Council for Scientific and Industrial Research developed in 1970 a new instrument for identifying minerals underground. The leader of the team of scientists who developed the instrument, Dr. Alan W. Wylie, said in Melbourne at the beginning of October that the equipment was the first of its kind in the Western world, although he believed that the Soviet Union had developed a similar earth probe. The Australian probe with a radioactive core is lowered into a test hole in order to bombard the surrounding earth with neutrons. Reflected wavelengths were fed into a computer which by analysing them identified the surrounding minerals.

East Kilbride, Scotland. Site work on a £6 million centre shopping development in the new town of East Kilbride is to begin in March 1971. The centre, which will occupy 6 acres, will include a centrally

Eisenhower Memorials. Mrs. Mamie Eisenhower beside the statue of her late husband on the campus at Gettysburg College. It was unveiled on his birthday, October 14.

heated covered shopping mall with an exhibition area; two- and three-storey shopping blocks; a 15-storey office block; a large department store; a 60-bedroom hotel incorporating a conference centre; and a three-deck car park, with space for 1,500 cars. There will be segregation of vehicles and pedestrians. The whole scheme, to be built on similar lines to the Yorkdale plaza in Toronto, is due to be completed in 1974.

Eisenhower Memorials. A statue of the late President Eisenhower was unveiled on the Gettysburg College campus on Oct. 14. Sculpted by Norman Annis, professor of art at the college, the statue stands in front of the office which Eisenhower used in his post-presidential years.

Eisteddfod. The Royal National Eisteddfod was held at Ammanford at the beginning of August 1970. The crown went to Bryan Davies, a schoolmaster from Ruabon, Denbighshire, for 10 poems about the people and places in the Amman valley, called "Pictures on a Canvas". Mr. Davies drew on memories of his childhood and youth for his work. There was a record entry of 37 for this competition. The bardic chair was awarded to Thomas Evans for his 300-line poem in strict metre on "The Wild Boar", the set subject, which attracted 10 entries. The chair won by Mr. Evans was one of the most modern in design to be awarded by the Eisteddfod;

Eisteddfod. At the 1970 Royal National Eisteddfod at Ammanford, Carmarthenshire, the popular Welsh singer Mari Hopcyn (better known as Mary Hopkin) was initiated into the Bardic circle as "a Welsh girl who has won European fame as an interpreter of contemporary folk music".

more than 6 ft. high, it was made of white laminated plastic and lined in green and red felt.

ELDO. All British participation in the European Launcher Development Organization ended in 1970, when the Blue Streak rocket was replaced as the first stage of ELDO's experimental Europa satellite launchings by a French booster. ELDO was formed in 1962 on British initiative to develop a satellite launcher based on the Blue Streak, with French and German upper stages. Member states were Great Britain, West Germany, Italy, Belgium, France, the Netherlands, and Australia. In 1966 Great Britain, which was paying 40 per cent of the bill, threatened to withdraw unless the cost was more evenly distributed, and in 1968 the government confirmed that Great Britain would withdraw entirely by 1971. No ELDO launching from Woomera, the Australian rocket range, had been successful, and Great Britain decided to concentrate its space efforts on co-operation with ESRO. See ESRO.

Electric Bicycle. A Japanese electrical company, Sanyo Electric, showed its latest product, an electric bicycle, in February 1970. The bicycle is powered by twenty 12-amp-hour batteries, which are rechargeable, runs for approximately 30 miles on one charge, and achieves speeds of up to 13 miles per hour. It is 5 ft. 2 in. long, 2 ft. wide, and 4 ft. 1 in. high.

Electric Cars. The Sony Corporation of Japan announced in April 1970 that it had developed a fuel battery system with a power rating of 100 W to 20 kW, by employing fine-grained zinc and a special electrode structure which allows repeated use of fuel. A regulated quantity of fine pulverized zinc in a fuel tank is transferred into the electrolyte-fuel in a mixture tank, and then pumped to electrolyte distributors. A 5–20 kW battery mounted on a car can operate at about half the cost of petrol.

Mass production of a small electric runabout car started in October at a plant at Creuzwald in France. The car is designed to carry one or two people and light equipment inside factories and hospitals, at ports, airports, and shipyards, and in recreation centres and holiday camps, and is also useful for transporting elderly or physically handicapped people. It has no steering wheel, no pedals, and no gear change, but is operated solely by an all-purpose lever. Powered by two small electric motors, one for each rear wheel, it can reach a speed of just over 11 m.p.h., and can run for about 6 hours on its batteries. The factory is capable of turning out 150 cars a day, and is manufacturing three versions. One is a single-seater with a platform for transporting objects; another is a single-seater with a second (removable) seat, which can be adapted for running on public roads; and the third is a more comfortable type specially fitted out for use in normal road traffic.

Electricity, Generation of. A new concept of fuelling a power station was put forward by the U.K. Central Electricity Generating Board in February 1970 and approved by the ministry of technology a month later. It is the idea of dual firing, partly by pulverized solid fuel and partly by natural (North Sea) gas. The gas will be supplied on an "interruptible" basis—i.e. the station will run on gas most of the time but, at the Gas Council's request, will turn over to solid fuel at periods of peak gas consumption. The station to be adapted will be Hams Hall C, near Birmingham, formerly wholly coal-fired. It will take between 240 and 250 million therms of gas per year, and is expected to be in use during the winter of 1970–71. During the same month of February, four coal-burning power stations received ministry of technology approval for conversion to oil.

The C.E.G.B. announced in January 1970 that it plans to build a large nuclear power station at Stourport, Worcs, which is on the river Severn about 15 miles W. of Birmingham. The station, which would have an initial output of 1,300 megawatts, could have cost £150 million by the time of its completion in the late 1970s. Already proposed was a nuclear station at Connah's Quay, on the estuary of the Dee.

On July 29 the Board announced plans for a fourth new oil-fired power station, to cost about £250 million, at Killingholme, Lincs. The station will be sited near new oil refineries on the south bank of the Humber, and will burn between 5 and 6 million tons of fuel oil a year. It will be dominated by an 850-ft. chimney, one of the largest in Europe, and will be built in two phases, work probably starting early in 1972. All four planned stations—Killingholme, Millbrooks (Cornwall), Ince "B" (Cheshire), and Littlebrook "D" (Kent)—represent potential business to the oil industry of between 10 and 11 million tons a year.

Plans for Northern Ireland's first pumped storage hydro-electric scheme, to cost £12 million, were announced by the ministry of commerce at the beginning of June. This major development is to take place near Newry, co. Down, and work is scheduled to be completed in 1976. The pumped storage system involves pumping water at "non-peak" hours from a lower to an upper reservoir, ready to be released back into the lower reservoir for the immediate generation of electric power at peak periods. The lower reservoir in the project is Camlough Lake, and the upper reservoir is being built on the northern slope of Slieve Gullion. The level of Camlough Lake is to be raised some 12 ft., and 550 million gallons of water will be circulated between the two reservoirs to produce power at peak periods. Two reversible pumping and generating units will each be capable of producing 115 megawatts.

It was announced in March 1970 that the North of Scotland hydro-electric board is to build a nuclear power station, costing £85–£110 million at Stake Ness, near Banff, on the Moray Firth. The project will comprise two reactor and generator units, the first to come into operation by 1977, and the second by 1978. The station will have a capacity of 950–1,250 megawatts. Up to 2,000 men will be employed on its 98-acre site at the peak of construction, and between 300 and 350 permanent staff will be needed.

The largest nuclear power station in Italy, and one of the largest in the world, is to be built on the Po plain, between Piacenza and Cremona. The station will have a guaranteed output of 780,000 kW, which could well be increased to 800,000 kW. The 150,000 million lire plant will be of the monoblock type, with one reactor, one turbine, and one generator.

Electron Microscope. The development of an improved electron microscope which completely eliminates the need for complicated hand adjustments, and is therefore simple to operate, was announced by a Japanese manufacture of electronic machinery in January 1970. The company, Hitachi Ltd., said that nearly 1,000 of these highly efficient instruments had already been exported, including 560 to the U.S.A. and 240 to Europe. Of the 10 microscopes it plans to produce each month, five will be exported.

Ellis Island, New York. Early in the summer of 1970 squatters belonging to NEGRO (National Economic Growth and Reconstruction Organization) seized this 27½-acre island in New York harbour and occupied

Electric Cars. The anti-pollution movement gave considerable stimulus to the production of experimental battery-driven cars in 1970, especially in the U.S.A. and Japan where atmospheric pollution of the cities is at its worst. Above, left: in this U.S. General Motors model, with a top speed of 60 m.p.h. and a range of 150 miles, lead-acid batteries are carried in a tray attached to the front bumper (upper) and zinc-air batteries in the boot; right, the Japanese Nissan car has its batteries under the floor (lower). Below: the revolutionary metal fuel battery system developed by the Sony Corporation of Japan.

it for 13 days. In August it was announced that they had been given a special-use permit by the National Park Service to return to the island and proceed with their plans to turn it into a rehabilitation centre for 2,500 drug addicts. The permit, which allows the organization to remain on Ellis Island for five years, will probably be renewed after that period. Ellis Island was the notorious immigration control point through which 16 million immigrants into the U.S.A. passed between 1892 and

1954. The old buildings, now in decay, are to be repaired and redecorated; electricity will be installed and plumbing renewed, and the undergrowth surrounding the buildings will be cleared. Members of NEGRO, a self-help group whose main purpose is to generate economic growth and job opportunities for negroes, started work on the island during the summer.

Elm Trees. Because of the rapid spread of Dutch elm disease in the U.K. a London

conference, attended by 200 tree experts, was called by the forestry commission in October. The outbreak of the disease, spread by the elm bark beetle, had reached crisis proportions. In 1968 an unusually high number of trees were already affected, and the disease had continued to spread at an alarming rate. Tens of thousands of elms in Gloucestershire, Worcestershire, Kent, and Essex had been stricken. Once affected, a tree has to be cut down and burnt, for newly dead trees are the beetle's most prolific breeding grounds. In Basildon, Essex, an area badly affected, the local council decided to spend several thousand pounds on importing a breed of wasp from Austria in what was described as a "long-shot hope" of combating the beetle. This wasp lays its eggs in the beetle larvae, killing off the young beetle grub.

Embryology. Drs. A. B. Mukherjee and M. M. Cohen succeeded in obtaining fully developed mammalian offspring from eggs fertilized outside the body in experiments carried out at the New York State University during 1970. They removed eggs from a mouse's ovary and fertilized them in the laboratory by mixing and incubating them with sperm extracted from the uteri of other female mice after they had mated. After fertilization, the egg cells grew into embryos in test-tubes until the stage was reached when they could be surgically implanted into the uteri of other mice; from 23 implants 11 apparently normal offspring developed. It was possible to identify them from the normal offspring of their foster-mothers because of their different coat colour. This was the first time that such offspring have been obtained from eggs artificially fertilized outside the body.

Emigration and Immigration. Figures published by the U.K. Registrar General in September 1970 showed that immigration into the U.K. fell in 1969 to 206,000 compared with 222,000 in 1968, chiefly because of a smaller intake from the Commonwealth, particularly from India, Pakistan, and Ceylon. The number of people leaving the U.K. rose to 293,000 in 1969, compared with 278,000 in 1968; 71,000 emigrated to Australia, compared with 55,000 who went there in 1968. There was therefore a net outflow of 87,000, an increase of 31,000 over the 1968 outflow.

Immigrants from India, Pakistan, and Ceylon totalled 32,000, compared with 40,000 in 1968; from "black" Africa 15,000, compared with 22,000; and from the West Indies 10,000, compared with 11,000. The number of emigrants from the U.K. to "black" Africa was 15,000, while 100,000 went to India, Pakistan, and Ceylon, and 9,000 to the West Indies. The number of people from the professional and managerial group who emigrated was 55,000, about the same number as in 1968 and 1967, but the "brain drain" was smaller because of an increased inflow, particularly of returning former emigrants. The report did not give figures for traffic between the U.K. and the Republic of Ireland, but it was estimated that about 25,000 Irish moved to the U.K. between mid-1968 and mid-1969.

During the first 10 months of 1970 the number of Commonwealth immigrants continued to fall. There was a 20·5 per cent decrease on the figures for the similar period in 1969, the actual figures being 31,604 in 1969 and 25,144 in 1970. In the same 10-month period of 1970, 5,621 U.K. passport holders from East Africa were admitted, compared with 5,253 in the corresponding period of 1969.

Figures given by the U.K. Registrar General on March 10, 1970, for the first time contained an analysis of births by birth-place of parents, and showed that nearly 12 per cent of the 405,000 births registered in the second and third quarters of 1969 in England and Wales were to mothers born outside the United Kingdom. The following table shows births by mothers' country of origin for the middle six months of 1969:

United Kingdom	351,982
Republic of Ireland	12,887
India and Pakistan	10,014
Africa	2,634
West Indies	8,042
Malta, Gibraltar, and Cyprus	1,557
Remainder of new Commonwealth	1,267
Australia, Canada, and New Zealand	1,104
Foreign	10,197
Not stated	5,312
Total	404,996

These figures show that new-Commonwealth-born people in Great Britain, although forming only 2 per cent of the population, account for 5·8 per cent of the births (in some areas the figure is 16·3 per cent). This is largely due to the fact that a high proportion of immigrants are of child-bearing age. In the Greater London boroughs of Brent, Hammersmith, Haringey, Islington, Kensington and Chelsea, and the City of Westminster at least half the births registered in the second and third quarters of 1969 were to mothers

born outside Great Britain, many of them from the Republic of Ireland and foreign countries as well as from new Commonwealth countries. Outside Greater London, the following local authority areas recorded substantial proportions of births to mothers born in the new Commonwealth countries: Wolverhampton 25 per cent; Slough 24 per cent; Huddersfield 23 per cent; Warley 21 per cent; Birmingham 20 per cent; Bradford 20 per cent; Dewsbury 20 per cent; and Leamington Spa 20 per cent.

Australia. In the year ending March 31, 1970, the number of new permanent settlers arriving in Australia was 137,426, a decrease of over 38,000 on the previous year's figure, which had been a record, but near the average number of arrivals over the preceding 5 years. Of the total, over half came from the U.K. Of other nationalities the largest number were of Yugoslav origin, followed by Italians, Greeks, Americans, Turks, and Czechoslovaks.

Figures made public by the Australian immigration department in Canberra on Oct. 30 showed that more than 3,000 people of Asian nationality were granted Australian citizenship in the financial year 1969–70. A detailed analysis showed that almost 900 of these Asians were from countries outside the Commonwealth (the biggest group being formerly Chinese nationals) and the remaining 2,400 came from Asian countries within the Commonwealth (the biggest group being formerly Indian nationals) or were British subjects. A migration study published during the summer indicated that people born in Egypt are among Australia's most stable migrants. The Egyptian-born are relatively well settled, and much less likely to leave than the British, Germans, Dutch, Italians, Maltese, Greeks, or Yugoslavs.

New Zealand. The N.Z. immigration minister announced on Feb. 9, 1970, that the government had introduced measures to increase immigration from Great Britain to ease New Zealand's labour shortage. The measures included halving the employer's 50 per cent contribution to immi-

grants' fares; the abolition of the requirement that subsidy-scheme British immigrants must have specific skills; and the removal of the 4,250 annual quota of subsidy-scheme immigrants. These measures were introduced because the number of immigrants had fallen from about 35,000 annually to about 25,000 in 1968 and 1969. Indeed, figures published in March 1970 showed that, during the year ending February 1970, there was a net migration loss of 4,076. In a further attempt to encourage immigration the assisted passage scheme, hitherto limited to British citizens, was in 1970 extended to include workers from Holland, Germany, France, Belgium, Italy, Switzerland, and the U.S.A.

ESRO (European Space Research Organization). Agreed upon in 1962 by the six European members of ELDO, plus Denmark, Spain, Sweden, and Switzerland, ESRO, which designs satellites and not rockets, came into being in 1964 and fired its first instruments into space in 1966. European rockets in use by ESRO include the British Black Arrow and French Diamant, but all the Organization's satellites until 1970 had been launched by U.S. rockets from U.S. soil. Great Britain decided in 1968 to leave ELDO and concentrate on ESRO. It was hoped to create a European communications satellite system, but this aspect of space utilization is monopolized by Intelsat (International Satellite Organization), which is managed by the American-dominated Comsat (Communications Satellite Corporation). All ESRO members belong to Intelsat; in 1970 it appeared that no separate European communications satellite was likely to be developed.

A serious threat to the continued existence of ESRO was posed in November 1970 by France's refusal to pay her 20 per cent share of the £4,300,000 budget intended to cover experimental, aeronautical, and communications satellites. This was part of the French campaign to revise ESRO's programme in order to concentrate upon practical applied uses of satellites rather than purely scientific uses

Esso Northumbria. This 253,000-ton tanker, the biggest ship ever built in the United Kingdom, is seen leaving the Tyne in February 1970.

—a point of view shared by West Germany and Belgium but not by Great Britain. The French then proposed in December that each member country should be allowed to participate in only those aspects of the ESRO programme in which it was interested, and to this end wrung from the governing council agreement that the existing convention, which binds all members to participate in all programmes, could be denounced by any country up to June 1971.

Eurovision Song Contest. The 1970 contest, held in Amsterdam on March 21, was won by the Irish entry "All Kinds of Everything", sung by Dana, an 18-year-old Londonderry schoolgirl, whose real name is Rosemary Brown. The song was written by Derry Lindsay and Jackie Smith, from Dublin. The British entry "Knock, Knock, Who's There?" sung by Mary Hopkin, took second place. Only 12 countries took part in the competition.

Examinations. Statistics published by the Joint Matriculation Board in February 1970 showed that in the U.K., although 4,000 more "O" level papers were taken by boys than girls in 1969, the girls obtained 14,000 more passes. In the "A" level examinations boys passed 66 per cent of them, and girls almost 70 per cent. Only just over half the boys passed "O" level English, compared with well over two thirds of the girls. In Physics and Chemistry fewer than half of the 2,700 boys passed, compared with 61 per cent of the 2,100 girls. All the 12 girls who took Welsh passed, but only two of the four boy entrants did so. In general, the pass rate tends to be higher in subjects where there are only a few entrants. For example, Greek was taken by only 417 candidates, and there was a 78 per cent pass rate. The Board reported a marked swing away from the sciences and towards the arts.

F-310. This is the code name of a petrol additive which has been developed by the Chevron Research Company in California. It is claimed that the additive, which is the result of 15 years' research work at the company's main laboratories at Richmond, California, will not only act as a detergent, so helping to restore the engine to its original maximum performance and efficiency, but will also substantially reduce pollution by exhaust fumes. F-310; so-named because it was the 310th formula tried during research, contains a number of previously developed additives with the addition, as its major ingredient, of a polybutene amine, a hydrocarbon with nitrogen. It was reported that a number of pursuit cars from the fleet of the Los Angeles sheriff's department showed a reduction of 42 per cent in carbon mon-

Farnham, Surrey. Sir Bernard Miles and Sir Michael Redgrave (right) studying a model of the theatre to be built at Farnham in 1971–72. It will be called the Redgrave Theatre.

oxide exhaust emission and of 24 per cent of unburnt hydrocarbons after the first six tankfuls of petrol containing the additive had been used; it is also suggested that a reduction in petrol consumption is achieved, particularly when the engine is idling. Extensive field tests also were carried out at the Chevron central laboratories at Pernis, near Rotterdam. Before the official launching of the additive in Great Britain on July 1, 1970, F-310 was demonstrated to audiences of motor manufacturers and other experts who reported their belief in the claims made by the company for the new product.

Farnham, Surrey. In March 1971 work will start here on a new £250,000 theatre to be named the Redgrave Theatre, in honour of Sir Michael Redgrave. It is hoped that the theatre will open in September 1972. It will replace the existing Castle Theatre, where a repertory company has played for the past 25 years. Its area of 14,400 sq. ft. will include a workroom, rehearsal room, green room, dressing rooms, offices, and a licensed bar and cafeteria. Designed by Frank Rutter, F.R.I.B.A., the new air-conditioned theatre will seat 350 in a "wide and shallow" auditorium. It will have no proscenium arch. An appeal for a fund to defray the cost of the building was announced on Oct. 15.

Ferro-Cement Boats. It was reported in September 1970 that the Italian company, Nervi and Bartoli of Rome, headed by the engineer Pier Luigi Nervi, had just completed two diesel-engined boats in ferro-cement for the U.N. Food and Agricultural

Organization. The boats are to be used on Lake Nasser, Egypt, to demonstrate fishing techniques and act as prototypes for building similar craft. One boat is 33 ft. long, weighs $3\frac{1}{2}$ tons, and is equipped with a 16 h.p. engine, and the other is 25 ft. long, weighs 2 tons, and has an 8 h.p. engine. Dr. Nervi's process, said to be the least expensive form of marine construction, uses several layers of reinforcing mesh combined with steel rods, covered with a thin layer of cement. When hardened, the hull—which need be only three quarters of an inch thick—is waterproof, fire-resistant, rot-proof, resistant to vibration, and impervious to shipworms. The craft are particularly suitable for countries where wood is scarce, but sand, wire-mesh, and cement readily available.

Film and Television Arts, Society of. This British body was formed in 1970 from a combination of the British Film Academy and the Guild of Television Producers and Directors. Its awards for film and television performances and productions were presented at the London Palladium on March 8, 1970, in a televised ceremony introduced by David Frost. See under Film Awards; Television Awards.

Film Awards. The 1969 awards by the American Motion Picture Academy of Arts and Sciences (Oscars) were announced in April 1970. The best film of 1969 was *Midnight Cowboy*, and its director, John Schlesinger, won the award for best director; it also received the award for best screenplay written directly for the screen. The best actress award went to Maggie Smith for her performance in *The*

Prime of Miss Jean Brodie, and the best actor award to John Wayne for his role in *True Grit*. The best supporting actress was Goldie Hawn for her part in *Cactus Flower*, and the best supporting actor Gig Young for his performance in *They Shoot Horses, Don't They? Butch Cassidy and the Sundance Kid* took four Oscars—best screenplay, best cinematography, best original score, and best song (*Raindrops Keep Fallin' on My Head*) by Burt Bacharach. *Hello, Dolly!* also took four awards—for best music score, best sound, best art direction, and best set decoration. Among the other awards were:

Best costume—*Anne of the Thousand Days*.

Best foreign language film—*Z* (which also won the best film editing award).

Best documentary feature—Arthur Rubinstein, for *The Love of Life*.

Best short subject documentary—*Czechoslovakia 1968*.

Best short subject cartoon—*Its Tough to be a Bird*.

Special awards were made to Cary Grant, for "sheer brilliance in the acting business", and to George Jessel, who received the Jean Hersholt Humanitarian Award for devotion to worthy causes.

At the British Society of Film and Television Arts awards presentation on March 8, 1970, at the London Palladium, twelve of the awards went to two films. *Midnight Cowboy* was chosen as best film of the year, and also won the best direction award for John Schlesinger, the best actor award for Dustin Hoffman, the most promising newcomer award for John Voight, and the best screenplay and the best film editing awards for Waldo Salt and Hugh Robertson respectively. *Oh, What a Lovely War!* received the United Nations award, and also gained the best sound-track award for Don Challis and Simon Kaye, the best costume award for Anthony Mendleson, the best art direction award for Don Ashton, the best cinematography award for Gerry Turpin, and the best supporting actor award for Sir Laurence Olivier. The best actress award went to Maggie Smith for *The Prime of Miss Jean Brodie*, and the best supporting actress award to Celia Johnson for her part in the same film. The Anthony Asquith award for the most original film music went to the Greek composer Mikis Theodorakis for his score for *Z*.

The U.S. Film Critics' Guild in its fourth annual ballot, held on Jan. 4, 1970, voted the French film *Z* the best of 1969, and named François Truffaut as the year's outstanding director for his film *Stolen Kisses*. The British actresses Vanessa Redgrave (*Isadora*) and Maggie Smith (*The Prime of Miss Jean Brodie*) shared the best actress award, and Sian Phillips was voted best supporting actress for her role in *Goodbye, Mr. Chips*. Best actor was John Voight (*Midnight Cowboy*), and best supporting actor John Nicholson (*Easy Rider*).

Other film awards made in 1970 included the David di Donatello awards for an Italian and a non-Italian film (Sophia Loren and Nino Manfredi, and John

Schlesinger and Dustin Hoffman (*Midnight Cowboy*), respectively), and the Italian *Maschera d'Argento* award for services to the cinema to Anne Heywood (Great Britain).

The New York film critics announced their awards for 1970 on Dec. 28. Glenda Jackson received the best actress award for her part in *Woman in Love*, and George C. Scott the best actor award for his part in *Patton*. Chief Don George received the best supporting actor award for his role in *Little Big Man*, and Karen Black the best supporting actress award for her part in *Five Easy Pieces*. *Five Easy Pieces* was judged the best film of the year, and its director, Bob Rafelson, received the best director award. The award for the best screen writer went to Eric Rohmer for *My Night at Maud's*.

On Jan. 1, 1971, the U.S. National Board of Review of Motion Pictures announced that *Patton* had been chosen as the best motion picture of 1970, and *The Wild Child* the best foreign-language film.

Fire-fighting. The Rand Institute in New York is studying ways to make the New York City fire department more efficient, and in December Dr. Edward Blum of the Institute reported that biochemists had developed a "slippery water" that more than doubles firemen's ability to extinguish blazes. "Slippery water" contains polyethylene oxide, which increases the flow of water through a hose by 70 per cent, and doubles the reach of the stream. The chemical is inexpensive and can be stored in a plastic bag. Mechanical feeders inject small amounts in powder form into the water as it passes from hydrant to pump. It allows the use of hoses which are much lighter and more easily manageable than the normal bulky, heavy ones. The "slippery water" was tested for 14

months in New York City under actual fire-fighting conditions.

Fireworks. In the annual report of the U.K. inspectors of explosives, published in August 1970, it was stated that the total number of injuries from fireworks fell from 2,537 in 1968 to 1,636 in 1969, the lowest figure since records were first kept in 1962. There were 240 serious injuries in 1969, compared with 392 in 1968, a decrease of nearly 40 per cent. The report attributed the improvement to helpful publicity by the press and broadcasting services, leading to the exercise of greater care in the period about Nov. 5. Previously (in April), the minimum age of children to whom fireworks may be sold had been raised from 13 to 16 years. In the summer, the Northern Ireland government went even further and introduced regulations under the Explosives Act 1970 permanently prohibiting the use or sale of fireworks except under licence or for certain navigational, safety, or industrial purposes. Licences are given to allow organized fireworks displays to be held on special occasions, but individual "back garden" fireworks were completely banned.

Fleas. Early in 1970 a fossilized flea, about 120 million years old, was unearthed by scientists from Monash University at Koonwarra in southern Gippsland, Victoria, Australia. The flea had apparently fallen off its host, drowned in the lake, floated to the edge, and then settled into the sediment which eventually built up to form the siltstone which preserved it. This primeval flea had much longer feelers on its head, longer and differently bristled legs, and a slightly longer body than its modern counterpart. Its long thin legs and long feelers suggest that it lived on the outer surface of a sparsely haired animal. Al-

Fire-fighting. The latest U.S. fire-engine is "Big John", brought into use in Chicago in 1970. Its double hose can be linked with 21 pumps to shoot water to an immense height.

though no direct evidence has been found of any furred animals living in Australia more than 20 million years ago, the Koonwarra flea indicates the probable existence of marsupials 100 million years before. Only two fossil fleas had been discovered previously, both near the Baltic Sea. Their age was put at about 40 million years and, unlike the Koonwarra flea, their anatomical structure was quite modern.

Flood Control. In March 1970 the nine provinces of the Tuscany region of Italy announced their unanimous decision to install a computer with the primary task of controlling the flow of the river Arno and its tributaries. The decision was inspired by the flood disasters in Florence and Grosseto in 1966. The computer, which is to be installed at Florence, with terminals in the other eight provinces, will calculate the height and volume of water in various stretches of the river, giving minimum and maximum warnings of 6 and 30 hours respectively, and will control the opening and shutting of drainage canals and conduits which carry off excess water. The project, launched in 1967, was worked out by technicians at the national university centre of electronic computation at Pisa; and geologists, engineers, and mathematicians, after taking many photographs of the basins of the rivers Arno, Magra, and Ombrone, planned the computer. Information gathered from apparatus installed at many points will be transmitted to the computer by radio, and its conclusions will be shown on luminous panels, television screens, and teleprinters. The computer, which will cost 400 million lire per year, will also be available for the automation of administrative and technical services in the provinces, ranging from the registration of births, marriages, and deaths to hospital management and road construction.

Flucloxacillin. This is the name of a new form of penicillin developed by the Beecham research laboratories at Betchworth, Surrey. When information about the new antibiotic was given in November, scientists at the laboratories said that it was at least as effective as other isoxazoyl penicillins against penicillin-resistant bacteria, and not so easily knocked out by proteins in the blood; that it can be taken by mouth instead of by injection; and that one dose is as effective as two doses of the normal semi-synthetic penicillin used in Great Britain.

Fluorel. This is the name of a fireproofing chemical produced in the U.S.A. arising from work in the space programme. The product is a co-polymer, containing two fluorides, that becomes more resistant to heat and deterioration as temperature increases. It can protect materials against temperatures as high as 2,200°F in a 100 per cent oxygen atmosphere, over twice as high as those at which they would normally catch fire. Fluorel can be sprayed

on surfaces such as those found in the home, in car interiors, in hospital operating rooms, in aircraft cabins, and in other places where fire risk is high. It is also produced in a solid form, as a foam, and as a paint.

Folkestone, Kent. British Rail announced in April that it plans to build a second cross-Channel ferry terminal at Folkestone harbour. The scheme will cost £1 million for the buildings, and a further £6½ million for two ferries to operate services to Boulogne and Calais. The terminal will open in 1972.

Food and Drink. An experiment to analyse flavours and determine what makes up the characteristic taste of food was conducted during the summer of 1970 by a team at La Trobe University, at Melbourne, Victoria. The project involved the use of a computer which was programmed to help to identify new substances. Prof. J. B. Morrison of the university's chemistry department said that it is now possible to identify the pure chemicals making up a flavour, and to produce synthetic flavours which could not be distinguished from those of real food. He also hopes to be able to make completely new flavours, and said that the use of synthetic flavours is becoming increasingly important because it is likely that "everyone will be eating processed sawdust by the year 2000". A new language is needed to describe taste sensation, and La Trobe University's chemistry department is trying to invent new words to describe flavours.

Consumption. According to a statistical survey of food consumption in Great Britain for the years 1966–69, published by the ministry of agriculture on July 30, 1970, consumption of all types of beef was 46·9 lb. per head in 1969, compared with 45·1 lb. in 1968, and consumption of mutton and lamb was 21·6 lb. per head in 1969, compared with 23·2 lb. in 1968. The latter was the lowest figure since 1952. The amounts of pork and poultry consumed continued to increase, and rose by 1·2 lb. and 1 lb. per head respectively between 1968 and 1969. Cheese consumption at 11·3 lb. per head in 1969 was almost ⅓ lb. higher than in 1968. Sales of cream, which have almost doubled over the past 10 years, rose from 2½ lb. per head in 1966 to 3 lb. in 1969.

Beer consumption increased by 6·5 pints per head to a total of 21·6 gallons in 1969. Since 1966 beer consumption had gone up by almost 11 pints per head. Wine drinking increased steadily to 6·7 pints a head in 1968, but fell to 6·4 pints in 1969. Consumption of spirits remained steady at 2·5–2·6 proof pints per head during the period under review.

In New Zealand during 1969 beer and stout production (69,270,000 gallons) was 1·7 per cent higher than that brewed in 1968; consumption per head rose from 24·3 gallons in 1968 to 24·5 in 1969. In 1969, Australians drank an average of 25·7 gallons per head.

Football. The Ford Motor Company's Sporting League, offering £100,000 in prize money among the 92 football clubs in the Football League, came into operation in the 1969–70 season. The competition is based on a system of points awarded for goals scored at home (1 point) and away (2 points), with deductions for infringements (5 points deducted for each player "booked", and 10 for each player sent off). The first prize is £50,000, and the second £30,000; other awards total £20,000.

In addition to these prizes, all of which must be devoted to ground improvements, the Football League and Ford will nominate certain charities each year to share the Ford Sporting League charity gift of £20,000.

Fossils. It was reported in July that scientists exploring Lake Callabonna, a salty depression in the S. Australian desert, had struck a huge field of giant fossils. Hundreds of skeletons of Ice Age diprotodons, the largest known marsupial in the world, were found lying on the surface of the lake-bed, in groups of 20–30 about 6 miles apart. The diprotodon has been identified only in Australia and in New Guinea.

In November scientists at a field camp about 350 miles from the Amundsen–Scott South Pole station confirmed that a 10-in. skeleton, found by a member of a team of geologists and palaeontologists, was that of a 200-million-year-old cynodont reptile. These four-legged, carnivorous creatures had dog-like teeth, and are closely related to the most primitive mammals. The discovery of the skeleton was another piece of evidence confirming the continental drift theory that parts of South America, India, Australia, and Antarctica once formed a solid land mass (see also page 56).

Foulness, Essex. In their preliminary report on Dec. 18, six of the seven members of the Roskill Commission recommended that Foulness should not be the site of London's third airport. They stated that they were "reluctantly obliged" to reject Foulness partly because, in the event of its being a failure, an enormous burden would fall on the taxpayer, partly because the area is badly served by high-speed transport links, and partly because of the inevitable destruction of wild life and the coastline. The seventh member of the Commission, Prof. Colin Buchanan, the transport expert, favoured Foulness.

Argument for and against the choice of Foulness had waxed strong during 1970. In March the South-East Planning Council told the Commission that the balance of advantage pointed clearly towards the choice of Foulness. Southend and south Essex would provide the city site to support it. Not only would an airport at Foulness cost about £35 million less to build than one at any of the other three suggested sites, but it would also provide 65,000 jobs in the area where the highest male unemployment rate of 4·2 per cent compared with

1 per cent at Cublington, 1·4 per cent at Nuthampstead, and 1·5 per cent at Thurleigh. The council also said that the costs of noise and the harmful impact on recreational facilities would be £2½ million less at Foulness than at Thurleigh, £9 million less than at Cublington, and £16 million less than at Nuthampstead. A survey submitted in the same month by Political and Economic Planning, an independent research organization, was also largely in favour of Foulness. It said that the real choice lay between a third "London" airport there, or a new "national" airport at Thurleigh, Bedfordshire. It claimed that the Roskill Commission's cost-benefit study had failed to make a comprehensive comparison of the four suggested sites, and had not taken the regional advantages of Foulness into account. Like the S.E. Planning Council, it noted the substantial unemployment rate in the Foulness area, and also pointed out that, while local authorities near Cublington, Thurleigh, and Nuthampstead all opposed an airport in their areas, those in Essex had nearly all welcomed the Foulness siting. The Thames Estuary Development Company—a consortium of private interests, the Port of London Authority, and Southend Corporation—reported to the Roskill Commission in March that their experiments, costing £250,000, had shown that reclamation of 18,000 acres on the Maplin Sands for an airport and seaport at Foulness was possible; it would also reduce flooding in the Thames by a tenth of a foot. The number of people affected by aircraft noise at Foulness would be 50,000 fewer than elsewhere. It was also stated that, if necessary, enough private finance had been promised to pay for the entire £182 million scheme without calling on the taxpayer. Experts advising the Commission agreed that Foulness would be the best site as regards noise. Their figures were calculated from effects on house property values and the cost of capital losses on house sales, from sound-insulating costs, and from effects on recreational activities and loss of enjoyment. For Foulness the noise cost on this basis was set at £22 million, compared with £28 million for both Thurleigh and Cublington, and £47 million for Nuthampstead.

On the other hand, the same experts declared that the construction of an airport at Foulness would cost at least £11 million more than at Thurleigh, Nuthampstead, or Cublington. It would cost £599 million to build houses at Foulness for the envisaged 65,000 workers by the year 2000—which was £15 million more than at Nuthampstead, £11 million more than at Thurleigh, and £13 million more than at Cublington—and transport costs between the airport and airport city would also be the highest of the four. The estimated total net costs were for Foulness £4,651 million; for Nuthampstead £4,434 million; for Thurleigh £4,419 million; and for Cublington £4,416 million. Both BOAC and BEA made it clear that they do not favour Foulness. BEA stated that it was

the least well placed site in relation to London, envisaged a possible hazard from sea birds, and also pointed out that sea air would corrode aircraft. BOAC, which operates about 54 per cent of its flights in a westerly or north-westerly direction, pointed out that flights from Foulness would take longer, and that Foulness had no secondary traffic catchment areas. If forced to choose from the four suggested sites, BOAC preferred Thurleigh. Finally, the Action Committee Against Foulness Airport reported in April that, as people became more aware of how the siting of an airport at Foulness would affect them, more than 50,000 had indicated opposition. In order to join existing air routes aircraft would have to turn inland on take-off, and the noise would affect densely populated areas in Southend and north Kent. Agricultural land would be lost by the provision of vast new surface communication systems made necessary by the remoteness of the site. The Committee also referred to the hazards not only from bird strikes but also from fog and mist.

Fowl Pest. What was to become a serious U.K. epidemic of this disease of poultry broke out in Essex on Aug. 24, 1970. By Dec. 29 there had been 3,111 outbreaks, involving over 20 million birds, of which nearly 7 million were lost. The minister of agriculture announced on Oct. 29 that field trials with live fowl-pest vaccine were to start immediately in parts of East Anglia; this was the first time that a live vaccine had been authorized in the U.K.

Frankfort on Main, W. Germany. The world's largest aircraft hangar, 900 ft. long, 110 ft. high, and 300 ft. wide, built by the German national airline, Lufthansa,

was inaugurated at Frankfort airport on Oct. 2. The hangar, which cost about £1¾ million, will accommodate six Boeing-747 jumbo jet airliners, or 14 Boeing-737s, and will be used for the maintenance of Lufthansa, Air France, Alitalia, and Sabena aircraft. It is heated by 39 miles of hot-water pipes, and is claimed to have the world's biggest doors, each of which weighs 160 tons.

"Galaxy." This is the name of the world's first electronic measuring machine dealing automatically with the visual examination and analysis of star photographs. A British invention, the £110,000 machine is installed at the Royal Observatory, Edinburgh. Linked to a 16-in. telescope and to a computer, "Galaxy" permits the analysis and examination of large quantities of astronomical information in a fraction of the time required by conventional methods. Photographs taken by a telescope show the images of tens of thousands of stars, and measurements of their positions and strengths give astronomers much valuable information. Because of the great numbers and complexity of the images it had, until the introduction of the new machine, been possible for astronomers to examine only a few hundred selected stars in each photograph. "Galaxy" finds the images of all the stars in a photograph, and measures their positions, sizes, and densities. Work on the machine started at Edinburgh in 1964. It is planned to install a similar machine in the Royal Greenwich Observatory, Herstmonceux, Sussex, in 1971.

Freud. This statue by Oscar Nemon of the great psychoanalyst Sigmund Freud was unveiled at the Swiss Cottage library in north-west London in October 1970. Freud's great-grandchildren (children of the writer Clement Freud) were present at the unveiling. Freud came to London in 1938 after the German annexation of Austria, and died the following year in a house in the Swiss Cottage district.

Gaming Act. When the U.K. 1968 Gaming Act came into effect on July 1, 1970, the number of local authority areas in which the licensing of gaming clubs is permitted was 41. In addition, the Gaming Board granted certificates of consent to 165 applicants for casino gaming, and 1,798 for bingo; these have to apply for actual licences to local magistrates.

Gas. The development of a new gas burner which will operate without modfication on town gas, natural gas, propane, or butane was announced by Dunlop in March 1970. A spokesman for the company said that the matrix gas burner had been developed with the difficulties of conversion from town gas to natural gas in mind. The burner is made from a new rigid metal foam called Retimet.

George Medal. Awards in 1970 of this British medal for bravery were as follows:
January: Lt. Robert James Burns, Australian navy, for rescuing survivors of the U.S. destroyer *Frank E. Evans* in June 1969, when a collision between the Australian aircraft carrier *Melbourne* and the *Frank E. Evans* during combined naval exercises in the South China Seas cut the latter in two and killed 74 U.S. seamen.
February: Private Shawn James, aged 21, of the 3rd Battalion, Light Infantry, for outstanding courage and steadiness on Oct. 11, 1969, in the Shankill area of Belfast, when under fire from a mob of over 1,500.
April: Major G. R. Fletcher, second in command of the Explosive Ordnance Disposal Unit, Royal Engineers, and his sergeant-major, Warrant Officer Class II S. D. Hambrook, for gallantry in October 1969 in dealing in London with an "outstandingly dangerous" war-time German parachute mine, containing 1,500 lb. of explosive, by steaming out the explosive with the fuse system still intact, which took 14 hours.
September: Two Glasgow police officers, Inspector Arthur Hyslop and Constable John Campbell, for bravery in a fight with a gunman earlier in 1970, after which two policemen had died.
See also under Albert Medal.

Gipsies. The U.K. minister of housing and local government said on Jan. 27, 1970, that local authorities in England and Wales must implement part 2 of the Caravan Sites Act of 1968 from April 1970, and provide camping sites for gipsies in their area. Although over 20 permanent sites for gipsies have been built since 1965, the National Gipsy Council estimated that at least another 200 were needed to give adequate accommodation to the 20,000 gipsies and nomads in the country.

Giro. On May 14, 1970, the U.K. National Giro announced a new scheme under which employees who have their wages paid directly into a Giro account will get free cash-on-demand facilities at two named post offices, and receive Giro stationery free. Employers participating in the scheme pay 5p a week for each weekly paid employee, or £1 a year for each monthly paid employee. Normal Giro account holders have to pay 4p for each cash withdrawal and 42½p for a package of transfer forms, Girocheques, and postage-paid envelopes.

Glass. The U.K. Glass and Metal Holdings in partnership with the Continental group, Soldig, announced in April 1970 that they had developed a new chemical process to toughen glass. In the normal expensive long-heat method the size and thickness of the glass that can be treated are limited, and it is also made too rigid for some uses. The new process, which consists of immersing glass in certain chemicals, allows it to withstand enormous blows without shattering and to be bent as easily as Perspex. In a demonstration, a head-on collision between two cars was simulated; both were badly damaged, but the treated windscreens remained intact.

Glen Strathallan. In fulfilment of the dying wish of her former owner, this training ship was scuttled outside Plymouth Sound in May 1970. The *Glen Strathallan*, 330 tons, was built as a trawler and later converted to a 150-ft. yacht. When her owner, Tubby Colvin, died in 1954, he left her to his mother and she on her death in the following year left the yacht to the Shaftesbury Homes and *Arethusa* Training Ship, on condition that the vessel should be sunk when her useful life was over. At first *Glen Strathallan* was used as an additional classroom for the *Arethusa*, and then, in 1960, she was chartered by the King Edward VII Nautical Training College as a sea-going ship for training deck cadets, in which capacity she made 192 voyages. When she developed defects too costly to repair it was decided to sink her, and, one month later, the steel-hulled ship began a new chapter in her life as Great Britain's first underwater "classroom" for training divers. Lying 50 ft. deep on the sea-bed, her position marked by a green conical buoy, she is being used by divers on courses organized by the School for Nautical Archaeology at Plymouth. The men come from the services, the British Sub-Aqua Club, and other diving groups, and during 4-day courses they try out underwater photography and study marine growth and the rate of break-up of the ship.

Golden Eagle. It was revealed on July 31, 1970, that a pair of golden eagles had bred successfully in the Lake District, the first recorded in England, it is thought, for about 200 years. After the adult birds were first seen in a remote valley in March, the Nature Conservancy and the Royal Society for the Protection of Birds, with support from the Lake District Naturalists' Trust and the Cumbrian police, kept up a continuous guard over the area until an eaglet was hatched.

Gove Peninsula. At Gove Peninsula on the Arnhem Land coast of Australia a $A310 million bauxite-alumina development had to be redesigned in 1970 because on the site originally planned for an office block and factory complex stands an ancient banyan, a sacred tribal tree of the aborigines. The company recognized the reverence for the tree, and the new design both incorporates and protects it.

Great Barrier Reef. A joint Federal and Queensland State three-man royal commission to examine the danger of oil drilling to the Great Barrier Reef was announced by the Federal government of Australia on May 5, 1970. The commission's enquiries cover the entire area of the Reef from low-water mark on the mainland to the outer line of the reef and the area outside and adjacent to the outer line of reefs. The commission's terms of reference require it to assess the risk of an oil or gas leak in exploratory and production drilling for petroleum, and the probable effects of such a leak and of subsequent remedial measures on the reefs, the coastline, and the area's ecological and biological life; to discover if any localities within the prescribed area exist where the effects of drilling would cause so little detriment that it can be permitted, and what their geographical limits are; to examine existing safety precautions in such localities and recommend any additional conditions if necessary; and to assess what benefits would accrue to the State of Queensland and other parts of the Commonwealth from exploration or drilling for petroleum in the area.

Great Britain. On June 23, 1970, the *Great Britain*, Brunel's 1,400-ton iron ship, the first to be screw-propeller driven, arrived in Avonmouth Docks, Bristol, at the end of an 8,000-mile journey on a pontoon from the Falkland Islands. She was greeted by the cheers of hundreds of dockers and the sound of ships' sirens as tugs eased her through the lock gates. Here members of the *Great Britain* project committee, formed in September 1968, civic leaders, and Jack Hayward, the British businessman who gave £150,000 so that the ship could be brought back to Bristol, watched her approach.

Thus began the last stage of the world's longest salvaging operation. The *Great Britain* was the largest, though not the heaviest, load ever ferried by pontoon. To raise the ship from Sparrow Cove, in the Falkland Islands, where she was beached in 1886 after rounding the Horn, the pontoon, 240 ft. long, 80 ft. wide, and 15 ft. deep, and divided into 15 water-tight compartments, was sunk near her by letting water into the compartments. Then the *Great Britain* was towed over the pontoon and made fast, and compressed air was blown into each pontoon compartment, so raising it under the ship. She was then towed to Port Stanley, where on April 23 the governor of the Falkland Islands formally handed over the

Great Britain. The hulk of Brunel's historic iron ship, which had lain in the Falkland Islands since 1886, was towed 8,000 miles on a pontoon (left) to Bristol in 1970. As she was hauled to the dock where she was launched in 1843, she passed under Brunel's Clifton suspension bridge.

Crown wreck to the salvage firms, which brought her home via Montevideo.

On July 5, as thousands of people lined the banks of the Avon, the ship was towed up the river, passing under Brunel's Clifton suspension bridge, to Canon's Marsh wharf, Bristol, and, with the Duke of Edinburgh and Jack Hayward aboard, she entered on July 19 the dry dock where she was launched on July 19, 1843. Here the work of restoring her to her original launching condition is being carried out. It is expected to take at least two years, and the committee aim to raise £100,000 by 1971, and a further £250,000 in the following year. To aid the towing operation the three wooden masts added between 1882 and 1886 were removed; when restored, she will have six masts and a funnel. It is planned to restore the external part of the ship to its original appearance, and reconstruct the public rooms and to install facsimile engines. The forward part will be converted for community and educational purposes. Her final resting place has not, as yet, been decided. She may remain in Bristol, or she may be anchored in the Thames, near the Tower of London.

Guam. On June 22, 1970, a number of dignitaries and priests from Japan took part in religious ceremonies at the Memorial Park in Yigo, Guam. It was on this site that the last battle for Guam was fought in 1944 when the Americans reoccupied the island captured by the Japanese in 1941. During the ceremonies a 100-ft. peace memorial tower was unveiled.

Hanover, West Germany. A new exhibition hall, said to be the largest in the world, was constructed here for the 1970 Hanover Fair, held from April 25 to May 3. The Z-shaped hall has a surface area of approximately 81,222 sq. ft., and is constructed on pillars, the basement providing a car park for 2,359 cars. On the roof a bungalow town of 752 offices and apartments, all hexagonal and arranged in groups, has been built. The streets include a shopping centre with restaurants.

Haworth, Yorkshire. The Keighley town council agreed in October to a proposal put forward by the West Riding county council that part of the village of Haworth, famous for its association with the Brontës, should be declared a conservation area. Strict control is to be exercised over all advertising in an area of half a mile around Haworth's main street and the parsonage where the Brontë sisters lived with their father and brother.

Health Centre. A new £500,000 British United Provident Association medical centre providing facilities for a rapid and thorough health check as well as a comprehensive pathological service able to deal with 20,000 people a year, was opened near King's Cross station, London,

on April 30, 1970. Described as one of the most advanced in the world, the centre uses a time-saving question-and-answer computer to complete an introductory dossier on each new patient. The data derived from X-rays are mechanically recorded, and results from the blood-testing equipment, in which electronically active tubes allow all biochemical and haematological tests to be made quickly and accurately, are also computerized. Every doctor who sends a patient to the centre receives a full printed report within 48 hours of the patient's attendance. The fee for a total screening including diagnostic report is £25 (£22 to a BUPA subscriber).

Heart Disease. The medical director of the National Heart Foundation of Australia, Dr. Ralph Reader, said on April 30, 1970, that heart diseases are costing Australia over $A700 million a year from loss of productivity, premature deaths, invalidism, and cost of medical services. In the Foundation's annual report it was stated that 57,000 deaths (about 55 per cent of all deaths) occur annually from heart disease, and that some 65,000 people in the prime of life—between 30 and 59 years of age—are affected by coronary heart disease. In addition, about 1·2 million suffer from high blood pressure, and many thousands more are affected by other forms of potentially fatal heart and blood-vessel diseases. A computerized survey carried out by the Royal Australian College of General Practitioners and the Pharmaceutical Research Services of Australia of 700,000 instances of illness showed a surprising predominance of females over males treated for heart diseases, women outnumbering men by 14,000 to 8,500.

Henry Stokes Memorial Medal. This award, presented every 3 years by the Geologists' Association, was given in February 1970 to Dr. Ian Cornwall, of the University of London Institute of Archaeology. Dr. Cornwall is a specialist in the study of the environment of ancient man in Britain and Mexico, and he was awarded the medal for his outstanding work in this field. Previous holders of the award include Dr. Louis B. Leakey, the palaeontologist, and Dr. Kenneth Oakley, of the Natural History Museum, London.

Heroes. The winner of a competition to select the 25 greatest heroes in history, organized by the British Parliamentary Group for World Government and the World Confederation of Organizations of the Teaching Profession, was announced on Dec. 1. He is Daniel Jaussaud, aged 20, a student teacher at the *École Normale*, Digne, France, and his prize was a trip round the world. His selection of heroes, in alphabetical order, was: Avicenna (the Islamic philosopher), Simon Bolivar, Buddha, Charlemagne, Marie Curie, Henri Dunant, Einstein, Erasmus, St. Francis of Assisi, Galen, Gandhi, Gutenberg, Hippocrates, Jesus Christ, Martin Luther King, Lincoln, Marx, Michelangelo, Sir Thomas More, Pasteur, Plato, Rousseau, Schweitzer, Tolstoy, and Leonardo da Vinci. The competition was intended to focus the attention of teachers, parents, and students on the need for a greater sense of world community and how education could encourage it, and entrants had to list men or women ''the knowledge of whom would be likely to encourage world understanding''.

Heveningham Hall, Halesworth, Suffolk. The U.K. minister of housing and local government announced on April 17, 1970, that Heveningham Hall had been purchased for the nation. This 18th-century house contains a fine collection of furniture, and is surrounded by 477 acres of land, including grounds laid out by Capability Brown.

Himet. This is the name of an iron-enriched product with an iron content of over 90 per cent to be produced in Western Australia. It was announced in March 1970 that a plant is to be built at Dampier by a corporation set up with capital from Australia, Japan, West Germany, Canada, and the U.S.A. Completion of the plant is due in 1972.

Historic Buildings. The U.K. minister of housing and local government announced on Feb. 3, 1970, that 50 additions to the statutory list of buildings of special architectural or historical interest had been made. The additions include two department stores (Peter Jones in Sloane Square, London, and Simpson's, Piccadilly), and four London Underground stations (Sudbury Town, Arnos Grove, Southgate, and Oakwood), all designed by Dr. Charles Holden and all completed between 1930 and 1934. Other additions are the gorilla house and penguin pool at London Zoo, Norwich City Hall, the *Daily Express* building in Fleet Street, the science block at Marlborough College, Boot's factory at Beeston, Notts, the Finsbury Health Centre, London, and Dudley Zoo.

In March the minister announced grants totalling £520,710 for the repair and maintenance of 99 historic buildings. The largest single amount was £50,000 to support a 10-year programme of repairs to Blenheim Palace, and the second largest, £32,500, for the Royal Albert Hall, London, which is appealing for £500,000 for restoration work. Other grants were £26,900 to Knole, near Sevenoaks, Kent; £14,960 to Stowe School, Bucks; £2,625 to Norman Manor House, Boothby Pagnell, near Grantham, Lincs; £1,156 to Barham Windmill, Barham, Kent; £1,500 to the Spread Eagle Hotel, Thame, Oxfordshire; £1,000 to 84, Plymouth Grove, Manchester, once the home of Mrs. Gaskell, the Victorian novelist, and now to be used as a club for overseas students of Manchester university; and £500 to Sandleford Priory, Newbury, Berks. Since the grants system was introduced in 1954, £6,484,703 has been made available for 1,337 buildings.

Holidays. A British Tourist Authority survey, published in March 1970, showed that the number of holidays spent by British holiday-makers in Britain in 1969 was 30·5 million, and the cost £600 million (representing an increase over 1968 of 500,000 and £30 million). Holidays abroad increased by 750,000 to 5·75 million, costing £390 million, an increase of about £70 million. The total of £990 million (which includes fares) was a record for holiday spending. The most popular holiday region in Great Britain was the South-West, which attracted 22 per cent of the total number of holiday-makers. This was followed by the South (15 per cent), Wales (13 per cent), Scotland (12 per cent), the North-West (11 per cent), the East (10 per cent), the South-East (9 per cent), the North-East (8 per cent), the Midlands (6 per cent), and London (3 per cent). July and August were the most popular months, 63 per cent of the total taking their holidays then. The next most popular months were June (16 per cent), September (11 per cent), and May (6 per cent). The average length of holiday was just over 10 nights, and the average cost £21 per person.

Fifty-three per cent of all holidays abroad were package or inclusive holidays, 59 per cent involving air travel from Great Britain. Spain was the most popular country, attracting 32 per cent of holiday-makers, followed by France and Eire (10 per cent each), Italy (9 per cent), Austria and Germany (6 per cent each), and Switzerland (5 per cent). The average cost of a holiday abroad was £68 per person, an increase of £6 over 1968, and the average length of the holiday was 14·9 nights.

Honours. The 1970 New Year honours list included the creation of four life peers:

Hanover, W. Germany. The roof of the huge exhibition hall built for the 1970 Hanover Fair accommodates a bungalow town of 752 offices and apartments, with its own shopping centre.

Capt. Terence O'Neill, prime minister of Northern Ireland from 1963 to May 1969; Sir Frank Kearton, chairman of Courtauld's; John Beavan, political editor of the *Daily Mirror*; and Lady Masham for her social services and work for the handicapped. Among the artists, authors, musicians, poets, and broadcasters honoured, Noël Coward, actor and composer, and William Glock, controller of music at the BBC, both received knighthoods; Sir Alan Herbert was made a Companion of Honour; Kenneth More, actor, Malcolm Arnold, composer and conductor, Roy Fuller, professor of poetry at Oxford, Maggie Smith, actress, and Joan Plowright (Lady Olivier), actress, all received the C.B.E.; Kenny Lynch, entertainer, John Arlott, sports commentator and writer, and Pete Murray, disc jockey, received the O.B.E.; the athletes Lillian Board and Don Thompson were awarded the M.B.E. Other knighthoods were conferred on Dr. Walter Adams, director of the London School of Economics; Prof. Alfred Ayer, professor of logic at Oxford University; Hubert Bennett, architect to the Greater London Council; Sydney Green, the trade union leader; and Lt.-Col. James Carreras, managing director of Hammer Films. Among the many Australians knighted were Professor E. W. Titterton, professor of nuclear physics at the Australian National University; Vernon Treatt, Q.C., chief commissioner of the city of Sydney; and Senator M. C. Cormack, for long political and public service. More than 300 other Australians received awards. In New Zealand Te Ata-I-Rangi-kaahu Ariki nui, "Queen of the Maoris", was awarded the D.B.E. for outstanding services to her people.

Nine new life peers were announced on June 2, 1970. All were former M.P.s, five Labour and four Conservative. The five Labour life peers are Emanuel Shinwell, Sir Eric Fletcher, Sir Barnett Janner, James Hoy, and Joseph Slater; and the four Tories Nigel Birch, Sir Edward Boyle, Sir John Vaughan-Morgan, and Priscilla, Lady Tweedsmuir.

In the birthday honours published on June 13, 1970, four life peers were created: Sir Laurence Olivier (first actor to receive a peerage, who had several times declined the honour); Sir Max Rosenheim, president of the Royal College of Physicians; Lord Wheatley, Scottish law lord; and Cyril Hamnett, chairman of the Co-op Press. New knights included Prof. George Catlin; Norman Reid, director of the Tate Gallery; Charles Forte, restaurateur extraordinary; Jack Longland, educationist and broadcaster; Arnold Weinstock, architect of the gigantic G.E.C.–A.E.I.–E.E. combine; Ralph Freeman, of Freeman Fox, engineers of the Forth and Severn Bridges; Julian Hodge, financier; Kenneth McColl Anderson, Australian minister for supply; William Alexander Dargie, chairman of the Australian Commonwealth art advisory board; and William Collins the publisher. The K.B.E. was conferred on the Most Rev. Philip Nigel Warrington, Primate of Australia and Archbishop of Brisbane. Three new Dames were Mrs. Margaret

Cole, widow and co-author of the late G. D. H. Cole, the economist and novelist; Elizabeth Ackroyd, director of the Consumer Council; and Peggy van Praagh, co-director with Robert Helpmann of the Australian Ballet. Actors, actresses, and musicians honoured included Sir Frederick Ashton (C.H.) on his retirement from direction of the Royal Ballet, Dame Sybil Thorndike (C.H.), Richard Burton (C.B.E.), Henry Hall (C.B.E.), the violinist Hugh Bean (C.B.E.), Janet Baker (C.B.E.), and Moira Anderson (O.B.E.), the actresses Jessie Matthews, Judi Dench, Nyree Dawn Porter, and Margaret Tyzack (all O.B.E.), Richard Hearne (Mr. Pastry) for services to handicapped children (O.B.E.), and three members of the Amadeus String Quartet not previously honoured (all O.B.E.). Literary figures honoured were Phyllis Bentley (O.B.E.) and Robert Gittings (C.B.E.), and the C.B.E. was given to John Schlesinger, director of the film *Midnight Cowboy*. Gordon Banks, the England goalkeeper, and David Broome, the show-jumping champion, both received the O.B.E., Stan Mellor, the jockey, the M.B.E., and Jock Stein, manager of Celtic F.C., the C.B.E. The television personality David Frost, and the *Daily Mirror* columnist Donald Zec, were among the O.B.E.s. Among the 50 people honoured for services to export were F. R. J. Britten and N. D. Norman, joint managing directors of the Britten-Norman aircraft firm which makes the successful "Islander" aircraft, and Peter Wilson, auctioneer, the chairman of Sotheby's, who were all made C.B.E. Four new Knights of the Garter were installed on June 15—Lords Chandos and Cobbold, Sir Edmund Bacon, and Sir Cennydd Traherne.

Harold Wilson's resignation honours list was published on Aug. 7. The list of 37 names included eight life peerages. These were awarded to George Brown, former deputy leader of the Labour party; John Diamond, former chief secretary to the Treasury; Anthony Greenwood, former minister of housing; Jennie Lee, former minister in charge of the arts; Alice Bacon, former minister of state for education; Eirene White, former minister of state in the Welsh office; Harold Davies, former parliamentary private secretary to Mr. Wilson; and Julian Snow. Knighthoods were conferred on Joseph Kagan, founder and chairman of Kagan Textiles (the "Gannex" makers); Harry Nicholas, general secretary of the Labour party; Leslie Lever, former Labour M.P.; Kenneth Selby, chairman of the Bath and Portland Group; Dr. Joseph Stone, Mr. Wilson's personal doctor; Trevor Lloyd-Hughes, Mr. Wilson's press secretary 1964–69; and John Desmond Brayley, chairman of Canning Town Glass Works. Sara Barker, former national agent of the Labour party, who had for some time acted as general secretary for the party, was made Dame Commander of the Order of the British Empire, and Mrs. Marcia Williams, previously Mr. Wilson's political secretary and now his private secretary, received the C.B.E.

Others who received the C.B.E. included George Hall, former chief press officer; Mrs. Marjorie Halls, whose late husband, Michael, was Mr. Wilson's principal private secretary; and two Transport House officials, Percy Clark, director of publicity, and Ronald Haywood, national agent.

Prof. John Cawte Beaglehole, of New Zealand, an authority on Captain Cook, was admitted to the Order of Merit on March 20.

Horses. It was reported in January 1970 that 52-year-old Monty, believed to be the oldest horse in the world, had died at Wagga Wagga, New South Wales, Australia. The horse, a draught breed, stood 17 hands high, and lived on an unusual diet which included lettuce sandwiches, cake, biscuits, and pudding. Its jaws were sent to the Melbourne University for preservation.

Hotels. In January 1970 it was announced by the Hilton Hotels Corporation that the construction of a 45-storey tower adjoining the New York Hilton was planned for completion early in 1972; this tower, by adding 1,250 guest rooms to the 2,150-room hotel, will make the hotel the largest in the world. On Jan. 30, 1970, U.S. Trans World Airlines purchased a $1\frac{1}{2}$-acre site in Holland Park, London, for £1$\frac{1}{4}$ million. T.W.A. plans to erect a 600-bedroom hotel on the site, to cater for jumbo-jet passengers. It was disclosed on Sept. 25 that Aer Lingus, the Irish national airline, had acquired a £1$\frac{1}{2}$ million site off Kensington High Street, London, on which an 850-room hotel will be built at a cost of between £6 million and £7 million. Construction will start in 1971.

An international computerized hotel-booking service was launched in London on May 7, 1970. Under this system a hotel reservation can be booked in seconds for hotels in Great Britain or the U.S.A., by making a call to reservation offices which will be set up in Birmingham, Glasgow, London, and Manchester. The enquiry will be fed by direct high-speed lines into the National Coal Board's two IBM360/50 computers at Cannock, Staffordshire, which are programmed to register all the rooms available in those hotels subscribing to the system, and to make immediate firm bookings. The computerized part of the operation takes only 15 seconds.

Housing. Figures published by the U.K. department of the environment on Nov. 26 showed that the total number of dwellings completed between January and October 1970 was 289,000, a decrease of nearly 4 per cent below the 1969 figure for the same period. Although fractionally more council dwellings were built, the number of houses and flats completed for owner-occupiers fell by over 8 per cent.

Australia. A report, the result of a 12-month survey, prepared by the Australian Housing Industry Association, a national organization of the building industry, banks, building societies, and estate agents, was presented to the Federal

Hovercraft. The Hoverhornet, a light single-seater runabout hovercraft made at Peterborough, England, sells at about £400. It can be carried on the roof of a car.

already shown that a twin-track 200-mile inter-city hovertrain with four interchanges should be both clean and quiet, and cost little more than a motorway of equivalent capacity.

Hydrofoil. The world's largest hydrofoil, *Queen of the Waves,* a 250-passenger vessel, was delivered by Westermoen Hydrofoil A/S, of Mandel, south Norway, to a shipowner in Bergen, at the beginning of October 1970. The vessel, which has a speed of 36·5 knots, will be used for tourist traffic between Las Palmas and Tenerife in the Canary Isles.

Ice. Two scientists at the University of Toledo, Ohio, U.S.A., reported in January 1970 that they had made a new form of ice two and a third times as dense as ordinary ice. They succeeded in forming it in their laboratory at a temperature of −277 deg F (−136 deg C). Ice of this kind could play an important role in the physical make-up of some planets and comets, for the heads of comets are known to be made up of ice particles (see page 38).

Icons. Among a consignment of 500 icons sold by the Soviet government to a London dealer in May 1970, three were found to have a second painting underneath. When the top, 18th-century icon of one of these was being peeled away the restorer found a third, showing Abraham sacrificing his son, sandwiched between the upper and lower, which X-rays had failed to reveal. By using special solvents the restorer hoped to save all three icons.

Illiteracy. The United Nations published figures on Sept. 7, 1970, showing that the number of people in the world who could neither read nor write had increased from 735 million in 1960 to 783 million in 1970. But because of the great increase in the total population, this figure actually represents a reduction in the percentage of illiterates.

According to a lecturer at the Nottingham University institute of education, about 20 per cent of British undergraduates read too badly to cope with university courses. At teachers' training colleges the percentage is even higher. A reading speed of 450–500 words a minute is necessary, he said, and the average student's speed is 180–250 words a minute.

treasurer and the minister for housing on March 5, 1970. It stated that over 60,000 Australian families were living in substandard accommodation, the majority being forced to do so because they have neither the resources nor the income to obtain better accommodation. The report said that while there had been a substantial increase in the number of dwellings built in the past 10 years, the number of flats far exceeded that of houses. In 1969 the number of flats built was 366·5 per cent greater than the 1960 total, while the number of detached houses rose by only 12 per cent. In 1969 a total of 130,687 houses and flats was completed, but the minimum requirement was for 143,000. It was estimated that by 1972 Australia would need a minimum of 156,000 dwellings annually, rising to 183,000 in 1977.

Hovercraft. A single-seater runabout hovercraft called the Hoverhornet was demonstrated at the Hover-Air factory at Whittlesey, Peterborough, in March 1970. The Hoverhornet will travel over land, swamp, mud-flat, sand, water, snow, and ice, and is light enough to be carried on the roof of a small car. Easy to repair and maintain, it is available in two models, the

standard selling at £400, and the de luxe selling at £425. Another air-cushion vehicle, the Hoverover, manufactured by Canahover in Ottawa, Ontario, is also designed in two versions—one for commercial use and one for sports and recreation. Both have fibreglass bodies and an aluminium and steel frame and base. The commercial version, which has a speed of up to 50 m.p.h. and a payload of 600 lb. on water and 1,000 lb. on land, can be used for surveying, prospecting, and similar activities that require transport over terrain unsuitable for either boats or wheeled vehicles.

Hovertrain. The U.K. department of trade and industry commissioned in 1970 a £36,000 study of two possible hovertrain routes—one between London's Heathrow and Gatwick airports, and the other between London and Manchester. When this was announced in November it was stated that a prototype capable of 500 m.p.h. was being built, which will make its first run on a specially constructed track at Earith, Hunts, in February or March 1971. Three miles of test track near Cambridge was already under construction, and later it is intended to extend its length to 8 miles. Studies by outside consultants had

Immingham, Lincs. On March 20, 1970, the British Transport Docks Board's new £5½ million deep-water oil terminal at Immingham on the Humber was officially opened. The installation is the only terminal on the Humber able to accommodate tankers of up to 250,000 tons. It

Hydrofoil. The 160-ton *Queen of the Waves,* the largest hydrofoil in the world, was built in Norway for ferry traffic in the Canary Islands. It can carry 250 passengers.

incorporates a 4,500-ft.-long jetty with 68,000 ft. of pipeline, and is expected to handle about 10 million tons of crude oil and refined products in 1970. Plans for developing an £11½ million bulk-handling terminal at Immingham were announced in February. The National Coal Board have already developed the site as a coal-exporting terminal, at a cost of £5½ million, and the British Steel Corporation is to spend £6 million on the building of an ore-handling complex to take vessels of up to 70,000 tons at the same site. In the first instance the terminal should be able to handle about 9 million tons of outward-bound coal and incoming ore, and it will later be expanded to take more. It is expected to become fully operational during 1972.

Incas. It was stated in August 1970 that Dr. Thomas Barthel, a German anthropologist, had succeeded in deciphering the signs of the Incas, previously thought to be purely decorative. Dr. Barthel found that the small, coloured squares on wooden beakers made by the Incas contained the names of their gods as well as astronomical and calendar information. The signs, which accompany pictures of birds, plants, and geometrical symbols, resemble those still used today in Chinese ideographs.

Income and Expenditure. The U.K. National Income Blue Book for 1970, published on Sept. 10, 1970, stated that in 1969 salaries and wages rose by 7½ per cent, reduced by income tax to slightly less than 6 per cent. Personal spending rose by 5½ per cent, but this was virtually accounted for by price rises of over 5 per cent. The GNP of £38,600 million represented £700 for every man, woman, and child in the U.K. (£665 in 1968); the total real value of goods and services produced increased by less than 2 per cent. An analysis of the items on which personal incomes were spent in 1969 compared with 1959 was as follows:

	1959 (per cent)	1969 (per cent)
Food (excluding meals in restaurants, etc.)	25·8	20·9
Alcoholic drink	5·7	6·4
Tobacco	6·6	5·9
Housing	9·7	12·5
Fuel and light	4·3	5·0
Clothing and footwear	9·5	8·4
Purchase, running cost of cars, motor-cycles	5·7	8·0
Household durable goods	5·3	4·1
Other goods	9·3	9·4
Travel, entertainment and other services	18·2	19·4

The decline in the purchasing power of the pound over the same 10 years was shown as follows:

1959	. . . .	£1
1960	. . . .	99p
1961	. . . .	96p
1962	. . . .	93p
1963	. . . .	91p
1964	. . . .	88p
1965	. . . .	84p
1966	. . . .	81p
1967	. . . .	79p
1968	. . . .	76p
1969	. . . .	72p

Another official publication showed how each £1 was spent in 1969:

Food	21p
Housing	13p
Clothing and footwear . . .	8p
Alcohol	6p
Tobacco	6p
Fuel and light	5p
Buying cars and motor-cycles.	3p
Other durable goods . . .	4p
Other goods	15p
Other services	19p

According to figures published by the U.K. government in "Earnings in Great Britain, April 1970", the average earnings of the British breadwinner in 1970 amounted to over £30 a week, although there were still 300,000 men and 2,600,000 women earning less than £15 a week. Male manual workers earned £26·80 on average, and most white-collar workers were in the £20–£30 bracket. The best paid manual workers were printers on newspapers and periodicals, two thirds of whom earned over £30 a week. The 8½ million women workers earned an average of £16·80.

The Paris headquarters of the Organization for Economic Co-operation and Development, which has 22 member countries, in March 1970 published some interesting comparisons in household expenditure in 1968, the most recent year for which statistics were available. Per 1,000 inhabitants Sweden had 489 telephones (second only to 540 per 1,000 in the U.S.A.), 246 passenger cars, and 289 television sets. The Swedes also spent more than any other country in the world on education (7·4 per cent of their gross national product) and built more homes (12·7 per 1,000 inhabitants) than any other European country. Ireland, however, consumed 3,470 calories of food per head per day, compared with 3,170 calories in the Netherlands and France, 3,150 in Denmark and Great Britain, 3,140 in the U.S.A., and 2,460 in Japan. Norway easily led the world in the consumption of electricity, with 13,354 kilowatt-hours per head of population annually, compared with 6,532 kWh in the U.S.A., 6,320 in Sweden, 3,745 in Switzerland, and 3,481 in Great Britain.

The report also stated that, in terms of overall national wealth, the U.S.A. led the world with $4,380 per capita income. The Swedish average was $3,230, followed by Canada with $3,010, Switzerland with $2,790, and Denmark with $2,540. Among the lowest average

incomes were those in Spain ($770), Portugal ($530), and Turkey ($350).

Italy. A sample survey of the consumption of the average Italian family, carried out by the Institute of Statistics in 1968, was published early in 1970. It showed that the family spent an average of 15,420 lire a week on food (the actual figure varies from 16,583 in central Italy to 16,479 in north-west Italy, 16,330 in north-east Italy, and 13,263 in southern Italy and the islands). About 28 per cent of this weekly sum was spent on meat, consumption of which continues to rise, and only 13 per cent on bread. Expenditure on home maintenance, including fuel and electricity, averaged 28·2 per cent of income, on transport 17·8 per cent, and on clothing 16·7 per cent.

Indian Princes. A bill to remove from the former princes of India the special privileges and privy purses they have enjoyed since the formation of the Union in 1947 was passed by the lower house of parliament in Delhi by a narrow majority, but was rejected in September by the upper house when it failed by one vote to secure the necessary two-thirds majority. The cabinet thereupon decided to withdraw recognition of the princes by a presidential order, and the princes, numbering 278, received individual notification of their reduction in status from ruler to commoner. In return, the Concord of Princes decided to appeal to the supreme court on the grounds that the cabinet's action was unconstitutional. On Dec. 15 the court ruled that it was indeed unconstitutional, and that the princes' privy purses were property which was their fundamental right.

Industrial Relations. The new U.K. government published its proposed industrial laws on Oct. 5 in an 11,000-word consultative document. Among the main proposals were: collective agreements to be legally binding, unless the parties say otherwise; secret ballots to be held in serious disputes, and a "cooling off" period of 60 days to elapse before a strike is held; the "closed shop" to be outlawed, and workers to have the right to refuse to join a trade union; large firms to give regular shareholder-type reports to workers; 6 weeks' dismissal notice for workers after 10 years' service, and 8 weeks' after 15 years', and appeals against unfair dismissal to be dealt with by new industrial courts; these new courts to deal with all industrial offences, with fines collected through the county courts; appointment of a registrar of trade unions and employers' federations to ensure that their rules are up to standard and are kept; and the giving of a statutory basis to the Commission on Industrial Relations, which would retain its present responsibilities.

The Industrial Relations Bill, published on Dec. 3, incorporated all these proposals and, in addition, specified the financial penalties payable by a trade union or an employer who takes part in unfair

Instant Building by Inflation

A feature of recent years has been the increasing use of inflatable structures as portable headquarters, exhibition halls, and the like. The trend grew and spread during 1970. At right is a plastic church, 50 ft. long, which can be inflated in 5 minutes; it was demonstrated at the *Europlastique 70* exhibition in Paris. Below, left, is an inflated tent-like cover used to make an outdoor swimming pool into an indoor one during the winter, at Dillenburg, Hesse, W. Germany.

In these days of swift "bushfire" campaigns and rapidly changing theatres of war, military headquarters buildings need to be easily transportable as well as quickly constructed and dismantled. Below, right, is a mobile air control headquarters designed for use at an American air force base in Europe. In a comparatively small container it can be flown by helicopter to the site, and there quickly inflated, the sides of the container forming solid walls.

The largest air dome ever used for exhibition purposes in Great Britain (right) was erected in front of Euston station, London, in September. Manufactured by a Scottish firm, it was 150 ft. long, 60 ft. wide, and 30 ft. high, and covered an area of 9,000 sq. ft. The exhibition that it housed dealt with the involvement of international industry in contemporary culture as expressed in its links with architecture, design, the graphic arts, and literature—a grandiose theme for which, some thought, an inflated building was particularly apt.

A highly practical "blown-up" plastic building was the temporary postal sorting office (below) erected by the British Post Office at Twickenham, Greater London, to deal with the rush of Christmas mail. It covered an area of 7,500 sq. ft. The exterior view shows the main entrance; others were at the sides. Inside (right) transparent panels in the roof admitted daylight, supplemented by fluorescent tubes, and there was ample room for handling the 400,000 parcels that passed through the building.

industrial practices. The compensation scale laid down for the guidance of the new National Industrial Relations Court ranges from a limit of £5,000 for a union with less than 5,000 members to a limit of £100,000 for one with more than 100,000. Employers will have to pay an individual who successfully complains of unfair industrial practice or unfair dismissal a maximum of 2 years' pay or £4,160, whichever is the less.

Infanticide. Statistics published by the U.K. Registrar General on March 12, 1970, showed that the number of babies dying a violent death in England and Wales increased by over 50 per cent between 1848 and 1966, the last year for which figures were available, although the overall risk of dying in the first year of life has been reduced by one eighth in the last 100 years. In 1966, babies' violent deaths were due to fractured skulls, strangulation, stabbing, and drowning. Between 1848 and 1872 1 per cent of infant deaths were attributed to accident, poisoning, and violence; with a total mortality rate of about 150 per thousand live births, violent death accounted for 1·5 per thousand. Between 1964 and 1966 4 per cent of infant deaths were attributed to the same causes; with a total infant mortality of 19 per thousand live births, violent death accounted for 0·8 per thousand. In 1848–1872 about two thirds of infant deaths were caused by accidental suffocation; this was still true in 1966 when, out of the 132 deaths due to smothering, 18 occurred in the parents' bed (described as "overlaying") and 284 from inhaled vomit.

Invalid Carriages. From Sept. 29, 1970, small battery-driven cars, travelling at no more than 4 m.p.h. and occupied by handicapped people, are allowed to use pedestrian pavements in the U.K. No age or licence restrictions apply. These exemptions from certain parts of the Road Traffic Act were contained in regulations made under the Chronically Sick and Handicapped Persons Act (see p. 335).

Iron Age. At the suggestion of the British Association's research committee on ancient agriculture and the Council for British Archaeology, an experimental Iron Age farmstead is to be established on a hilltop at Little Butser, near Petersfield, Hampshire. The farmstead, a complex of round houses and enclosures, will be built with prehistoric-type tools, and stocked with sheep and cattle similar to those raised over 2,000 years ago. Three Kerry oxen, the closest equivalent to Iron Age beasts, will be trained to pull ploughs of the period. The project is to be carried out under the guidance of 20 scientists, biologists, and archaeologists. The Research Council announced its intention of raising the initial outlay of £35,000, and it was estimated that the annual cost of maintaining the farmstead would be £10,000.

Isle of Dogs. On March 6, 1970, this 618-acre "island" with a population of 11,000 in the East End of London, declared itself independent, severing all links with the Tower Hamlets borough council, the local authority, and electing its own government. The Isle of Dogs is not strictly an island, but a peninsula in Poplar, virtually cut off by the West India Docks. An indication that the people living there were tired of receiving no answers to their complaints about poor bus services, inadequate shops and schools, and general lack of social amenities, had been given on March 1, when the rebels cut their links with London by blocking two bridges to the "island". On March 6 they set up their rebel regime, the Independent Citizens' Council, after the government had ignored a demand to recognize their independence. A president and two prime ministers, one a Thames lighterman and the other a stevedore, were elected; the appointment of a foreign minister was to be made at a later date. One of the rebels' first actions was to take over an empty school, and they announced that their future policies included better transport and education facilities, to provide which they demanded £10,000 a year from Tower Hamlets council.

Although the British government did not recognize the existence of the new regime, the Post Office was apparently quick to do so, for a letter from Mexico addressed to the "Isle of Dogs Government, Government House" was promptly delivered. (The letter contained a request for a photograph of the president, and asked if the islanders intended to issue new sets of stamps.)

On March 7, hundreds of the island's citizens gathered in the streets, and it was apparent that not all of them welcomed their newly declared republican status. Many remained loyal to Tower Hamlets, and planned to make their peace with the mainland. The president, unruffled by threats of civil war and secure in Government House (a fourth-floor flat in Glengall Grove), gave a press conference, at which he revealed that he would pay his first state visit to the Home Office on March 11. Meanwhile, the Tower Hamlets borough council was not slow to come forward with plans to cure the "ills" of the island, for on March 10 it announced proposals which could double the population, improve amenities, and solve schooling, transport, and shopping difficulties. This seemed to satisfy the "rebel government", and no more was heard of the shortest-lived independent republic in history.

Islington, London. Michael Sobell, a retired industrialist, on April 6, 1970, laid the foundation stone of the youth sports and recreational centre which will bear his

Isle of Dogs. A comic-opera episode of March 1970 in the East End of London was a "declaration of independence" by the Isle of Dogs. Above: the "national flag", held up by the two "prime ministers" after they had invaded County Hall, h.q. of the Greater London Council.

name at Isledon Road, Islington, North London. The centre is being built under the aegis of the Variety Club of Great Britain, of which Mr. Sobell is a member, through the £1 million donation he gave the Club for the project. When completed, the centre will incorporate a main arena for tennis, badminton, and five-a-side football, an ice rink, a sports hall, 10 squash courts, a gymnasium, and other facilities.

Ivor Novello Awards. These awards, sponsored by the Songwriters' Guild of Great Britain, are presented annually to those responsible for the writing, publishing, and exploitation of works which in the opinion of the judges represent outstanding contributions to British popular and light music. The 1969 awards, presented on May 10, 1970, went to the following:

Special award for "outstanding services to British music"—Sir Noël Coward.

Most performed work of the year—"Ob-La-Di, Ob-La-Da" (John Lennon and Paul McCartney).

Record issued in 1969 which achieved the highest certified British sales—"Get Back" (John Lennon and Paul McCartney).

British international song of the year—"Love Is All" (Les Reed and Barry Mason).

British songwriter of the year—Tony Macauley.

Best British song, musically and lyrically—"Where Do You Go to, My Lovely" (Peter Sarstedt).

Most contemporary song—"Melting Pot" (Roger Cook and Roger Greenaway).

Best score from film or musical play—Michael Lewis, for *The Madwoman of Chaillot*.

Outstanding light orchestral arranger or composer—Ernest Tomlinson.

Jerusalem. The discovery of a 2,000-year-old city underneath Jerusalem was announced in February 1970. The city disappeared in A.D. 70, when the Romans sacked Jerusalem and destroyed the Herodian temple. Excavations, described as the first attempt to uncover the city, were carried out by the Israeli ministry of religious affairs under the direction of Rabbi Dov Perla. They revealed stone-walled passages of the Hasmonean era, which extend to the gates of walled Jerusalem, some of them a mile away; and new stretches of the Wailing Wall.

Journalism Awards. The I.P.C. national press awards, the Hannen Swaffer awards, were announced on April 16, 1970. Anthony Grey, Reuter's correspondent in Peking, who was held prisoner for three years by the Chinese, was named Journalist of the Year, and the 100-guinea award for News Reporter of the Year went to Mary Holland of the *Observer* for her reporting from Northern Ireland. The other awards were:

Young Journalist of the Year—Raymond

Jerusalem. Part of the newly discovered stretch of the Wailing Wall in the 2,000-year-old city found underneath Jerusalem in 1970. The ancient city was destroyed by the Romans in A.D. 70—disastrous date in Jewish history.

Fitz-Walter (Bradford *Telegraph and Argus*).

International Reporter of the Year—Murray Sayle (*Sunday Times*).

Provincial Journalist of the Year—Eric Forster (Newcastle *Evening Chronicle*).

Critic of the Year—Alexander Walker (*Evening Standard*).

Descriptive Writer of the Year—Michael Frayn (*Observer*).

Sports Writer of the Year—Hugh McIlvanney (*Observer*).

Woman's Page Journalist of the Year—Felicity Green (*Daily Mirror*).

Campaigning Journalist of the Year—Ken Gardner (*People*).

Special award—Sir Neville Cardus.

Granada Television's "What the Papers Say" awards had been presented on Jan. 14, 1970. The recipients were:

Newspaper of the Year—*The Guardian*.

"Writer we always read"—Vincent Mulchrone (*Daily Mail*).

Photographer of the Year—Don McCullin (for pictures of Biafra in *Sunday Times* magazine).

Reporter of the Year—Michael Hornsby (*The Times*).

Other journalists to be honoured in 1970 included M. Hubert Beuve-Mery, founder of *Le Monde*, who received the Institute of Journalists' gold medal on Oct. 13; and American Seymour Hersh, who won both the Pulitzer prize for reporting and the Worth Bingham prize for distinguished reporting in 1969.

Kangaroos. In Melbourne, Australia, on May 3, 1970, a band of demonstrators marched through the city streets protesting against the killing of the country's kangaroos. The demonstrators, most of them members of the Save Our Kangaroo Committee, carried banners condemning the slaughter of kangaroos, and drawing attention to the fact that an average of 42,000 are killed each week.

Kawasaki, Japan. In 1970 the Kawasaki municipal government embarked on a gigantic five-year project, costing a total of 70,000 million yen, to create an artificial island in Tokyo Bay off the city, on which to create a new port and build factories. The planned artificial island of over 1,000 acres will be made 750 yards from the city, and will have 20 berths for 15,000-ton ships, 11 berths for 5,000-ton ships, and six berths for 700-ton ships, with loading zones, warehouses, and other port facilities. Three hundred and eighty-six acres will be reserved for the re-location of factories. The island will be linked to Kawasaki city by undersea highway tunnels and will eventually be connected to a new traffic artery planned to run along the northern coast of Tokyo Bay.

Kennedy Memorials. A bust of the late president of the U.S.A. was unveiled at John F. Kennedy House, a block of flats on the Greater London Council's Silwood Estate at Rotherhithe, London, on March 26, 1970. The bust is the work of a former art student, now a lorry driver, Tom Winter, who spent 18 months modelling it in plastic wood. Experts were so favourably impressed by it that the G.L.C.'s Arts and Recreation Committee decided to meet the cost of casting it in more durable material, and providing a plinth. The bust was cast in fibreglass resin reinforced with fabric, and coloured bronze.

Kennet and Avon Canal. The entrance lock to this canal, which has been restored at a cost of £1,500, was officially opened on May 16, 1970. The Kennet and Avon Canal Trust intends to restore the whole length of the 55-mile waterway, which connects the Severn with the Thames, as a recreational or pleasure strip, and also for working use if it proves a practicable proposition. It was completed in 1810 by the famous canal builder, John Rennie, and last used along its entire length in 1955. Since then many of its 79 locks have fallen into disuse.

Kilkeel, Northern Ireland. Plans for the modernization of the harbour at this co. Down village, Northern Ireland's main sea-fishing base, were announced in March 1970. Under a two-year improvement scheme, costing £650,000, extensive excavations will be carried out to double the size of the inner harbour basin, and provide accommodation for 75 vessels, compared with the present 46. Both the inner and outer harbours will be dredged to a sufficient depth to allow the largest boats to remain afloat at all states of the tide, which will permit much increased mobility of the fishing fleet.

Kolyma, River. It was reported in the Soviet press on Nov. 30 that the Soviet government had authorized the construction of a hydro-electric dam on the Kolyma river, in the extreme north of the Soviet Union. The dam, which will be 420 ft. high, will provide "thousands of millions of kilowatts per hour" to the northern goldfield.

Koyagi Island, Japan. On Aug. 18, 1970, the Japanese government approved a plan for the construction at Koyagi Island in the Bay of Nagasaki of a dock capable of building 1,000,000-ton tankers. The dock, which a transport ministry spokesman said will be the largest in the world, is due for completion by September 1972.

Kuching, Sarawak. In September 1970 the biggest and most modern hospital in east Malaysia, with facilities for training its own para-medical personnel, was opened at Kuching. Australia, through her foreign aid programme, contributed $A300,000 towards the hospital, which cost $A5 million, and planning, design, and supervision of construction were provided by Australian experts under the Colombo plan. A further two blocks of six storeys each are to be built at a cost of $A2 million.

Lancashire. The U.K. minister of housing and local government announced in March that he had made the final designation order for the building of a central Lancashire "new town", based on Preston, Leyland, and Chorley, and covering an area of 35,000 acres. It will have an eventual population of 430,000, making it the largest new town in the country. Its name is to be chosen by local people; the minister expressed a preference for Redrose, a name which, he said, would symbolize Lancashire's renaissance.

Land Registry. The U.K. Stationery Office has placed an order for an IBM 360/40 computer system for H.M. Land Registry. When information about the computer was given in July it was stated that the immediate loading would be over 2 million name records and details of over 3 million charges relating to them. Each day, 1,000 new entries and about 300 alternatives or deletions are made. At present, daily enquiries in respect of conveyancing and

other legal operations, on these files of charges, indexed under owner's names and relating to unregistered land in England and Wales, are in the region of 12,000, but by 1980, when about $3\frac{1}{2}$ million names are on file concerning $5\frac{1}{2}$ million charges, enquiries will have risen to about 24,000 per day. The new system, which will be one of the largest data banks in Government service, will provide a rapid search and registration service. It is scheduled to be fully operational in the spring of 1973.

Lara Lake, Victoria, Australia. In 1966 when the landslide at Aberfan, South Wales, killed 114 people, most of them schoolchildren, children from the Lara Lake primary school raised about £47 which they sent to the village as a contribution towards rebuilding the school. In 1969, when the Lara Lake school was burnt down in bushfires it was the turn of the Aberfan children to help the Australians, and they collected and sent them £106. These gestures drew the two communities closer together, and they exchanged national flags, which were raised over the two schools. The Australian ceremony took place in the early summer of 1970.

Lasers. American scientists of the AVCO Everett Research Laboratory, Everett, Mass., reported in April 1970 that they had developed the world's most powerful continuous-beam laser, capable of producing 30 kW in a very narrow beam, and 60 kW in a more divergent beam, values which are about three times more powerful than the most powerful continuous-beam lasers at present in operation. The AVCO laser was described at the annual meeting of the American Physical Society as resembling a rocket engine comprising two small chambers separated by a nozzle. A gas composed of nitrogen and carbon dioxide is heated in one chamber to about 3,000°F, and shot through the nozzle into the second chamber at supersonic speed. The carbon dioxide molecules become extremely "excited", and some of them eventually "lase", or emit photons, which are focused by mirrors into a coherent beam of light.

A new type of dye laser which can be used in spectroscopy, photo-chemistry, and medicine, developed by the department of pure and applied physics of Queen's University, Belfast, was shown at the annual physics exhibition in London in March. In this new laser, concentration of the beam of light is caused by passing it through a liquid substance. Even at its present early stage of development it can be used for the detection of atmospheric pollution, and for measuring airport visibility in fog and snow conditions. It has the unique advantage that it will produce light at any colour from ultra-violet to infra-red.

Bell Telephone Laboratories in Murray Hill, New Jersey, U.S.A., announced on Sept. 1 the development of a low-cost, pocket-sized infra-red laser which operates on battery power. It was stated that its single, high-frequency light beam could

carry hundreds of thousands of telephone calls, television signals, or other communication messages. Existing lasers are bulky, fragile, and expensive, but this new laser, when perfected and ready for commercial use within two or three years, will be as small as a cigarette lighter, will last a lifetime, and will cost only a few dollars.

Applications. It was reported in a January 1970 issue of the American journal *Aviation Week and Space Technology* that the introduction of laser-guided bombs into the Vietnam war had led to a great improvement in accuracy, for of the nearly 1,000 bombs guided by this method 700 had hit their targets. A laser beam is pointed at a target by a forward air controller or ground observer, and the guided weapon is launched from an aircraft to home on to the indicated spot.

The development by Great Britain's Atomic Weapons Research Establishment at Aldermaston of a surgical laser knife which can cut without causing bleeding was announced in August. The light beam, which seals the wound as it cuts, is as easy for surgeons to use as a ball-point pen, and is about the same size.

In October a team of researchers in forensic medicine at the faculty of medicine of Kiramoto University, Kyushu, Japan, claimed to have developed a laser-beam apparatus which can pinpoint the exact time of a person's death. The apparatus consists of a steel box about 40 in. wide, $8\frac{1}{2}$ in. high, and $4\frac{1}{2}$ in. deep. A cornea from the dead person's eye is placed between laser transmitting and receiving devices, and the laser beams passing through it are transformed by a phototube into an electric current which actuates a dial showing the degree of cornea opacity. (Cornea opacity is a recognized sign of death.) By this method time of death can be accurately estimated to within one hour. Time of death estimated by normal visual examination can often be wrong by as much as 10 hours, because the condition of the body can vary greatly according to age, physical constitution, and other factors.

The world's first laser lighthouse went into operation at Point Danger on Australia's east coast in 1970. The lighthouse, which guides shipping on the main eastern coast sea lanes, is installed on top of a 60-ft. memorial commemorating Captain Cook's voyage 200 years ago. It is claimed that it could revolutionize lighthouse construction throughout the world.

Law Reform. A U.K. Law Commission report incorporating a draft for a Wild Creatures and Forest Laws bill was published in August. It recommended drastic alterations in the ancient laws pertaining to forests and reduction of the royal prerogatives over wild creatures. It proposed the abolition of the forestal rights of the Crown for hunting and preserving game, which still apply to Windsor Forest, the New Forest, and the Forest of Dean, but said that the office of the verderers of the New Forest and the Forest of Dean, and timber rights, whether enjoyed by the

Lifeboats. The R.N.L.I.'s first glass-reinforced-plastic-hulled inshore rescue boats were ordered in 1970. The boats are capable of a speed of 22 knots.

Crown or by a subject, should remain. It also proposed the abolition of the Crown's prerogative right to royal fish, such as whales and sturgeon taken in British waters or found on the shore, which the Queen had indicated she no longer wishes to retain. But the royal right to swans would remain.

Lea Valley. Part of the Lea Valley regional park, a sports and social centre, was under construction at Picketts Lock, Enfield, in 1970. The centre, which will have a total usable area of 150,000 sq. ft., will consist of a gymnasium, swimming pool, rifle and archery ranges, eight squash courts, an indoor bowling green, and a two-court sports hall equipped for a variety of games. A separate section will contain a general-purpose hall which can be used for roller skating, dances, meetings, and exhibitions, while the surrounding area will have an 18-hole golf course and soccer pitches. The cost will be £1¼ million.

Leeds, Yorkshire. Work on two 25-storey, 228-ft.-high blocks of flats, which will be the tallest buildings in Leeds, began in September 1970. The buildings, 5 ft. taller than the pinnacle of the Leeds town hall, and situated on the Cottingley Hall estate, will cost £1 million; they contain 196 four-person and 96 two-person flats, as well as two caretakers' flats. They are due for completion by early 1972. A 21-storey shop and office block, to cost an estimated £3 million, is to be built on the Albion Street and Bond Street site in central Leeds now occupied by Yorkshire Post Newspapers. The ground and first floors will provide 75,000 sq. ft. of shops and storage space, and the upper floors nearly 100,000 sq. ft. of office space. The top floor will be about 200 ft. above street level. When this development, planned to fit into new traffic routes, was announced in August it was stated that demolition of the existing buildings will start in 1971.

Legal Advice Centre. The first British neighbourhood law centre, designed to provide round-the-clock legal advice for those unable to afford a lawyer, was opened on July 17, 1970, in a converted shop in North Kensington, London. The project has the support of the Law Society, the Bar Council, the Lord Chancellor's office, and both the Labour and Conservative Societies of Lawyers, and will receive funds—£4,000 in its first year and £2,500 in its second and third year—from the City Parochial Foundation and the Pilgrim Trust. Anyone living in the neighbourhood who has a legal problem is entitled to seek advice at the centre and, if it is quickly solved, will pay no fee. In other cases he will be referred to a private solicitor, if he is deemed able to afford it, or helped to apply for legal aid. The centre employs a full-time salaried solicitor, and about 40 solicitors and some barristers attend part-time. A night service is provided to deal with emergencies.

Libraries. The Ferguson collection, regarded as one of the world's greatest collections of books, manuscripts, maps, and pamphlets on Australia and the Pacific, was bought by the Australian National Library for $A300,000 at the beginning of 1970. The collection was assembled by Sir John Ferguson, president of the Library Trustees of N.S.W., 1963–67, who died in May 1969. The collection includes an original manuscript journal kept by Lt. James Burney in 1772–73 while on Captain Cook's second voyage.

Lifeboats. The 104th operational inshore rescue station of the Royal National Lifeboat Institution was opened at Minehead, Somerset, in 1970. Its inflatable 15-ft. rescue boat can carry 20 people and reach a speed of 20 knots. The Institution's first inshore rescue boat to have a glass-reinforced-plastic hull was demonstrated on September 30. Four of these boats, each costing about £4,000 and capable of a speed of 22 knots, have been ordered by the R.N.L.I. In 1969, R.N.L.I. inshore boats were launched 1,205 times, and saved 541 lives.

Life Expectation. Statistics in the U.K. Registrar General's quarterly return published in November showed that the expectation of life at birth had risen by 0·7 of a year to 68·7 years for boys, and by 1·2 years to 74·9 years for girls, over the past three years. In England and Wales, 70 per cent of men and 82 per cent of women can expect to live to the age of 65, and at that age a man has a life expectation of 12 years and a woman of 15·9 years.

Linmap. This is the name of a computerized system of presenting census, survey, and other data in the form of maps printed out directly by a computer, developed by a British government department and described in October 1970. About 8 million items of information from the 1966 5 per cent sample census are now held on magnetic tape; they comprise not information about individuals but about 380 categories of data down to ward and parish level. The interaction of social factors such as income, car ownership, age distribution, and housing can be shown more clearly by a printed map than by complicated tables of statistics. At a cost as low as £50 it is now possible for local authorities, companies, and other organizations to relate their market, opinion-poll, and factory-location surveys to national census information.

Literary Awards. Among the many awards made to writers in 1970 were the £5,000 Booker prize for the best novel of 1969 to Bernice Rubens for *The Elected Member* (the Booker was not awarded for 1970); the £300 Schlegal-Tieck prize to Eric Mosbacher for his translation from the German of Alexander Mitscherlich's *Society Without a Father*; the W. H. Heinemann 1969 awards to Brian Fothergill for *Sir William Hamilton*, Ronald Blythe for *Akenfield*, and Nicholas Wollaston for *Pharaoh's Chicken*; the Winifred Holtby award to Ian McDonald for *The Humming Bird Tree*; the Hawthornden prize for the best work of imaginative literature published in 1969 to Piers Paul Read for *Monk Dawson*; the Duff Cooper memorial prize (1969) to John Gross for *The Rise and Fall of the Man of Letters*, and (1970) to Enid McLeod for *Charles of Orleans, Prince and Poet*; the Robert Pitman £1,000 prize to John Hemming for *The Conquest of the Incas*; the John Llewelyn Rhys memorial prize to Angus Calder for *The People's War: Britain 1939–45*; the Alice Hunt Bartlett award for 1969 for the poet whom the Poetry Society most wishes to encourage to Tom Raworth for *The Relation Ship*; the 1970 James Tait Black memorial prize for the best novel published in 1969 to Elizabeth Bowen for *Eva Trout*, and for the best biography to Lady Antonia Fraser for *Mary Queen of Scots*; the *Guardian* award for children's fiction to Kathleen M. Peyton for her trilogy, *Flambards*, *The Edge of the Cloud*, and *Flambards in Summer* (*The Edge of the Cloud* also won the British Library Association's Carnegie medal for the most distinguished work in children's books published in the U.K. in 1969); the Eleanor Farjeon award for services to children's literature to Mrs. Kaye Webb, editor of *Puffin Books*; the 1970 Australian science fiction achievement award, for the best international work of science fiction published during 1969, to Italo Calvino for *Cosmicomics*; the 1970 Cholmondeley awards for poets to Edward Brathwaite (West Indies), Douglas Livingstone (Natal) and Kathleen Raine (Great Britain); the Scottish Arts Council's special award of £1,000 to Hugh MacDiarmid (Dr. C. M. Grieve) for his "unique and continuing contribution to Scottish letters", and bursaries of £1,000 each to Robert Nye, author of children's books, poems, plays, and a novel *Doubtfire*, and Pete Morgan, author of a book of poems *A Big Hat or What*; the *grand prix* of the Académie Française to Julien Green for his "total literary output"; the Freiherr von Stein foundation's Shakespeare prize to "Britain's most controversial author", Harold Pinter; the Prix Goncourt to Michel Tournier for *Le Roi des Aulnes* (The Erl King); the Prix Theophraste Renaudot to Jean Freustie for *Isabelle ou l'arrière Saison*; the Prix Femina to François Nourissier for *La Crève*; the Prix Medicis to Camille Bourniquel for *Sélinoute ou la Chambre Imperiale*, and for the best foreign novel published in French to Luigi Malerba (Italy) for *Salto Mortale* (*Le Saut de la Mort*, The Death Jump); the Prix Interallié to Michel Deon for *Les Poneys Sauvages*; the Kate Greenaway award for illustrations to children's books to Helen Oxenbury for *The Quangle Wangle's Hat* and *The Dragon of an Ordinary Family*; the Mystery Writers of America's principal award to Dick Francis for *Forfeit*, their "Edgar" for the best "fact crime" book of 1969 to Herbert B. Ehrmann for *The Case That Will Not Die*, and their Edgar Allan Poe award for the best mystery story for young people to Winifred Finlay for *Danger at Black Dyke*; the 1969 Scott-Moncrieff prize for the best translation into English of a French 20th-century work of fiction, poetry, criticism, history, biography, or travel jointly to W. G. Corp for his translation of *L'Espagnol* by Bernard Clavel, Maj.-Gen. Richard Barry for *The Suez Expedition 1956* by Gen. Beaufre, and Mrs. Elaine P. Halperin for *The Other Side of the Mountain* by Michel Bernanos; the 1970 U.S. national medal for literature, with cash prize of about £2,000, to Robert Penn Warren for *All the King's Men*; the U.S. Francis Parkman prize to Theodore Wilson for *The First Summit*; the American national book award to Dr. T. Harry Williams for his biography of the late Governor Huey P. Long of Louisiana; the Luther King poetry prize to Alfredo Bonazzi, who was sentenced in 1960 to a 24-year term in prison for murder; the Queen's gold medal for poetry to Prof. Roy Fuller; the W. H. Smith £1,000 award to John Fowles for *The French Lieutenant's Woman*; the Rothman's award for Australian literature to George Johnston for *Clean Straw for Nothing* (which also

won the Australian $A1,000 Miles Franklin award and the Moomba prize); the Weickhardt award to T. G. H. Strehlow for *Journey to Horseshoe Bend*; the Sydney Myer charity trust awards for Australian poetry to Thomas W. Shapcott for *Inwards to the Sun*, and J. M. Couper for *The Book of Bligh*; the Victorian chamber of automotive industries award for an Australian pictorial and documentary work to Hal Missingham for *My Australia*; the State of Victoria short story awards to Frank Moorhouse for *Dell Goes into Politics*, Stretin Bozic for *At Half-Mast*, and Len Moore for *The Yoke Is Off*; the State of Victoria short story awards for young writers to Philip McIntosh for *Memory of an Afternoon in Falling*, Michael Middleton for *A Sword in a Fist*, and Bruce R. Davis for *Story of a New Colonist*; the 1970 Mary Gilmore award to Keith Antill's unpublished novel, *Mom in the Ground.*

Lloyd George, Earl. On July 27, 1970, a memorial to the late Earl Lloyd George, the British statesman who died in 1945, was unveiled in Westminster Abbey, London, by the Prince of Wales. The ceremony was attended by the leaders of all three political parties represented in the House of Commons.

Lobsters. During the summer of 1970 the marine biological institute in Heligoland started breeding experiments with a million lobster larvae. They are placed in a large submersible plastic container which is washed with nutrient plankton by tidal currents. Later, artificial feeding stuff is added to the sea water, and its temperature is raised to 60°F. It is expected that this new breeding and feeding method should produce lobsters from 1 to 2 ft. long in three years, instead of the 10–12 years required under natural conditions.

Loch Morar, Inverness-shire. A team of scientists based at London University in November released their findings on the apparent existence of a whole family of "monsters" in Scotland's deepest lake, in *Loch Morar Survey, 1970*. The loch, on the west coast, is 12 miles long, and over 1,000 ft. deep at its deepest point. The report contained 27 "authenticated reports" of the existence of at least one and possibly a whole family of unknown species. The creatures are reported to be of massive size, with an eel- or snake-like head and neck, and to travel at high speed through the water, with humps sometimes protruding above the surface. Reports from people who claim to have seen the creatures said that they vary in colour from black to grey and greeny-brown. The report, which called for a full-scale investigation of the loch, said that the creatures appeared to frequent shallow water, and that nothing in the results of the biological survey had "so far ruled out the possibility that a large predatory species could be supported in the loch".

Loch Ness Monster. Dr. Robert H. Rines, president of the Belmont Academy of

Applied Science, Mass., said in September, after spending two weeks with U.S. colleagues and researchers of the Loch Ness Phenomena Investigation Bureau, that he believed that several Loch Ness monsters exist. Sonar readings made after "sex lures" (essences of such creatures as eels, sea cows, and other mammals and fish that might be related to the monster) were put into the water provided, he claimed, proof of a family of creatures "many many times" larger than the largest fish known to live in the loch. The investigation team, who are planning a 20-year search programme starting in 1971, have built up a picture of the monsters from sonar results, eye-witness accounts, and photographs. They say that they are white, average 30–40 ft. in length, have a small head and long slender neck but a bulky body, can move through the water at about 10 m.p.h., and may be blind, through living at depths below 200 ft.

Lomonosov Gold Medals. The Soviet Academy of Sciences announced in January 1970 that the 1969 Lomonosov gold medals, instituted in 1959 for annual award to one Soviet and one foreign scientist, had been given to Professor Julio Natta (Italy) for work in polymer chemistry, and Academician Nikolai Semyonov (U.S.S.R.) for achievements in physical chemistry.

London. *City.* The removal of the Stock Exchange from its old premises in Throgmorton Street into an adjacent new tower block took place in 1970 in two stages, at the beginning of February and at the end of April. The decision to rebuild the Stock Exchange was taken in 1961, the plans were finally approved in 1965, and demolition of the eastern side of the old building began in July 1966. It is on this site that the new 26-storey tower block has been erected. On the site which has been vacated a new market floor, a public relations block containing access to a much larger visitors' gallery, and new premises for Algemene Bank Nederland N.V. will be built. It is hoped that the whole project will be completed by the latter part of 1972, when the total redeveloped site area will be 62,858 sq. ft. The estimated cost, excluding the acquisition of freeholds, is approximately £11 million.

Work started in March 1970 on a £7 million international telephone exchange, Mondial House, on a $2\frac{1}{2}$-acre site between the Thames and Upper Thames Street, close to Cannon Street station. The largest exchange of its type in Europe, and probably in the world, it will have nine storeys and extensive basements, and will accommodate a staff of 2,000. It is expected that the 150-ft.-high building will be completed by 1972, and that the exchange will come into service by 1974–75. Mondial House will be linked to the existing main international exchange at Faraday Building in Queen Victoria Street, and to a new exchange nearing completion in Wood Street, Cheapside (see also p. 64).

London. The £40 million rebuilding of 65 bombed acres in the Barbican area of the City of London at last began to take shape in 1970, when the "city within a city" was shown to the world's press in September. Above: Lauderdale Tower, one of the three 43-storey blocks of flats. Right: upper, other new flats, overlooking an artificial lake; lower, the City of London Girls' School, already open.

The Lord Mayor laid the foundation stone of the south block of the Central Criminal Court (the Old Bailey) on May 4, 1970. Under the stone he placed an aluminium cylinder containing the day's copy of *The Times*, the latest edition of the *City Press*, a set of coins in current use, and a set of decimal coins. The block, the second and final phase of a £7 million development scheme, will contain 12 new courts, accommodation for judges, barristers, jurors, staff, and female prisoners, a public restaurant, and an underground car park. It is due for completion in the spring of 1972. The east wing, which represented the first phase of the plan, was handed over to the corporation of London in April 1969.

A garden on the site of St. Mary Aldermanbury, the City church removed stone by stone and rebuilt on the campus of Westminster College, Fulton, Missouri, as a Churchill memorial, was officially opened in April. It cost £20,000 to prepare.

Plans for a 600-ft.-high tower block proposed for a $2\frac{1}{2}$-acre site between Bishopsgate and Old Broad Street were placed on exhibition in London on Jan. 13, 1970. Costing £15 million, the proposed building, the new headquarters of the National Westminster Bank, would house 4,000 workers in 45 storeys. Objections that the office block would overshadow St. Paul's Cathedral were raised in parliament, but building permission was given during the summer.

In July the Worshipful Company of Plaisterers placed a contract, worth nearly £1 million, for the building of a livery hall to replace its premises destroyed during the Second World War. The building, which will include a 12-storey office block, is to be erected at the junction of London Wall and Aldersgate, and is due for completion in March 1972. The livery company will occupy the lower level, and will have a separate entrance building with a master's room and housekeeper's flat and a two-storey livery hall; its headquarters will include a hall to seat 300 people, committee and council rooms, and kitchens. The Worshipful Company of Plaisterers, one of London's 84 livery companies, was founded in 1501.

Riverside. On July 14 the Greater London Council and Tower Hamlets borough council outlined plans to create a small "new town" in the Wapping area of London's dockland. The area stretches from the edge of St. Katharine's Dock development near the Tower of London to King Edward VII Park, Shadwell, in the east; and from the Thames to the Highway, the widened east–west road. It includes 103 acres of Port of London Authority land, and most of the 35 acres of dock basins will have to be filled in. The plan envisages homes to house about 12,000 people, a $1\frac{1}{2}$-mile continuous riverside walk linking open spaces, loop roads off the Highway for local traffic, footpaths linking the riverside with shopping centres and with Watney Street market, new schools, a polytechnic building, and a further education centre.

Permission in principle for what will be the biggest hotel in Europe to be built on a 5-acre site of Hay's Wharf by Tower Bridge on London's South Bank was given by Southwark borough council on Nov. 4. The plans provide for 1,700 bedrooms, to accommodate over 3,000 guests. The hotel, which will have a 600-ft. river frontage, will be U-shaped, with high terraced wings. Its own landing-stage is proposed for passengers who have arrived at Heathrow airport and been transported to some point such as Kew Bridge, and thence down the Thames by hydrofoil.

On the recommendation of the Royal Fine Art Commission the Greater London Council decided to abandon its plans for a 15-storey 170-ft.-high tower block on the Westminster Bridge roundabout for a six-sided building only half as high. The latter will hold 1,540 staff, the same number as the block originally planned. When this was announced in February 1970 it was stated that the new building will be linked with County Hall by an enclosed bridge over York Road. The exterior will be of light-coloured cast-stone panels, alternating with continuous bands of aluminium-framed windows. The cost is estimated at £3,615,000.

Plans to create a formal garden overlooking the Thames on a corner of the St. Thomas's Hospital site, by the end of Westminster Bridge, were announced at the beginning of March 1970. The garden will be 30 ft. above ground level, at the same height as the bridge, and this elevation will be achieved by building a concrete platform above the hospital car park. It will also be necessary to build a high wall facing the terrace of the Palace of Westminster, but it is planned to use this for a hanging garden.

South. During the summer of 1970 archaeologists uncovered an early 17th-century Lambeth Delft pottery workshop near the Thames in Montague Close, Southwark. Described as one of the most important industrial sites found in Great Britain, the workshop is thought to be the earliest Delftware pothouse to be excavated; its location has been confirmed by documentary evidence.

London's largest court, a £1 million complex designed by the architects' department of the Metropolitan Police, was opened in Kimpton Road, Camberwell, in July 1970. Work on the air-conditioned building, which contains four magistrates' courts and one juvenile court, began in 1964. There are eight lifts, a staff restaurant, and a top floor which houses probation officers. Similar court complexes are planned for other areas of London.

North. The first £5 million stage of Enfield council's £9¼ million town centre redevelopment at Edmonton Green was opened to the public on Sept. 1. It consists

of 175,000 sq. ft. of shopping area; 55,000 sq. ft. of offices; two housing blocks of 188 flats each; and 1,000 car spaces in two multi-storey parks. There will be a permanent market in the Market Square at the centre of the traffic-free shopping precinct, and the shops overlooking the square are on two levels. The facilities include two supermarkets, a department store, post office, electricity offices, two public houses, and more than 100 shop units of various sizes. The second stage will include more shops, flats, and another 2,000 car-parking spaces. Work on this latter stage began in 1970, and is expected to take two or three years; it will include an indoor swimming pool and an entertainment centre. The entire development will cover 61 acres.

West End. The 2½-mile-long Western Avenue extension, known as Westway, was opened on July 28. Great Britain's longest elevated road, it runs from the White City via the Harrow Road flyover to Marylebone Road, linking central London with the A40 trunk road to South Wales. Work started on the road, which cost £30 million, in September 1966.

A new cafeteria in St. James's Park, a £60,000 pavilion-like building replacing the old brick Cake House erected in 1922, was opened on Feb. 23, 1970. The new Cake House has room for 72 people inside, and a further 58 on the outer terrace, which is protected by a red and white awning. The building is shaped like a circular tent, with a conical roof supported by a series of shaped polished white concrete and Portland stone beams. It was designed by architects of the ministry of public building and works. The cleaning of

Left: London's largest local court, in Camberwell; it contains four magistrates' courts and one juvenile court. Below: the gigantic interchange at the White City whence the 2½-mile elevated Westway runs to Marylebone.

Marble Arch began on Aug. 28, and was completed by the end of September. The Arch, designed in 1828 to form a gateway to the forecourt of Buckingham Palace, was taken to its present position at the north entrance to Hyde Park in 1851.

Two tower office blocks form the centre of a redevelopment scheme for the 2½-acre site bounded by Cambridge Circus, St. Giles High Street, Charing Cross Road, and Shaftesbury Avenue. The proposed development, announced on March 9, 1970, will begin in the latter part of 1971, and take about three years to complete. One of the office blocks will face Cambridge Circus; 260 ft. high, with 20 storeys, it will provide about 130,000 sq. ft. of offices. The other block, 118 ft. tall, with 11 storeys, will provide about 125,000 sq. ft. of office space facing Charing Cross Road. The plans also include private flats, shops, and car-parking facilities, with landscaped gardens on the flat roof of garages along New Compton Street. The total cost of the scheme is estimated at £10 million.

In July the Greater London Council announced a £140 million scheme designed to "revitalize" the West End by remodelling almost 100 acres round Covent Garden. It proposed a one-way traffic system along the Strand, with eastbound traffic carried on an underground road parallel to the Strand along the line of Maiden Lane, and a link road running from Charing Cross Road to the Strand across the site of the Coutts Bank triangle. The central area round Covent Garden would be encircled by a loop road, much of it underground. Other proposals include traffic-free settings for the National Gallery

and St. Martin-in-the-Fields, and the preservation of two theatres, Wyndham's and the New, which it had earlier been suggested should be demolished.

A rebuilding plan for a half-acre site at the corner of King's Road and Jubilee Place, Chelsea, was announced in August. The developers propose to increase shopping space by building up to 30 small shops and kiosks on three levels, and, above the terraced roof of these shopping storeys, a block of 24 flats crowned by two penthouses. The 19th-century building called the Pheasantry, which stands on the site, is listed as being of historic merit; it is planned to retain its façade, entry courtyard, triumphal arch, balustraded wall, and a large studio on the first floor for use as a restaurant.

It was announced in September that the ministry of housing and local government had given consent for the building of a new London air terminal, combined with an hotel of at least 500 bedrooms, at Hammersmith Broadway. The £6 million com-

plex, sited on 4½ acres, will include 15 restaurants, and conference facilities for 2,000 people.

In August the U.K. ministry of housing and local government confirmed that the Lyric Theatre, Hammersmith, is to be demolished to make way for a development scheme. The 82-year-old theatre is on the statutory list of buildings of special architectural or historical interest because of the fine decorative interior plaster work; most of this will be taken down and stored, and, where this is impossible, moulds will be made and stored.

Transport. The Greater London Council announced on Feb. 4, 1970, that it had granted London Transport £2 million for improving bus and underground services. Just over half this money, the council's first grant to London Transport after taking control on Jan. 1, will be spent on extending the Victoria Line to Brixton. A further £50,000 is to be spent on erecting a translucent plastic roof over the bus forecourt at Victoria Station. Covering 12,000 sq.

Right: the new Knightsbridge Barracks, home of the Household Cavalry; the 270-ft. tower block dominates Hyde Park. Below: the charming new Cake House (opened in February), shaped like a tent, in St. James's Park.

yds., it will offer protection to the 20 million passengers using the station each year. Other projects on which the rest of the money may be spent include the improvement of bus shelters at Victoria and London Bridge stations, additional escalators at Waterloo Station, and reconstruction work at older and more seriously congested tube stations.

London Airport (Gatwick). The British Airports Authority announced on April 24, 1970, that it is planning to spend about £75 million on a development scheme for Gatwick Airport, in order to make it capable of handling about 20 million passengers a year by 1980, compared with the present 3 million a year. The plans include extending the existing runway to a length of 11,500 ft.; building a second runway of 8,500 ft.; enlarging the terminal buildings; and extending the land area of the airport to the north and west by 850 acres to a total of 2,300 acres.

London Airport (Heathrow). The world's first airliner hangar specially designed to house the Boeing-747 jumbo jet was formally handed over to BOAC at Heathrow on March 12, 1970. The hangar cost £4 million, covers 3½ acres, and can accommodate two of the aircraft at a time. A new international arrivals building costing £2 million was opened to passengers on June 1, 1970. The terminal, which has a total floor area of 100,000 sq. ft., is connected to a new loading and unloading pier by a 900-ft. two-channel passage with a moving walkway that has a speed of up to 180 ft. a minute. A new departure route for aircraft leaving Heathrow came into use on March 5, 1970, for a trial period. The new route takes airliners slightly farther to the west, away from the built-up areas of Egham, Englefield Green, and Virginia Water, and nearer to Windsor Castle.

A royal pavilion is to be part of a scheme for the airport's north side, announced by the British Airports Authority on Feb. 4, 1970. It will be used for state occasions and as a special lounge for visiting heads of state and governments. The scheme also includes a new hotel, expected to have at least 500 or 600 rooms, offices, and car parks. The whole redevelopment area, covering 30 acres adjoining the Bath Road, is expected to cost over £25 million.

The ministry of transport announced in November that a £15 million extension of the Piccadilly Line of the London Underground to Heathrow had been approved. A 3½-mile rail link will be built from Hounslow West station to the airport. The scheme will not receive a government grant, and apart from a £3,750,000 grant from the Greater London Council the cost will have to be met by higher fares.

Londonderry, N. Ireland. A preliminary blueprint for a 128-acre sports complex costing £1½ million was approved by the city's development commission in the autumn of 1970. The complex will have an indoor sports centre with a swimming pool; seven soccer pitches, two of them

Long Beach. The new mile-long six-lane Queen's Way bridge between the port and the city.

all-weather; two Gaelic football pitches, one all-weather; and rugby, hockey, cycling, bowling, and tennis facilities. The scheme also envisages a motel-boatel, a marina, riverside walks, a boating lake, and a ski slope. It was announced in May that Londonderry is to have a second bridge over the river Foyle. To cost £4,600,000, it will be built entirely of concrete. It is expected to be in use by 1975–76.

Long Beach, California. A new six-lane bridge, called Queen's Way Bridge, was officially opened here in the autumn of 1970. The mile-long bridge, which links the city to the port of Long Beach, provides for a traffic flow of 4,000 cars per hour. It cost $13,300,000.

Longevity. Shirali Muslinova, who lives in the high mountain settlement of Barzavu, Azerbaijan, U.S.S.R., claimed in 1970 to be 165 years old. He attributed his long life to regular physical work, meals at regular times, no smoking, and no drinking of alcohol. He still leads an active life and is a keen gardener. Married three times, he has 23 children, and countless grandchildren and great grandchildren.

MacRobert Prize. This annual £25,000 prize and gold medal for an outstanding innovation which has enhanced national prestige in the field of engineering and technology were awarded for the first time in 1970. It was announced in January that the joint winners were Freeman Fox and Partners, designers of the Forth and Severn Bridges, and Rolls-Royce, for the Pegasus jet engine. The award is made from one of six charitable trusts endowed by Lady MacRobert of Dounside before her death in 1954.

Mail Transport. In November the Posttechnisches Zentralamt in Darmstadt, W. Germany, published details of a new electrically driven system for transporting mail underground from post office to post office. "Trains" about 16 ft. long, powered by two 3 kW motors, travel through asbestos-concrete tubes at speeds of up to 25 m.p.h. There are no rails, and the wheels are set radially in the tube at an angle of 90 degrees to each other, which allows them to ride up the walls of the tube when the train negotiates a curve. About 10,000 letters can be carried in special compartments coupled at the back and front of the train, which can be braked mechanically. Tests carried out on a trial loop in Darmstadt showed that the system was silent and vibration-free and, because of its flexibility, could easily be laid underneath a city.

Madrid. Twin 250-ft.-high towers, which form the cores of a new building, dwarf the Christopher Columbus memorial column in Colon Square. The floors will be cantilevered out from the towers on the "umbrella" principle.

Man. Excavations in the Lake Rudolf area of Kenya unearthed in 1970 the earliest hominid remains yet found and the earliest man-made tools. The *Australopithecus* hominid fossils date back variously to 3 million and between 5 and 6 million years ago, and the tools to 2,600,000 years ago. The tools comprised quartzite flakes that were shaped into various specialized forms. If the tools were made by australopithecines, then *Homo habilis*, discovered by Dr. Leakey in 1964, was not, as supposed, the first tool-maker, since *Australopithecus* antedated him.

Mangere, Auckland, N. Zealand. It was announced in April 1970 that a new $NZ6½ million bridge is to be constructed here to cross Auckland harbour. To be built in three stages, it will have eight traffic lanes, and a pedestrian way and cycle track under one of the outside lanes. This will be the first bridge in New Zealand designed to metric measurements.

Marbles. The world marbles championship, held at Tinsley Green, near Crawley, Sussex, on March 27, 1970, was won for the 14th consecutive year by the Toucan Terribles, a Crawley factory team. Len Smith, captain of the team, individual world champion for the past 11 years, retained the title after defeating his son, Alan, himself twice holder of the award, in the final. The championship at Tinsley Green dates back to the days of the Spanish Armada, when two men contested the hand of a young woman, and, having tried all other sports without a victory for either, decided that the winner of a marbles game should have the maiden. Since then it has been an established tradition for the marbles championships to be played at Tinsley Green on Good Friday.

Marine National Park. Australia's first marine national park is to be established in New South Wales, and will include about 700 acres of the south Pacific Ocean bed near Bouddi States Park in the Gosford area. When the N.S.W. premier gave this information on September 18 he said that the park would extend between Gerrin Head and Third Point for about a quarter of a mile out to sea. The National Parks and Wildlife service will carry out an investigation of the sea-bed, tabulating all fish and marine growth, and make facilities available to encourage the use of the area for scientific research. The public will be given the opportunity to see underwater scenery and marine life by the establishment of underwater nature trails (these are already used in the Virgin Islands National Park). At a later stage an underwater visitors' centre, a scuba diving system, and an underwater walkway will all be considered.

Maritime Trust. This new trust to preserve ships of historical value was launched on Feb. 19, 1970, by the Duke of Westminster. The purpose of the Trust is declared to be to "discover, repair, and preserve for the nation vessels of historic,

scientific, or technical interest, and to arrange for their berthing at suitable sites ashore or afloat". Prince Philip is president of the Trust, and the Duke of Westminster chairman; the council includes the Earl of Antrim (chairman of the National Trust), Viscount Runciman of Doxford (chairman of the National Maritime Museum), and Admiral Sir Deric Holland-Martin (chairman of the Imperial War Museum). The Trust's first purchase, the last of the old West Country topsail trading schooners, the *Kathleen and May*, was made in June. The three-masted wooden vessel, built at Connah's Quay, Flintshire, in 1900, by Ferguson and Baird, traded in the Bristol Channel and the Irish Sea before being laid up in the 1950s. The Trust bought her for £2,800 from Capt. Paul Davis, who found her lying derelict at Southampton in 1967 and had failed to raise the £7,000 he estimated he would need to make her seaworthy again. It is intended to restore the ship to her original state, with exact replicas of the original masting, rigging, and sails. She is at present berthed in the river Torridge at Appledore, North Devon.

Martin Luther King Memorial. The Martin Luther King Memorial Fund and Foundation announced its first plans in March 1970. They include an employment agency to help black people to secure good jobs; information bureaux throughout Great Britain to provide guidance on legal and social problems; financial help to racial integration schemes, such as playgroups, and to cultural centres and business developments. The biggest project is a national educational programme aimed at all ages, classes, creeds, and colours, with the aim of encouraging mutual tolerance.

Medals. It was announced in Salisbury, Rhodesia, on Aug. 19 that a new set of 30 Rhodesian awards and honours had been devised to replace those of British origin. The Victoria Cross is being replaced by a Grand Cross of Valour.

Melbourne, Victoria, Australia. Many new building plans for Melbourne were made public in 1970. Further details about the Broken Hill Proprietary headquarters building disclosed that there will be a small shopping complex half-way up the building; that the roof has been designed for future use as a heliport; and that there will be parking space for about 300 cars in a seven-storey annexe. But its 503 ft. will be easily surpassed by a 650-ft. hotel and office block, which, it was announced in July, is to be built in the centre of the city. This $A40 million 53-storey building, which will be Australia's tallest building, 18 ft. taller than the Australia Square tower in Sydney, will house a 445-bed luxury hotel in its first 24 storeys, and the remaining 29 storeys will provide office accommodation. Work will start in 1971, and the building is expected to be completed in 1975. In June it was reported that in 1970 the city council had issued permits for buildings in the Golden Mile

business area valued at $A107,585,000, double the value of the previous record building permit year 1966, and three times the value of the permits issued in 1969. This building boom has two centres: one bounded by Collins, Queen, Bourke, and King Streets, where buildings are being put up by banks, insurance companies, and big public companies; and the other bounded by Collins, Russell, Bourke, and Spring Streets, where huge hotel and entertainment complexes are being built. Among other new buildings will be a 30-storey office block to be built over the Jolimont railway station and yards. This $A8½ million construction will include a shopping area and large car park.

A new stadium with one of the best playing surfaces in the country, for Australian Rules Football, which draws the biggest crowds of any sport in Australia, was opened at the beginning of the summer of 1970. The $A3 million first stage of the Victoria Football League Park has seating for 70,000, and will eventually be developed to accommodate 150,000 in comfort. By 1974 the stadium will have been considerably expanded and a new high-speed freeway from Melbourne will run right to its gates.

On July 1, John Gorton, the Australian prime minister, opened the new airport at Tullamarine, outside Melbourne. The airport, which cost £23 million, can operate 24 hours a day, unlike that at Sydney, where an overnight curfew operates to protect residential areas from aircraft noise.

Melbourne's first festival of the performing arts opened on October 16, 1970, and lasted for two weeks. Ballet, theatre, music, films, and art were represented at venues mainly within the new arts centre. Although described as "of modest proportions", this first season of the kind in Melbourne is expected to be developed in the future.

Menai Bridge. The Britannia rail bridge across the Menai Strait between Bangor and Anglesey, damaged by fire in May 1970 and out of use since then, will be repaired at a cost of £3¼ million and re-opened by July 1971, according to a British Rail statement on Sept. 15. Lattice steel arches will support the over-water spans, and a three-lane road deck (to cost a further £3 million) will be built over the railway track. While the bridge was closed the port of Holyhead was more or less out of action. Caernarvon replaced it as a container ship terminal for services to Belfast and Dublin, and passenger crossings were transferred to Heysham, Lancs. The bridge was designed by Robert Stephenson and built in 1850. The fire, accidentally started by two boys hunting with a newspaper "torch" for bats, cost British Rail £2 million in revenue lost while the bridge was closed.

Mersey, River. The 1½-mile-long, 34-ft.-diameter tunnel forming the second roadway under the Mersey between Liverpool and Birkenhead was completed on March 4, 1970, when the tunnelling machine cut through the last section of rock on the Liverpool side. It is expected that the tunnel will be opened in the spring of 1971. Work on a duplication of the tunnel, alongside the present one, which will result in the opening to motorists of eight traffic lanes under the Mersey, started in 1970.

Meteorites. It was announced in Washington on Dec. 2 that a meteorite which fell to earth in 1969 93 miles north of Melbourne, Australia, had brought what was thought to be the "first conclusive proof of extra-terrestrial chemical evolution, the chemical process which preceded the origin of life". This was the opinion of Dr. Cyril Ponnamperuma, head of a U.S. research team at the N.A.S.A. Ames Centre in California, after scientists had reported finding traces of amino acids in fragments of the meteorite. The opinion was received with some scepticism by the former professor of inorganic chemistry at the University of New South Wales, Prof. D. P. Mellor, who said he needed more evidence. The head of Melbourne University's school of geology, Prof. J. F. Lovering, said that he believed the meteorite to be an asteroid which had left an orbit somewhere between Mars and Jupiter, and that it probably weighed at least a ton when it entered the earth's atmosphere. A great deal of the meteorite would have burnt or broken away upon entry. The biggest fragments hit the earth at over 32,000 m.p.h., while others

landed in an area 7 miles by 2 miles near Murchison. Prof. Lovering also said that tests made on samples at Melbourne University showed that the meteorite had an unusually high water and carbon content, whereas other meteorites tested at the university had had almost no water content.

It was announced in December that the world's largest known meteorite crater, 60 miles in diameter, had been located inside the Arctic Circle in the Krasnoyarsk region of Soviet Siberia.

Metrication. The first report of the U.K. Metrication Board, *Going Metric—the First Five Years*, was published on May 13, 1970. In pursuit of the aim to make Great Britain metric by 1975, changes envisaged include altering petrol pumps as soon as possible to serve litres instead of gallons. (The idea of converting, by 1973, 250,000 miles-per-hour speed-limit signs to kilometres-per-hour was abandoned in December.) In the construction industry, where over a million people are employed in 80,000 firms, a substantial amount of new work is already being designed in metric units, and the report said that by 1972 virtually all new projects in the public sector should be so designed, and hoped for similar progress in the private sector. In the engineering industries, where $3\frac{1}{2}$ million people are employed, progress is encouraging, and the pace is expected to accelerate in 1971. The Board hopes retailers will start to measure milk

and beer in metric quantities during 1972–1973. It stated that a scheme for the metric sizing of shoes had been agreed in principle by the footwear industry, and that from 1973 the Inland Revenue would use metric units to assess rates. The principal new units facing ordinary consumers will be the metre (39·37 inches), the kilogramme (2·205 lb.), and the litre (about $1\frac{3}{4}$ pints).

Mr. Gorton, prime minister of Australia, said on Jan. 19, 1970, that by the end of the 1970s all Australian weights and measures would be converted to the metric system. A Metric Conversion Board will be set up to plan, guide, and facilitate the conversion. In New Zealand, primary-school children will be taught only the metric system of measurement from the middle of 1971. When this was announced in October 1970 it was also stated that the metric system will be used in teachers' training colleges from the middle of 1972, and that secondary schools will change to the system at the beginning of 1973. During the summer of 1970 the Papua–New Guinea house of assembly passed a bill providing for the progressive introduction of the metric system, which it is hoped will be completed by 1980.

Miami, Florida, U.S.A. Two of five berths at the artificial island port, called Dodge Island, created off Miami, were completed in August 1969, and in 1970 the whole port was opened. Record activity was reported at the $30 million port, which is

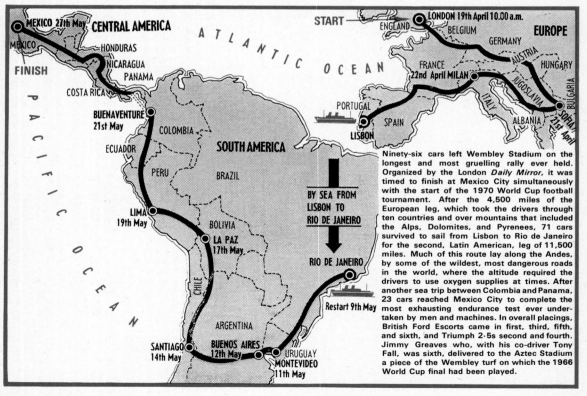

Ninety-six cars left Wembley Stadium on the longest and most gruelling rally ever held. Organized by the London *Daily Mirror*, it was timed to finish at Mexico City simultaneously with the start of the 1970 World Cup football tournament. After the 4,500 miles of the European leg, which took the drivers through ten countries and over mountains that included the Alps, Dolomites, and Pyrenees, 71 cars survived to sail from Lisbon to Rio de Janeiro for the second, Latin American, leg of 11,500 miles. Much of this route lay along the Andes, by some of the wildest, most dangerous roads in the world, where the altitude required the drivers to use oxygen supplies at times. After another sea trip between Colombia and Panama, 23 cars reached Mexico City to complete the most exhausting endurance test ever undertaken by men and machines. In overall placings, British Ford Escorts came in first, third, fifth, and sixth, and Triumph 2·5s second and fourth. Jimmy Greaves who, with his co-driver Tony Fall, was sixth, delivered to the Aztec Stadium a piece of the Wembley turf on which the 1966 World Cup final had been played.

Sir Alf Ramsey (left) started the Rally at Wembley Stadium on April 19. Manager of the England World Cup soccer team, he was also in Mexico when the Rally finished. The European leg took the drivers south-eastwards across the Continent as far as Sofia. On the way they passed through Vienna (right), visiting the famous Schoenbrunn Palace, seen here in the background.

After completing 4,500 miles across Europe and back, the 71 surviving cars were carried in the British freighter *Derwent* from Lisbon to Rio de Janeiro, where the Rally re-started on May 9. Left: some of the cars parked on the quayside at Rio. Right: the day after the official end of the Rally, the 23 finishers drove in triumph along the Mexico City boulevards to the Aztec Stadium.

Left: the victorious women drivers—left to right, Alice Watson (Scotland), Rosemary Smith (Ireland), and Ginette Derolland (France), winners of the ladies' section and the 1,300–1,600 c.c. class. Right: the overall winners, Hannu Mikkola (Finland) and co-driver Gunnar Palm (Sweden).

Molokai, Hawaii. Kualupuu reservoir, lined with nylon-reinforced butyl rubber sheeting.

said to be the most advanced on the U.S. east coast.

Migraine. The City of London migraine clinic, which provides a free service for City businessmen and employees suffering from migraine, was formally opened by Princess Margaret on May 19, 1970. Money for the clinic is being provided by the Migraine Trust, founded by the late Lord Brain in 1966, and the venture has the co-operation of St. Bartholomew's Hospital. The clinic is open 5 days a week, can treat between 20 and 30 patients a day, and can give immediate help to victims suffering from an attack. Expert diagnosis can decide whether the illness is, in fact, migraine or, for example, diabetes, which was revealed to be the cause of severe headaches in 2 per cent of patients examined in a recent study. The premises are two converted houses in Bartholomew Close, near Aldersgate station. Running the clinic cost £17,000 in 1970.

Milton Keynes, Bucks. The master plan for Milton Keynes, this great "new city" in north Buckinghamshire, was published on March 17, 1970. It showed that the estimated cost of building the city had risen by £100 million to £700 million since the publication of the interim plan. The master plan confirmed the principles originally laid down, with a unified health service, a grid pattern of roads, and "campus" style schools. Milton Keynes, which will cover 25,000 acres, is planned to provide homes and jobs for 70,000 newcomers by 1981, and for 150,000 by the early 1990s, when its total population will be 250,000. Some uncertainty about the planning and progress of the city is due to the possibility that the Roskill Commission may choose either Thurleigh or Cublington as the site for London's third airport; the choice of either of these places would seriously harm the new community. Nevertheless, work started on the city on Aug. 26, when the first earth was ceremonially moved, on the A5, a mile south of Stony Stratford, one of the three towns that will become part of the city.

"Miss World." At the Royal Albert Hall, London, on Nov. 20 Miss Grenada, Jennifer Hosten, a 22-year-old air hostess, was judged winner of the 1970 "Miss World" competition. Pearl Jansen (Miss Africa South) was runner-up, Irith Lavi (Miss Israel) third, Maj Johansson (Miss Sweden) fourth, and Jillian Jessup (Miss South Africa) fifth.

Molokai, Hawaii. The Kualapuu reservoir here was dedicated early in 1970. The world's largest reservoir to be lined with nylon-reinforced butyl-rubber sheeting, Kualapuu has a water storage capacity of 1,419 million gallons. The lining was installed in less than 2 months at less than one third of the cost of the traditional concrete construction methods. The reservoir is designed to irrigate 16,000 acres of land which has lain fallow through lack of water.

Monici. This is the name of a new musical instrument capable of producing a variety of percussion sounds, yet light and compact enough to be readily portable. Its eponymous inventor is André Monici, a

French cellist. The instrument produces its sounds by striking 13 steel strings with ordinary drum sticks, and selects the desired diameter and tension of the strings and the method by which they are hit. Electromagnetic pick-ups with ferrite cores feed the vibrations into an amplifier. Stability of pitch is achieved by the use of a solid and rigid metallic double frame.

More, Sir Thomas. The Japanese Thomas More Association was founded in Tokyo in December 1969 to encourage the Japanese people to study and take an interest in the British saint. It was reported in February 1970 that the new organization already had 50 members, and that it planned to publish an annual bulletin, and hold regular meetings culminating in a series of celebrations in 1978, the year of the 500th anniversary of More's birth.

Morecambe Bay, Lancs. Alternatives to the scheme for a full barrage across the bay from Hest to Furness to conserve water for N.W. England were being studied by the U.K. Water Resources Board in 1970. The first alternative would provide twin barrages across the mouths of the rivers Kent and Leven, with a pumped storage reservoir off the Cartmel peninsula. In the second, the pumped storage reservoir would extend south from near Jenny Brown's Point towards Bolton-le-Sands. The third provides for river barriers within the mouths of the two rivers and two pumped storage reservoirs, one on the Morecambe side of the Silverdale coast and the other off the Cartmel peninsula. The latter two schemes would involve the building of sea defence walls that would create "polders" along part of the sea front at Morecambe. The barrages would rise 15 ft., and the reservoir dykes would be between 25 and 40 ft., above high water. In the first two schemes, roads would be built across the barrages to link Furness with the M6 motorway. In the third, the dams across the rivers would not be conveniently sited for a through road across them.

"Miss World." The finalists in the 1970 contest were, left to right, Miss Israel (3rd), Miss South Africa (5th), Miss Grenada (1st), Miss Africa South (2nd), and Miss Sweden (4th).

Morwellham, Devon. In 1970, to mark European Conservation Year, the derelict port of Morwellham, 20 miles N. of Plymouth, underwent conversion into a centre for recreation and education. The project was started by the Dartington Amenity Research Trust with financial aid from the Countryside Commission, and work by an international team of volunteers began in the spring and continued throughout the summer. The centre was opened to the public in July, and by the beginning of December had been visited by over 18,000 people.

Morwellham was once a busy and prosperous port, for it was the highest point to which vessels of 10 ft. draught could navigate the tidal Tamar river, and it was also easy to transport ore to the village by the Tavistock canal, which was completed in 1817. Tin mining in the area began in Tudor times, and was followed by copper mining in the late 18th century. In 1844 the Devon Great Consols Mine was discovered, and during the next 30 years vast quantities of arsenic, copper ore, and other minerals were shipped from Morwellham. But by the end of the century the port's heyday was over. The Tavistock canal fell into disuse with the coming of the railways; the markets for arsenic and copper fell away; and the port became a quiet village.

The new centre includes a museum containing rock samples, mining tools, and a model of the port as it was at the height of the village's boom period. A lecture-room and library are to be built, as well as a hostel and camp-site for field study groups. Nature trails pass through old mineral workings, and those interested in industrial archaeology can see many other relics and reminders of Morwellham's past.

Moscow. The first of 14 supermarkets to be built during 1970 by the Italian consortium SIRCE, which represents several Italian contractors, was opened in Moscow in May 1970. This Western-style supermarket is open only to foreigners, but the other 13 will be available to Russians.

Motherhood. According to World Health Organization statistics for 1966 for 36 countries, published in March 1970, Sweden was the safest country in the world in which to have a baby, for there deaths ascribed to pregnancy, childbirth, and confinement numbered only 11·3 per 100,000 live births. Figures for other countries in ascending order were: Northern Ireland 17·8, Denmark 19·2, Netherlands 20·4, Scotland 24·9, Norway 25·4, England and Wales 26·2, Belgium 27·8, Republic of Ireland 28·9, U.S.A. 29·1, Finland 30·9, France 31·1, Poland 32·6, New Zealand 36·6, Switzerland 41, Austria 41·2, Hong Kong 43·3, Singapore 49·4, Israel 51·9, West Germany 65·1, West Berlin 72·8, Italy 77, Portugal 83·1, Japan 93, Mauritius 108·1, Costa Rica 110·3, Venezuela 117·4, El Salvador 121·1, Trinidad and Tobago 129·7, Mexico 151·8, Ceylon 239·3, Colombia 240·3, and Chile 271·8.

Motoring Awards. Left to right, with trophies: Graham Hill, Keith Duckworth, Jackie Stewart.

Motoring Awards. At the R.A.C. Club on Feb. 11, 1970, former world champion Graham Hill was presented with the Campbell Memorial Trophy for the outstanding performance in any form of motor competition during the calendar year, having won the Monaco Grand Prix five times. Two other R.A.C. awards were presented on the same occasion: Keith Duckworth was given the Dewar Trophy for the design of the Ford Formula 1 engine, which has retained the supremacy of British engineering in Grand Prix racing; and Jackie Stewart was presented with the Hawthorn Memorial Trophy as the British or Commonwealth driver placed highest in the 1969 world championship.

Motoring Offences. A U.K. Home Office report published on July 29, 1970, showed that drink-and-driving convictions during 1969 numbered 26,392, an increase of 5,435 on the 1968 figure. According to the ministry of transport, this rise did not necessarily indicate more drunken driving, but only that more offenders were caught. In 1969 there were 1,461,207 prosecutions for all motoring offences, a decrease of 11,672 on 1968. Convictions for speeding dropped by 29,678 to 248,647, but convictions for defective tyres (1969 was the first full year since the "tread" regulation came into force) increased from 24,541 in 1968 to 41,808 in 1969. Magistrates' courts' fines rose from a total of £7,883,963 in 1968 to £8,323,467 in 1969, and fines imposed by higher courts from £44,141 to £57,183.

From Sept. 1, 1970, the fixed penalty of £2 for committing certain offences was extended to the whole of England and Wales, and the number of offences covered by the system increased from two to six. The offences named in the new order are going the wrong way down a one-way street, making a U-turn where it is forbidden, certain lighting and parking offences, and failing to display a valid excise licence. Under the fixed penalty system a motorist can pay the £2 penalty instead of facing prosecution in the courts.

Motor Vehicles (Italy). From 1900 to 1968, the last year for which final figures are available, annual production of motor vehicles in Italy rose from 300 to 1,663,648. These figures were given in September 1970, when it was also stated that in 1968 Lombardy registered the greatest number of new vehicles (253,573), followed by Piedmont (157,412), Latium (125,305, of which 105,285 were in Rome), and Emilia-Romagna (106,457). The decennial increase in the number of motor vehicles on the roads was from 11 in 1899 to 6,353 in 1909, 34,833 in 1919, 222,394 in 1929, 391,463 in 1939, 486,200 in 1949, 2,087,771 in 1959, and 8,976,558 in 1968. (These figures did not include vehicles with special registrations, such as the diplomatic corps, armed forces, police, etc.) The Italian car industry showed a constant growth in exports, for Italy exported 6 vehicles in 1900, 11,320 in 1920, 14,266 in 1940, 203,935 in 1960, and 687,141 in 1968. Of this last figure, 466,277 went to other European countries, 156,990 to the U.S.A., 34,376 to Africa, 17,817 to Asia, and 9,370 to Oceania. Cars imported into Italy totalled 199 in 1900 and 194,627 in 1968, of which 190,675 came from member states of the European Common Market.

Mount Whaleback. The Mount Newman mining company in Western Australia released at the beginning of April 1970 figures for its first year of iron-ore operations in the Mount Whaleback area. They showed that almost 6½ million tons of iron ore were shipped out of Port Hedland, most of it to Japan, and the rest chiefly to steel mills in Great Britain, France, Belgium, and the Netherlands, although some also went to steel mills in Australia.

Museums. It was announced in July that the Natural History Museum, South Kensington, is to have a new £1,350,000 wing to house one of the world's largest collection of fossils. The L-shaped five-storey wing will be on the Exhibition

Museums. The new National Army Museum, completed in May 1970, stands next to the Royal Hospital, Chelsea, London (home of the "Chelsea pensioners").

Road side of the museum, adjoining the geological section and facing Cromwell Road. The site of the new building is occupied by the war-time headquarters of the Civil Defence, and, because its densely reinforced 6-ft.-thick concrete walls would be too expensive to demolish, it will be incorporated into the new air-conditioned structure, providing a basement where electron and optical microscopy can be carried out. The whole of the new extension will be of reinforced concrete, with pre-cast columns and bronzed window-frames. At the eastern end of the wing an octagonal tower, containing offices and small laboratories, will be topped by a glass rotunda for growing mosses and ferns. A nine-storey extension to the existing north block is also to be built in Exhibition Road.

Details of the new £1 million National Army Museum which has been built next door to the Royal Hospital, Chelsea, London, were given in May 1970. Designed by Lord Holford, the building is the first purpose-built museum erected in London in this century. Illustrating the army's development from the formation of the militias in 1573 until 1914, it will be opened to the public in the summer of 1971. The setting up of a museum at Bow Street Police Station was announced in February 1970. To be called the Metropolitan Police Historical Museum, it will display London policemen's clothing and equipment over the last 140 years, including the swallow-tail uniforms, top hats, and gloves worn in the time of Sir Robert Peel, the founder of the force. The removal of the National Transport Museum from Clapham, London, to the railway museum at York was postponed once again in 1970, when it was officially stated on October 7 that the rail enthusiasts of southern England had been given six months to find an alternative site in London.

The concept of the open-air folk museum, popular in Scandinavia, spread to England in February 1970 when the establishment of such a museum at

Beamish, 6 miles S.W. of Newcastle upon Tyne, was approved by the local authorities. To be sited in the 270 acres of farmland and grounds of Beamish Hall, the museum will contain exhibits showing the development of local lead and coal mining, and iron and steel working, but will chiefly be an open-air panorama of social history.

A private, non-profit making museum of U.S. space achievements, at Huntsville, Alabama, was described in June 1970. It has an open-air space and rocket centre, expected to attract 200,000 visitors annually, as well as an exhibition building. The largest exhibit on show is the Saturn 5 Moon rocket, and the tallest of the other rockets at the museum is a Saturn 1B. There is also a replica of a moon crater, with an Apollo lunar module. For the past 10 years, launch vehicles essential to the Apollo and other space missions have been designed and developed at the Marshall Space Flight Centre at Huntsville. Russia honoured the first astronaut, Yuri Gagarin, who was killed in an air crash in 1969, by opening, on April 5, 1970, a museum near Smolensk.

A unique cart museum was formally opened at La Mancha, Spain, in the autumn. The building is in the shape of a *bombo* (a word of Moorish origin meaning a big drum) such as for centuries was used to house agricultural implements and harness in this part of Spain. It was erected by the last surviving craftsman to know the secrets of the *bombo*'s construction. The museum houses a collection of farm carts and farm animal trappings.

Music Awards. The first prize in the international Tchaikovsky piano competition, awarded in Moscow on June 23, 1970, was shared between John Lill (Great Britain) and Vladimir Krainev (U.S.S.R.), both aged 26. Each pianist received a gold medal and 2,500 roubles (£1,163). The winner of the eighth international Chopin piano competition, held in Warsaw in October, was Garrick Ohlsson, aged 22, of New York, the first American ever to

win the prize. The second prize went to Mitsuko Uehida (Japan) and the third to Peter Paleczny (Poland).

The Composers' Guild of Great Britain announced in August 1970 a posthumous award for "Composer of the Year 1969" to Roberto Gerhard, for his outstanding contribution to British music during the last year of his life, particularly his Symphony No. 4, *Libra and Gemini*. Gerhard died in January 1970.

Mutrah, Muscat and Oman. Work on the first stage of a new port at Mutrah began in 1970, and is due for completion in 1972. A £2 million contract for the work, which includes the erection of 1,650 ft. of armoured rockfill breakwater, 1,000 ft. of lighter quay, two transit sheds, and passenger, administration, and security buildings, was awarded by the Sultanate of Muscat and Oman to a consortium of Belgian, French, Dutch, and Spanish companies. The port was designed by the London consulting engineers, Sir William Halcrow and Partners, in association with John R. Harris, architects and planners.

n

Naples, Italy. Because of the caving-in of many of the city's streets which had been occurring for over a year, the authorities had to close Naples airport early in 1970. The reason for the cave-ins is that the 2,400-year-old city is built on loose, sandy soil over hundreds of caves. The situation has been aggravated by the failure of an ancient sewer system to carry away water following heavy downpours, and by uncon-

Naples. A typical cave-in in a Naples street, the Via Aniello Falcone. Over 4,000 cave-ins have occurred in the city since 1968.

trolled building development that has increased pressure on the subsoil. Since 1966, 18 people have been killed and over 40 injured in more than 4,000 separate cave-ins in Naples.

Naracoorte, S. Australia. The discovery of one of the richest deposits of Ice Age animal bones in a cave at Naracoorte was reported in July, following an inspection of the 200-ft.-long and 50-ft.-wide fossil bed by Dr. R. A. Tedford, curator of vertebrate palaeontology at the American Museum of Natural History, New York. Dr. Tedford said that the deposits provided "an unprecedented view of the type of animals that lived in the Pleistocene age", and that the discovery might provide an answer to the question why so many large forms of animal life became extinct. The largest of the bones were those of an extinct herbivorous animal about the size of a cow; others were of a marsupial lion and a giant kangaroo.

National Gallery, London. Plans and models of a proposed northern extension to the National Gallery were put on show at the gallery on July 1, 1970. The extension covers a half-acre site at the rear of the gallery, bounded by Orange Street and St. Martin's Street at the west end. Along this west side a pedestrian way is planned, leading from Trafalgar Square to Leicester Square. The extension adds an extra 10 rooms to the exhibition area, increasing the wall space by 25 per cent; gives an additional 50 per cent hanging space on the ground floor for the reserve collection; and provides new laboratories and offices. The building—the result of 4 years' work by government architects—is contemporary in design but harmonizes with the main building, which was constructed in 1832–1837. Renovations to the existing gallery, including new air-conditioning, are also planned. It is estimated that the project will take about $3\frac{1}{2}$ years to complete, and cost £1·2 million.

National Insurance Act. The first legislative measure to be introduced by the Conservative government, the National Insurance (Old Persons' and Widows' Pensions and Attendance Allowance) Act

was passed on July 23, 1970. It provided the following new benefits: retirement pensions of £4·85 a week for married couples, and £3 a week for single persons, who had been too old to be covered by the National Insurance scheme when it was introduced on July 5, 1948 (to be paid from Nov. 4, 1970); a widow's pension of £1·50 to a woman if she was aged 40 or over at the time of her husband's death, and the introduction of a sliding scale for widows between 40 and 50, reaching the full £5 pension at that age (to be paid from April 1971); and, for severely disabled people, a special attendance allowance of £4 a week for those needing day and night or continual supervision (to be paid from April 1972).

National Trust. On Jan. 11, 1969, the Trust issued a statement showing that in 1969 the total membership was 177,000, compared with 90,000 in 1959. During the ten-year period the amount of land protected in England, Wales, and Northern Ireland increased from 275,000 acres to 420,000 acres. In 1959 the Trust protected 160 miles of coastline, and by 1969 this had increased to 280 miles, largely thanks to Enterprise Neptune, the campaign launched by the Duke of Edinburgh in 1965. By 1969, £1$\frac{1}{2}$ million of the £2 million sought by the campaign had been raised.

The first National Trust country park in the North of England is being planned for an 18-acre site at Fell Foot, Windermere, in the Lake District. The outline plan, announced on Oct. 5, provides for a café, information centre, chalets, a shop, a boatstore, caravan sites, two car parks, and a launching point. The site has a quartermile frontage on Lake Windermere.

National Youth Theatre. Work on the 510-seat Shaw Theatre, intended to be the home of the National Youth Theatre, continued during 1970. It will form part of the St. Pancras library building in Euston Road, London. A model was unveiled by the founder and director of the National Youth Theatre, Michael Croft, on May 3, when he outlined plans to provide for both professionals and amateurs at the theatre. A professional group, called the

Dolphin Company, formed with a nucleus of five or six actors, will present six or seven productions each year during a 40-week season, while the normal amateur activities of the Youth Theatre continue. An appeal to raise £200,000 to finance the productions at the theatre was officially opened on May 4, when hundreds of past and present members of the Theatre staged a rally on the site of the new theatre.

Natural Gas. Discoveries of deposits of natural gas in the North Sea continued to be made in 1970. They included a strike by the Hamilton group about 80 miles from Middlesbrough, the most northerly find yet announced in the U.K. sector of the continental shelf; a strike by Conoco in April about 18 miles from the Humber; another by Conoco-N.C.B. in July about 40 miles from the Norfolk coast, 13 miles S.W. of Viking field and 12 miles N. of Leman Bank; and a find in the Dutch sector, about 53 miles N.W. of Den Helder, by the Shell-Esso group in August.

Delivery. The Gas Council-Amoco and Shell-Esso groups are to lay and share a 100-mile network of large-capacity underwater pipelines to carry gas from the Leman and Indefatigable fields to the shore terminal at Bacton, Norfolk. When this was announced in February 1970 it was stated that three separate 30-in.-diameter lines are planned. One, to run from the Indefatigable field via the Leman field to the terminal, is to be built in two stages in 1970–71, and another, running 30 miles to Bacton from the Leman field, will be laid in 1973. The capacity of these two lines is expected to be more than 1,000 million cu. ft. of gas per day. The third pipe, 5 miles long, will be laid to link the two lines connecting the Leman field to the shore terminal.

In July British Petroleum signed a 20-year contract worth over £100 million with the Gas Council for deliveries of North Sea natural gas from B.P.'s West Sole field, 40 miles from the mouth of the Humber. The agreement covers a production rate of 150 million cu. ft. per day, at the fixed price of 2·9d a therm for this minimal annual contract, and 2·025d a

Natural Gas. This vast £14 million gas treatment plant has sprung up in desert country in the Zagros Mountains foothills in south Iran.

therm for additional quantities. B.P. also obtained government consent to use some of its own North Sea gas at its chemicals plant near Hull—the first time an oil company had been permitted to take direct delivery of sea gas.

Plans to develop and put into production the Conoco-National Coal Board Viking field off the Lincolnshire coast were announced on Oct. 8. The cost of £50 million will cover building a producing platform and laying an 82-mile 28-in. undersea pipeline—the longest in the North Sea—to carry the gas to a terminal to be built at Mablethorpe. The platform will be used to drill 10 wells. First deliveries are planned for October 1972, and output should eventually average over 500 million cu. ft. per day.

During 1970 the work of laying a 67-mile natural gas pipeline of 36-in. diameter from Yelverton, near Norwich, Norfolk, to the London area, via Stowmarket and Braintree, was carried out. The work, which started at the southern end, involved about 130 crossings, including 17 thrust-borings under roads, 80 open-cut crossings of roads, and 6 river and 19 stream crossings.

Storage. On Aug. 9 the Gas Council announced plans for a £4 million storage plant to hold liquefied natural gas on a 40–50-acre site near Tower Colliery at Hirwarn, near Aberdare, Glamorgan. The plant, the first in Wales, will have two insulated tanks, each 150 ft. in diameter and capable of holding 20,000 tons of liquid gas. Intended to provide additional security of supply to gas users in S. Wales and the Severn basin area of England, the plant will be operating by 1972.

Safety. Because of the number of accidents in homes converted to the use of natural gas the U.K. government promised that an inquiry into its safety would be made. It was announced in March 1970 that an independent inquiry would be carried out by Professor Frank Morton, professor of chemical engineering at Manchester University. Professor Morton's report was published in August. It stated that natural gas was no more dangerous to use than town gas, but stressed the importance of ventilation, recommending that national building regulations and other controls for the provision, design, and installation of flues and permanent ventilation should be strengthened. The report also recommended that gas boards should be given authority to enter premises and inspect installations, and suggested that a joint safety committee of the fuel and electricity supply industries should be formed to consider promoting the safe use of all fuels and electricity.

Australia. A survey of Australia's mineral developments, details of which were given in March 1970, showed that large-scale use of natural gas in Australia began in 1969, during which year total commercial consumption amounted to 9,374,500,000 cu. ft., compared with 215,800,000 cu. ft. in 1968. The first commercial use of gas from Bass Strait began in April 1969, and commercial use from this source during

the year totalled 4,476,900,000 cu. ft. Supplies to Brisbane from the Roma field in Queensland commenced in March 1969, and the total commercial use in Queensland during 1969 amounted to 3,917,000,000 cu. ft. In South Australia commercial use of natural gas began in November 1969, and total use during November and December was 741,700,000 cu. ft. From the Barrow Island field in Western Australia, 238,900,000 cu. ft. were used as field and plant fuel in connection with the production of crude oil.

Further discoveries of natural gas were announced during 1970. They included what was believed to be the largest gas flow ever recorded in Australia. Magellan Petroleum's Palm Valley No. 2 well, in Amadeus Basin 80 miles W. of Alice Springs, was reported to be flowing at a rate of 69·7 million cu. ft. per day through a 2¾-in. choke at a depth of 6,559 ft. Surface data suggested that the Palm Valley gas field could be 20 miles long and 5 miles wide. Other significant discoveries were a strike by the Sydney-based oil exploration company, Exoil No Liability, in the Surat Basin in Queensland at the rate of 3 million cu. ft. per day, reported in February; a new find by Bridge Oil in June about 160 miles W. of the Moonie oilfield in southern Queensland, at the rate of 8,850,000 cu. ft. per day; a strike in June at the Grafton Range No. 15 well, N.E. of Roma, at the rate of 3½ million cu. ft. per day; and another in August at Roma, south Queensland, itself, with a flow of 4¼ million cu. ft. per day.

Melbourne became in 1970 the first Australian city wholly converted to the use of natural gas. When this was announced in December it was stated that the Victorian Gas and Fuel Corporation had converted appliances in the last of 1,000 homes in the western suburb of Altona, and that almost half a million households in Melbourne were then connected to natural gas.

Natural gas from the Dongara field in Western Australia is to be used to supply Perth and the big industrial centre of Kwinana. West Australian Petroleum, the firm which discovered the field about 250 miles N. of Perth, said in July that it intended to set up a company to build a pipeline which will cost about $A20 million and should be completed by the end of 1971. The Dongara field is believed to contain sufficient reserves for at least 15 years.

Russia. The international gas conference, meeting in Moscow in June 1970, was told by a Soviet minister that Russia's proven natural gas reserves are the largest in the world, prospecting having increased them by 50 per cent in two years, and that Russian fuel policy is being directed away from coal towards gas and oil. Natural gas already accounts for 20 per cent of total fuel consumption, and there are nearly 40,000 miles of gas pipelines in the Soviet Union. The chief reserves are in Western Siberia (about 57 per cent of the total) and under the Central Asian deserts

—both areas in which exploitation is difficult and both remote from areas that need the gas.

Russia has signed contracts to supply natural gas to Italy, France, and West Germany, chiefly in barter arrangements of gas in exchange for pipelines. Delivery of 100,000 million cu. metres of gas to the Austrian–Czech border, from which Italy has to build her own 230-mile pipe, is due to start in 1973. Russia already supplies gas to East Germany, Czechoslovakia, and other Iron Curtain countries, at a price over twice that ruling in Western Europe. Russian exports in 1970 totalled between 2 and 3 per cent of her total production.

Spain. A strike of high-quality natural gas was made by a Spanish rig off San Carlos de la Rapita in August. The strike was made about a mile from a smaller one made in 1969, and found at a depth of about a mile.

Nature Reserves. A major wildlife project 40 miles E. of Vienna and extending along the March river on Austria's border with Czechoslovakia was opened on June 1, 1970, by President Franz Jonas of Austria and Prince Bernhard of the Netherlands. The site includes some of the most beautiful river and forest landscape in central Europe, with woodlands, meadows, swamps, and ponds, containing a wide variety of both flora and fauna. Birds found there include cormorants, herons, egrets, cranes, curlews, warblers, black storks, and, nesting in trees, white storks.

Great Britain. Eleven nature reserves were created in Northumberland on June 25, 1970, when the head of the Forestry Commission in the north-east of England formally handed over agreements to the chairman of the Northumberland and Durham Naturalists' Trust. Of these additional reserves, which cover about 800 acres, three are in the Coquet valley, above Rothbury. The largest of them, above Harbottle village, consisting of over 350 acres, includes the Drake Stone, a huge sandstone boulder; a further 60 acres are in the valley of the Holystone burn, containing several rare plants; and the third reserve is Holystone North Wood, a 36-acre oak wood. The other eight reserves consist of unspoiled areas of sphagnum bog in the Roman Wall country in the west of the county.

On Oct. 1 a wildlife reserve of 33 acres of nightingale wood in the Mendip Hills was opened. The area, part of the several-hundred-acre Asham Wood, is semi-natural woodland believed to have been afforested in the 19th century. Wild daffodils, lily of the valley, Solomon's seal, meadow saffron, wild cherry ash, and whitebeam are all found here.

In November the Nature Conservancy declared that the Avon Gorge, Somerset is to be a national nature reserve. The Gorge, on the western side of Bristol, is famous for its fine carboniferous limestone cliffs which rise steeply for about 300 ft., as well as for its interesting plants and animals. The National Trust owns the western slopes on the Somerset side of the river above and below the Clifton suspension bridge, as well as a large part of Leigh Woods, the plateau overlooking the gorge. This property covers 156 acres, and under an arrangement made by the Trust to strengthen the conservation of this area it will now be managed by the Nature Conservancy. Leigh Woods consist chiefly of oak species with ash, wych elm, small-leaved lime, hornbeam, and two species of whitebeam which occur nowhere else in the world. There are also 110 different kinds of mosses and liverworts. An Iron Age hill fort, known as Stokeleigh Camp, lies in the centre of the reserve, and part of the drystone wall that surrounded its ramparts has been excavated. An extension of 12 acres of open woodland, scrub, and moorland, including a small reservoir, to the Yarner Wood reserve in Devon, and an extension of 487 acres of rocky heather-covered slopes to Rhinog national nature reserve in Merionethshire, were also announced in November.

The Central Electricity Generating Board announced on Nov. 24 that a 200-acre nature reserve is to be created in the West Midlands within a loop of the river Tame, on the site of Hams Hall power station, near Coleshill. The Board said that over 120 bird species, including many rarely seen in Great Britain, had already been observed on the site.

Northern Ireland. Eleven new reserves in Northern Ireland were declared by the minister of development at the beginning of September. There are relatively few woodlands remaining in Northern Ireland which display native tree species in their natural environments, and five of the new reserves contain the best of these. They are: Brean Forest, a 50-acre woodland in Glenshesk, North Antrim; Castle Archdale Forest, three islands in lower Lough Erne, displaying mature and regenerated woodland; Correl Glen Forest, mixed deciduous woodland on the uplands near Lough

Navar, co. Fermanagh; Marble Arch Forest, ashwood in a limestone gorge in co. Fermanagh; and Rostrevor Forest, a 40-acre oak wood in co. Down. The other reserves are Slieveanorra Forest, bog sites in co. Antrim; Killeter Forest, in co. Tyrone, which displays bog development; Lough Naman in co. Fermanagh, showing a western maritime bog type; Portrush, a two-acre stretch of rock on the foreshore, of geological interest; Randalstown Forest, containing valuable shoreline vegetation and the home of wildfowl and fallow deer; and Quoile Pondage, formerly a tidal estuary, now fresh water.

Nervous System. Prof. Geoffrey Burnstock, professor of zoology at Melbourne University, announced in December that he and his team had discovered in the human body a previously unknown nervous system which appears to be a third unit of what is called the autonomous nervous system regulating the stomach, lungs, and other organs. It had previously been thought that the autonomous system consisted of only two units—the sympathetic and para-sympathetic nerves. Prof. Burnstock said that the structure of the third unit had been traced, and the team believed that they had identified the chemical messenger which relays its impulses. The discovery has important implications both for understanding the nervous control of organs, and for greater effectiveness in the use of drugs in certain nervous diseases.

New York. On July 20 a hydrofoil, *Gateway Flyer*, made its inaugural run down the East River from 90th Street to Manhattan. This latest form of transport provided for New Yorkers travels at speeds of up to 35 m.p.h.; the fare is $3·75 for a single journey, or $110 for a monthly season ticket with a guaranteed seat.

A fourth daily newspaper, the *Daily Mirror*, began publication in New York on Dec. 7, 1970.

The discovery of the remains of a Dutch colonial stockade in Kingston, New York, by a team of archaeologists, was announced in July. It was acclaimed by experts as the oldest find of a European fortification in New York State. The discovery, which will help archaeologists to learn more about how the Dutch lived and defended themselves in the 17th century, consists of nine post holes which showed that the irregularly laid out posts of the stockade were about 8–10 in. in diameter.

Nhulunbuy, Northern Territory, Australia. Work on this new mining township on the Gove peninsula began early in 1970. The company developing the bauxite deposits here expects that the town will have a population of 4,000 by 1974. Three of Australia's largest construction companies won contracts worth $A35 million to build Nhulunbuy; they will erect over 500 houses and flats, a shopping centre, a community hall, a 64-bed hospital, a police station, and a primary school with 21 classrooms. It is expected that work will be completed by the end of 1972.

Nickel. Minutes after the official lifting in June of a 4-month-old ban on the pegging of Crown land, a great rush for claims was made in the nickel belt of Western Australia. Prospectors arrived on motor bikes, in cars, and in helicopters to stake their claims, while many of the large mining companies evaded the race by having their prospecting crews camp on their claims overnight. Security men, armed with shotguns, were employed to prevent claim-jumping. Particularly heavy prospecting was reported in the Laverton area, near the huge 1968 Poseidon strike at Mount Windarra, and in the Mount Clifford area, where it was reported that at least 1,500 prospectors were pegging claims, the first of them lodged less than 2½ hours after the ban was lifted.

New York. Trans World Airline's Flight Wing 1 at Kennedy airport (foreground) is the first terminal in the U.S.A. to be designed to handle the Boeing 747 jumbo jet. The complex in the background is Flight Wing 2.

The premier of Western Australia announced in September that Australia's biggest nickel-mining company, Western Mining Corporation, plans to establish a nickel smelter at Kalgoorlie at a cost of $A30 million. By-products of the smelter will include cobalt, copper, and platinum.

Nobel Prizes. The 1970 Nobel prizes were awarded as follows:

Peace: Dr. Norman Ernest Borlaug, a U.S. plant biologist, for his development of new types of wheat.

Chemistry: Prof. Luis Leloir, of Buenos Aires University, for work on carbohydrates.

Physics: shared by Prof. Louis Neel of Grenoble University for work on magnetohydrodynamics, and Prof. Hannes Alfven of Sweden for work on magnetism.

Medicine: shared by Prof. Sir Bernard Katz of the University of London, Prof. Ulf von Euler of the Karolinska Institute, Sweden, and Prof. Julius Axelrod of the National Institute of Health, Bethesda, Maryland, U.S.A., for their independent discoveries in the search for remedies for nervous and mental disturbances.

Literature: Alexander Solzhenitsyn (U.S.S.R.) for the "ethical force with which he has pursued the indispensable traditions of Russian literature".

The Nobel memorial prize for Economics, donated by the Bank of Sweden, was awarded to Prof. Paul Samuelson of the Massachusetts Institute of Technology for his development of scientific analysis in economic theory.

Noise Abatement. The design director of the U.K. Road Research Laboratory told a University of Surrey conference on urban environment on Sept. 17, 1970, that at present traffic noise causes discomfort to 46 per cent of urban British homes—a figure that will rise to 61 per cent by 1980 if the forecast increase in number of vehicles is realized. A reduction of 5 decibels would lower that 61 per cent to 30 per cent, and one of 10 decibels would reduce it to 10 per cent, but to attain the latter a major programme of research and development would have to be started now. Otherwise, sound insulation will have to be incorporated in the design of all buildings from 1975 onwards. The "official" definition of "comfort" in this connection is that people should be able to hold a conversation in rooms fronting a main road with the windows open.

The first supplies of pocket-size noise-measuring meters, specially miniaturized to a U.K. ministry of transport specification, were distributed to police and traffic wardens in September, from when cars and lorries were reported for noise infringements. Costing £10, the meters can also be bought by the public, who can use them for reporting their own noise nuisances, including aircraft noise. The meter is the smallest of its kind to be commercially produced.

The first report of the U.K. Noise Advisory Council, published in April 1970, declared that the 1960 Noise Abatement Act was inadequate to deal with present-day conditions, and in December the Council set up a working group to consider what measures are necessary to strengthen the law. The act, which applies to all sources of noise other than that made by aircraft, places responsibility for abatement upon local authorities. The Council found that, although many cases of industrial noise had been tackled, a large number of local authorities have been less active in this matter than is desirable.

Norwich, Norfolk. A commission into the use of the city's churches, set up in 1967 by the bishop of Norwich, published its report on Jan. 23, 1970. It suggested that 24 of the 30 medieval churches in the centre of Norwich could be closed and used as concert halls, public libraries, health centres, and clubs for old people, and, as a last resort, those churches that are not required and have little historical value should be demolished and the sites sold for development. It also suggested that the money spent on ancient churches with small congregations in the centre of the city should be used to strengthen the work of churches in new housing areas in the suburbs.

It was announced in October that gold and silver plate belonging to parish churches in Norfolk are to be housed and displayed in a treasury specially built in Norwich cathedral. This is the third cathedral treasury to be presented by the Goldsmiths' Company, the others being at Lincoln and Winchester.

Nottingham, University of. On Oct. 6, 1970, the first new medical school in Great Britain since 1893 was opened at Nottingham University. The new school will make it possible for the intake of students to be increased by stages to 160 a year, and possibly, later, to 192 a year. Equipment and buildings cost about £1,400,000.

Nova. In July 1970, a British schoolmaster and well-known amateur astronomer, George Alcock, was scanning the night sky through binoculars from a deck-chair in his back garden when he located a nova (exploding star) never seen before. The nova, several thousand light years away, was confirmed by experts in America and Japan, who used high-powered telescopes, and by the Royal Observatory.

Mr. Alcock's discovery, entered in the record book as Nova Scuti, is his third important sighting. In 1959 he discovered two comets in 6 days (both of them are named after him), and in 1967 he sighted Nova Delphinus.

Nobel Prizes. Portraits of all the winners of the Nobel prizes in 1970 are given here. Left: Dr. Norman Ernest Borlaug (Peace). Right: Alexander Solzhenitsyn (Literature). Below, left to right: Prof. Luis Leloir (Chemistry); Prof. Louis Neel (joint Physics); Prof. Sir Bernard Katz, Prof Ulf von Euler, and Prof. Julius Axelrod (joint Medicine); Prof. Paul Samuelson (Bank of Sweden Economics award); and Prof. Hannes Alfven (joint Physics). The photo below was taken at the presentation ceremony at Stockholm on December 10. Solzhenitsyn, the Russian author, declined to leave the U.S.S.R. Borlaug received his prize later in Oslo.

Oceanology. One of the many 5-person teams who spent 2 weeks 50 ft. below the surface of Lameshur Bay, St. John I., Virgin Is., in Tektite II (left) during 1970 was a group of women aquanauts (right), seen here in their living quarters.

Novello, Ivor. It was announced in October that a memorial plaque to this British actor and composer was to be placed in the crypt of St. Paul's Cathedral. The plaque will show the profile of the creator of *The Dancing Years, King's Rhapsody,* and many other musical comedies, plays, and songs, as well as his name and the dates of his birth and death. It will also be engraved with a four-line verse written by Mrs. Lyne Maury, who for some years has been campaigning for some posthumous honour for Ivor Novello. The plaque is to be unveiled on March 6, 1971, the twentieth anniversary of his death.

Nuthampstead, Herts. On Aug. 12, at the end of the Roskill Commission inquiry—the longest public inquiry ever held in Great Britain—into the site of the third London airport, it was stated that the airport would not be built here, the case against it being, in the view of W. A. Bagnall, Q.C., counsel for the Commission, "overwhelming".

Oceanology. On April 1, 1970, a seven-month U.S. programme of marine research carried out from an underwater habitat, Tektite II, began in waters adjacent to St. John Island in the Virgin Island group in the Caribbean Sea. Four American scientists and an engineer were lowered 50 ft. below the surface to begin a 14-day mission in Tektite II, which consists of two interconnected vertical cylinders 18·1 ft. high and 12·5 ft. in diameter mounted on

a ballasted base. There are two compartments in each cylinder. One cylinder has the crew quarters on the lower deck, and the bridge or control room on the upper deck. The second houses the engine room on its upper deck, and below it the "wet room" which, being open to the sea, gives divers easy access to and from the habitat. A 4·5-ft. diameter tunnel connects the two cylinders. During the programme a total of 17 missions were carried out, 10 of them at 50 ft. and 7 at 100 ft., and 62 scientist-aquanauts, engineers, and doctors took part in them. The project was a co-operative one, involving the U.S. government, private industry, and universities under the leadership of the department of the interior.

An experimental undersea vessel, the *Argyronète,* is to be built jointly by the French Petroleum Institute and the *Centre National pour l'Exploitation des Océans.* Details of this 91·87-ft.-long and 22·31-ft.-wide vessel were given in February 1970. Its normal diving depth is 1,000 ft., but it can go as deep as 2,000 ft. The forward part, comprising three-quarters of the submarine, will be of conventional design, with a crew of six men living under normal atmospheric pressure. There will be a water-tight chamber separated by a lock in the stern which can be put under the same pressure as the surrounding water. When the submarine settles on the ocean floor frogmen will be able to go out through a lower hatch, and when they return to the vessel will undergo decompression inside the chamber during the journey back to port. The upper deck will carry a releasable sphere which, in an emergency, could contain the entire crew and carry them up to the surface. The *Argyronète* will have a surface range of about 400 nautical miles and a cruising

speed of 6 knots, and will be able to remain submerged on the sea-bed for 3 days. The prototype will cost about 20 million francs, and will be ready to operate in 1972. Plans are being made for the construction of an initial series of four submarines of this type—one for the Mediterranean, another for the North Sea, a third for the Gulf of Mexico, and a fourth to be available wherever it is needed.

An undersea "marine home" in which four aquanauts can live for as long as 30 days at a depth of 328 ft. below the surface was completed for the first time in 1970. It was made in Japan at the Kobe shipyard and engine works of Mitsubishi Heavy Industries. The habitat, 36 ft. long, 15 ft. wide, and 21 ft. high, was built for the science and technology agency, which plans to use it for the development of Japan's continental shelf. The aquanauts will enter a decompression chamber installed on the mother ship on the ocean's surface before being transferred by underwater lift to the habitat anchored to the sea bed. The craft, which will have colour television in the living quarters, will be linked to the mother ship by wireless telephone, and will have circulated "artificial air", made up of a mixture of 87 per cent helium, 10 per cent nitrogen, and 3 per cent oxygen, installed with a special gas control to prevent air pollution. The aquanauts will not be allowed to drink liquor, smoke, or use any form of fire in the underwater dwelling.

Oil. *Discoveries.* The excitement of new oil discoveries shifted in 1970 from Alaska to the North Sea, where Phillips Petroleum announced on April 27 that it had made a significant strike in the Norwegian sector, 185 miles S.W. of the Norwegian

Oil. Historic photo of the buoy marking the drill-hole in the North Sea Ekofisk field.

coast and 200 miles E. of Aberdeen. A test well had produced up to 2,000 barrels a day of high-quality, low-sulphur-content oil. The site of the discovery was named the Ekofisk field, and more news of its importance was soon given. In May it was stated that the reserves in the area amount to about 1,000 million tons, and in June that production of 10,000 barrels a day of the highest-quality crude oil could be expected at first. It was confirmed in July that Ekofisk, about 6·3 miles by 3·5 miles in extent, is one of the largest off-shore oilfields in the world, and two more wells had by the end of August proved the immense extent of its reserves. Production from Ekofisk will begin in the spring of 1971, and at first the oil will be transported by tankers. Later, a pipeline, probably to the Scottish coast, will be laid. By that time, probably in 1973 or 1974, production will have reached 100,000 barrels a day.

Other exploration-licence holders with concessions adjoining the Ekofisk field accelerated their own drilling efforts, and it became apparent that the area forms a gigantic oilfield: the Amoco-Noco group reported in September an important strike 6 miles N.E. of Ekofisk, and named it Erg-fisk; Phillips announced two weeks later another substantial strike 25 miles W. of Ekofisk; and in October, Amoco Europe made a large strike 15 miles from Ekofisk. Later in October, B.P. found oil in the British sector of the North Sea about 110 miles E.N.E. of Aberdeen; a test well drilled to over 11,000 ft. was flowing at 4,700 barrels a day, and the crude was of the same high quality, with low sulphur content. On Dec. 1, Phillips announced another rich find, 5 miles W. of Ekofisk, with an estimated yield of 10,000 barrels a day.

Earlier, in May, a 2,000-barrels-a-day strike had been made in the Dutch sector of the North Sea about 115 miles N. of Amsterdam, and in July Esso had found oil in smaller quantities N.W. of Stavanger, Norway. Strikes in other parts of the world included a second discovery by B.P. in Alaska, 30 miles from Prudhoe Bay, in the Kuparuk river formation, announced on April 28; a 3,000-barrels-a-day test-well flow off the coast of Qatar in the Persian Gulf by AGIP in June; a major discovery off the coast of Ghana by Signal Oil and its associates in July; and a significant strike in the N.E. corner of South Australia, about 500 miles N. of Adelaide, by Bridge Oil in July.

Prospecting. The U.K. ministry of technology announced on June 8 that 30 new prospecting licences had been granted to 24 companies for oil and gas exploration in the North and Irish Seas, mostly in areas off Scotland. The new areas cover 8,000 sq. miles in 94 blocks. Only 11 of the 42 Irish Sea blocks offered by the government had been taken up by the oil industry. A Texas company, Pennzoil (U.K.), was given permission on Sept. 16 by the West Sussex county council to drill for oil at Ford airfield near Littlehampton, and at Middleton-on-Sea near Bognor. Some believe that a gigantic oil field underlies the English Channel, stretching inland on both sides. In July, it was stated that nearly 300 prospecting licences covering more than 50,000 sq. miles are current in New Zealand. In addition, in territorial waters to the 3-mile limit a further 25 licences cover about 130,000 sq. miles of New Zealand's continental shelf.

Consumption. Figures given by the Institute of Petroleum's information service in June 1970 showed that inland oil consumption in the U.K. (excluding bunker fuel deliveries for ships engaged in foreign trade) in 1969 reached the record figure of 89,342,950 tons, an increase of 7·9 per cent over the 82,828,586 tons consumed during 1968. Deliveries of gas oil, diesel oil (other than for road transport), and fuel oils accounted for 43,741,125 tons of the total, and were 10·4 per cent higher than in 1968. Motor spirit accounted for 13,231,476 tons of total consumption (3·3 per cent over the 12,807,521 tons used in 1968), while heavier commercial road transport usage of derv (diesel-engine road vehicle) fuel caused a rise of 4·7 per cent, deliveries totalling 4,791,201 tons. Demand for aviation fuels increased by 4·2 per cent to 3,298,009 tons, and there was a 9·8 per cent rise in requirements for naphtha, deliveries of which totalled 11,073·057 tons.

Information published by the Petroleum Information Bureau of Australia in 1970 showed that in 1968–69 consumption in Australia of all petroleum products totalled 6,032 million gallons, including 2,049 million gallons of petrol. A comparison of consumption with refinery production showed that in the same year, after deducting exports, Australian refineries met 93·3 per cent of the national demand, compared with 95·9 per cent in 1967–68.

The Bureau also stated that, throughout the world, consumption of petroleum products in 1968 increased by 8·9 per cent over the 1967 figure, considerably outstripping population growth; but there is no likelihood of a world shortage of oil, for while during 1968 producers took nearly 15,000 million barrels of oil from the earth, prospectors found sufficient crude oil deposits to enlarge the world's proved reserves by nearly three times that amount. At the beginning of 1969 world reserves stood at 457,000 million barrels, of which Middle East countries accounted for 60 per cent.

Refining. Work on a £16 million lubricating oil complex at B.P.'s Llandarcy refinery in South Wales began in the summer of 1970. It will replace existing units and raise output by 100,000 tons a year—about double the present output. The complex is due for completion early in 1972. Shell (U.K.) announced on Jan. 28, 1970, that the company plans to build a £20 million major process unit at its Shell Haven oil refinery, Essex. When completed in 1974, it will increase the refinery's processing capacity from 10 million tons a year to 13¼ million tons. But what is believed to be Great Britain's biggest single industrial investment project, a £225 million expansion programme at Carrington and Stanlow, Cheshire, was announced by the Shell group on Jan. 15, 1970. The programme will double the company's chemical production in Great Britain, boost oil-refining capacity, and produce a £40–£50 million a year balance of payments saving. £150 million is to be spent on chemicals expansion, £120 million of this sum at Carrington and £30 million at Stanlow. The remaining £75 million will be spent on expanding facilities at Stanlow, which will make the site into the largest oil refinery in the country. The new plants are due for completion by 1973, when they will produce an additional 1 million tons of chemical products each year, with a value of over £125 million.

Olympic Games. The central feature of the 1972 Olympic Games site, a former airfield 3 miles from Munich, W. Germany, will be a tree-planted hill, 200 ft. high and half a mile round, formed by bomb rubble from the city. A 20-storey skyscraper building, two apartment blocks of 12 and 14 storeys, and many houses to provide accommodation for the 12,000 athletes, coaches, trainers, managers, and 2,000 umpires, had already been built by early 1970. Another complex will house 4,000 newspaper and television reporters, and 2,000 technicians. The huge stadium will hold 80,000 spectators, none of whom will be further than 300 yds. from the events. By the time the athletes arrive on Aug. 26, 1972, a new tube line, a new suburban rail line, and two autobahns will have been constructed, and 5,000 fully grown lime trees planted to provide landscaping. The dining-room will hold 3,200 people, and television monitors are to be installed at the entrance to show where there are empty tables. In July it was

risen to 48,988,000 by the middle of 1970, an increase of 161,000 over 1969. The estimated populations of the regions were:

Region	Population 1970	Increase over 1969
North	3,360,000	14,000
Yorkshire and Humberside	4,812,000	1,000
North-west	6,789,000	19,000
East Midlands	3,363,000	14,000
West Midlands	5,178,000	33,000
East Anglia	1,673,000	16,000
South-West	3,764,000	33,000
Wales	2,734,000	9,000

In the South-east the population was 17,316,000, an increase of 21,000 on the 1969 figure. Greater London's population fell by 91,000 to 7,612,000, but that of the Outer Metropolitan area rose by 66,000 to 5,291,000 and of the remainder by 46,000 to 4,413,000.

The U.K. Registrar General's quarterly return, published in September 1970, stated that the population of England and Wales is expected to rise by only 9,700,000 between 1969 and 2001, which is 2,300,000 less than the expected total given in 1969. The decline is caused by revised assumptions about fertility, for the latest opinion was that the sharp difference between the number of children born to women marrying before they are 20 and to those in the 20–24 age group is levelling out.

Earlier figures, published by the U.K. Central Statistics Office in February 1970, showed that the population of Great Britain was estimated in June 1969 as 55,534,000, a quarter of a million more than in 1968. This growth was ''more than accounted for'' by increases in the numbers of people aged under 14 years and over 64 years, since the number in the 15–64 age group fell slightly. The figures showed that there were 28,550,000 females, compared with 26,984,000 males, but that the surplus females were in the 44-and-over age group.

Australia. According to figures given by the federal statistician in December, Australia's population at the end of June 1970 was 12,551,000, an increase of 255,000 since June 1969. Australia's most populous State, New South Wales, had 4,566,900, Victoria 3,443,900, Queensland 1,799,300, South Australia 1,164,700, Western Australia 979,700, Tasmania 392,500, Northern Territory 71,300, and Capital Territory 133,100. Official figures published in Canberra in March 1970 gave the population of Australia's capital cities, at June 1969, as Sydney 2,712,000, Melbourne 2,372,000, Brisbane 833,400, Adelaide 808,600, Perth 635,500, Hobart 147,800, Canberra 119,200, and Darwin 30,200.

New Zealand. Figures given in March 1970 showed that of New Zealand's total population at the end of 1969, 43 per cent were under the age of 21. The country's population total for the year ending March 31, 1970, was 2,820,814, an increase of 1·4 per cent over the 1969 total.

U.S.A. According to the 1970 decennial census the total population of the U.S.A. is now 204,765,770, including some 1,500,000 Americans overseas as soldiers, federal employees, and their families. The resident population showed an increase of 13·3 per cent over the 1960 total. Of all the regions the South enjoyed the greatest growth, its population increasing by 8 million to nearly 63 million. Next was the West, with California the most populous single state, increasing by over 4 million to nearly 20 million. The fastest growing state, proportionately, was Arizona. The preliminary figures for the twelve largest cities were as follows:

City	1970 Census (in thousands)	1960 Census (in thousands)	Percentage Change
New York	7,772	7,782	− 0·1
Chicago	3,325	3,550	− 6·3
Los Angeles	2,782	2,479	+ 12·2
Philadelphia	1,927	2,003	− 3·8
Detroit	1,493	1,670	− 10·6
Houston	1,213	938	+ 29·3
Baltimore	895	939	− 4·7
Dallas	836	680	+ 22·9
Washington	746	764	− 2·4
Indianapolis	743	476	+ 56·1
Cleveland	739	876	− 15·6
Milwaukee	710	741	+ 4·2

Soviet Union. Preliminary returns published in April 1970 of a census held in January 1970 showed that the U.S.S.R. then had a population of 241,748,000, nearly 33 million more than the 1959 census total. During the 11 years between the censuses there were 51,500,000 births, and 18,600,000 deaths. The 1970 returns showed that there were 130,400,000 men and 111,300,000 women; that 56 per cent of the population lived in towns, compared with 48 per cent in 1959; and that the population of Moscow had risen by 17 per cent since 1959 to a total of 7,061,000. Ten cities —Moscow, Leningrad, Kiev, Tashkent, Baku, Kharkov, Gorky, Novosibirsk, Kuibyshev, and Sverdlovsk—now have a population of over a million, and 33 cities have a population of over half a million. The figures showed considerable movement of populations: Kazakhstan, in Central Asia, for example, showed a natural growth of 8,600,000 and an influx of 1,200,000 from other Soviet republics.

Porcelain. At Sotheby's auction rooms, London, on July 7, 1970, a Meissen service, of 62 pieces, sold in 43 lots, fetched £68,250, the highest price ever paid for a porcelain service. The top price for an individual piece was £4,200 for a painted bowl of 1740, the only dated piece in the service.

Portsmouth, Hants. A revised plan for the reshaping and rebuilding of the city's centre, prepared by Viscount Esher, was presented to the city council on July 16. The 7-year building programme, estimated to cost £25 million (including £14 million for public buildings), includes civic, cultural, and educational buildings, offices for

letting, and a students' hostel. The plan diverts town traffic round a new circuit feeding three car parks which are connected to a pedestrian network, and makes Commercial Road, formerly a through traffic route, into a pedestrian precinct. There will also be a new Guildhall Square and Station Square, and a small Theatre Square. A curved pedestrian mall will lead to an art gallery and museum related to the existing law courts and college of art, and large extensions are planned for the polytechnic college.

Port Talbot, Glamorgan. On May 12, 1970, the Queen inaugurated the £20 million British Transport Docks Board tidal harbour at Port Talbot. Linked with the £18 million basic oxygen steel-making plant of the British Steel Corporation, the harbour is believed to be the most modern ore-importing and steel-making development in the world. At the ceremony, the Queen unveiled a sundial calibrated to give the time in Port Talbot and in six other major seaports in different parts of the world.

Pozzuoli, Italy. This city, 6 miles W. of Naples, and near Mount Vesuvius, was reported in March 1970 to have risen at least 28 inches since the autumn of 1969, suffering damage estimated at $1\frac{1}{2}$ billion lire. Early in March, tremors, said to have been so slight that 70,000 residents did not even feel them, caused further damage. Nevertheless, 10,000 of the city's inhabitants were reported to have fled when the first tremors occurred. The authorities decided to serve evacuation orders on families living in an 11th-century Spanish castle in the centre of old Pozzuoli, and also to evacuate part of a slum area. On receiving the orders hundreds of slum-dwellers demonstrated outside the city hall. As the city rose, the water level in the harbour fell, and the port authority had to undertake dredging operations to clear the harbour mouth for ferries which link the city with islands in the Bay of Naples. The type of earth movement which is affecting Pozzuoli is called ''Bradyseism'' or ''slow earthquake''. The town is no stranger to volcanic convulsions. It frequently suffered from them during the Middle Ages, particularly in 1198 and 1538.

Presbyterian Church (Australia). On Sept. 10 the general assembly of the Presbyterian Church of Australia adopted a national constitution which gave the Church power to unite with other Australian denominations and approved the establishment of a board of ecumenical missions and relations which will represent the assembly in ecumenical negotiations. The principle that women might be ordained as ministers was accepted. The number of candidates for the ministry had fallen from 263 to 157 since 1967, and a reduction of about 2 years in the course of training for candidates over the age of 30 who had previous experience working in the church was recommended.

Prices and Incomes Board. The new Conservative government of the U.K. announced on Nov. 2, 1970, that the National Prices and Incomes Board, set up in 1965, is to be wound up in the spring of 1971, and replaced by three new review bodies. The latter will advise the government on the pay of people in public service who have no negotiating machinery of their own, viz. chairmen and board members of the nationalized industries, the judiciary, senior civil servants, senior officers of the armed forces and ''such other groups as might be appropriately considered with them'', the armed forces generally, and doctors and dentists. The new bodies will be serviced by an Office of Manpower Economics (OME), which will not be part of the government machine and will make independent reports. The Prices and Incomes Board was set up to carry into practice the agreement of the employers' organizations and the T.U.C. to co-operate with the government in reviewing the general movement of prices and incomes, and in deciding whether particular rises were in the national interest. After operating for the first 6 months on a voluntary basis, the Board was given statutory powers to collect information and call witnesses. In August 1966, the Board's powers were again increased when an act was passed compelling all U.K. trade unions and employers to refer proposed increases in prices or pay, or pay claims, to it.

Prince of Wales Countryside Award. Prince Charles announced the introduction of this award in Cardiff on Feb. 19, 1970, when, as chairman of Countryside in 1970 Committee for Wales, he was launching European Conservation Year in the principality. The award, which consists of a plaque decorated with a green and white crest, and described by the Prince as being ''vandal-proof'', will go to statutory and voluntary organizations which have made a distinctive contribution towards improving the general quality and beauty of the Welsh environment during 1970.

Prints. The results of the 1969 annual survey of the best-selling colour reproduction of the year in the U.K., conducted by the Fine Art Trade Guild, were announced on Feb. 4, 1970. The first place in the popularity poll of *new* reproductions went to *Burnished Gold*, a painting of boats at anchor under a sunset, by Victor E. Elford. W. F. Burton's *Oyster Beds* came second, and third was *Spring Fields* by R. N. Folland. Of the top ten new reproductions, six were seascapes. The survey also listed the first five pre-1969 reproductions in order of popularity: they were *The Hay Wain* by Constable, *Blue Waterfall* by A. Palmero, *Sunny Cove* by Ellenshaw, *The Great Race from China to London* by H. Scott, and *Flatford Mill* by Constable.

Prisons. On March 31, 1970, the director-general of the U.K. prison service announced plans for a £15 million refurbishing and building programme for the country's jails, phased over the next 20 years. The work will be done by the prisoners themselves. At Lewes prison, Sussex, prisoners completely rebuilt a wing destroyed by fire in August 1968. The work, which included knocking down the old structure, complete redecoration, and modernizing cell furnishings, cost £30,000 instead of the estimated £75,000 that outside contractors would have charged. Much of the equipment, including the furnishings, was made by prisoners in workshops at various prisons. This work at Lewes is an example of what it is planned to carry out during the major programme. The men selected to take part in the scheme will come from the middle- and long-term prisoners. They will be taught building and decorating, and then transported to new sites to build cells and essential amenities. This work completed, they will become inmates of the new prison, and continue other building operations. Eighty-five of Great Britain's 120 prisons will receive the ''do-it-yourself'' treatment. At present, the prison service has the greatest number of obsolete buildings of any service; of the daily prison population of 37,000, 25,000 are accommodated in mainly outdated 19th-century prisons, 5,000 in hutted camps, and only 7,000 in up-to-date premises. On Aug. 24 the director-general saw another example of self-help when he opened a centrally heated three-storey cell block at Ashwell jail, Rutland, built in 2 years by the prisoners. They received double their normal weekly wages for the work, which included bricklaying, painting, tiling, plumbing, glazing, and concrete and electrical work, and saved £22,500, including wages and materials. The block will house an extra 100 men, each in a separate room.

Because of severe overcrowding of prisoners in England and Wales—the total reached the record number of 40,265 at the end of November 1970—the new Long Lartin prison, near Evesham, Worcs, is to be opened earlier than was planned. Early in 1971 it will take up to 320 low-escape category prisoners in the last months of their sentence. The £3½ million prison is due for completion in 1972, and then will take prisoners who have a high escape risk or are dangerous to the community. The main cell-locking system will be electronically controlled from a central point, which will add to security and ease the duties of the prison staff. Each prisoner will have a key to his centrally heated cell, allowing him some privacy, and he will also be paid for his work in cash, instead of by credit. Average earnings will start at about 70p a week, but some men will be able to earn up to £1·50.

The U.K. Home Office announced on Sept. 30 that Holloway, the largest women's prison in the country, opened in 1852, is to be rebuilt on its present site at an estimated cost of £5–6 million. It will be the first urban prison site to be developed while remaining operational. The building, which started in December 1970, will take over 7 years. Holloway will then be essentially a hospital rather than a house of correction. It is proposed to increase the number of doctors and nursing staff, and to find better ways of restraining difficult prisoners, women being more prone to violence than men when in prison. The basis will be units of 14–16 prisoners, who will be encouraged to discuss their problems with each other and with a group psychiatrist. It is also intended to concentrate on vocational training, with as much skilled work as possible. Each prisoner will have a key to her own bed-sitting-room, and there will be no bars on windows. In Great Britain, there are about 1,000 women and girls in custody compared with 39,000 men and boys. Holloway's population in 1970 numbered between 350 and 400; the new prison will accommodate up to 500.

A report by the U.K. advisory council on the penal system, published on Feb. 12, 1970, recommended a wide-ranging review of all existing methods of treating young offenders aged 17 and over. An end to close-crop haircuts in detention centres was among the recommendations. The report also said that there was a strong case for providing television and radio as an educational source, as well as newspapers and the time to read them.

Scotland. Figures given in the Scottish home and health department's report on prisons in Scotland in 1969, published in December 1970, showed there were a record number of people in prison, and a record number of daily admissions during the year. A total of 19,620 men, women, and young people were admitted, about two thirds of them for sentences of 6 months or less, and half of these for non-payment of fines. The average prison population was 4,834, an increase of almost 7 per cent over 1968, and provisional figures for 1970 showed a further increase, to 5,200.

Australia. On March 17, 1970, the Queensland parliament introduced legislation which, for the first time in Australia, allows a court, at its discretion, to order a short sentence to be served over a series of week-ends rather than continuously. Such sentences are intended mainly for offenders who have a steady employment record and, if married, a stable family life, and whose offences are not too serious. Prison administrators are concerned by the large number of people given short prison sentences, which cause loss of employment and victimization of wives and children; these problems will be overcome by serving a series of weekends, the maximum number of which is 26. A prisoner sentenced to this form of detention reports voluntarily to jail after midday on Friday, and serves from 40 to 48 hours. On June 16, the N.S.W. State cabinet authorized similar legislation under which an offender could be gaoled from 7 p.m. on Friday to 4.30 p.m. on Sunday. Such a sentence is imposed only where the offence is punishable by imprisonment, and where the offender is male, aged at least 18, and has not served a previous prison sentence other than by default. The sentence can be from 3 to 12 months. The scheme will probably be in operation by the beginning of 1971.

Prostoglandins. A symposium of scientists from all over the world discussed in New York in September 1970 the possible uses of the chemical compounds known as prostoglandins. The compounds, numbering 14 in all, are produced in many glands and tissues of the human body, in which their main effect seems to be contraction of the uterus. Discovered and named in the 1930s, they were not seriously examined until 1956 and experimental work with them did not begin until 1964. As well as causing uterine contraction (which could bring about abortion and thus substitute for contraception), the prostoglandins are said to be able to lower blood pressure by dilatation of blood vessels, prevent thrombosis by arresting blood-clotting, and even decongest catarrh-blocked nostrils. As yet insufficient evidence exists regarding their side-effects and they have not been synthesized, but intensive research by U.S. drug houses is expected to produce a usable version of the substances in the form of a pill or powder within perhaps 5 years.

Protein. Details of the discovery of a cheap source of high-value protein obtainable from carbohydrates were given in May 1970. Small quantities of the substance had been prepared at the Rank-Hovis-McDougall research laboratory at High Wycombe, Bucks, where during the previous 4 years £1 million was spent on developing it. The process involves the continuous culture of a yeast-like microorganism obtained from carbohydrate-rich crops such as cassava, potatoes, sugar, and yams. The end product is a creamy white powder with no marked flavour, which has a biological value roughly twice that of beef. The National Research Development Corporation agreed to contribute £500,000 over a 3-year period towards the construction of a large-scale pilot plant for producing the substance at the rate of a quarter to half a ton per week. As only 3 oz. are required each day by a working adult, the powder should prove a valuable inexpensive addition to world food supplies.

A whole-milk biscuit which took the New Zealand dairy board almost 5 years to develop is to be made available to the protein-short countries in the world's developing regions. The biscuit, a small rectangular slab with a 24 per cent protein content, is fortified with minerals and vitamins, and contains the equivalent of almost 6 oz. of whole milk. Two biscuits would provide about 36 per cent of the recommended daily protein intake of young children, 50 per cent of the daily requirement of the main vitamins except for vitamin C, and some 12 per cent of the necessary calorie intake. Trials of the biscuit, which is made in six flavours, have been carried out in 12 countries, and in all cases have resulted in increased weight

and height. In Western Samoa, medical authorities conducted a 13-week trial with about 90 children and reported that the children gained an average of 1·2 lb. and that the skin infection from which almost half the children suffered at the start of the trial decreased to 18 per cent. When details of the biscuit were given in November it was stated that while New Zealand was willing to share the manufacturing methods with a potential manufacturer without any charge, it would not allow any commercial use of the product, which was essentially devised as a medium of aid.

The invention of a "protein sequinator" was announced in July. This is a machine which determines the structure of proteins 200 times faster than previous methods. Invented by Dr. Pehr Edman of the St. Vincent's school of medical research, Melbourne, Australia, with the help of a research technician, Geoffrey Begg, the sequinator determines protein structure by analysing the sequence of amino acids from which proteins are made. The scientists expect that it will enable them to determine within 20 years the structure of all known proteins, a task which using older methods would take about 2,000 years. Dr. Edman has offered blueprints of the machine, free of profit, to scientists all over the world.

Public Schools Commission. This British government-appointed body, which began work in March 1966, published its second report, made under the chairmanship of Prof. David Donnison, in March 1970. It proposed that direct-grant schools (those which receive a direct grant from central government for providing places for local authorities in fee-paying grammar schools) should either become comprehensive, or become independent without state aid, or close. In England and Wales in January 1968, the 178 direct-grant schools, which include such famous names as Haberdashers' Aske's, Manchester Grammar School, Leeds Grammar, and Bristol Grammar, had 101,236 pupils, 60 per cent of whom were paid for by local authorities, and 37 per cent fully or partly by their parents. There were 29 broadly comparable grant-aided schools in Scotland. The report created the expected furore, and several of the best-known schools stated that they would close rather than go comprehensive. But on the return of the Conservatives in the general election in July the whole question of comprehensive schools was thrown again into the melting-pot, and it was clear that the direct-grant schools would be reprieved.

Pulitzer Prizes. The 1970 Pulitzer prizes, announced on May 4, 1970, included the following:

Drama—Charles Gordone for *No Price to Be Somebody.*
Music—Charles Wuorinen for a musical composition composed on an electronic synthesizer.
Editorial writing—Philip L. Geyelin, of the *Washington Post.*
History—Dean G. Acheson for *Present*

at the Creation: My Years in the State Department.
Fiction—Jean Stafford for *Collected Stories.*
Biography—T. Harry Williams for *Huey Long.*
Poetry—Richard Howard for *Untitled Subjects.*
General non-fiction—Erik T. Erikson for *Gandhi's Truth.*
The journalism prizes included:
International reporting—Seymour Hersh for report on alleged My Lai massacre.
Local reporting, general—Thomas Fitzpatrick of the *Chicago Sun-Times.*
Local reporting, special—Harold Eugene Martin of the Montgomery (Ala.) *Advertiser.*
National reporting—William J. Eaton of the Chicago *Daily News.*
Cartoons—Thomas F. Darcy of *Newsday.*
Spot news photography—Steve Starr of the Albany bureau of the Associated Press.
Feature photography—Dallas Kinney of the Palm Beach (Fla.) *Post.*

A new category for criticism or commentary was set up in 1970, and Ada Louise Huxtable, architecture critic of the *New York Times,* became the winner of the first Pulitzer prize for distinguished criticism, and Marquis W. Childs of the *St. Louis Post-Dispatch* won the award for distinguished commentary. The gold medal, given for meritorious public service, went to *Newsday.*

Pulsars. A new theory to account for these mysterious heavenly objects which emit regular radio pulses was put forward by three astronomers at Princeton University, U.S.A., in June 1970. They agree that pulsars are probably concentrations of matter remaining as debris after a star explosion, but suggest that when the explosion takes place a pulsar is propelled away from the site at a speed of several hundred miles per second. In this theory, a pulsar is one of a pair of stars circling each other and held together by mutual gravitational pull; when one of the pair explodes, the other, no longer held by gravitation, flies off into space. The theory helps to explain the strange spread of pulsars through space, and also the fact that the oldest pulsars (those with the slowest rate of pulses) are the farthest from the chief star concentrations in the galaxy. See also p. 41.

Queen Elizabeth. On June 25, 1970, it was announced that, as the American firm which bought the ex-Cunard liner *Queen Elizabeth* and towed her to Fort Lauderdale, Florida, for use as a tourist attraction had gone bankrupt, the famous liner was again up for sale. In October, a bid of £1,333,000 at an auction at Fort Lauderdale made Mr. C. Y. Tung, Chinese shipping magnate of Formosa and Hong Kong, the new owner of the liner. Mr. Tung said that he would spend up to £2 million on re-fitting the vessel as a cruise ship, and that he hoped later on to turn her into a floating university. On October 11, it was announced that Commodore Geoffrey Marr, her former master, was to interrupt his retirement to take charge of the vessel once more on the trip from Florida, where she has lain idle for two years, to Hong Kong—a 10,000-mile voyage taking 6 weeks via Curaçao, Cape Town, Ceylon, and Singapore.

Further details of Mr. Tung's plans for the liner were given in December, when it was stated that negotiations for turning the ship into a combination cruise ship and floating university (to be called "Seawise University") had been completed with Chapman College, a private co-educational school with 1,300 pupils, 35 miles S.E. of Los Angeles, California, U.S.A. The college will be responsible for the new university pupils' studies, and it is thought that eventually the *Queen Elizabeth* will carry as many as 1,800 students on round-the-world trips. A spokesman for Chapman College said that it is hoped to get the project under way by September 1971, with a group of 400–600 undergraduates, who will sail from Los Angeles. Tuition fees will be £468, and the fare will range from £1,020 to £1,187. There will be about 30 teachers, and over 80 courses will be offered.

Queen Mary. Work on the former Cunard liner progressed during 1970 at Long Beach, California, U.S.A., where the *Queen Mary* is being converted into a floating museum and convention centre. It was announced in March that cost had increased from the first estimate of £2 million to at least £13,300,000.

Queen's Award to Industry. The fifth annual list of companies that have won these awards for achievement in the export field, or for technological innovation, or for both, was published in April 1970. From the 1,200 entrants, 104 received awards, 74 of them for exports and 25 for technology. Five companies—Courtaulds, Dunlop, Elliot Flight Automation, Hawker Siddeley Aviation, and Imperial Chemical Industries—gained recognition for their successes in both fields. Forty-seven of the winners had won awards in previous years; nine of them in two earlier years; six in three; and two—I.C.I. and Rolls-Royce—in all four. I.C.I. is the only company to have won awards each year for both exports and technology. Those who received the award for export achievement covered a wide field, ranging from light aircraft (Britten-Norman) to toys (Lesney Products); caravans (Astral Caravan) to china (Doulton Fine China); whisky (John Dewar and, for the third time, John Walker) to machine tools (Norton Machine); Irish tweeds (Walker Caledon) to fibre-glass boats (Westerly Marine Construction). One of the youngest firms to win the award for export achievement was Henley Forklift, for their mechanical handling equipment; this company was started by two young men in a Coventry garage in 1966, and by 1970 employed 120 people. Among the award winners for techno-

logical innovation were British Ropes (steel ropes), Pilkington Brothers (production of tinted glass), British European Airways (automatic landing of aircraft), and W. E. Sykes (gear-cutting machinery). A new company, Hudswell Yates Developments, with only 22 employees and 4 years in business, also received this award for its fully automatic pipe-laying system.

As recommended in the report of a special committee under Lord McFadzean, published on May 29, 1970, the award is to be extended to include "invisible" exporters. The committee, set up in December 1969 to review the working of the award, made 24 recommendations, all of which were accepted by the government. As a result, the number of companies winning awards is expected to rise by 25 per cent. The "invisible" exporters will include companies earning foreign currency by services (banking, insurance, contracting, brokerage), transport, tourism, and the professions. Non-manufacturing merchants who are engaged solely in exporting are now eligible, but component manufacturers who are only "indirect" exporters and the mere holders of portfolio investments overseas will not be eligible.

Queen's Fellowships. The establishment, to commemorate the 1970 royal tour of Australia, of five international fellowships to be awarded annually for study in the field of marine science at the Australian institute of marine science, Townsville, the James Cook University of North Queensland, or any other approved university or research establishment, was announced by John Gorton, the Australian prime minister, on May 3, 1970.

r

Rabies. The U.K. ministry of agriculture reported on March 1, 1970, that a 3-year-old black mongrel bitch, imported from Pakistan on May 30, 1969, and released from quarantine kennels at Purleigh, near Maldon, Essex, on Nov. 30, 1969, had died of rabies at Newmarket on Feb. 27, 1970, 2 days after falling ill. Another dog belonging to the same owner and imported at the same time, although pronounced "perfectly healthy", was destroyed. The two animals, which were both at the same quarantine kennels, had been released a month before the government extended the quarantine period from 6 to 8 months following the rabies outbreak at Camberley, Surrey, in October 1969. As a result of these cases, from March 12 the importing of dogs and cats into Britain was prohibited, and the period of quarantine for animals already in the country was extended from 8 to 12 months. The ban applied to all canine and feline animals, including pets owned by servicemen now abroad; those taken abroad by people on holiday; and animals imported by zoos. Animals from Northern Ireland, Eire, and

the Isle of Man were not subject to the ban. A committee of inquiry was set up to examine the country's policy on rabies and, until it had given its report, the minister said, the ban and extended quarantine would remain in force. On March 6, Australian health authorities extended for an indefinite period the ban, introduced in October 1969, on imports of cats and dogs from the U.K. and Ireland.

On July 14, 1970, the ministry lifted the restrictions imposed on dogs in the Camberley area of Surrey after the October 1969 case of rabies. They were allowed out without leads or muzzles 3 months earlier than had been expected, the danger of their developing the disease after 9 months being regarded as minimal. But owners whose dogs might have had contact with the dog that died of rabies, were asked to keep a close watch on their pets, and a ministry veterinary surgeon paid a monthly visit to all dogs until the 12-month period had elapsed.

The committee of inquiry published an interim report on Aug. 17. It recommended that the ban on dog and cat imports should be lifted, and that dogs and cats which had been in quarantine for 9 months or more should be released. The remainder should be vaccinated to build up immunity before imports were resumed, and then released as soon as they had completed 9 months' quarantine. It proposed that any new outbreak in quarantine kennels should be followed by an increase in the quarantine period for other animals there, and that during this period no other animals should be admitted, and those released in the previous 2 weeks should be recalled. The committee did not recommend removing the ban on other susceptible animals, including zoo animals. The minister of agriculture accepted the recommendations, and the importation of cats and dogs was allowed again from Sept. 16.

Race Relations. According to figures issued by the U.K. department of employment and productivity on Feb. 26, 1970, about 40 cases of racial discrimination in British industry were revealed during the first year of operation of the Race Relations Act. Of a total of 819 complaints received by the department, 186 were referred to the appropriate industry conciliation machinery, and the rest were passed on to the Race Relations Board. Only 5 per cent of the complaints were upheld. Over half the complaints came from Greater London and the home counties, and a quarter from the Midlands. Most complaints were made against employers, although 14 were directed at trade unions for allegedly not giving immigrant workers as much support as other trade union members. It was found that the great majority of coloured workers who complained of discrimination had been refused jobs or dismissed for reasons other than the colour of their skin.

On the second anniversary of the U.K. Race Relations Act on Nov. 26, 1970, its provisions were extended to cover employers of not more than 10 workers, instead of the previous 25. Small boarding houses and lodging houses were also brought within its scope. Previously they had been judged "small premises" if there was not normally accommodation for more than 12 persons other than the landlord's household; from Nov. 1970 this number was reduced to 6.

Radio Telescopes. A new radio telescope went into operation at Ootacamund, southern India, in April 1970, and within 14 days had detected five new radio sources in the heavens. Built under the direction of the Tata institute of fundamental research, Bombay, the cylindrical telescope, which is located on a slope, is constructed on 24 equidistant steel towers spanning a horizontal distance of 1,712 ft. The two ends of each of its parabolic frames are 97 ft. apart, and over a thousand 1,712-ft.-long parallel stainless steel wires make up the radio reflecting surface. The entire surface can be rotated as a unit through an angle of 140 degrees with electrical and mechanical equipment designed and made in India. The telescope was reported to have a sensitivity about four times that of the 250-ft. dish at Jodrell Bank.

Ramaciotti Foundation. In Sydney, Australia, on Aug. 13, 1970, Vera Ramaciotti signed the deed establishing the Clive and Vera Ramaciotti Foundation for medical research and charities. When she sold the Theatre Royal site in Sydney for $A7½ million on Sept. 25, 1969, she decided to give $A6 million of it to be used in this way. The foundation is divided into two portions—$A4 million to be confined to objectives in N.S.W., and $A2 million for similar objectives over the whole country.

Raphael. Officials of the National Gallery, London, disclosed on July 14, 1970, that the Gallery's three-quarter length portrait by Raphael of Pope Julius II, previously thought to be a copy of an identical painting in the Uffizi gallery in Florence, was, in fact, the original. X-ray examination of the 450-year-old panel and subsequent cleaning had not only revealed the number

Ramaciotti Foundation. Miss Vera Ramaciotti, founder of this $A6 million foundation.

Raphael. Portrait of Pope Julius II discovered in 1970 to be a genuine Raphael.

118 at the bottom left-hand corner (a number which corresponds with the number of the picture in an inventory taken in 1693) but also alterations which Raphael made while work on the painting was in progress. Art experts estimated that the painting is now worth between £1 million and £5 million.

Rats. A 4-year attempt to cordon off the area in Montgomeryshire and Shropshire where the rats have become resistant to the poison Warfarin was abandoned by the U.K. ministry of agriculture in September 1970, and immediate fears were expressed that the rats would invade near-by towns and cities in the Midlands. The rats carry the organism of a form of jaundice called Weil's disease. Attempts to discover a new rat poison, which would not harm pets or farm animals, had involved the investigation of 75 different chemical compounds, but only three of these showed promise of being effective against the "super-rats".

Regiments, British. The U.K. government announced on Aug. 6 that it planned to create "mini-regiments", comprising 120 officers and men, of the regiments due to be phased out by March 1972. The most famous regiment to be thus saved was the first battalion of the Argyll and Sutherland Highlanders, due to be disbanded on Nov. 30, 1970. The Gloucestershire Regiment and the Royal Hampshire Regiment were due to amalgamate on Sept. 5, 1970; the new plan allows the Hampshires to become a "mini-regiment", while the Gloucesters remain at full strength. The 4th Battalion, the Royal Anglican Regiment (the Queen's Division) was reduced to company strength on Sept. 30, 1970, and 4th Battalion, the Queen's Regiment (the Queen's Division) to company strength on Dec. 31, 1970. The Royal Scots Greys (2nd Dragoons) and the 3rd Carabiniers (Prince of Wales's Dragoon Guards), decided to amalgamate in the

second half of 1971 under the name of Royal Scots Dragoon Guards. The 14th Light Regiment of the Royal Artillery is to go into "suspended animation" by July 31, 1971. One field squadron and two field support squadrons of the Royal Engineers will be reduced to squadron strength on March 31, 1972; 2nd Battalion, Scots Guards (the Guards Division) to company strength on March 31, 1971; and 3rd Battalion, the Royal Green Jackets (the Light Division) to company strength (March 31, 1972). All these regiments will form the nucleus of new regiments if Great Britain ever needs to increase her army.

River Pollution. In December, Pres. Nixon ordered the setting up of a federal system to control the dumping of industrial waste and effluents into U.S. rivers and streams. By July 1971 all industrial plants must obtain government permission to allow pollutants to escape into rivers. They will first have to submit details of their waste, and a permit will be granted if the waste is not considered harmful. Firms polluting rivers without a permit will be fined $2,500 (£1,042) per day during the continuance of the pollution, and those misrepresenting the nature of their waste in order to obtain a permit will be fined up to $10,000 and the signatory of the false application will face a prison sentence.

Roads. In W. Germany plastic foam is replacing the gravel traditionally used under motorways for loadbearing and frost insulation. The use of a rigid polymethane foam, which is sprayed at a rate of 100 sq. ft. a minute and hardens into a 1¼-in. layer ready for the application of the top course of the road, has led to a considerable saving in costs. About 2,000 lorry-loads of gravel are normally required to lay a 2-ft.-deep bed under each mile of road; the 38½ tons of plastic needed for the same length of road can be taken to the site by five road tankers.

Road Safety. *Regulations.* Under regulations laid before the U.K. parliament on Jan. 27, 1970, all new vehicles will have from 1973 to be fitted with "dual intensity" stop lamps and rear indicators, which give a brighter light in day time and reduce dazzle at night. The regulations also make the fitting of stop lamps and direction indicators obligatory from Jan. 1, 1971; from this date, amber-coloured stop lamps will be illegal on all vehicles, but semaphore arms, and flashing lights that are white at the front and red at the rear, will be allowed on all pre-1965 vehicles.

Draft regulations requiring heavy motor vehicles to carry new rear markings to make them more conspicuous at night and in poor daylight were outlined by the U.K. ministry of transport on March 24, 1970. Vehicles or combinations 13 metres (42 ft.) or less in length will have to be fitted with a plate or plates, of alternate red fluorescent and yellow reflective material, while those over that length will have to bear a plate or plates with the words "Long Vehicle" in black lettering on a yellow reflective background with a red fluorescent border. The plates must be fitted by April 1, 1971.

More draft regulations—circulated on April 7, 1970—proposed that zigzag road markings indicating safety zones on each side of zebra crossings should replace the existing approach studs. The new markings would make the crossing more visible to approaching drivers and indicate the area in which vehicles must not halt, park, or wait and in which, on the approach side of the crossing, overtaking is prohibited. They would also indicate to pedestrians the area in which they should not cross the road other than on the crossing itself, for studies had shown that it was three times more dangerous to cross the road within 20 yds. of a crossing than on the crossing.

New limits on hours of driving and duty came into force in the U.K. on March 15, 1970, for drivers of public service vehicles. From that date, drivers were forbidden to do more than $5\frac{1}{2}$ hours continuous duty without a break, and no more than 11 hours in any one day. A limit of 72 hours' duty a week, subject to a limit of 132 hours a fortnight, was also laid down.

Heavy Vehicles. A report prepared by the road research laboratory for the U.K. ministry of transport, based on an analysis of 275 fatal accidents to people in cars and light vans investigated by coroners in England and Wales, was published in May 1970. It found that heavy lorries were ten times more likely to be involved in the death of a motorist than vehicles such as cars and light vans. In the 275 accidents examined, heavy lorries were involved in 147. Motorists who crash into a lorry are likely to receive more than one injury severe enough to cause death. The report said that, while little could be done to protect car occupants in head-on collision with a lorry, a great deal could be done to reduce the number of deaths caused by cars running into the backs of lorries. It recommended that the rears of lorries should be modified to stop "under-running" accidents; that lorries be made more conspicuous with more powerful rear lights and brighter colours that must be kept clean; and that drop tailboards must not be permitted to obscure rear lights. The report said that about 400,000 heavy lorries could be modified at a cost of only about £50 each.

Devices. A February 1970 report by the U.K. road research laboratory suggested that car windscreen surrounds should be recessed in order to reduce the risk of head injuries caused by glass fragments left embedded in the surround after a crash. Investigations showed that of 418 occupants of cars with toughened glass windscreens detained in hospital with head injuries, 15 per cent of injuries were caused by the windscreen, and nearly half of these by the head impacting on fragments of glass retained in the windscreen surround. The report also stated that, since thinner windscreen glass was introduced in

British cars in 1968, the incidence of facial bone fractures had declined.

Scotland Yard stated in March 1970 that a special skid-resistant epoxy-resin surface sprayed on to roads had reduced accidents to pedestrians at 20 selected crossings in London by 87 per cent. At these points, rear-end collisions had been eliminated, and at road junctions where similar experiments were carried out this type of collision had been reduced by 73 per cent. At road junctions, wet road accidents were reduced by 72 per cent, and accidents in which a driver lost control of his vehicle by 70 per cent. Both the police and the Greater London Council were reported to be so satisfied with these results that the system, which involves spraying the road for 200 ft. on either side of the approaches to road junctions, and for 40 ft. on either side of pedestrian crossings, is to be extended throughout London.

An electronic device designed to prevent multi-vehicle crashes on motorways was announced in March 1970 to be in the early stages of development in Great Britain and the U.S.A. The device, known as Headway control, works on the radar principle. Infra-red rays, transmitted ahead by a car, are bounced back by a special reflector fitted on the back of the vehicle in front, and the device gives either a visual or an audible warning whenever the car closes to less than a safe distance of the vehicle in front.

Information about a new system for protecting rear-seat passengers in car crashes, produced by Firestone in the U.S.A., was given in August. Within one thirtieth of a second of an impact a shock-absorbing blanket, stored in the back of the front seat, is thrown over the rear-seat passengers from their knees to shoulders, so holding them firmly in place. The manufacturers claim that the blanket will operate at speeds as low as 10 m.p.h., and that is it capable of restraining four large men at speeds as high as 44 m.p.h. (see also p. 108).

France. On March 18, 1970, the French government announced a 100 kilometre per hour (68 m.p.h.) speed limit on 8,700 miles of national motorways, in an attempt to reduce road deaths. Other measures announced at the same time included the setting up of a national register of all motor vehicle drivers, and a list of dangerous drivers; quicker help for those injured in road accidents; improved road signs; and the elimination of 400 motorway danger spots. Figures showed that 14,248 people were killed on French roads in 1968, the last year for which complete figures were available.

Australia. On July 9, State and Commonwealth transport ministers meeting in Port Moresby finalized agreement on the introduction of seven further safety features for incorporation in new motor vehicles sold in Australia. The new rules call for non-tinted safety glass (to be provided by July 1, 1971); burst-proof door latches and hinges (Jan. 1, 1971); stronger seat mountings (Jan. 1, 1971);

rear vision mirrors (Jan. 1, 1972); padded sun visors (Jan. 1, 1972); energy-absorbing instrument panels (Jan. 1, 1973); and clearly located instruments (Jan. 1, 1973). Existing requirements for the fitting of seat belts in new vehicles were altered to permit the installation of retractor-type belts, which are considered to encourage greater usage by vehicle occupants.

Under the Road Safety Act which passed the State of Tasmania legislative council and house of assembly on Dec. 17 drivers were forbidden to drive after taking any alcoholic drink, during the first year that they hold a licence.

New Zealand. The national Roads Board in Wellington decided in April 1970 that in future fibreglass lamp-posts will be used on motorways instead of steel or concrete poles. The Board was told that 35-ft.-high fibreglass poles are about one twelfth the weight of similar concrete poles, and are accordingly less dangerous if struck by cars.

Roman Catholic Church. The 1970 Catholic Directory showed a decline in the estimated Roman Catholic population of England and Wales from the 1968 figure of 4,143,800 to 4,050,200 in 1969. The U.S. 1970 Directory showed a similar decline in the United States for the first time in this century. The 1969 figure of 47,872,089 was 1,149 less than in 1968. The number of baptisms fell from 1,095,162 in 1968 to 1,086,848 in 1969, and the number of converts to Roman Catholicism declined from 102,865 in 1968 to 92,670 in 1969, the lowest for 24 years. Statistics published by the Vatican on Feb. 8, 1970, showed that the number of young men in Western countries training to become priests had fallen by almost 20,000 in 3 years. A survey of 41 nations showed there were 146,996 seminarists at the end of 1968 compared with over 166,000 in 1965.

There seems little doubt that the decline in candidates for the priesthood is due to the Vatican's continued insistence on the celibacy of the clergy. Yet the Vatican announced on Feb. 9, 1970, that Roman Catholic priests throughout the world would in future be asked to renew their vows of celibacy and obedience once a year. This demand, sent to bishops in a letter from the Vatican's Congregation for the Clergy on Nov. 4, 1969, but withheld from publication until February 1970, is thought to have been made because of the increasing agitation by Dutch Roman Catholic clergy and laity against the celibacy law. A Dutch ecclesiastical report published on Jan. 6, 1970, and submitted to a meeting of the fifth pastoral council of the Dutch Catholic church recommended the abolition of the oath of celibacy for priests, and claimed that there is a link between compulsory celibacy and the shortage of priests. The next day, the 106 delegates passed by overwhelming majorities four proposals in favour of allowing priests to marry, and 12 days later the Dutch conclave of bishops issued a statement that the country's Roman

Catholic community would be better off if married men were permitted to be ordained priests, and if priests who had married could be readmitted to the Church.

Holland was not the only country to feel strongly on this subject. The results of a survey conducted over 6 years by Father Silvano Burgalassi, director of the socio-religious research centre at Pisa, and professor of sociology at Rome's Lateran University, were published in November. They showed that the majority of Italian Roman Catholic clergy are also against compulsory celibacy. Father Burgalassi questioned over 4,500 Italian priests, and found that between 30 and 50 per cent favoured optional celibacy; that between 10 and 20 per cent might marry if compulsory celibacy was abolished; that about 30 per cent accepted the compulsory rule; and that 10 per cent considered it to be a matter of secondary importance.

The question was referred to again in a Vatican decree on the first total reform of education standards for Roman Catholic priests since 1556, published on March 16, 1970. The decree stated that seminaries should put more stress on teaching about Christian unity, sex, and atheism. The 10,000-word document, written with the help of bishops from all over the world, reaffirmed the Church's teaching on the celibacy of priests, but said that, if the choice of celibacy was to be truly free, the priest must ''rightly appreciate the good sides of married life''. Traditional seminary practices confirmed by the document included periods of silence, daily mass and prayer, preparation for the vows of poverty and chastity, and the classical curriculum stressing Latin, Greek, history, literature, philosophy, and theology.

A more independent attitude towards the authority of the Church was evident in Australia where, in May, 400 priests and bishops met at St. Joseph's College, Hunter's Hill, Sydney, to consider the proposal, first put forward at Coogee in October 1969, to form a National Association of Priests. During the 3-day conference six study commissions covered problems of the inner life of the priest; the involvement of priests in secular and social problems; in-service training for clergy; the application of the gospel in modern Australia; the improvement of communications in the Church; and the future of the ministry. At the end of the conference it was voted that a national body of some kind should be formed, and a seven-member committee was elected to work towards this end.

Women. Among new regulations decreed by Pope Paul, and revealed on Aug. 19, were some affecting the life of all nuns, execept those living in cloisters. Nuns are now able to come and go freely from their convents without seeking previous permission to do so from their superiors, but, although they do not have to account for their movements outside convents, the new rules stated that bishops and superiors must maintain

overall vigilance. It was also ruled that bishops need no longer carry out a month-long investigation designed to establish whether a potential nun was being forced or deceived into entering a nunnery, the Vatican assuming that women seeking to enter a religious order feel they have a vocation for the life.

A papal decree published on Sept. 7 allows women who wish to dedicate themselves to God without entering a convent to take vows of virginity and be formally consecrated by a bishop, while continuing to live in the world. The rite, said the document containing it, will unite them ''ultimately with the Lord'' and make them ''more completely available for the service of the Church''.

At the end of September the Pope proclaimed St. Teresa of Avila a Doctor of the Church, and on Oct. 4 St. Catherine of Siena, the patron saint of Italy, was also elevated to the same position. The other 29 Doctors of the Church, officially defined as illustrious persons for their sanctity of life, orthodoxy of faith, and eminent wisdom in sacred things, are all men. They are given the title Doctor by special decree of the Church, and the inclusion of women for the first time is seen as part of the Pope's declared policy of giving women greater recognition.

Inter-marriage. The Vatican announced on April 29, 1970, that from Oct. 1, 1970, non-Catholics marrying Catholic spouses would no longer have to promise to bring up their children as Roman Catholics. Although the Catholic partner in a mixed marriage will be expected to pass on his or her faith to the children, he or she will no longer face automatic excommunication and the refusal of sacraments in the event of failure to do so. These penalties were also lifted from those Catholics who had previously incurred them. But Roman Catholic priests are forbidden to share in

wedding ceremonies in other churches, and a second marriage ceremony in a church of another faith before or after a wedding in a Catholic church is also prohibited. Another change in the rules is that, while Roman Catholics may still not marry non-Catholics without special dispensation, this will now be granted by the local bishop instead of by the Vatican.

Cardinals. The Vatican announced on Nov. 23 that the Pope had ruled that cardinals over the age of 80 would not be allowed to vote for his successor, and were not to belong to departments of the Roman Curia (the Church's central government body). This was the first time in Roman Catholic history that an age limit had been set. The ruling affected 25 of the 127 members of the Sacred College of Cardinals (11 Italian, 3 French, 2 Spanish, 2 Portuguese, 1 German, 1 Scottish, 1 Irish, 1 American, 1 Brazilian, 1 Argentine, and 1 Mexican), all of whom had to retire on Jan. 1, 1971, when the order came into force. The Pope also asked cardinals heading Curia departments to submit their resignations when they reach the age of 75; he would then decide, according to the circumstances of each case, whether or not to accept them.

Rome. As work on the new £850,000 British embassy building on a site next to the Porta Pia gateway here continued during 1970, restoration work costing £20,000 on a 400–500-yard section of the Rome city wall of A.D. 275 was also undertaken. The 30-ft. wall stands on one of the boundaries of the site, and its face is technically on British territory. Built by the emperor Aurelian, the wall is one of the largest Roman monuments ever to be restored by the U.K. ministry of public building and works. The Italian labour team, directed by Alan Griffiths of the ministry's ancient monument branch, had

Rome. Remains of the ancient Imperial city revealed by chance in 1970 by workmen digging in the centre of the city midway between the Trevi fountain and the Via Veneto.

to remove plant growth and dig out tree roots by hand before strengthening the wall with matching bricks. The embassy building, due for completion in the spring of 1971, replaces the embassy blown up by Zionist terrorists in 1947. Built round a courtyard, the new building will have two storeys of offices raised above an open ground floor, with an outside staircase from the courtyard leading to the principal rooms on the first floor. As each successive floor overhangs the one below, shade from the strong sun is provided. The embassy was designed by Sir Basil Spence.

During the autumn, workmen digging on a site in the centre of the city midway between the Trevi fountain and the Via Veneto struck an old wall about 24 ft. below the surface. Further digging by archaeologists revealed mosaics, columns, statues, and a street—remains spreading over three centuries of imperial Rome. The ruins are to be roofed over.

Roskill Commission. This U.K. commission appointed in May 1968 to investigate the suggested sites for London's third airport issued a summary of its report on Dec. 8, 1970. Six of its seven members favoured the choice of Cublington, Bucks (see under Cublington).

They had received a report from their own independent experts, published on Feb. 4, 1970, assessing the potential agricultural loss to the nation of each of the four short-listed sites. In terms of the least loss to agriculture it put the sites in the following order: Cublington, Bucks; Thurleigh, Beds; Nuthampstead, Herts; and Foulness, Essex. The report, prepared by a research team at Wye College, University of London, said that, although the choice of Foulness would cause the loss of the smallest number of acres, much of the 18,150 acres involved was Grade I agricultural land. It was estimated that a total of 25,000 acres would be needed for the airport and the urban development associated with it.

The British Airports Authority was reported in May to have found none of the four sites satisfactory, because ''they are all too far from London''. If forced to choose, it favoured Cublington, Bucks, but only as the least disadvantageous. It found Foulness the worst, because of its inaccessibility, the possibility of conflict with European air traffic control, the hazard of bird strikes, and because the Authority had grave doubts about the meteorology of the site. Thurleigh was condemned because, although potentially the most profitable to the Authority, it was the farthest from London and would depend on a substantial volume of traffic from outside the South-Eastern region. Cublington was found to be marginally preferable to Nuthampstead, because it would involve the closure of only Luton airport, whereas the choice of Nuthampstead would require the closing of both Luton and Stansted.

Rotterdam, Holland. The 340-ft.-high ''Euromast'' tower built here in 1960 has been extended by 266 ft. by the addition of a ''space tower''. This consists of a hollow steel tube, 8 ft. in diameter, with an engine room mounted at the top. By using cables a steel ring is pulled up and down the outside of the tube, and an observation cabin, carrying 32 people, fixed to it rotates upwards and downwards in a spiral movement as the ring is raised and lowered.

Royal Albert Hall, London. A centenary appeal to raise £500,000 to restore and preserve the Royal Albert Hall was launched on Feb. 13, 1970. The corporation which, under a royal charter of 1866, owns and controls the hall, decided to make this appeal to the millions who have visited it. The aim is to restore it to, and possibly improve upon, the condition it was in when it was completed in 1871.

Royal Flying Doctor Service. It was announced in June that the radio network of the Royal Flying Doctor Service in Australia is to be modernized, the first major change since it was set up in 1928. The 12 bases of the service will be re-equipped to ease radio congestion. Australia's flying doctor service, the biggest of its type in the world, provides emergency medical services for more than 5,000 outposts in the country, and is also a vital part of outback communications. Design and installation of the new radio network is expected to have been completed by the middle of 1972.

Royal Institute of Chartered Surveyors. On June 8, 1970, the Chartered Land Agents' Society and the Chartered Auctioneers' and Estate Agents' Institute amalgamated with the Royal Institute of Chartered Surveyors, so creating a new body with over 40,000 corporate and student members from Great Britain's surveyors, land and estate agents, and auctioneers. The unification is intended to reduce the number of qualifications in the profession, to help promote higher standards of education and training, and to help chartered surveyors to give an increasingly efficient and comprehensive service. The R.I.C.S., the largest and oldest of the three bodies, was formed in 1868, the C.A.E.A.I. in 1886, and the C.L.A.S. in 1902. They took the first step towards amalgamation by forming a chartered land societies' committee in 1964.

Royal Navy. A tradition regularly observed in the Royal Navy for 278 years was celebrated for the last time on July 31, 1970, when the last rum ration was issued to the ratings. At noon, as ''Up spirits'' was piped, the last tots were ladled from the brass-bound casks bearing the words ''God Bless Our Queen''. The decision to abolish the naval rum issue—also issued to Royal Marine other ranks—had been announced in the House of Commons on Dec. 17, 1969, with effect from Aug. 1, 1970, on the advice of the Admiralty board. As the alcoholic content

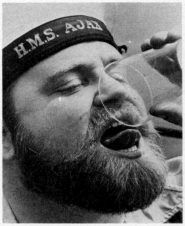

Royal Navy. The last drop of the daily rum ration was swallowed on July 31, 1970.

of the daily issue was equivalent to slightly more than four measures of spirit, it was regarded as being ''no longer compatible with the high standards of efficiency required, now that the individual's tasks in ships are concerned with complex, and often delicate, machinery and systems, on the correct functioning of which people's lives may depend''. The £2,700,000 saved by the abolition of grog is to be paid into a new fund for the benefit of naval ratings and Royal Marine other ranks. As part of ''a more liberal approach to the Seventies'' new rules on the length of sailors' hair and sideburns were issued by the Navy in July. Sailors are now allowed to grow their hair fuller than in the past, but must still have it cut so that it is always neat and tidy. Sideburns may be grown to the bottom of the ear.

S

Sadler's Wells. The governors of Sadler's Wells Theatre in Rosebery Avenue, London, assumed direct control of the theatre from the Sadler's Wells Trust on April 1, 1970. The Trust continues to run Sadler's Wells Opera at the London Coliseum, as it has since August 1968. The theatre will be used to stage opera, ballet, and drama by ''worthy visiting companies'', both British and foreign. The governors estimate that the cost of running the theatre will be between £25,000 and £45,000 annually, the economic rent being £1,800 a week.

St. Crispin's Reef, Cairns, North Queensland. It was announced in July that a group of Australian businessmen plan to build a 200-bed hotel on an artificial Great Barrier Reef. To create the island, a 400-ft.-diameter circle of precast concrete segments will be laid on the reef, and filled with sand pumped from the sea-bed.

Saints. On May 18, 1970, the Pope confirmed his 1969 announcement that 40 Roman Catholic martyrs of England and Wales were to be proclaimed saints, so ending a campaign for their canonization which English Roman Catholics had maintained for over 300 years. On Oct. 25 the 40 martyrs were duly canonized in St. Peter's, Rome, in the presence of 10,000 pilgrims from the English- and Welsh-speaking world. The martyrs are priests, laymen, and women who died for their religious convictions under England's penal anti-Catholic laws between 1535 and 1679. The best known are the poet Edmund Campion, executed at Tyburn in 1581, and Philip Howard, Earl of Arundel, who died in the Tower of London in 1595. During the ceremony the Pope was presented with some relics of the martyrs, among them a piece of the rope with which Campion was hanged. When the intended canonization was first announced in 1969 the Archbishop of Canterbury deplored it as "harmful to the ecumenical cause", but in May the Pope declared that he did not intend that "cause should be given for mutual contumely and accusation". At the October ceremony those present bore in mind those Protestant martyrs who died for their faith under England's Catholic queen Mary I, and the inclusion of some Anglican hymns stressed the doctrine common to both communions. The Church of England was officially represented at the ceremony.

A Vatican ordinance issued on Aug. 21 ruled that no nation, region, city, diocese, or association could have more than one patron saint. Great Britain will be allowed to keep her three saints—St. George for England, St. Andrew for Scotland, and St. David for Wales—as it is recognized that the country is made up of three nations.

Sandringham, Norfolk. On July 20, 1970, the Queen's scenic driveway here was opened to the public as the first part of a plan to open 8,000 acres of the royal estate as a country park. Together with a loop road to reduce traffic hazards, the single asphalted track, along which parking bays have been made to take about 100 cars, cost £10,000. A 2-mile nature trail, intended to show how natural vegetation has been combined with planting for both beauty and timber production, was opened on the same day. Some of the oldest trees along the trail date back to 1863, when the Sandringham estate was created.

San Francisco, U.S.A. A modern luxury housing development for American negroes was completed here in 1970. Called "Martin Luther King Square", after the outstanding leader of the negro struggle for civil rights who was assassinated in April 1968, the project cost $2 million and includes 60 tower buildings and 50 flats. Another new building opened during 1970 was the Roman Catholic St. Mary's Cathedral which came into use in October.

Satellites. Figures given by NASA's satellite situation report in June showed that by April 30, 1970, man had flung 4,396 objects into space, of which 1,859 were still there. The remaining 2,537 had "decayed" in orbit and faded from the view of trackers. The U.S.A. and U.S.S.R. lead the world both in number of objects launched and in objects still flying. The U.S.A. had 1,407 objects still in orbit, and 937 had decayed; the U.S.S.R. had 404 still in orbit, and 1,583 had decayed.

Scammonden Bridge, Yorkshire. This bridge at Scammonden, a village 6 miles W. of Huddersfield, the biggest single-span fixed-arch structure of its kind in the U.K., was opened on May 18, 1970. Crossing over the deepest motorway (M62) cutting in Europe—180 ft. at its maximum point—the bridge has a 410-ft. span and a total deck length of 656 ft. It took 18 months to build.

Scarborough, Ontario, Canada. Early in 1970, under a $4·1 million contract awarded to Mitchell Construction Company (Canada), work started on the first phase of a telecommunications centre here. The building, measuring 124 ft. by 237 ft., is of five storeys and provision has been made for adding a further four storeys at some future date. Two adjoining buildings are involved in the project, which includes a 500-ft.-high microwave transmission tower. The centre is due for completion in February 1971.

Schools TV. The Inner London Education Authority, which makes its own television programmes for schools, polytechnics, colleges, youth centres, and centres of adult education, moved its TV head-quarters and studios to the former Tennyson School, Battersea, in March 1970. In 1970–71, 400 programmes will be created, including some for the 5–7-year-olds and some for trainee teachers. The programmes, which are received in 1,200 schools and nearly 150 other educational centres, are written and produced by teachers released from their classrooms for up to 2 years. By the autumn of 1970 an audience of almost a million was watching the I.L.E.A. programmes.

Scientology. This psycho-religious sect brought a libel action in November 1970 against Geoffrey Johnson-Smith, M.P. for East Grinstead (where its h.q., Saint Hill Manor, is situated), for repeating on television derogatory remarks about scientologists made in the House of Commons. The suit was lost on Dec. 21, and the plaintiffs were faced with legal costs estimated at between £50,000 and £75,000. They decided not to appeal, and also stated that they would withdraw other actions pending against the East Grinstead urban district council, three of its former councillors, and another M.P.

Scorpions. The world's first antivenene for a scorpion's bite was developed in 1970 by Drs. Hervé and Catherine Rochat, working at St. Vincent's School of Medical Research, Melbourne. The French couple used the protein sequenator (see under Protein) in their research. When the

San Francisco. Martin Luther King Square, a modern luxury housing development for negroes, completed in 1970.

antidote becomes fully available it is expected that it will save thousands of scorpion victims who die every year in India, Africa, the Middle East, and Mexico.

Scouting. The 1970 Scout Association census showed a membership in the U.K. of 539,340. Cub scouts had the largest increase in membership, which went up by 4,978 over the 1969 figure to a total of 254,839. Scout section numbers went up by 2,167 to a total of 190,546, but Venture Scout numbers decreased by 227 to 21,471. Scout groups numbered 11,357. Of the young people in the youth service age range of 14–21 those catered for by the Scout movement totalled 83,080, an increase of 2,047 over 1969. Public notice was drawn to the Venture Scout mobile emergency aid teams which are equipped to help in cave-rescue, fire-fighting, air disasters, first-aid, and aid to the disabled, when the Chief Scout, Sir Charles Maclean, inspected them for the first time at Chelsea Barracks, London, on March 15, 1970.

A new "world badge" to emphasize the internationalism of scouting has been adopted for wear from Jan. 1, 1971. Over 40 overseas scout associations agreed to adopt the new badge, and a period of 3 years has been allowed for the change-over.

A jamboree, the last official event of the Captain Cook bicentenary celebrations, was held on a 500-acre site at Leppington, near Liverpool, New South Wales, from Dec. 29, 1970, to Jan. 9, 1971. During the jamboree, 12,000 Scouts from Australia and 20 other countries ate 144,000 sausages, 18,000 lb. of chops, 9,000 lb. of steak, 24,000 frankfurters, 96,000 eggs, 9,000 lb. of butter, and 29,000 loaves, and drank 108,000 pints of milk. The Australian army lent the Scouts $A500,000 worth of equipment, including tents, field cookers, and a 72-bed field hospital.

Segrave Trophy. The announcement that Bruce McLaren had been awarded the 1969 Segrave Trophy for his "outstanding performance in winning every race in the 1969 Canadian-American Challenge Cup series in cars of his own design and construction" was about to be made at the time of his fatal accident on June 2. In a simple ceremony at the Brands Hatch racing circuit, Kent, on July 16 his widow, Pat, received the award. The trophy, in memory of record-breaker Sir Henry Segrave (1896–1930), is an annual award made to the British subject who accomplishes the most outstanding demonstration of the possibilities of transport by land, air, or water.

Severn River. Work on a 10-ft. tunnel under the Severn to carry a 400,000-volt power line for the national super grid was carried out during 1970. Costing £4 million, the tunnel, which passes diagonally under the new Severn Bridge, was bored through 12,000 ft. of rock 90 ft. beneath the river bed.

Seville, Spain. It was reported in August that archaeologists had discovered within 5 miles of the centre of Seville the foundations of the Roman city of Italica, founded at the time of Publius Cornelius Scipio Africanus c. 206 B.C. The find consists mainly of the foundations of a number of small town houses, square in shape, and, one layer above them, the foundations of much larger houses with mosaics. In one of the foundations the skull of a bull, believed to have been part of a ritual sacrifice to invoke protection for the house, was found in perfect condition. The survey was conducted by five archaeologists from Seville University.

Seville is to have its own underground railway by 1975, according to an announcement made in November. Initially it will be only 5 miles long. Work will start in 1972, the state paying 60 per cent of the cost and the rest being borne by the city council. The railway is the latest step in a large public works programme for the south-west, one of the country's fastest growth areas. Seville will be the third Spanish city to have an underground railway; Madrid and Barcelona already have "tubes".

Sheep. According to the Commonwealth bureau of census and statistics, Australia pastured 181,312,000 sheep and lambs at March 1970. New South Wales, with 72,900,000, had the largest State total, followed by Victoria (33,355,000), Western Australia (33,300,000), South Australia (19,916,000), Queensland (16,951,000), and Tasmania (4,648,000). The total was nearly 7 million more than 1969's. All States recorded increases except Queensland, where drought was responsible for a decrease of nearly 4 million.

During the 1969–70 wool season (July 1 to June 30) 5,600,702 bales of wool were sold at auction in Australia. Although this total was 393,597 more than that for the preceding 12 months, lower prices presented a disappointing overall picture for the woolgrower. The average price for the 12 months was 37·55 cents—a fall of almost 16 per cent on the previous season's return, and the lowest for 22 years. The total amount realized was $A652,169,663 compared with $A724,634,356 for the preceding year. Japan was the largest buyer, taking about a third of the offering. Other large buyers were the U.K., Italy, France, Russia, Belgium, and Germany.

Shipbuilding. Figures published on April 22, 1970, in the 1969 annual report of Lloyd's Register of Shipping showed that between 1960 and 1969 Japan was the world's leading shipbuilding nation, completing 49·7 million tons gross of ships in the period. The U.K. and West Germany were the second largest, completing 11·1 million tons gross each. The launching of a record 19 million tons gross in 1969 brought the total output of the world's shipyards for the decade to 122 million tons gross. The world fleet, currently over 211 million gross tons, has doubled since 1956.

In the year 1969 alone, Japan retained her place as the leading shipbuilding nation, with 48·2 per cent of the world market, and with gross tonnage of 9,303,453 tons launched. West Germany came second with gross tonnage launched of 1,608,545 tons; Sweden was third, with 1,292,884 tons; the U.K. fourth, with 1,039,516 tons; and France fifth, with 791,193 tons. Ships ordered by British owners from foreign yards totalled 2,142,680 tons gross, the highest ever recorded. British yards launched a total of 385,000 tons for foreign owners. On a world basis, bulk carrier production fell by 815,684 tons to 4,823,049 tons, representing 25 per cent of the total world tonnage launched, but world oil tanker tonnage reached a record 9,325,810 tons, 2·7 million tons more than in 1968.

Shipping. On June 30, 1969, the world's merchant fleets, classified under flags, were headed by Liberia with 29,215,000 gross tons; followed by Japan with 23,987,000; U.K. with 23,844,000; Norway with 19,679,000; the U.S.A. with 19,590,000; the Soviet Union with 13,705,000; Greece with 8,581,000; and Italy with 7,038,000.

Figures published by Lloyd's Register in September showed that the total tonnage lost by the world's shipping fleets in 1969 was 824,978 tons gross, the second highest amount ever recorded, and 64,531 tons more than that lost in 1968. The Shell super-tanker *Marpessa*, 104,373 gross tons, the largest ship ever lost, was included in the 1969 figures, and this ship, together with three other large vessels, accounted for 29 per cent of the total tonnage lost. Tonnage listed as "missing" amounted to 10,637 tons, while tonnage totally lost through fire was, at 266,498 tons, the highest figure ever recorded, and an increase of 90,535 tons on the 1968 figure. The number of ships lost was 327.

Shoes. John Dalton, director of a Melbourne, Australia, footwear company, stated on June 2, 1970, that he had applied for a world patent of a process used in developing a new type of shoe which through its sole dissipates the static electricity that is built up in the body. The sole was designed for use in places where precautions should be taken to prevent the accumulation of body electricity, such as operating theatres and plants and laboratories making explosives, volatile liquids, and gases.

Silver. A Charles I inkstand was sold at Christie's, London, on July 1 for £78,000, the highest price ever paid at auction for a piece of silver, and three times the previous record price paid for an English piece. The inkstand, dated 1639, weighs 172 oz., and is 16½ in. wide. In 1893, when it was last auctioned by Christie's, it fetched £446.

Singapore. The Ocean Steamship Co. and the Capital and Counties Property Co.

Singapore. Montage showing how the new 28-storey office tower will look in 1973.

announced on September 22 that work on the construction of a £10 million building complex on Singapore's waterfront was to start immediately. The complex includes a 390-ft.-high, 28-storey office tower, which is planned for completion by the end of 1973.

Skynet. This is the name of the British system of military communications by satellite. It was reported in January 1970 that during the acceptance trials of Skynet I it was proved that low-cost dish-aerials only 3 ft. wide could be used by ships for picking up the satellite signals. This means that, by the late 1970s, most British ships, aircraft, and army ground units will be able to send and receive messages via space relay stations. A development in electronic amplifiers had also eliminated the refrigeration previously needed, so that the equipment can work at atmospheric temperatures. The stabilizer for the aerial has also undergone development; the mounting of the small dishes for shipborne use employs a modified version of the inertial stabilization system developed for the Black Arrow rocket.

Skynet I was built in the U.S.A. to British specifications. It was announced on Oct. 1 that Great Britain will build her own next generation of Skynet satellites. Marconi Space and Defence Systems in Portsmouth will be responsible for constructing two satellites under a ministry of technology contract, including the entire electronics system, and the manufacture, assembly, and testing of the complete package. Some major components, only available in the U.S.A., will still be provided by the U.S. Philco-Ford Corporation. Both of the new satellites will be launched

from Cape Kennedy on a Thor-Delta rocket in the summer of 1973.

Smoking. The year 1970 saw the usual publication of reports on the dangers to health of smoking, especially cigarette-smoking. One of the most strongly worded of such denunciations was contained in the tenth annual report on the nation's health, published on Oct. 22, of the chief medical officer of the U.K. department of health and social security. Smoking, he said, was no "harmless indulgence" but the biggest single avoidable menace to health in contemporary life in Great Britain, causing, all told, "perhaps 10 times as many deaths as did road accidents and nearly as many deaths as all cancers unrelated to smoking put together". Expert analysis of deaths from lung cancer, chronic bronchitis, and ischaemic heart disease, all associated with cigarette-smoking, showed that some 80,000 people probably died prematurely from these diseases in England and Wales each year, and about 100,000 in the whole of the U.K. Allowing for the fact that these deaths included a high proportion of older people, there were still enough deaths in the working age groups to cause the loss each year of 190,000 working years of man-power. The amount of working time lost from illness due to cigarette-smoking could not be estimated, but it must be responsible for the greater part of the 38,600,000 days of sickness absence certified in 1969 as being due to bronchitis. The abolition of cigarette-smoking would thus not only be of enormous benefit to health, but also would add hundreds of millions of pounds to the economy each year.

A similar statement on the cost of smoking had been made by Dr. Keith Ball, consultant cardiologist at the Central Middlesex Hospital, who claimed that cigarette-smoking costs the National Health Service about £43 million a year. In a letter to the *Lancet*, published at the beginning of July, he estimated that about 8,000 beds—4·5 per cent of the total of hospital beds—were occupied every day by patients who were in hospital because they were suffering from the effects of smoking. This, he said, was "the equivalent of all the beds in the 12 London teaching hospitals. Every 800-bed hospital would, on this calculation, use a fully staffed ward of 36 beds solely for the results of cigarette smoking." On May 15 the World Health Organization had endorsed a world-wide campaign against cigarette-smoking, during which doctors and other health workers were asked to refrain from smoking as an example to others. It called for restrictions on advertising, and asked governments to make it compulsory for cigarette packets to carry warnings of the health hazards.

Claims that cigar smoke is less harmful than cigarette smoke were once again disproved in 1970. The U.K. Tobacco Research Council reported in June that nicotine from cigars was more likely to affect blood pressure than cigarette nicotine; experiments with cats showed that

cigar smoke caused a slow rise in blood pressure, while cigarette smoke had very little effect. In November the Council stated that smoke from small cigars had a greater tumour-producing effect than that of cigarettes prepared from normal flue-cured cigarette tobacco. Smoke condensate is believed to contain the principal cancer-producing element of tobacco. Laboratory tests, which involved painting this condensate on to the skins of mice, showed no difference in the cancer-producing effect of cigarettes with or without acetate filters, but revealed that the addition of copper, potassium, and sodium nitrate to ordinary cigarettes reduces their cancer-producing effect.

The repeated warnings of the health hazards of cigarette-smoking seemed to have some effect in the U.S.A. but none in Great Britain. The U.S. department of agriculture reported in March 1970 that cigarette-smoking in the U.S.A. fell from 546,000 million cigarettes in 1968 to 528,000 million in 1969, a decrease of 3 per cent. This was the greatest drop in any year since 1963–64, when government concern over the relation of smoking to lung cancer was first disclosed. During 1969, the average American smoker consumed 3,993 cigarettes, compared with 4,186 in 1968. This was the first time in at least 10 years that per capita consumption had fallen below 4,000 cigarettes per year. In contrast, a report issued by the Tobacco Research Council in January 1970 showed that 121,800 million cigarettes were smoked in Great Britain in 1968, an increase of 2,900 million over the 1967 figure. The amount of tobacco smoked was, however, reduced by more than 221 million lb. owing to the increase in the number of filtered and smaller cigarettes. In 1968, there were nearly 13,600,000 men and 9,300,000 women smokers in Great Britain. Unskilled men smoked more than professional men. Construction workers smoked 156 cigarettes a week, followed by transport workers (155) and farmers and fishermen (110). The number of teenage girls who started to smoke as soon as they began work was shown to be increasing: in 1961 the average 15-year-old girl was smoking four cigarettes a week, and in 1968 this had risen to eight a week. In 1958, girls aged 16–19 smoked 17 cigarettes a week, and by 1968 were smoking 37. In 1961, 15-year-old boys smoked an average of 13 cigarettes a week, and in 1968 this figure had risen to 19.

Aversion Therapy. The January 1970 issue of the *British Medical Journal* contained a report of an experiment carried out by Dr. M. A. Hailton Russell, of the Institute of Psychiatry's addiction research unit at Maudsley Hospital, to help smokers overcome their addiction to cigarettes. The experiment consisted of seating each of 14 patients at a desk on which were placed an ashtray, matches, and cigarettes. Two electrodes were strapped to each patient's arms, and when at a prearranged signal the instruction was given to stub out his cigarette any hesitation in doing so caused

Snowy Mountains. The last and biggest part of this gigantic Australian hydro-electric and irrigation scheme—Tumut 3 power station—will be supplied with water through six pipelines each 18 ft. 3 in. in diameter and 1,600 ft. long. A small section of one is seen here.

him to receive an electric shock of up to 250 volts. After three sessions the patients had reduced their smoking from an average of 21·5 cigarettes a day to 1·4 a day. Three started smoking again at 1, 3, and 4 months respectively after the treatment ended; six stopped smoking altogether; and five stopped taking the treatment.

Snowy Mountains. The construction of Australia's biggest dam, the Talbingo, part of the Snowy Mountains scheme which, when completed, will provide water for irrigation in Victoria, New South Wales, and South Australia, was completed on Sept. 20. The last major dam in the scheme, Talbingo is 530 ft. high and 3,000 ft. across, and took 2 years to build at a cost of $A27 million.

Snuff. Figures given in August by the British Society of Snuff Grinders, Blenders, and Purveyors showed that there is a world rise in snuff-taking. This led to a fourfold increase in the export values of basic and blended British snuffs between 1962 and 1969. The duty-free value of exported snuffs was stated to be £250,000 each year, compared with £1¼ million in terms of home sales.

Sonning Prize. This annual Danish award of £8,730 was given in 1970 to Dr. Max Tau, Norwegian writer and humanist, for his achievements as a spokesman for European culture and for peace.

South-East England. A team of U.K. government and local planners, and the region's economic planning council, in a report, *Strategic Plan for the South-East*, published on June 30, 1970, forecast that by the turn of the century there might be 4½ million extra people living in the area, which already contains 17 million, a third of Great Britain's population. In order to accommodate this increase at satisfactory environmental standards, the team believed that future development of the region's towns and cities might require 600–700 of its 10,500 sq. miles. A map showing areas of outstanding beauty and agriculture was studied before the sites for post-1981 growth were chosen, since preservation of extensive areas of open country, including the metropolitan green belt, were considered essential. Unlike an

earlier report by the economic planning council, which foresaw continuous ribbon development along the main lines of communication from London, this plan recommends the development of a limited number of growth areas at varying distances from London, using existing or planned urban areas as the basis for growth.

Five major areas of growth are envisaged: south Hampshire (1,400,000 population by the end of the century); Milton Keynes-Northampton-Wellingborough (800,000); Reading-Wokingham-Aldershot-Basingstoke (between 1 million and 1,200,000); south Essex (about 1 million); and Crawley-Burgess Hill (500,000). Medium growth areas will also be required: these are Maidstone-Medway, Ashford, Eastbourne-Hastings, Bournemouth-Poole, Aylesbury, Bishop's Stortford-Harlow, and Chelmsford. In proposals for a regional communications network to link centres of population within the South-East and to provide for traffic between them and the rest of Great Britain two new routes were suggested. One would link the new city of Milton Keynes in north Bucks with Luton, Stevenage, Harlow, and south Essex, and connect south Essex with the Channel ports or Channel tunnel by way of Tilbury. The other would link Milton Keynes and growth areas at Reading, Wokingham, Aldershot, Basingstoke, and south Hampshire. A major part of the team's report concerned the problems of inner London, with its urgent housing needs and high cost of living. The team forecast a shortage of up to 100,000 homes in London in the years after 1981, and repeatedly emphasized the need for decentralization.

Southsea, Hants. Proposals for a multi-million-pound entertainment centre in the shape of a futuristic ship beached on the shore near Southsea Castle were considered by Portsmouth corporation's entertainment committee on Oct. 12. The stern of the "ship" would house a circular theatre to seat 1,500 people, which could also be used for conferences and functions, while the long "hull" would accommodate an amphitheatre for horse shows, sports activities, and "pop" festivals. A central bridge tower area would contain restaurants, bars and shops. There would also be a sea-water swimming pool.

British and Commonwealth Stamps issued in 1970

1st row. Malawi, 4d, Commonwealth Games; St. Kitts, 20 cents, 17th-century cannon; Papua and New Guinea, 5 cents, Nicolaus Miklouho-Maclay, Russian explorer; St. Vincent, 4 cents, soufrière bird.

2nd row. St. Lucia, 25 cents, centenary of the British Red Cross; Cook Islands, 5 cents, Royal visit and 5th anniversary of self-government; Barbados, 4 cents, International Education Year.

3rd row. Bermuda, 4 cents, Bermudiana; New Zealand, 2½ cents plus 1 cent Health, netball; Great Britain, 5d, Philympia 1970, Penny Black; Great Britain, 9d, rural architecture, Cotswold limestone.

4th row. (Above) Montserrat, 5 cents, brown pelican; (below) Canada, 6 cents, Eskimo art, "Enchanted owl"; British Solomon Islands, 8 cents, Christmas 1970; Zambia, 3 ngwee, preventive medicine; (above) Australia, 5 cents, International Grassland Conference; (below) India, 20 paise, centenary of the birth of Lenin.

5th row. The Gambia, 1d, Commonwealth Games; Turks and Caicos Islands, 1 cent, centenary of the death of Charles Dickens; Falkland Islands, 2s, return of *S.S. Great Britain*.

Stamps and Stamp-Collecting. The world record price for a single postage stamp, $280,000 (about £116,660), was paid at a New York auction on March 24, 1970, by an American dealer for the unique British Guiana 1-cent magenta stamp issued in 1856. The sale solved a mystery which had puzzled stamp-collectors for 30 years—the identity of the fortunate owner. He had bought the stamp anonymously for about £15,000 in 1940, but not until after the record-breaking New York sale was his name made public. He was Mr. Frederick T. Small, an Australian living in Florida, and the remainder of his large British Guiana collection was later sold at auction in London for £123,000.

For British stamp-collectors the most important event of 1970 was the international philatelic exhibition staged at Olympia, London, Sept. 18–26. Known as Philympia 1970, the exhibition was opened by the new minister of posts, Christopher Chataway, and commemorated by the issue of three special stamps. These reproduced in their original colours three famous British stamps of Queen Victoria's reign: the Penny Black of 1840,

Stamps. This is a stamp within a stamp—a Guyana 5 cents of 1967 depicting the unique British Guiana 1 cent of 1856. The latter was sold in March 1970 for £116,660.

NINTH COMMONWEALTH GAMES 1970
4d
MALAWI

20 cents
17th century garrison and ship gun
EⅡR
St.CHRISTOPHER·NEVIS·ANGUILLA

Miklouho-Maclay
5c
PAPUA & NEW GUINEA

Soufrière Bird
Myadestes genibarbis sibilans
EⅡR
4c
St.VINCENT

St. Lucia
25 CENTS
CENTENARY OF THE BRITISH RED CROSS

ROYAL VISIT — MARCH 1970
FIFTH ANNIVERSARY · AUGUST 1970 · SELF GOVERNMENT
EⅡR
5c
COOK ISLANDS

PRIMARY
UNITED NATIONS 25th ANNIVERSARY
INTERNATIONAL EDUCATION YEAR 1970
4c
BARBADOS

BERMUDA
BERMUDIANA
4 cents

1970
2½c POSTAGE
1c HEALTH
NEW ZEALAND

5d
Philympia 1970
POSTAGE
P ONE PENNY L
1840 first engraved issue

Cotswold limestone
9d

BROWN PELICAN
Pelecanus occidentalis
5 cents
MONTSERRAT

British Solomon Islands
CHRISTMAS 1970
8c

PREVENTIVE MEDICINE
CLEAN WATER
POSTAGE
ZAMBIA 3n

XI INTERNATIONAL GRASSLAND CONGRESS
5c
AUSTRALIA

Centennial of the Northwest Territories 1870
Le Centenaire des Territoires du Nord-Ouest 1970
Canada 6

भारत
INDIA
1870-1924
वी.आई. लेनिन V.I.LENIN
u.p.20

2/-
The Great Britain 1970
Falkland Islands

THE GAMBIA
1970
IX COMMONWEALTH GAMES
1d

1c
EⅡR
OLIVER TWIST
CENTENARY
TURKS & CAICOS ISLANDS

Foreign Stamps issued in 1970

1st row. German Democratic Republic, 10 plus 5 pfennigs and 25 plus 5 pfennigs (*se tenant*), rally of Young Pioneers, Cottbus.

2nd row. Turkey, 130 kurus, "Europa"; Nicaragua, 20 centavos, footballer (Djalma Santos, Brazil); Ireland, 9 pence, European Conservation Year.

3rd row. Dubai, 1 riyal, centenary of the death of Charles Dickens; U.S.A., 6 cents, centenary of the American Museum of Natural History, New York, African elephants.

4th row. Bulgaria, 5 stotinki, World Cup; Afghanistan, 1 afghani, International Education Year; Czechoslovakia, 30 heller, 25th anniversary of liberation from German occupation.

5th row. Argentina, 40 pesos plus 20 pesos, child welfare, flamingo; Rwanda "Republic, 50 centimes, African costumes, Tunisian girl; Poland, 60 groszy, Wroclaw town hall; Qatar, 3 dirhams, Expo 70, Japanese fisherman.

6th row. Rumania, 1·20 lei, world ice hockey championship; Mongolia, 80 mung, marmot; Paraguay, 20 centimos, World Cup.

---

the embossed Shilling Green of 1847, and the surface-printed Fourpence Carmine of 1855. Commemorative postmarks, each in three colours, were also used on mail posted at the exhibition post office. Notable among the exhibits, whose total value was estimated at £10 million, was the letter flown to the Moon in July 1969 by the American astronauts and postmarked there by their commander, Neil Armstrong, before being brought back to Earth. The major award at Philympia 1970 was won by a French collector, M. Roger Leouillet, for his display of French stamps issued between 1849 and 1870.

A link with the previous British international philatelic exhibition, held in the Royal Festival Hall, London, in 1960, was provided by the news that the principal award winner on that occasion, Reginald M. Phillips, of Brighton, had been appointed honorary curator of Britain's first university philatelic unit. This is being established at the University of Sussex as a centre for seminars, research, and other philatelic activities. Mr. Phillips is already well known to stamp-collectors as the founder of the National Postal Museum, the nucleus of which was his own valuable collection of Victorian stamps.

Another important international event commemorated by the issue in Britain of three special stamps was the ninth commonwealth Games held in Edinburgh in July. The Games were publicized by similar issues in other Commonwealth countries, among them the Gambia, Malawi, and Swaziland. Britain's first decimal currency stamps were placed on sale in June, their face values being 10p, 20p, and 50p. They had the same size and design as the three sterling high-value stamps, 2s. 6d., 5s., and 10s., which they replace, with the profile portrait of the Queen by Arnold Machin, R.A. A series of four stamps illustrating British rural architecture was issued in February, and there were new issues to mark various anniversaries, including the bicentenary of the

birth of William Wordsworth, the 150th anniversary of the birth of Florence Nightingale, the centenary of the death of Charles Dickens, and, of particular interest to patriotic Scots, the 650th anniversary of the Declaration of Arbroath, which affirmed Scotland's determination to preserve her independence.

The centenary of Dickens's death was the occasion for the issue of commemorative stamps in many Commonwealth countries. Most designs featured characters from his novels, Mr. Pickwick and Oliver Twist being the most popular choices. Beethoven, born in 1770, and Lenin, born in 1870, were portrayed on dozens of stamps from many countries, and a handsome series of six large stamps was issued in Australia to mark the bicentenary of Captain Cook's exploration of the east coast. The 25th anniversary of the foundation of the United Nations was celebrated in about a hundred countries by appropriate issues, and other special stamps publicized the fact that 1970 was designated as International Education Year and European Conservation Year. Of the year's other main international events, Expo 70, held at Osaka, Japan, and the World Cup football tournament, in Mexico during June, brought varied and attractive issues from many countries. Among the most striking of the football series was that from Nicaragua, which featured eleven of the world's greatest players chosen as a team by a panel of leading sports writers. The crown agents for overseas governments and administrations, who market stamps on behalf of nearly seventy Commonwealth and associated countries, scored a notable victory with the announcement that, beginning with the football series, they would also be marketing the stamps of Nicaragua, the first foreign Latin American country to grant them a philatelic contract.

The usual issue of "Europa" stamps in the same basic design, made annually by members of the Conference of European Posts and Telecommunications, had as its main feature a motif by the noted Irish abstract artist Louis le Brocquy. The motif, consisting of 24 closely woven threads forming a circular sun-like pattern, symbolized the close co-operation among members of the C.E.P.T. and recalled that Le Brocquy is also a designer of tapestries. The year 1970, he declared, saw the production of both his smallest work of art, the postage stamp design, and his largest, a 30-sq.-metre tapestry commissioned by an Irish firm.

A noticeable development during 1970 was the increased use of special hand-stamped postmarks to publicize such local events as exhibitions, trade fairs, flower shows, conferences, and the activities of voluntary organizations. The last day of trolley-bus services in Walsall, Staffs, the centenary of the Derbyshire county cricket club, sixty years of scouting in Conway, North Wales, and the Royal Society of Health conference at Edinburgh were among dozens of events commemorated by postmarks and souvenir envelopes. The

centenary of the British plain postcard, first placed on sale on October 1, 1870, was marked by an exhibition staged in London by the Postcard Association, whose members also issued a commemorative picture postcard portraying the six British monarchs who have reigned since 1870. At the same time the Post Office announced that because of the diminishing demand for them, reply-paid postcards, first sold in 1882, were being withdrawn from use.

C. W. HILL

Starfish. The depredations of the crown-of-thorns starfish (*Acanthaster planci*), which is attacking and destroying coral islands throughout the S.W. Pacific, and particularly Australia's Great Barrier Reef, continued to exercise the minds of marine biologists and conservationists in 1970. In May, a six-man committee, jointly sponsored by the Australian government and the Queensland State government, inspected the damage done by the starfish in the Cairns and Innisfail areas, using glass-bottomed boats. They reported that much of the coral on reefs badly damaged by the pest was growing again. Prof. R. J. Walsh, chairman of the committee, said that while he and his colleagues had been impressed by the extent of the regeneration of the coral, a process which appeared to have started between 6 months and 3 years before, further inspections of the Great Barrier Reef would be necessary before it would be possible to tell how far it extended. A much less optimistic view was taken by Dr. Robert Endean, a zoology reader at Queensland University, who said on June 1 that within 12 months the starfish would kill much of the coral on the 2,000-mile-long reef, and that on Lodestone reef, near Townsville, 980 miles N. of Brisbane, a research team estimated that there were about 15 million starfish along a stretch of about 3 miles.

The same serious view of the situation was expressed in October in a report of what was described as the most comprehensive detailed investigation ever undertaken of the starfish plague on the Great Barrier Reef. This report, by a team of zoologists at Queensland University, said that at least one quarter of the Reef was already devastated, and another 120 miles could be devastated by 1975. Of 110 reefs inspected by the team, only 14 were free of the starfish. One reef left by the starfish in 1967 had shown only 1 per cent regeneration of the coral, and the team estimated that it could take up to 40 years for some areas to return to normal. It was also reported that the plague was continuing to move south at an accelerating rate.

The starfish was reported in August to be growing in numbers in the waters of Papua-New Guinea. The assistant director for research in the department of agriculture said that it had been found in large numbers on a reef off Port Moresby, and that other colonies had been found in widely separated areas. Administration officials expressed their fear that the starfish will upset the balance of marine life

Steel. The largest ever steel forging—396,600 lb. and 53 ft. long—is a rotor for a nuclear-powered electricity generator in Alabama.

in coastal waters, jeopardizing the livelihood of coastal villagers who rely entirely on food from the sea.

A new means of controlling the starfish was suggested by Dr. Yasuo Suehiro, director of the Aburatsubo marine park aquarium and professor emeritus of Tokyo University, who discovered that it is vulnerable to copper ions produced by dissolving copper salt in water. In March 1969 Dr. Suehiro took part in an ocean survey conducted by the government of Queensland. Asked to develop a method of killing the starfish, on his return to Japan he first experimented with electric currents along a wire stretched through the water, but, although it killed starfish which came into contact with it, it would be extremely costly to install. He then found that the starfish were vulnerable to copper ions. He filled a perforated vinyl pipe with a powdered copper compound mixed with gelatine and gum arabic; the pipe was submerged, and when the contents slowly dissolved and flowed through the holes, approaching starfish either turned away or were killed. If the method were to be adopted in the Great Barrier Reef the pipe would have to be laid about 100 ft. deep on the sea bottom. Coral polyps and fishes would suffer no harm from the copper ion solution, and it is claimed that this method would cost less than one tenth of the expense of installing a protective electric fence.

Stetson Hat Company. This American firm, which produced its first hats in 1865, announced in December that it will stop production early in 1971, because millions of Americans now prefer to go bare-headed. John Batterson Stetson founded the firm on his return from a trip to the West. His first hat was the "10-gallon" Western, which has been worn by American notables from presidents to cowboy film actors.

Still's Disease. A January 1970 report from the British Arthritis and Rheumatism Council stated that almost three quarters

of the children suffering from Still's disease, a crippling form of arthritis which causes limb distortion, will now be able to lead a comparatively normal adult life, thanks to the use of steroid drugs of the cortisone type. It is believed that in the U.K. about 5,000 children are affected by the disease, and that there are 100,000 adults who had it when children. The treatment does not cure, but successfully controls, the disease.

Stoneleigh, Warwickshire. It was stated in January 1970 that developments costing a total of £1½ million were planned for the National Agricultural Centre here. Of this sum, £750,000 would be spent on technical demonstrations; £290,000 for development capital; £250,000 on services, including roads and drainage; £110,000 for communications, education, and a conference centre; and £75,000 for a permanent export exhibition. On Jan. 15, an appeal was launched for funds by the Royal Agricultural Society of England, which has spent £750,000 of its own money on the project.

Strathblane, Scotland. The projected building of a £9 million tourist and conference centre on a 400-acre site at Strathblane, 15 miles S.E. of Loch Lomond, was announced on Sept. 23, 1970. The plans provide for a 300-room multi-storey luxury hotel; a conference hall seating about 2,500 people; exhibition and sports centres; an 18-hole championship golf course; and a large nature reserve. The golf course will be the first in the world to be laid out with filming and television in mind. Near the hotel, which will form the centre-piece of the plan, there will be stables for riding and pony trekking, and an artificial dry ski-run.

Strikes. In 1969 strikes cost the Netherlands 10,000 working days and Italy 20 million (the highest number in Western Europe). France lost 2·2 million working days, compared with 150 million in 1968. In Great Britain, 1969 was the worst year

for strikes since the war, with the exception of 1957. During 1969, 6,772,000 days were lost, compared with 4,690,000 in 1968; and the total number of stoppages rose to 3,021 from 2,378 in 1968. The industries worst hit were coal-mining, engineering, motor manufacturing, docks, and administrative services, and those least affected were transport—both road and rail—bricks, potteries and glass, and shipbuilding. The motor industry, with 1,635,000 days lost, accounted for a quarter of the total; there were 274 strikes in the industry, including six major stoppages. The mining industry's strike figures rose from 54,000 days lost in 1968 to 1,039,000 in 1969, the prime factor being an unofficial strike in October which was the largest single stoppage for 25 years. These British figures, however, were dwarfed by the losses due to strikes in 1970, for in the first 10 months alone, 8,828,000 days were lost, and 1,520,000 workers were involved in 3,491 stoppages. The engineering industry was the worst affected, suffering a loss of 1,549,000 working days in the 10 months. The 1970 strike total, when known, will certainly prove to be the worst since the General Strike of 1926.

Figures given in Canberra on Dec. 3, 1970, showed that Australia had a record number of 775 industrial disputes in the 3 months ending Sept. 30, with an estimated loss in wages of $A8·4 million compared with $A3·5 million in the same quarter of 1969. New South Wales accounted for more than half the national total with 404 disputes (compared with 336 in the same period of 1969), while Victoria had 130 (compared with 112). Both these figures were the highest recorded for any quarter. Queensland had 113 disputes (compared with 65), South Australia 45 (compared with 21), Western Australia 29 (compared with 22), and Tasmania 23 (compared with 9). Manufacturing industries accounted for 390 of the disputes, the building and construction industries for 79, stevedoring for 134, road and air transport for 22, and shipping services for 16. Workers involved totalled 579,000, compared with 301,000 in the June quarter (and 136,000 in the September quarter of 1969), while a total of 667,100 working days were lost, compared with 759,000 in the June quarter (and 284,800 in the 1969 September quarter).

Strontium-90. Figures given in the annual report of the Letcombe laboratory of the British Agricultural Research Council, published in June 1970, showed that strontium-90 levels in milk in Great Britain in 1969 were lower than in any year since 1961, and about 10 per cent lower than in 1968. The ratio of strontium-90 to calcium in milk was only a quarter of the contamination of 1964 after the large-scale nuclear tests of 1961 and 1962.

Students. Figures given by the U.K. department of education and science in August 1970 showed that the total of full-time students at universities in Great Britain was 211,485 in 1968–69, compared with 200,121 in 1967–68; and the number of part-time students was 21,197, compared with 19,378. Of the full-time students, 152,913 were men and only 58,572 (27·7 per cent) were women. The number of undergraduates was 173,510, compared with 164,653 in 1967–68; and the number of postgraduates was 37,784, compared with 35,019 in 1967–68. The balance of 191 students (449 in 1967–68) were taking courses "not of a university standard". In 1968–69 the proportion of science students declined by 0·7 per cent to 55·8 per cent, and there was a corresponding increase in the proportion of arts students.

The number of first degrees obtained in Great Britain was 41,685 in 1967–68, compared with 36,256 in 1966–67. There was a rise of 11·8 per cent in engineering and technology degrees, of 19 per cent in science, and of 21·6 per cent in social, administrative, and business studies, and a decrease of 2·1 per cent in the number of agriculture, forestry, and veterinary science degrees obtained. The number of higher degrees increased from 7,909 in 1966–67 to 9,713 in 1967–68. Full-time teaching and research staff paid directly from university funds increased from 25,353 in 1967–68 to 26,067 in 1968–69.

In September 1970 full-time students on maximum grants at London, Oxford, and Cambridge had their grants raised from £395 to £420, while maximum grants for students at other universities were increased from £360 to £380. The maximum for students living at home was increased from £290 to £305. The new awards will cost £6 million in a full financial year, bringing the total annual cost of students' grants to £140 million.

Italy. Figures given in June 1970 showed that, at the University of Rome, registrations since 1934 had increased six times, including undergraduates and those registered externally. The increase was especially high in the faculty of mathematics, physics, and natural science, where numbers rose from 2,347 students in 1950–51 to 8,081 in 1967–68; in the faculty of philosophy and letters, from 3,336 students to 9,114; in the faculty of political science, from 584 to 3,135; and in the faculty of economic and commercial science, from 3,614 to 11,768. At the end of 1969, students at Rome University were registered as follows: law, 7,251; political science, 3,496; economic and commercial science, 10,066; statistical science, 2,096; philosophy and letters, 8,129; teacher's college, 6,824; medicine and surgery, 7,799; mathematics, physics, and natural science, 5,587; pharmaceutics, 824; engineering, 9,110; architecture, 3,937; civil aviation and space engineering, 169. At least 30,000 additional students were registered between January and June 1970, bringing the total number in the University of Rome to approximately 100,000.

Australia. The Australian Federal government announced at the beginning of February 1970 increases in the allowances to overseas students who visit Australia under certain exchange programmes. The new allowances are $A1,670 a year for students, and $A2,140 for research fellows. The new rates apply to overseas students coming under the Colombo plan, the special African assistance plan, the Australian pacific assistance programme, the Australian international award scheme, and the Seato civilian training scheme.

Submarines. The 3,500-tons nuclear-powered submarine, H.M.S. *Churchill*, left the Vickers yard at Barrow-in-Furness on March 6, 1970, to begin a month of sea trials. The *Churchill* was Great Britain's ninth nuclear-powered submarine, and the seventh such to be built by the Vickers shipbuilding group. She was commissioned in July. On the following day (March 7), Great Britain's tenth nuclear-powered submarine, H.M.S. *Courageous*, was launched from the same yard at Barrow-in-Furness.

The £17 million U.S. deep submergence rescue vehicle (DSRV), launched in January 1970, is capable of diving to a depth of 5,280 ft. with a crew of three, and can rescue 24 men at a time from a disabled submarine. The DSRV, which uses a computer to guide it to a stricken vessel, has a "skirt" hanging beneath it, which is locked over the submarine's hatch. The water in the submarine is then pumped out, and the men can pass to safety.

A new world record for submarine escape was set on July 16, 1970, when a team of 13 men of the Royal Navy surfaced off Malta from the submarine *Osiris*, 1,610 tons, moving at 3 knots at a depth of 525 ft. On July 20, the same men broke their own record when they escaped from a depth of 600 ft. from the same submarine moving at the same speed. The team, consisting of 12 instructors from the escape training tank at H.M.S. *Dolphin*, Gosport, wore rubber

Submarines. Record escapee breaks surface.

suits incorporating a cotton fabric hood with a plastic facepiece. They were released one by one from a flooded escape tower, two of which are fitted in every British submarine. While in the tower the man breathes air supplied from the submarine and, on his way to the surface, he uses the air trapped in his hood. The previous record of 500 ft. was set up by Royal Navy personnel in July 1965. The new record proved that it is possible to escape from submarines bottomed anywhere on the continental shelf.

Suicide. Figures assembled by the Samaritans, a lay organization for helping the depressed and potentially suicidal, published on July 15, 1970, showed that, while in 1967 their seven London area branches dealt with 5,999 cases, in 1969 the same branches dealt with 11,641 cases. New "crisis assistance" stations opened at Kingston and Lewisham were consulted by 569 people. A spokesman for the Samaritans said the figures for Greater London were proportionately higher than for the rest of Great Britain because of "pressure and loneliness". The busiest of the London branches in 1969 was at St. Stephen's, Walbrook, in the City, which dealt with 6,697 cases. The U.K. Registrar-General's statistical

pure sugar

Sugar. The new international sugar mark adopted in December 1970.

review, also published on July 15, gave the total of suicides in England and Wales in 1968 as 4,584, the lowest figure since 1952.

Sunbury, Melbourne, Australia. The restoration of a homestead and farm, Emu Bottom, built in 1836 by a pioneer, George Evans, was completed in February 1970, and the building was officially opened to the public on Feb. 16. The farm was purchased by Mr. and Mrs. Hedley Elliot in 1967, and, assisted by the National Trust of Australia which classified Emu Bottom as being of extreme importance, to be preserved at all costs, they totally restored the original building. The house is fitted with utensils and furniture of the period, and the land is to be cultivated by horse plough, and the crops sown by hand—the same methods as used by George Evans.

Sunday Review. This is the name of a new Australian Sunday newspaper which began publication in Melbourne in October 1970. The newspaper concentrates on stories behind the week's news in politics, science, literature, education, finance, and other fields, and circulates throughout the eastern States.

Supplementary Benefits. New supplementary benefits for 2,700,000 U.K. pensioners in need of assistance were announced on May 15, 1970. On Nov. 2, when the benefits came into effect, a single householder received an additional increase of 40p a week, bringing the total to £8·50. These benefits will cost about £70 million each year. In addition, the income limits of people qualifying for rebate of local rates was raised from £9 to £10 per week for a single person, and from £11 to £12·25 a week for married couples; this order took effect on Oct. 1, but applications based on the new limits were eligible from Aug. 1.

Swaffham, Norfolk. It was reported in November that 16 Saxon skeletons dating from the 6th century A.D. had been discovered by archaeologists here. They included warriors with shields and iron knives, and women with amber beads and necklaces. The most interesting was that of a 6-foot warrior lying face downwards with feet outstretched, and arms bent up towards his chest; a shield was lying over his head and shoulders, and he had been armed with a small iron knife.

Swindon, Wilts. Work on a new £6½ million shopping centre which will occupy a 13-acre site on the western side of Regent Street, Swindon, started on Dec. 17. The centre will have a traffic-free ground-level area linked by a walkway to a car-parking block for 700 cars, with a small area of parkland between the car park and the main shops. Vehicles will deliver their goods to a service area at third-storey level, and the goods will be taken by lifts to shops on the lower floors. A central feature of the centre will be a covered piazza, to be called Brunel Plaza.

Sydney, New South Wales, Australia. Several sets of statistics published during 1970 emphasized the speed and extent of the building going on in the N.S.W. capital city. The Sydney Water Board, for example, stated in July 1970 that the value of building projects completed in its Sydney-Wollongong area in the 1969–70 financial year exceeded the $A500 million mark for the first time. The actual value of $558,694,296 was an increase of $82,143,071 on the figure for the previous year. The total number of completed jobs (new buildings, alterations and additions to existing buildings) was also a record. The main increase in activity was again in the building of flats, but the number of houses built, altered, or added to also increased. The average price of new houses was $11,120, nearly 10 per cent more than in the previous year. In August, a survey by the property consultant firm of Jones, Lang, Wootton, indicated that the annual production of office space in the central business district increased from 557,000 sq. ft. in 1969 to 1,207,150 sq. ft. in 1970. It forecast further increases of 1,926,950 sq. ft. in 1971, over 2,631,500 sq. ft. in 1972, and more than 1,373,000 sq. ft. in 1973. This will bring the net production of office space in the central district in 1957–73 to 16,547,100 sq. ft. In 1970, the largest supplier of office space in the city was the Bank of New South Wales, with 260,000 sq. ft.; in 1971 it will be the I.A.C. building, with 200,000 sq. ft. The north shore is also increasing its office space, for the amount built there between 1968 and 1971 will be 2,544,000 sq. ft.

On June 18, the N.S.W. Club building in Bligh Street was sold at auction for a record $A421 per sq. ft., beating the previous record of $A406 per sq. ft. paid by the government insurance office for Kay House in October 1968. The four-storeyed sandstone club building, which also contains a basement, covers 8,780 sq. ft., and the purchase price was $A3·7 million. The building will be demolished in 2 years'

time, and an office block built on the site.

Work began on Sept. 7 on fitting the huge glass walls of Sydney's $A85 million Opera House. The work, costing between $4 and $5 million, is the last remaining major exterior feature of the Opera House, and will take a year to complete; it consists of sealing openings of four large walls and two small shells with 67,000 sq. ft. of glass about three quarters of an inch thick. The glass wall of the main concert hall shell opening, facing the harbour, will be 80 ft. high and up to 140 ft. wide, and will contain 11,500 sq. ft. of glass. The semi-transparent laminated glass, imported from France and specially designed and structurally tested, is supported by 120 structural steel bars. The glass walls will not only make the building weatherproof, but also reduce outside sound to an acceptable level. It has been found structurally impossible to install escalators in the building, and lifts will be used instead. The latest estimate for the completion date of the Opera House is November 1972.

William Tyree, of Sydney, the founder and managing director of a group of companies which manufacture a wide range of machinery for electrical engineering, announced in June his intention to spend $A1 million on establishing a medical and scientific research foundation. Its first project will be the setting up of a health screening service in Sydney, to which patients would be referred by their doctors for health checks and diagnostic tests. The results would be processed by computers and returned to the patient's doctor. The service, to be known as "Medicheck", will be one of the most modern in the world, and should be able to deal with about 2,000 patients per month. The new foundation will also provide $A20,000 a year for the endowment of a chair in the school of electrical engineering in the University of New South Wales. Further funds will be devoted to the rehabilitation of disabled people in industry.

An unusual ceremony took place on

Sydney Express. Arrival of this large container ship at Fremantle in November.

June 17, 1970, when the ashes of Special Sergeant Harry Ware, founder of the New South Wales Police Rescue Squad, were scattered from the police launch *Nemesis* at the foot of the Gap, an indentation in the precipitous cliffs near South Head of Sydney Harbour, notorious for suicides. Sergeant Ware, who died on April 24, 1970, saved more than 80 lives and recovered more than 300 bodies, many of them from the Gap area. Members of the Police Rescue Squad, which was headed by Sergeant Ware from 1946 until his retirement in 1962, formed a guard of honour at the top of the cliffs. Harry Ware, who was presented with the British Empire Medal by King George VI in 1952, was responsible for the design of all the equipment used by the Squad today in its cliff rescues.

Mrs. Margaret Mary Sleeman, aged 36, who started her career in August 1949 as a temporary office assistant in the justice department, became Australia's first woman stipendiary magistrate on July 27 when she received her commission in Sydney. During the 21 years since her first job Mrs. Sleeman has become a solicitor, has been maintenance clerk in Burwood, assistant clerk of petty sessions at Bankstown, chief clerk of divorce, relieving chamber magistrate, and in April 1970 became a coroner.

Sydney Express. The world's biggest container ship, the *Sydney Express*, 27,000 tons, was launched at the Blöhm and Voss shipyard in Hamburg on Feb. 16, 1970. Capable of carrying more than 1,500 20-ft.-long containers, she began to operate between Europe and Australia in November.

t

Tachograph. It was announced in Brussels on Jan. 27, 1970, that by 1978 all long-distance lorries and coaches registered in Common Market countries will have their log-books replaced by this instrument, which keeps a check on the number of hours worked and distances driven by crews. Regulations for using these instruments were drawn up by the end of June 1970. All new lorries registered in the Common Market countries will have to be fitted with a tachograph from 1975.

Teeth. A U.K. government survey on adult dental health in England and Wales in 1968 was published in March 1970. It showed that the condition of the nation's teeth has improved under National Health Service treatment. Less than 4·6 per cent now lose their teeth before the age of 30 compared with 11 per cent in 1945, and although 37 per cent of the population had lost all their teeth, nearly half lost them before the Health Service began. The survey showed some remarkable difference in dental care in different regions. In London and the South-East, 72 per cent of

people over the age of 16 have some of their natural teeth remaining, compared with 66 per cent in the Midlands and East Anglia, 57 per cent in Wales and the South-West, and only 54 per cent in the North. In London there is one dentist to every 2,850 patients; in the North, one to every 6,140; and in Wales, one to every 6,340. Differences in the dental health of social groups were also revealed: 46 per cent of manual workers and their families have total tooth loss, compared with only 27 per cent of non-manual workers and their families. This situation worsens for both groups the farther north they live. It was also shown that the proportion of women who lose all their teeth is higher than for men in all areas. The survey deduced that, as soft foods now make up a high proportion of our diet, the original role of the teeth is of less importance than formerly. It also noted a general extreme reluctance to wear dentures.

Telescopes. A specialized telescope for studying the Sun went into operation in the U.S.A. in 1970. Called a solar vacuum tower telescope, it is the first of a new generation of instruments to study solar energy processes. Perched on a 9,200-ft. mountain peak overlooking Alamogordo, New Mexico, it is 365 ft. long, 227 ft. of it being housed in a vertical shaft below the ground and the remainder enclosed in a conical tower. A unique feature is that the interior is pumped free of air so that the distortion caused when the Sun's rays heat air currents is minimized, the the image has greater stability. As a further means of sharpening the image, the outside temperature of the tower is controlled by painting it with reflecting paint, and pipes embedded in the concrete circulate cooling water. Sunlight enters the telescope through a 32-in.-diameter quartz aperture at the top of the tower, and falls on to two flat mirrors arranged to reflect the light straight down the tube. A 64-in. focusing mirror, 183 ft. below ground level, directs the sunlight back up the

Telescopes. Zelenchuk observatory, U.S.S.R.

shaft to instruments mounted on a platform at about ground level. An 11-ton pool of mercury near the top of the tower provides friction-free support for the optical assembly, which rotates to follow the Sun across the sky. The new telescope, the latest addition to an observatory operated by the Cambridge research laboratories, will make a special study of sun-spots and flares, which cause electrical disturbances in the Earth's atmosphere.

The installation of the world's largest telescope (236-in. mirror) at the Zelenchuk observatory in the northern Caucasus continued in 1970. Made in Leningrad, it was transported here in 1968. The observatory that will house it is over 1½ miles above sea level.

Television Awards. At the 1970 Montreux festival of light entertainment TV on April 30, 1970, the Golden Rose was won by the Czechoslovak programme *Six Fugitives*, which also won the City of Montreux's prize for "the most comic work" and the press jury prize. The Silver Rose went to Columbia Broadcasting System for the Anne Bancroft show, *Annie, the Women in the Life of a Man*. The Bronze Rose was taken by the Norwegian entry, *Bedside Story*. At the sixth international competition for television news and documentary coverage held in Cannes in May 1970, Great Britain won the live reporting award with the BBC's programme of the Investiture of the Prince of Wales, and the U.S. National Education Television network took the filmed coverage prize for *The Trial—the City of Denver against Laureen Watson*. The 3-day festival brought together 36 documentaries, including nine in colour, from 25 television organizations in 18 countries. The Italia prize for drama at the Florence television festival, announced in September, went to the third episode of *The Six Wives of Henry VIII*, which featured Anne Stallybrass as Jane Seymour and starred Keith Michell as the king; this programme was shown on BBC 2 early in 1970.

Individual awards to British television, given by the Society of Film and Television Arts, were presented on March 8, 1970, at the London Palladium. They were won by the following:

Actor of the Year—Edward Woodward.
Actress of the Year—Margaret Tyzack.
Light Entertainment Personalities of the Year—Eric Morecambe and Ernie Wise.

Production drama awards went to Christopher Morahan, Verity Lambert, and Paul Watson, while the ITN production team for the second year running gained the Factual Programmes award for "News at Ten". In light entertainment, Yvonne Littlewood and Mark Stuart both gained production awards. Specialized programme awards went to "The Blue Peter" team; to Fred Burnley for "Omnibus"; to Tony Abbot for script-writing; and to John Terraine for general production. The Richard Dimbleby award was given to Sir Kenneth (now Lord) Clark for his "Civilization" series of programmes. "Monty Python's Flying Circus" was given a special award for production, and Terry Gilliam received an allied craft award for his graphics for the show. Richard Cawston's "Royal Family" gained the Desmond Davis award. On April 21, the Australian entertainer Rolf Harris was named television personality of the year by the U.K. Radio Industries Club, and Val Doonican radio personality of the year.

Tennis Courts. A new type of meter was introduced in the U.K. in 1970 to collect the fees and to time the hire periods for public tennis courts. The device is coin-operated: when the appropriate coins are inserted in the slot the net can be winched up to its correct position, and 5 minutes before the end of the time the net is automatically let down. The first of the new meters were installed at Bromley, Kent.

seals, statues, figurines, and carved steatite bowls, extending over a period of about 4,000 years. These finds have led the professor to the view that, instead of single units of urban life in the Mesopotamia area, there were in fact a series of trade colonies engaged in far-flung and often complicated economic transactions.

Territorial Waters. The U.S. state department's legal adviser announced on Feb. 18, 1970, that the U.S.A. would support a 12-mile territorial sea limit as part of a new international effort to resolve legal disputes over ocean resources. The 12-mile limit is recognized by about 40 nations. The previous U.S. view had supported the old 3-mile limit, while recognizing a 9-mile fishing zone beyond it.

Thalidomide. On April 30, 1970, the West German government approved a £22 million foundation to help the estimated

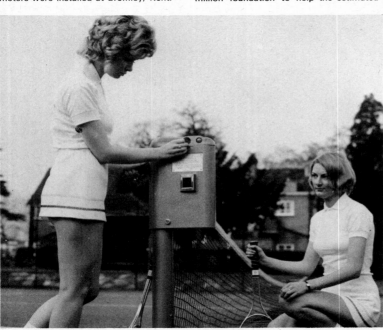

Tennis Courts. "Parking meter" for hiring a public tennis court at Bromley, Kent.

Tepe Yakya, Iran. During excavations in August 1970 at Tepe Yakya, a 65-ft.-high mound in the Soghun valley 156 miles S. of Kerman, S.E. Iran, archaeologists led by Prof. C. C. Lamberg-Kariovsky found tablets bearing some of the earliest writing known. The writing on the tablets, which recorded economic transactions, is the same as that on the proto-Elamite tablets found at Susa, and Prof. Lamberg-Karlovsky dated them at about 3200 B.C. They throw new light on the extent and development of the world's first urban culture, showing that a civilization parallel to that of Mesopotamia was developing in S.E. Iran, the two being linked by trade. Earlier excavations during the summer had revealed cylinder seals, stamp

2,000 German children born handicapped through their mothers' use of the drug thalidomide during pregnancy, and other handicapped children living in the republic. Chemie Grünenthal, the manufacturers of the drug, agreed to contribute £11 million to the foundation, and later offered a further £4 million compensation to 300 adults suffering from nervous disorders attributed to thalidomide. The £22 million foundation will provide for individual compensation of up to £4,560 for each child, in addition to a maximum monthly allowance of £44 for life. The government is to contribute the rest of the money. The trial of Chemie Grünenthal and its directors was finally abandoned on Dec. 18, after 283 days, spread over 2½ years, without

a verdict being passed. The defence had applied to the court for the case to be dropped, quoting the United Nations charter of human rights which gives a defendant a right to expect a verdict within a reasonable time. The application was supported by the prosecution. Both felt, and the court agreed, that the principal aims of the trial had been achieved through the payment of compensation to victims of the drug.

In the United Kingdom actions on behalf of thalidomide-deformed children against Distillers Co. (Biochemicals) Ltd., who distributed the drug, continued throughout the year. Agreed damages of £12,000 were awarded to a boy, £2,000 to his mother, and £800 to his father in February; a total of £369,709 to 18 children and their parents in March; a total of £485,528 to 28 children and their parents in July; and a total of £157,638 to nine children and their parents in December. These last cases brought the number dealt with by settlement to 69. The judge said that two outstanding cases were due to come before the court in 1971, and that it was hoped a trust would be set up by Distillers Co. to help the remaining 300 thalidomide children who had not yet brought proceedings before the court. By Dec. 18 over £1 million had been paid in agreed damages by the company.

A report, "The Challenge of Thalidomide", published on Sept. 21, said that thalidomide children born in Great Britain show a remarkable ability to keep pace with other children in spite of their handicaps. Their school work had proved better than expected, and the report said that it appeared that "quite a number" would go on to universities, colleges of education, or technical colleges. While about 20 per cent of the 500 deformed children will need special care, it was thought that over half will be able to attend ordinary secondary or grammar schools. As all thalidomide children will have to depend on their intellectual ability in finding employment, educational environment is of much greater importance to them than to normal children. The report recommended a six-point plan for helping them, to include opportunities for pre-school education; provision of a more challenging, enriched educational environment; consideration of a change of school, either from a special school to an ordinary school or vice versa; long-term plans for secondary education and after; anticipation of problems in adolescence by the immediate setting-up of a psychological counselling service both for parents and children; and re-examination of all children within the next 3 years, and again a year before leaving school.

Thames, River. A plan to erect a Thames barrier to protect London from flooding was announced on Jan. 19, 1970. The plan was put together by a G.L.C. team working under a government policy committee, set up in 1968 under the chairmanship of Lord Kennet following a report on London's flood problems by Prof.

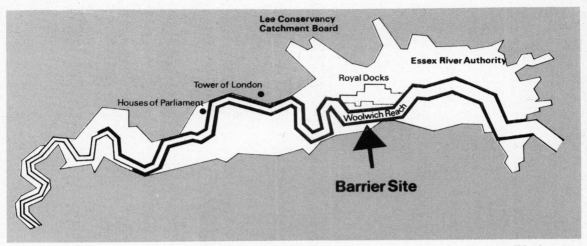

Thames. Uncoloured area is the part of riverside London needing flood protection: heavy line shows where wall-raising will be done.

Herman Bondi. It recommends the construction of a barrier incorporating tide control in the Woolwich-Limehouse area, and the scheme would include the building of walls and banks downstream to give equal protection to the whole of London. The barrier would be raised during normal conditions of a rising tide, and dropped to hold back the water when the tide falls. The amenities of the river would be improved, as the tide would be prevented from ever falling below half-tide level upstream, and this would make the Thames navigable above Woolwich at all times. Opportunities would be provided for developing a riverside park with walks built on terraces below the present embankment level. Water-sport facilities could be provided for Tower Hamlets and Southwark, and a water stadium with a rowing course at Chelsea Reach, beside Battersea Park. The work would take between 7 and 11 years to complete, and would cost £50 million.

The leader of the Greater London Council announced on Dec. 15 that, as an interim measure until the major flood barrier was built at Woolwich Reach, the council would spend £5$\frac{1}{4}$ million on immediate emergency flood-protection schemes which would raise the flood defences along 27 miles of the Thames by 18 in. The Victoria Embankment walls will be strengthened with concrete blocks and raised, and on the South Bank, to preserve amenity and the views, Perspex sheeting will be used to reinforce the railings where these have been raised. Where necessary, walls and banks will be raised from Chiswick to Purfleet on the North Bank, and from Wandsworth Park, Putney, to beyond Thamesmead at Erith on the South Bank. Work will start early in 1971, and is expected to be completed in 21 months.

The chairman of the Thames Conservancy Board announced on May 14, 1970, that boreholes are to be sunk in the western Thames valley, and used to pump up 100 millions gallons of water a day from underground sources when the level of the Thames drops during summer drought. The scheme is the first of its kind in the world, will cost between £6 million and £8 million, and will take 10 years to develop.

On March 4, 1970, the Greater London Council announced plans for a £29 million tunnel under the Thames between Barking and Thamesmead. The proposed tunnel would be 811 yds. long, and have eight lanes. If work starts in 1972–73 the tunnel will be open by 1976.

Tigers. It was announced by the Nepal government in December that hunting tigers for sport is to be banned from March 1, 1971. The order was made to prevent the extinction of the tiger, whose numbers are decreasing rapidly.

Tin. The first instrument in the world that can automatically assay the tin content of ore down a 50-ft. borehole, developed by British scientists, was demonstrated in November. Named the "borehole logger", the instrument contains a small amount of the man-made radio-active element americium-241, which gives out rays that excite X-rays in the tin-containing ore. The latter are measured in a portable probe which states the result as a simple percentage of tin in the ore. The borehole logger costs £2,350, and, at the time of the demonstration, it was reported that 15 were already in production.

Titian. At the beginning of 1970 the parish priest of the village of Vaiano, near Cremona, Italy, discovered the missing third *Coronation of Christ* by Titian (Tiziano Vecellio, 1477–1576) hidden in his church. The 5 ft. by 6 ft. painting, described as "a radiant, magnificent masterpiece", and authenticated by Prof. Marcello Bonomi, is quite beyond price. One of the other paintings forming the trio is in the Louvre, and the other in the art gallery at Munich. Although it was thought the picture should be placed under guard, possibly in the Uffizi gallery in Florence, the priest who made the find refused to let it leave his church, where, watched over only by Sunday school teachers and choirboys, it hangs above the altar.

Tokyo, Japan. The world trade centre here was formally opened in March 1970. Japan's tallest building, it is almost 500 ft. high and comprises 40 storeys with three basement floors. It incorporates new building systems as safeguards against fire, earthquakes, and typhoons. The centre houses trade organizations, airline and other transport firms, foreign exchange banks, a customs office, and a post office. It also includes foreign trade showrooms, retail shops, and restaurants, and on the 40th floor there is an observation lounge.

Construction work on the new Tokyo international airport, covering an area of 2,630 acres about 38 miles east of Tokyo, went into full swing in April 1970, with the target of partial opening to air traffic in April 1971. The overall plan envisages sufficient facilities to handle 16 million international passengers and 1·4 million tons of international cargo—predicted for 1986. There will be two main runways, plus a cross-wind runway. In addition, two one-way taxiways will be constructed along the inside of each of the three runways to facilitate the movement of aircraft. Passenger and cargo terminal buildings and aircraft parking areas will be arranged in a 740-acre area surrounded by the three runways, and aircraft maintenance facilities will be built on the eastern edge. The parking areas will be capable of accommodating a total of 230 planes in terms of the DC-8 class—namely, 96 passenger planes, 18 cargo planes, 110 night-time planes and six planes during "run-up" (for checking engine performance).

Two "new towns", Narita and Chiba, are to be built near by, and travelling facilities to the new airport include a planned super-express railway similar to the New Tokaido Line, a monorail, and

Tokyo. The new 17-storey Imperial Hotel opened on March 10, in good time for Expo 70. It contains 900 bedrooms, 10 restaurants, four bars, and several conference halls.

screen auditorium, and a 30-acre nature trail. Three special awards for outstanding examples of tourist enterprise during European Conservation Year were also made. They were given to the city of Sheffield, for its Abbeydale industrial hamlet; to Tewkesbury borough council, for restoration of medieval shops and other projects; and to the Crofters' Commission, for its Highland village 1970 project.

Spain. The number of foreign visitors to Spain in 1969 was 21,700,000, compared with just over 19 million in 1968. The greatest number of visitors, 8,210,000, were from France, followed by 2,600,000 from Great Britain. Others included nearly 2 million from Portugal, just over 900,000 from the U.S.A., and nearly 16,000 from Cuba. The number of Spaniards who went abroad in 1969 reached a record total of 4,150,700.

Israel. A record number of tourists, 194,000 visited Israel in the first 6 months of 1970. The previous highest figure for a 6-month period was 188,900 in 1968, which was about 2·7 per cent lower than the 1970 figure.

Australia. The 1970 annual report of the Australian Tourist Commission in September stated that the tourist industry earned Australia $A119 million in 1969, $9 million more than in 1968. The spectacular rise was due to spending by U.S. servicemen on rest and recreation leave.

New Zealand. New Zealand's income from tourism during the year ended March 31, 1970, totalled $NZ26,023,000, a $29\frac{1}{2}$ per cent increase over the previous year. There was a $17\frac{1}{2}$ per cent increase in number of visitors.

Tours, France. During November, volunteers planted 8,000 trees and shrubs on a 26-acre island near Tours, known as Île de la Prairie. The work, which took only 6 hours, was part of a project for a future park.

extensions of and connections to the new express-way roads now being constructed around Tokyo. The total cost of the new airport is estimated at £233 million.

Tourism. On Dec. 28, 1970, the International Union of Official Travel Organizations published in Geneva a survey of world tourism which showed that a record number of 167 million tourists travelled during 1970, spending a record sum of £6,500 million. This was a 9 per cent increase on the 1969 number of tourists, and an 11 per cent increase in the amount that they spent. The survey stated that the number of tourists during the decade 1960–70 had more than doubled.

Great Britain. Figures given in the British Tourist Authority's first annual report, published on Sept. 21, 1970, showed that over 5 million people visited Great Britain in 1969. The largest number came from the U.S.A.—1·3 million, a 35 per cent increase over the 1968 figure, and the highest ever annual increase. There was also a record number of over $2\frac{1}{2}$ million visitors from European countries, an increase of 20 per cent in 1968. About 800,000 came from France, 500,000 from Germany, over 300,000 from the Netherlands and over 200,000 from Belgium and Luxemburg, and nearly 200,000 from Italy. Visitors from more distant countries included 60,000 from Japan and the same number from South Africa, 25,000 from Mexico, about 22,500 from Brazil, and about 20,000 from Argentina. In addition there were 750,000 visitors from the Republic of Ireland. Tourists spent £355 million in Great Britain, an increase of 26 per cent over the 1968 figure, and, with fares paid to British air

and shipping lines, the total tourist earnings rose to £475 million, an increase of almost £100 million over 1968. In 1969 tourism was Great Britain's fourth largest earner of foreign exchange.

The British Tourist Authority's "Come to Britain" trophy for 1970 was awarded to Landmark, the £190,000 centre opened by the Duke of Edinburgh at Carrbridge, Inverness-shire, in June 1970. The centre, the first of its kind in Europe, was designed to increase enjoyment and understanding of the Scottish Highlands; it includes an exhibition hall, restaurant, shops, a multi-

Tours, France. In November, volunteers planted on the Ile de la Prairie 8,000 trees and shrubs in 6 hours, for a future park.

Traffic Control. On this suburban highway in Washington, D.C., one lane is kept for buses, which drive rapidly past the jammed ranks of private cars in the other lanes.

Traffic Control. All traffic on British motorways will come under computer control by 1972 following the award of a contract to G.E.C.-Elliott's Traffic Automation division by the ministry of transport in January 1970. The system will cover 800 miles of motorway, including 200 miles not yet constructed. Ten computers, working in pairs, at centres to be built at Hook, Hants, Perry Barr, Birmingham, Almondsbury, Glos, Westhoughton, Lancs, and Scratchwood, Herts, will operate illuminated traffic signs at one-kilometre intervals on urban motorways, and three-kilometre intervals on country motorways. The signs will show no symbol in normal conditions, but in bad weather, or in the vicinity of an accident, road-works or other hazard, will show an advised speed limit of 20, 30, 40, 50, or 60 m.p.h. The signals will be mounted on overhead gantries on urban motorways and on the central reservation of rural motorways. They will have red flashing stop signals, and the symbols will be accompanied by the alternate flashing of upper and lower pairs of amber lights. Following a series of warning signals, an octagon with a diagonal bar will be shown to indicate that the road is clear. The computers will receive their data from police using teletype machines.

Traffic Wardens. A "Functions of Traffic Wardens" order by the U.K. Home Office came into force on Jan. 1, 1971. The order authorizes wardens in certain situations to stop cars and ask drivers for names and addresses, makes it an offence for motorists to ignore the signal of a warden on point-duty, and allows wardens to replace policemen to man car pounds.

Tropical Diseases. In May 1970 the Wellcome Trust announced a £1 million Anglo-American scheme for stimulating research into tropical diseases. The scheme, which aims to provide long-term support for young scientists interested in this field of research, will be operated jointly with the London School of Hygiene and Tropical Medicine and the Harvard School of Public Health.

Tunnels. On May 5, 1970, the Swiss prime minister inaugurated work on the 9-mile-long Gotthard road tunnel, which will be the longest tunnel in Europe, if not in the world. Its construction, which is scheduled for completion in 1977, will involve the removal of 1·3 million tons of rock. Two large Swedish excavating machines will be used, and this work is expected to proceed at the rate of 50—65 ft. per day. The tunnel will have a single broad roadway in each direction, flanked by a footpath, will be brightly lit, and will be air-conditioned by continuous fresh air pumped through four shafts. The highway police will control the traffic flow by means of closed-circut television, and it will also be regulated by traffic lights installed every 250 yds, and, in case of accidents, lay-bys will be located every 800 yds. Parallel with the main tunnel an emergency one will be built, with access passages into it every 250 yds. The present road to and through the Gotthard pass follows the contours of the mountain and involves 26 sharp curves and many very steep gradients, so that in the busy summer season, when traffic reaches some 14,000 vehicles a day, inevitable traffic jams occur, while in the winter months the road is frequently blocked by snow and ice. The

new tunnel will provide an all-year-round route for commercial and other traffic between northern Italy and the rest of Western Europe. (See also p. 123.)

(See also p. 123.)

Europe's first double-decker tunnel for trucks and cars was opened at Wuppertal, West Germany, on Oct. 2. The tunnel, which cost about £4 million and took 6 years to construct, links this north German industrial city to the Ruhr valley auto-bahn system, cutting the average travelling time to Düsseldorf from 45 to 15 minutes. Named after the Kiesberg mountain through which it passes, the tunnel consists of a 915-yd.-long upper deck leading out of the city, and a 1,140-yd.-long lower deck leading into the city.

uv

Ulster '71. This festival, to be held in N. Ireland in 1971, will be the biggest of its kind in the U.K. for 20 years. It will include a huge Expo-style exhibition and exhibition park in Belfast; a big tourist campaign throughout the world; a series of festival fortnights in towns and villages in N. Ireland; a special programme of international sporting events; and an ambitious programme of the arts. The Belfast exhibition, which will be held in the Botanic Gardens from mid-May to mid-September, covering 37 acres, will mirror N. Ireland's past, present, and future. It will occupy over 20,000 sq. ft. on two floors in a new building, which will afterwards be used as a physical education centre for Queen's University. A prominent feature of the building will be massive sculptured hexagonal forms, inspired by the Giant's Causeway, two of which will form the entrance and exit. The first and second sections of the exhibition will be devoted to a history of N. Ireland; the third to the

Ulster '71. Symbol of the Northern Ireland festival and exhibition.

achievements of famous citizens; and the fourth to the re-creation of an outdoor scene, with the sights and sounds of the sea, hills and forests. Another section will deal with the future. The exhibition park will include a large-scale funfair, an arena for pageants, displays, and sporting attractions with seating for 6,000 people, and a children's play centre. Five brightly coloured domes will house subsidiary exhibitions, entertainments, and a restaurant.

Universities. An international university of art, with campuses at Florence and Venice, was inaugurated on Oct. 4. It will provide seminars, lecures, and laboratory facilities for investigating the function of art in contemporary society. The restoration and conservation of works of

Vatican City. The building at right is the first to be erected in the modern style in the Vatican City. Opened in June 1970, it houses a museum of antiques and the missionary and ethnological museum. The building opposite is the Vatican picture gallery.

art will be studied in the laboratories, a natural consequence of the fact that the suggestion of the university came from Prof. Carlo Ludovico Ragghianti in 1966, following the floods which devastated the two cities and damaged many of their art treasures.

The Lord Mayor of London opened on Nov. 9 a £3½ million estension to the City University, the first stage of a £12 million development plan. The extension includes a new five-level electrical and electronic engineering block, a new library on two floors, and offices. The City University, which has about 2,400 students, began its life as the City Polytechnic in 1891, later became Northampton Polytechnic Institute and later still a college of advanced technology, and in 1966 was given a university charter. The next stages of the development plan include the building of a new civil and mechanical engineering block, two more halls of residence, and a business studies centre on a site near the Tower of London.

Bath University of Technology is to include a grassed open-air theatre seating 600 people in a major landscaping scheme announced in May 1970. The £25,000 scheme also includes a 2-acre lake, a series of small lakes, a fountain, bridges, a small botanical garden, and the planting of hundreds of shrubs and trees, including pines, maples, willows, wild cherries, and redwoods. There will be a continuous programme of landscaping at the University, the whole concept being to preserve the natural characteristics of Claverton Down on which it stands.

It was announced on May 21, 1970, that Clare College, Cambridge, founded in 1326, had decided to admit women students into residence as from October 1972. Clare is the third Cambridge men's college to admit women, the other two being Churchill and King's.

New England College, New Hampshire, U.S.A., announced on Oct. 7 that it had bought Tortington Park School buildings, on the Duke of Norfolk's Arundel estate, as its British campus. The co-educational university will open in September 1971 with 200 American students, who will pay about £1,350 a year to study there. It will offer the usual American college degree courses in the liberal arts and sciences.

The first students to graduate from the University of Papua-New Guinea received their degrees at a ceremony in Port Moresby on Aug. 18, 1970. The degrees were presented to 10 graduate and four post-graduate students.

Uranium. Three discoveries of uranium ore of great value were made in Australia during 1970. The first—one of the world's largest and richest deposits of uranium—of about 55,000 tons, worth $A700 million, in the first of three lenses alone—was announced in September 1970. The site is at Nabarlek, 150 miles E. of Darwin, Northern Territory, Australia, and the strike was made in July by Queensland Mines Ltd. Easy to mine since it is close to the surface, the yield was estimated at up to 1,300 lb. of uranium oxide per ton of ore—100 times the yield that is considered commercially worth while. The strike length is 3,600 ft., and its average width 300 ft. It was announced on Sept. 17 by the Australian prime minister John Gorton that foreign participation in Queensland Mines Ltd. (and in Kathleen Investments which owns 50 per cent of Queensland Mines shares) will be limited by law to 15 per cent, and that any individual holding in either company would be limited to 5 per cent. Mr. Gorton said that it would not be in the national interest for control over the huge uranium discovery to pass into other than Australian hands.

Also in July, the Brisbane-based group, Exoil, Transoil, and Petromin, announced that drilling tests near Lake Frome in South Australia had indicated a uranium deposit with reserves of at least 200,000 tons. This deposit is 20 miles E. of those at Mt. Painter, and the ore body is at a depth of 400 ft., with an average thickness of 13 ft. The third strike, 140 miles S. of Darwin, was announced at the beginning of November by Peko Wallsend, who said it could be the largest found in Australia. Preliminary evidence suggested that it would yield 70,000 long tons of uranium oxide.

Variety Club Awards. The 1969 awards to actors and actresses by the Variety Club of Great Britain were announced and presented on March 10, 1970. They were:

Show business personality of 1969—Danny La Rue.

Stage actor—Leonard Rossiter, for his performance in *Arturo Ui.*

Stage actress—Margaret Leighton, for her performance in *Antony and Cleopatra.*

Film actor—Nicol Williamson, for his performance in *Inadmissible Evidence.*

Film actress—Glenda Jackson, for her performance in *Women in Love.*

BBC-TV personality—Eric Robinson, for his presentation of light music in the series *Records for You* and *Melodies for You.*

ITV personality—Ronnie Barker for *Hark at Barker* and performances in the David Frost programmes.

Most promising artiste—Polly James, for her performance in the stage musical *Anne of Green Gables.*

A special award was made to Bernard Delfont for services to the entertainment industry.

Vatican City. The Pope announced on Sept. 15, 1970, that all the armed forces of the Vatican City, except the 50 members of the Swiss Papal Guard were to be disbanded. They number about 700 in all, in the Guard of Honour or Noble Guard, the Palatine Guard, and the Pontifical Gendarmerie; most of the last named will be absorbed in a new force formed to help the Swiss Guard with police and guard duties. The announcement was made 100 years after the last military action by Vatican forces, on Sept. 20, 1870, when with French troops they unsuccessfully resisted a Piedmontese army that captured Rome, ending the Pope's temporal power and uniting Italy for the first time. The Swiss Guard, established in 1506, still wear on ceremonial occasions the yellow and blue uniforms designed by Michelangelo.

Vegetable Oils. A ban on the use of specially treated vegetable oils, called brominated oils, in soft drinks was announced by the U.K. minister of agriculture on Jan. 23, 1970. The oils have been used for many years in soft drinks like orange juice, barley water, and lemon squash to give a cloudy effect. While there is no evidence that their use has led to any harmful effects on human beings, recent experimental work in Canada has shown that some rats treated with doses of 100 times the normal human intake developed heart lesions. Parallel research work by the British industrial biological research association at Carshalton, Surrey, on the accumulation of bromine in body tissues produced similar results.

Victoria, Gozo, Malta. The government of Malta announced in May 1970 that a £2 million contract had been awarded for the construction of a general hospital at Victoria. The hospital will consist of a series of single- and double-storey buildings, made from local stone, and linked together by corridors. There will be a total floor area of some 210,000 sq. ft., and accommodation for some 360 patients in the general medical and surgical wards, maternity wards, psychiatric wards, outpatients department, and accident and emergency sections. There will also be an X-ray department, and pathology facilities.

Victoria Cross. A Victoria Cross awarded to Sepoy (later Captain) Ishar Singh, of the 28th Punjab Regiment on April 10, 1921, fetched an auction record price of £2,000 at Sotheby's, London, on June 24. Only five Victoria Crosses were awarded between the two World Wars, four of them in Indian campaigns.

Vicuna. The importation into Great Britain of the hair and skin of the vicuna, a rare South American relative of the camel and llama, was banned from Oct. 27, 1970. The result of a campaign by the World Wildlife Fund, the ban was introduced to help the animal to survive, for there are thought to be fewer than 10,000 vicunas in existence.

Volcanoes. In February 1970 a volcano in Hokkaido, the most northerly of the four main islands of Japan, was put up for sale by its owner, Nasao Mimatsu, who had bought it for about £30 over 20 years ago. The 1,480-ft. mountain of lava named the Showa Shinzan (new mountain of Showa) was thrown up during 1944 and 1945. It is about 45 miles S.W. of Sapporo, capital of Hokkaido.

Wages. Official figures issued in the U.K. on Jan. 29, 1970, showed that the average weekly earnings of adult male manual workers in a wide range of industries, including manufacturing, construction, road transport, and public administration, was £24·82 in October 1969. This was 8 per cent higher than in October 1968. In the year 1969–70, weekly earnings in Australia rose almost 9 per cent, giving an average weekly wage of $A75 (£34·70) to each employed man. Average wages in the various States were $77·40 per week in New South Wales, $77 in Victoria, $74·90 in Western Australia, $70 in Tasmania, $69·90 in South Australia, and $65·40 in Queensland. These figures were published by the bureau of census and statistics on Aug. 26, 1970. In New Zealand average weekly earnings have increased by 61 per cent in the last 10 years. During the 6 months ending April 1970, average overtime hours, 3·2 a week, were at a record level, and 20 minutes above the average in April 1969. Average ordinary time hourly rates of pay had risen 5½ cents, and overtime rates 11¾ cents, in the previous 12 months. Average weekly earnings, including overtime and bonus payments, in all surveyed industries were $NZ47·85 (£22·33) in April 1970, compared with $44·29 in April 1969. In 1960 the figure was $29·73. The 1969–70 increase was 8 per cent, compared with 6·9 per cent in 1968–69, and 3·1 per cent in 1967–68.

"Walls of China", N. Mildura, N.S.W. The discovery of the oldest human bones ever found in Australia was announced in January 1970. The bones, which are expected to provide clues to the date of man's first arrival on the continent, were found accidentally in 1969 by a research geologist of the National University, Canberra, who was working in an area between Mildura and Ivanhoe in southwestern New South Wales known as the "Walls of China" and once part of an extensive lake system that vanished about 15,000 years ago. The bones were those of a young woman who had been cremated and buried between 25,000 and 32,000 years ago. With the bones were stone tools, and the remains of fish, animals, and eggs, evidently used for food. An archaeologist said that the relics are about twice as old as a skull found in

Queensland, previously the oldest human relic found in Australia. This skull showed a mixture of the characteristics of the modern aborigine with those of Java man, who lived from a quarter to half a million years ago.

Wash, The. A report of the U.K. water resources board, published on Sept. 10, 1970, suggested that 15 per cent of the area of the Wash, the 330 sq. mile, shallow inlet on the E. coast of England, could be converted into reservoirs for supplying water to S.E. England. It proposed the creation of three or four reservoirs, enclosed by 30-ft.-high "bunds" or banks, between the mouths of the Great Ouse and Welland rivers. The first, on the foreshore west of the Great Ouse, would hold 14,000 million gallons and supply 100 million gallons a day; at a cost of about £24 million, it could be constructed and in service by 1983–84. A total of 240 million gallons a day could be supplied by all four reservoirs together, which would contain 44,000 million gallons and cost £140 million. A barrage right across the Wash was considered impracticable.

Washington, co. Durham. Permission for a £10 million town centre covering 11 acres at Washington new town was given by the U.K. government at the beginning of August. The first stage, due for completion by April 1973, will include 273,000 sq. ft. of shopping space; nearly 1 million sq. ft. of commercial and professional offices; a health centre with regional hospital board and industrial health service facilities; restaurants; public houses; a careers office; and a citizen's advice bureau, with council of social service accommodation, information centre, and rent office. The centre will also include a library and swimming pool, and an initial 1,200 car-parking spaces. Future developments will include a cinema, hotel, dance hall, magistrates' court, probation office, adult arts centre, youth centre, technical education centre, and labour exchange. Recreational facilities, including a sports hall, games hall, art centre, and a £300,000 swimming pool, will also be provided. Washington will be one of nine regional computer centres, which will be fully operational, with a staff of about 6,000, by 1977.

Water Storage. An Australian scientist has developed an insoluble compound which, he claims, when spread over water storage areas will cut evaporation by at least 30 per cent. The scientist, Dr. G. T. Barnes of the University of Queensland, said in March 1970 that the compound was based on pure alcohol; an additive increases the spreading rate over water 10 times and reduces the risk that wind will break it up. He said that the compound could be used ultimately to save millions of gallons of water now wasted in Australia through evaporation.

Weapons. A world record auction price of £21,000 for a sword was paid at

Sotheby's in London on March 23, 1970, for a swept-hilted jewelled rapier of 1606 by Israel Schuech, from the Saxon royal collection. This was seven times higher than the previous world record price. Another record price at the same sale was paid for a wheel-lock ball-butt pistol of the last quarter of the 16th century, which originally came from the armoury of the electors of Saxony and had recently been housed in the *Historisches Museum* in Dresden. It fetched £5,800.

Weather Forecasting. In the 1970 annual report of the U.K. meteorological office it was reported that an order had been placed for a new giant U.S. computer, an IBM 360/195, one of the most powerful in the world. The price is about £5 million. The computer should make it possible to give more detailed forecasts up to 36 hours ahead, including the amount and distribution of rainfall likely to occur over the British Isles and Western Europe, and to give reliable, less detailed forecasts of the weather for up to a week ahead. Reports from Great Britain, Ireland, Iceland, Greenland, and four weather ships in the Atlantic will be collected and added to observations made by merchant shipping and aircraft which are in communication with the meteorological office's h.q. at Bracknell, Berks, where the machine will be installed during 1971. A new automated computer-controlled system is also being installed there, the first stage of which, involving automation of the telecommunications centre, will be completed by the beginning of 1971. Later phases will lead to the gradual automation of the whole national meteorological data-gathering network. The number of inquiries received by the meteorological office from industry in 1969 was a record 1,610,000 and from aviation 1,440,000. Calls on the automatic telephone weather service reached the record number of 12,400,000.

Weedkiller. The U.K. forestry commission stated in April 1970 that it had suspended the use of the weedkiller 2,4,5-T (trichlorophenol), which had been used extensively for clearing undergrowth, following allegations that it had caused serious harm to both human beings and animals. The allegations included the birth of deformed babies, impotence among some agricultural workers, and paralysis among animals. The chemical had already been banned by the U.S.A. (including its use as a defoliant in the Vietnam war), on evidence that it could cause harm to pregnant women and unborn animals.

Wells, Somerset. A conservation scheme for Wells, to include the cathedral, cathedral green, bishop's palace, vicar's close, and many of the old streets, was approved by the city council on Jan. 26, 1970. A relief road to skirt the city on its northern boundary was also recommended, and a tree preservation order on certain woodland approved. The centre of Wells will be under strict planning control.

Windsor. Princess Margaret watching dolphins' antics at the new Windsor safari park.

Wembley, Greater London. The construction of London's first purpose-built conference centre began here, beside Wembley Stadium, during 1970. The centre, which will seat about 2,000 people, will include facilities for exhibitions. The scheme includes a 500,000 sq. ft. distribution centre, a 300-bedroom hotel, and parking space for about 5,000 cars and 1,000 coaches. It will cost an estimated £1 million, and is due for completion in 1972.

Whaling. When the June talks of the international whaling commission ended in London on June 29 it was announced that agreement on stricter whale catch limits for the North Pacific had been reached. For the 1971 season, the catch of sperm whales is limited to 3,551, 10 per cent less than the 1970 catch. The fin whale catch was reduced to 1,308, also a 10 per cent reduction on the 1970 figure, and the sei whale limit reduced by 15 per cent to 4,710. The quota of 2,700 "blue whale units" in the Antarctic remained unchanged.

Whyalla, S. Australia. A new 55,000-deadweight-ton ore ship *Yarra River*, launched in January 1970, was built in the record time of 29 weeks for the Australian National Line at Whyalla shipyards, by the Broken Hill Proprietary Co. Ltd. The previous best time for the construction of a similar vessel was 36 weeks. *Yarra River*, the 50th vessel constructed by BHP, is about 740 ft. long and has a maximum draft of 41 ft.; her turbine engines are designed to produce 16,500 h.p., giving a service speed of about 16 knots. On Jan. 15, the minister for shipping and transport went to Whyalla to lay the keel of the *Amanda Miller*, which will be the biggest ship ever built in Australia. The cost of this 62,000-ton tanker is estimated at $A15 million. It will be the most technologically advanced vessel operating on the Australian coast; it will have a fully automated, unmanned engine-room controlled from the bridge by computer, and

will be moored by using closed circuit television, an automatic recorder measuring the distance from the wharf.

Windsor, Berks. On March 31, 1970, Princess Margaret officially opened the Royal Windsor safari park, which lies in 140 acres off the Bracknell–Windsor road. In 1966, the late circus impresario, Billy Smart, deciding that this was an ideal spot to show wild animals, purchased St. Leonard's House, which stands in the park. There is a long history of a building standing on this hill site. Before the 1700s it was a workman's cottage; in 1756 William Pitt built a mansion there, which was rebuilt in 1771, and again in 1782 when Sir Francis Tress-Barry bought the estate. Work on the safari park started on March 1, 1969, and the first car drove through the entrance 4 months later. The park has a selection of wild life from all corners of the globe, including baboons, lions, elephants, giraffes, camels, ostriches, sea lions, and zebras, as well as a large collection of birds. One of the chief attractions is the dolphinarium, where the animals provide a spectacular entertainment. There is also a pet's corner, children's corner, a tree walk with leopards and aviaries, a chimpanzee house, and a mouse village.

Wine. Australia produced a record estimated total of 63,100,000 gallons of wine during the 12 months ending June 30, 1970—an increase of 11,200,000 gallons over the figure for 1968–9, which was itself a record. Total exports for 1969–70 were 1,322,000 gallons. Canada was the main market, followed by Great Britain, Papua and New Guinea, New Zealand, Hong Kong, Singapore, Japan, the U.S.A., and 60 other countries.

Woburn, Beds. The Bedfordshire county chief planner announced on July 7, 1970, that Woburn is to be protected by designation as a conservation area. The British council for archaeology has described it as one of the most important historic towns in Great Britain, with a street pattern that has remained basically unchanged since the last century. The conservation proposals will limit development to about 40 new houses within the built-up area, and ensure that this development is in keeping with the compact nature of the small town.

The "wild animal kingdom", claimed to be one of the largest game reserves outside Africa, was opened at Woburn Abbey, in 350 acres of the Duke of Bedford's estate, on May 19, 1970. Among the 400 animals are zebras, cheetahs, wildebeeste, giraffes, oryx, elephants, rhinoceroses, and lions. Precautions against accidents include double electric gates to the lion enclosure, look-out posts everywhere manned by game wardens armed with shotguns, and repeated reminders to visitors to keep car windows closed. The charge to drive through the reserve is £1 per car.

Woolwich, Greater London. The old dockyard here is to be developed for homes and public recreation under a scheme put forward by Taylor Woodrow Property Ltd. When this was announced in December it was stated that the company would aim to create a community containing its own schools as well as social and recreational facilities. The dockyard, which was founded by Henry VIII, was closed in 1869 when the war office took it over for storage use, and in 1969 the 23-acre site was purchased from the ministry of defence by Greenwich council.

Woomera, S. Australia. It was announced on Dec. 2 that Woomera is to be abandoned as an effective rocket-launching range. The next Europa rocket will be launched in the autumn of 1971 from the French range at Kourou, French Guiana, following an agreement signed between ELDO and the French government. The main advantage of Kourou is that rockets can be fired in an easterly direction, gaining a 1,000 m.p.h. "bonus" from the Earth's rotation; similar firings from Woomera would send rockets on a course directly over Sydney.

Wye, River. The U.K. Countryside Commission announced on Sept. 21 that the Wye valley had been designated an area of outstanding natural beauty. The area, covering about 124 sq. miles in Gloucestershire, Herefordshire, and Monmouthshire, extends from Chepstow to near Hereford, and includes several tourist attractions, including Tintern Abbey and Symond's Yat. The Wye valley is the 28th such designated area in England and Wales, and brings their total area to 4,550 sq. miles.

xyz

X-Rays. Details of a new portable industrial X-ray machine, designed by Soviet engineers, were given in March 1970. Although it weighs only a little over 4 lb., and uses tubes smaller than a match-box and a tiny, high-voltage battery, it generates rays that can penetrate $\frac{1}{2}$ in. of metal to reveal defects in pipes and welds. It replaces much less accurate magnetic and ultrasonic systems previously used for this task.

York. Work on an £8 million, 1,000-bed hospital here is expected to start in October 1971. It was announced in April 1970 that the hospital will be built on a vacant plot of land alongside the existing Bootham Park hospital. The first of three stages will provide 342 beds for acute patients, 72 of which will be allocated to children, and also major diagnostic, treatment, and service facilities for the complete hospital, including emergency, out-patient, X-ray, pathology, and operating departments. Staff accommodation, workshops, and a hospital chapel will also form part of the first stage.

Youth Hostels Association. The Y.H.A. of England and Wales reported in October that the previous membership record of 228,069 (1948) had been broken in 1970, when members numbered 234,087. It is thought that the increase of 12,655 over 1969 was due to far-reaching changes in policy, which included brightening up hostels and improving facilities and communications.

A new four-grade system of charges for the use of Y.H.A. hostels came into force on Jan. 1, 1971. The nightly fee of 30p for adults remained unaltered at 68 hostels classified as "simple", but at 156 designated as "standard" the charge was increased to 35p. To stay at a "superior" hostel costs 40p per night, and a few "special hostels", which have central heating and baths, charge up to 60p. The charges have been raised to keep pace with increased maintenance, heating, lighting, and other costs. Hostellers under the age of 21 will continue to pay lower rates. The Association has 256 hostels.

Youth Hotel. An 800-bedroom youth hotel and community centre for males and females is being built to replace the present London central Y.M.C.A. hostel and club premises off Tottenham Court Road, built in 1912. Information about the building was given at the beginning of August 1970. It will consist of four towers rising from a low podium which, together with the lower floors, will contain a library, lounges, meeting rooms, sports halls, a swimming pool, a chapel, shops, a restaurant, and a basement car park for 200 vehicles.

Zeya Dam. Work on this Russian hydroelectric power project, with a design capacity of 1,470,000 kW, was carried out during 1970. The station is sited on the middle reaches of the Zeya river, at a point where the Saktakhan and Tuhuringra mountain ranges form what are known as the Zeya Gates. The low-cost power provided by the project will operate metallurgical, engineering, and timber-chemical works, as well as supply farms; it will also enable the eastern sector of the Trans-Siberian railway to be electrified. The dam will prevent the menace of flooding over nearly 1 million acres of fertile land in the Amur region and Khabarovsk territory. A huge 2,500 sq. km. reservoir will be formed in an area of coniferous forest, and work on tree felling has already begun; while concrete is poured into the future dam a housing community, the nucleus of a future town, is also being built.

Zoos. Taronga Park Zoo, Sydney, N.S.W., is spending over $A200,000 on improvements, details of which were announced in September. A large area is being rebuilt to provide a walk-through aviary, an elaborate series of waterfowl ponds, and a nocturnal house where animals normally active only at night can be observed by visitors during the daytime. The new aviary, which was completed by the autumn of 1970, is 110 ft. high and 60 ft. long, and formed by two soaring parabolic arches covered with wire mesh. Visitors, who enter and leave through revolving doors, see the birds without any barrier, and elaborate landscaping gives the birds a simulated natural habitat in which to fly and perch.

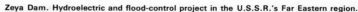
Zeya Dam. Hydroelectric and flood-control project in the U.S.S.R.'s Far Eastern region.

INDEX

This Index comprises references to all the important subjects mentioned or illustrated in pages 5–288 of the Year Book. "Names in the News" and "Fact Digest", which are arranged in alphabetical order, are not indexed here.

Page references to illustrations are in italic type; where an illustration is in the same page as its related text it is not separately noted. Dates refer to the section "The Year 1970 in Headlines" in pages 6–29. The abbreviation f.p. ("facing page") refers to illustrations in the plate facing the page given. Names beginning with Mc are entered as if spelt Mac, and names beginning with St. are entered as if spelt Saint in full.